THE JOSLIN DIABETES
GOURMET COOKBOOK

THE
JOSLIN DIABETES GOURMET COOKBOOK

Heart-Healthy, Everyday Recipes for Family and Friends

Bonnie Sanders Polin, Ph.D., and Frances Towner Giedt

with the Nutrition Services Staff at Joslin Diabetes Center

Foreword by Edward Horton, M.D.

Medical Director, Joslin Diabetes Center

BANTAM BOOKS

NEW YORK • TORONTO • LONDON • SYDNEY • AUCKLAND

Library of Congress Cataloging-in-Publication Data

Polin, Bonnie Sanders, 1941–
The Joslin Diabetes gourmet cookbook : heart-healthy, everyday
recipes for family and friends / Bonnie Sanders Polin and Frances
Towner Giedt, with the nutrition services staff at Joslin Diabetes
Center ; foreword by Edward Horton.
p.   cm.
Includes index.
ISBN 0-553-08760-6
1. Diabetes—Diet therapy—Recipes.   2. Low-fat diet—Recipes.
3. High-fiber diet—Recipes.   I. Giedt, Frances Towner.   II. Joslin
Diabetes Center.   III. Title.
RC662.P63   1993
616.4′620654—dc20   93-25887
                                                                 CIP

CONTENTS

FOREWORD

As a former president of the American Diabetes Association and the American Society for Clinical Nutrition, and as the new Medical Director of Joslin Diabetes Center in Boston, it gives me great pleasure to write the Foreword to what I consider to be a unique culinary resource for people with diabetes—and for anyone who is trying to eat meals that are simultaneously delicious, elegant, and healthy.

There are many cookbooks on the market that offer lower fat, lower cholesterol, and lower sugar recipes with varying degrees of success in the taste department. What makes this book unique is that in a single volume the reader obtains both a wealth of nutritional information plus over four hundred gourmet recipes that put this dietary information into practice with flair. To achieve this unusual accomplishment, Joslin's expert nutrition counseling staff has worked with Bonnie Polin, Ph.D., and Frances Giedt, two women with diabetes who share both a passion for good food and a strong desire to maintain a normal and at times demanding lifestyle while managing their disease.

The book they have created is full of inviting recipes—recipes for foods that will never leave you with the feeling that you've been cheated at a meal simply because you have diabetes. They are simply wonderful meals and will suit anyone who enjoys cooking and good food—whether you have a medical condition like diabetes or not.

In the last few years, a great level of consensus has developed in the medical and nutritional communities about what is included in a healthy diet for anyone who has diabetes or heart disease or who is trying to minimize the risk of developing heart problems, adult-onset diabetes, or cancer. The American Diabetes Association, the American Heart Association, and the American Cancer Society all agree that each of us needs to decrease the amount of saturated fats in our diet, eat adequate but not excessive amounts of protein, and increase the amount of complex carbohydrates and fiber we eat.

By targeting people with diabetes, this book contains many recipes that are also good for those trying to prevent heart disease and cancer or those who wish to keep their weight down to prevent or control obesity-related diseases including adult-onset diabetes, hypertension, hyperlipidemia, gout, and osteoarthritis. But because the recipes in this book taste so good, they can be used for the whole family and on even the most festive occasions.

When reading the nutritional and medical information briefly presented in this book, keep in mind that it does not replace other information on diabetes or healthy lifestyles that you obtain from your own health-care team. We at Joslin always encourage our patients with diabetes to learn as much as they can about their condition so they can assume more active and informed roles in their care. To become skilled in self-management, people with diabetes need to know not only about diet, but how regular exercise, weight control, frequent blood sugar monitoring, and oral medications or insulin can play a role in managing their condition. You can live a healthy, happy, full life with diabetes if you learn all you can, work closely with your health-care team, and participate in regular educational opportunities to keep up-to-date on your medical care. We hope the recipes in this book will help you achieve these goals!

Bon appétit!

Edward S. Horton, M.D.
Professor of Medicine, Harvard Medical School
Medical Director, Joslin Diabetes Center

A FEW WORDS FROM THE AUTHORS

Two days before my forty-first birthday I found myself in an endocrinologist's office being told that I had Type I (insulin-dependent) diabetes. My husband, a physician, was present, but neither of us was prepared for the months of mourning for our respective losses that would accompany that diagnosis.

I was immediately taught how to inject myself with insulin and was given an 1,800-calorie exchange diet—a low-fat, low-salt meal plan for eating at regular intervals and in modest portions. On that day I became a member of a sizable minority of people who need special diets, and my family became one of more than 13 million people in the United States with a diabetic member. The losses for me were significant in terms of ease in structuring my professional, personal, and social life. I was forced to become almost obsessive about food, which had been a pleasure in the past, as it now took on aspects of a life-and-death issue in my mind. I worried about mealtimes, quantity of food, preparation, and the exchanges.

For some time I, a psychologist and practicing mental health professional, had treated patients who had experienced loss of health, a relationship, or a loved one. I found myself going through the same well-documented and familiar phases attributed to loss and the inevitable lowered self-esteem. Unfortunately, my family also had to reconcile the loss of the mother/wife they had always thought of as strong and available. First there was a period of denial: "How can I have diabetes? I feel fine." "I really was trying to lose all of that weight." "That doctor is wrong. All I need to do is cut out sugar and I'll be fine." Worse, like many with Type I diabetes, I went into a short period of remission (sometimes called the "honeymoon period"), which allowed me to "test" to see if I really had the "big D."

Another part of my early reaction to loss was more magical. This is where we may bargain with God or try "treatments" read about or heard about. We magically rationalize our not keeping doctor's appointments and minimize our symptoms. It's during this time that we and our families blame others, look for cures, and take little responsibility for ourselves. In the next phase, anger and sadness, many people seem to get lost. We feel angry that we are ill and that part of our life has been stolen from us, and we feel sad because of this loss and our fears for our future health. At times during this process I felt like a rubber ball bouncing out of control.

Finally, there is a working-through time that allows one to come out of this tunnel of depression as a whole person once again, one who just happens to have a chronic disease. For many, including me, the first step toward this resolution was a conscious decision that, diabetes or not, I wanted to live a meaningful life.

My family and I were aware of this mourning process, so fleeting feelings of alienation, anger, hopelessness, and helplessness were not permitted to destroy us. We all have grown more empathetic to others' needs and have become emotionally stronger for the experience.

Additionally, I was fortunate enough to become a patient of Dr. Gordon Weir, an alumnus of my husband's college who was at that time the assistant medical director at the Medical College of Virginia and later became a researcher and medical director at Joslin Diabetes Center. His research on Type II (non-insulin-dependent) diabetes was well known, but it was his kindness and support as well as the time we spent together discussing all aspects of diabetes that helped me sustain my decision to live the best and healthiest life I could.

For this reason I am both grateful and proud that Dr. Weir supported the writing of this book and that Joslin Diabetes Center, an affiliate of Harvard Medical School, of which he was then medical director, became our collaborator in this project.

In the process of regaining my self-esteem I found that one thing lacking in the community was a really creative and inspiring cookbook. My monthly cooking magazines contained recipes loaded with fats, sugars, and protein. I could not consider restaurant food safe, nor was it very tasty when all the sauces were omitted. Travel could become a nightmare. From my perspective cookbooks for people with diabetes were dull. Cooking at home and being able to eat wonderful, diverse, and safe meals became very important indeed. Thus the idea for this book was born. Colleagues and friends agreed on the need for a gourmet cookbook for people with diabetes. So with a lot of family support I submitted the idea for this book to our publisher. At that time I was introduced to Fran Giedt, my co-author, who has become a respected friend.

My goal in writing this book has always been to free those on special diets from feeling imprisoned by their disease—by modifying recipes in such a way that everyone can enjoy them. Being able to cook the newest dishes and a variety of styles allows one to dine and entertain beautifully. This not only helps to minimize feelings of being different but also instills pride in oneself that can extend to other aspects of life. As we feel more in control, we may be able to better control our diabetes.

To all readers who have family members or friends with special dietary needs and to those of you who have diabetes, I wish you *bon appétit*. Enjoy and please decide to take good care of yourselves.

BONNIE
Tulsa, Oklahoma

When I was first approached by Bantam Books to join Bonnie in writing this cookbook, I questioned how two strangers from different parts of the country could successfully co-author a cookbook. Later, when I met Bonnie in the Manhattan offices of our publisher, I was immediately taken by how similarly we thought and expressed ourselves, particularly about food. It was clear that, although not a food writer by profession, Bonnie really understood the chemistry of food and most certainly the boredom that special diets inflict on most people with diabetes. Before the meeting was over, we were finishing each other's sentences, and I felt as if this was a friendship of years, not hours. Now, hundreds of recipes later, after days huddled in a hotel room planning the book, countless hours on the telephone, and weekly parcels of manuscript back and forth between Connecticut and Oklahoma, I am convinced that our collaboration on this book was meant to be.

My close association with Joan Hill, R.D., C.D.E., director of Nutrition Services at Joslin Diabetes Center, Boston, during the writing of this book has given me new understanding of the critical role that nutrition plays in controlling diabetes. From our first meeting at Joslin in Boston, she and her staff have played a pivotal role in helping us shape this book in such a way that it both pleases the palate and meets the special dietary concerns that all people with diabetes face.

I was diagnosed as having Type II diabetes in the summer of 1988. Depression set in immediately, followed by anger at myself for letting this happen. One of my college degrees is in foods and nutrition with graduate work in dietetics. Since I'd had gestational diabetes during my second pregnancy, I knew I was a likely candidate for diabetes later in life. But food had become my life! As a cookbook author and food consultant to restaurants and food manufacturers for years, if I wasn't writing about food, I was developing recipes and eating the results.

I'd convinced myself that I cooked healthfully—after all, I always used fresh ingredients rather than processed foods and lots of fresh herbs rather than salt. I was also using eggs, butter, heavy cream, and lots of olive oil. No wonder my medical tests showed high levels of cholesterol, elevated blood pressure, and alarming levels of blood glucose—all of which were brought under control with my new proper diet.

As I switched to cooking low-fat, high-fiber dishes, it became apparent to me that what I was missing most was to be able to pick up a new best-selling cookbook or the latest issue of a food magazine to try out someone else's recipes. If this was true for me, it had to be true for millions of others who have diabetes or were cooking for someone with diabetes. It's very depressing to have to cook separately for anyone who requires a special diet. How much better it would be if everyone could and would eat the same food.

Like Bonnie, I found that the cookbooks for those with diabetes were lacking. Where were the arugula, sun-dried tomatoes, balsamic vinegar, and couscous? I have a passion for wonderful food, and when I cook for my family or friends, they expect the best. So it was back to doing what I do best, developing recipes, this time for people with diabetes. I hope you and everyone at your table love the results and enjoy our efforts in good health.

FRAN
Wilton, Connecticut

ABOUT JOSLIN DIABETES CENTER

Joslin Diabetes Center is the oldest freestanding institution in the United States dedicated solely to diabetes research, patient care, and patient and professional education. It was founded in 1898 in Boston by Elliott P. Joslin, M.D., a dedicated pioneer who believed that the patient was an integral part of the diabetes treatment team. He and those who treat patients at the center today believe people with diabetes need to understand the condition and its treatment because the patients are in charge of their own care day by day.

Joslin is located in a seven-story building that takes up an entire city block in Boston's famous Longwood Medical Area of Harvard-affiliated hospitals and institutions. In addition to its affiliation with Harvard Medical School, Joslin Diabetes Center is closely associated with some of the most well-respected hospitals in Boston and throughout the nation. More than 170,000 patients have been seen at the Boston Joslin Diabetes Center.

In 1921 Dr. Joslin's friends and colleagues, the Canadians Dr. Charles Best and Dr. Frederick Banting, discovered insulin. Dr. Joslin and his medical colleague Howard F. Root, M.D., were the first to use the new wonder drug in New England.

Dr. Joslin and the clinicians and researchers who have followed him at what is now the Joslin Diabetes Center have developed some of the most important treatments for diabetes in the postinsulin era.

These include

- New treatments for diabetic women during pregnancy—techniques that have brought the fetal survival rate for Joslin pregnancies from 54 percent to over 96 percent.
- Laser surgery for treating diabetic eye disease—saving the sight of countless thousands of diabetics.
- Tight control of blood sugars as the best means of treating patients with diabetes and preventing long-term complications. This treatment regimen— unpopular with patients and physicians alike when first introduced more than

sixty years ago—has now evolved into insulin replacement programs that are the treatment of choice for physician experts working with diabetic patients.

- Means of identifying who will develop Type I diabetes years before actual symptoms appear. Researchers are now trying different treatments to see if they can prevent the disease from developing entirely.

Dozens of Joslin clinicians—including endocrinologists, ophthalmologists, renal specialists, exercise physiologists, podiatrists, psychiatrists, psychologists, social workers, nurses, dietitians, and others—provide total quality care every day to patients facing the disease and its complications. Joslin's cadre of scientists conducts basic and clinical research that is improving treatment for people with diabetes—and may one day actually prevent the disease altogether. New discoveries by Joslin's internationally acclaimed researchers are immediately translated into improvements in care by its equally prestigious, award-winning clinicians.

Since 1987 Joslin has expanded its ability to treat patients with diabetes by establishing affiliated clinics around the country. You will find listings for the Joslin Diabetes Center and its affiliates in Appendix 3.

A NOTE FROM THE NUTRITION SERVICES STAFF AT JOSLIN DIABETES CENTER

As nutrition practitioners in diabetes care dealing with all kinds of clients through the life cycle—parents of the two-year-old picky eater, the rebellious adolescent, someone's 65-year-old dad who just can't give up his ice cream, or the young woman planning pregnancy—we feel privileged to be working at Joslin. Today research and clinical care at Joslin Diabetes Center in Boston is continuing the tradition of excellence that Dr. Joslin launched nearly a century ago.

In 1898, nearly twenty-five years before the discovery of lifesaving insulin, Elliott P. Joslin, M.D., opened a medical practice in Boston's Back Bay. Harvard educated and trained, Dr. Joslin treated individuals with a wide variety of ailments, but his strongest interest was in diabetes, a disease that was then untreatable and usually fatal. In the early twentieth century, Dr. Joslin's diabetic patients literally had to starve to remain alive.

It was in Dr. Joslin's 1913 edition of his textbook that he stated, "The instruction of the patient should not end with urinary tests: it should include didactic and practical instruction in the preparation of his diet." While many things related to diabetes management, such as monitoring techniques and dietary recommendations, have changed over the years, that Joslin philosophy has remained a constant.

The Joslin concept of diabetes care emphasizes Dr. Joslin's long held belief, stated more than 60 years ago, that "the patient is his own nurse, doctor's assistant and chemist." Long before it was fashionable to include patients in health-care decisions, the Joslin patient was an integral part of the diabetes treatment team. At Joslin patients have always received and will always receive the education they need—about diet, about medication, about exercise, and about complications—to manage the disease as well as possible.

Joslin's commitment to keeping patients intimately involved in day-to-day treatment decisions was part of our reason for developing a Joslin cookbook. Today people with diabetes can eat a wide variety of delicious foods. In fact there are very few things that a person with diabetes cannot eat occasionally, with proper planning.

If you or someone in your family has diabetes, we hope this book will help bring back into your lives the enjoyment around the dinner table that may be missing because of diabetes. We also hope that knowing about and making certain modifications to your eating program recommended in this book will help you minimize the risk of developing long-term complications.

There is a wealth of information in this book: how to reduce your total fat intake as well as cholesterol and saturated fat, what you can do to satisfy your "sweet tooth," how to reduce the protein in your diet, and much more. The hundreds of wonderful, mouthwatering recipes in this book have been developed using the latest information available about food and its effects on managing diabetes. Bonnie Polin and Fran Giedt have done an exceptional job of proving that food can still be delicious and need never be boring or repetitive just because someone has this disease. Our working together has been, I believe, an educational experience for us all. Bonnie and Fran have learned more about managing their diabetes, and we've been challenged to produce even more inventive meals for patients.

All of us in the Nutrition Services Department at Joslin thank Bonnie and Fran for helping us once again show people with diabetes how to live well with this disease.

JOAN HILL, R.D., C.D.E.
Director of Nutrition Services
Joslin Diabetes Center

And the Nutrition Services Staff:
JULIE MARCIL, M.A., R.D., C.D.E.
JILL WEST, R.D., C.D.E.
GEOFF GALLANT, R.D., C.D.E.
ANNA MARIA BERTORELLI, M.B.A., R.D., C.D.E.
ROBERTA LAREDO, R.D.
EMMY FRIEDLANDER, M.S., R.D., C.D.E.
MARIA IOCCO
Communications Director:
JULIE RAFFERTY

INTRODUCTION

MANAGING DIABETES

You may be reading this cookbook because you are one of the 13 million Americans who has diabetes. Maybe you are looking at it because your husband, wife, or best friend has been diagnosed with the condition. Or you may be picking up this book because someone in your family has diabetes and you've been told that you are more likely to develop it as a result—particularly if you are overweight and over 40.

Whatever your reasons, you want to know more about diabetes—and especially what people with diabetes can eat. While this book is not an exhaustive text on diabetes, here are some basic facts about the disease that you should know.

Two Major Types of Diabetes

Diabetes is a disease in which your body fails to make adequate use of food energy. Food energy in the form of sugar or glucose can't make its way into the body's cells, builds up in the bloodstream, and is passed in the urine.

Not all diabetes is the same, however. There are actually two major forms of the disease.

Type I Diabetes

About 300,000 Americans have Type I or juvenile-onset diabetes. This type of diabetes occurs primarily in children or young adults, although it can develop, as Bonnie discovered from firsthand experience, at any age. People with this form of diabetes do not make any insulin, a vital hormone produced by the pancreas that enables us to convert food into energy. People with undiagnosed Type I diabetes will lose weight, be constantly thirsty, and urinate frequently as the body tries to rid itself of the unused glucose.

People with Type I diabetes treat this condition with daily insulin injections to replace the insulin their bodies no longer produce. They should follow a meal plan and exercise program devised with their health-care team. They also need to monitor their blood glucose levels several times each day to be sure that their medication, diet, and exercise program is keeping their blood sugars in control—ideally within the range of 80 to 140 mg/dl.

Research now shows that people develop Type I diabetes because their bodies destroy the insulin-producing cells in their pancreas. Studies at Joslin and elsewhere suggest that one day we actually may be able to prevent the disease by stopping that destructive process using drugs or other means.

TYPE II DIABETES

People who develop diabetes when they are over 40 often have what is called Type II or adult-onset diabetes, although Type II diabetes sometimes occurs in younger people who are usually overweight. About 12.7 million Americans have this form of diabetes. People with Type II diabetes usually produce some insulin, but either it is not enough to meet their needs or for some reason the insulin that is produced does not properly signal the cells to allow glucose to enter.

Frequently people who develop Type II diabetes are overweight. Scientists believe that being overweight may make the body less able to use the insulin it produces correctly. There are substances called *insulin receptors* on the body's cells that enable insulin to do its work. Researchers suspect that either there aren't enough receptors on hand to handle the workload in people with Type II diabetes or perhaps the Type II patient's receptors are defective in a way that prevents them from functioning properly. When they are overweight, this situation is exacerbated.

To treat Type II diabetes, people need to increase their exercise and follow a meal plan devised with their health-care team. Frequently weight loss will bring blood sugars back into a more normal range. If you have Type II diabetes, you may also take pills called *oral hypoglycemic agents*, which help the body make and use insulin more effectively. People with Type II diabetes will also need to monitor their blood glucose levels at home on a regular basis to make sure that their medical program is keeping their before-meal blood sugars in the target range—ideally 80 to 140 mg/dl.

In some cases people with Type II diabetes need insulin injections because diet, weight loss, exercise, and pills alone simply aren't enough to adequately help the body use the insulin it produces. Also, researchers believe that sometimes over a period of years the amount of insulin a person with Type II diabetes produces decreases—the pancreas just starts to tire out from all the years of pumping out more insulin that your body uses less effectively. For whatever reason, you simply need more insulin.

Diabetes Frequently Is Undiagnosed

Amazingly, only about half of the people who have diabetes know it. This is because Type II diabetes frequently can develop with few or no obvious symptoms. This happens probably because people with this form of the disease are still producing some insulin, which enables them to convert some of what they eat into energy. People with Type I diabetes need prompt medical care as soon as the first symptoms of uncontrolled blood sugar develop (page xvii). In contrast, people with Type II diabetes can actually live for months or years not knowing they have the disease or not treating it properly, and still feel generally all right.

Symptoms and Risk Factors for Diabetes

You are more likely to develop Type II diabetes if you are

- over 40
- more than 20 percent above your ideal body weight
- related to anyone who has diabetes
- Afro-American, Hispanic, or Native American
- a woman and have given birth to a baby that weighed more than nine pounds at birth (or if you weighed more than nine pounds at birth)

The warning signs of diabetes include

- excessive thirst
- excessive hunger
- frequent urination
- blurred or changing vision
- unexplained weight loss
- tiredness
- tingling or numbness in the legs, feet, or fingers
- sometimes there are no symptoms (for Type II diabetes)

Diabetes Runs in Families

While many people who develop diabetes have no history of the disease in their families, people who have relatives with diabetes are more likely to develop it themselves. If you have Type II diabetes, your immediate relatives should be checked regularly for signs of high blood sugars. Research shows that the risk of developing Type II diabetes is lower if you maintain your proper weight and exercise regularly. This improves the efficiency with which your body uses insulin. So urge your family members to join you in exercising and losing weight.

If Type I diabetes runs in your family, research such as studies done by Joslin's immunology section now shows that signs of the disease can be picked up using special testing up to eight years before actual symptoms develop. Researchers at Joslin and elsewhere are just beginning new treatments that may enable us to prevent Type I diabetes in susceptible individuals.

Untreated or Poorly Treated Diabetes Can Cause Life-Threatening Problems

People who have been told they have diabetes—particularly those with Type II diabetes—may not follow their physician's medical advice about diet and medication because they feel okay. But unfortunately, untreated or poorly treated high blood sugars can take their toll, resulting in serious complications—heart disease, blindness, kidney disease, nerve damage, or blood vessel disease in an extremity requiring amputation of a foot or a toe.

Things You Can Do to Minimize Your Risk of Complications

Scientists aren't precisely sure what causes diabetic complications. Yet they do have some clues, and the clinicians at Joslin believe that there are a lot of things people with diabetes can do to prevent or at least minimize their problems.

Prevent Chronic High Blood Sugar

Eye disease and kidney disease, strokes, heart attacks, and amputations may result—at least in part—from damage to blood vessels caused by chronically high blood sugars. While scientists don't know exactly why, they have observed the following:

- Chronically high blood sugars can cause blood vessels in the retina of the eye, for example, to weaken and bulge out, causing leakage and swelling. In more advanced stages of diabetic eye disease, abnormal, numerous fragile blood vessels grow and may ultimately rupture and bleed, interfering with the passage of light in the eye. High blood sugars may also damage the blood vessels in the kidney, impairing its ability to filter waste products and ultimately leading to end-stage kidney disease requiring dialysis or kidney transplantation.
- Chronically high blood sugars seem to accelerate the rate at which gradual thickening of the walls of the blood vessels (atherosclerosis) occurs. So, while atherosclerosis and the resulting poor circulation are common in older people, chronically high blood glucose levels seem to intensify the risk.

- Chronically high blood sugars seem to damage the nerves, causing painful nerve damage or "neuropathy" in the hands, legs, and feet or causing damage to the nerves that control bodily functions such as digestion, bladder control, or penile erection.

The Diabetes Control and Complication Trial (DCCT), a nationwide ten-year study involving over 1,400 patients at twenty-nine sites around the U.S.—including Joslin, looked to see just how important keeping blood sugars under control is in preventing complications. The results of that study, released in June 1993, showed that it is very important. Those individuals who kept their blood sugars as close to normal as possible using intensified diabetes management techniques reduced their risk of diabetic eye disease by 76 percent, their risk of kidney disease by 35–56 percent, and their risk of nerve damage by 60 percent.

Get Regular Checks for Early Signs of Complications

Watching for and acting on early signs of problems is crucial if the full force of these complications is to be prevented. People with diabetes can do many things in this regard.

Joslin and the American Academy of Ophthalmology urge yearly eye exams by a physician who recognizes and treats diabetic eye disease so that eye problems can be identified early. Advances over the past two decades have greatly increased the chances for successfully treating eye problems. Recently the Early Treatment of Diabetic Retinopathy Study (ETDRS), a five-year study funded through the National Institutes of Health at twenty-one centers throughout the U.S., demonstrated that early recognition and prompt treatment of changes in the eye due to diabetes can significantly reduce the risk of vision loss.

Joslin also urges regular testing of the urine for early signs of kidney damage. Many recent and ongoing studies are examining the significance of small amounts of protein in the urine due to diabetic kidney damage—called *microalbuminuria*. Preventive treatments (lower-protein diets and control of high blood pressure) may be initiated when early signs of kidney damage, such as microalbuminuria, are detected.

Joslin also urges people with diabetes to have regular checks of the circulation to their feet and heart. Careful examination of the feet by a physician and podiatrist and watchful self-care by the individuals can help detect foot problems before they become more serious. Regular heart examinations, including electrocardiograms and perhaps an exercise "stress" test, are also recommended. People with diabetes often do not have the "classic" signs of heart problems such as chest pain (angina) and may need to rely on detection of these problems through such testing procedures.

Lower the Fat Levels in Your Blood

Complications like heart disease, strokes, and blood vessel disease leading to amputations seem to occur more frequently if blood levels of cholesterol and bad fats (called *low-density lipoproteins* and *triglycerides*) are high. People with diabetes are more likely to have high cholesterol and fat levels than nondiabetics. Fat and cholesterol levels facilitate plaque buildup in blood vessels. The vessels narrow, slowing circulation. Clot formation also becomes more likely, leading to stroke or vessel blockage.

To minimize your risk of developing these problems, make sure your physician is testing regularly to measure the levels of fat and cholesterol in your blood—cholesterol levels over 200 mg/dl are cause for concern, as are LDL levels above 130 mg/dl and HDL levels below 35 mg/dl. Triglycerides over 200 are also cause for concern. (More on this later.) Following a low-fat diet that your health-care team recommends for you can help to lower the levels of fat and cholesterol in your blood. You may need to take blood-fat-lowering medication if diet alone does not correct the problem, however.

Keep a Check on High Blood Pressure

People with diabetes are more likely to have high blood pressure than nondiabetics. High blood pressure increases the risk of cardiovascular disease—in essence, the increased pressure on the arteries can damage the tissues in your body, including vital organs. High blood pressure also speeds up atherosclerosis.

Again, scientists are not sure why people with diabetes are more prone to high blood pressure. It may be either a cause or an effect of the increased tendency people with diabetes have to develop kidney complications—people with diabetic kidney disease usually have high blood pressure, and people with diabetes and high blood pressure seem to be more likely to develop kidney problems. Being overweight seems to increase the risk for hypertension as well—and many people with Type II diabetes are overweight, so there is probably some connection there, although again researchers are not sure which is the chicken and which is the egg. Be assured that the relationships among diabetes, high blood pressure, and high blood fat levels and their contribution to the development of atherosclerosis are an active area of scientific research.

So, people with diabetes need to be tested regularly for signs of high blood pressure—readings above 140/90 mmHg. Treat high blood pressure, if it develops, with diet to achieve weight loss. Medications may be added if necessary. Recent research has called into question the prevailing wisdom that a low-sodium diet may help lower blood pressure. Some studies suggest that not everyone who has high blood pressure is salt sensitive. Your doctor may recommend a low-salt diet to see if it helps lower your blood pressure. All of the recipes in this book, except a few so noted, are considered low in salt. If cutting back on salt doesn't seem to help, you may be able to incorporate more salt in your diet. Weight loss will almost certainly lower your blood pressure.

Keep an Eye on Protein

Recent research has begun to question whether eating too much protein may be connected to the development of kidney disease. Most Americans eat too much animal protein. Try to make protein the accompaniment and not the focus of your meal. We are encouraging you to reduce your intake to no more than 6 ounces per day and to use more vegetable protein sources, as they are thought to affect your kidney function differently. We encourage you to use the grain options in this cookbook to change the way you plan your meals.

Heredity—What You Can't Control

Recent research at Joslin and elsewhere suggests that genes dictate why some people with diabetes are more likely to develop complications than others. Scientists are trying to pinpoint the genes that control this increased susceptibility. Someday physicians may use some form of gene manipulation to lower the risk of developing certain complications. In the meantime, keeping blood sugars under control, watching for signs of high blood pressure and high fat levels in the blood, and working with your health-care team to identify problems early are the best things you can do to minimize complications.

Risk of Developing Complications If You Have Diabetes

People with diabetes are:

- More than four times as likely to go blind than nondiabetics. Diabetes is the leading cause of new blindness in adults.
- Nineteen times more likely to develop kidney disease. One-third of all cases of end-stage kidney disease develop in people with diabetes.
- Twenty-eight times more likely to have a lower-extremity amputation.
- Two to four times as likely to develop heart disease or have a stroke than nondiabetics.

DIET IN DIABETES MANAGEMENT

Some people believe that diabetics simply have to avoid eating "sugary" foods and take medication to manage their disease. Not so! It's eating the right foods at the right times in coordination with your medication and exercise program—and losing weight if you are overweight—that will result in lower blood sugars and better health.

The recipes in this book were developed with people who have either Type I or Type II diabetes in mind. The recipes are lower in saturated fat, lower in salt, higher in fiber, and lower in sugars than the recipes you may find in many cookbooks. The reasons for these differences, as discussed earlier, are to minimize the increased risks for serious health problems that people with diabetes face. We will talk more about how and why these changes are recommended throughout this book.

The recipes in this book are intended to be used in conjunction with a meal plan or some form of dietary instruction provided by your health-care team. We assume that your physician and others helping you manage your diabetes have mapped out a strategy with you for incorporating food into your diabetes treatment program. It is not enough simply to eat the foods described in this book in whatever quantity and whenever you want. That will do little to manage your blood sugars and will not help you lose weight if that is one of the goals of your diabetes treatment program. So talk to your doctor and your dietitian!

DEVELOPING AN EATING PROGRAM

At Joslin Diabetes Center and in many private diabetes specialists' practices, patients work with a registered dietitian (R.D.) to develop an individualized meal plan to help them balance the food they eat with medication. The meal plan takes into account the patient's likes and dislikes and allows for a great deal of flexibility so the patient has choices each day and at each meal.

Percentage of Calories from Fat

The daily guideline is 30 percent of calories from fat. An entire day's meal plan should not derive more than 30 percent of the calories from fat—*not* 30 percent of the calories per recipe or per meal. The percentage of calories from fat listed in each recipe in this book is a guideline to alert you when a recipe contains a relatively high percentage of fat so that the rest of that meal and that day's meals can compensate for a relatively rich dish. Be sure to check the total calories, because sometimes a recipe is so low-calorie that the fat percentage looks exorbitant when, in fact, it's just a gram or two. The total grams of fat are the crucial information. On a 2,000-calorie daily allowance, for instance, you want to keep your fat grams below 67.

A dietitian can help you achieve the following nutritional goals:

- Eat less fat and substitute vegetable fat for animal fat whenever possible.

  If you have Type II diabetes and are overweight, this is particularly important because it will help you lose weight. Every gram of fat contains nine calories, while every gram of carbohydrate or protein contains four calories. If 30 percent of your diet comes from fat, you are consuming fewer calories than if 50 percent of your diet comes from fat.

  Also, animal fat tends to encourage clogging of the arteries, which can lead to coronary artery disease and stroke. Switching to vegetable fats helps lower the level of bad fats and cholesterol in the bloodstream, reducing the risk of heart and blood vessel problems.
- Eat more complex carbohydrates (breads, grains, beans, vegetables), especially if they are high in fiber.

  Fiber-rich breads, fruits, and vegetables help you feel full without overloading on calories so you can lose weight more easily. Fiber also slows the rise of blood sugar after meals. Eating more fiber (35 to 50 grams) on a daily basis may lead to an overall reduction in blood glucose levels, decreasing your need for insulin or oral medications and helping you prevent long-term complications. Soluble fibers also lower the levels of bad fats in the bloodstream.
- Eat less sugars. Foods that contain sugars like sucrose, corn syrup, and dextrose will cause your blood sugar to rise rapidly.
- Use less salt if you have high blood pressure. While there is conflicting research about the value of reducing the amount of sodium you eat if you have high blood pressure, at Joslin we believe that it is better to be safe now than sorry later. So, if patients have high blood pressure—as many people with diabetes do—we show them how to eat deliciously while consuming less salt to see if that will help bring their blood pressure down.

Keeping the preceding principles in mind, a dietitian can develop a meal plan to balance the amount and the timing of your meals with your insulin (the insulin your body is producing and/or the insulin you are injecting) to keep your blood sugar as close to normal as possible.

MEAL PLANNING IF YOU TAKE INSULIN

Coordinating mealtimes and the amount and type of food eaten is especially important for people taking insulin. Different types of insulin build up to their peak level of activity in the bloodstream over different periods of time. If there isn't enough glucose in your bloodstream for the insulin to interact with during these times because you haven't eaten when and what you are supposed to, your blood sugar may dip too low.

Short-acting insulin begins to act within 30 minutes after injection and is at its peak action—i.e., moving the most glucose into cells—two to four hours after injection. Intermediate-acting insulin, like NPH or Lente, begins acting one to two hours after injection and peaks between six and twelve hours after injection. Long-acting insulin begins to act in 4 to 6 hours and peaks in 18 to 24 hours.

The amount of insulin, the types used alone or in combination, and when you inject them will be determined by your doctor. Whichever injection schedule you and your doctor agree on, you and your dietitian will need to develop a meal plan that works well with it.

Exercise can also affect how quickly and how strongly your insulin works. Exercise lowers blood glucose levels, and unplanned exercise may therefore cause an unexpected low-blood-sugar reaction if adjustments are not made. Such a reaction may cause you to feel light-headed, sweaty, dizzy, and you may even faint. These symptoms can be alleviated only by eating more food. But if you eat more food just to offset that low-blood-sugar reaction, you may find a few hours later that you ate too much, and for this or for other reasons your blood sugar may rebound too high. This will begin a vicious cycle of trying to get your blood sugar back into a normal range. This is one of the reasons that following a meal plan can be so important.

Your eating patterns may have to be altered if you are embarking on a new exercise program, if you are sick, or when you travel across time zones. Ask your dietitian for help in adjusting to these situations.

MEAL PLANNING IF YOU DON'T TAKE INSULIN

If you are not taking insulin, a rigid, exact eating schedule may be less important. Your body is still producing some insulin, which serves as a cushion that prevents you from experiencing extreme lows and highs in blood sugar.

Usually weight loss is the top priority for people with Type II diabetes not on insulin. Using the recipes in this book won't help bring your blood sugars under control if you eat too much food. Eating recipes that are high in fat will also prevent you from losing the weight you need so your body can use the insulin it is producing more effectively.

Therefore, you should also follow an eating program devised with your health-care team, although your goals may be a little different from those of the individual on insulin. Your meal plan may focus on eliminating or greatly reducing high-fat, high-calorie items from your diet and replacing them with lower-fat foods. Its emphasis on high-fiber foods may be driven by your dietitian's desire both to slow blood glucose rise and to show you how you can eat a lot of food, feel more full, and still lose weight because you are consuming fewer overall calories.

If you are on oral agents, be sure to eat fairly regularly and don't skip meals.

Although low blood sugars are less common than in people who are taking insulin, reactions still can occur and are more likely if you eat irregularly.

Again, your eating schedule may require alterations if you start a new exercise program, are sick, or find that you need to go on insulin for a while to get your diabetes under control. Ask your dietitian for help in adjusting to these and other similar situations that may arise.

THE GLYCEMIC INDEX

Recent nutrition research has shown that certain types of foods can cause your blood sugar to rise at more rapid rates than other foods. The food lists used in conjunction with your meal plan—which begin on page 472—are developed with this fact in mind. In developing a meal plan your dietitian will take into account how quickly certain foods or combinations of foods will enter your bloodstream. Your dietitian will develop a meal plan to keep your blood sugars at a fairly constant level.

HOW IS AN EATING PLAN DEVELOPED?

Your dietitian will strive to develop a meal plan that contains a healthy ratio of 50 to 60 percent carbohydrate, 12 to 20 percent protein, and no more than 25 to 30 percent fat.

In doing so the dietitian will take into account the following:

- Your goals: Are you looking to lose weight, gain weight, or maintain your current weight?
- Your medication: Are you taking insulin or oral medications? If so, how much, and when does the action of your medication peak?
- Your medical condition: Do you have any other medical problems? If you have kidney disease, for example, your dietitian may prescribe a low-protein diet.
- Your lifestyle and preferences: Are you a vegetarian? When do you exercise?

A Joslin meal plan, like the sample on the next page, shows the number of servings or choices you have at mealtime. The choices come from the six food groups listed in Appendix 1. Using the food lists, your dietitian will help you consistently distribute the nutrients you need over each day's meals, while at the same time giving you freedom to choose the foods you want to eat from each list.

Each section of the food lists contains measured amounts of foods that are roughly equal in nutritional value and calories. The items on a given list are interchangeable because all contain about equal proportions of carbohydrate, protein, and fat and will affect your blood sugar in a similar way.

INCORPORATING THE RECIPES IN THE BOOK INTO YOUR MEAL PLAN

You can easily incorporate the recipes in this cookbook into your meal plan. At the end of each recipe is listed the number of exchanges in each serving of a particular food when prepared as directed. Simply use those exchanges in your meal plan-

---

Sample Meal Plan

Dietitian: _____

Phone: _____

CHO: _____

PRO: _____

FAT: _____

MEAL

Breakfast	Morning Snack	Lunch	Afternoon Snack	Dinner	Evening Snack
Time_____	Time_____	Time_____	Time_____	Time_____	Time_____
No. of Choices		No. of Choices		No. of Choices	
Milk_____		Milk_____		Milk_____	
Fruit_____		Fruit_____		Fruit_____	
Bread/ Starch_____		Bread/ Starch_____		Bread/ Starch_____	
Meat_____		Meat_____		Meat_____	
Fat_____		Fat_____		Fat_____	

---

ning. So, if you can eat one milk, one vegetable, one fruit, two bread/starch, two meat, and one fat at lunch, then you can eat one portion of the Albuquerque Chicken and Corn Soup (page 60), plus other foods from the food list that equal the one milk, one vegetable, one fruit, and one fat exchanges remaining on your meal plan for lunch.

How else will this book help you eat well with diabetes? At the end of each recipe Joslin's nutritionists have calculated how much fat, sodium, cholesterol, and other nutrients are in the recipes for those of you watching these. The calories per serving of a given recipe are also shown, so if your doctor has instructed you to eat no more than 1,800 calories per day, for example, you know how many calories a particular recipe will contribute to that 1,800-calorie limit. Each of the recipes shows you the percentage of fat per serving to help you stay within the recommended guideline that no more than 30 percent of your daily calories come from fat. In the section on fat and cholesterol beginning on page 447, we give you some additional guidelines for using this information in meal planning.

JOSLIN EXCHANGES

This cookbook uses the Joslin Diabetes Center Food Lists and Exchanges, located in Appendix 1, which are similar in most ways to those provided by the American Diabetes Association (ADA). Dr. Joslin first developed food lists to help people with diabetes in the 1930s. In 1954 the ADA also developed food lists. For many years these food lists were quite different, each organization believing that its lists more accurately reflected the effects food has on blood sugars.

Over the years Joslin and ADA exchanges have become similar. In most instances what Joslin calls an exchange is the same as for the ADA. The major differences are that the ADA does not have a nonfat meat category and Joslin's combination foods are different. Joslin's portion sizes in the food lists are slightly different, and Joslin counts fractions of nutrients in making calculations. Joslin lists tofu as a low-fat meat; the ADA has it listed as a medium-fat meat. Joslin counts peanut butter as a medium-fat meat plus a fat, where the ADA has it listed as a high-fat meat. Joslin lists pork tenderloin as a low-fat meat. On the ADA list it is considered a medium-fat meat.

If you have been given a meal plan with exchanges based on the ADA's exchanges, you can, with confidence, use the exchanges listed at the end of these recipes in the same way as you would use ADA exchanges. If you have questions, just ask your dietitian.

How This Book Is Organized

The introduction to *The Joslin Diabetes Gourmet Cookbook* contains essential information on the management of diabetes and its relation to diet. After the recipe section, beginning on page 3 which is arranged seasonally, spring to winter, you'll find important nutritional information on fiber, sugar and sugar substitutes, fat and cholesterol, salt, and alcohol, as well as valuable information on fresh herbs, savvy shopping, kitchen basics, and healthy cooking techniques. Appendix 1 provides the Joslin Diabetes Center Exchange List.

NUTRITION INFORMATION

Our recipes contain nutrition information calculated by Nutrition Services at Joslin Diabetes Center, Boston, using the most current data available from N-Squared Computing (Version 7.0), the United States Department of Agriculture, and direct from the manufacturer when necessary. Nutrition information is given for calories; grams of protein, carbohydrate, fat (including percent of calories from fat), and fiber; and milligrams of cholesterol, sodium, and potassium.

If an ingredient is listed with an alternative, the figures are calculated using the first choice. Recipes using stock are based on the stock recipes given in this book. To obtain similar sodium counts, use a salt-free broth, canned or homemade.

THE JOSLIN DIABETES
GOURMET COOKBOOK

APPETIZERS AND DRINKS

Unless we are entertaining guests, we seldom bother with appetizers or hors d'oeuvres beyond a few crudités (raw or barely cooked vegetables) to keep our appetite under control as we prepare the meal. If we're entertaining, though, we like to offer a variety of drinks with tidbits to nibble on as everyone arrives. Sometimes we skip the appetizers and serve something warm and enticing, like crêpes, as a first course at the table.

Most of these appetizers are also appropriate as a snack or light meal. The majority are simple to prepare; all are easy on your meal plan.

Crudités and Dips

Crudités are standard fare at our homes for predinner cocktail time. Light and healthful, they offer even those on the strictest of diets a chance to munch without guilt.

We change our crudités with the seasons. A spring arrangement might include asparagus, sugar snap peas, and tiny young string beans, all of which benefit from a 30-second dip in boiling water. In summer there's a rainbow of bell peppers (ranging from orange to red to deep purple), bright red and yellow cherry tomatoes, fennel, and summer squashes in all shapes and colors. Winter offerings might include baby turnips, daikon radish, cauliflower, broccoli, bok choy, and mushrooms.

Other favorite crudités include cucumbers (particularly the English, or hothouse, variety), zucchini, celery, carrots, jícama (a southwestern root vegetable), red radishes, Belgian endive leaves, scallions (green onions), snow peas, and cooked artichoke leaves.

Choose the best vegetables available at the produce market, using a mixture of colors and tastes. Cut the larger vegetables into slices or strips; separate leaves. Arrange the vegetables in a pretty basket, bunching those of one kind together. Add sprigs of fresh herbs as a garnish to make an appealing still life.

Sauces or dips look irresistible served in hollowed-out vegetables. For example, a purple or Savoy cabbage, a large white pattypan squash, a giant bell pepper, an acorn or butternut squash, a giant zucchini, a large head of radicchio, or a small pumpkin can be hollowed out to hold the dip.

Note: most dips taste better when made at least an hour ahead so their full flavor can develop.

Chili and Lime

Crudités taste so good that we often opt for just a dusting of seasoning—in this case a dip into fresh lime juice and a dusting of chili salt. Strips of jícama, turnip, daikon radish, or red and yellow bell peppers are particularly good served this way.

½ cup (118 ml) fresh lime juice
2 tablespoons (30 ml) chili powder
1 teaspoon (5 ml) salt

Pour lime juice into a small bowl. Combine chili powder and salt in another small bowl. To eat, dip crudités into the lime juice, then into the chili powder mixture.

MAKES 6 SERVINGS

Per serving: calories, 14 ◆ protein, trace ◆ carbohydrate, 3 g ◆ fat, trace (calories from fat, 22%) ◆ dietary fiber, 1 g ◆ cholesterol, 0 mg ◆ sodium, 382 mg ◆ potassium, 72 mg
Joslin Exchanges: free

Lemon Pepper Variation

Dip the crudités into ½ cup (118 ml) lemon juice and then a mixture of 1 teaspoon (5 ml) salt and 1 tablespoon (15 ml) coarsely ground pepper.

SERVES 6

Per serving: calories, 8 ◆ protein, trace ◆ carbohydrate, 2 g ◆ fat, trace (calories from fat, 3%) ◆ dietary fiber, trace ◆ cholesterol, 0 mg ◆ sodium, 356 mg ◆ potassium, 38 mg
Joslin Exchanges: free

Curry Dip

5 scallions, white part and 1 inch (2.5 cm) green, thinly sliced
olive oil cooking spray
1 tablespoon (15 ml) curry powder

1 cup (236 ml) plain nonfat yogurt
1 tablespoon (15 ml) finely chopped golden raisins

In a skillet sprayed with cooking spray, sauté scallions over low heat until they wilt. Add curry powder; blend well. Remove skillet from heat. Stir curried scallion mixture into yogurt. Add raisins. Chill and serve.

MAKES ABOUT 1 CUP (236 ML)

Per 2-tablespoon (30 ml) serving: calories, 22 ◆ protein, 2 g ◆ carbohydrate, 4 g ◆ fat, trace (calories from fat, less than 1%) ◆ dietary fiber, trace ◆ cholesterol, 1 mg ◆ sodium, 22 mg ◆ potassium, 101 mg
Joslin Exchanges: free

Fresh Herb Dip

½ cup (118 ml) plain nonfat yogurt
½ cup (118 ml) low-fat (1%)
  cottage cheese
1 garlic clove, minced
2 tablespoons (30 ml) prepared
  horseradish
¼ cup (59 ml) finely chopped fresh
  flat-leaf parsley
1 tablespoon (15 ml) chopped
  fresh dill or to taste
freshly ground pepper to taste

In a food processor or blender, combine yogurt and cottage cheese until smooth. Stir in garlic, horseradish, parsley, and dill. Add a generous grinding of pepper. Chill before serving.

MAKES ABOUT 1½ CUPS (354 ML)

Per 2-tablespoon (30 ml) serving: calories, 14 ◆ protein, 2 g ◆ carbohydrate, 1 g ◆ fat, trace (calories from fat, less than 1%) ◆ dietary fiber, trace ◆ cholesterol, trace ◆ sodium, 74 mg ◆ potassium, 50 mg
Joslin Exchanges: free

Fresh Vegetable Dip

1 cup (236 ml) low-fat (1%)
  cottage cheese
¼ cup (59 ml) finely chopped
  scallion, white part and 1 inch
  (2.5 cm) green
¼ cup (59 ml) finely minced red
  bell pepper
¼ cup (59 ml) finely minced green
  bell pepper
½ cup (118 ml) finely minced fresh
  mushrooms
1 garlic clove, minced
1 small fresh jalapeño chili, seeded
  and minced (optional)
freshly ground pepper to taste
pinch of dry mustard

In a food processor or blender, process cottage cheese until smooth. Stir in vegetables, garlic, jalapeño, pepper, and mustard. Chill before serving.

MAKES ABOUT 2½ CUPS (590 ML)

Per 2-tablespoon (30 ml) serving: calories, 11 ◆ protein, 2 g ◆ carbohydrate, 1 g ◆ fat, trace (calories from fat, less than 1%) ◆ dietary fiber, trace ◆ cholesterol, 1 mg ◆ sodium, 47 mg ◆ potassium, 27 mg
Joslin Exchanges: free

Ginger Tofu Dip

1 pound (450 g) soft tofu, drained
3 scallions, white part only, chopped
1 tablespoon (15 ml) minced fresh ginger
2 garlic cloves, minced
2 tablespoons (30 ml) low-sodium soy sauce
½ teaspoon (2.5 ml) dark sesame oil

In a food processor or blender, combine all ingredients. Process until smooth. Cover and chill for 1 hour before serving.

MAKES ABOUT 1¾ CUPS (413 ML)

Per 2-tablespoon (30 ml) serving: calories, 34 ◆ protein, 3 g ◆ carbohydrate, 1 g ◆ fat, 2 g (calories from fat, 53%) ◆ dietary fiber, trace ◆ cholesterol, 0 mg ◆ sodium, 82 mg ◆ potassium, 45 mg
Joslin Exchanges: free

Asian Dip

1 cup (236 ml) yogurt cheese (page 11)
1/4 pound (115 g) soft tofu
1 tablespoon (15 ml) low-sodium soy sauce
1 tablespoon (15 ml) chopped fresh ginger
2 garlic cloves, minced

1 4-inch (10 cm) length of lemongrass, white part only, chopped, or 2 teaspoons (10 ml) grated lemon zest
1 8-ounce (225 g) can water chestnuts, drained and chopped
chopped fresh flat-leaf parsley for garnish

Place all ingredients except water chestnuts and parsley in a food processor or blender. Process until smooth. Transfer to a small bowl; stir in water chestnuts. Cover and refrigerate for several hours to allow flavors to blend. When ready to serve, garnish with chopped parsley.

MAKES ABOUT 2 CUPS (472 ML)

Per 2-tablespoon (30 ml) serving: calories, 22 ◆ protein, 2 g ◆ carbohydrate, 3 g ◆ fat, trace (calories from fat, less than 1%) ◆ dietary fiber, trace ◆ cholesterol, trace ◆ sodium, 48 mg ◆ potassium, 59 mg
Joslin Exchanges: free

Salsa Fresca

2 large fresh tomatoes, about 1 pound (450 g), diced
1 small onion, about 2 ounces (60 g), diced
1/3 cup (78 ml) chopped fresh cilantro (fresh coriander)
1 tablespoon (15 ml) chopped fresh oregano or 1 teaspoon (5 ml) crushed dried

2 garlic cloves, minced
1 tablespoon (15 ml) seeded and minced fresh jalapeño chili
2 tablespoons (30 ml) fresh lime juice
1/8 teaspoon (.6 ml) salt (optional)

In a small bowl, combine all ingredients. If made ahead, cover and refrigerate for up to 2 days.

MAKES ABOUT 2 CUPS (472 ML)

Per 2-tablespoon (30 ml) serving: calories, 10 ◆ protein, trace ◆ carbohydrate, 2 g ◆ fat, trace (calories from fat, less than 1%) ◆ dietary fiber, 1 g ◆ cholesterol, 0 dietary fiber, 1 g ◆ cholesterol, 0 mg ◆ sodium, 20 mg ◆ potassium, 87 mg Joslin Exchanges: free

Pico de Gallo

Of the many versions of *pico de gallo*, the most typical contain jícama, the sweet, crunchy root vegetable. The name (literally "rooster's beak") refers to the style of eating the chunks of relish with the fingers, the way a rooster pecks corn. Serve with Flour Tortilla Chips (page 371).

In larger portions this could be served as a salad.

1 cup (236 ml) peeled and diced
   jícama
½ green bell pepper, about 3
   ounces, seeded and minced
¼ cup (59 ml) minced onion
½ cup (118 ml) diced cucumber,
   peeled and seeds removed

1 teaspoon (5 ml) olive oil
1 tablespoon (15 ml) fresh lime
   juice
¼ teaspoon (1.25 ml) crushed dried
   oregano leaves
freshly ground pepper to taste

Combine vegetables. Whisk together oil, lime juice, oregano, and pepper. Pour over vegetables; toss to coat evenly.

MAKES ABOUT 1 CUP (236 ML)

Per 2-tablespoon (30 ml) serving: calories, 29 ◆ protein, 1 g ◆ carbohydrate, 4 g ◆ fat, 1 g (calories from fat, 31%) ◆ dietary fiber, trace ◆ cholesterol, 0 mg ◆ sodium, 2 mg ◆ potassium, 63 mg Joslin Exchanges: free

---

MEXICAN SUPPER

◆

Pico de Gallo (page 9) with Flour Tortilla Chips (page 371)

Halibut Grilled in Corn Husks with Salsa (page 140)

Grilled Corn on the Cob (page 306)

Cantaloupe Graníta (page 435)

Per serving: 470 calories (11% fat)
Joslin Exchanges: 4 low-fat meat, 2 bread/starch, 1 vegetable, 1 fruit

Skinny Guacamole

Like most Americans, we love the buttery texture and addictive taste of avocados. Since they're high in fat, we've slimmed down this popular dip with plain nonfat yogurt cheese so that we can enjoy it also—in moderation.

Serve the guacamole piled on cactus leaves (if they're available) and offer Flour Tortilla Chips (page 371) for dipping.

1 ripe avocado, halved and pitted
1 tablespoon (15 ml) fresh lime juice
1 medium-size tomato, about 4 ounces (115 g), peeled, seeded, and chopped
2 tablespoons (30 ml) chopped red onion

2 tablespoons (30 ml) chopped fresh cilantro (fresh coriander)
1 small fresh jalapeño chili, seeded and minced
½ cup (118 ml) yogurt cheese (page 11)
¼ teaspoon (1.25 ml) salt (optional)
freshly ground pepper to taste

Using a spoon, scoop avocado pulp into a bowl. Add lime juice. With a fork, coarsely mash avocado. Stir in tomato, onion, cilantro, jalapeño, and yogurt cheese. Season with salt and pepper. Serve within an hour at room temperature.

MAKES ABOUT 2 CUPS (472 ML)

Per 2-tablespoon (30 ml) serving: calories, 39 ◆ protein, 1 g ◆ carbohydrate, 2 g ◆ fat, 3 g (calories from fat, 69%) ◆ dietary fiber, trace ◆ cholesterol, 0 mg ◆ sodium, 40 mg ◆ potassium, 94 mg Joslin Exchanges: 1 fat

Yogurt Cheese

American cooks are just beginning to discover the versatility of yogurt. This ancient recipe from the Mediterranean produces a creamy white cheese that can be low in fat or nonfat, depending on the yogurt you use. Use yogurt cheese in recipes that call for cream cheese or sour cream. Traditionally the yogurt is drained in a cheesecloth bag or a colander lined with a double layer of cheesecloth, but a coffee filter is easier to use.

coffee filter or double thickness of cheesecloth

2 cups (472 ml) plain low-fat or nonfat yogurt

Line a sieve with a coffee filter or cheesecloth; suspend sieve over a deep bowl. Place yogurt in filter and refrigerate for several hours or overnight to allow whey to drip out. When the yogurt has thickened to the texture of a soft cream cheese, scrape the yogurt away from the filter, transferring it to a resealable plastic container. Discard liquid in bowl. Refrigerate for up to 1 week, discarding any accumulated liquid before using.

MAKES ABOUT 1 CUP (236 ML)

Per 1-tablespoon (15 ml) serving (made with low-fat yogurt): calories, 13 ◆ protein, 2 g ◆ carbohydrate, 1 g ◆ fat, trace (calories from fat, less than 1%) ◆ dietary fiber, 0 g ◆ cholesterol, 0 mg ◆ sodium, 0 mg ◆ potassium, 0 mg Joslin Exchanges: free

Per 1-tablespoon (15 ml) serving (made with nonfat yogurt): calories, 10 ◆ protein, 2 g ◆ carbohydrate, 1 g ◆ fat, 0 g (calories from fat, 0%) ◆ dietary fiber, 0 g ◆ cholesterol, 0 mg ◆ sodium, 0 mg ◆ potassium, 0 mg Joslin Exchanges: free

Belgian Endive with Goat Cheese and Figs

Extravagant looking but surprisingly low in calories, these hors d'oeuvres are a snap to make. Fresh figs are available from June through October. At other times of the year, use thin strips of roasted red pepper (page 100) or sun-dried tomatoes (packed dry without oil), plumping them first in hot water according to the package directions.

2 large or 3 small heads of Belgian endive, about 6 ounces (180 g)
5 ounces (140 g) fresh low-fat goat cheese
2 teaspoons (10 ml) skim milk
½ teaspoon (2.5 ml) freshly ground pepper
½ teaspoon (2.5 ml) fresh lemon juice
½ teaspoon (2.5 ml) grated lemon zest
6 fresh ripe green figs, about ½ pound (225 g), quartered, or thin strips of roasted red pepper or plumped sun-dried tomatoes (not packed in oil)
fresh thyme leaves for garnish

Cut 24 outer leaves from endive heads; reserve remainder for salads. Rinse; wrap in paper towels and chill for at least 1 hour.

With a mixer, beat together goat cheese and milk until smooth. Stir in pepper, lemon juice, and lemon zest. Spread about 2 teaspoons (10 ml) cheese mixture onto the bottom of each endive leaf using a pastry bag, small spoon, or spatula. Garnish each with a quarter of fresh fig, strip of roasted pepper, or strip of sun-dried tomato. Sprinkle with fresh thyme leaves. Cover and chill for up to 3 hours before serving.

MAKES 6 SERVINGS

Per 4-piece serving: calories, 84 ◆ protein, 3 g ◆ carbohydrate, 12 g ◆ fat, 4 g (calories from fat, 42%) ◆ dietary fiber, 1 g ◆ cholesterol, 17 mg ◆ sodium, 133 mg ◆ potassium, 211 mg

Joslin Exchanges: 2 vegetable, 1 fat (with figs), *or* 1 vegetable, 1 fat (with roasted peppers or plumped sun-dried tomatoes)

Pickled Vegetables

Pickled vegetables, available in specialty food stores, make delicious calorie-wise nibbling. They're simple to make in small quantities at home, at a fraction of the cost—and without sugar or salt. Pack the raw or crisp cooked vegetables into a jar with some herbs, spices, and a hot vinegar solution; then refrigerate. Your pickled vegetables are ready to eat that day and will keep for up to 1 week. Arrange the vegetables in a shallow rimmed plate or serving bowl—a great finger food.

Pickled Carrots

1 pound (450 g) baby carrots, peeled

½ teaspoon (2.5 ml) dried dill weed
1 teaspoon (5 ml) mustard seed

Pickling Solution

¾ cup (177 ml) cider vinegar
½ cup (118 ml) water

½ teaspoon (2.5 ml) pickling spices
12 peppercorns

Trim carrots so they will fit vertically ¾ inch (2 cm) below the rim of a wide-mouth pint glass jar. In a large skillet, cook carrots in water to cover until crisp-tender, about 5 minutes. Drain. Loosely pack carrots vertically into a clean wide-mouth pint glass jar along with dill weed and mustard seed. In a small saucepan, combine ingredients for pickling solution. Bring to a boil. Pour hot liquid over carrots to cover, reserving any extra liquid. Seal with lid and refrigerate. If needed, add reserved liquid after carrots are chilled to keep carrots covered with liquid. Use within 1 week.

MAKES 1 PINT (472 ML); 10 SERVINGS

Per serving: calories, 28 ◆ protein, 1 g ◆ carbohydrate, 6 g ◆ fat, trace (calories from fat, less than 1%) ◆ dietary fiber, 1 g ◆ cholesterol, 0 mg ◆ sodium, 16 mg ◆ potassium, 169 mg Joslin Exchanges: free

Pickled Asparagus

Follow the recipe, using about 1½ pounds (675 g) pencil-thin asparagus, tough ends trimmed off, in place of the carrots. Cook in boiling water until barely tender, about 5 minutes. Drain, immerse in ice water, then drain again. Pack asparagus vertically into jar along with 4 fresh tarragon sprigs in place of the dill and mustard seed. Fill jar with hot pickling solution. Refrigerate; use within 1 week.

MAKES 1 PINT (472 ML); 10 SERVINGS

Per serving: calories, 24 ◆ protein, 2 g ◆ carbohydrate, 4 g ◆ fat, trace (calories from fat, less than 1%) ◆ dietary fiber, 1 g ◆ cholesterol, 0 mg ◆ sodium, 6 mg ◆ potassium, 114 mg
Joslin Exchanges: free

Pickled Green Beans

Follow the recipe, using about ¾ pound (340 g) small green beans, ends trimmed, in place of carrots. Cook beans in boiling water until barely tender, about 3 minutes. Drain, immerse in ice water, then drain again. Pack beans in jar vertically along with 2 small dried red chili peppers and 1 teaspoon (5 ml) cumin seed *or* 1 teaspoon (5 ml) dried dill weed instead of the dill and mustard seed. Fill jar with hot pickling solution. Refrigerate; use within 1 week.

MAKES 1 PINT (472 ML); 10 SERVINGS

Per serving: calories, 13 ◆ protein, 1 g ◆ carbohydrate, 4 g ◆ fat, trace (calories from fat, less than 1%) ◆ dietary fiber, 1 g ◆ cholesterol, 0 mg ◆ sodium, 2 mg ◆ potassium, 130 mg
Joslin Exchanges: free

Pickled Okra

Follow the recipe, using about ¾ pound (340 g) fresh okra, about 3 inches (8 cm) long, in place of carrots. Trim stems, taking care not to cut into the okra itself. Place 1 peeled garlic clove, 1 teaspoon (5 ml) dill seed, 1 teaspoon (5 ml) celery seed, ¼ teaspoon (1.25 ml) mustard seed, and 1 small dried hot red chili in jar in place of dill and mustard. Pack okra vertically in jar. Fill jar with hot pickling solution. Refrigerate; use within 1 week.

MAKES 1 PINT (472 ML); 10 SERVINGS

> **Per serving:** calories, 13 ◆ protein, 1 g ◆ carbohydrate, 4 g ◆ fat, trace (calories from fat, less than 1%) ◆ dietary fiber, trace ◆ cholesterol, 0 mg ◆ sodium, 12 mg ◆ potassium, 136 mg
> Joslin Exchanges: free

Vegetarian Chopped Liver

We used to make chopped liver, complete with rendered chicken fat and lots of hard-cooked eggs. Since it's very high in saturated fat and calories, it's no longer allowed on our diet. Here's a mock chopped liver you'll be able to share with friends.

1 medium-size eggplant, about ¾ pound (340 g)
olive oil cooking spray
2 medium-size onions, about ½ pound (225 g), chopped
1 garlic clove, minced
2 hard-cooked large egg whites
½ teaspoon (2.5 ml) salt (optional)
freshly ground pepper to taste
white wine vinegar to taste

Preheat broiler. Peel and slice eggplant ½ inch (1.5 cm) thick. Place eggplant on a nonstick baking sheet and broil on both sides until tender, about 10 minutes on each side. Coarsely chop; set aside.

Lightly spray a nonstick sauté pan with cooking spray. Add onions and garlic; sauté over medium-low heat until onions are soft and browned, about 6 minutes. Place onion mixture, chopped eggplant, and egg whites in a food processor or blender. Process until smooth. Add salt and pepper. Add white wine vinegar to taste, starting with about 1 teaspoon (5 ml). Refrigerate. Let stand at room temperature for 30 minutes before serving. Serve with melba toast or toast points.

MAKES ABOUT 2 CUPS (472 ML)

> **Per ¼-cup serving:** calories, 16 ◆ protein, 1 g ◆ carbohydrate, 4 g ◆ fat, trace (calories from fat, 4%) ◆ dietary fiber, trace ◆ cholesterol, 0 mg ◆ sodium, 74 mg ◆ potassium, 88 mg
> Joslin Exchanges: free

Mediterranean Stuffed Bread

This slimmed-down version of *pan bagna*, a popular sandwich that's sold from little stands along the beaches of the French Riviera, makes a terrific hors d'oeuvre or addition to a summer picnic.

Literally a salad in a loaf of bread, it must be made ahead and chilled so that the flavors mingle. Be sure to buy the best French bread available. If you're on a low-sodium diet, leave out the capers.

1 large baguette, about 1 pound (450 g)

4 medium-size tomatoes, about 1¼ pounds (570 g), peeled and chopped

4 scallions, white part and 1 inch (2.5 cm) green, finely chopped

1 green bell pepper, about 6 ounces (180 g), seeded and chopped

1 tablespoon (15 ml) drained capers (optional)

2 tablespoons (30 ml) finely chopped fresh flat-leaf parsley

1 tablespoon (15 ml) chopped fresh mint or 1 teaspoon (5 ml) crushed dried

1 teaspoon (5 ml) fresh thyme leaves or ¼ teaspoon (1.25 ml) crushed dried

freshly ground pepper to taste

juice of 1 lemon

1 teaspoon (5 ml) Dijon mustard

1 tablespoon (15 ml) olive oil

1 small garlic clove, minced

Cut the baguette in half lengthwise and scoop out part of the bread to create a shell. Break the insides into small pieces. Combine with tomatoes, scallions, green pepper, and capers.

In a small bowl, whisk together parsley, mint, thyme, pepper, lemon juice, mustard, olive oil, and garlic. Pour over vegetable mixture; toss. Spoon the mixture into bottom half of bread, packing down firmly. Top with other bread half. Press bread halves together and wrap tightly in plastic wrap or aluminum foil. Chill for several hours or overnight. To serve, slice into 6 equal portions for a sandwich or into 12 equal portions for an hors d'oeuvre.

MAKES 6 TO 12 SERVINGS

Per sandwich serving:
calories, 266 ◆ protein, 9 g ◆ carbohydrate, 46 g ◆ fat, 6 g (calories from fat, 20%) ◆ dietary fiber, 1 g ◆ cholesterol, 0 mg ◆ sodium, 641 mg ◆ potassium, 329 mg Joslin Exchanges: 3 bread/starch, ½ fat

FALL TAIL-GATE PICNIC

◆

*Country Pâté (page 36) with Water Biscuits
and Melba Toast*

Mediterranean Stuffed Bread (page 16)

Mixed Pickled Vegetables (page 13)

Basket of Fresh Apples, Pears, and Grapes

Per serving: 517 calories (21% fat)
Joslin Exchanges: 2 low-fat meat, 4 bread/starch, 1 fruit, ½ fat

Crostini

Crostini are thin slices of toasted peasant bread. Sometimes they are piled high with intensely flavored vegetable toppings. Hardly any work for the cook, they make a terrific hors d'oeuvre, snack, or light lunch. Here we've added garlic to the crostini and your choice of three toppings.

1 narrow loaf of Italian or French bread, about 1 pound (450 g)	**2 garlic cloves, peeled and cut in half**

Preheat oven to 350° F (180° C) (or use the toasting element of a toaster oven).

Slice the bread into 20 ¼-inch-thick (.75 cm) slices. Lay on a baking sheet and toast until bread begins to color, 10 to 15 minutes, turning once. Remove from oven and rub while still hot with a cut clove of garlic. Set aside. Store in an airtight container at room temperature for up to 2 days.

MAKES 20 PIECES

Per piece: calories, 65 ◆ protein, 2 g ◆ carbohydrate, 13 g ◆ fat, trace (calories from fat, 0%) ◆ dietary fiber, trace ◆ cholesterol, 0 mg ◆ sodium, 115 mg ◆ potassium, 18 mg
Joslin Exchanges: 1 bread/starch

Crostini with Smoky Eggplant

1 large eggplant, about 1 pound (450 g)
2 plum tomatoes, about ½ pound (225 g), peeled, seeded, and chopped
½ pound (225 g) fresh mushrooms, chopped
½ cup (118 ml) onion chopped
2 garlic cloves, minced
juice and grated zest of ½ lemon
2 tablespoons (30 ml) olive oil
2 tablespoons (30 ml) chopped fresh flat-leaf parsley
½ teaspoon (2.5 ml) ground cumin
freshly ground pepper to taste
20 *crostini* (preceding recipe)

Preheat broiler. Prick skin of eggplant and place on a baking sheet. Broil about 4 inches (10 cm) from source of heat, turning every 5 minutes, until eggplant is charred and soft. Remove from heat and allow to cool. Remove skin; chop pulp finely and combine with remaining ingredients except *crostini*. Cover and refrigerate for several hours. To serve, bring to room temperature. Top *crostini* with eggplant mixture.

MAKES 10 SERVINGS

Per 2-piece serving: calories, 178 ◆ protein, 6 g ◆ carbohydrate, 32 g ◆ fat, 3 g (calories from fat, 15%) ◆ dietary fiber, 1 g ◆ cholesterol, 0 mg ◆ sodium, 234 mg ◆ potassium, 276 mg Joslin Exchanges: 2 bread/starch, 1 vegetable

Crostini with Roasted Peppers

2 tablespoons (30 ml) white wine vinegar
2 tablespoons (30 ml) olive oil
2 scallions, white part only, thinly sliced
2 tablespoons (30 ml) chopped fresh herbs (basil, thyme, or tarragon) or 2 teaspoons (10 ml) crushed dried
2 tablespoons (30 ml) chopped fresh flat-leaf parsley
freshly ground pepper to taste
2 tablespoons (30 ml) dried currants
2 roasted red bell peppers (page 100), chopped
2 roasted yellow bell peppers (page 100), chopped
20 *crostini* (page 17)

In a bowl, whisk together vinegar, olive oil, scallions, herbs, and parsley. Add pepper and currants. Toss peppers in dressing and refrigerate for several hours to marinate.

To serve, bring to room temperature. Top *crostini* with pepper mixture.

MAKES 10 SERVINGS

> **Per 2-piece serving:** calories, 184 ◆ protein, 6 g ◆ carbohydrate, 34 g ◆ fat, 3 g (calories from fat, 14%) ◆ dietary fiber, 1 g ◆
>
> cholesterol, 0 mg ◆ sodium, 232 mg ◆ potassium 128 mg
> Joslin Exchanges: 2 bread/starch

Crostini with Spicy Hummus

1 16-ounce (450 g) can chick-peas, drained and liquid reserved
juice of 2 lemons
3 tablespoons (45 ml) tahini*
2 garlic cloves, crushed
1 teaspoon (5 ml) ground cumin

2 tablespoons (30 ml) olive oil
20 *crostini* (page 17)
paprika for garnish
finely chopped fresh parsley for garnish

To make hummus, process the chick-peas, lemon juice, tahini, garlic, cumin, and olive oil in a food processor or blender, adding enough of the reserved liquid to obtain a soft, creamy consistency. Transfer to a bowl, cover, and chill until ready to serve.

To serve, spread hummus on *crostini*. Dust with paprika and garnish with a little parsley.

MAKES 20 SERVINGS

> **Per 1-piece serving:** calories, 133 ◆ protein, 5 g ◆ carbohydrate, 21 g ◆ fat, 3 g (calories from fat, 20%) ◆ dietary fiber, trace ◆ cholesterol
>
> 0 mg ◆ sodium, 232 mg ◆ potassium, 125 mg
> Joslin Exchanges: 2 bread/starch

* Tahini is a thick paste made of ground sesame seeds used in Middle Eastern cooking. It's available in health food stores and the ethnic section of some supermarkets.

DIM SUM

The literal Chinese translation of dim sum is "light to the heart." Dim sum is just that, offering delicious hors d'oeuvre or light meal options for people with diabetes.

Here are some slimmed-down versions of dim sum dumplings, using purchased wonton wrappers, available in the produce section of most supermarkets, plus a variety of flavorful dipping sauces. Working with wonton wrappers is a snap—just fill a few at a time, keeping the rest of the wrappers under a damp paper towel or plastic wrap so that they don't dry out.

Turkey Dim Sum

Be sure the ground turkey doesn't include turkey skin. Check the label or purchase a turkey breast and have your butcher grind it fresh after removing the skin.

6 dried tree ear or other Asian dried mushrooms
30 wonton wrappers
1 pound (450 g) freshly ground turkey
1/3 cup (78 ml) chopped scallion, white part and 1 inch (2.5 cm) green
1 tablespoon (15 ml) minced fresh cilantro (fresh coriander) or fresh flat-leaf parsley

1 tablespoon (15 ml) minced fresh ginger
1/4 cup (59 ml) minced canned water chestnuts
1/4 cup (59 ml) minced canned bamboo shoots
2 tablespoons (30 ml) low-sodium soy sauce
1 large egg white
1 tablespoon (15 ml) cornstarch

Soak dried mushrooms in warm water to cover for 30 minutes. Drain and mince. Discard soaking liquid.

Meanwhile, using kitchen shears or a sharp knife, trim off corners of each wonton skin to form a circle. In a large bowl, combine mushrooms, turkey, scallions, cilantro, ginger, water chestnuts, bamboo shoots, soy sauce, egg white, and cornstarch.

Place 1 tablespoon (15 ml) of the filling in center of each wonton wrapper. Gather up the sides around the filling, making small pleats around the dumpling to shape the skin to the filling, leaving the top open with the filling showing. Gently squeeze the skin against the filling and flatten the bottom.

Place the dumplings on a damp cloth or piece of parchment paper in the bottom of a Chinese bamboo steamer placed over a wok (or lay a piece of parchment paper over a wire rack set in a large skillet). Cover and steam over boiling water for 20 minutes.

MAKES 30 DUMPLINGS

Per 2-dumpling serving:
calories, 79 ◆ protein, 5 g ◆ carbohydrate, 10 g ◆ fat, 2 g (calories from fat, 22%) ◆ dietary fiber, trace ◆ cholesterol, 8 mg ◆ sodium, 159 mg ◆ potassium, 69 mg
Joslin Exchanges: 1 bread/starch

Shrimp and Scallop Dim Sum

¾ pound (340 g) medium-size shrimp, peeled and deveined
¾ pound (340 g) scallops
⅓ cup (78 ml) minced canned bamboo shoots
⅓ cup (78 ml) minced canned water chestnuts
1 tablespoon (15 ml) minced fresh ginger

⅛ teaspoon (.6 ml) five-spice powder
¼ teaspoon (1.25 ml) hot red pepper flakes
1 teaspoon (5 ml) minced fresh cilantro (fresh coriander) or fresh flat-leaf parsley
30 wonton wrappers

Mince shrimp and scallops. Combine with remaining ingredients except wrappers.

With your fingers, lightly dampen the edge of a wonton wrapper. Place 1 tablespoon (15 ml) filling along the center bottom. Roll once; turn in sides of the wrapper. Continue rolling to form a tight package. Repeat, filling remaining wonton wrappers.

Place dumplings, seam side down, on a damp cloth or piece of parchment paper in the bottom of a Chinese bamboo steamer placed over a wok (or lay a piece of parchment paper over a wire rack set in a large skillet). Cover and steam over boiling water for 15 minutes.

MAKES 30 DUMPLINGS

Per 2-dumpling serving:
calories, 78 ◆ protein, 8 g ◆ carbohydrate, 10 g ◆ fat, 1 g (calories from fat, 11%) ◆ dietary fiber, trace ◆ cholesterol, 32 mg ◆ sodium, 124 mg ◆ potassium, 126 mg
Joslin Exchanges: 1 bread/starch, 1 low-fat meat

Shiitake Mushroom Dim Sum

2 cups (472 ml) minced fresh shiitake mushrooms

2 scallions, white part and 1 inch (2.5 cm) green, minced

1 cup (236 ml) minced Chinese cabbage

1½ tablespoons (22.5 ml) minced fresh ginger

2 drops of dark sesame oil

⅛ teaspoon (.6 ml) five-spice powder

¼ teaspoon (1.25 ml) hot red pepper flakes

1 tablespoon (15 ml) minced fresh cilantro (fresh coriander) or fresh flat-leaf parsley

1 tablespoon (15 ml) low-sodium soy sauce

30 wonton wrappers

Combine all ingredients except wrappers. Stir-fry in a well-seasoned wok or non-stick skillet over high heat until all liquid is evaporated.

Using kitchen shears or a sharp knife, trim off corners of each wonton skin to form a circle. Moisten the edges of 1 wrapper with water. Place 1 tablespoon (15 ml) filling on half of the circle, leaving a ¼-inch (.75 cm) border. Fold the other half of the wrapper over and seal the edges. Make pleats around the edge by folding over tiny sections of the sealed edge to form a border. Repeat, filling remaining wonton wrappers.

Place the dumplings on a damp cloth or piece of parchment paper in the bottom of a Chinese bamboo steamer placed over a wok (or lay a piece of parchment paper over a wire rack set into a large skillet). Cover and steam over boiling water for 10 to 12 minutes.

MAKES 30 DUMPLINGS

Per 2-dumpling serving: calories, 45 ◆ protein, 2 g ◆ carbohydrate, 9 g ◆ fat, trace (calories from fat, less than 1%) ◆ dietary fiber, trace ◆ cholesterol, 0 mg ◆ sodium, 110 mg ◆ potassium, 55 mg Joslin Exchanges: ½ bread/starch

Lemon-Chili Peanut Dipping Sauce

¼ cup (59 ml) fresh lemon juice
1 tablespoon (15 ml) honey
2 garlic cloves, peeled
¼ cup (59 ml) creamy peanut
  butter (no sugar added)

¼ cup (59 ml) low-sodium soy
  sauce
1 red jalapeño chili, stemmed and
  seeded

Place all ingredients in a food processor or blender. Puree until smooth. Serve at room temperature.

MAKES ABOUT 1 CUP (236 ML)

Per 1-tablespoon (15 ml) serving: calories, 34 ◆ protein, 1 g ◆ carbohydrate, 3 g ◆ fat, 2 g (calories from fat, 53%) ◆ fiber, trace ◆ cholesterol, 0 mg ◆ sodium, 158 mg ◆ potassium, 41 mg
Joslin Exchanges: free

Hot Mustard Dipping Sauce

¼ cup (59 ml) powdered Chinese
  mustard
⅓ cup (78 ml) water
3 tablespoons (45 ml) white wine
  vinegar

3 tablespoons (45 ml) low-sodium
  soy sauce
2 garlic cloves, minced

In a small bowl, combine all ingredients, mixing well to form a smooth sauce. Let sit for at least 1 hour before serving at room temperature.

MAKES ABOUT 1 CUP (236 ML)

Per 1-tablespoon (15 ml) serving: calories, 8 ◆ protein, 1 g ◆ carbohydrate, 1 g ◆ fat, trace (calories from fat, less than 1%) ◆ fiber, 0 g ◆ cholesterol, 0 mg ◆ sodium, 114 mg ◆ potassium, 10 mg
Joslin Exchanges: free

Plum Dipping Sauce

2 garlic cloves, peeled
1 tablespoon (15 ml) minced fresh ginger
¼ cup (59 ml) balsamic vinegar

½ cup (118 ml) plum fruit spread (no sugar added)
3 tablespoons (45 ml) hoisin sauce*

Combine all ingredients in a food processor or blender. Puree to a smooth sauce. Serve at room temperature.

MAKES ABOUT 1 CUP (236 ML)

Per 1-tablespoon (15 ml) serving: calories, 31 ◆ protein, trace ◆ carbohydrate, 8 g ◆ fat, trace (calories from fat, 0%) ◆ dietary fiber, trace ◆ cholesterol, 0 mg ◆ sodium, trace ◆ potassium, 3 mg Joslin Exchanges: free

* You'll find this sweet and spicy sauce, sometimes called Peking sauce, in Asian markets and many large supermarkets. Refrigerate any leftover sauce in a tightly sealed glass bottle; it'll keep indefinitely.

Spicy Dipping Sauce

¼ cup (59 ml) dry sherry
¾ cup (177 ml) low-sodium soy sauce
1 tablespoon (15 ml) finely minced fresh ginger

¼ teaspoon (1.25 ml) five-spice powder

Combine all ingredients in a small saucepan. Bring to a boil; cook for 3 minutes. Strain into a small bowl. Cool to room temperature.

MAKES ABOUT 1 CUP (236 ML)

Per 1-tablespoon (15 ml) serving: calories, 8 ◆ protein, 1 g ◆ carbohydrate, 1 g ◆ fat, trace (calories from fat, 0%) ◆ fiber, 0 g ◆ cholesterol, 0 mg ◆ sodium, 417 mg ◆ potassium, 2 mg Joslin Exchanges: free

A DIM SUM MEAL

◆

Hot and Sour Crab Soup (page 50)

Turkey Dim Sum (page 20)

Shrimp and Scallop Dim Sum (page 21)

Shiitake Mushroom Dim Sum (page 22)

Assorted Dipping Sauces (pages 23–24)

Cucumber Salad (page 89)

Sliced Mango with Lime

Per serving: 469 calories (20% fat)
Joslin Exchanges: 2½ low-fat meat, 3 bread/starch, 1 vegetable, 1 fruit

Middle Eastern Lamb Balls with Fresh Mint Chutney

Make these savory lamb balls for your next party. To serve them at their best, you can prepare them ahead of time, reheating to piping hot just before serving.

The Fresh Mint Chutney is also delicious with grilled chicken or fish, spooned over cooked vegetables, or as a dip with raw vegetables.

Middle Eastern Lamb Balls

6 scallions, both white and green parts, finely chopped

1 tomato, about 5 ounces (140 g), peeled, seeded, and finely chopped

1 cup (140 g) fine bulgur

¼ cup (59 ml) chopped fresh flat-leaf parsley

¼ cup (59 ml) chopped fresh mint or 4 teaspoons (20 ml) crushed dried

½ teaspoon (2.5 ml) hot red pepper flakes or to taste

1 teaspoon (5 ml) ground coriander

1 teaspoon (5 ml) ground cumin

½ teaspoon (2.5 ml) salt (optional)

½ teaspoon (2.5 ml) freshly ground pepper

1 large egg, lightly beaten

1 pound (450 g) lean ground lamb

In a large bowl, combine all ingredients and mix well. Using about 1 tablespoon (15 ml) of the lamb mixture, form into small balls.

Preheat oven to 450° F (230° C). Place lamb balls in a shallow roasting pan. Bake for 10 to 15 minutes or until browned. Remove from pan and drain on paper towels. If made ahead, reheat in a low oven before serving. Serve hot, providing wooden picks and a bowl of Fresh Mint Chutney for dipping.

MAKES ABOUT 48 BALLS

Per 4-ball serving (lamb balls only): calories, 77 ◆ protein, 9 g ◆ carbohydrate, 4 g ◆ fat, 3 g (calories from fat, 35%) ◆ dietary fiber, trace ◆ cholesterol, 43 mg ◆ sodium, 116 mg ◆ potassium, 150 mg
Joslin Exchanges: 1 medium-fat meat

Fresh Mint Chutney

1 cup (236 ml) packed fresh mint leaves

1 cup (236 ml) packed fresh flat-leaf parsley, stems removed

4 garlic cloves, peeled and quartered

3 scallions, white part and 1 inch (2.5 cm) green, chopped

2 tablespoons (30 ml) chopped fresh hot green chilies (serrano or jalapeño)

2 tablespoons (30 ml) fresh lemon juice

¾ cup (177 ml) plain nonfat yogurt

In a food processor or blender, whirl all ingredients until smooth. Serve or cover and chill up to 1 week.

MAKES ABOUT 1¹/₄ CUPS (295 ML)

Per 2-tablespoon serving:
calories, 9 ◆ protein, 1 g ◆ carbohydrate, 2 g ◆ fat, trace (calories from fat, less than 1%)

◆ dietary fiber, trace ◆ cholesterol, trace ◆ sodium, 9 mg ◆ potassium, 70 mg
Joslin Exchanges: free

CREPES

We're very fond of crêpes, those light, paper-thin pancakes filled with savory or sweet concoctions that allow the savvy cook to use leftovers or stretch small amounts of food to feed many. We like to serve them as an elegant first course, as the main dish for breakfast or lunch, as a savory side dish, or filled with something sweet for a light dessert.

It takes a little practice to make crêpes—you'll probably throw out the first one or two—but once you master the technique you'll want to keep them on hand in the refrigerator (they'll keep for up to three days) or frozen between layers of wax paper for longer storage and thawed in the microwave when needed.

The possibilities for fillings are endless. Here are a few of our favorites for elegant first courses.

Basic Crêpes

1¹/₂ cups (354 ml) skim milk
2 large eggs
¹/₄ teaspoon (1.25 ml) salt
(optional)

1 cup (125 g) unbleached flour
butter-flavored cooking spray

Place milk, eggs, and salt in a blender or food processor. Add flour; process for 30 seconds. Scrape down sides and process for another 10 seconds, until smooth. Let batter rest for 30 minutes.

Lightly spray an 8-inch (20 cm) nonstick skillet or crêpe pan with cooking spray and place over high heat. When hot, add 3 tablespoons (45 ml) batter and tilt pan so batter spreads evenly to cover the entire bottom of the pan.

Cook until crêpe appears dry and edge is lightly browned, about 30 to 45 seconds. Turn over and cook for another 30 seconds. Turn cooked crêpe onto a plate. Continue making crêpes until all batter is used.

MAKES 12 CREPES

> **Per 1-crêpe serving:** calories, 58 ◆ protein, 3 g ◆ carbohydrate, 9 g ◆ fat, 1 g (calories from fat, 16%) ◆ dietary fiber, trace ◆ cholesterol, 36 mg ◆ sodium, 71 mg ◆ potassium, 71 mg Joslin Exchanges: ½ bread/starch

Chicken or Shrimp Crêpes

For a different taste, you can serve this filling in cornmeal crêpes (page 33).

butter-flavored cooking spray
½ cup (118 ml) finely chopped onion
½ cup (118 ml) finely chopped green bell pepper
6 fresh mushrooms, finely chopped
1 tablespoon (15 g) margarine
1 cup (236 ml) skim milk
¼ cup (59 ml) dry white wine or chicken stock (page 45)
1 tablespoon (15 ml) cornstarch
dash of salt (optional)
freshly ground pepper to taste
1 tablespoon (15 ml) minced fresh herbs (tarragon with chicken; thyme with shrimp) or 1 teaspoon (5 ml) crushed dried

1 cup (172 g) chopped cooked chicken or 1 cup (172 g) cooked baby shrimp
12 cooked crêpes (preceding recipe)
¼ cup (11 g) fresh bread crumbs
¼ cup (25 g) grated Parmesan cheese
2 tablespoons (30 ml) chopped fresh flat-leaf parsley

In a nonstick skillet sprayed with cooking spray, sauté onion, bell pepper, and mushrooms over low heat until wilted and reduced by half, about 8 minutes. Set mixture aside.

In a 2-quart (2 l) pot, melt the margarine. Mix together the milk, wine, cornstarch, salt, and pepper; add to margarine. Cook, stirring constantly, over medium heat until mixture is smooth and thick, about 5 minutes. Add mushroom mixture, herbs, and chicken or shrimp; stir to combine well.

Preheat oven to 350° F (180° C). Working with one crêpe at a time, put 1 tablespoon (15 ml) chicken or shrimp mixture in the center of each crêpe. Fold each side over toward the center. Place filled crêpes, seam side down, in a baking dish just large enough to hold them in one layer.

Mix together bread crumbs, Parmesan cheese, and parsley. Sprinkle over rolled crêpes. Bake for about 10 minutes or until heated through and lightly browned. Serve immediately.

MAKES 12 SERVINGS

Per 1-crêpe serving (made with chicken): calories, 130 ◆ protein, 10 g ◆ carbohydrate, 14 g ◆ fat, 4 g (calories from fat, 27%) ◆ dietary fiber, trace ◆ cholesterol, 50 mg ◆ sodium, 158 mg ◆ potassium, 202 mg Joslin Exchanges: 1 low-fat meat, 1 bread/starch

Per serving (chicken filling alone): calories, 72 ◆ protein, 6 g ◆ carbohydrate, 5 g ◆ fat, 3 g (calories from fat, 38%) ◆ dietary fiber, trace ◆ cholesterol, 14 mg ◆ sodium, 87 mg ◆ potassium, 131 mg Joslin Exchanges: 1 low-fat meat

Per 1-crêpe serving (made with shrimp): calories, 119 ◆ protein, 9 g ◆ carbohydrate, 14 g ◆ fat, 3 g (calories from fat, 22%) ◆ dietary fiber, trace ◆ cholesterol, 63 mg ◆ sodium, 172 mg ◆ potassium, 194 mg Joslin Exchanges: 1 low-fat meat, 1 bread/starch

Per serving (shrimp filling alone): calories, 61 ◆ protein, 6 g ◆ carbohydrate, 5 g ◆ fat, 2 g (calories from fat, 29%) ◆ dietary fiber, trace ◆ cholesterol, 27 mg ◆ sodium, 101 mg ◆ potassium, 123 mg Joslin Exchanges: 1 low-fat meat

---

BRUNCH ON THE PORCH

◆

Spa Bloody Mary (page 42) or Red Pepper Sunrise (page 41)

Shrimp Crêpes (page 28)

Tropical Salad with Chervil Dressing (page 101)

Irish Oatmeal Scones with Dried Cherries (page 391)

Espresso with Lemon Twists

Per serving: 305 calories (14% fat)
Joslin Exchanges: 1 low-fat meat, 2 bread/starch, 1 vegetable, 1 fruit

Crêpes with Curried Peppers

This recipe calls for tamarind paste, a very sour flavoring used in East Indian, Middle Eastern, and Indonesian cuisines—much as we use lemon juice. You'll find it in Asian and other specialty food markets (see Appendix 2). Additional grated lemon zest is an acceptable substitute.

2 teaspoons (10 ml) canola oil
2 scallions, white part only, chopped
2 garlic cloves, minced
1 small tomato, about 3 ounces (85 g), peeled, seeded, and finely chopped
2 red bell peppers, about ¾ pound (340 g), seeded and sliced ¼-inch (.75 cm) thick

1 yellow bell pepper, about 6 ounces (180 g), seeded and sliced ¼-inch (.75 cm) thick
1 tablespoon (15 ml) minced fresh ginger
1 4-inch (10 cm) length of lemongrass, white part only, chopped, or 2 teaspoons (10 ml) grated lemon zest

1 teaspoon (5 ml) tamarind paste
1 tablespoon (15 ml) curry
   powder or to taste
¼ teaspoon (1.25 ml) celery seed

¼ teaspoon (1.25 ml) hot red
   pepper flakes
12 cooked crêpes (page 27)
butter-flavored cooking spray

Place oil in a sauté pan over low heat. Add scallions and sauté for 2 minutes. Add garlic and tomato; sauté until scallions and garlic are wilted, about 5 minutes. Add peppers, ginger, lemongrass, tamarind paste, curry powder, celery seed, and red pepper flakes. Cook for 5 minutes, until peppers are tender but still crisp and liquid is reduced.

Working with one crêpe at a time, place 2 tablespoons (30 ml) pepper mixture in center of each crêpe. Roll crêpes up jelly-roll fashion. Arrange crêpes seam side down in a shallow baking dish lightly sprayed with cooking spray.

When ready to serve, preheat oven to 350° F (180° C). Bake crêpes for 10 minutes, until lightly browned and heated through. Serve immediately.

MAKES 12 SERVINGS

Per 1-crêpe serving: calories, 74 ◆ protein, 3 g ◆ carbohydrate, 11 g ◆ fat, 2 g (calories from fat, 24%) ◆ dietary fiber, 1 g ◆ cholesterol, 36 mg ◆ sodium, 73 mg ◆ potassium, 133 mg
Joslin Exchanges: 1 bread/starch

Per serving (filling only): calories, 31 ◆ protein, 1 g ◆ carbohydrate, 4 g ◆ fat, 2 g (calories from fat, 58%) ◆ dietary fiber, 1 g ◆ cholesterol, 0 mg ◆ sodium, 4 mg ◆ potassium, 125 mg
Joslin Exchanges: free

Fennel and Shiitake Mushroom Crêpes

Cooked fresh fennel (also called *finocchio*) has a very mild, almost elusive flavor of anise, which combines splendidly with the smoky flavor of the mushrooms. Other wild mushrooms or cultivated mushrooms could be used in place of shiitake.

This filling would also be delicious as a low-calorie vegetable side dish, stuffed into a giant mushroom cap or artichoke bottom and baked at 375° F (190° C) for 15 to 20 minutes, until heated through.

1 fennel bulb, about ¾ pound
   (340 g)
2 teaspoons (10 ml) olive oil
1 medium-size red onion, about 3
   ounces (85 g), chopped
1 garlic clove, minced
½ pound (225 g) fresh shiitake
   mushrooms, cleaned and
   chopped
2 tablespoons (30 ml) chopped
   fresh flat-leaf parsley

1 tablespoon (15 ml) fresh thyme
   leaves or 1 teaspoon (5 ml)
   crushed dried
freshly ground pepper to taste
½ teaspoon (2.5 ml) salt (optional)
1 tablespoon (15 ml) white wine
   vinegar
12 cooked crêpes (page 27)
butter-flavored cooking spray

Trim the fennel stalks down to the bulb; trim the bottom. Peel off any wilted or hard outer layers. Slice crosswise into thin strips. Set aside.

In a large nonstick sauté pan, heat olive oil over low heat. Add onion and sauté for 3 minutes, until onion is soft but not brown. Add garlic and fennel; cook, stirring occasionally, for 10 to 15 minutes, until fennel and onions are tender. Add mushrooms, raise heat to medium-high, and cook, stirring frequently, until mushrooms are wilted and liquid is absorbed, about 4 minutes. Add herbs, pepper, salt, and vinegar.

Working with one crêpe at a time, put 2 tablespoons (30 ml) vegetable filling on one quadrant of each crêpe. Fold the crêpe in half over filling and fold it in half again to form a triangle. Arrange crêpes on a baking dish lightly sprayed with cooking spray.

When ready to serve, preheat oven to 350° F (180° C). Bake for 10 minutes, until lightly browned. Serve immediately.

MAKES 12 SERVINGS

Per 1-crêpe serving: calories,
82 ◆ protein, 4 g ◆
carbohydrate, 13 g ◆ fat, 2 g
(calories from fat, 21%) ◆
dietary fiber, trace ◆ cholesterol,
36 mg ◆ sodium, 161 mg ◆
potassium, 276 mg
Joslin Exchanges: 1 bread/starch

Per serving (filling alone):
calories, 24 ◆ protein, 1 g ◆
carbohydrate, 4 g ◆ fat, 1 g
(calories from fat, 37%) ◆
dietary fiber, trace ◆ cholesterol,
0 mg ◆ sodium, 90 mg ◆
potassium, 205 mg
Joslin Exchanges: free

Southwestern Vegetable Crêpes

Stone-ground cornmeal (you can use yellow or blue) gives these crêpes a crunchy texture and a hint of sweet corn flavor. We like them stuffed with vegetables, but you can also use one of the other crêpe fillings. The vegetable filling could be tossed with cooked pasta for a light meal.

Cornmeal Crêpes

1½ cups (354 ml) skim milk
2 large eggs
¼ teaspoon (1.25 ml) salt (optional)
¾ cup (94 g) unbleached flour

¼ cup (35 g) stone-ground yellow or blue cornmeal
1 tablespoon (15 ml) chili powder
butter-flavored cooking spray

Place milk, eggs, and salt in a blender or food processor. Add flour, cornmeal, and chili powder. Process for 30 seconds. Scrape down sides and process for another 10 seconds, until smooth. Let batter rest for 30 minutes before using.

Lightly spray an 8-inch (20 cm) nonstick skillet or crêpe pan with butter-flavored spray and place over high heat. When hot, add 3 tablespoons (45 ml) batter and tilt pan so batter spreads evenly and covers the entire bottom of the pan.

Cook until crêpe appears dry and edge is lightly browned, about 30 to 45 seconds. Turn over and cook another 30 seconds. Turn cooked crêpe onto a plate. Continue making crêpes until all batter is used.

MAKES 12 CREPES

Per 1-crêpe serving: calories, 61 ◆ protein, 3 g ◆ carbohydrate, 9 g ◆ fat, 1 g (calories from fat, 15%) ◆ fiber, 1 g ◆ cholesterol, 36 mg ◆ sodium, 78 mg ◆ potassium, 88 mg
Joslin Exchanges: ½ bread/starch

Vegetable Filling

1 tablespoon (15 ml) olive oil

3 scallions, white part only, thinly sliced

2 garlic cloves, minced

2 tomatoes, about ½ pound (225 g), peeled, seeded, and chopped

3 small Japanese or Italian white eggplants, about 5 ounces (140 g) each, cut into 1-inch (2.5 cm) cubes

3 cups (708 ml) cauliflower florets

1 fresh jalapeño or serrano chili, seeded and minced

¾ teaspoon (3.75 ml) ground cumin

1 tablespoon (15 ml) chopped fresh cilantro (fresh coriander)

½ teaspoon (2.5 ml) turmeric

½ teaspoon (2.5 ml) ground ginger

1 teaspoon (5 ml) tamarind paste

1 tablespoon (15 ml) fresh lemon juice

½ teaspoon (2.5 ml) salt (optional)

butter-flavored cooking spray

6 tablespoons (90 ml) plain nonfat yogurt

fresh cilantro (fresh coriander) sprigs for garnish

Heat oil in a heavy nonstick skillet over low heat. Add scallions; sauté until wilted but not browned, about 4 minutes. Add garlic, vegetables, chili, spices, tamarind paste, lemon juice, and salt. Cover and cook over low heat until vegetables are tender but still crisp, about 20 minutes. Stir occasionally.

Remove vegetables from skillet; set aside. Reduce any liquid in skillet over high heat until it forms a syrup. Return vegetables to pan. Remove from heat and stir to coat vegetables; keep warm.

Working with one crêpe at a time, mound about 3 tablespoons (45 ml) vegetable mixture on half of each crêpe. Fold crêpe gently over the filling. Repeat with remaining crêpes.

Place crêpes in a single layer in a baking pan lightly sprayed with cooking spray.

When ready to serve, preheat oven to 350° F (180° C). Bake crêpes for 10 minutes or until heated through. With a long spatula, transfer 1 crêpe to each of 12 heated serving plates. Garnish each plate with ½ tablespoon (7.5 ml) yogurt and a cilantro sprig.

MAKES 12 SERVINGS

Per 1-crêpe serving: calories, 97 ◆ protein, 5 g ◆ carbohydrate, 15 g ◆ fat, 3 g (calories from fat, 28%) ◆ dietary fiber, 1 g ◆ cholesterol, 36 mg ◆ sodium, 181 mg ◆ potassium, 341 mg
Joslin Exchanges: 1 bread/starch

Per serving (filling alone): calories, 37 ◆ protein, 2 g ◆ carbohydrate, 5 g ◆ fat, 1 g (calories from fat, 24%) ◆ dietary fiber, 1 g ◆ cholesterol, trace ◆ sodium, 103 mg ◆ potassium, 252 mg
Joslin Exchanges: 1 vegetable

Blue Corn Blinis with Fresh Corn Relish

These feathery light blinis make a terrific first course. If blue cornmeal is not available at your specialty food store, you can get it by mail order (see Appendix 2) or substitute yellow cornmeal.

Poblano chilies (called *ancho* in their dried form) are thick-walled, very dark green or red triangle-shaped chilies with a long tip. When roasted, they impart a mild to medium-hot smoky flavor. If you can't find them, you can substitute milder Anaheim chilies, or use a green bell pepper and a jalapeño.

6 tablespoons (90 ml) skim milk, heated to 110° F (43° C)
1 ¼-ounce (7 g) package active dry yeast
2 teaspoons (10 ml) sugar
¼ cup (31 g) unbleached flour
¼ cup (35 g) blue cornmeal
1 large egg yolk
1 teaspoon (5 ml) margarine at room temperature
2 large egg whites, beaten to stiff peaks
½ cup (118 ml) fresh cilantro (fresh coriander) leaves
2 tablespoons (30 ml) plain low-fat yogurt
1 ounce (30 g) low-fat goat cheese, crumbled

boiling water
1 cup (77 g) fresh corn kernels (about 1 large ear) or defrosted frozen corn kernels
1 red bell pepper, about 6 ounces (180 g), roasted (page 100), peeled, seeded, and finely diced
2 poblano peppers, roasted (page 100), peeled, seeded, and finely diced
¼ cup (59 ml) finely diced onion
1 tablespoon (15 ml) balsamic vinegar
¼ teaspoon (1.25 ml) salt (optional)
freshly ground pepper to taste
vegetable cooking spray

In a medium-size bowl, combine milk, yeast, and sugar. Let sit at room temperature until foamy, about 10 minutes. Whisk in flour and cornmeal until batter is smooth. Beat in egg yolk and margarine. Fold in beaten egg whites and ¼ cup (59 ml) cilantro leaves. Set aside at room temperature. In a small bowl, combine yogurt and goat cheese. Set aside.

In another small metal bowl, pour boiling water over corn kernels. Let sit for 3 minutes. Drain in a colander. Return corn to bowl and combine with peppers and onion. Add balsamic vinegar, salt, and pepper. Set aside.

Spray a heavy-bottomed 6-inch (15 cm) skillet with cooking spray. Place over medium-high heat. Pour ¼ cup (59 ml) batter into skillet and cook blini until golden, about 2 minutes. Turn and cook for another 2 minutes. Transfer blini to a heated plate and keep warm. Repeat until all batter is cooked.

To serve, place a blini on each of 6 serving plates. Top with some of the corn relish and yogurt sauce. Scatter remaining cilantro leaves over as a garnish. Serve at once.

MAKES 6 SERVINGS

> **Per serving:** calories, 113 ◆ protein, 5 g ◆ carbohydrate, 18 g ◆ fat, 3 g (calories from fat, 24%) ◆ dietary fiber, 3 g ◆ cholesterol, 39 mg ◆ sodium, 159 mg ◆ potassium, 244 mg Joslin Exchanges: 1 bread/starch

Country Pâté

A classic recipe for this pâté would be loaded with pork fat, cognac, and whole eggs. Our lean version is a winner, perfect for a picnic or as a first course for a splendid dinner. Slice the pâté very thinly and serve with a basket of water biscuits, melba toast, or French bread.

1 boneless, skinless chicken breast, about ½ pound (225 g)
1 teaspoon (5 ml) cognac (optional)
1 pound (450 g) lean ground turkey
1 pound (450 g) lean ground veal
¼ cup (59 ml) fresh thyme leaves or 1 tablespoon (15 ml) crushed dried
¼ cup (59 ml) chopped fresh sage or 1 tablespoon (15 ml) crushed dried
1 teaspoon (5 ml) salt (optional)
1 teaspoon (5 ml) freshly ground pepper or to taste

1 garlic clove, minced
2 scallions, white part only, finely minced
4 large egg whites, beaten
1 pound (450 mg) fresh spinach, washed and stems removed
boiling water
¾ pound (340 g) turkey bacon, boiled in water for 10 minutes and drained on paper towels
dash of ground nutmeg
3 bay leaves
salad greens for garnish
cornichons for garnish

Preheat oven to 325° F (165° C).

Slice chicken breast into thin strips. Toss with cognac and marinate for 15 minutes. Meanwhile, combine ground meats, thyme, sage, salt, pepper, garlic, scallions, and egg whites. Place spinach leaves in a colander. Pour boiling water over spinach to wilt leaves. Drain and squeeze dry in paper towels. Line bottom and sides of a 9½- by 5- by 3-inch (24- by 13- by 8-cm) loaf pan with bacon, letting some hang over sides. Tightly pack one-third of meat mixture into pan. Arrange chicken strips on top. Cover with another third of meat mixture, packing tightly. Arrange spinach over meat; sprinkle with nutmeg. Cover with final third of meat mixture, mounding top slightly. Top with bay leaves and cover with overhanging edges of bacon. Cover with aluminum foil, pressing foil snugly onto edges of pan to completely seal pâté.

Set loaf pan in a larger pan and place in lower third of oven. Pour enough boiling water into outer pan to come halfway up the sides of the loaf pan. Bake for 2½ hours.

When pâté is done, remove loaf pan from boiling water bath. Remove foil and drain off all fat. Discard bacon. Replace foil on top of pâté.

The pâté is now ready to be pressed for several hours to force out any remaining interior fat and to compress meat for easy slicing. To do this, place another loaf pan or a board of suitable size on top of pâté. Place two bricks (or an equivalent weight of canned goods) in second loaf pan or atop board. Refrigerate for 24 hours.

To serve, remove weights and unmold, scraping off any fat that remains. Let pâté come almost to room temperature before slicing. Arrange on a serving platter lined with greens. Garnish with cornichons sliced into fans.

MAKES 1 LOAF: 20 COCKTAIL SERVINGS OR 10 FIRST-COURSE SERVINGS

> **Per cocktail serving:** calories, 111 ◆ protein, 15 g ◆ carbohydrate, 1 g ◆ fat, 5 g (calories from fat, 40%) ◆ dietary fiber, trace ◆ cholesterol, 30 mg ◆ sodium, 189 mg ◆ potassium, 241 mg
> Joslin Exchanges: 2 low-fat meat

DRINKS

Whether or not to drink alcoholic beverages is an important decision that can be made only by you, your physician, and your registered dietitian. Alcohol can directly influence blood glucose control, blood fat levels, and weight control. Alcohol consumption provides "empty calories," approximately 96 calories for 1½ ounces (45 ml), costing 3 fat exchanges. We'd rather use our calories and fat exchanges elsewhere so we opt for nonalcoholic drinks. We do use wine and small amounts of other alcoholic beverages in cooking, since almost all of the alcohol evaporates during the cooking process, leaving behind the flavor.

The following nonalcoholic drinks contain carbohydrate from fruit, in liquid form, that is quickly absorbed by the body, which may quickly affect your blood sugar levels.

Remember that diabetics should attempt to combine fruit with a protein source to slow down the absorption in the bloodstream of the natural sugar (fructose) from the fruit. So the following fruit-based beverages are for snacks, appetizers, or mealtime and should not be consumed by themselves. They are also appropriate before vigorous exercise.

Cantaloupe Slush

⅓ cup (78 ml) diced cantaloupe
⅓ cup (78 ml) unsweetened
   pineapple juice

crushed ice
1 whole strawberry for garnish

In a food processor or blender, puree cantaloupe and pineapple juice until smooth. Pour into a goblet over crushed ice. To decorate glass, slash unhulled strawberry about halfway through and perch on glass rim.

MAKES 1 SERVING

Per serving: calories, 65 ◆ protein, 1 g ◆ carbohydrate, 16 g ◆ fat, trace (calories from fat, less than 1%) ◆ dietary fiber, trace ◆ cholesterol, 0 mg ◆ sodium, 6 mg ◆ potassium, 274 mg
Joslin Exchanges: 1 fruit

Cranberry Mist

½ cup (118 ml) low-calorie
   cranberry juice
1 cranberry clove tea bag
ice

about ⅓ cup (78 ml) chilled club
   soda
1 fresh mint sprig for garnish

In a small saucepan, bring cranberry juice to a boil over medium heat. Add tea bag. Remove from heat and let steep for 10 minutes. Cool to room temperature. Fill a tall glass with ice. Pour cranberry tea mixture over ice. Fill glass with club soda. Garnish with mint.

MAKES 1 SERVING

Per serving: calories, 24 ◆ protein, trace ◆ carbohydrate, 6 g ◆ fat, trace (calories from fat, less than 1%) ◆ dietary fiber, 0 g ◆ cholesterol, 0 mg ◆ sodium, 55 mg ◆ potassium, 35 mg
Joslin Exchanges: free

Herb Spritzer

1 large fresh herb sprig (orange mint, lemon balm, pineapple sage, peppermint, or rose geranium)

crushed ice
about ¾ cup (177 ml) sparkling mineral water or club soda

Using your fingers, gently bruise the herb sprig to release its volatile oils. Drop sprig into a champagne flute or tall glass half filled with crushed ice. Fill glass with sparkling water.

MAKES 1 SERVING

Per serving (club soda): calories, 0 ◆ protein, 0 g ◆ carbohydrate, 0 g ◆ fat, 0 g ◆ dietary fiber, 0 g ◆ cholesterol, 0 mg ◆ sodium, 37 mg ◆ potassium, 4 mg
Joslin Exchanges: free

Hot Orange Spiced Cider

⅓ cup (78 ml) fresh orange juice
5 cloves
2 cups (472 ml) apple cider

2 apple cinnamon spice tea bags
whole cinnamon sticks for garnish
grated orange zest for garnish

In a large saucepan, combine orange juice, cloves, cider, and tea bags. Place over low heat and bring to a simmer. Cook for 10 minutes. Pour hot cider into heated mugs; discard cloves and tea bags.

Garnish each mug with a cinnamon stick and a sprinkling of grated orange zest.

MAKES 4 SERVINGS

Per serving: calories, 68 ◆ protein, trace ◆ carbohydrate, 17 g ◆ fat, trace (calories from fat, less than 1%) ◆ dietary fiber, trace ◆ cholesterol, 0 mg ◆ sodium, 4 mg ◆ potassium, 142 mg
Joslin Exchanges: 1 fruit

Orange-Tangerine Mimosa

1 orange
2 tangerines

about ⅓ cup (78 ml) chilled
sparkling mineral water, seltzer,
or club soda

Juice the fruits using a hand or electric juicer; blend together. Divide the juice between 2 goblets. Fill with mineral water.

MAKES 2 SERVINGS

Per serving: calories, 37 ◆ protein, 1 g ◆ carbohydrate, 9 g ◆ fat, trace (calories from fat, less than 1%) ◆ dietary fiber, trace ◆ cholesterol, 0 mg ◆ sodium, 1 mg ◆ potassium, 107 mg
Joslin Exchanges: ½ fruit

Peach Sparkler

⅓ cup (78 ml) chopped peeled fresh
peaches
⅔ cup (156 ml) chilled sparkling
mineral water

1 fresh peach slice impaled on a
wooden skewer for garnish
1 fresh mint sprig for garnish

In a blender or food processor, puree fruit and mineral water until smooth. Pour into a chilled stemmed glass. Garnish with peach slice and mint.

MAKES 1 SERVING

Per serving: calories, 37 ◆ protein, 1 g ◆ carbohydrate, 10 g ◆ fat, trace (calories from fat, less than 1%) ◆ dietary fiber, 1 g ◆ cholesterol, 0 mg ◆ sodium, 5 mg ◆ potassium, 167 mg
Joslin Exchanges: ½ fruit

Raspberry Slush

½ cup (62 g) fresh raspberries,
  rinsed
½ cup (118 ml) fresh orange juice

3 ice cubes
about 1 cup (236 ml) chilled
  sparkling mineral water

Place raspberries (reserve a few for garnish), orange juice, and ice cubes in a blender. Puree until smooth. Pour into 2 tall glasses, filling halfway. Add mineral water to fill each glass. Float reserved berries in drinks.

MAKES 2 SERVINGS

Per serving: calories, 43 ◆ protein, 1 g ◆ carbohydrate, 10 g ◆ fat, trace (calories from fat, less than 1%) ◆ dietary fiber, 2 g

◆ cholesterol, 0 mg ◆ sodium, 4 mg ◆ potassium, 171 mg
Joslin Exchanges: 1 fruit

Red Pepper Sunrise

1 large red bell pepper, about 6
  ounces (180 g)
1 cup (236 ml) crushed ice
½ cup (118 ml) buttermilk
1 tablespoon (15 ml) fresh lemon
  juice

¼ teaspoon (1.25 ml) hot red
  pepper flakes or to taste
paprika for garnish
dill pickle spears for garnish

Preheat broiler. Cut pepper in half lengthwise. Place cut side down on a baking sheet. Broil about 4 inches (10 cm) from heat for about 10 minutes, until skin is charred. Remove from oven. Place bell pepper in a plastic bag and let stand until cool. Remove and discard skin and seeds. Coarsely chop pepper. Place in a food processor or blender along with ice, buttermilk, lemon juice, and red pepper flakes. Process until smooth. Pour into chilled mugs. Garnish with paprika; add a dill pickle spear to each mug.

MAKES 2 SERVINGS

Per serving: calories, 59 ◆ protein, 3 g ◆ carbohydrate, 11 g ◆ fat, 1 g (calories from fat, 15%) ◆ dietary fiber, 2 g ◆

cholesterol, 2 mg ◆ sodium, 67 mg ◆ potassium, 327 mg
Joslin Exchanges: 2 vegetable

Spa Bloody Mary

ice
½ cup (118 ml) low-sodium
  vegetable juice cocktail
½ teaspoon (2.5 ml) prepared
  horseradish
½ tablespoon (7.5 ml) fresh lemon
  juice

¼ teaspoon (1.25 ml)
  Worcestershire sauce
dash of Tabasco sauce or to taste
dash of celery salt (optional)
 1 celery rib with leaves for garnish
freshly ground pepper to taste

Fill a highball glass with ice. Combine remaining ingredients except celery and pepper. Pour over ice. Garnish with celery and sprinkle generously with pepper.

MAKES 1 SERVING

> **Per serving:** calories, 35 ◆ protein, trace ◆ carbohydrate, 8 g ◆ fat, trace (calories from fat, less than 1%) ◆ dietary fiber, 3 g ◆ cholesterol, 0 mg ◆ sodium, 115 mg ◆ potassium, 429 mg
> Joslin Exchanges: 1 vegetable

Strawberry Yogurt Cooler

 1 cup (128 g) sliced strawberries,
  crushed
½ cup (118 ml) plain nonfat yogurt

1 cup (236 ml) sparkling mineral
  water, seltzer, or club soda

Combine ingredients in a blender or food processor; process until smooth. Pour into chilled glasses and serve.

MAKES 2 SERVINGS

> **Per serving:** calories, 54 ◆ protein, 4 g ◆ carbohydrate, 10 g ◆ fat, trace (calories from fat, less than 1%) ◆ dietary fiber, trace ◆ cholesterol, 1 mg ◆ sodium, 70 mg ◆ potassium, 271 mg
> Joslin Exchanges: ½ nonfat milk

SOUPS

Whether it's a serious soup sturdy enough to be supper or a light first course of broth and vegetables that takes the edge off our appetites before the main course, homemade soups enjoy an important place in our cuisine. They're a snap to prepare and can make something delicious from leftover bits and vegetables too exhausted for the salad bowl.

A rich, savory stock is the essence of a wonderful soup, and nothing you can buy is as good as the stock you make yourself. Most commercial stocks (sold in cans or cubes) have additives and are very salty. Look for no-salt-added canned broths. Commercial stock sold in cans also contains fat, so you need to chill it first and discard the surface fat.

We make stock on days when we're working on a project that will keep us home for most of the day. Beef, chicken, and vegetable stock do take some time to cook (fish stock takes only 30 minutes), but they need little attention, and since stocks freeze very well it's easy to keep homemade soup stock on hand. Be sure to leave room at the top of the freezer container for expansion. If freezer space is at a premium, you can reduce the stock further and freeze it in ice cube trays. Pack the cubes in a freezer bag and use them as needed.

Beef Stock

Ask your butcher to crack the bones for stock making. For an even richer flavor, return the strained stock to the stove and reduce it further.

5 pounds (2.25 kg) mixed beef and veal bones (marrow, knuckle, and shin)

2 large onions, about ½ pound (225 g), peeled and cut in half

1 leek, white part only, well rinsed and cut into large pieces

2 carrots, scrubbed and cut into large chunks

2 celery ribs with leaves, cut into large pieces

4 garlic cloves, peeled

about 6 quarts (5.5 l) water

5 fresh thyme sprigs or 1 teaspoon (5 ml) crushed dried

6 fresh flat-leaf parsley sprigs

1 bay leaf

8 peppercorns or to taste

Preheat oven to 400° F (205° C).

Place bones in a single layer in a large roasting pan. Scatter onions, leek, carrots, celery, and garlic among bones. Roast for 1 hour, until bones and vegetables begin to brown.

Transfer bones and vegetables to a large stockpot. Add water to cover, about 6 quarts. Bring to a vigorous boil. Skim and discard foam that rises to the top. Reduce to a simmer. Add remaining seasonings and cook, uncovered, for 6 hours.

Strain through a fine sieve or a colander lined with cheesecloth. Discard solids. Return stock to stove and boil slowly until reduced to 2 quarts (2 l). Set aside to cool to room temperature. Skim off any fat that rises to top. Refrigerate, covered tightly, or freeze.

MAKES 2 QUARTS (2 L)

Per 1-cup serving: calories, 24 ◆ protein, 1 g ◆ carbohydrate, 5 g ◆ fat, trace (calories from fat, 4%) ◆ dietary fiber, 1 g ◆ cholesterol, 0 mg ◆ sodium, 32 mg ◆ potassium, 97 mg Joslin Exchanges: free

Chicken Stock

We depend on this richly flavored stock for soups and sauces. Whenever we buy a whole chicken and are cutting it up for breasts, thighs, and legs, we freeze the rest. It doesn't take long to accumulate 3 pounds (1.35 kg).

3 pounds (1.35 kg) chicken bones, such as wings, necks, and backs
2 onions, peeled and stuck with 1 clove
1 garlic clove, peeled
1 carrot, peeled and sliced
1 celery rib with leaves, cut into large pieces

4 quarts (3.75 l) water
6 peppercorns
1 bay leaf
4 fresh flat-leaf parsley sprigs
1 fresh thyme sprig or ¼ teaspoon (1.25 ml) crushed dried
¼ teaspoon (1.25 ml) salt (optional)

Place chicken bones, onions, garlic, carrot, celery, and water in a large stockpot. Bring to a boil; skim and discard foam that rises to the top. Add remaining ingredients. Reduce heat to simmer. Cover and cook for 2½ hours, skimming occasionally to remove any foam. Strain through a fine sieve or a colander lined with cheesecloth; discard solids. Set aside to cool, uncovered, to room temperature. Remove all fat that rises to the surface. Store in sealed container in refrigerator for as long as 3 days or freeze.

MAKES 4 QUARTS (3.75 L)

Per 1-cup serving: calories, 13 ◆ protein, trace ◆ carbohydrate, 3 g ◆ fat, trace (calories from fat, 6%) ◆ dietary fiber, trace ◆ cholesterol, 0 mg ◆ sodium, 46 mg ◆ potassium, 63 mg
Joslin Exchanges: free

Fish Stock

Use bones from nonoily fish (halibut, bass, snapper, or any other white fish) for this wonderful stock. Your fish market will usually give you the bones.

1 pound (450 g) fish bones, rinsed and cut into chunks
1 medium-size white onion, about 3 ounces (85 g), peeled and quartered
1 leek, white part only, well rinsed and sliced
1 celery rib with leaves, sliced
8 shallots, sliced
2 garlic cloves, sliced
1 quart (1 l) water

4 fresh flat-leaf parsley sprigs
2 fresh thyme sprigs or ½ teaspoon crushed dried
2 small fresh tarragon sprigs, or ½ teaspoon crushed dried
2 2-inch (5 cm) strips of lemon zest
1 teaspoon (5 ml) fennel seed
4 peppercorns
1 cup (236 ml) dry white wine

Combine fish bones, onion, leek, celery, shallots, garlic, and water in a large stockpot or heavy saucepan. Bring to a boil over medium heat. Skim off all foam that rises to the surface. Add parsley, thyme, tarragon, lemon zest, fennel seeds, and peppercorns. Cover, reduce heat, and simmer for 15 minutes.

Add wine and continue to simmer for 15 minutes. Strain through a fine sieve or a colander lined with cheesecloth. Discard solids. Cool to room temperature. Store in a sealed container in refrigerator for up to 24 hours or freeze.

MAKES 1 QUART (1 L)

Per 1-cup serving: calories, 23 ◆ protein, 1 g ◆ carbohydrate, 5 g ◆ fat, trace (calories from fat, 6%) ◆ dietary fiber, 1 g ◆ cholesterol, 0 mg ◆ sodium, 16 mg ◆ potassium, 107 mg Joslin Exchanges: free

Vegetable Stock

The wonderful flavor of the vegetables is intensified by roasting them for this savory stock. Use this broth as a substitute for chicken or beef stock.

1 large carrot, scrubbed and cut into large chunks
1 large leek, white part only, well rinsed and cut into large pieces
1 large onion, about ½ pound (225 g), cut into 8 pieces
2 large celery ribs with leaves, coarsely chopped
1 cup (236 ml) coarsely chopped fresh fennel bulb
1 cup (236 ml) coarsely chopped tomato

¾ pound (340 g) fresh spinach, rinsed and trimmed
2 fresh thyme sprigs or ½ teaspoon (2.5 ml) crushed dried
4 fresh flat-leaf parsley sprigs
2 bay leaves
½ teaspoon (2.5 ml) salt (optional)
4 whole peppercorns or to taste
10 cups (2.5 l) water

Preheat oven to 400° F (205° C).

Arrange carrot, leek, onion, celery, and fennel in a shallow roasting pan. Roast for 30 to 45 minutes, until vegetables begin to brown.

Transfer vegetables to a stockpot or large heavy saucepan. Add remaining ingredients; bring to a boil. Reduce heat and simmer, uncovered, for 30 minutes. Remove pot from stove and let sit for another 30 minutes.

Strain stock through a fine sieve or a colander lined with cheesecloth. Discard vegetables. Return stock to the stove and reduce at a slow simmer to 1 quart (1 l).

MAKES 1 QUART (1 L)

Per 1-cup serving: calories, 25 ◆ protein, 1 g ◆ carbohydrate, 5 g ◆ fat, trace (calories from fat, 7%) ◆ dietary fiber, 1 g ◆ cholesterol, 0 mg ◆ sodium, 304 mg ◆ potassium, 182 mg Joslin Exchanges: free

A Quick Cup of Soup

Whenever we make stock we make extra to freeze in 1-cup (236 ml) portions. Once frozen, these are removed from their containers and stored in zip-lock bags. Then, whenever we want a cup of soup for a quick solo meal, all we have to do is defrost the stock in the microwave. While it's defrosting, we rummage through the fridge and pantry for whatever ingredients we have on hand for the soup.

Here are some ideas:

Curried Asparagus Soup

To 1 cup (236 ml) chicken stock (page 45), add 1 cup (236 ml) leftover cooked asparagus, 1/2 to 1 teaspoon (2.5 to 5 ml) curry powder, 1/3 cup (78 ml) evaporated skim milk, and a splash of fresh lemon juice. Process in a food processor or blender until smooth. Reheat on stove or chill in freezer for 20 minutes. Pour into a mug or soup bowl. Top with a generous grinding of pepper.

MAKES 1 SERVING

> **Per serving:** calories, 116 ◆ protein, 11 g ◆ carbohydrate, 18 g ◆ fat, 1 g (calories from fat, 7%) ◆ dietary fiber, 3 g ◆ cholesterol, 3 mg ◆ sodium, 163 mg ◆ potassium, 662 mg
> Joslin Exchanges: 1 low-fat meat, 1 bread/starch

Quick Barley Soup

In a small saucepan, combine 1 cup (236 ml) beef stock (page 44), 1 small minced garlic clove, 1 cup (236 ml) chopped fresh vegetables (combination of carrots, green beans, celery, and/or peeled tomatoes), 1 minced scallion, 1 small bay leaf, freshly ground pepper to taste, and 1 tablespoon (15 ml) pearl barley. Simmer until barley is tender, about 15 minutes.

MAKES 1 SERVING

> **Per serving:** calories, 128 ◆ protein, 6 g ◆ carbohydrate, 27 g ◆ fat, 1 g (calories from fat, 4%) ◆ dietary fiber, 12 g ◆ cholesterol, 0 mg ◆ sodium, 287 mg ◆ potassium, 724 mg
> Joslin Exchanges: 2 bread/starch

Carrot Soup

In a small saucepan, combine 1 cup (236 ml) chicken stock (page 45), 2 tablespoons (30 ml) minced onion, 1 small new potato (1 ounce/30 g), scrubbed and diced but not peeled, ⅛ teaspoon (.6 ml) ground cumin, ⅓ cup (78 ml) chopped carrot, and freshly ground pepper to taste. Simmer until potato is tender, about 10 minutes. Puree in a food processor or blender until smooth. Return soup to saucepan. Reheat. Serve warm in a mug or soup bowl with a sprinkling of chopped fresh dill or snipped chives.

MAKES 1 SERVING

Per serving: calories, 55 ◆ protein, 1 g ◆ carbohydrate, 13 g ◆ fat, trace (calories from fat, 4%) ◆ dietary fiber, 2 g ◆ cholesterol, 0 mg ◆ sodium, 62 mg ◆ potassium, 348 mg
Joslin Exchanges: 1 bread/starch

Spaghetti Soup

In a small saucepan, combine 1 cup (236 ml) chicken stock (page 45); ¼ cup (59 ml) leftover cooked green beans; ¼ cup (59 ml) diced zucchini; 4 cherry tomatoes, halved; 1 tablespoon (15 ml) minced onion; ½ small garlic clove, minced; ¼ cup (59 ml) leftover cooked spaghetti; and ⅛ teaspoon (.6 ml) crushed dried basil. Heat through; serve with a sprinkling of grated Parmesan cheese.

MAKES 1 SERVING

Per serving: calories, 80 ◆ protein, 3 g ◆ carbohydrate, 17 g ◆ fat, 1 g (calories from fat, 6%) ◆ dietary fiber, 3 g ◆ cholesterol, 0 mg ◆ sodium, 57 mg ◆ potassium, 371 mg
Joslin Exchanges: 1 bread/starch

Hot Tomato Soup

In a food processor or blender, combine 1 cup (236 ml) vegetable stock (page 47) and ½ cup (118 ml) peeled, seeded, and chopped fresh tomatoes (or drained canned Italian plum tomatoes). Process until smooth. Pour into a small saucepan. Bring to a simmer over medium heat. Stir in ⅛ teaspoon (.6 ml) ground ginger and a dash of Tabasco sauce. Pour into a mug and top with 1 tablespoon (15 ml) plain low-fat yogurt.

MAKES 1 SERVING

Per serving: calories, 33 ◆ protein, 2 g ◆ carbohydrate, 6 g ◆ fat, 1 g (calories from fat, 13%) ◆ dietary fiber, 1 g ◆ cholesterol, 1 mg ◆ sodium, 251 mg ◆ potassium, 364 mg
Joslin Exchanges: 1 vegetable

Turkey Soup

In a small saucepan, combine 1 cup (236 ml) chicken stock (page 45), 4 cherry tomatoes, halved; ¼ cup (59 ml) diced zucchini; ¼ cup (59 ml) diced carrot; ¼ cup (59 ml) diced celery; 1 tablespoon (15 ml) minced onion; and ¼ cup (59 ml) chopped cooked turkey meat. Simmer for 10 minutes. Add freshly ground pepper to taste and serve.

MAKES 1 SERVING

Per serving: calories, 91 ◆ protein, 12 g ◆ carbohydrate, 8 g ◆ fat, 2 g (calories from fat, 14%) ◆ dietary fiber, 3 g ◆ cholesterol, 24 mg ◆ sodium, 86 mg ◆ potassium, 536 mg Joslin Exchanges: 1 low-fat meat, 1 vegetable

Hot and Sour Crab Soup

Our revised version of this classic Chinese soup works for those of us watching our cholesterol intake. The dried mushrooms, sometimes called *winter mushrooms,* are available in Asian markets. You can substitute dried cloud ear or tree ear mushrooms, which may be easier to find. All are very meaty.

4 dried black mushrooms
5 cups (1.25 l) chicken stock (page 45)
2 cups (472 ml) coarsely chopped fresh spinach leaves
2 scallions, white part and 1 inch (2.5 cm) green, chopped
1 tablespoon (15 ml) Chinese cooking wine or dry sherry (optional)
2 to 3 tablespoons (30 to 45 ml) rice vinegar, to taste

1 tablespoon (15 ml) low-sodium soy sauce
2 tablespoons (30 ml) cornstarch
¼ cup (59 ml) water
½ teaspoon (2.5 ml) freshly ground pepper or to taste
3 drops of dark sesame oil
¼ cup (59 ml) egg substitute
1 cup (236 ml) cooked crabmeat, picked over
chopped scallions for garnish

Cover mushrooms with warm water; let stand for 30 minutes. Drain; strain and reserve soaking liquid. Squeeze mushrooms dry; cut into julienne strips. Bring stock and reserved mushroom liquid to a simmer in a large pot. Add mushrooms, spinach, and scallions to stock. Simmer for 5 minutes.

Stir in wine, vinegar, and soy sauce. Mix cornstarch with water and stir into soup. Cook, stirring constantly, until slightly thickened. Turn off heat. Add pepper and sesame oil. Stirring continuously, slowly pour egg substitute into soup. Add crabmeat; stir well. Ladle into hot soup bowls. Garnish with chopped scallions.

MAKES 6 SERVINGS

Per 1½-cup (354 ml) serving: calories, 66 ◆ protein, 6 g ◆ carbohydrate, 7 g ◆ fat, 2 g (calories from fat, 27%) ◆ dietary fiber, 1 g ◆ cholesterol, 23 mg ◆ sodium, 277 mg ◆ potassium, 286 mg Joslin Exchanges: ½ low-fat meat, ½ bread/starch

Curried Potato Chowder

A delicious potato soup made without cream or butter.

olive oil cooking spray
2 large onions, about 1 pound (450 g), thinly sliced
1 garlic clove, minced
⅛ teaspoon (.6 ml) sugar
3 cups (708 ml) beef stock (page 44)
2 large russet potatoes, about 2 pounds (900 g), peeled and diced

¼ cup (59 ml) dry white wine
1 tablespoon (15 ml) curry powder
½ teaspoon (2.5 ml) dry English mustard
1 cup (236 ml) plain nonfat yogurt, drained
grated lemon zest for garnish
thin cucumber slices for garnish

In a large nonstick covered skillet that has been lightly sprayed with cooking spray, cook onions and garlic over low heat until onions wilt, about 15 minutes. Stir frequently. Uncover, stir in sugar, and continue to cook, stirring often, until onions begin to brown.

Meanwhile, in a large saucepan, bring stock to a boil. Add potatoes, reduce heat to a simmer, and cook until potatoes are tender when pierced with a fork, about 15 minutes. Add onions. Add wine to skillet; stir to loosen any browned bits. Add wine mixture to potato mixture. Return soup to a simmer. Cook for another 5 to 10 minutes, until potatoes begin to fall apart and soup thickens. Stir in curry powder and dry mustard. Remove soup from stove; stir in yogurt. Return soup to stove;

heat through. Do not allow to boil. Ladle into hot soup plates; garnish with grated lemon zest and cucumber slices.

MAKES 8 SERVINGS

Per 1-cup (236 ml) serving:
calories, 137 ◆ protein, 4 g ◆
carbohydrate, 30 g ◆ fat, trace
(calories from fat, less than 1%) ◆
dietary fiber, 3 g ◆ cholesterol, 1
mg ◆ sodium, 45 mg ◆
potassium, 610 mg
Joslin Exchanges: 2 bread/starch

Corn Chowder Variation

Omit curry powder, dry mustard, and plain nonfat yogurt. Chop onions and potatoes into small dice. Cook as directed until potatoes are just tender. Add ½ cup (118 ml) fresh corn kernels or defrosted frozen corn just before serving. Garnish each serving with 1 tablespoon (15 ml) chopped cooked turkey bacon.

MAKES 8 SERVINGS

Per 1-cup (236 ml) serving:
calories, 129 ◆ protein, 3 g ◆
carbohydrate, 30 g ◆ fat, trace
(calories from fat, less than 1%) ◆
dietary fiber, 1 g ◆ cholesterol, 1
mg ◆ sodium, 36 mg ◆
potassium, 541 mg
Joslin Exchanges: 2 bread/starch

 # Fresh Cream of Pea Soup

Make this soup in late spring, when fresh peas are in the market. Other times, substitute defrosted frozen tiny peas.

Serve the soup cold in summer, garnished with fresh mint.

1½ cups (354 ml) vegetable stock
(page 47) or chicken stock
(page 45)
2 pounds (900 g) fresh peas,
shelled, or 2 cups (472 ml)
frozen peas
¼ cup (59 ml) chopped fresh mint
or 1 tablespoon (15 ml) crushed
dried

2 cups (472 ml) evaporated skim
milk
2 tablespoons (30 ml) cornstarch
pinch of ground nutmeg
freshly ground pepper to taste
4 scallions, white part only,
chopped
6 tablespoons (90 ml) plain
nonfat yogurt, drained

In a large saucepan, bring stock to a boil. Add peas, mint, and scallions; reduce to a simmer and cook, covered, until peas are tender, 10 to 15 minutes (5 minutes for frozen peas). Puree in batches in a food processor or blender until smooth.

In a medium-size bowl, combine evaporated milk and cornstarch; mix well. Add to hot soup. Return to stove and simmer until thickened, about 5 minutes. Season with nutmeg and pepper. Ladle into hot soup bowls. Serve with a small dollop of yogurt.

MAKES 6 SERVINGS

Per 1-cup (236 ml) serving: calories, 128 ◆ protein, 10 g ◆ carbohydrate, 21 g ◆ fat, trace (calories from fat, less than 1%) ◆ dietary fiber, 1 g ◆ cholesterol, 4 mg ◆ sodium, 167 mg ◆ potassium, 433 mg Joslin Exchanges: ½ nonfat milk, 1 bread/starch

---

CELEBRATING SPRING

◆

Fresh Cream of Pea Soup (page 52)

Bajan Chicken Brochettes (page 186)

Basmati Rice with Parsley and Lemon (page 288)

Fresh Strawberries with Balsamic Vinegar (page 430)

Per serving: 511 calories (22% fat)
Joslin Exchanges: 3 ½ low-fat meat, 2 bread/starch, 2 vegetable, 1 fruit, ½ nonfat milk

Tortilla Chicken Soup with Lime

One of our favorites, this soup gets its spirited flavor and aroma from the lime and cilantro. If you don't like cilantro, you can use fresh mint for a different but equally good flavor.

1 ¹/₂-pound (225 g) skinless and boneless chicken breast
1 tablespoon (15 ml) dry white wine (optional)
2 fresh flat-leaf parsley sprigs
2 slices of fresh lime
3 corn tortillas
olive oil cooking spray
1 quart (1 l) chicken stock (page 45)
2 to 3 garlic cloves, to taste, peeled and pressed
3 to 4 tablespoons (45 to 59 ml) fresh lime juice, to taste
¹/₄ cup (59 ml) evaporated skim milk
1 tablespoon (15 ml) cornstarch
¹/₂ teaspoon (2.5 ml) freshly ground pepper or to taste
¹/₄ cup (59 ml) chopped fresh cilantro (fresh coriander) or fresh mint

In a heavy nonstick skillet, poach chicken breast in simmering water to cover along with white wine, parsley sprigs, and lime slices until chicken is tender, about 10 minutes. Drain, discarding poaching liquid. Shred cooked chicken; set aside.

Meanwhile, preheat oven to 400° F (205° C). Cut each tortilla into thin strips. Lightly spray a baking sheet with cooking spray. Arrange tortilla strips in a single layer on baking sheet. Bake until crisp, about 5 to 7 minutes. Remove from oven; set aside.

In a large saucepan, bring stock, garlic, and lime juice to a boil. Reduce heat and simmer for 10 minutes. Combine skim milk and cornstarch. Stir into soup. Heat until slightly thickened, about 4 minutes. Add shredded chicken and pepper; heat through. Divide tortilla strips among 4 heated soup plates. Ladle soup over tortilla chips. Sprinkle with chopped cilantro.

MAKES 4 SERVINGS

Per 1¹/₂-cup (354 ml) serving:
calories, 159 ◆ protein, 15 g ◆ carbohydrate, 16 g ◆ fat, 4 g (calories from fat, 23%) ◆ dietary fiber, 2 g ◆ cholesterol, 32 mg ◆ sodium, 132 mg ◆ potassium, 286 mg
Joslin Exchanges: 1¹/₂ low-fat meat, 1 bread/starch

Cream of Watercress Soup

Here we've lightened a year-round favorite, using plain nonfat yogurt instead of the more traditional heavy cream. Fresh spinach can be substituted for watercress.

1 quart (1 l) chicken stock (page 45)	¼ teaspoon (1.25 ml) salt (optional)
¼ cup (59 ml) minced onion	½ cup (118 ml) plain nonfat yogurt
2 bunches of watercress, trimmed	freshly ground pepper to taste

In a large saucepan, bring chicken stock to a boil over high heat. Add onion and watercress. Reduce heat, cover, and simmer for 5 to 10 minutes, until watercress is tender. In a food processor or blender, puree mixture until smooth. Stir in salt, yogurt, and pepper. Serve warm or cover, chill for up to 1 day, and serve cold.

MAKES 4 SERVINGS

Per 1½-cup (354 ml) serving: calories, 24 ◆ protein, 3 g ◆ carbohydrate, 4 g ◆ fat, trace (calories from fat, less than 1%) ◆ dietary fiber, trace ◆ cholesterol, 1 mg ◆ sodium, 215 mg ◆ potassium, 263 mg
Joslin Exchanges: 1 vegetable

Roasted Yellow Pepper Soup

Roasting the peppers intensifies the flavor of this colorful soup. Whenever we roast peppers, we do a few extra to refrigerate or freeze for future use. Substitute red peppers for equally flavorful results.

2 large yellow bell peppers, about 1 pound (450 g), roasted and peeled (see page 100)	1 small celery root, about ¼ pound (115 g), peeled and chopped
1 large onion, about ½ pound (225 g), chopped	6 cups (1.5 l) chicken stock (page 45)
2 large potatoes, about 1 pound (450 g), peeled and cut into ½-inch (1.5 cm) chunks	4 teaspoons (20 ml) olive oil
2 large carrots, about ½ pound (225 g), peeled and sliced	4 teaspoons (20 ml) unsalted sunflower seeds

Cut peppers into large chunks. In a large soup pot, combine peppers with onion, potatoes, carrots, celery root, and chicken stock. Bring to a boil, cover, and simmer until carrots and potatoes are very tender, about 20 to 25 minutes.

In a food processor or blender, in batches, puree vegetables and stock until smooth. Return soup to stove; heat through. Ladle into hot soup plates. Drizzle each serving with ½ teaspoon (2.5 ml) olive oil and sprinkle with ½ teaspoon (2.5 ml) sunflower seeds.

MAKES 8 SERVINGS

Per 1-cup (236 ml) serving: calories, 114 ◆ protein, 2 g ◆ carbohydrate, 20 g ◆ fat, 3 g (calories from fat, 24%) ◆ dietary fiber, 1 g ◆ cholesterol, 0 mg ◆ sodium, 61 mg ◆ potassium, 508 mg
Joslin Exchanges: 1 bread/starch

Creamy Gazpacho

A particularly refreshing soup for hot weather, this easy-to-make gazpacho is best made in late summer, when the tomatoes are vine ripened and luscious. Serve it in small cups or mugs with a scallion swizzle stick as a starter for dinner or in bowls for a light lunch.

1 medium-size cucumber, about ½ pound (225 g), peeled, seeded, and coarsely chopped
1 medium-size red onion, about 3 ounces (85 g), coarsely chopped
2 garlic cloves, chopped
2 large fresh tomatoes, about 1 pound (450 g), peeled, seeded, and coarsely chopped
1 cup (236 ml) tomato juice
2 tablespoons (30 ml) tomato paste
1 cup (236 ml) chicken stock (page 45)

2 cups (472 ml) plain low-fat yogurt
pinch of cayenne pepper
3 tablespoons (45 ml) chopped scallion for garnish
3 tablespoons (45 ml) finely chopped red bell pepper for garnish
3 tablespoons (45 ml) finely chopped toasted almonds for garnish

Place cucumber, onion, garlic, and tomatoes in a food processor. Process to a smooth puree (you may need to do this in batches). Pour mixture into a large bowl. Stir in tomato juice, tomato paste, chicken stock, yogurt, and cayenne. Blend well. Chill for at least 6 hours. Stir well before serving. Ladle into small soup cups or mugs. Garnish the center of each cup with small mounds of scallion, red pepper, and almonds.

MAKES 12 SERVINGS

Per ¹/₂-cup (118 ml) serving: calories, 54 ◆ protein, 3 g ◆ carbohydrate, 7 g ◆ fat, 2 g (calories from fat, 33%) ◆ dietary fiber, 1 g ◆ cholesterol, 2 mg ◆ sodium, 128 mg ◆ potassium, 280 mg
Joslin Exchanges: ¹/₂ nonfat milk

FAMILY REUNION

◆

Creamy Gazpacho with Scallion Swizzles (page 56)

Lemon Pepper Breadsticks (page 396)

London Broil with Sun-Dried Tomato Sauce (page 231)

Vegetable Terrine (page 315)

Fresh Peach Cake (page 411)

Per serving: 530 calories (30% fat)
Joslin Exchanges: 3 medium-fat meat, 3 bread/starch, 1 vegetable, ¹/₂ nonfat milk

Spicy Seafood Gazpacho

Gazpacho is getting bolder, and good cooks everywhere are creating intriguing new recipes for this Spanish cold soup. Our version is a meal in a bowl and has a southwestern accent.

Serve with a tossed salad and crusty bread for an easy, light summertime meal.

 2 quarts (2 l) water
juice of 1 lemon
 1 fresh thyme sprig or ¼ teaspoon (1.25 ml) crushed dried
 1 parsley sprig
30 large fresh shrimp, about 1 pound (450 g)
18 small fresh clams
 4 ripe but firm tomatoes, about 1 pound (450 g), peeled and seeded
 2 cucumbers, about 1 pound (450 g), peeled and seeded
 1 small onion, about 3 ounces (85 g)
 1 celery rib
 1 garlic clove, peeled
 1 large red bell pepper, seeded

 1 Anaheim chili, seeded (optional)
 2 tablespoons (30 ml) fresh lime juice
 2 tablespoons (30 ml) fresh lemon juice
 2 teaspoons (10 ml) olive oil
 ½ cup (118 ml) chopped cilantro (fresh coriander)
 ¼ teaspoon (1.25 ml) salt (optional)
freshly ground pepper to taste
 ¼ teaspoon (1.25 ml) ground cumin
 ⅛ teaspoon (.6 ml) Tabasco sauce or to taste
cilantro (fresh coriander) sprigs for garnish

In a large saucepan, bring water to a boil. Add lemon, thyme, parsley, and shrimp. Shrimp are done when they rise to the top, about 2 minutes. Remove shrimp with a strainer. Peel and devein. Pour out and reserve cooking liquid, leaving 1 cup (236 ml) in pot. Discard thyme and parsley.

With a stiff brush, scrub clams under running water to remove any sand. Add clams to cooking liquid in pot. Cover and steam over medium-high heat until clams open, about 6 minutes, discarding any unopened clams. Remove clams from shells. Wash out clam shells, taking care not to break them apart; set aside for later use. Add clam cooking liquid to reserved shrimp cooking liquid. Cover and chill seafood.

Either by hand or in a food processor, finely chop all vegetables. Add 2 cups (472 ml) reserved cooking liquid, lime juice, lemon juice, olive oil, cilantro, salt, pepper, cumin, and Tabasco sauce. Chill for 3 hours.

To serve, ladle gazpacho into 6 large chilled soup plates. Arrange 5 shrimp and 3 clams (placed back in the reserved clean clam shells) on each serving. Garnish with cilantro sprigs.

MAKES 6 SERVINGS

Per 2-cup (472 ml) serving: calories, 113 ◆ protein, 13 g ◆ carbohydrate, 10 g ◆ fat, 3 g (calories from fat, 23%) ◆ dietary fiber, 1 g ◆ cholesterol, 91 mg ◆ sodium, 222 mg ◆ potassium, 474 mg Joslin Exchanges: 2 low-fat meat, 2 vegetable

Cucumber Buttermilk Soup

The simplicity of this cooling soup makes it a favorite in summer when cooking should be light and easy.

2 medium-size cucumbers, about 1 pound (450 g), peeled
2 scallions, white part only, chopped
2 cups (472 ml) buttermilk
1¾ cups (413 ml) chicken stock (page 45)
¼ teaspoon (1.25 ml) salt (optional)

freshly ground pepper to taste
1 tablespoon (15 ml) fresh lemon juice
paper-thin slices of unpeeled cucumber for garnish
grated lemon zest for garnish

Cut peeled cucumbers in half lengthwise. Using a small spoon, scoop out and discard seeds. Coarsely grate cucumber using a hand grater or food processor.

In a large bowl, combine grated cucumbers, scallions, buttermilk, chicken stock, salt, pepper, and lemon juice. Mix well. Cover and refrigerate for several hours, until well chilled. Stir well before serving. Garnish each serving with a thin cucumber slice and a light sprinkling of grated lemon zest.

MAKES 6 SERVINGS

Per 1-cup (236 ml) serving: calories, 43 ◆ protein, 3 g ◆ carbohydrate, 6 g ◆ fat, 1 g (calories from fat, 20%) ◆ dietary fiber, 1 g ◆ cholesterol, 3 mg ◆ sodium, 189 mg ◆ potassium, 259 mg Joslin Exchanges: 1 vegetable

LUNCH IN THE GARDEN

◆

Cucumber Buttermilk Soup (page 59)

Shrimp Salad with Grapes (page 144)

Chive Popovers (page 388)

Honeydew Granita (page 435)

Per serving: 390 calories (23% fat)
Joslin Exchanges: 3 low-fat meat, 3 vegetable, 1 bread/starch, 1 fruit

Albuquerque Chicken and Corn Soup

A southwestern treat with vivid color and a hint of cumin and cilantro (fresh coriander). Remember this whole-meal soup when fresh corn is at the farmer's markets. In the winter, use defrosted frozen corn.

1 3-pound (1.35 kg) frying chicken, cut up
2 quarts (2 l) chicken stock (page 45)
1 large onion, about ½ pound (225 g), stuck with 2 cloves
1 large carrot, about ½ pound (225 g), peeled and cut into 3 pieces
1 large celery rib with leaves, cut into 3 pieces
2 whole garlic cloves, peeled
1½ teaspoons (7.5 ml) crushed dried thyme
1 teaspoon (5 ml) ground cumin
1 bay leaf
freshly ground pepper to taste
3 cups (708 ml) corn kernels
1 large red bell pepper, about ½ pound (225 g), seeded and chopped
2 cups (472 ml) cooked white rice
⅓ cup (78 ml) chopped fresh cilantro (fresh coriander) or fresh flat-leaf parsley

In a large soup pot, combine chicken, stock, onion, carrot, celery, garlic, thyme, cumin, bay leaf, and pepper. Bring to a boil. Reduce heat to a simmer and cook until chicken is tender, about 40 minutes. Skim off any foam and fat. Remove chicken; cool and chop the meat into bite-size pieces. Discard bones and skin. Remove and reserve vegetables. Discard cloves and bay leaf.

In a food processor or blender, puree 1½ cups (354 ml) corn kernels with the reserved onion, carrot, celery, and garlic and ½ cup (118 ml) of the soup broth. Return corn mixture to the soup pot along with the remaining 1½ cups (354 ml) corn kernels, chopped chicken meat, bell pepper, cooked rice, and ¼ cup (59 ml) chopped cilantro. Simmer for another 15 minutes. Taste for seasoning, adding more cumin and pepper if needed. Ladle into hot soup plates; garnish with remaining cilantro.

MAKES 8 SERVINGS

Per 2-cup (472 ml) serving: calories, 234 ◆ protein, 20 g ◆ carbohydrate, 29 g ◆ fat, 5 g (calories from fat, 19%) ◆ dietary fiber, trace ◆ cholesterol, 51 mg ◆ sodium, 95 mg ◆ potassium, 345 mg Joslin Exchanges: 2 low-fat meat, 2 bread/starch

Peach Soup

A perfect summer beginning (or ending—you could serve this in stemmed goblets as dessert). Be sure that the peaches are fully ripened. Nectarines can be substituted.

3 large ripe peaches, about 1 pound (450 g)
3 tablespoons (45 ml) fresh orange juice
3 tablespoons (45 ml) fresh lemon juice

½ cup (118 ml) crème fraîche (page 428)
4 fresh mint sprigs for garnish

Peel and pit peaches; cut into chunks. In a food processor or blender, puree peaches with orange juice and lemon juice. Add crème fraîche; mix until smooth. Serve or cover and chill for up to 1 day. Garnish with mint. Stir before using.

MAKES 4 SERVINGS

Per 1-cup (236 ml) serving: calories, 74 ◆ protein, 2 g ◆ carbohydrate, 17 g ◆ fat, 1 g (calories from fat, 12%) ◆ dietary fiber, 1 g ◆ cholesterol, 2 mg ◆ sodium, 21 mg ◆ potassium, 324 mg Joslin Exchanges: 1 fruit

---

FAMILY SUPPER

◆

Grilled Chicken Breasts

with Smoky Barbecue Sauce (page 174)

Grilled Corn on the Cob (page 306)

Buttermilk Slaw (page 94)

Peach Soup (page 61)

Per serving: 394 calories (23% fat)
Joslin Exchanges: 3 low-fat meat, 3 vegetable, 1 bread/starch, 1 fruit

Yellow Tomato Bisque with Fiery Tomato Ice

A great flavor combination—hot yellow tomato soup topped with a scoop of fiery tomato ice. This ice would be terrific in a cold carrot soup or the Roasted Yellow Pepper Soup (page 55).

If your market doesn't have yellow tomatoes, of course you can use red tomatoes.

Fiery Tomato Ice

1½ cups (354 ml) tomato juice
½ cup (118 ml) firmly packed
    fresh cilantro (fresh coriander)
    or fresh mint leaves

2 tablespoons (30 ml) seeded and
    minced fresh jalapeño chilies
freshly ground pepper to taste

Soup

1 tablespoon (15 ml) olive oil
½ cup (118 ml) chopped onion
¼ cup (59 ml) finely chopped carrot
¼ cup (59 ml) finely chopped celery
2 garlic cloves, minced
3 pounds (1.35 kg) yellow or red tomatoes, peeled, seeded, and chopped
1 medium-size russet potato, about 5 ounces (140 g), peeled and chopped

3 cups (708 ml) chicken stock (page 45)
1 bay leaf
¼ teaspoon (1.25 ml) freshly ground pepper or to taste
3 parsley sprigs
6 cilantro or fresh mint sprigs for garnish

Combine tomato juice, cilantro, chilies, and pepper. Pour into a 9-inch (23 cm) square cake pan, cover tightly with foil, and freeze until solid, 1 hour or longer.

Let ice stand at room temperature until you can break it into chunks with a heavy spoon. Whirl chunks in a food processor or beat with a mixer until mixture forms a smooth slush. Return to cake pan and freeze for another 30 to 45 minutes.

Meanwhile, heat olive oil in a large heavy saucepan over low heat. Add onion, carrot, celery, and garlic. Sauté until onion is limp but not browned, about 4 minutes. Add tomatoes, potato, stock, bay leaf, pepper, and parsley. Lower the heat to simmer and cook, stirring occasionally, for 30 minutes. Remove and discard bay leaf and parsley.

In a food processor or blender, puree soup until smooth (you may need to do this in batches). Return soup to the stove; reheat and keep hot.

To serve, remove ice from freezer. Let stand at room temperature for a few minutes, until you can easily scoop it with an ice cream scoop or large spoon.

Ladle hot soup into heated soup plates. Shape ice into 6 equal scoops. Quickly place 1 scoop in the center of each soup serving with a sprig of cilantro alongside. Serve at once.

MAKES 6 SERVINGS

Per 1½-cup (354 ml) serving: calories, 111 ◆ protein, 3 g ◆ carbohydrate, 21 g ◆ fat, 3 g (calories from fat, 24%) ◆ dietary fiber, 2 g ◆ cholesterol, 0 mg ◆ sodium, 269 mg ◆ potassium, 814 mg
Joslin Exchanges: 1 bread/starch, ½ fat

Per ¼-cup (59 ml) serving (ice alone): calories, 14 ◆ protein, 1 g ◆ carbohydrate, 3 g ◆ fat, trace (calories from fat, less than 1%) ◆ dietary fiber, 1 g ◆ cholesterol, 0 mg ◆ sodium, 220 mg ◆ potassium, 163 mg
Joslin Exchanges: free

Shrimp Gumbo

This southern stewlike soup needs only a salad to complete a meal for a cool autumn evening.

2   medium-size onions, about ½ pound (225 g), chopped
2   garlic cloves, pressed or minced
1   large green bell pepper, about ½ pound (225 g), seeded and chopped
1   teaspoon (5 ml) olive oil
2   tablespoons (16 g) unbleached flour
1   quart (1 l) fish stock (page 46)
1   pound (450 g) fresh plum tomatoes, peeled and chopped
5   ounces (140 g) fresh okra, stems removed and sliced, or ½ 10-ounce (285 g) box frozen sliced okra

gumbo filé powder (optional)
1   teaspoon (5 ml) Worcestershire sauce
1   small bay leaf
½   teaspoon (2.5 ml) crushed dried thyme
cayenne pepper to taste
¾   pound (340 g) medium-size shrimp, peeled and deveined
1   cup (236 ml) hot cooked rice

In a large nonstick saucepan over low heat, sauté onions, garlic, and green pepper in oil until onions are wilted, about 5 minutes. Sprinkle with flour and cook, stirring constantly, until flour turns a deep golden brown color. Slowly add fish stock, stirring constantly. Add remaining ingredients except shrimp, rice, and filé powder. Simmer, uncovered, for 30 minutes, skimming foam as necessary.

Just before serving, add shrimp and simmer until shrimp turn pink, about 5 minutes. Serve immediately, ladling each portion over ¼ cup (59 ml) hot rice in a soup bowl. Sprinkle with filé powder.

MAKES 4 SERVINGS

Per 2-cup (472 ml) serving: calories, 205 ◆ protein, 15 g ◆ carbohydrate, 32 g ◆ fat, 2 g (calories from fat, 10%) ◆ dietary fiber, 5 g ◆ cholesterol, 98 mg ◆ sodium, 699 mg* ◆ potassium, 854 mg
Joslin Exchanges: 1 low-fat meat, 2 bread/starch

* Not recommended for low-sodium diets, except for occasional use only.

Red Lentil Soup

This is our version of the lentil soup served at Rancho la Puerta, a health spa in Tecate, Mexico. Using red lentils instead of the usual brown ones speeds up the cooking time. Red lentils are available in Indian markets and natural food stores.

While the soup cooks, make a vegetable salad, and you have a meal.

½ pound (225 g) red lentils
2 quarts (2 l) water
1 tablespoon (15 ml) olive oil
1 medium-size onion, about 3 ounces (85 g), chopped
1 medium-size tomato, about 6 ounces (180 g), peeled, seeded, and coarsely chopped
1 medium-size green bell pepper, about 6 ounces (180 g), seeded and chopped
4 garlic cloves, minced
1 large leek, white part only, well rinsed and thinly sliced

1 fresh jalapeño or serrano chili, seeded and minced
1 teaspoon (5 ml) ground cumin
1 quart (1 l) vegetable stock (page 47)
¼ teaspoon (1.25 ml) salt or to taste
¼ teaspoon (1.25 ml) freshly ground pepper or to taste
¼ cup (59 ml) chopped fresh flat-leaf parsley for garnish
¼ cup (59 ml) thinly sliced scallion, white part only, for garnish

In a large saucepan, simmer lentils in water until tender, about 10 minutes. Drain.

In a large soup pot, heat olive oil over medium heat. Add onion, tomato, bell pepper, garlic, leek, chili, and cumin. Sauté until vegetables are limp, about 5 minutes. Add lentils and vegetable stock. Cook for 5 minutes. Season with salt and pepper. Ladle into hot soup bowls. Garnish with parsley and scallions.

MAKES 6 SERVINGS

Per 1-cup (236 ml) serving: calories, 147 ◆ protein, 9 g ◆ carbohydrate, 24 g ◆ fat, 3 g (calories from fat, 18%) ◆ dietary fiber, 6 g ◆ cholesterol, 0 mg ◆ sodium, 139 mg ◆ potassium, 505 mg
Joslin Exchanges: 1½ bread/starch, ½ low-fat meat

Wild Mushroom Soup

In the fall our local markets are filled with several varieties of fresh wild mushrooms. If your store doesn't have fresh wild mushrooms, you can get the woodsy flavor by substituting 1 ounce (30 g) dried mushrooms, soaked in hot water for half an hour, and ½ pound (225 g) fresh cultivated mushrooms.

2 teaspoons (10 ml) olive oil
½ pound (225 g) fresh wild mushrooms, a mixture of chanterelles, shiitake, porcini, morels, or whatever is available, sliced
2 shallots, chopped
1 small onion, about 3 ounces (85 g), chopped
1 medium-size potato, about 5 ounces (140 g), peeled and finely chopped
1 carrot, about 5 ounces (140 g), peeled and finely chopped

1 quart (1 l) chicken stock (page 45) or vegetable stock (page 47)
½ tablespoon (7.5 ml) fresh lemon juice
1 tablespoon (15 ml) chopped fresh parsley
½ teaspoon (2.5 ml) fresh thyme leaves or ¼ teaspoon (1.25 ml) crushed dried
¼ teaspoon (1.25 ml) Tabasco sauce or to taste
½ teaspoon (2.5 ml) salt (optional)
freshly ground pepper to taste

Heat oil in a large nonstick skillet. Add mushrooms, shallots, and onion; sauté over low heat until mushrooms are tender and all liquid has evaporated, about 7 minutes.

Using a food processor, finely chop mushroom mixture. Transfer to a large soup pot. Add potato, carrot, and stock. Bring to a boil; reduce heat to simmer and cook until vegetables are tender, about 15 to 20 minutes.

Stir in lemon juice, parsley, thyme, and Tabasco sauce. Simmer for another 5 minutes. Add salt and pepper. Ladle into hot soup plates.

MAKES 6 SERVINGS

Per 1-cup (236 ml) serving: calories, 79 ◆ protein, 3 g ◆ carbohydrate, 15 g ◆ fat, 2 g (calories from fat, 22%) ◆ dietary fiber, 1 g ◆ cholesterol, 0 mg ◆ sodium, 218 mg ◆ potassium, 541 mg Joslin Exchanges: 1 bread/starch

Chinese Turkey and Cellophane Noodle Soup

A delicate yet highly flavored soup that uses Chinese rice stick noodles, sometimes labeled *Chinese vermicelli*, found in the Asian section of many supermarkets. The noodles must be soaked prior to cooking.

Serve with Snow Pea and Pearl Onion Salad (page 108) and offer tangerines for dessert.

½ pound (225 g) ground turkey
2 tablespoons (30 ml) rolled oats
½ teaspoon (2.5 ml) minced fresh ginger
1 garlic clove, minced
1 scallion, white part plus 1 inch (2.5 cm) green, minced
¼ cup (59 ml) chopped canned water chestnuts

2 ounces (60 g) Chinese rice stick noodles
5 cups (1.25 l) chicken stock (page 45)
1 tablespoon (15 ml) low-sodium soy sauce
⅛ teaspoon (.6 ml) dark sesame oil
chopped scallions for garnish

In a small bowl, combine turkey, oats, ginger, garlic, minced scallion, and water chestnuts. Using about 1 tablespoon (15 ml) of the turkey mixture, form into small balls. Drop turkey balls into a pot of simmering water, cover, and cook for 10 minutes. Drain.

Meanwhile, break rice stick noodles into 2-inch (5 cm) lengths. Soak according to package directions. In a large pot, bring stock to a boil. Add turkey balls and noodles. Simmer for 5 minutes. Add soy sauce and sesame oil. Ladle into hot soup bowls. Garnish with chopped scallions.

MAKES 4 SERVINGS

Per 1½-cup (354 ml) serving: calories, 135 ◆ protein, 14 g ◆ carbohydrate, 17 g ◆ fat, 1 g (calories from fat, less than 6%) ◆ dietary fiber, 1 g ◆ cholesterol, 35 mg ◆ sodium, 221 mg ◆ potassium, 265 mg Joslin Exchanges: 1½ low-fat meat, 1 bread/starch

Tomato Pasta Soup

At the first hint of frost we're quick to pick the last of the tomatoes and make a pot of soup that's perfect fare for a chilly evening. Make the soup with canned Italian plum tomatoes in winter.

Ditalini are tiny, very short tubes of macaroni. More common elbow macaroni can also be used.

Serve the soup with Green Chili Scones (page 390) and a light dessert for a simple, satisfying soup meal.

½ cup (85 g) dried cannellini beans, rinsed and picked over

1 quart (1 l) chicken stock (page 45) or vegetable stock (page 47)

1 large leek, white part only, well rinsed and thinly sliced

2 medium-size onions, about ½ pound (225 g), chopped

1 celery rib, thinly sliced

1 garlic clove, minced

1 cup (236 ml) peeled, seeded, and chopped fresh tomatoes or chopped, drained, canned Italian plum tomatoes

1 large red bell pepper, about ½ pound (225 g), seeded and chopped

2 tablespoons (30 ml) dry red wine (optional)

½ teaspoon (2.5 ml) salt (optional)

¼ teaspoon (1.25 ml) freshly ground pepper

½ cup (60 g) ditalini or elbow macaroni

1 tablespoon (15 ml) olive oil

6 tablespoons (90 ml) shredded fresh basil for garnish

1 tablespoon (15 ml) freshly grated Parmesan cheese for garnish

Place beans and cold water to cover in a medium-size saucepan. Bring to a boil over high heat; cook for 2 minutes. Remove from heat, cover, and let sit for 1 hour.

Meanwhile, in a heavy soup pot, heat ¼ cup (59 ml) stock over medium heat. Add leek, onions, celery, and garlic; cook for 5 to 8 minutes, stirring frequently, until vegetables are tender but not browned. Drain beans, discarding soaking liquid; add beans to soup pot along with remaining chicken stock, tomatoes, red bell pepper, wine, salt, and black pepper. Bring to a boil, cover, and reduce heat to simmer. Cook for 1 hour, until beans are tender. Add macaroni and continue to simmer until pasta is just tender, about 10 minutes.

Ladle into hot soup plates. Drizzle each serving with ½ teaspoon (2.5 ml) olive oil, 1 tablespoon (15 ml) shredded fresh basil, and ½ teaspoon (2.5 ml) grated Parmesan cheese.

MAKES 6 SERVINGS

Per 1½-cup (354 ml) serving: calories, 143 ◆ protein, 6 g ◆ carbohydrate, 25 g ◆ fat, 3 g (calories from fat, 18%) ◆ dietary fiber, 3 g ◆ cholesterol, 0 mg ◆ sodium, 226 mg ◆ potassium, 517 mg

Joslin Exchanges: 1½ bread/starch

Baby Pumpkin Soup

Pint-size pumpkins make charming individual containers for this soup made without cream. Use miniature pumpkins such as Munchkin or Jack Be Little.

4 baby pumpkins, about 6 to 8 ounces (180 to 225 g) each
1 cup (236 ml) dry white wine
1 fresh thyme sprig or ¼ teaspoon (1.25 ml) crushed dried
½ bay leaf
1 cup chopped well-rinsed leek, white part only
2 garlic cloves, minced
2 teaspoons (10 ml) olive oil
¾ cup (177 ml) chicken stock (page 45)
¼ teaspoon (1.25 ml) salt (optional)
¼ teaspoon (1.25 ml) freshly ground pepper or to taste
toasted pumpkin seeds for garnish

Cut off tops of pumpkins. Scrape out and discard seeds and strings from pumpkins. Using a short, sharp knife, hollow out pumpkins to leave ½-inch-thick (1.5 cm) shells. Reserve pumpkin pulp.

In a large saucepan, bring wine, thyme, and bay leaf to a boil. Add pumpkin shells, cover, and simmer until slightly softened, about 20 minutes. Remove shells from pan; keep warm. Reserve cooking liquid.

Meanwhile, in a large saucepan, sauté leeks and garlic in olive oil over low heat until leeks and garlic are limp but not browned. Add stock, reserved pumpkin, salt, and pepper. Simmer for 20 minutes, until pumpkin is very tender when pierced with a fork. Remove from heat and transfer to a food processor or blender. Puree until smooth. Thin soup with reserved pumpkin-cooking liquid to desired consistency.

Fill pumpkin shells with hot soup. Garnish with toasted pumpkin seeds. Serve at once.

MAKES 4 SERVINGS

Per ³/₄-cup (177 ml) serving: calories, 69 ◆ protein, 1 g ◆ carbohydrate, 12 g ◆ fat, 3 g (calories from fat, 30%) ◆ dietary fiber, 2 g ◆ cholesterol, 0 mg ◆ sodium, 154 mg ◆ potassium, 123 mg
Joslin Exchanges: 2 vegetable, ¹/₂ fat

FALL DINNER PARTY

◆

Baby Pumpkin Soup (page 69)

Italian Pork with Creamy Polenta (page 251)

Braised Broccoli Rabe (page 340)

Poached Pears with Roasted Plum Sauce (page 436)

Per serving: 495 calories (21% fat)
Joslin Exchanges: 3 low-fat meat, 3 vegetable, 1¹/₂ bread/starch, 2 fruit

Root Vegetable Soup

This velvety and intensely flavored soup is easy to make and perfect for starting special cold-weather meals. Root vegetables never tasted so delicious.

Yukon Gold potatoes are becoming quite popular and more readily available. We love their buttery texture, but if you can't find them, substitute any white potato.

3 shallots, minced
1 large onion, about ¹/₂ pound (225 g), thinly sliced

1 small celery root, about ³/₄ pound (340 g), peeled and thinly sliced

2 medium-size Yukon Gold or
   white potatoes, about 10 ounces
   (285 g), peeled and coarsely
   chopped
2 small parsnips, about 5 ounces
   (140 g), peeled and thinly sliced
1 carrot, about 3 ounces (85 g),
   peeled and thinly sliced

½ teaspoon (2.5 ml) ground
   coriander
5 cups (1.25 l) chicken stock
   (page 45)
½ teaspoon (2.5 ml) salt (optional)
freshly ground pepper to taste
snipped fresh chives for garnish

In a large soup pot, combine shallots, onion, celery root, potatoes, parsnips, carrot, coriander, and chicken stock. Bring to a boil; reduce heat and simmer for 35 to 40 minutes, until vegetables are very tender. Puree in blender or food processor until smooth. (You may need to do this in batches.) Return soup to the pot. Add salt and pepper to taste. Serve hot, sprinkling chives on each portion.

MAKES 8 SERVINGS

Per 1-cup (236 ml) serving:
calories, 66 ◆ protein, 2 g ◆
carbohydrate, 16 g ◆ fat,
trace (calories from fat,

3%) ◆ dietary fiber, 3 g ◆
cholesterol, 0 mg ◆ sodium, 208
mg ◆ potassium, 426 mg
Joslin Exchanges: 1 bread/starch

Black Bean Soup with Chili Chutney

The humble elements of this soup make a flavorful main course with a spicy twist. Fresh mint can be used instead of cilantro in the chutney.

Serve this soup with Winter Vegetable Salad with Yogurt Garlic Dressing (page 112). Offer frozen grapes (popped into the freezer for about 3 hours) for dessert.

1 tablespoon (15 ml) olive oil
2 large onions, about 1 pound (450
   g), chopped
3 garlic cloves, minced
2 celery ribs, including some
   leaves, chopped
1 carrot, about 3 ounces (85 g),
   chopped
½ pound (225 g) dried black beans,
   rinsed and picked over
⅛ teaspoon (.6 ml) cayenne pepper
   or to taste

1 teaspoon (5 ml) ground cumin
2 quarts (2 l) chicken stock
   (page 45)
½ teaspoon (2.5 ml) salt (optional)
2 tablespoons (2.5 ml) fresh lemon
   juice
2 fresh jalapeño chilies, seeded
   and coarsely chopped
½ cup (118 ml) loosely packed
   fresh cilantro (fresh coriander)
   or mint leaves

Heat oil in a large soup pot over low heat. Add onions and garlic; sauté until onions are limp but not browned. Add celery, carrot, beans, cayenne pepper, cumin, and chicken stock. Bring to a boil over high heat; reduce heat, cover, and simmer for 2 to 2½ hours, until beans are very tender.

Whirl soup in a food processor or blender (you may need to do this in batches) until smooth. Return soup to pan; add salt and 1 tablespoon (15 ml) lemon juice. Reheat; keep hot.

Meanwhile, in a clean food processor or blender, make chili chutney by combining jalapeños, remaining 1 tablespoon (15 ml) lemon juice, and cilantro or mint. Process to a coarse puree.

Ladle soup into hot soup plates. Top each serving with some of the chili chutney.

MAKES 8 SERVINGS

Per 1-cup (236 ml) serving: calories, 124 ◆ protein, 6 g ◆ carbohydrate, 21 g ◆ fat, 2 g (calories from fat, 15%) ◆ dietary fiber, 4 g ◆ cholesterol, 0 mg ◆ sodium, 194 mg ◆ potassium, 445 mg
Joslin Exchanges: 1 vegetable, 1 bread/starch

Creamed Onion Soup

A terrific soup for a cold winter day. Vegetarians can substitute vegetable stock (page 47) for the chicken stock.

butter-flavored cooking spray
2 large onions, about 1 pound (450 g), thinly sliced
⅔ cup (156 ml) dry white wine
1⅓ cups (314 ml) chicken stock (page 45)
2 tablespoons (30 ml) chopped fresh basil or 2 teaspoons (10 ml) crushed dried
1 teaspoon (5 ml) fresh thyme leaves or ¼ teaspoon (1.25 ml) crushed dried
1½ tablespoons (22.5 ml) cornstarch
1½ cups (354 ml) evaporated skim milk
chopped scallions, including some greens, for garnish

Lightly spray a large nonstick saucepan with cooking spray. Place over low heat; add onions, cover, and cook, stirring frequently, until onions are wilted, about 15 minutes. Add wine, stock, and herbs. Simmer, covered, for 20 minutes. Stir together cornstarch and evaporated milk, mixing well. Add to onion soup. Return soup to a simmer, stirring until thickened. Ladle into hot soup bowls; garnish with chopped scallions.

MAKES 4 SERVINGS

Per 1-cup (236 ml) serving: calories, 147 ◆ protein, 8 g ◆ carbohydrate, 22 g ◆ fat, 3 g (calories from fat, 18%) ◆ dietary fiber, 2 g ◆ cholesterol, 4 mg ◆ sodium, 130 mg ◆ potassium, 528 mg Joslin Exchanges: 1 nonfat milk, 2 vegetable

Hearty Beef Vegetable Soup

A French combination called *petite marmite*, this is a rich combination of broth, vegetables, and meat traditionally served in individual deep kettle-shaped soup crocks. It's particularly enjoyable in winter.

½ pound (225 g) very lean boneless beef, such as rump or bottom round roast
1 quart (1 l) beef stock (page 44)
1 bay leaf
1 tablespoon (15 ml) fresh thyme leaves or 1 teaspoon (5 ml) crushed dried
3 carrots, about ½ pound (225 g), peeled and cut into chunks
3 celery ribs, cut into 1½-inch (4 cm) pieces

2 medium-size onions, about ½ pound (225 g), coarsely chopped
2 small turnips, about 6 ounces (180 g), peeled and cut into chunks
1 small cabbage, about 1 pound (450 g), cored and cut into 6 wedges
6 thin slices of French bread, toasted
3 tablespoons (19 g) grated Parmesan cheese

Trim the beef of all visible fat, thinly slice, and sauté in a nonstick skillet over medium heat until lightly seared. Place in a large soup pot along with stock, bay leaf, and thyme. Bring to a simmer and cook for 45 minutes, skimming off any foam that rises to the top. Add vegetables; continue to simmer for 45 minutes. Remove bay leaf.

Preheat broiler. Ladle soup into 6 individual deep bowls. Top with French bread; sprinkle each bread slice with ½ tablespoon (7.5 ml) Parmesan cheese. Place under broiler to brown the cheese. Serve at once.

MAKES 6 SERVINGS

Per 1-cup (236 ml) serving: calories, 271 ◆ protein, 14 g ◆ carbohydrate, 32 g ◆ fat, 10 g (calories from fat, 33%) ◆ dietary fiber, 2 g ◆ cholesterol, 29 mg ◆ sodium, 370 mg ◆ potassium, 756 mg
Joslin Exchanges: 2 bread/ starch, 1 medium-fat meat, 1 fat

APRÈS-SKI DINNER

◆

Hearty Beef Vegetable Soup (page 73)

Walnut Raisin Whole-Wheat Peasant Bread (page 399)

Orange and Onion Salad (page 106)

Baked Pears (page 441)

Per serving: 556 calories (29% fat)
Joslin Exchanges: 1 medium-fat meat, 3 bread/starch, 2½ fruit, 2 fat

Seafood Chowder

A hearty fish soup that's perfect on a cold winter's night. We used orzo, the tiny rice-shaped pasta, but you can also use brown rice.

1 tablespoon (15 ml) olive oil
1 medium-size onion, about ¼ pound (115 g), chopped
2 celery ribs, diagonally sliced

1 small red bell pepper, about ¼ pound (115 g), seeded and chopped
1 medium-size leek, white part only, well rinsed and thinly sliced

2 carrots, peeled and diagonally
  sliced
3 garlic cloves, chopped
½ teaspoon (2.5 ml) crushed dried
  basil
½ teaspoon (2.5 ml) crushed dried
  thyme
¼ teaspoon (1.25 ml) crushed
  dried oregano
¼ teaspoon (1.25 ml) freshly
  ground pepper or to taste
2½ cups (590 ml) bottled clam juice

1 15-ounce (425 g) can plum
  tomatoes with liquid, coarsely
  chopped
¼ teaspoon (1.25 ml) cayenne
  pepper or to taste
⅓ cup (60 g) orzo or rice
½ pound (225 g) medium-size
  shrimp, peeled and deveined
½ pound (225 g) sea scallops
1 6½-ounce (195 g) can chopped
  clams, drained
2 tablespoons (30 ml) chopped
  fresh basil or flat-leaf parsley for
  garnish

Heat oil in a large heavy saucepan over medium heat. Add onion, celery, bell pepper, leek, carrots, and garlic. Sauté until onions are limp, about 5 minutes. Add basil, thyme, oregano, pepper, clam juice, tomatoes, and cayenne pepper. Bring to a boil. Reduce heat and simmer until slightly thickened, stirring occasionally, about 30 minutes.

In a medium-size saucepan, cook orzo in boiling water until just tender, stirring occasionally, about 8 minutes. Drain. Set aside.

Add shrimp and scallops to chowder; cook for 4 minutes, until shrimp are pink and scallops are no longer opaque. Add clams; heat through.

Divide orzo among 6 heated soup plates. Ladle chowder over orzo and sprinkle with chopped basil.

MAKES 6 SERVINGS

Per 1½-cup (354 ml) serving:
calories, 196 ◆ protein, 17 g ◆
carbohydrate, 24 g ◆ fat, 4 g
(calories from fat, 18%) ◆
dietary fiber, 2 g ◆ cholesterol,
61 mg ◆ sodium, 365 mg ◆
potassium, 702 mg
Joslin Exchanges: 1½ low-fat
meat, 1½ bread/starch

FIRESIDE SUPPER WITH FRIENDS

◆

Mâche (page 87) in Radicchio Cups with Classic Vinaigrette

(page 114)

Sun-Dried Tomato and Garlic Breadsticks (page 397)

Seafood Chowder (page 74)

Baked Apples (page 441) with Crème Fraîche (page 428)

Per serving: 488 calories (22% fat)
Joslin Exchanges: 1½ low-fat meat, 2½ bread/starch, 1½ fruit, ½ nonfat milk,
1 fat

Persian Bean and Noodle Soup

This is a very filling main-course soup, full of fiber and complex carbohydrates, so keep the salad and dessert course light.

¼ cup (45 g) dried chick-peas
¼ cup (45 g) dried small white beans
¼ cup (45 g) dried small red beans
¼ cup (45 g) dried black-eyed peas
2 cups (472 ml) chopped onion
2 leeks, white part and 1 inch (2.5 cm) green, well rinsed, and thinly sliced
6 garlic cloves, minced
1 tablespoon (15 ml) olive oil

¼ cup (45 g) lentils
2 quarts (2 l) chicken stock (page 45) or vegetable stock (page 47)
6 ounces (180 g) wide noodles (such as pappardelle or tagliatelle)
1 teaspoon (5 ml) turmeric
¼ teaspoon (1.25 ml) freshly ground pepper or to taste
¼ cup (59 ml) chopped parsley

3 tablespoons (45 ml)) chopped
  fresh mint or 1 tablespoon (15
  ml) crushed dried
3 tablespoons (45 ml) chopped
  fresh dill or 1 tablespoon (15 ml)
  dried dill weed

1 tablespoon (15 ml) chopped
  fresh fennel or 1 teaspoon (5 ml)
  fennel seed

Wash and pick over dried beans. Place in a large pot with water to cover. Bring to a boil over high heat; reduce heat to simmer and cook for 2 minutes. Remove from heat and allow to soak for 1 hour. Drain.

Meanwhile, in a large soup pot, sauté onions, leeks, and garlic in olive oil over low heat until onions are limp. Add lentils, drained beans, and stock. Cook, uncovered, over low heat until beans begin to get tender, about 1 hour.

Add noodles to the soup along with turmeric, pepper, and herbs. Continue to cook for 6 to 8 minutes, until noodles are tender. Ladle into hot soup plates.

MAKES 8 SERVINGS

Per 1½-cup (354 ml) serving: calories, 193 ◆ protein, 8 g ◆ carbohydrate, 35 g ◆ fat, 3 g (calories from fat, 14%) ◆ dietary fiber, 3 g ◆ cholesterol, 0 mg ◆ sodium, 104 mg ◆ potassium, 483 mg Joslin Exchanges: 1 vegetable, 2 bread/starch

Beef Barley Soup

A hearty meal in a bowl that needs only a bit of warmed bread and a fresh green salad for a comforting soup supper.

2 pounds (900 g) beef shin bones,
  all fat and membranes removed
¾ pound (340 g) lean boneless
  round steak, chopped into ½-
  inch (1.5 cm) cubes
1 quart (1 l) beef stock (page 44)
3½ cups (826 ml) water
½ cup (118 ml) dry red wine
½ cup (118 ml) chopped celery
½ cup (118 ml) chopped carrot
1 cup (236 ml) chopped onion
1 garlic clove, minced

1 teaspoon (5 ml) crushed dried
  thyme
1 bay leaf
1 rutabaga, about ½ pound (225
  g), peeled and coarsely chopped
1 medium-size leek, white part
  only, well rinsed and chopped
½ pound (225 g) fresh
  mushrooms, sliced
1 cup (180 g) fine or medium
  pearled barley

In a large soup pot, combine all ingredients except barley. Bring to a boil over medium heat. Reduce heat to simmer; cook for 2 hours, skimming off surface fat as necessary. Remove shin bones. Add barley and continue to cook 15 to 20 minutes, until barley is tender.

MAKES 6 SERVINGS

Per 1½-cup (354 ml) serving: calories, 242 ◆ protein, 17 g ◆ carbohydrate, 37 g ◆ fat, 3 g (calories from fat, 11%) ◆ dietary fiber, 2 g ◆ cholesterol, 32 mg ◆ sodium, 79 mg ◆ potassium, 773 mg
Joslin Exchanges: 1 medium-fat meat, 1 vegetable, 2 bread/starch

Winter Vegetable Soup

Humble vegetables—leeks, onions, carrots, parsnips, tomatoes, and spinach—with a complex carbohydrate and fiber boost from lentils, split peas, and small white beans, cooked in an herb broth, make a savory soup that's sure to chase away the winter chill.

The Sage and Onion Focaccia (page 394) would be splendid with this soup. Offer pears and a small wedge of Italian Fontina for dessert.

½ pound (225 g) leeks
1 cup (236 ml) chopped onion
1 tablespoon (15 ml) olive oil
½ pound (225 g) carrots, peeled and diagonally sliced
½ pound (225 g) parsnips, peeled and chopped
2 tablespoons (25 g) lentils
2 tablespoons (25 g) dried split peas
2 tablespoons (25 g) dried small white beans
5 small fresh thyme sprigs or 1 teaspoon (5 ml) crushed dried

½ teaspoon (2.5 ml) freshly ground pepper or to taste
2 quarts (2 l) chicken stock (page 45)
1 pound (450 g) canned Italian plum tomatoes, drained and chopped
5 ounces (140 g) fresh spinach, well rinsed, stems discarded
½ cup (118 ml) fresh flat-leaf parsley leaves, loosely packed

Trim leeks, leaving 1 inch (2.5 cm) of green. Cut leeks in half lengthwise and rinse well under running water, then thinly slice them.

In a large soup pot, sauté leeks and onion in oil over medium heat for 5 minutes, until onions are soft but not browned. Add carrots, parsnips, lentils, split peas, white beans, thyme, black pepper, and stock. Bring to a boil; reduce heat to simmer, cover, and cook for 45 minutes, stirring occasionally. Add tomatoes and continue to simmer for 15 minutes, until white beans are tender. Add spinach and cook until spinach is wilted, about 3 minutes. Ladle into heated soup plates, discarding thyme sprigs. Scatter parsley leaves on top and serve.

MAKES 8 SERVINGS

> **Per 1-cup (236 ml) serving:** calories, 118 ◆ protein, 4 g ◆ carbohydrate, 22 g ◆ fat, 2 g (calories from fat, 15%) ◆dietary fiber, 3 g ◆ cholesterol, 0 mg
>
> ◆ sodium, 173 mg ◆ potassium, 668 mg Joslin Exchanges: 1½ bread/ starch

White Bean Soup

This homey soup is great for a crowd. Topped with a bell pepper and red onion relish, it's full of interesting contrasts in flavors and textures.

2 cups (340 g) dried white beans, such as Great Northern
6 cups (1.5 l) cold water
¼ teaspoon (1.25 ml) salt (optional)
2 slices of turkey bacon, chopped
2 large onions, about 1 pound (450 g), chopped
2 garlic cloves, minced
1 celery rib with leaves, chopped
5 cups (1.25 l) chicken stock (page 45)
2 bay leaves
1½ tablespoons (22.5 ml) fresh thyme leaves or 1½ teaspoons (7.5 ml) crushed dried

1 cup (236 ml) dry white wine
¼ cup (59 ml) balsamic vinegar
2 cups (472 ml) evaporated skim milk, mixed with 2 tablespoons (30 ml) cornstarch
freshly ground pepper to taste
¼ cup (59 ml) chopped red bell pepper for garnish
¼ cup (59 ml) chopped green bell pepper for garnish
¼ cup (59 ml) chopped red onion for garnish

Rinse and pick over beans. Soak beans overnight in cold water to cover. Or bring to a boil, simmer for 1 minute, remove from heat, cover, and let stand for 1 hour. Drain beans.

Place beans, 6 cups (1.5 l) cold water, and salt in a large soup pot. Bring to a boil over high heat. Reduce heat to simmer and cook, stirring occasionally, for 40 minutes, until beans are tender. Drain and reserve beans; discard cooking liquid.

In the same soup pot, combine turkey bacon, onions, garlic, celery, herbs, and stock. Bring to a boil; reduce heat to simmer and cook, covered, for 45 to 50 minutes. Add wine and vinegar; continue to cook for 15 minutes. Add reserved beans, evaporated milk mixed with cornstarch, and pepper. Simmer for 15 minutes, stirring frequently, until beans are quite tender and soup has thickened. Discard bay leaves.

Combine bell peppers and red onion. Ladle soup into hot soup plates and garnish each serving with a heaped tablespoon (15 ml) of the bell pepper/onion mixture.

MAKES 8 SERVINGS

Per 1½-cup (354 ml) serving: calories, 227 ◆ protein, 15 g ◆ carbohydrate, 40 g ◆ fat, 1 g (calories from fat, 4%) ◆ dietary fiber, 4 g ◆ cholesterol, 5 mg ◆ sodium, 226 mg ◆ potassium, 816 mg Joslin Exchanges: 1 low-fat meat, 2 bread/starch, 2 vegetable

---

A KITCHEN SUPPER

◆

Country Pâté (page 36) with Assorted Mustards

White Bean Soup (page 79)

Warm Grapefruit and Orange with Sherry Sauce (page 437)

Per serving: 443 calories (22% fat)
Joslin Exchanges: 3 low-fat meat, 2 bread/starch, 2 vegetable, 1 fruit

Chicken and Rice Soup in a Pot

We remember seeing "chicken in a pot" on menus of ethnic New York City restaurants of our youth. This is a healthier rendition of that dish, lower in fat and salt. Make the soup ahead to allow time for the fat to congeal so it can be removed easily.

1 quart (1 l) chicken stock
(page 45)
2 cups (472 ml) water
1 pound (450 g) chicken breasts
with bones and skin
1 small sweet potato, scrubbed
1 small turnip, scrubbed
1 large carrot, peeled

1 celery rib
1 large onion, peeled
1 fresh dill sprig or ¼ teaspoon
(1.25 ml) dried dill weed
1 bay leaf
6 to 8 peppercorns, to taste
1 cup (236 ml) cooked rice or
kasha (buckwheat groats)

In a large soup pot, combine all ingredients except rice or kasha. Bring to a boil, skimming foam from surface as it accumulates. Lower heat, cover, and simmer for 1 hour, until chicken and vegetables are very tender.

Remove chicken and all vegetables. Strain soup through a strainer lined with cheesecloth. Return soup to pot. Thinly slice celery and carrot. Finely chop chicken, discarding skin and bones. Return celery, carrot, and chicken to the pot. (Save sweet potato, turnip, and onion for another use.) Place soup in refrigerator or freezer. Fat will rise to the surface; remove it with a spoon. To serve, reheat soup, adding rice or kasha.

MAKES 6 SERVINGS

Per 1½-cup (354 ml) serving: calories, 143 ◆ protein, 19 g ◆ carbohydrate, 11 g ◆ fat, 2 g (calories from fat, 14%) ◆ fiber, 1 g ◆ cholesterol, 48 mg ◆ sodium, 82 mg ◆ potassium, 258 mg
Joslin Exchanges: 2 low-fat meat, 1 bread/starch

Italian Fish Soup

This light and delicate soup should be made with low-fat, firm-fleshed white fish fillets such as haddock, hake, pollack, or tilefish. Perfect for midweek entertaining, the soup cooks in 30 minutes. Make the rest of the meal the night before. Be sure to include some fresh fennel in the basket of crudités.

2 medium-size onions, about ½ pound (225 g), chopped
2 to 3 garlic cloves, to taste, minced
1 teaspoon (5 ml) olive oil
1 quart (1 l) fish stock (page 46)
1 bay leaf
1 tablespoon (15 ml) chopped fresh basil or 1 teaspoon (5 ml) crushed dried
1 teaspoon (5 ml) fresh thyme leaves or ¼ teaspoon (1.25 ml) crushed dried

1 28-ounce (790 g) can low-sodium Italian plum tomatoes, chopped
1 pound (450 g) firm-fleshed white fish fillets, cut into 1-inch (2.5 cm) strips
freshly ground pepper to taste
lemon slices for garnish
shredded fresh basil for garnish
4 teaspoons (20 ml) grated Parmesan cheese for garnish

In a large, heavy nonstick saucepan over low heat, sauté onions and garlic in oil until onions are wilted, about 5 minutes. Add stock, bay leaf, basil, and thyme. Simmer for 10 minutes, skimming foam as necessary.

Add tomatoes and fish. Simmer until fish is done, another 8 to 10 minutes. Do not overcook. Add pepper and serve. Garnish each portion with lemon slices, shredded basil, and a teaspoon (5 ml) of Parmesan cheese.

MAKES 4 SERVINGS

Per 2-cup (472 ml) serving: calories, 162 ◆ protein, 19 g ◆ carbohydrate, 15 g ◆ fat, 3 g (calories from fat, 17%) ◆ fiber, 3 g ◆ cholesterol, 66 mg ◆ sodium, 144 mg ◆ potassium, 813 mg
Joslin Exchanges: 3 low-fat meat, 2 vegetable

MIDWEEK WINTER SOUP PARTY

◆

Crudités with Lemon and Pepper (page 5)

Rosemary and Raisin Focaccia (page 394)

Italian Fish Soup (page 82)

Fresh Pineapple Upside-Down Polenta Cake (page 413)

Per serving: 452 calories (23% fat)
Joslin Exchanges: 3 low-fat meat, 3 vegetable, 2½ bread/starch

SALADS

Low in calories and high in fiber, salads are a godsend for dieters. They can be dazzling and full of exciting, satisfying flavor, but as we all know, they can also be full of hidden calories from dressings and salad extras that are high in fat and sodium. This is particularly true at salad bars, not always a healthful choice at the food market or a restaurant. Potato salad slathered with mayonnaise, bacon bits, chopped eggs, shreds of cheese, cubes of avocado, pasta salad covered with oil—all can add hundreds of fat calories to an otherwise healthful plate of lettuces and vegetables. Add salad dressing at 80 to 100 calories per tablespoon (15 ml) and you've spent several days' worth of fat allowances on one salad. So it's important to know how to make your own dressings and select items for your salads that fit into your meal plan.

One rule for creating really good salads is to follow the seasons—forget winter tomatoes, for instance. Even in this age of hothouses and interhemispheric jet freight, the best salad ingredients are usually those in the local market.

THE GREENS

Most salads start with cold, crisp greens. Pick the freshest available, choosing them for looks, taste, and texture. After washing greens thoroughly in cold water to remove any sand or silt, wrap them in paper towels, tuck them into a plastic bag (don't seal it), and store in the refrigerator until you need them. You can also rinse and refrigerate the greens in a colander to dry and crisp.

Be sure the greens are dry, then tear or cut them into bite-size pieces.

These are some of our favorites:

Arugula

A staple in restaurants on both coasts of the United States and throughout Europe, arugula (also called *rocket*) is now readily available in supermarkets year-round. It can also easily be grown in the home garden. Resembling large radish leaves in texture and appearance, arugula's pungent and peppery flavor is excellent by itself and makes a lively addition to other greens. Choose leaves that are deep bright green with no evidence of yellowing; use within a day or two. The pretty blossoms are edible too. Combine with mild lettuce such as Boston or Bibb.

Beet Greens

Strip the leaves away from the stems of tiny beet greens. Wash the leaves thoroughly. Cut the scarlet stems into 2-inch (5 cm) lengths. Blanch in boiling water until tender, about 4 minutes. Refresh under running cold water. Combine this year-round green with any mild green.

Belgian Endive

The mildest member of the chicory family, these pearly-pale spear-shaped heads add elegance and flavor to salads. Select heads that are firm and crisp, with tightly furled leaves and pale yellow-green tips. Belgian endive is available September through May; use within a day or two of purchase. Cut out the bitter conical core with a paring knife to separate the leaves. Use whole, cut into fine strips, or cut crosswise to form crescents. Combine with watercress, arugula, radicchio, Bibb, Boston, or loose-leaf lettuces.

Cabbage

This year-round salad green includes the familiar red cabbage frequently used as a filler in restaurant salads; Chinese or Napa cabbage with its large, crinkled, light green leaves; bok choy (Chinese white cabbage) with large ivory-white stalks and dark green, white-veined, rounded leaves; and savory, a mild-flavored loose head of crinkled leaves varying from dark to pale green. Kale, a cabbage cousin, has frilly deep green leaves tinged with shades of blue or purple. All add interesting taste and texture. Combine with bean or alfalfa sprouts.

Dandelion Greens

No longer just a nuisance in your spring lawn, dandelion greens have become a year-round greenhouse item that's milder in flavor than the wild variety. (You can also eat your own *if* your lawn has not been treated with pesticides or fertilizers.)

Use the smallest leaves for salads (mixed with loose-leaf lettuces), cooking the larger leaves like spinach. Dandelion greens are particularly delicious when used with warm dressings made with intense oils such as walnut or hazelnut. Combine with loose-leaf lettuce and butterheads (Boston, Bibb, and limestone).

Edible Flowers

Flowery "sallets" were eaten by Elizabethans. In 1699 English diarist John Evelyn wrote of "sallets" containing the flowers of caper, orange, and nasturtium plants. We still use nasturtiums, as well as calendula petals, rose petals, violets, chive blossoms, scented geraniums, pansies or violas, bee balm, lavender, hyssop, and pineapple sage. Use only flowers that are sold as "edible flowers" at a produce market (never eat flowers from a commercial florist) or pick your own flowers from your garden. *Be certain that the flowers you use are pesticide-free. Don't use flowers you don't know about; if in doubt, call your local poison control center. Be sure that your children also know the difference between safe and unsafe flowers.* They're available sporadically throughout the year at the produce market. Use with any mixed greens.

Frisée

This hard-to-find frizzy version of standard curly endive is a visual show-off. The heads are flattened with feathery narrow leaves that range in color from ivory to deep chartreuse. The bittersweet taste enlivens almost any mixture of salad greens and stands on its own as a backdrop for warm seafood and poultry salads. Frisée is expensive, so be sure to select the head carefully, making sure there are no brown leaves you'll pay for and then have to discard. Use within a few days, cutting off the base and separating the leaves. Frisée is available sporadically year-round, with peak season from June through October. Combine with arugula and baby lettuces.

Herbs

Finely chopped or used as whole leaves, fresh herbs add a nice bite to salads. We can't imagine a summer green salad without a handful of fresh chervil, parsley, or basil. Other herbs to try are chives, mint (be sure to check out the fruit varieties—apple, pineapple, orange), fennel, borage, purslane (check in Greek markets for this fleshy-leaved herb), parsley (both flat-leaf and curly), and sweet marjoram. Use strong herbs such as tarragon and sage with some restraint. Don't forget the blossoms: the flowers of basil, borage, chive, marjoram, thyme, sage, and rosemary can all be used for interesting flavor and splashes of color. We've also adopted the Middle Eastern tradition of putting out small plates of fresh herbs—mint, basil, tarragon, cilantro, parsley—to be eaten along with the meal. The herbs freshen the palate and add extra flavor to the dishes served. Fresh herbs can be found at various times of the year, depending on the herb, with the more common herbs like parsley, thyme, sage, rosemary, cilantro, and basil available all of the time.

Loose-Leaf Lettuce

All types of loose-leaf lettuces, once the prize of the home gardener and farmer's markets, are now widely available year-round. We like the soft and ruffly pale green or bronze-red oak leaf types. Select heads that are not waterlogged; use within two days. Combine with watercress, arugula, and radicchio.

Mâche

Also called *corn salad, lamb's lettuce, lamb's tongue,* or *field salad.* Although it grows wild in some parts of the country, this is a "gourmet" green to most of us, pricey and hard to find. We love its nutlike flavor and buy the violet-shaped bright green leaves whenever we can. Mâche is very delicate; use within a day of purchase. It's available sporadically throughout the year. Best alone—serve it with a light vinaigrette, piled into a radicchio leaf.

Market Lettuce

The most familiar lettuces: iceberg, the Ford of lettuces and salad bars; butterheads (Boston, Bibb, and limestone); and reliably crunchy and sweet-tasting romaine (also called *cos lettuce*), the only lettuce for Caesar salad. All are readily available year-round from supermarkets, farmer's markets, and can be easily grown in the garden. Combine with spinach, arugula, radicchio, and watercress.

Mesclun

This mixed green treat from the south of France is easy to grow in the home garden (see Appendix 2 to order seeds by mail), and is now being marketed from coast to coast in gourmet produce markets and some supermarket chains. A blend of 8 to 12 varieties of baby lettuce leaves, savory herbs, edible petals, and wild greens, it's a ready-to-serve salad, needing only a light vinaigrette. Mesclun is very delicate; use the same day it's purchased or picked. Our markets offer different mesclun mixes throughout the year. Serve alone.

Mizuna

A member of the mustard family, this sprightly green with fernlike leaves has a nippy flavor and is becoming more readily available at farmer's markets and Asian produce markets. It's easily grown in the home garden (see Appendix 2 to order seeds by mail). Select bright green leaves that are four to five inches long. Available sporadically throughout the year. Combine with Bibb, Boston, and loose-leaf lettuces.

Radicchio

This red-leafed version of Italian chicory is now readily available year-round in produce markets and many supermarkets. Radicchio di Verona grows in a small, loose head similar to butterhead lettuce with burgundy-red leaves with white ribs. Radicchio di Treviso has narrow, tuliplike, pink to red leaves with white ribs. Both varieties have a slightly bitter flavor. We love it as a solo green, but radicchio also adds a vibrant splash of color and a slight bite to mixed salads. It can be grilled, sautéed, or baked and served as a warm salad.

Radish leaves

Don't overlook this lively-flavored green that would otherwise end up in the compost heap. Select only the tiniest leaves for best flavor. Just a few leaves can do wonders for a mixed green salad. Available year-round.

Spinach

Choose baby spinach leaves for salads (the grown-up leaves are tough and are best cooked). The leaves should be dark green and crisp and, depending on the variety, will be curled or smooth with a nice fresh fragrance. Use spinach throughout the year alone or mixed with almost any other green.

Sprouts

These make a great finish for a mixed green salad or whole-meal salad of seafood or poultry. We are particularly fond of radish and alfalfa sprouts, but bean sprouts, mustard sprouts, and daikon sprouts also add a bit of bite. Select sprouts with no signs of yellowing at the seeds. Use within a day or two of purchase, snipping off the roots of large sprouts. Fresh sprouts are available throughout the year; combine with just about any green.

Watercress

This member of the mustard family is sold in small bouquets throughout the year. Watercress has small, crisp, dark green leaves with a peppery bite. Refrigerate in a plastic bag for up to 5 days. Wash and shake dry just before using. Combines well with Boston, loose-leaf lettuces, and Belgian endive. Often used alone.

Favorite Green Combinations

Most of the time we eat a salad with lunch and dinner, sprinkling a little fresh lemon juice, balsamic, or red wine vinegar onto the greens. Here are our favorite combinations.

Spring:
- mixed baby lettuces (red oak leaf, green oak leaf, ruffly red) and edible flowers
- radicchio, Belgian endive, and fennel
- dandelion, Boston, and spinach
- arugula and Bibb

Summer:
- Bibb, Boston, and radish sprouts
- beet greens and baby lettuces (Boston, ruffly green, green oak leaf)
- red oak leaf, Boston, basil, chervil, dill, mint, and parsley
- Boston and baby nasturtium leaves

Fall:
- spinach and bean sprouts
- red cabbage, green cabbage, bok choy
- frisée and green leaf lettuce
- mesclun mixture of dandelion, red oak leaf, watercress, arugula, radicchio, frisée, parsley, and mint

Winter:
- watercress and Belgian endive
- mâche and radicchio
- dandelion, arugula, and Bibb
- spinach and watercress

Cucumber Salad

This salad should be served as soon as it's made, while the flavors are still bright. To serve as a light lunch or snack, spoon the cucumbers over sliced tomatoes into whole-wheat pita bread.

2 large cucumbers, about 1 pound (450 g), peeled and seeded

2 small fresh hot red chilies, seeded and minced

1 garlic clove, minced

2 tablespoons (30 ml) chopped fresh cilantro (fresh coriander) or dill

3 tablespoons (45 ml) fresh lime juice

Shred cucumbers. In a large bowl, combine cucumbers, chilies, garlic, cilantro, and lime juice. Toss lightly to mix. Serve immediately.

MAKES 4 SERVINGS

Per serving: calories, 25 ◆ protein, 1 g ◆ carbohydrate, 6 g ◆ fat, trace (calories from fat, 7%) ◆ dietary fiber, 1 g

◆ cholesterol, 0 mg ◆ sodium, 4 mg ◆ potassium, 256 mg
Joslin Exchanges: 1 vegetable

Asparagus Salad with Dill Vinaigrette

A springtime delight. Don't bother peeling asparagus unless the spears are very large or past their prime. If you don't have a microwave to wilt the bell pepper, drop it into boiling water for 30 seconds. Drain and refresh under cold running water.

1 pound (450 g) fresh asparagus
1 medium-size red bell pepper, about 6 ounces (180 g), seeded and cut into thin strips
2 tablespoons (30 ml) white wine vinegar
2 tablespoons (30 ml) olive oil
1/2 teaspoon (2.5 ml) Dijon mustard
1 tablespoon (15 ml) chopped parsley

1/2 tablespoon (7.5 ml) chopped fresh dill or 1/2 teaspoon (2.5 ml) dried dill weed
1 tablespoon (15 ml) minced shallot or minced scallion, white part only
freshly ground pepper to taste
2 hard-cooked large egg whites, chopped

Snap off woody ends of asparagus. Rinse under cold water. Peel if necessary. Cook in 3 to 4 inches (8 to 10 cm) boiling water until just tender (1 to 2 minutes for tiny spears, 3 to 5 minutes for small spears, 5 to 8 minutes for medium-size spears, and 10 to 12 minutes for large). Drain and refresh in ice-cold water. Place red pepper strips in a microwave dish. Cook on HIGH power, covered, for 20 seconds to wilt.

Prepare dressing by whisking together vinegar, olive oil, mustard, parsley, dill, shallot, and pepper. Toss with cooled asparagus.

Arrange asparagus on 6 chilled salad plates. Decorate with red pepper and chopped egg white.

MAKES 6 SERVINGS

Per serving: calories, 72 ◆ protein, 3 g ◆ carbohydrate, 5 g ◆ fat, 5 g (calories from fat, 60%) ◆ dietary fiber, 1 g ◆

cholesterol, 0 mg ◆ sodium, 33 mg ◆ potassium, 184 mg
Joslin Exchanges: 1 vegetable, 1 fat

Endive Salad with Beet Vinaigrette

Serve this tart salad as a refreshing first course before roasted poultry or meat.

The dressing is also excellent spooned over split heads of baby lettuces or a slice of delicate Vidalia onion (or other sweet variety such as Walla Walla, Maui, or Texas 1015 Supersweet). Taste the onion first to be sure it really *is* sweet.

3 Belgian endives, about 9 ounces (250 g), washed, cored, and cut into 1-inch (2.5 cm) rounds
2 hard-cooked large egg whites chopped

1 tablespoon (15 ml) minced fresh tarragon or flat-leaf parsley

Beet Vinaigrette

2 teaspoons (10 ml) Dijon mustard
3 tablespoons (45 ml) red wine vinegar
3 tablespoons (45 ml) water
½ teaspoon (2.5 ml) sugar
1 garlic clove, peeled and quartered

¼ teaspoon (1.25 ml) freshly ground pepper or to taste
3 tablespoons (45 ml) olive oil or canola oil
1 cup (236 ml) finely chopped cooked or drained canned beets

Divide endive among 6 salad plates. In a food processor or blender, combine mustard, vinegar, water, sugar, garlic, and pepper. Process until smooth. With motor running, slowly add oil and process until blended. Stir in beets. Spoon over endive. Sprinkle with chopped egg white and tarragon.

MAKES 6 SERVINGS

Per serving: calories, 98 ◆ protein, 3 g ◆ carbohydrate, 7 g ◆ fat, 7 g (calories from fat, 65%) ◆ dietary fiber, 1 g ◆ cholesterol, 0 mg ◆ sodium, 75 mg ◆ potassium, 357 mg Joslin Exchanges: 1 vegetable, 1 fat

Per 1-tablespoon (15 ml) serving (dressing alone): calories, 36 ◆ protein, trace ◆ carbohydrate, 2 g ◆ fat, 4 g (calories from fat, 82%) ◆ dietary fiber, trace ◆ cholesterol, 0 mg ◆ sodium, 18 mg ◆ potassium, 51 mg Joslin Exchanges: 1 fat

Mixed Spring Vegetable Salad with Curry Dressing

This salad depends on tender baby vegetables, but if you can't find them in your market, use standard-size vegetables and cut them into small pieces.

½ pound (225 g) baby carrots, peeled
½ pound (225 g) baby turnips, peeled
boiling water
½ pound (225 g) French green beans (very thin string beans), trimmed
½ pound (225 g) baby beets, trimmed
2 scallions, white part and 2 inches (5 cm) green, chopped
½ cup (118 ml) nonfat yogurt cheese (page 11)

1 tablespoon (15 ml) olive oil
1 teaspoon (5 ml) curry powder or to taste
1 garlic clove, minced
1 teaspoon (5 ml) Dijon mustard
3 tablespoons (45 ml) white wine vinegar
⅛ teaspoon (.6 ml) Worcestershire sauce
¼ pound (115 g) fresh mushrooms, cleaned

In a vegetable steamer over boiling water, steam carrots and turnips until just tender, about 5 minutes. Remove from steamer; set aside. In the same steamer, steam beans for 2 to 3 minutes, until just tender. Remove from steamer; set aside. Repeat process, steaming beets until just tender, about 10 minutes. Remove beets; peel and set aside.

In a small bowl, whisk together remaining ingredients except mushrooms. Toss together vegetables and mushrooms. Arrange on a serving platter. Serve dressing in a small bowl (if you're entertaining, use a hollowed-out cabbage to hold the dressing).

MAKES 8 SERVINGS

Per serving: calories, 68 ◆ protein, 3 g ◆ carbohydrate, 11 g ◆ fat, 2 g (calories from fat, 26%) ◆ dietary fiber, 1 g ◆ cholesterol, 0 mg ◆ sodium, 44 mg ◆ potassium, 388 mg
Joslin Exchanges: 2 vegetable

Apple Slaw

Use Granny Smith, Cortland, Gravenstein, or Rhode Island Greening apples for this delicious slaw.

4 cups (1 l) shredded green cabbage
3 tart apples, about 1 pound (450 g), cored and grated or thinly sliced
2 celery ribs, sliced
¼ cup (59 ml) golden raisins

1 cup (236 ml) plain low-fat yogurt
freshly ground pepper to taste
dash of salt (optional)
2 teaspoons (10 ml) fresh lemon juice
½ teaspoon (2.5 ml) celery seed

In a large bowl, combine cabbage, apples, celery, and raisins. Whisk together yogurt, pepper, salt, lemon juice, and celery seeds. Pour over cabbage mixture; toss.

MAKES ABOUT 12 SERVINGS

Per ½-cup (118 ml) serving: calories, 61 ◆ protein, 2 g ◆ carbohydrate, 11 g ◆ fat, 1 g (calories from fat, 15%) ◆ dietary

fiber, 1 g ◆ cholesterol, 1 mg ◆ sodium, 23 mg ◆ potassium, 196 mg
Joslin Exchanges: 1 fruit

A FAMILY DINNER

◆

Family Turkey Loaf with Savory Gravy (page 221)

Mashed Turnips with Roasted Garlic (page 361)

Apple Slaw (page 93)

Irish Soda Bread (page 392)

Per serving: 360 calories (20% fat)
Joslin Exchanges: 2 low-fat meat, 1 vegetable, 2 bread/starch, 1 fruit

Buttermilk Slaw

Sometimes we make this crunchy slaw with red cabbage or bok choy (Chinese white cabbage)—or a combination of all three.

4 cups (1 l) shredded green
  cabbage
¹/₃ cup (78 ml) chopped red onion
2 carrots, peeled and shredded
¹/₄ cup (59 ml) chopped fresh flat-
  leaf parsley
1 teaspoon (5 ml) curry powder

¹/₄ cup (59 ml) reduced-calorie
  mayonnaise
¹/₄ cup (59 ml) buttermilk
1 tablespoon (15 ml) cider vinegar
dash of Tabasco sauce
¹/₂ teaspoon (2.5 ml) salt (optional)
freshly ground pepper to taste

In a large bowl, combine cabbage, red onion, carrots, and parsley. Whisk together remaining ingredients. Pour over cabbage mixture; toss. Refrigerate for 1 hour before serving.

MAKES ABOUT 6 SERVINGS

Per 1-cup (236 ml) serving:
calories, 40 ◆ protein, 2 g ◆
carbohydrate, 8 g ◆ fat, 1 g
(calories from fat, 13%) ◆

dietary fiber, 1 g ◆ cholesterol, 1
mg ◆ sodium, 216 mg ◆
potassium, 299 mg
Joslin Exchanges: 1 vegetable

Confetti Coleslaw

Coleslaw is a classic American food that's often made with mayonnaise-based or sweet vinegar dressings. Our flavorful version saves on calories and complements most grilled seafood, poultry, and meat.

4 cups (1 l) shredded green
  cabbage
¹/₂ cup (118 ml) chopped green bell
  pepper
¹/₂ cup (118 ml) chopped red bell
  pepper
2 scallions, white part and 2
  inches (5 cm) green, finely
  chopped

2 celery ribs, finely sliced
freshly ground pepper to taste
¹/₂ teaspoon (2.5 ml) salt (optional)
¹/₂ teaspoon (2.5 ml) celery seed
1 teaspoon (5 ml) Dijon mustard
2 tablespoons (30 ml) rice wine
  vinegar
3 tablespoons (45 ml) olive oil

In a large bowl, combine cabbage, bell peppers, scallions, and celery. Whisk together remaining ingredients. Pour over cabbage mixture; toss. Refrigerate for 1 hour before serving.

MAKES 12 SERVINGS

> **Per ½-cup (118 ml) serving:** calories, 44 ◆ protein, 1 g ◆ carbohydrate, 3 g ◆ fat, 4 g (calories from fat, 67%) ◆ dietary fiber, 1 g ◆ cholesterol, 0 mg ◆ sodium, 105 mg ◆ potassium, 129 mg
> Joslin Exchanges: ½ vegetable, 1 fat

Summer Melon Ribbons with Balsamic Vinaigrette

When the sun is hot and melons are plentiful, this is a particularly refreshing salad. The sweet flavor of the paper-thin ribbons of melon is intensified by the balsamic vinegar dressing.

½ 3-pound (1.35 kg) cantaloupe, seeded

½ 3-pound (1.35 kg) honeydew melon, seeded

1 small head of Boston lettuce, leaves separated

Balsamic Vinaigrette

1 medium-size red onion, about 5 ounces (140 g), halved and thinly sliced

2 tablespoons (30 ml) olive oil

freshly ground pepper to taste

2 tablespoons (30 ml) balsamic vinegar

Cut each melon half into quarters and peel. With a vegetable peeler, slice melons into paper-thin ribbons. Chill until ready to use. Wash and crisp lettuce.

Separate onion into rings. Heat oil in a heavy skillet; add onion and sauté over low heat until onions are limp, about 4 minutes, stirring frequently. (Do not let onions brown.) Stir in pepper and balsamic vinegar.

Divide lettuce leaves among 6 salad plates. Arrange melon ribbons on lettuce. Top each with one-sixth of the onion mixture.

MAKES 6 SERVINGS

Per serving: calories, 96 ◆ protein, 1 g ◆ carbohydrate, 14 g ◆ fat, 5 g (calories from fat, 44%) ◆ dietary fiber, 1 g ◆ cholesterol, 0 mg ◆ sodium, 14 mg ◆ potassium, 389 mg
Joslin Exchanges: 1 fruit, 1 fat

Cherry Tomato and Pepper Salad with Lemon Vinaigrette

You can make this colorful salad using red cherry tomatoes and a yellow pepper or yellow cherry tomatoes and a red pepper. The vinaigrette can also be used on a warm white bean or lentil salad.

1 pound (450 g) red or yellow cherry tomatoes
½ yellow or red 6-ounce (180 g) bell pepper, seeded and cut into thin strips

1 large Belgian endive, about ¼ pound (115 g) leaves separated and sliced crosswise into crescents
8 leaves of green leaf lettuce, washed and dried

Lemon Vinaigrette

2 tablespoons (30 ml) fresh lemon juice
1 teaspoon (5 ml) grated lemon zest
2 tablespoons (30 ml) olive oil
1 garlic clove, minced

⅛ teaspoon (.6 ml) curry powder
1 scallion, white part only, chopped
freshly ground pepper to taste
½ teaspoon (2.5 ml) Dijon mustard

In a bowl, combine tomatoes, bell pepper, and endive. Prepare dressing by whisking all ingredients together. Pour over tomatoes; toss. Spoon onto chilled salad plates lined with a lettuce leaf.

MAKES 6 SERVINGS

Per serving: calories, 71 ◆ protein, 2 g ◆ carbohydrate, 7 g ◆ fat, 5 g (calories from fat, 64%) ◆ dietary fiber, 1 g ◆ cholesterol, 0 mg ◆ sodium, 22 mg ◆ potassium, 335 mg
Joslin Exchanges: 1 vegetable, 1 fat

Per 1-tablespoon (15 ml) serving (dressing alone): calories, 43 ◆ protein, trace ◆ carbohydrate, 1 g ◆ fat, 5 g (calories from fat, 92%) ◆ dietary fiber, trace ◆ cholesterol, 0 mg ◆ sodium, 6 mg ◆ potassium, 12 mg
Joslin Exchanges: 1 fat

Carrot and Cucumber Chat

Chat is a cool but spicy Indian salad. Particularly suited for warm weather, this lively salad combination can also be stuffed into pita bread for a snack or light lunch.

¼ cup (59 ml) white wine vinegar
2 teaspoons (10 ml) sugar
1 teaspoon (5 ml) mustard seed
½ teaspoon (2.5 ml) cumin seed
¼ teaspoon (1.25 ml) salt (optional)
1 teaspoon (5 ml) hot red pepper
   flakes or to taste
freshly ground pepper to taste

1 small onion, about 3 ounces
   (85 g), coarsely chopped
1 large carrot, about 5 ounces
   (140 g), peeled and shredded
2 medium-size cucumbers, about 1
   pound (450 g), peeled, halved
   lengthwise, seeded, and thinly
   sliced
¼ cup (59 ml) chopped fresh mint

In a food processor or blender, combine vinegar, sugar, mustard seed, cumin seed, salt, red pepper flakes, pepper, and onion. Process until onion is finely minced.

In a large bowl, combine carrot and cucumbers. Pour on dressing; toss to mix well. Cover and chill for at least 30 minutes and up to 4 hours. Sprinkle with mint just before serving.

MAKES 6 SERVINGS

Per serving: calories, 34 ◆ protein, 1 g ◆ carbohydrate, 8 g ◆ fat, 1 g (calories from fat, 10%) ◆ dietary fiber, 1 g ◆ cholesterol, 0 mg ◆ sodium, 96 mg ◆ potassium, 221 mg
Joslin Exchanges: 1 vegetable

Garden Salad with Balsamic Yogurt Dressing

A terrific combination of garden-fresh vegetables readily available throughout most of the year (in winter, use thinly sliced plum tomatoes). The balsamic yogurt dressing is tangy and bursting with fresh herb flavor.

8 cherry tomatoes, cut in half
4 large celery ribs, thinly sliced
1 green bell pepper, about 6 ounces (180 g), seeded and cut into 1-inch (2.5 cm) squares
1 sweet onion (Vidalia, Walla Walla, Maui, Texas 1015 Supersweet), about 5 ounces

(140 g), quartered and thinly sliced
8 radishes, trimmed and thinly sliced
2 tablespoons (30 ml) chopped fresh chervil or flat-leaf parsley for garnish

Balsamic Yogurt Dressing

3 tablespoons (45 ml) olive oil
2 tablespoons (30 ml) balsamic vinegar
2 tablespoons (30 ml) plain nonfat yogurt
1/4 teaspoon salt (1.25 ml) (optional)

1/4 teaspoon (1.25 ml) freshly ground pepper or to taste
1 tablespoon (15 ml) finely chopped fresh tarragon or 1 teaspoon (5 ml) crushed dried

Place vegetables in a bowl. In a small bowl, whisk together dressing ingredients. Toss vegetables with dressing to coat evenly. Arrange vegetables on 8 serving plates. Sprinkle with chervil. Serve immediately.

MAKES 8 SERVINGS

Per serving: calories, 73 ◆ protein, 1 g ◆ carbohydrate, 6 g ◆ fat, 5 g (calories from fat, 62%) ◆ dietary fiber, 1 g ◆ cholesterol, trace ◆ sodium, 99 mg ◆ potassium, 263 mg
Joslin Exchanges: 1 vegetable, 1 fat

Per 1-tablespoon (15 ml) serving (dressing alone): calories, 51 ◆ protein, trace ◆ carbohydrate, 1 g ◆ fat, 5 g (calories from fat, 89%) ◆ dietary fiber, trace ◆ cholesterol, trace ◆ sodium, 70 mg ◆ potassium, 16 mg
Joslin Exchanges: 1 fat

IMPROMPTU DINNER PARTY

◆

Steamed Fish Fillets (page 122) with Fresh Pineapple Salsa

(page 124)

Couscous with Chives (page 281)

Garden Salad with Balsamic Yogurt Dressing (page 98)

Blueberries and Crème Fraîche (page 428)

Per serving: 490 calories (28% fat)
Joslin Exchanges: 3 low-fat meat, 1 vegetable, 1½ bread/starch, 1½ fruit, ½
nonfat milk, 1 fat

Roasted Peppers with Tarragon Vinaigrette

Fresh peppers with bright vivid colors are available year-round. We like to mix the
colors for an eye-catching salad.

Roasted peppers (page 100) have a rich, intense flavor. We keep a supply on
hand in the refrigerator to use in salads and as a garnish.

Tarragon Vinaigrette

1½ tablespoons (22.5 ml) white
   wine vinegar
1½ tablespoons (22.5 ml) olive oil
 2 teaspoons (10 ml) fresh
   tarragon leaves or ½ teaspoon
   (2.5 ml) crushed dried
freshly ground pepper to taste
 ¾ teaspoon (3.75 ml) Dijon
   mustard

Peppers

 2 small red bell peppers, roasted
   (see box on next page)
 2 small yellow bell peppers,
   roasted
 2 small orange or purple bell
   peppers, roasted
 8 leaves of red leaf lettuce
 4 fresh tarragon sprigs for
   garnish

Prepare vinaigrette by whisking together all ingredients. Pour over peppers; toss gently. Arrange 3 pepper halves (one of each color) on chilled salad plates lined with lettuce leaves. Garnish with a sprig of fresh tarragon.

MAKES 4 SERVINGS

Per serving: calories, 93 ◆ protein, 2 g ◆ carbohydrate, 10 g ◆ fat, 6 g (calories from fat, 53%) ◆ dietary fiber, 1 g ◆ cholesterol, 0 mg ◆ sodium, 16 mg ◆ potassium, 309 mg
Joslin Exchanges: 2 vegetable, 1 fat

Roasted Peppers

Preheat broiler. Place bell peppers in a shallow baking pan. Place under broiler about 2 to 3 inches (5 to 8 cm) from source of heat; broil until skins are charred, turning occasionally. Remove peppers from oven and place in a plastic bag; steam for 15 minutes. Remove and cool until you can handle them easily. Peel peppers; cut in half lengthwise. Remove and discard seeds. Cover and refrigerate for up to 3 days. If you're going to use the peppers in a cooked dish, wrap tightly in plastic wrap, seal, and freeze for up to 1 month.

Greek Salad

Could anything be simpler or better? In summer, when tomatoes are at their peak, this can take the place of a vegetable.

In winter, make a smaller version with plum tomatoes that have been ripened for a few days at room temperature or more quickly in a brown paper bag at room temperature.

2 large tomatoes, about 1 pound (450 g), cut into chunks
1 large green bell pepper, about ½ pound (225 g), seeded and cut into 1-inch (2.5 cm) squares
1 large cucumber, about ½ pound (225 g), peeled, halved lengthwise, seeded, and sliced
6 fresh mushrooms, thinly sliced
1 small red onion, about 3 ounces (85 g), thinly sliced
6 Greek-style olives, such as Kalamata
2 tablespoons (30 ml) olive oil
2 tablespoons (30 ml) fresh lemon juice

1 garlic clove, minced
½ tablespoon (7.5 ml) fresh
  oregano leaves or ½ teaspoon
  (2.5 ml) crushed dried

freshly ground pepper to taste
2 tablespoons (30 g) crumbled feta
  cheese

In a large bowl, combine tomatoes, bell pepper, cucumber, mushrooms, onion, and olives. Whisk together olive oil, lemon juice, garlic, oregano, and pepper. Pour over tomato mixture; toss lightly. Sprinkle with cheese. Serve immediately.

MAKES 6 SERVINGS

Per serving: calories, 98 ◆ protein, 2 g ◆ carbohydrate, 10 g ◆ fat, 7 g (calories from fat, 57%) ◆ dietary fiber, 1 g ◆ cholesterol, 4 mg ◆ sodium, 143 mg ◆ potassium, 519 mg
Joslin Exchanges: 2 vegetable, 1 fat

Tropical Salad with Chervil Dressing

The refreshing dressing for this salad is the inspiration of Steve Wilkins of Fine Bouche, a country restaurant in Connecticut. The dressing is particularly good on tropical fruit. Also try it on a warm salad of steamed small red potatoes and slivered red onion.

If you can't find fresh chervil in your produce market, you might want to grow it from seed (chervil grows easily in a pot) for this and other uses. Its feathery leaves possess a subtle anise-tarragon flavor that almost becomes addictive. Use chervil in green salads; sprinkle it onto poached fish or into a baked potato—you won't miss the butter. Substitute fresh parsley for a different taste.

When papaya or mango is not available, you can substitute kiwifruit or bananas—or just use the pineapple and strawberry combination alone.

1 large head of frisée, about ½
  pound (225 g), or Boston lettuce,
  leaves separated
1 cup (236 ml) fresh pineapple
  chunks

1 cup (236 ml) fresh papaya
  chunks
1 mango, chopped
1 cup (150 g) fresh strawberries,
  hulled and halved

Chervil Dressing

3 tablespoons (45 ml) fresh chervil
  leaves
juice of 1 lemon
2 tablespoons (30 ml) fresh
  grapefruit juice

1 teaspoon (5 ml) low-sodium soy
  sauce
3 tablespoons (45 ml) peanut oil
1/8 teaspoon (.6 ml) hot red pepper
  flakes or to taste

Divide frisée among 8 salad plates. Arrange fruit on frisée. In a food processor or blender, combine dressing ingredients. Blend until smooth. Drizzle dressing over salad and serve.

MAKES 8 SERVINGS

Per serving: calories, 68 ◆ protein, 2 g ◆ carbohydrate, 13 g ◆ fat, 2 g (calories from fat, 26%) ◆ dietary fiber, 1 g ◆ cholesterol, 0 mg ◆ sodium, 32 mg ◆ potassium, 275 mg Joslin Exchanges: 1 fruit
Per 1-tablespoon (15 ml)

serving (dressing alone): calories, 48 ◆ protein, 2 g ◆ carbohydrate, 3 g ◆ fat, 4 g (calories from fat, 66%) ◆ dietary fiber, trace ◆ cholesterol, 0 mg ◆ sodium, 47 mg ◆ potassium, 89 mg Joslin Exchanges: 1 fat

Star Fruit and Swiss Chard Salad

Fresh fruit flavor infuses this interesting salad. Star fruit (carambola), a juicy, tart, plum-flavored fruit, looks like a five-pointed star when it's sliced crosswise.

Available from summer's end to midwinter, star fruit has become one of our favorite fruits—we love its exotic flavor, and 1½ star fruits is only 1 fruit exchange. Choose firm fruit that has a bright, even color. Those with greening on the ribs need to be ripened at room temperature. Once ripe, refrigerate in a tightly closed plastic bag for up to a week.

If star fruit is not available, you can substitute orange sections. Small inner leaves of crisp romaine can be used instead of Swiss chard.

1/2 pound (225 g) Swiss chard or
  small romaine leaves, washed
2 star fruits (carambolas), thinly
  sliced, or 2 oranges, sectioned
1 small red onion, about 3 ounces
  (85 g), very thinly sliced

1 yellow bell pepper, about 6
  ounces (180 g), seeded and cut
  into thin strips
1 tablespoon (15 ml) fresh lemon
  juice

1 tablespoon (15 ml) fresh orange
  juice
1 garlic clove, minced

2 tablespoons (30 ml) olive oil
freshly ground pepper to taste

Remove chard stems; trim and discard woody bottoms. Coarsely chop stems and
leaves. Place in salad bowl along with star fruit, onion, and bell pepper.

In a small bowl, whisk together remaining ingredients. Pour over salad; toss.

MAKES 6 SERVINGS

Per serving: calories, 86 ◆
protein, 2 g ◆ carbohydrate, 11
g ◆ fat, 5 g (calories from fat,
46%) ◆ dietary fiber, 3 g ◆

cholesterol, 0 mg ◆ sodium, 81
mg ◆ potassium, 317 mg
Joslin Exchanges: 1 vegetable,
$\frac{1}{2}$ fruit, 1 fat

Asian Pear and Grapefruit Salad

A refreshing flavor combination to go with any spicy food. If Asian pears are
unavailable, use Bosc pears.

1 Asian or Bosc pear, about $\frac{1}{4}$
  pound (115 g), thinly sliced
juice of $\frac{1}{2}$ lemon
1 medium-size pink grapefruit,
  about $\frac{3}{4}$ pound (340 g), peeled
  and sectioned
1 medium-size red onion, about 5
  ounces (140 g), halved and
  thinly sliced lengthwise

1 bunch of watercress, washed
juice of 1 lemon
2 tablespoons (30 ml) white wine
  vinegar
3 tablespoons (45 ml) canola oil
$\frac{1}{8}$ teaspoon (.6 ml) hot red pepper
  flakes or to taste

Place pear slices in lemon juice to prevent darkening. Place in a salad bowl along
with grapefruit and onion. Remove any large stems from watercress; add leaves to
the bowl.

In a small bowl, whisk together lemon juice, vinegar, oil, and hot pepper flakes.
Pour over salad and toss.

MAKES 4 SERVINGS

Per serving: calories, 109 ◆
protein, 2 g ◆ carbohydrate, 14
g ◆ fat, 5 g (calories from fat,
41%) ◆ dietary fiber, trace ◆

cholesterol, 0 mg ◆ sodium, 8
mg ◆ potassium, 221 mg
Joslin Exchanges: 1 fruit, 1 fat

Spinach and Fennel Salad with Tarragon Dressing

We're particularly fond of spinach salads, and this is one of our favorites. You can vary the fruit garnish from season to season. Instead of pomegranate seeds, try fresh raspberries, strawberries, or sliced red grapes.

The dressing is also excellent on sliced tomatoes or a salad of sliced fresh mushrooms.

8 cups (2 l) lightly packed torn small spinach leaves, about ½ pound (225 g), washed and dried
1 fennel bulb, about 1 pound (450 g), thinly sliced crosswise
½ pound (225 g) fresh mushrooms, sliced
1 large firm Bosc or Red Bartlett pear, about 5 ounces (140 g)

½ cup (118 ml) water
1 tablespoon (15 ml) fresh lemon juice
2 tablespoons (30 ml) pomegranate seeds for garnish (optional)
1 slice of turkey bacon, cooked and crumbled, for garnish

Tarragon Dressing

3 tablespoons (45 ml) olive oil
2 tablespoons (30 ml) balsamic vinegar
1 teaspoon (5 ml) Dijon mustard

1 tablespoon (15 ml) chopped fresh tarragon or 1 teaspoon (5 ml) crushed dried
freshly ground pepper to taste
1 tablespoon (15 ml) egg substitute

Place spinach, fennel, and mushrooms in a large salad bowl. Core and slice pear. Dip in water mixed with lemon juice to prevent darkening. Place in salad bowl.

To prepare dressing, mix together oil and vinegar. Stir in mustard, tarragon, and pepper. While whisking, slowly add egg substitute. Pour over salad and toss. Garnish each serving with pomegranate seeds and bit of crumbled bacon.

MAKES 6 SERVINGS

Per serving: calories, 137 ◆ protein, 4 g ◆ carbohydrate, 16 g ◆ fat, 8 g (calories from fat, 52%) ◆ dietary fiber, 1 g ◆ cholesterol, 2 mg ◆ sodium, 82 mg ◆ potassium, 728 mg
Joslin Exchanges: 1 bread/ starch, 2 fat; or 3 vegetable, 2 fat

Per 1-tablespoon serving (dressing alone): calories, 67 ◆ protein, trace ◆ carbohydrate, 1 g ◆ fat, 7 g (calories from fat, 94%) ◆ dietary fiber, 0 g ◆ cholesterol, 0 mg ◆ sodium, 17 mg ◆ potassium, 18 mg
Joslin Exchanges: 1 fat

Belgian Endive and Watercress Salad

This is a lighter version of the wonderful salad served at the Jockey Club in Washington, D.C.

2 Belgian endives, about ½ pound (225 g), leaves separated
½ pound (225 g) watercress, washed and tough stems removed
6 ounces (180 g) fresh mushrooms, thinly sliced
1 teaspoon (5 ml) Dijon mustard
3 tablespoons (45 ml) olive oil
2 tablespoons (30 ml) white wine vinegar

freshly ground pepper to taste
2 tablespoons (30 ml) egg substitute
2 tablespoons (30 ml) finely chopped fresh tarragon, basil, or parsley for garnish (optional)
8 leaves of Boston lettuce, washed and crisped

Cut endive crosswise into crescents. Tear watercress into bite-size pieces. Place endive, watercress, and mushrooms in a large salad bowl.

Whisk together mustard, olive oil, vinegar, pepper, and egg substitute. Pour over salad mixture; toss. Arrange salad on 8 chilled salad plates lined with lettuce leaves. Sprinkle with chopped tarragon.

MAKES 8 SERVINGS

Per serving: calories, 65 ◆ protein, 2 g ◆ carbohydrate, 3 g ◆ fat, 6 g (calories from fat, 76%) ◆ dietary fiber, 1 g ◆ cholesterol, trace ◆ sodium, 37 mg ◆ potassium, 308 mg
Joslin Exchanges: 1 vegetable, 1 fat

Orange and Onion Salad

We love the unique flavor combination of oranges and onions. Here a hot balsamic ginger dressing and ruby-colored radicchio leaves add a new dimension to this exciting first course.

8 small leaves of radicchio (about 1 small head), washed and crisped
2 navel oranges, about 1¼ pounds (570 g)
1 small red onion, about 3 ounces (85 g), thinly sliced

½ cup (118 ml) balsamic vinegar
1 garlic clove, minced
1 tablespoon (15 ml) minced fresh ginger
4 teaspoons (20 ml) olive oil
freshly ground pepper to taste

On each of 4 salad plates, arrange 2 radicchio leaves to form a cup. With a small sharp knife, cut peel and white membrane from oranges. Cut oranges crosswise into ¼-inch-thick (.75 cm) slices. Arrange orange slices and red onion in radicchio cups.

In a small nonstick skillet, combine vinegar, garlic, ginger, and oil. Cook over medium-low heat until garlic is soft, about 3 minutes. Pour hot dressing over salad. Sprinkle with pepper. Serve immediately.

MAKES 4 SERVINGS

Per serving: calories, 119 ◆ protein, 1 g ◆ carbohydrate, 19 g ◆ fat, 5 g (calories from fat, 34%) ◆ dietary fiber, 1 g ◆ cholesterol, 0 mg ◆ sodium, 8 mg ◆ potassium, 411 mg
Joslin Exchanges: 1 fruit, 1 fat

Cauliflower and Tomato Salad with Horseradish Dressing

Steamed and then tossed with a zippy dressing, cauliflower makes a light and lovely winter salad. Plum tomatoes are the best variety to buy in cold months; ripen them at room temperature in a closed paper bag.

For a more formal presentation, line a large serving plate with lettuce leaves. Arrange cauliflower florets on lettuce in the shape of the cauliflower head. Top with tomato and pass dressing on the side.

1³/₄ pounds (790 g) cauliflower, cut into florets

¹/₂ pound (225 g) fresh plum tomatoes

¹/₃ cup (78 ml) nonfat yogurt cheese (page 11)

1 to 2 tablespoons (15 to 30 ml) prepared horseradish, to taste

1 teaspoon (5 ml) Dijon mustard

2 tablespoons (30 ml) white wine vinegar

1 garlic clove, minced

freshly ground pepper to taste

2 tablespoons (30 ml) canola oil

8 leaves of red leaf lettuce, washed and dried

Steam cauliflower until crisp-tender, about 5 minutes. Refresh under cold running water. Dip tomatoes in boiling water for 60 seconds. Refresh under cold running water, peel, seed, and chop.

Combine remaining ingredients except lettuce, whisking until smooth. Pour over cauliflower and tomatoes; toss. Serve on lettuce-lined salad plates.

MAKES 6 SERVINGS

Per serving: calories, 92 ◆ protein, 4 g ◆ carbohydrate, 10 g ◆ fat, 5 g (calories from fat, 50%) ◆ dietary fiber, 1 g ◆ cholesterol, 0 mg ◆ sodium, 62 mg ◆ potassium, 563 mg Joslin Exchanges: 2 vegetable, 1 fat

Citrus Salad with Cumin Vinaigrette

This salad offers a cooling contrast to fiery entrees. It's also a good choice for winter buffets.

1 large pink grapefruit, about ³/₄ pound (340 g), peeled and sectioned

1 large navel orange, about 10 ounces (285 g), peeled and sectioned

1¹/₄ pound (570 g) jícama, peeled and cut into slices about ¹/₃ inch (.85 cm) thick

¹/₂ cup (118 ml) loosely packed fresh cilantro (fresh coriander) or fresh mint leaves

1 2-ounce (60 g) fresh hot chili, seeded and sliced crosswise

2 tablespoons (30 ml) fresh lime or lemon juice

2 tablespoons (30 ml) olive oil

1 garlic clove, minced

¹/₄ teaspoon (1.25 ml) ground cumin

¹/₈ teaspoon (.6 ml) ground ginger

¹/₈ teaspoon (.6 ml) chili powder

freshly ground pepper to taste

¹/₈ teaspoon (.6 ml) Worcestershire sauce

8 leaves of red leaf lettuce, washed and crisped

In a large bowl, combine grapefruit, orange, jícama, cilantro, and chili. Whisk together remaining ingredients except lettuce. Pour over jícama and citrus; toss. Arrange salad on chilled plates lined with lettuce leaves.

MAKES 4 SERVINGS

Per serving: calories, 120 ◆ protein, 2 g ◆ carbohydrate, 19 g ◆ fat, 5 g (calories from fat, 34%) ◆ dietary fiber, 1 g ◆ cholesterol, 0 mg ◆ sodium, 7 mg ◆ potassium, 294 mg Joslin Exchanges: 1 fruit, 1 fat

Snow Pea and Pearl Onion Salad

Crisp-tender snow peas and tiny pearl onions combine with a sesame dressing to make this terrific winter salad. To save time you can use frozen pearl onions, which are already peeled.

- 6 ounces (180 g) snow peas, ends trimmed and strings removed
- ½ pound (225 g) pearl onions
- ½ teaspoon (2.5 ml) dark sesame oil
- 2 tablespoons (30 ml) canola oil
- 2 tablespoons (30 ml) rice vinegar
- 1 teaspoon (5 ml) low-sodium soy sauce
- 1 to 2 garlic cloves, to taste, mashed
- ⅛ teaspoon (.6 ml) dry English mustard
- 2 teaspoons (10 ml) toasted sesame seeds (page 440)
- 6 ounces (180 g) fresh spinach leaves, washed
- 2 scallions, white part and 1 inch (2.5 cm) green, chopped, for garnish

Blanch snow peas for 1 to 2 minutes, until just tender and still bright green. Refresh under cold running water. Cut a small X in the root end of each onion. Drop into a pan of boiling water; cook for 10 minutes until tender but firm. Drain and plunge into cold water. Slip skins off onions and place in a salad bowl along with snow peas.

Whisk together sesame oil, canola oil, vinegar, soy sauce, garlic, dry mustard, and sesame seeds. Pour over snow peas and onions; toss. Arrange spinach leaves on 6 chilled salad plates. Spoon snow peas and onions onto spinach. Top with scallions.

MAKES 6 SERVINGS

Per serving: calories, 84 ◆ protein, 2 g ◆ carbohydrate, 7 g ◆ fat, 6 g (calories from fat, 62%) ◆ dietary fiber, 1 g ◆ cholesterol, 0 mg ◆ sodium, 60 mg ◆ potassium, 285 mg Joslin Exchanges: 1 vegetable, 1 fat

Broccoli and Cauliflower Salad

For an enticing hearty salad year-round, toss broccoli and cauliflower florets in a mellow herb dressing.

3 cups (708 ml) broccoli florets
3 cups (708 ml) cauliflower florets
1 cup (236 ml) plain nonfat yogurt
2 scallions, white part and 1 inch (2.5 cm) green, chopped
1 garlic clove, minced
¼ teaspoon (1.25 ml) Dijon mustard
1 tablespoon (15 ml) tarragon or white wine vinegar

1 tablespoon (15 ml) fresh tarragon leaves or 1 teaspoon (5 ml) crushed dried
1 tablespoon (15 ml) canola oil
¼ cup (1.25 ml) chopped parsley
8 leaves of radicchio, washed and crisped
finely chopped red bell pepper for garnish

Steam broccoli and cauliflower over boiling water until barely tender when pierced, about 5 minutes. (Or place broccoli and cauliflower in a covered microwave-safe dish. Sprinkle with 2 tablespoons water. Cover and cook on HIGH for 3 to 5 minutes, until crisp-tender.) Refresh under cold water; drain well.

Meanwhile, in a food processor or blender, combine remaining ingredients except radicchio and bell pepper. Pulse until blended. Pour over vegetables; toss to coat evenly.

Arrange salad on chilled salad plates lined with radicchio leaves. Garnish with chopped bell pepper.

MAKES 8 SERVINGS

Per serving: calories, 52 ◆ protein, 4 g ◆ carbohydrate, 6 g ◆ fat, 2 g (calories from fat, 32%) ◆ dietary fiber, 2 g ◆ cholesterol, 1 mg ◆ sodium, 40 mg ◆ potassium, 344 mg
Joslin Exchanges: 1 vegetable

A FALL LUNCH WITH A FRIEND

◆

Broccoli and Cauliflower Salad (page 109)

Open-Face Sandwich of Sliced Plum Tomatoes, Arugula, and

Low-Fat Goat Cheese on French Bread

Warm Grapefruit and Orange with Sherry Sauce (page 437)

Iced Tea with Fresh Mint

Per serving: 351 calories (18% fat)
Joslin Exchanges: 1 medium-fat meat, 2 vegetable, 2 bread/starch, 1 fruit

Jerusalem Artichoke Salad with Sun-Dried Tomato Vinaigrette

You may find Jerusalem artichokes labeled *sunchokes* in your market. This strange-looking knobby winter vegetable is not an artichoke, nor is it from Jerusalem. It's actually the brown-skinned tuber from a variety of sunflower; the name is derived from the Italian word for sunflower, *girasole*. Regardless of the convoluted origin of the name, we love the sweet, nutty flavor of Jerusalem artichokes in this salad.

Be sure to use dry-packed sun-dried tomatoes from California for the dressing. The "freezer trick" to crumble dried tomatoes was given to us by a sun-dried tomato manufacturer. The crumbled tomatoes are also great as a topping for soups, pasta, or baked potatoes.

1 pound (450 g) Jerusalem artichokes, peeled and cut into thin strips

1 fennel bulb, about 1 pound (450 g)

½ pound (225 g) fresh mushrooms, sliced

1 red bell pepper, about 6 ounces (180 g), seeded and sliced into thin strips

1 ounce (30 g) sun-dried tomatoes
  (packed dry)
2 tablespoons (30 ml) balsamic
  vinegar
2 garlic cloves, minced
2 scallions, white part only,
  minced

1 tablespoon (15 ml) chopped
  fresh basil or 1 teaspoon (5 ml)
  crushed dried
3 tablespoons (45 ml) olive oil
½ teaspoon salt (optional)
freshly ground pepper to taste
8 leaves of Boston lettuce, washed
  and crisped

Place Jerusalem artichokes in a large bowl. Trim fennel bulb; cut crosswise into thin strips. Add to artichokes along with mushrooms and peppers. Toss.

To prepare vinaigrette, set aside 6 sun-dried tomatoes. Simmer remaining tomatoes in water to cover for 5 minutes. Drain and finely chop. Whisk together chopped tomatoes, vinegar, garlic, scallions, basil, olive oil, salt, and pepper. Pour over artichoke mixture. Toss and marinate for 2 hours.

Just before serving, place reserved sun-dried tomatoes in the freezer for 5 minutes. Arrange salad on lettuce leaves. Remove tomatoes from freezer; finely crumble with hands or a rolling pin. Sprinkle on salad and serve.

MAKES 8 SERVINGS

Per serving: calories, 137 ◆ protein, 3 g ◆ carbohydrate, 21 g ◆ fat, 5 g (calories from fat, 35%) ◆ dietary fiber, 1 g ◆ cholesterol, 0 mg ◆ sodium, 142 mg ◆ potassium, 498 mg Joslin Exchanges: 1 bread/starch, 1 fat

---

WINTER SOUP AND SALAD PARTY

◆

Jerusalem Artichoke Salad with Sun-Dried Tomato

Vinaigrette (page 110)

Seafood Chowder (page 74)

Poached Pears with Crème Fraîche (page 428)

Per serving: 430 calories (25% fat)
Joslin Exchanges: 1½ low-fat meat, 2½ bread/starch, 1 fruit, ½ milk, 1 fat

Winter Vegetable Salad with Yogurt Garlic Dressing

The garlic dressing perfectly complements a colorful toss of raw vegetables in this spectacular winter salad.

1 small bunch of broccoli, about ¾ pound (340 g)
1 small head of cauliflower, about ¾ pound (340 g)
1 small zucchini, about 3 ounces (85 g), thinly sliced
1 small red bell pepper, about ¼ pound (115 g), seeded and cut into thin strips

8 red radishes, thinly sliced
1 small onion, about 3 ounces (85 g), thinly sliced and separated into rings
¼ cup (59 ml) chopped fresh parsley for garnish

Yogurt Garlic Dressing

1 cup (236 ml) plain low-fat yogurt
1 teaspoon (5 ml) fresh lemon juice
½ teaspoon (2.5 ml) grated lemon zest

2 garlic cloves, minced
½ teaspoon (2.5 ml) freshly ground pepper or to taste

Cut broccoli florets into bite-size pieces; cut stalks into paper-thin slices. Cut cauliflower florets into bite-size pieces.

In a large salad bowl, combine broccoli, cauliflower, zucchini, red pepper, radishes, and onion.

In a small bowl, whisk together dressing ingredients. Pour over vegetables; toss to coat evenly. Sprinkle with chopped parsley and serve.

MAKES 8 SERVINGS

Per serving: calories, 52 ◆ protein, 4 g ◆ carbohydrate, 9 g ◆ fat, 1 g (calories from fat, 12%) ◆ dietary fiber, 1 g ◆ cholesterol, 2 mg ◆ sodium, 41 mg ◆ potassium, 453 mg
Joslin Exchanges: 2 vegetable
Per 1-tablespoon (15 ml)

serving (dressing alone): calories, 10 ◆ protein, 1 g ◆ carbohydrate, 1 g ◆ fat, trace (calories from fat, 18%) ◆ dietary fiber, trace ◆ cholesterol, 0 mg ◆ sodium, 10 mg ◆ potassium, 36 mg
Joslin Exchanges: free

Warm Brown Rice, Red Cabbage, and Kale Salad

Brown rice is rich in fiber, vitamins, and minerals. Presoaking the rice speeds up the cooking time. The nutty flavor of the rice is heightened by the addition of walnuts and walnut oil.

Serve this winter salad as an accompaniment to any simple fish or chicken dish— or solo for a light vegetarian meal.

½ cup (118 ml) long-grain brown rice

1½ cups (354 ml) water

3 tablespoons (45 ml) red wine vinegar

¾ pound (340 g) red cabbage, shredded

1 pound (450 g) kale, stems removed and chopped

1 teaspoon (5 ml) crushed dried mixed Italian herbs

½ teaspoon (2.5 ml) salt (optional)

2 tablespoons (30 ml) walnut oil

2 tablespoons (30 ml) finely chopped walnuts, about 10 walnut halves

In a small saucepan, bring rice and 1 cup (236 ml) water to a boil. Turn off heat and let stand, covered, for 2 hours. When you're ready to cook, bring to a boil. Reduce heat and cook, covered, for 10 minutes, until water is absorbed and rice is tender. Keep warm.

Meanwhile, in a medium-size saucepan, bring ¼ cup (59 ml) water and 2 tablespoons (30 ml) red wine vinegar to a boil. Add shredded cabbage, reduce heat, and simmer for 5 to 8 minutes, until cabbage is crisp-tender and liquid is absorbed. Keep warm.

In another medium-size saucepan, combine kale and ¼ cup (59 ml) water. Bring to a boil, reduce heat, and simmer until kale is tender, about 15 minutes. Keep warm.

In a large bowl, combine warm rice, cabbage, and kale. Add herbs, salt, walnut oil, and remaining 1 tablespoon (15 ml) red wine vinegar. Toss lightly to mix. Sprinkle with chopped walnuts; serve warm.

MAKES 8 SERVINGS

Per serving: calories, 85 ◆ protein, 2 g ◆ carbohydrate, 9 g ◆ fat, 5 g (calories from fat, 49%) ◆ dietary fiber, 3 g ◆ cholesterol, 0 mg ◆ sodium, 154 mg ◆ potassium, 258 mg
Joslin Exchanges: 2 vegetable, 1 fat

VEGETARIAN SUPPER

◆

Curried Asparagus Soup (page 48)

Warm Brown Rice, Red Cabbage, and Kale Salad (page 113)

Gingerbread (page 414)

Per serving: 318 calories (28% fat)
Joslin Exchanges: 1 low-fat meat, 2 vegetable, 2 bread/starch, 1 fat

DRESSINGS

Most bottled low-calorie, low-fat dressings are also low on taste. Here are some of our favorite flavor-packed dressings:

Classic Vinaigrette

The sparkling mineral water cuts the calories of this basic vinaigrette.

5 tablespoons (75 ml) red wine
   vinegar
5 tablespoons (75 ml) sparkling
   mineral water
5 tablespoons (75 ml) extra-virgin
   olive oil

1 tablespoon (15 ml) minced
   shallots
1 teaspoon (5 ml) Dijon mustard
freshly ground pepper to taste
sodium-free herb seasoning (page
   115) to taste

Whisk ingredients together until well combined. Make fresh; it loses its effervescence within an hour or so.

MAKES ABOUT 1 CUP (236 ML)

**Per 1-tablespoon (15 ml)
serving:** calories, 39 ◆ protein,
trace ◆ carbohydrate, trace ◆
fat, 4 g (calories from fat, 96%)

◆ dietary fiber, trace ◆
cholesterol, 0 mg ◆ sodium, 5
mg ◆ potassium, 3 mg
Joslin Exchanges: 1 fat

Sodium-Free Herb Seasoning

Commercial sodium-free herb seasonings can be purchased in the spice section of your supermarket, but many contain a salt substitute that can be harmful to some people. It's easy and cheaper to make your own. Use it as a salt replacement on salads, vegetables, fish, and sprinkled into baked potatoes.

> 2 tablespoons (30 ml) crushed dried basil
> 1 tablespoon (15 ml) crushed dried tarragon
> 1 tablespoon (15 ml) crushed dried mint
> 1 tablespoon (15 ml) crushed dried thyme
> 1 tablespoon (15 ml) dried dill weed

Combine all ingredients and store in a spice jar away from light.

Creamy Honey Dijon Dressing

½ cup (118 ml) plain nonfat yogurt
½ cup (118 ml) buttermilk
2 tablespoons (30 ml) Dijon mustard
1 tablespoon (15 ml) fresh lemon juice
1 tablespoon (15 ml) honey

Combine all ingredients and whisk until smooth. Refrigerate for up to 2 days.

MAKES ABOUT 1⅓ CUPS (314 ML)

Per 1-tablespoon (15 ml) serving: calories, 20 ◆ protein, 1 g ◆ carbohydrate, 3 g ◆ fat, trace (calories from fat, 14%) ◆ dietary fiber, trace ◆ cholesterol, 1 g ◆ sodium, 60 mg ◆ potassium, 52 mg
Joslin Exchanges: free

Creamy Italian Dressing

2 tablespoons (30 ml) olive oil
½ cup (118 ml) plain low-fat yogurt
1 tablespoon (15 ml) fresh lemon juice
1 garlic clove, minced
¼ teaspoon (1.25 ml) crushed dried oregano

½ teaspoon (2.5 ml) crushed dried basil
¼ teaspoon (1.25 ml) crushed dried thyme
2 tablespoons (30 ml) chopped fresh flat-leaf parsley

Mix ingredients together until well blended. Refrigerate for up to 2 days.

MAKES ABOUT 1 CUP (236 ML)

Per 1-tablespoon (15 ml) serving: calories, 20 ◆ protein, 1 g ◆ carbohydrate, 1 g ◆ fat, 2 g (calories from fat, 81%) ◆ dietary fiber, trace ◆ cholesterol, trace ◆ sodium, 5 mg ◆ potassium, 23 mg
Joslin Exchanges: free

Creamy Orange Dressing

½ cup (118 ml) plain low-fat yogurt
2 tablespoons (30 ml) fresh orange juice

1 teaspoon (5 ml) grated orange zest

Mix all ingredients and chill for at least 2 hours. To be used with fresh fruit or poultry. Refrigerate for up to 2 days.

MAKES ABOUT ⅔ CUP (156 ML)

Per 1-tablespoon (15 ml) serving: calories, 9 ◆ protein, 1 g ◆ carbohydrate, 1 g ◆ fat, trace (calories from fat, 21%) ◆ dietary fiber, trace ◆ cholesterol, trace ◆ sodium, 8 mg ◆ potassium, 33 mg
Joslin Exchanges: free

Curry Dressing

½ cup (118 ml) plain low-fat yogurt
1 teaspoon (5 ml) curry powder or
  to taste
½ teaspoon (2.5 ml) minced fresh
  ginger

dash of ground cinnamon
freshly ground pepper
⅛ teaspoon (.6 ml) salt (optional)

Mix all of the ingredients well. Chill well before serving. Keeps for 2 days.

MAKES ABOUT ½ CUP (118 ML)

**Per 1-tablespoon (15 ml)
serving:** calories, 18 ◆ protein,
2 g ◆ carbohydrate, 3 g ◆ fat,
trace (calories from fat, 6%) ◆

dietary fiber, trace ◆ cholesterol,
1 mg ◆ sodium, 89 mg ◆
potassium, 81 mg
Joslin Exchanges: free

Garlicky Cheese Dressing

1 cup (236 ml) low-fat (1%)
  cottage cheese
2 garlic cloves, peeled and cut into
  quarters
2 shallots, peeled and cut into
  quarters
1 teaspoon (5 ml) Dijon mustard

1 tablespoon (15 ml) mixed fresh
  herbs (thyme, chives, parsley,
  tarragon, basil, dill)
freshly ground pepper to taste
⅛ teaspoon (.6 ml) salt (optional)
2 to 3 tablespoons (30 to 45 ml)
  skim milk

In a food processor or blender, combine all ingredients. Blend until smooth, thinning with skim milk as desired. Refrigerate for up to 2 days.

MAKES ABOUT 1¼ CUPS (295 ML)

**Per 1-tablespoon (15 ml)
serving:** calories, 12 ◆ protein,
2 g ◆ carbohydrate, 1 g ◆ fat,
trace (calories from fat, 15%) ◆

dietary fiber, trace ◆ cholesterol,
1 mg ◆ sodium, 65 mg ◆
potassium, 23 mg
Joslin Exchanges: free

Asian Variation

Omit Dijon mustard and fresh herbs. Add 1 tablespoon (15 ml) minced fresh ginger, 2 tablespoons (30 ml) fresh cilantro (fresh coriander) leaves, and ⅛ teaspoon (.6 ml) dark sesame oil. Proceed as directed.

MAKES ABOUT 1¼ CUPS (295 ML)

Per 1-tablespoon (15 ml) serving: calories, 11 ◆ protein, 2 g ◆ carbohydrate, 1 g ◆ fat, trace (calories from fat, 12%) ◆ dietary fiber, trace ◆ cholesterol, 1 mg ◆ sodium, 61 mg ◆ potassium, 23 mg
Joslin Exchanges: free

Blue Cheese Variation

Omit Dijon mustard and fresh herbs. Add 1 tablespoon (15 ml) fresh lemon juice and 2 ounces (60 g) blue cheese. Proceed as directed.

MAKES ABOUT 1¼ CUPS (295 ML)

Per 1-tablespoon (15 ml) serving: calories, 21 ◆ protein, 2 g ◆ carbohydrate, 1 g ◆ fat, 1 g (calories from fat, 42%) ◆ dietary fiber, trace ◆ cholesterol, 5 mg ◆ sodium, 100 mg ◆ potassium, 26 mg
Joslin Exchanges: free

Ranch Dressing

½ cup (118 ml) plain low-fat yogurt
¼ cup (59 ml) reduced-calorie mayonnaise
¼ cup (59 ml) fresh lemon juice
½ teaspoon (2.5 ml) grated lemon zest
1 garlic clove, minced

1 tablespoon (15 ml) chopped parsley
1 tablespoon (15 ml) chopped chives
⅛ teaspoon (.6 ml) freshly ground pepper or to taste

Combine all ingredients with a whisk; chill for up to 2 days.

MAKES ABOUT 1 CUP (236 ML)

**Per 1-tablespoon (15 ml)
serving:** calories, 16 ◆ protein,
trace ◆ carbohydrate, 1 g ◆ fat,
1 g (calories from fat, 61%) ◆

dietary fiber, trace ◆ cholesterol,
2 mg ◆ sodium, 5 mg ◆
potassium, 24 mg
Joslin Exchanges: free

Russian Dressing

½ cup (118 ml) plain low-fat yogurt
¼ cup (59 ml) buttermilk
juice of ½ lemon
½ teaspoon (2.5 ml) prepared
    horseradish or to taste

1 teaspoon (5 ml) Dijon mustard
1 tablespoon (15 ml) tomato paste
½ teaspoon (2.5 ml) Worcestershire
    sauce
dash of Tabasco sauce

Mix all ingredients; chill for at least 2 hours and up to 2 days.

MAKES ABOUT 1 CUP (236 ML)

**Per 1-tablespoon (15 ml)
serving:** calories, 8 ◆ protein,
1 g ◆ carbohydrate, 1 g ◆ fat,
trace (calories from fat, 19%) ◆

dietary fiber, trace ◆ cholesterol,
1 mg ◆ sodium, 25 mg ◆
potassium, 36 mg
Joslin Exchanges: free

Spicy Gazpacho Dressing

1 cup (236 ml) peeled, seeded, and
    diced fresh tomatoes
⅓ cup (78 ml) tomato juice
¼ cup (59 ml) cider vinegar
¼ cup (59 ml) fresh lemon juice
⅓ cup (78 ml) olive oil
1 garlic clove, minced
¼ cup (59 ml) minced fresh
    cilantro (fresh coriander)

¼ cup (59 ml) minced red bell
    pepper
1 fresh jalapeño chili, seeded and
    minced
⅛ teaspoon (.6 ml) freshly ground
    pepper or to taste
¼ teaspoon (1.25 ml) crushed dried
    thyme
¼ teaspoon (1.25 ml) salt (optional)

Mix ingredients together until well blended. Refrigerate for up to 2 days.

MAKES ABOUT 2 CUPS (472 ML)

**Per 1-tablespoon (15 ml)
serving:** calories, 24 ◆ protein,
trace ◆ carbohydrate, 1 g ◆ fat,
2 g (calories from fat, 75%) ◆

dietary fiber, trace ◆ cholesterol,
0 mg ◆ sodium, 17 mg ◆
potassium, 38 mg
Joslin Exchanges: free

Sweet and Sour Poppy Seed Dressing

½ cup (118 ml) minced sweet onion
(Vidalia, Walla Walla, Maui, or
Texas 1015 Supersweet)
⅓ cup (78 ml) white wine vinegar
1 tablespoon (15 ml) honey
1 tablespoon (15 ml) fresh lemon
juice

3 tablespoons (45 ml) olive oil
1 tablespoon (15 ml) poppy seeds
1 teaspoon (5 ml) paprika
1 teaspoon (5 ml) dry mustard
1 tablespoon (15 ml) chopped
fresh tarragon

Whisk ingredients together until well combined. Refrigerate for up to one day.

MAKES ABOUT 1⅓ CUPS (314 ML)

**Per 1-tablespoon (15 ml)
serving:** calories, 25 ◆ protein,
trace ◆ carbohydrate, 2 g ◆ fat,
2 g (calories from fat, 72%) ◆

dietary fiber, 1 g ◆ cholesterol, 0
mg ◆ sodium, trace ◆
potassium, 15 mg
Joslin Exchanges: free

FISH AND SHELLFISH

Great taste isn't all you get from eating fish—not only is it usually low in calories and fat, but some of the fats fish does contain, Omega-3 oils, may be a defense against some health problems. Recent medical studies suggest that eating certain types of fish can reduce your risk of heart disease by helping to lower blood cholesterol and blood pressure, counter arthritis, and stimulate the immune system, among other desirable effects. The best sources of Omega-3s are tuna, mackerel, bluefish, salmon, rainbow trout, lake trout, shad, and pompano. Canned fish such as tuna, salmon, mackerel, and sardines are also good sources (buy these fish packed in water to minimize your fat intake).

Increased enthusiasm for fish of course means higher price tags at the seafood markets. However, there are affordable alternatives to swordfish, salmon, lobster, and king crab. Freshly caught fish, in varieties unheard of just a few years ago, is readily available almost everywhere.

Fish is very perishable, so it's important to know how to buy and store it. Get to know your fishmonger. You'll want to shop where the fish is very fresh and properly displayed. A good display includes fillets in individual pans surrounded by ice, with whole fish displayed under ice. Fresh fish does not have a strong odor. If a seafood market has a strong "fishy" smell, shop elsewhere.

When you're buying whole fish, look for bright, clear, bulging eyes. The fish should have vivid color with no skin tears or blemishes. When you're buying steaks or fillets, look for moist flesh with a translucent sheen. Take fish home promptly. Pat dry with paper towels; wrap in plastic wrap, then aluminum foil. Store in the coldest part of the refrigerator and cook it the same day.

Always wash your hands after handling raw fish. Wash all surfaces and utensils that the raw fish touched to avoid possible cross-contamination. For example, don't use a knife to cut a piece of raw fish and then use that knife to cut vegetables for a salad.

Before cooking, scrub bivalves (clams, mussels, oysters, and scallops) under cold running water to prevent the meat from being contaminated when the shells are opened. Discard any bivalve that fails to open after cooking.

To determine how long to cook fish, use the "Canadian Rule" from the Canadian Department of Fisheries: the total cooking time of any fish is 10 minutes per inch (2.5 cm) measured at the thickest part, plus or minus any fraction. This works for whole fish, steaks, and fillets, regardless of the cooking method. Double the time for frozen fish.

Steaming Fish

An excellent way to cook fish fillets (flounder, sole, orange roughy, cod, scrod, salmon, red snapper, etc.), is by steaming, adding no fat calories. A Chinese steamer is ideal for this, but if you don't have one, you can improvise by using a wire rack (one you would use for cooling cookies or cakes) that is large enough to hold the fillets in a single layer and that extends just beyond the sides of the skillet. Lay a doubled sheet of heavy-duty aluminum foil over the rack, folding the edges back several times to form a ridge around the fish. Cut several slashes in the foil to allow the juices to escape. Place the rack over a large skillet filled with about 1 inch (2.5 cm) water. Cover the fish with more foil or a large lid and steam until done, 10 minutes per inch.

To microwave fish fillets, tuck the thinner ends of each fillet under the center, folding the fillet into thirds. Arrange fillets seam side down around the outer edge of a shallow microwave-safe dish, leaving the center open. Cover and cook on HIGH for 3½ to 6 minutes or until the fish flakes when pressed with a fork. Let stand, covered, for 2 minutes.

Fish Sauces

Although other chapters offer recipes (see index) for sauces, relishes, and salsas that can be used with steamed or microwaved fish, here are some other quick embellishments for four 5-ounce (140 g) cooked fish fillets (the calories and nutrient values are calculated for sole or flounder only and will vary slightly with other types of fish, but not enough to affect the exchanges).

Cold Cucumber Sauce

Drain 1 cup (236 ml) plain nonfat yogurt for 3 hours (see yogurt cheese, page 11). Combine with 2 cucumbers, peeled, seeded, and finely chopped. Stir in 1 tablespoon (15 ml) fresh lemon juice, 1 teaspoon (5 ml) white wine vinegar, 1 teaspoon (5 ml) prepared horseradish, 1 teaspoon (5 ml) Dijon mustard, and freshly ground pepper to taste. Nap each of 4 well-chilled steamed 5-ounce (140 g) fish fillets with ⅓ cup (78 ml) sauce. Garnish each fillet with ⅛ teaspoon (.6 ml) drained capers and a fresh dill sprig.

MAKES 4 SERVINGS

Per serving (with fish): calories, 148 ◆ protein, 24 g ◆ carbohydrate, 9 g ◆ fat, 1 g (calories from fat, 6%) ◆ dietary fiber, 1 g ◆ cholesterol, 46 mg ◆ sodium, 103 mg ◆ potassium, 655 mg Joslin Exchanges: 3 low-fat meat, ½ nonfat milk

Per ⅓ cup (78 ml) serving (sauce alone): calories, 61 ◆ protein, 5 g ◆ carbohydrate, 9 g ◆ fat, trace (calories from fat, less than 1%) ◆ dietary fiber, trace ◆ cholesterol, 0 mg ◆ sodium, 46 mg ◆ potassium, 221 mg Joslin Exchanges: ½ nonfat milk

Italian Mushroom Sauce

Thinly slice 5 ounces (140 g) fresh porcini* or cultivated mushrooms. In a medium-size nonstick skillet, combine mushrooms, 3 tablespoons (45 ml) dry white wine, ¼ cup (59 ml) minced red onion, 1 tablespoon (15 ml) minced flat-leaf parsley, 1 minced garlic clove, and 1 tablespoon (15 ml) fresh lemon juice. Sauté over medium heat, stirring occasionally, until mushrooms and onion are very soft and all liquid has evaporated. Stir in 1 teaspoon (5 ml) tomato paste, a pinch of crushed dried thyme, and ⅓ cup (78 ml) beef stock (page 44). Spoon over four 5-ounce (140 g) steamed fish fillets.

MAKES 4 SERVINGS

Per serving (with fish): calories, 103 ◆ protein, 20 g ◆ carbohydrate, 4 g ◆ fat, 1 g (calories from fat, 8%) ◆ dietary fiber, 1 g ◆ cholesterol, 46 mg ◆ sodium, 80 mg ◆ potassium, 627 mg Joslin Exchanges: 3 low-fat meat

Per ⅓-cup (78 ml) serving (sauce alone): calories, 16 ◆ protein, 1 g ◆ carbohydrate, 3 g ◆ fat, trace (calories from fat, 9%) ◆ dietary fiber, 1 g ◆ cholesterol, 0 mg ◆ sodium, 17 mg ◆ potassium, 188 mg Joslin Exchanges: free

* Fresh porcini mushrooms are available in specialty food shops in the spring and fall. They are quite meaty and woodsy flavored.

Red Onion Confit

Thinly slice 1 large red onion; separate into rings. In a medium-size saucepan, cook onions along with 2 teaspoons (10 ml) light brown sugar and ¼ cup (59 ml) dry red wine over medium heat until onions begin to caramelize. Stir occasionally. Add ¼ cup (59 ml) red wine vinegar. Bring to a boil, stirring constantly. Spoon over four 5-ounce (140 g) steamed fish fillets.

MAKES 4 SERVINGS

Per serving (with fish): calories, 118 ◆ protein, 19 g ◆ carbohydrate, 8 g ◆ fat, 1 g (calories from fat, 7%) ◆ dietary fiber, trace ◆ cholesterol, 38 mg ◆ sodium, 77 mg ◆ potassium, 522 mg
Joslin Exchanges: 3 low-fat meat, 1 vegetable

Per ¼-cup (59 ml) serving (confit alone): calories, 31 ◆ protein, 1 g ◆ carbohydrate, 8 g ◆ fat, trace (calories from fat, less than 1%) ◆ dietary fiber, 1 g ◆ cholesterol, 0 mg ◆ sodium, 3 mg ◆ potassium, 99 mg
Joslin Exchanges: 1 vegetable

Fresh Pineapple Salsa

In a small bowl, combine 1 cup (236 ml) diced fresh pineapple, ¼ cup (59 ml) minced red onion, 3 tablespoons (45 ml) chopped fresh mint, 1 teaspoon (5 ml) balsamic vinegar, and a dash of Tabasco sauce. Spoon onto four 5-ounce (140 g) steamed fish fillets.

MAKES 4 SERVINGS

Per serving (with fish): calories, 134 ◆ protein, 24 g ◆ carbohydrate, 6 g ◆ fat, 1 g (calories from fat, 7%) ◆ dietary fiber, trace ◆ cholesterol, 58 mg ◆ sodium, 83 mg ◆ potassium, 320 mg
Joslin Exchanges: 3 low-fat meat, ½ fruit

Per ⅓-cup (78 ml) serving (salsa alone): calories, 24 ◆ protein, trace ◆ carbohydrate, 6 g ◆ fat, trace (calories from fat, less than 1%) ◆ dietary fiber, trace ◆ cholesterol, 0 mg ◆ sodium, 1 mg ◆ potassium, 64 mg
Joslin Exchanges: ½ fruit

Sesame Scallion Sauce

Sprinkle four 5-ounce (140 g) steamed fish fillets with 2 tablespoons (30 ml) low-sodium soy sauce, 1 tablespoon (15 ml) toasted sesame seeds (page 440), and 4 scallions, including some green, chopped.

MAKES 4 SERVINGS

Per serving (with fish):
calories, 106 ◆ protein, 20 g ◆ carbohydrate, 1 g ◆ fat, 2 g (calories from fat, 17%) ◆ dietary fiber, 1 g ◆ cholesterol, 46 mg ◆ sodium, 335 mg ◆ potassium, 457 mg
Joslin Exchanges: 3 low-fat meat

Per 2-tablespoon (30 ml) serving (sauce alone): calories, 20 ◆ protein, 1 g ◆ carbohydrate, 1 g ◆ fat, 1 g (calories from fat, 49%) ◆ dietary fiber, trace ◆ cholesterol, 0 mg ◆ sodium, 278 mg ◆ potassium, 23 mg
Joslin Exchanges: free

Yogurt Mustard Sauce

In a small bowl, combine ⅓ cup (78 ml) plain nonfat yogurt with 1 tablespoon (15 ml) Dijon mustard and ⅛ teaspoon (.6 ml) cayenne pepper. Spoon sauce onto four 5-ounce (140 g) steamed fish fillets.

MAKES 4 SERVINGS

Per serving (with fish):
calories, 124 ◆ protein, 25 g ◆ carbohydrate, 2 g ◆ fat, 1 g (calories from fat, 7%) ◆ dietary fiber, trace ◆ cholesterol, 58 mg ◆ sodium, 146 mg ◆ potassium, 310 mg
Joslin Exchanges: 3½ low-fat meat

Per 1½-tablespoon (22.5 ml) serving (sauce alone): calories, 14 ◆ protein, 1 g ◆ carbohydrate, 2 g ◆ fat, trace (calories from fat, 20%) ◆ fiber, trace ◆ cholesterol, trace ◆ sodium, 64 mg ◆ potassium, 54 mg
Joslin Exchanges: free

Portuguese-Style Cod

Cod is the most popular fish worldwide. Like other lean, white fish, fresh cod is mild in flavor with a delicate flesh that flakes apart readily when cooked. Any other member of the cod family—scrod, pollack, haddock, whiting, hake, or cusk—can be used in our version of this flavorful fish dish.

Although the Portuguese would probably use dried salted codfish, we used fresh cod with typical Portuguese ingredients for cooking fish: tomatoes, green peppers, onions, and cumin. We added the eggplant for extra flavor and substance.

Serve with rice seasoned with cumin, chopped parsley, and freshly ground pepper.

1 eggplant, about 1 pound (450 g)
1 quart (1 l) water
½ cup (118 ml) dry white wine
juice of ½ lemon
1 large celery rib with leaves, cut into 4 pieces
2 flat-leaf parsley sprigs
1 bay leaf
2 peppercorns
1½ pounds (675 g) fresh cod fillets, cut into 2- to 3-inch (5 to 8 cm) squares
1 large onion, about 6 ounces, chopped
1 tablespoon (15 ml) olive oil

1 garlic clove, minced
1 large green bell pepper, about ½ pound (450 g), seeded and chopped
4 fresh plum tomatoes, about ¾ pound (340 g), peeled, seeded, and chopped, or 1½ cups (354 ml) chopped drained canned low-sodium Italian plum tomatoes
¼ teaspoon (1.25 ml) ground cumin
½ teaspoon (2.5 ml) salt (optional)
freshly ground pepper to taste
olive oil cooking spray

Preheat oven to 350°F (180°C).

Place eggplant on a baking sheet and bake for 30 minutes, until tender when pierced with a knife. Remove from oven; peel and chop.

Meanwhile, in a large heavy skillet, bring water and wine to a simmer over low heat. Add lemon juice, celery, parsley, bay leaf, peppercorns, and cod. Partially cover with a lid or piece of aluminum foil; gently poach until fish is tender, about 15 minutes.

In a separate skillet, sauté onion in olive oil over low heat until onion is wilted, about 5 minutes. Add garlic, green pepper, and tomatoes; cook, uncovered, until tomatoes are cooked but all vegetables still hold their shape, about 15 minutes. Season with cumin, salt, and pepper.

Increase oven temperature to 400°F (205°C). Spray a deep casserole with cooking spray. Place a layer of the cooked eggplant on the bottom. With a slotted spoon, remove fish from poaching liquid and place on top of eggplant. Spoon tomato sauce over fish; cover and bake until hot and bubbly, about 10 minutes.

MAKES 4 SERVINGS

Per serving: calories, 220 ◆ protein, 26 g ◆ carbohydrate, 20 g ◆ fat, 5 g (calories from fat, 20%) ◆ dietary fiber, 2 g ◆ cholesterol, 47 mg ◆ sodium, 381 mg ◆ potassium, 1,167 mg Joslin Exchanges: 3 low-fat meat, 3 vegetable

Poached Sole with Citrus and Herbs

Fillet of sole, napped with a citrus herb sauce, is one of those entrees that you'll turn to year-round.

Orange roughy, flounder, or red snapper could be cooked in the same manner.

¼ cup (59 ml) chicken stock (page 45)	1¼ pounds (570 g) fillet of sole, rinsed
3 tablespoons (45 ml) fresh orange juice	⅓ cup (78 ml) snipped chives, slivered fresh basil leaves, chopped fresh mint, or chopped flat-leaf parsley
2 tablespoons (30 ml) fresh lemon juice	
2 tablespoons (30 ml) fresh grapefruit juice	

In a large nonstick skillet, combine stock and fruit juices. Cover and bring to a boil. Add fish fillets. Cover and simmer gently for 4 to 6 minutes, until fish flakes easily when tested with a fork. Transfer fillets to a heated serving platter; keep warm.

Boil pan juices, uncovered, over high heat for 2 to 3 minutes, until reduced to about ¼ cup (59 ml). Spoon sauce over fillets. Top with fresh herbs and serve immediately.

MAKES 4 SERVINGS

Per serving: calories, 101 ◆ protein, 18 g ◆ carbohydrate, 4 g ◆ fat, 1 g (calories from fat, 8%) ◆ dietary fiber, trace ◆ cholesterol, 50 mg ◆ sodium, 182 mg ◆ potassium, 493 mg Joslin Exchanges: 2½ low-fat meat

A SPRING SUPPER

◆

Endive Salad with Beet Vinaigrette (page 91)

Poached Sole with Citrus and Herbs (page 127)

Basmati Rice (page 288)

Roasted Mixed Vegetables (page 326)

Mixed Fresh Fruit with Grated Lime Zest and

Chopped Fresh Mint

Per serving: 407 calories (29% fat)
Joslin Exchanges: 2½ low-fat meat, 1 bread/starch, 3 vegetable, 1 fruit, 1 fat

 Stir-Fried Tuna

Bok choy, red bell peppers, fresh ginger, and Asian seasonings give fresh tuna steaks a lively flavor in this easy stir-fry meal. It's served in shallow bowls over brown rice.

1 tablespoon (15 ml) cornstarch
⅓ cup (78 ml) dry sherry
2 tablespoons (30 ml) low-sodium soy sauce
½ cup (118 ml) chicken stock (page 45)
½ teaspoon (2.5 ml) dark sesame oil
½ teaspoon (2.5 ml) hot red pepper flakes or to taste
2 tablespoons (30 ml) canola oil

1 garlic clove, minced
1 tablespoon (15 ml) minced fresh ginger
1 pound (450 g) bok choy, coarsely chopped
1 large red bell pepper, seeded and cut into 2-inch (5 cm) squares
8 scallions, white part and 1 inch (2.5 cm) green, cut into 1-inch (2.5 cm) lengths

1½ pounds (675 g) fresh tuna,
sliced ¼ inch (.75 cm) thick, cut
into 6 equal pieces
2 cups (472 ml) hot cooked
brown rice (page 288)

1 tablespoon (15 ml) toasted
sesame seeds (page 440)

In a small bowl, combine cornstarch, sherry, soy sauce, chicken stock, sesame oil, and red pepper flakes. Set aside.

Heat 1 tablespoon (15 ml) canola oil in a wok or large skillet over high heat. When oil is hot, add garlic, ginger, bok choy, bell pepper, and scallions. Cook, stirring, until scallions are bright green and bok choy begins to wilt, about 2 minutes. With a slotted spoon, transfer vegetables to a bowl. Set aside.

Add remaining 1 tablespoon (15 ml) canola oil to wok. Lay tuna slices in a single layer in pan. Cook for 30 seconds. Turn over and continue to cook until browned on the outside but still pink in the center, about 1 minute. Transfer tuna to a plate.

Stir cornstarch mixture. Add to wok; bring to a boil. Return vegetables and tuna to wok; gently stir-fry until vegetables and tuna are hot, about 1½ minutes. Spoon ⅓ cup (78 ml) hot cooked brown rice into each of 6 shallow bowls. Top with vegetables and tuna. Sprinkle with sesame seeds.

MAKES 6 SERVINGS

Per serving: calories, 246 ◆ protein, 23 g ◆ carbohydrate, 22 g ◆ fat, 7 g (calories from fat, 26%) ◆ dietary fiber, 1 g ◆ cholesterol, 38 mg ◆ sodium, 259 mg ◆ potassium, 654 mg Joslin Exchanges: 3 low-fat meat, 1 bread/starch, 1 vegetable

Sautéed Shrimp with Fresh Tomato Sauce

Sautéed shrimp make a delightful year-round main course that's ready in minutes. Serve with basmati rice sprinkled with a few sliced almonds.

2 teaspoons (10 ml) olive oil
1 small onion, about 3 ounces (85
  g), peeled and coarsely grated
2 garlic cloves, minced
1½ pounds (675 g) large shrimp,
  peeled and deveined
juice of ½ lemon
2 fresh medium tomatoes, about
  ¾ pound (340 g), peeled,
  seeded, and chopped, or 1¼
  cups (295 ml) chopped drained
  canned Italian plum tomatoes

⅛ teaspoon (.6 ml) salt (optional)
¼ teaspoon (1.25 ml) cayenne
  pepper or to taste
½ teaspoon (2.5 ml) ground
  cumin
¼ cup (59 ml) chopped fresh basil

In a large nonstick skillet or wok, heat oil and sauté onion and garlic over low heat until onion is wilted, about 3 minutes. Add shrimp and sauté for about 30 seconds on each side. Add lemon juice, tomatoes, salt, cayenne pepper, and cumin. Continue to cook, stirring, for 1 minute. Stir in basil; serve immediately.

MAKES 4 SERVINGS

Per serving: calories, 187 ◆ protein, 27 g ◆ carbohydrate, 8 g ◆ fat, 5 g (calories from fat, 24%) ◆ dietary fiber, 1 g ◆ cholesterol, 197 mg ◆ sodium, 267 mg ◆ potassium, 482 mg Joslin Exchanges: 3 low-fat meat, 2 vegetable

Asian Variation

Omit lemon juice, tomatoes, salt, cayenne pepper, and cumin. To sautéed onion mixture, add shrimp; ½ pound (225 g) snow peas, strings removed; 1 medium-size red bell pepper, about 6 ounces (180 g), cut into thin strips; 2 tablespoons (30 ml) rice vinegar; 4 teaspoons (20 ml) low-sodium soy sauce; and a drop of dark sesame oil. Stir-fry for 3 minutes (the vegetables should still be crunchy and the shrimp just opaque in center). Stir in basil; serve immediately.

MAKES 4 SERVINGS

Per serving: calories, 200 ◆ protein, 28 g ◆ carbohydrate, 11 g ◆ fat, 5 g (calories from fat, 21%) ◆ dietary fiber, 1 g ◆ cholesterol, 197 mg ◆ sodium, 395 mg ◆ potassium, 471 mg Joslin Exchanges: 3 low-fat meat, 2 vegetable

Pesto Variation

Omit lemon juice, tomatoes, salt, cayenne pepper, and cumin. Mix together 1 tablespoon (15 ml) grated Parmesan cheese, 2 teaspoons (10 ml) crushed dried basil, 2 teaspoons (10 ml) minced fresh parsley, and 1 teaspoon (5 ml) olive oil. Add to sautéed onion mixture along with shrimp. Cook, stirring, until shrimp are just opaque in center, about 2 minutes. Stir in basil; serve immediately.

MAKES 4 SERVINGS

Per serving: calories, 186 ◆ protein, 27 g ◆ carbohydrate, 4 g ◆ fat, 6 g (calories from fat, 31%) ◆ dietary fiber, trace ◆ cholesterol, 198 mg ◆ sodium, 222 mg ◆ potassium, 305 mg Joslin Exchanges: 3½ low-fat meat

Grilled Fresh Tuna Niçoise

This is a slimmed-down version of Irena Chalmers and Rick Rogers's recipe from their book *Best Barbecues Ever*. It's a delicious change from a classic Niçoise, and we like our lightened version just as well.

Serve this springtime whole-meal salad with Lemon Pepper Breadsticks (page 396) and a light dessert.

Marinade

2 tablespoons (30 ml) fresh lemon juice
3 tablespoons (45 ml) olive oil
1 garlic clove, finely minced
½ teaspoon (2.5 ml) fresh thyme leaves or ¼ teaspoon (1.25 ml) crushed dried

¼ teaspoon (1.25 ml) freshly ground pepper or to taste

Salad

1½ pounds (675 g) tuna steaks, cut 1 inch (2.5 cm) thick

¾ pound (340 g) small new potatoes, scrubbed

3 scallions, white part only, thinly sliced

1 tablespoon (15 ml) dry white wine

½ pound (225 g) fresh asparagus, trimmed and cut into 1-inch (2.5 cm) pieces, or fresh green beans, trimmed

2 bunches of arugula, well washed and crisped

½ pound (225 g) cherry tomatoes, halved

1 tablespoon (15 ml) drained capers

Mix together marinade ingredients. Marinate tuna in mixture for 1 hour at room temperature.

Meanwhile, steam potatoes over boiling water until tender, about 10 minutes. (Or combine potatoes and ¼ cup (59 ml) water in a 6-cup (1.5 l) microwave-safe casserole. Cover tightly and cook on HIGH for 6 to 8 minutes, stirring once, until tender.) Toss potatoes with scallions and wine. Place in a large salad bowl.

In a small amount of boiling water, cook asparagus until just tender, about 3 minutes. Drain. Rinse under cold running water; drain again. [Or place asparagus and 1 tablespoon (15 ml) water in a shallow microwave-safe dish. Cover and microwave on HIGH for 2 minutes.] Add to potatoes.

Wash arugula; remove tough stem ends. Wrap washed leaves in paper towels and place in refrigerator.

Remove tuna from marinade, scraping off as much marinade as possible. Reserve marinade. Grill tuna over medium-hot coals, turning once, about 6 minutes. (Or broil under a preheated broiler, about 4 inches (10 cm) from source of heat) Slice tuna into strips. Add to potatoes and asparagus along with tomatoes, arugula, and reserved marinade. Toss. Arrange on serving plates. Sprinkle with capers.

MAKES 4 SERVINGS

Per serving: calories, 375 ◆ protein, 38 g ◆ carbohydrate, 24 g ◆ fat, 14 g (calories from fat, 33%) ◆ dietary fiber, 1 g ◆ cholesterol, 53 mg ◆ sodium, 102 mg ◆ potassium, 1,381 mg Joslin Exchanges: 4 low-fat meat, 1 vegetable, 1 bread/starch

Grilled Fish Veracruz

The combination of hot and refreshingly cool flavors lifts this grilled or broiled fish dish out of the ordinary. Serve with warmed flour tortillas to sop up the delicious sauce.

1½ pounds (675 g) firm white fish fillets, such as halibut or red snapper, ¾ to 1 inch (2 to 2.5 cm) thick, without skin
1 tablespoon (15 ml) olive oil
 ½ teaspoon (2.5 ml) celery seed
 ⅛ teaspoon (.6 ml) cayenne pepper or to taste
 ½ teaspoon (2.5 ml) dry mustard
 ¼ teaspoon (1.25 ml) ground ginger
 ⅛ teaspoon (.6 ml) allspice
 ½ teaspoon (2.5 ml) paprika
 ⅛ teaspoon (.6 ml) cumin
 ¼ teaspoon (1.25 ml) finely crushed bay leaf

2 medium-size tomatoes, about ½ pound (225 g), peeled, seeded, and chopped, or 1 cup (236 ml) drained canned low-sodium Italian plum tomatoes, chopped
2 scallions, white part only, chopped
½ cup (118 ml) chopped green bell pepper
2 tablespoons (30 ml) white wine vinegar
freshly ground pepper to taste
1 tablespoon (15 ml) chopped fresh oregano or 1 teaspoon (5 ml) crushed dried
1 lime, quartered

Cut fish into 4 equal portions. Brush with 1 teaspoon (5 ml) olive oil. In a small bowl, combine celery seed, cayenne, dry mustard, ginger, allspice, paprika, cumin, and bay leaf. Rub spice mixture on both sides of fish. Let stand for at least 15 minutes.

Meanwhile, in a large bowl, combine tomatoes, scallions, green pepper, vinegar, remaining 2 teaspoons (10 ml) olive oil, pepper, and oregano. Set aside.

Place fish on grill or under a preheated broiler, about 4 inches from source of heat. Grill or broil fish, turning once, until fish flakes when prodded with a fork, 3 to 5 minutes per side.

Arrange fish on a heated serving platter. Top with tomato mixture. Serve with lime wedges to squeeze over fish.

MAKES 4 SERVINGS

Per serving: calories, 229 ◆ protein, 35 ◆ carbohydrate, 5 g ◆ fat, 8 g (calories from fat, 31%) ◆ dietary fiber, 1 g ◆ cholesterol, 52 mg ◆ sodium, 94 mg ◆ potassium, 932 mg Joslin Exchanges: 4½ low-fat meat, 1 vegetable

MEXICAN BARBECUE

◆

Jícama with Chili and Lime (page 4)

Grilled Fish Veracruz (page 133)

Warm Flour Tortillas

Grilled Yellow Summer Squash (page 321)

Mixed Berries with Crème Fraîche (page 428)

Per serving: 542 calories (25% fat)
Joslin Exchanges: 4½ low-fat meat, 1 bread/starch, 3 vegetable, 1 fruit, ½ nonfat milk

Halibut Steaks Aïoli

Aïoli is a pungent garlic mayonnaise from the south of France that's served with fish, crudités, and steamed vegetables. We love it, but it's almost 100 percent fat. We've lightened the recipe, then used it as a marinade so that we can save on all those calories and fat exchanges without sacrificing the wonderful flavor.

Serve with Bulgur Pilaf (page 279).

2 garlic cloves, peeled and halved
2 tablespoons (30 ml) fresh rosemary leaves or 2 teaspoons (10 ml) crushed dried
¼ cup (59 ml) egg substitute
2 tablespoons (30 ml) fresh lemon juice

freshly ground pepper to taste
¼ cup (59 ml) olive oil
1¼ pounds (570 g) halibut steaks, cut ¾ to 1 inch (2 to 2.5 cm) thick
1 lemon, quartered

To make the sauce, in a food processor or blender, combine garlic, rosemary, egg substitute, lemon juice, and pepper. Process for 1 minute. With motor running, slowly add oil. Process until thick.

Place halibut in a shallow glass dish. Spoon aïoli over fish and turn once to coat both sides. Cover and refrigerate for at least 4 hours.

Grill or broil halibut 4 to 6 inches (10 to 15 cm) from source of heat or over medium-hot coals, turning once, until fish flakes when prodded with a fork, about 3 to 5 minutes per side. Baste occasionally with marinade during grilling. Serve with lemon wedges to squeeze over fish.

MAKES 4 SERVINGS

Per serving: calories, 287 ◆ protein, 30 g ◆ carbohydrate, 2 g ◆ fat, 17 g (calories from fat, 55%) ◆ dietary fiber, trace ◆ cholesterol, 44 mg ◆ sodium, 102 mg ◆ potassium, 686 mg Joslin Exchanges: 4 low-fat meat, 1 fat

 Grilled Red Snapper with Red and Green Peppercorn Sauce

Dry red and green peppercorns (dry-packed, not in brine) are available at specialty food stores and some supermarkets and are used for color here. This is a very simple but elegant dish.

While the fish cooks, grill some polenta (page 286) that you made earlier in the day and toss a salad. The peppercorn sauce can also be used over grilled chicken breasts.

Red and Green Peppercorn Sauce

2 tablespoons (30 ml) fresh lemon juice
1 tablespoon (15 ml) Dijon mustard
1 tablespoon (15 ml) canola oil
2 teaspoons (10 ml) red peppercorns
2 teaspoons (10 ml) green peppercorns
1 garlic clove, minced
½ cup (118 ml) chopped flat-leaf parsley
4 large scallions, both white and green parts, chopped

Fish

4 5-ounce (140 g) red snapper, halibut, or rockfish fillets, cut about ¾ inch (2 cm) thick

In a small bowl, combine sauce ingredients.

Grill or broil fish about 4 inches (10 cm) from heat source, brushing fish with sauce during grilling. Using a wide spatula, turn fish over when edges begin to turn opaque. Continue to grill until fish is opaque but still moist in thickest part, about 8 to 10 minutes altogether. Transfer fish to a heated serving platter; top with remaining sauce.

MAKES 4 SERVINGS

Per serving: calories, 128 ◆ protein, 19 g ◆ carbohydrate, 2 g ◆ fat, 5 g (calories from fat, 35%) ◆ dietary fiber, trace ◆ cholesterol, 50 mg ◆ sodium, 112 mg ◆ potassium, 629 mg Joslin Exchanges: 3 low-fat meat

Per serving (sauce alone): calories, 42 ◆ protein, 1 g ◆ carbohydrate, 2 g ◆ fat, 4 g (calories from fat, 85%) ◆ dietary fiber, 1 g ◆ cholesterol, 0 mg ◆ sodium, 55 mg ◆ potassium, 80 mg Joslin Exchanges: 1 fat

Grilled Tuna with Black Bean Salsa

Fresh tuna is becoming increasingly available year-round, and although it's a moderately fatty fish, it's one of our favorites for the grill. Fresh tuna is best cooked rare; overcooked tuna is dry and tough. Of course you can also grill tuna on a rack under an oven broiler.

The earthy flavor of the black beans complements the rich flavor of the fish. It can be made ahead, chilled, and returned to room temperature before serving. This salsa is also excellent with grilled chicken or turkey breast or as a stuffing for an omelet made with one egg plus one egg white.

1½ pounds (675 g) fresh tuna steaks, cut ½ inch (1.5 cm) thick
2 teaspoons (10 ml) olive oil

3 fresh lemon thyme sprigs or ½ teaspoon (2.5 ml) crushed dried thyme

grated zest of ½ lime
freshly ground pepper to taste

Black Bean Salsa (recipe follows)
1 orange, cut into 6 wedges

Marinate tuna in olive oil, thyme, and lime zest for 25 to 30 minutes before grilling. Season with pepper. Grill or broil over medium-hot coals, 4 inches (10 cm) from source of heat, for 2 to 3 minutes per side (center should be rare). Serve with Black Bean Salsa. Offer a wedge of orange to squeeze over tuna and beans.

MAKES 6 SERVINGS

Per serving (fish alone): calories, 105 ◆ protein, 20 g ◆ carbohydrate, trace ◆ fat, 2 g (calories from fat, 17%) ◆ dietary fiber, trace ◆ cholesterol, 38 mg ◆ sodium, 31 mg ◆ potassium, 378 mg
Joslin Exchanges: 3 low-fat meat

Black Bean Salsa

olive oil cooking spray
1 small red onion, unpeeled
1 medium-size red bell pepper
1 medium-size yellow bell pepper
1 small fresh jalapeño chili
1 large unpeeled garlic clove
1½ cups (354 ml) cooked black beans

1 teaspoon (5 ml) grated orange zest
1 tablespoon (15 ml) fresh lime juice
1 tablespoon (15 ml) olive oil
1 tablespoon (15 ml) minced fresh marjoram or 1 teaspoon (5 ml) crushed dried

Preheat oven to 375°F (190°C). Lightly spray a baking pan with cooking spray. Place unpeeled onion, bell peppers, jalapeño, and unpeeled garlic in pan; roast for 25 minutes. Remove from oven. Peel and dice onion. Peel and dice bell peppers, discarding seeds and core. Mince jalapeño, discarding seeds. Peel and mince garlic.

In a bowl, toss together beans and vegetables. Add orange zest, lime juice, olive oil, and marjoram. Serve at room temperature.

MAKES 6 SERVINGS

Per serving: calories, 95 ◆ protein, 4 g ◆ carbohydrate, 15 g ◆ fat, 3 g (calories from fat, 28%) ◆ dietary fiber, 1 g ◆ cholesterol, 0 g ◆ sodium, 2 mg ◆ potassium, 254 mg
Joslin Exchanges: 1 bread/starch

SUMMER SUNDAY SUPPER

◆

Cucumber Buttermilk Soup (page 59)

Grilled Tuna with Black Bean Salsa (page 136)

Grilled Radicchio (page 321)

Fresh Pineapple and Fresh Blackberries

Per serving: 330 calories (27% fat)
Joslin Exchanges: 3 low-fat meat, 1 bread/starch, 1 vegetable, 1 fruit

Scallop Brochettes with Lime and Chipotle Chilies

Canned chipotle chilies (smoked jalapeños) are sold in Mexican markets, many supermarkets, and by mail order (see Appendix 2). They add a smoky-hot flavor to the relish for this brochette of sea scallops.

  8 bamboo skewers
olive oil cooking spray
  4 shallots, minced
  2 scallions, white part only, chopped
¼ cup (59 ml) plus 3 tablespoons (45 ml) fresh lime juice
¼ teaspoon (1.25 ml) grated lime zest
  2 tablespoons (30 ml) olive oil
¼ pound (115 g) jícama, peeled and cut into thin strips

  2 tablespoons (30 ml) minced canned chipotle chilies
  2 tablespoons (30 ml) minced cilantro (fresh coriander)
1¼ pounds (570 g) sea scallops
  1 garlic clove, minced
½ teaspoon (2.5 ml) fresh thyme leaves or ⅛ teaspoon (.6 ml) crushed dried
⅛ teaspoon (.6 ml) salt (optional)
⅛ teaspoon (.6 ml) freshly ground pepper

Soak skewers for 30 minutes in water to cover. Meanwhile, in a nonstick skillet lightly sprayed with cooking spray, sauté shallots and scallions over low heat until shallots are soft but not browned, about 3 minutes. Remove from heat; stir in ¼ cup (59 ml) lime juice, lime zest, 1 tablespoon (15 ml) olive oil, jícama, chipotle chiles, and cilantro. Cover and refrigerate for at least 30 minutes.

Rinse scallops to remove any bits of shell or sand; pat dry with paper towels. Thread scallops onto skewers; lay in a shallow glass dish. Whisk together remaining 1 tablespoon (15 ml) olive oil, 3 tablespoons (45 ml) lime juice, garlic, thyme, salt, and pepper. Pour over scallops; marinate for 30 minutes.

Place scallops on a well-greased grill or broiler pan 4 to 6 inches (10 to 15 cm) from heat source or over medium-hot coals. Grill, turning once, until scallops are opaque throughout, about 5 to 7 minutes. Cut to test.

Place brochettes on a heated serving platter. Garnish with jícama chipotle mixture.

MAKES 4 SERVINGS

Per serving: calories, 198 ◆ protein, 19 g ◆ carbohydrate, 13 g ◆ fat, 8 g (calories from fat, 36%) ◆ dietary fiber, trace ◆ cholesterol, 35 mg ◆ sodium, 227 mg ◆ potassium, 512 mg Joslin Exchanges: 2½ low-fat meat, 2 vegetable

---

DINNER AL FRESCO

◆

Scallop Brochettes with Lime and Chipotle Chilies (page 138)

Grilled Eggplant (page 319) and Summer Squash (page 321)

Southwestern Focaccia (page 395)

Raspberry Sorbet (page 432)

Per serving: 404 calories (27% fat)
Joslin Exchanges: 2½ low-fat meat, 4 vegetable, 1 bread/starch, 1 fruit, ½ fat

Halibut Grilled in Corn Husks with Salsa

Grilling fresh fish in corn husks (available at specialty food stores and many supermarkets) adds an interesting, slightly smoky flavor to the fish. Dried herbs work wonderfully with this recipe, but if you have fresh, all the better; just use three times as much.

Accompany the fish with Grilled Corn on the Cob (page 306) or other grilled vegetables such as squash (page 321), or eggplant (page 319). We offer two salsas for the fish. If there's any Three-Pepper Salsa left over, add cold tomato juice for a quick, easy gazpacho for next day's lunch. The salsa is also excellent with chicken. The Roasted Tomatillo Sauce is also delicious. Tomatillos look like small green tomatoes with a papery husk; they've started turning up at supermarkets all over the country and are easy to grow in the garden. Both salsas can be made up to a day ahead. Bring to room temperature before serving.

1¼ **pounds (570 g) halibut or other firm-fleshed fish fillets such as salmon, mahimahi, mako shark, scrod, or turbot, skin removed**
dried corn husks
½ **tablespoon (7.5 ml) ground cumin**
½ **teaspoon (2.5 ml) crushed dried thyme**

½ **teaspoon (2.5 ml) crushed dried oregano**
¼ **teaspoon (1.25 ml) freshly ground pepper to taste**
Three-Pepper Salsa or Roasted Tomatillo Sauce (recipes follow)

Cut the halibut into small pieces, about 1½ inches (4 cm) square. Soak dried corn husks in hot water to cover until soft and pliable, about 15 minutes. Separate large husks, discarding torn ones. Combine cumin, thyme, oregano, and pepper. Sprinkle on halibut pieces.

Lay out one corn husk with the top (narrow part) pointed away from you. Place a piece of seasoned halibut in the middle of the husk. Wrap halibut, folding in sides, bottom, and top of the husk to completely enclose fish. Secure with a wet toothpick. Repeat process, wrapping each halibut piece.

Grill or broil, 4 inches (10 cm) from source of heat, over medium-hot coals for 10 to 12 minutes, about 10 minutes per inch (2.5 cm) of fish thickness, turning once or twice. Remove toothpicks. Serve halibut in corn husks, providing a large bowl for the discarded husks.

MAKES 4 SERVINGS

Per serving (fish alone): calories, 151 ♦ protein, 29 g ♦ carbohydrate, trace ♦ fat, 3 g (calories from fat, 20%) ♦ dietary fiber, trace ♦ cholesterol, 44 mg ♦ sodium, 74 mg ♦ potassium, 623 mg Joslin Exchanges: 4 low-fat meat

Three-Pepper Salsa

½ cup (118 ml) finely minced red bell pepper

½ cup (118 ml) finely minced yellow bell pepper

1 jalapeño chili, seeded and finely minced

¼ cup (59 ml) finely minced onion

1 tomatillo, husked and finely minced

1 garlic clove, finely minced

½ cup (118 ml) loosely packed cilantro (fresh coriander) leaves, chopped

1 teaspoon (5 ml) olive oil

1 tablespoon (15 ml) fresh lime juice

⅛ teaspoon (.6 ml) salt (optional)

⅛ teaspoon (.6 ml) freshly ground pepper or to taste

In a medium-size bowl, combine all ingredients; let sit for at least 30 minutes before serving.

MAKES ABOUT 2 CUPS

Per ¼-cup (59 ml) serving: calories, 19 ♦ protein, 1 g ♦ carbohydrate, 3 g ♦ fat, 1 g (calories from fat, 47%) ♦ dietary fiber, trace ♦ cholesterol, 0 mg ♦ sodium, 35 mg ♦ potassium, 99 mg Joslin Exchanges: free

Roasted Tomatillo Sauce

olive oil cooking spray

1 pound (450 g) tomatillos, husked

2 garlic cloves

1 small onion

2 drained canned green chilies

½ cup (118 ml) chopped fresh cilantro (coriander)

¼ teaspoon (1.25 ml) salt (optional)

1 teaspoon (5 ml) olive oil

1 tablespoon (15 ml) fresh lime juice

Preheat oven to 350°F (180°C). Lightly spray a roasting pan with cooking spray. Place tomatillos, unpeeled garlic, and unpeeled onion in pan. Roast for 25 to 30 minutes, until vegetables are very soft but not burned. Peel garlic and onion. Place tomatillos, garlic, onion, and remaining ingredients except lime juice in a food processor or blender. Blend until smooth, adding a little water as needed to make a smooth sauce. Add lime juice; blend for a few seconds. Serve at room temperature.

MAKES ABOUT 2 CUPS

Per ¼-cup (59 ml) serving:
calories, 25 ◆ protein, 1 g ◆ carbohydrate, 4 g ◆ fat, 1 g (calories from fat, 23%) ◆

dietary fiber, 1 g ◆ cholesterol, 0 mg ◆ sodium, 125 mg ◆ potassium, 149 mg
Joslin Exchanges: 1 vegetable

 ## *Grilled Gingered Swordfish with Fresh Fruit Relish*

This fish dish can be prepared in next to no time—a brief marinade in fresh ginger, followed by a few minutes on the grill while you prepare a snappy relish.

The Fresh Fruit Relish is also terrific alongside slices of roast chicken or turkey breast. We suggest using papaya for the relish, but if it's not available, substitute a mango, fresh peaches, nectarines, or red plums—or a combination of fruits.

4 teaspoons (20 ml) low-sodium soy sauce
2 tablespoons (30 ml) dry sherry
1 tablespoon (15 ml) finely minced fresh ginger

4 6-ounce (180 g) swordfish steaks, cut about 1 inch (2.5 cm) thick
Fresh Fruit Relish (see page 143)

In a small bowl, combine soy sauce, sherry, and ginger. Brush over swordfish steaks. Marinate for 15 minutes.

Meanwhile, prepare grill. Remove fish from marinade, reserving marinade. Grill or broil fish over medium-hot coals about 4 to 6 inches (10 to 15 cm) from source of heat for 7 to 10 minutes, turning once. Serve with Fresh Fruit Relish.

MAKES 4 SERVINGS

Per serving (fish alone):
calories, 168 ◆ protein, 27 g ◆ carbohydrate, 1 g ◆ fat, 5 g (calories from fat, 27%) ◆ dietary fiber, trace ◆

cholesterol, 52 mg ◆ sodium, 306 mg ◆ potassium, 395 mg
Joslin Exchanges: 4 low-fat meat

Fresh Fruit Relish

1 large firm but ripe papaya, about ³/₄ pound (340 g), or 1 large mango or 2 medium-size peaches or 2 medium-size nectarines
juice and grated zest of ½ lime
2 tablespoons (30 ml) rice vinegar
2 scallions, white part only, thinly sliced
3 tablespoons (45 ml) chopped cilantro (fresh coriander)
1 fresh jalapeño chili, seeded and minced

Cut papaya in half; scoop out and discard seeds. (Or cut mango, peaches, or nectarines in half. Remove pit.) Peel and cut into ¼-inch (.75 cm) cubes. In a small bowl, combine papaya or other fruit with remaining ingredients. Set aside until ready to serve.

MAKES 4 SERVINGS

Per serving: calories, 37 ◆ protein, 1 g ◆ carbohydrate, 10 g ◆ fat, trace (calories from fat, less than 1%) ◆ dietary fiber, 1 g ◆ cholesterol, 0 g ◆ sodium, 4 mg ◆ potassium, 264 mg
Joslin Exchanges: 1 fruit

BIRTHDAY BARBECUE

◆

Yellow Tomato Bisque with Fiery Tomato Ice (page 62)

Grilled Gingered Swordfish with Fresh Fruit Relish

(page 142)

Couscous with Steamed Peas

Lemon Chiffon Cake (page 407)

Per serving: 712 calories (30% fat)
Joslin Exchanges: 4 low-fat meat, 4½ bread/starch, 1 fruit, 1½ fat

Shrimp Salad with Grapes

A light and luscious supper when the weather is hot and sultry.

³/₄ cup (177 ml) low-fat (1%)
  cottage cheese
2 shallots, quartered
2 tablespoons (30 ml) chopped
  fresh dill
¹/₄ teaspoon (1.25 ml) freshly
  ground pepper or to taste
2 teaspoons (10 ml) Dijon mustard
1 tablespoon (15 ml) fresh lemon
  juice
¹/₈ teaspoon (.6 ml) Tabasco sauce
  or to taste
1 tablespoon (15 ml) olive oil
1 to 2 tablespoons (15 to 30 ml)
  skim milk if needed

1¹/₄ pounds (570 g) small shrimp,
  cooked, peeled, and deveined
2 hard-cooked large eggs (1 with
  yolk, 1 without), coarsely
  chopped
3 celery ribs, finely diced
¹/₄ cup (59 ml) chopped red onion
15 seedless green grapes, halved
12 large leaves of butter lettuce,
  washed and crisped
³/₄ pound (340 g) alfalfa sprouts
6 lemon wedges
6 fresh dill sprigs

In a food processor or blender, combine cottage cheese, shallots, dill, pepper, mustard, lemon juice, Tabasco sauce, and oil. Process until smooth, thinning dressing with milk if necessary (dressing should be the consistency of mayonnaise).

In a large bowl, combine dressing, shrimp, eggs, celery, red onion, and grapes. Mix gently. Cover and chill for up to 2 hours.

To serve, arrange 2 lettuce leaves on each of 6 chilled plates. Mound equal portions of alfalfa sprouts on lettuce; top with equal portions of shrimp salad. Garnish each with a lemon wedge and a dill sprig.

MAKES 6 SERVINGS

Per serving: calories, 181 ◆ protein, 25 g ◆ carbohydrate, 9 g ◆ fat, 6 g (calories from fat, 29%) ◆ dietary fiber, 1 g ◆ cholesterol, 159 mg ◆ sodium, 305 mg ◆ potassium, 415 mg Joslin Exchanges: 3 low-fat meat, 2 vegetable

---

SUPPER ON THE PORCH

◆

Chilled Fresh Cream of Pea Soup (page 52)

Shrimp Salad with Grapes (page 144)

Chive Popovers (page 388)

Nectarine Mousse (page 429)

Per serving: 483 calories (20% fat)
Joslin Exchanges: 3 low-fat meat, 2 vegetable, 2 bread/starch, 1 fruit, ½ nonfat milk

Fish and Shellfish in Parchment

Cooking in parchment or aluminum foil is an effortless way to prepare this elegant seafood entree. When the puffy package is opened, a cloud of heady aroma is released and a mélange of moist, sweet fish and a snappy tomato sauce is revealed. As the seafood cooks, cook some pasta to swirl into the flavorful sauce.

Cooking parchment is available in gourmet cooking shops, hardware stores, and many supermarkets. Look for it next to the wax paper. Wide (18 inches/46 cm) aluminum foil works just as well.

6 **shallots, finely minced**
6 **scallions, white part only, thinly sliced**
4 **teaspoons (20 ml) olive oil**

3 **large fresh tomatoes, peeled, seeded, and chopped, about 1 pound (450 g)**
⅓ **cup (78 ml) dry white wine**
juice of 1 lemon

⅓ cup (78 ml) chopped fresh parsley

1 teaspoon (5 ml) hot red pepper flakes or to taste

freshly ground pepper to taste

1¼ pounds (570 g) fresh flatfish fillets (turbot, sole, flounder, or red snapper), cut into 6 pieces

6 large shrimp, about 3 ounces (85 g), peeled and deveined

12 scallops, about ½ pound (225 g), rinsed and cut crosswise into 3 pieces each

6 thin slices of lemon

¾ pound (340 g) fresh angel hair pasta

3 tablespoons (45 ml) chopped fresh basil (optional)

In a heavy sauté pan over low heat, sauté shallots and scallions in 2 teaspoons (10 ml) olive oil until shallots are soft but not browned, about 4 minutes. Add tomatoes, wine, lemon juice, parsley, red pepper flakes, and a generous grinding of pepper. Cook, stirring frequently, until sauce thickens, about 5 minutes.

Preheat oven to 425°F (220°C). Cut 6 circles of parchment paper or aluminum foil 18 inches (46 cm) in diameter. Lay a fish fillet on one half of each parchment circle. Spoon sauce over fillets, dividing sauce equally. Flank each fillet with 1 shrimp and 2 cut scallops. Top with a lemon slice. Fold over parchment or foil and crimp edges to seal. Place on baking sheet; bake for 15 minutes.

Meanwhile, cook pasta in boiling salted water in a 6-quart (5.5 l) pot until just tender, about 2 minutes. Drain; toss with remaining 2 teaspoons (10 ml) olive oil. Keep warm.

Place parchment packets on serving plates. Break open and divide pasta among packets, tucking angel hair alongside seafood. Scatter fresh basil over seafood and pasta; serve at once.

MAKES 6 SERVINGS

Per serving: calories, 252 ◆ protein, 28 g ◆ carbohydrate, 23 g ◆ fat, 5 g (calories from fat, 17%) ◆ dietary fiber, 1 g ◆ cholesterol, 92 mg ◆ sodium, 152 mg ◆ potassium, 647 mg Joslin Exchanges: 3 low-fat meat, 1½ bread/starch

Grilled Swordfish with Pomegranate or Orange Sauce

Pomegranates are a labor-intensive fruit, but the unique flavor is well worth the effort needed to free the bright pink juicy seeds (page 236). Throughout the Mediterranean, pomegranate seeds and pomegranate syrup are used for cooking everything from duck to fish. Select a pomegranate that is heavy for its size with brightly colored skin.

Since pomegranates are available only from October to Christmas, the rest of the year you can make this dish using frozen pomegranate seeds (page 236) or chopped sections of a large orange with all rind and white pith removed.

Serve with Roasted Onions Balsamic (page 328) and some warm crusty bread.

2 garlic cloves, minced	1/4 cup (59 ml) chopped fresh mint
2 shallots, minced	or 1 tablespoon (15 ml) crushed
1 tablespoon (15 ml) olive oil	dried
1 cup (236 ml) bottled clam juice	seeds from 1 large pomegranate
juice of 1/2 lemon	1 1/2 pounds (675 g) swordfish
2 tablespoons (30 ml) dry white	steaks, 3/4 to 1 inch (2 to 2.5 cm)
wine (optional)	thick, cut into 4 portions
1/4 cup (59 ml) chopped flat-leaf	freshly ground pepper to taste
parsley	

In a heavy saucepan, sauté garlic and shallots in 2 teaspoons (10 ml) olive oil over low heat until garlic is soft but not browned, about 4 minutes. Add clam juice, lemon juice, and white wine. Increase heat to high and boil to reduce liquid by half. Add parsley, mint, and pomegranate seeds. Cook for 1 minute. Set aside; keep warm.

Rub fish with remaining 1 teaspoon (5 ml) olive oil. Season generously with pepper. Grill or broil fish 4 to 6 inches (10 to 15 cm) above a bed of hot coals, turning once until fish flakes easily when prodded with a fork, about 4 to 5 minutes per side.

Serve each fish portion with some of the sauce and pomegranate seeds.

MAKES 4 SERVINGS

Per serving: calories, 277 ◆ protein, 33 g ◆ carbohydrate, 12 g ◆ fat, 10 g (calories from fat, 32%) ◆ dietary fiber, trace ◆ cholesterol, 63 mg ◆ sodium, 279 mg ◆ potassium, 666 mg Joslin Exchanges: 4 low-fat meat, 1 fruit

Fish Poached in Romaine

Fish fillets wrapped in lettuce leaves are served with a sauce of aromatic vegetables and herbs for an extremely light elegant dish that can be completed in less than 30 minutes. The sauce is enriched at the last moment with a smidgen of unsalted butter—which we keep on hand in the freezer for just such uses.

4 large outer leaves of romaine lettuce
1¼ pounds (570 g) flounder, sole, or orange roughy fillets, cut into 4 pieces
freshly ground pepper to taste
4 small fresh tarragon sprigs
2 shallots, minced

2 leeks, white part only, well rinsed and cut into thin strips
1 celery rib, cut into 2-inch (5 cm) julienne strips
1 cup (236 ml) bottled clam juice
⅓ cup (78 ml) dry white wine
1 teaspoon (5 ml) frozen unsalted butter

Dip romaine lettuce in boiling water for 20 to 30 seconds, until wilted. Refresh under cold running water. Dry leaves on paper towels.

Place lettuce leaves, rib side up, on a flat surface. Using a small sharp knife, shave off back of center rib of each leaf (this is much easier than it sounds) to make them flat and flexible. Place a fish fillet lengthwise on each lettuce leaf. Season with a generous grinding of fresh pepper. Place a tarragon sprig on each fillet. Fold edges of lettuce up and over fish so that it is completely enclosed. Place fish in a single layer, seam side down, in a large heavy skillet.

Scatter shallots, leeks, and celery over fish packets. Add clam juice and wine to skillet. Bring to a simmer over low heat. Poach gently until fish is firm to the touch, about 10 minutes.

Transfer fish packets to a heated serving platter; keep warm. Bring poaching liquid to a boil over high heat and cook until reduced to about ½ cup (118 ml). Whisk in butter. Spoon sauce and vegetables over fish packets; serve immediately.

MAKES 4 SERVINGS

Per serving: calories, 143 ◆ protein, 21 g ◆ carbohydrate, 10 g ◆ fat, 2 g (calories from fat, 13%) ◆ dietary fiber, 1 g ◆ cholesterol, 49 mg ◆ sodium, 212 mg ◆ potassium, 640 mg Joslin Exchanges: 2½ low-fat meat, 2 vegetable

SPA SUPPER

◆

Mixed Baby Lettuces and Fresh Herbs with Lemon Vinaigrette

(page 96)

Fish Poached in Romaine (page 148)

Steamed New Potatoes

Roasted Tomatoes (page 330)

Fresh Persimmons on the Half Shell

Per serving: 352 calories (23% fat)
Joslin Exchanges: 2¹/₂ low-fat meat, 1 bread/starch, 3 vegetable, 1 fruit

Orange Roughy with Artichokes in Tomato Fennel Sauce

This popular New Zealand fish has tender white flesh and a tasty, mild flavor that's sparked by a striking combination of Mediterranean flavors of fresh fennel, tomato, and artichokes. You can also use flounder or sole. Serve with a side dish of polenta (page 286).

olive oil cooking spray
  3 scallions, white part only, finely chopped
  2 garlic cloves, minced

1 small fennel bulb, about ¹/₂ pound (225 g), finely chopped
¹/₄ pound (115 g) mushrooms, sliced

1 16-ounce (450 g) can plum
tomatoes, drained and coarsely
chopped

8 artichoke hearts, frozen or
canned in water

1 teaspoon (5 ml) crushed dried
oregano leaves

1 tablespoon (15 ml) crushed dried
basil leaves

⅛ teaspoon (.6 ml) hot red pepper
flakes or to taste

¼ cup (59 ml) dry white wine or ¼
cup (59 ml) bottled clam juice

4 5-ounce (140 g) orange roughy
fillets

In a large nonstick skillet lightly sprayed with cooking spray, sauté scallions, garlic, fennel, and mushrooms over low heat until vegetables are wilted, about 10 to 15 minutes. Add tomatoes, artichokes, herbs, red pepper flakes, and wine. Bring to a simmer and cook until reduced by a third.

Preheat oven to 425°F (220°C). Lightly spray a baking dish just big enough to hold the fish and tomato sauce with cooking spray. Place sauce in baking dish; arrange fish fillets on top. Lightly spray with cooking spray. Bake just until fish flakes when prodded with a fork, 5 to 8 minutes, depending on thickness of fish.

MAKES 4 SERVINGS

Per serving: calories, 182 ◆ protein, 24 g ◆ carbohydrate, 17 mg ◆ fat, 2 g (calories from fat, 5%) ◆ dietary fiber, 2 g ◆ cholesterol, 48 mg ◆ sodium, 284 mg ◆ potassium, 1,212 mg Joslin Exchanges: 2½ low-fat meat, 3 vegetable

Seafood Fajitas

Fajitas are usually made with steak or chicken, but when you use seafood, the make-it-yourself burrito becomes special fare for casual entertaining.

Pass the Salsa Fresca (page 8) and offer a side dish of Asian Pear and Grapefruit Salad (page 103).

¾ pound (340 g) shrimp

¾ pound (340 g) shelled, thawed
lobster meat from frozen lobster
tails, or use fresh crabmeat

¾ pound (340 g) sea scallops

1 large red bell pepper, about 6
ounces (180 g), seeded and cut
into julienne strips

1 large green bell pepper, about 6 ounces (180 g), seeded and cut into julienne strips
1 large onion, about ½ pound (225 g), cut in half and thinly sliced
1 tablespoon (15 ml) olive oil

juice of 1 lime
⅓ cup (78 ml) chopped fresh cilantro (fresh coriander)
16 8-inch (20 cm) flour tortillas, warmed

Lime Marinade

juice and grated zest of 1 lime
2 tablespoons (30 ml) olive oil
½ teaspoon (2.5 ml) Worcestershire sauce
1 teaspoon (5 ml) ground cumin
2 garlic cloves, pressed or minced

1 tablespoon (15 ml) fresh thyme leaves or 1 teaspoon (5 ml) crushed dried
½ teaspoon (2.5 ml) cayenne pepper or to taste
2 scallions, white part only, finely chopped

Peel and devein shrimp. Cut lobster meat into ½-inch (1.5 cm) squares. If scallops are large, cut into quarters. Place seafood in a shallow glass baking dish.

In a small bowl, combine marinade ingredients. Pour over seafood; toss to coat evenly. Marinate seafood for 30 minutes.

In a heavy nonstick sauté pan, sauté peppers and onion in olive oil until onions are just wilted but not browned, about 4 minutes. Add seafood and marinade; stir-fry until shrimp turns pink and lobster and scallops are cooked through, about 2 to 3 minutes. Stir in lime juice and cilantro. Serve with warmed tortillas.

MAKES 8 SERVINGS

Per serving: calories, 389 ◆ protein, 24 g ◆ carbohydrate, 45 g ◆ fat, 13 g (calories from fat, 30%) ◆ dietary fiber, 3 g ◆ cholesterol, 60 mg ◆ sodium, 178 mg ◆ potassium, 382 mg Joslin Exchanges: 2 low-fat meat, 3 bread/starch, 1 fat

Per serving (marinade alone): calories, 33 ◆ protein, trace ◆ carbohydrate, 1 g ◆ fat, 3 g (calories from fat, 81%) ◆ dietary fiber, trace ◆ cholesterol, 0 mg ◆ sodium, 4 mg ◆ potassium, 21 mg Joslin Exchanges: ½ fat

Microwave Oven–Poached Sole on Spicy Pipérade

Pipérade is a marvelous dish of peppers, tomato, garlic, and onion from the Basque region of France. Alive with the flavors of summer, it's traditionally made with lots of olive oil and simmered for an hour. Our low-fat version started in the microwave, using only 2 teaspoons (10 ml) of olive oil, cooks in half the time. The *pipérade* finishes on top of the stove while the sole poaches in the microwave.

We like to serve this spectacular dish with steamed small red potatoes. Also, try the *pipérade* with grilled chicken or slices of roasted turkey breast.

Spicy Pipérade

2 large garlic cloves, minced

1 medium-size onion, peeled and coarsely chopped

2 teaspoons (10 ml) olive oil

1 4-inch Anaheim chili, seeded and thinly sliced, or 2 tablespoons (30 ml) canned green chilies

1 medium-size red bell pepper, about 5 ounces (140 g), seeded and cut into thin strips

1 medium-size green bell pepper, about 5 ounces (140 g), seeded and cut into thin strips

1 pound (450 g) fresh tomatoes, peeled, seeded, and coarsely chopped, or 1 16-ounce (450 g) can low-sodium Italian plum tomatoes, drained and coarsely chopped

½ teaspoon (2.5 ml) salt (optional)

freshly ground pepper to taste

Place garlic, onion, and olive oil in a large glass casserole. Cover with casserole lid or wax paper. Microwave on HIGH for 5 minutes.

Add chili and bell peppers and microwave on HIGH for 5 minutes, until peppers are brightly colored.

Transfer onion-pepper mixture to a nonstick skillet. Stir in tomatoes, salt, and a generous grinding of pepper. Cook, uncovered, over low heat for 20 minutes, stirring occasionally.

MAKES 4 SERVINGS

Per serving: calories, 63 ◆ protein, 2 g ◆ carbohydrate, 12 g ◆ fat, 1 g (calories from fat, 14%) ◆ dietary fiber, 1 g ◆ cholesterol, 0 mg ◆ sodium, 147 mg ◆ potassium, 414 mg
Joslin Exchanges: 2 vegetable

Poached Sole

olive oil cooking spray
leaves from 4 flat-leaf parsley sprigs
leaves from 4 fresh lemon thyme
   sprigs or ³/₄ teaspoon (3.75 ml)
   crushed dried

4 5-ounce (140 g) sole, flounder, or
   orange roughy fillets
¹/₂ cup (118 ml) dry white wine
juice of ¹/₂ lemon
flat-leaf parsley leaves for garnish

Lightly spray bottom of a glass casserole dish with cooking spray. Distribute parsley and thyme leaves in casserole. Fold fish fillets into thirds, tucking thinner ends of each fillet under the thicker center. Arrange fillets, seam side down, around outer edge of dish, leaving center open. Pour wine and lemon juice over fillets. Cover with wax paper. Microwave on HIGH for 6 to 8 minutes, until fish flakes easily, rotating dish once.

    To serve, spoon *pipérade* onto a heated serving platter. Arrange poached sole on *pipérade*. Scatter parsley leaves on top and serve.

MAKES 4 SERVINGS

Per serving (fish alone):
calories, 87 ◆ protein, 18 g ◆ carbohydrate, 1 g ◆ fat, 1 g (calories from fat, 10%) ◆ dietary fiber, trace ◆ cholesterol, 49 mg ◆ sodium, 77 mg ◆ potassium, 264 mg
Joslin Exchanges: 2¹/₂ low-fat meat

Angel Hair with Shrimp

Thin strands of pasta mingle with garlicky shrimp for an elegant year-round dinner.

¹/₃ cup (78 ml) chopped shallot
6 garlic cloves, minced
1 tablespoon (15 ml) olive oil
1 cup (236 ml) bottled clam juice
¹/₄ cup (59 ml) dry white wine
¹/₂ cup (118 ml) chopped flat-leaf
   parsley
¹/₄ cup (59 ml) chopped fresh basil
   or 1 tablespoon (15 ml) crushed
   dried
1 teaspoon (5 ml) freshly ground
   pepper

2 medium-size fresh tomatoes,
   about ¹/₂ pound (225 g), peeled,
   seeded, and diced or 1 cup
   chopped, drained, canned
   tomatoes
¹/₂ teaspoon (2.5 ml) salt (optional)
9 ounces (250 g) fresh angel hair
   pasta or ¹/₂ pound (225 g) dry
   capellini
1 pound (450 g) medium-size
   shrimp, peeled and deveined

In a large nonstick skillet, sauté shallot and garlic in olive oil over low heat until shallot is wilted, about 4 minutes. Add clam juice, wine, parsley, basil, pepper, and tomatoes. Partially cover and simmer for 15 to 20 minutes.

When sauce is almost done, fill a 5- to 6-quart (4.75 to 5.5 l) pan with water, add salt, and bring to a boil. Add pasta and cook for 1 to 2 minutes (3 to 4 minutes for dry capellini), until just tender to bite. Drain well.

While pasta is cooking, add shrimp to simmering sauce. Cook, stirring, until opaque throughout, 3 to 4 minutes. Cut to test.

Divide pasta among 6 wide, shallow bowls. Spoon shrimp mixture over pasta.

MAKES 6 SERVINGS

> **Per serving:** calories, 160 ◆ protein, 15 g ◆ carbohydrate, 16 g ◆ fat, 4 g (calories from fat, 22%) ◆ dietary fiber, 1 g ◆ cholesterol, 101 mg ◆ sodium, 361 mg ◆ potassium, 296 mg Joslin Exchanges: 2 low-fat meat, 1 bread/starch

Foil-Baked Seafood

A splendid, easy way to prepare fish. Serve with Corn Pudding (page 305) and a tossed green salad.

4 5-ounce (140 g) sole, flounder, cod, or halibut fillets
8 medium-size shrimp, peeled and deveined
1/3 cup (78 ml) reduced-calorie mayonnaise
2 tablespoons (30 ml) Dijon mustard
1 garlic clove, minced
2 tablespoons (30 ml) fresh lime juice
1 teaspoon (5 ml) crushed dried tarragon

1 tablespoon (15 ml) Worcestershire sauce
1 tablespoon (15 ml) dry white wine
1 large fresh tomato, about 1/2 pound (225 g), peeled, seeded, and coarsely chopped
3 scallions, white part only, chopped
chopped parsley for garnish

Cut 4 pieces of aluminum foil, each large enough to hold a fillet. Arrange a fillet in center of each piece of foil. Lay 2 shrimp on top of each fillet.

In a small bowl, combine mayonnaise, mustard, garlic, lime juice, tarragon, Worcestershire sauce, and wine. Using a pastry brush, paint mayonnaise mixture on fish and shrimp. Divide tomato and scallion among the fillets.

Seal packets, crimping edges to make them airtight. Refrigerate for at least 30 to 35 minutes.

When ready to bake, preheat oven to 400°F (205°C). Place fish packets on a baking sheet. Bake for 10 to 20 minutes, 10 minutes per inch of thickness of fish. Unwrap to serve, garnishing each fillet with chopped parsley.

MAKES 4 SERVINGS

Per serving: calories, 190 ◆ protein, 24 g ◆ carbohydrate, 7 g ◆ fat, 7 g (calories from fat, 33%) ◆ dietary fiber, 1 g ◆ cholesterol, 85 mg ◆ sodium, 233 mg ◆ potassium, 671 mg Joslin Exchanges: 3 low-fat meat, 2 vegetable

Italian Variation

Place fish and shrimp on foil as directed. In a small bowl, combine ¼ cup (59 ml) chopped onion; ½ medium-size red bell pepper, cut into thin strips; ½ medium-size green bell pepper, cut into thin strips; 1 small minced garlic clove; ½ cup (118 ml) dry white wine; and ¼ teaspoon (1.25 ml) fennel seed. Spoon onion mixture over fish fillets. Seal packets, bake, and garnish as directed.

MAKES 4 SERVINGS

Per serving: calories, 119 ◆ protein, 23 g ◆ carbohydrate, 3 g ◆ fat, 1 g (calories from fat, 8%) ◆ dietary fiber, 1 g ◆ cholesterol, 79 mg ◆ sodium, 90 mg ◆ potassium, 527 mg Joslin Exchanges: 3 low-fat meat

Piccata Variation

Place fish and shrimp on foil as directed. In a small bowl, combine 1 small minced garlic clove, ½ cup (118 ml) dry white wine, 2 tablespoons (30 ml) fresh lemon juice, and 2 tablespoons (30 ml) chopped fresh parsley. Spoon wine mixture over fish fillets. Sprinkle each fillet with ¼ teaspoon (1.25 ml) drained capers. Seal and bake as directed. Unwrap to serve, garnishing each fillet with 2 thin slices of lemon.

MAKES 4 SERVINGS

Per serving: calories, 113 ◆ protein, 23 g ◆ carbohydrate, 1 g ◆ fat, 1 g (calories from fat, 9%) ◆ dietary fiber, trace ◆ cholesterol, 79 mg ◆ sodium, 96 mg ◆ potassium, 496 mg Joslin Exchanges: 3 low-fat meat

Yucatán Variation

Place fish and shrimp on foil as directed. In a small bowl, combine ½ cup fresh lemon juice, 2 tablespoons (30 ml) raisins, and 2 tablespoons (30 ml) canned chopped hot green chilies. Top fish with lemon juice mixture. Seal packets and bake as directed. Unwrap to serve, garnishing each fillet with ½ teaspoon (7.5 ml) toasted pine nuts (page 284).

MAKES 4 SERVINGS

Per serving: calories, 170 ◆ protein, 25 g ◆ carbohydrate, 12 g ◆ fat, 3 g (calories from fat, 16%) ◆ dietary fiber, 1 g ◆ cholesterol, 76 mg ◆ sodium, 96 mg ◆ potassium, 772 mg Joslin Exchanges: 3 low-fat meat, 2 vegetable

Lobster à l'Américaine

Fresh lobsters are expensive these days unless you live close to the source. However, for special occasions such as Christmas Eve dinner, we like to splurge on this version of the dish made famous by the Jockey Club in Washington, D.C.

2 2-pound (900 g) live lobsters or 4 1-pound (450 g) frozen lobster tails
1 tablespoon (15 ml) olive oil
1 medium-size onion, chopped
1 garlic clove, minced
1 tablespoon (15 ml) cognac (optional)
1 28-ounce (790 g) can Italian-style plum tomatoes, drained and chopped

1 cup (236 ml) bottled clam juice
½ cup (118 ml) dry white wine
1 tablespoon (15 ml) chopped fresh tarragon or 1 teaspoon (5 ml) crushed dried
1 small bay leaf

Kill lobsters by inserting a sharp knife crosswise where the head meets the shell to sever the spinal cord. Turn lobsters over and split them in half. (If this makes you queasy, have your fishmonger kill and split lobsters. Use within 2 hours.) Cut lobster into serving pieces; remove and reserve coral. Crack claws, cut through the underside of the tail, and remove lobster meat in large pieces. (If you're using frozen lobster tails, defrost in refrigerator for 24 hours. Cut through the underside of the tail, removing lobster meat in large pieces.) Reserve empty shells.

In a large heavy pot or pan big enough to hold lobster pieces, heat oil. Sauté lobster pieces over medium-high heat for 3 to 5 minutes, until they turn bright red; remove lobster pieces and keep warm.

Add onion and garlic to pot; sauté until wilted. Add remaining ingredients and empty lobster shells. Simmer for 25 to 30 minutes. Discard bay leaf and lobster shells. Add lobster, cover, and simmer for another 20 minutes. Just before serving, add reserved coral. Serve immediately.

MAKES 4 SERVINGS

Per serving: calories, 183 ◆ protein, 20 g ◆ carbohydrate, 18 g ◆ fat, 4 g (calories from fat, 20%) ◆ dietary fiber, 1 g ◆ cholesterol, 61 mg ◆ sodium, 953* ◆ potassium, 842 Joslin Exchanges: 2½ low-fat meat, 1 bread/starch

*Not recommended for low-sodium diets except as a once-a-year splurge.

CHRISTMAS EVE SUPPER

◆

Crudités with Fresh Herb Dip (page 6)

Lobster à l'Américaine (page 156)

Lemon Parsley Rice (page 289)

Steamed Broccoli

Bûche de Noël (page 409)

Per serving: 437 calories (22% fat)
Joslin Exchanges: 2½ low-fat meat, 3 bread/starch, 2 vegetable, 1 fat

Cod with Chinese Vegetables

A lovely light meal with a subtle blend of crunchy Chinese vegetables and delicately flavored fish.

You can use canned water chestnuts and bamboo shoots if fresh are not available.

1½ pounds (675 g) cod fillets, cut into bite-size pieces
1 teaspoon (5 ml) cornstarch
2 teaspoons (10 ml) peanut oil
1 tablespoon (15 ml) minced fresh ginger
2 garlic cloves, minced
½ pound (225 g) snow peas
2 scallions, including some green tops, thinly sliced
8 fresh water chestnuts, peeled and sliced
½ cup (118 ml) fresh bamboo shoots, sliced

1 ounce (30 g) dried mushrooms, soaked in warm water for 15 minutes, drained, and sliced, or 1 cup (236 ml) sliced fresh mushrooms
3 tablespoons (45 ml) white wine vinegar
2 tablespoons (30 ml) dry white wine
⅛ teaspoon (.6 ml) hot red pepper flakes
1 teaspoon (5 ml) low-sodium soy sauce
⅛ teaspoon (.6 ml) dark sesame oil

Sprinkle fish pieces with ½ teaspoon (2.5 ml) cornstarch. Heat peanut oil in a large heavy skillet. Add ginger and garlic; sauté for 2 minutes. Add fish and continue cooking until fish is just cooked through, about 2 minutes. Remove fish from skillet; keep warm.

Cut the snow peas into fine strips and cook in a pot of boiling water for 30 seconds. Drain and rinse under cold running water to stop the cooking. Drain again; set aside.

Add scallions to skillet along with remaining ingredients. Cook over high heat for 2 minutes. Dissolve remaining ½ teaspoon (2.5 ml) cornstarch in 1 teaspoon (5 ml) water. Add to skillet and cook for another 2 to 3 minutes, until thickened. Return fish to skillet and cook until fish is heated through.

Divide fish and vegetables among 4 serving plates. Top with snow peas. Serve at once.

MAKES 4 SERVINGS

Per serving: calories, 224 ◆ protein, 27 g ◆ carbohydrate, 20 g ◆ fat, 4 g (calories from fat, 16%) ◆ dietary fiber, 1 g ◆ cholesterol, 56 mg ◆ sodium, 122 mg ◆ potassium, 986 mg Joslin Exchanges: 3 low-fat meat, 1½ bread/starch

Salmon Mousse in Filo Bundles

You'll find filo dough, the paper-thin sheets of Greek pastry dough, in the freezer or dairy section at your supermarket. Filo is much lower in calories than the classic puff pastry alternative.

It's a bit tricky, but if you remember a few basics, you'll find it's easy to work with. To thaw, leave the package airtight in the refrigerator for about 8 hours; this minimizes accumulation of moisture, which can make the sheets gummy. When you're using it, keep the unbaked filo covered with a dampened kitchen towel and work with only one exposed sheet at a time. Filo will be flakier if layered with margarine or butter, but a light spritz with cooking spray works quite well, at a fraction of the calories and fat exchanges. You can refreeze what you don't use.

Here delicate sheets of filo dough envelop a smooth dilled fish mousse for a spectacular entree that's perfect for company or a special family dinner.

2 cups (472 ml) water
6 scallions, white part only
1 bay leaf
1 celery rib
4 slices of lemon
1 teaspoon (5 ml) crushed dried thyme
1 parsley sprig
1½ pounds (675 g) salmon fillets
1½ tablespoons (22.5 ml) chopped fresh dill or 1½ teaspoons (7.5 ml) dried dill weed

2 large egg whites
2 tablespoons (30 ml) egg substitute
freshly ground pepper to taste
1 teaspoon (5 ml) fresh lemon juice
6 sheets of frozen filo pastry, defrosted
butter-flavored cooking spray
1 small cucumber, peeled and very thinly sliced

In a large nonstick skillet, bring water to a boil. Add 2 scallions, bay leaf, celery, lemon slices, thyme, and parsley. Reduce heat to simmer. Add salmon, cover, and simmer very gently until salmon is just opaque in the center, 10 minutes for each inch of thickness measured at thickest part. Check occasionally to make sure that liquid is barely simmering.

Remove salmon from skillet; discard poaching liquid. When salmon is cool enough to handle, remove skin and any bones. Coarsely chop remaining 4 scallions. In a food processor or blender, combine salmon, scallions, dill, egg whites, egg substitute, pepper, and lemon juice. Process until smooth.

Preheat oven to 375°F (190°C). Working with one filo sheet at a time (keep remaining sheets covered with a damp paper towel to prevent drying out), lightly coat each sheet with cooking spray. Fold filo sheet in half crosswise to form a 13- by 8^1/$_2$-inch (33 by 21.5 cm) rectangle. Cut rectangle in half crosswise to form two 8^1/$_2$- by 6^1/$_2$-inch (21.5 by 16.5 cm) rectangles; lightly coat with cooking spray. Place ^{1}/$_2$ cup (118 ml) salmon mixture in center of each filo rectangle. Arrange cucumber slices on top of salmon mixture. Bring corners of filo to center, pinching together to form a bundle with a frilly top. Place bundles on a baking sheet. Lightly coat with cooking spray. Bake for 10 to 15 minutes, until puffed and lightly browned.

MAKES 6 SERVINGS

Per serving: calories, 181 ◆ protein, 21 g ◆ carbohydrate, 16 g ◆ fat, 3 g (calories from fat, 15%) ◆ dietary fiber, trace ◆ cholesterol, 44 mg ◆ sodium, 95 mg ◆ potassium, 439 mg Joslin Exchanges: 2^1/$_2$ low-fat meat, 1 bread/starch

---

NEW YEAR'S EVE DINNER

◆

Roasted Red Pepper Soup (page 55)

Salmon Mousse in Filo Bundles (page 159)

Pesto-Stuffed Mushroom Caps (page 352)

Roasted Tomatoes (page 330)

Lemon Tuiles with Apricot Mousse (page 439)

Per serving: 419 calories (26% fat)
Joslin Exchanges: 2^1/$_2$ low-fat meat, 2^1/$_2$ bread/starch, 2 vegetable, ^{1}/$_2$ fat

Chinese Steamed Whole Fish

Choose a whole flounder or a piece of grouper for this show-off entree. If you don't own a bamboo steamer, improvise using the steaming instructions on page 122. The rice wine, available in Asian markets and some supermarkets, is often labeled *Chinese Cooking Wine*.

Serve the fish with bowls of white rice (page 288).

1 2-pound (900 g) whole fish
2 tablespoons (30 ml) low-sodium soy sauce
1 tablespoon (15 ml) rice wine
2 tablespoons (30 ml) minced fresh ginger
2 garlic cloves, minced
½ cup (118 ml) thinly sliced shallot
⅛ teaspoon (.6 ml) dark sesame oil
½ cup (118 ml) bottled clam juice
½ cup (118 ml) lightly packed fresh cilantro (fresh coriander) leaves, coarsely chopped

3 cups (708 ml) chopped white cabbage
3 scallions, white part and 1 inch (2.5 cm) green, cut into 2-inch (5 cm) lengths and then into fine strips
1 small fresh hot red chili, seeded and cut into fine strips

Rinse fish well under cold running water. Score fish on both sides on a diagonal in a crosshatch pattern every inch (2.5 cm), cutting halfway to the bone. Steam in a bamboo steamer or on an aluminum foil–lined rack over simmering water until fish flakes, 10 minutes per inch of thickness.

Meanwhile, in a small saucepan, combine soy sauce, rice wine, ginger, garlic, shallot, sesame oil, clam juice, and half the cilantro. Simmer for 10 minutes.

Place chopped cabbage on a large platter. Top with fish. Pour on sauce and decorate with remaining cilantro, scallions, and chili. Serve immediately.

MAKES 6 SERVINGS

Per serving: calories, 123 ◆ protein, 22 g ◆ carbohydrate, 6 g ◆ fat, 1 g (calories from fat, 7%) ◆ dietary fiber, 1 g ◆ cholesterol, 49 mg ◆ sodium, 300 mg ◆ potassium, 657 mg Joslin Exchanges: 3 low-fat meat, 1 vegetable

CHINESE NEW YEAR

◆

Turkey Dim Sum (page 20) with Dipping Sauces

(pages 23–24)

Chinese Steamed Whole Fish (page 161)

Steamed White Rice (pages 287–288)

Tangerines and Almond Sugar Cookies (page 416)

Per serving: 514 calories (25% fat)
Joslin Exchanges: 3 low-fat meat, 3 bread/starch, 1 vegetable, 1 fruit, 1 fat

Crab Gumbo

Don't be intimidated by the long list of ingredients here; the dish is well worth the effort. The addition of vinegar keeps the okra from becoming stringy, and cooking the okra until just tender keeps it from becoming slippery (everyone's objection to okra).

Serve this gumbo over rice. Offer a bottle of Tabasco sauce for those who like their gumbo hotter. Filé powder, often used in Creole cooking, can be omitted if you don't have it.

2 whole ½-pound (225 g) chicken breasts, boned, skinned, and cut into 1-inch (2.5 cm) squares
olive oil cooking spray
1 large green bell pepper, about ½ pound (225 g), seeded and chopped
1 large onion, about ½ pound (225 g), chopped

2 garlic cloves, minced
3 cups (708 ml) drained canned plum tomatoes, slightly crushed
1 cup (236 ml) bottled clam juice
1 cup (236 ml) chicken stock (page 45)
2 bay leaves

3 parsley sprigs
1 tablespoon (15 ml) fresh thyme
   leaves or 1 teaspoon (5 ml)
   crushed dried
1 tablespoon (15 ml) white
   Worcestershire sauce
freshly ground pepper to taste
1 pound (450 g) large shrimp,
   peeled and deveined
16 cherrystone clams or 16 oysters,
    well scrubbed

1 pound (450 g) fresh okra, stems
   removed, sliced
1 tablespoon (15 ml) olive oil
1 teaspoon (5 ml) white wine
   vinegar
1 pound (450 g) lump crabmeat,
   picked over and cartilage
   removed
4 cups (1 l) hot cooked rice
filé powder to taste (optional)

Remove all visible fat from chicken. Sauté chicken in a large pot or Dutch oven that has been lightly sprayed with cooking spray over medium heat until chicken is browned, about 5 minutes. Add green pepper, onion, and garlic; cook until vegetables are wilted. Add tomatoes, clam juice, stock, bay leaves, parsley, thyme, Worcestershire sauce, and pepper. Cover and simmer for 30 minutes.

Add shrimp and clams; cover and simmer for another 5 minutes. Discard any unopened clams. Meanwhile, in a large skillet, sauté okra in olive oil and vinegar over low heat for 5 to 6 minutes. Add okra and any cooking liquid to gumbo along with crabmeat. Heat through.

Serve in heated bowls over ⅓ cup (78 ml) of hot cooked rice; remove bay leaves and parsley sprigs. Sprinkle each serving with a little filé powder if desired.

MAKES 12 SERVINGS

Per serving: calories, 242 ◆ protein, 23 g ◆ carbohydrate, 24 g ◆ fat, 6 g (calories from fat, 22%) ◆ dietary fiber, 2 g ◆ cholesterol, 105 mg ◆ sodium, 386 mg ◆ potassium, 518 mg Joslin Exchanges: 2½ low-fat meat, 1½ bread/starch

---

MARDI GRAS EVENING

◆

Pickled Okra (page 14)

Radicchio, Belgian Endive, and Fennel Salad

with Lemon Vinaigrette (pages 89 and 96)

Crab Gumbo (page 162)

Steamed Rice (page 287)

Grilled Bananas (page 434) with Crème Fraîche (page 428)

Per serving: 513 calories (26% fat)
Joslin Exchanges: 2½ low-fat meat, 2½ bread/starch, 1 vegetable, 1 fruit, 1 fat, ½ nonfat milk

Seafood Lasagne

All the hearty flavors of traditional lasagne, but at a fraction of the fat calories. Our version features a variety of seafood and two cheeses.

½ pound (225 g) lasagne noodles
olive oil cooking spray
2 garlic cloves, minced
3 scallions, white part only, chopped
6 ounces (180 g) fresh mushrooms, sliced
1 28-ounce (790 g) can crushed low-sodium Italian-style tomatoes

2 tablespoons (30 ml) chopped fresh basil or 2 teaspoons (10 ml) crushed dried
½ tablespoon (7.5 ml) chopped fresh oregano or ½ teaspoon (2.5 ml) crushed dried
⅛ teaspoon (.6 ml) fennel seed

⅛ teaspoon (.6 ml) freshly ground
  pepper or to taste
½ pound (225 g) medium-size
  shrimp, peeled and deveined
½ pound (225 g) sea scallops,
  quartered
¼ pound (115 g) fresh crabmeat,
  picked over
1 10-ounce (285 g) box frozen
  chopped spinach, thawed

1 15-ounce (425 g) container
  nonfat ricotta cheese
1 large egg white
⅓ cup (78 ml) chopped flat-leaf
  parsley
2 tablespoons (12 g) grated
  Parmesan cheese

Fill a 5- to 6-quart (4.75 to 5.5 l) pot with water and bring to a rapid boil. Add lasagne and cook until tender, about 10 minutes. Drain well.

In a large nonstick skillet lightly sprayed with cooking spray, sauté garlic, scallions, and mushrooms over low heat until vegetables are wilted, about 5 minutes. Add tomatoes, herbs, fennel seed, and pepper; simmer for 10 minutes. Add seafood to sauce. Continue to simmer until shrimp and scallops are opaque throughout, 3 to 4 minutes. Cut to test. Remove from heat; keep warm.

Squeeze as much liquid as possible from spinach. Mix spinach, ricotta, egg white, and parsley. Set aside.

Spread about ¼ cup (59 ml) seafood tomato sauce in the bottom of a shallow 2½- to 3-quart (2.5 to 2.75 l) baking dish. Arrange half the lasagne noodles over sauce. Spread half the ricotta mixture over lasagne. Top with half the sauce. Repeat layers, ending with sauce. Sprinkle with Parmesan cheese. Cover with aluminum foil. (At this point the lasagne can be refrigerated for up to 8 hours.)

Preheat oven to 350°F (180°C) for freshly made lasagne, 375°F (190°C) for refrigerated lasagne. Bake for 30 minutes. Remove foil; increase oven temperature to 375°F (190°C) for freshly made lasagne. Continue to bake, uncovered, for 15 to 20 minutes, until well browned and bubbling. Remove from oven and allow to rest for 10 to 15 minutes before serving.

MAKES 6 SERVINGS

Per serving: calories, 353 ◆ protein, 28 g ◆ carbohydrate, 49 g ◆ fat, 6 g (calories from fat, 15%) ◆ dietary fiber, 2 g ◆ cholesterol, 81 mg ◆ sodium, 634 mg* ◆ potassium, 1,083 mg Joslin Exchanges: 3 low-fat meat, 3 bread/starch

*Recipe not recommended for low-sodium diets except for occasional use.

FRIDAY NIGHT BUFFET

◆

Seafood Lasagne (page 164)

Radicchio Salad with Classic Vinaigrette (page 114)

Squash Ribbons with Garlic Lemon Sauce (page 356)

Frozen Grapes

Per serving: 569 calories (27% fat)
Joslin Exchanges: 3 low-fat meat, 2 vegetable, 3 bread/starch, 1 fruit, 1 fat

Friday Night Fish Stew

Our mothers might remember a fish stew made with freshly caught fish and vegetables. Originally the fish was cooked whole, and everyone was warned to watch out for the bones.

We prefer to use boneless fish fillets. The fish is still cooked until it literally falls apart. This dish is similar in flavor to the layered fish dish served in many Jewish homes on the Sabbath. Serve with a mixed green salad and offer fresh fruit for dessert.

2½ pounds (1.25 kg) firm-fleshed fish fillets, such as sea trout, tilefish, black bass, or grouper
2 teaspoons (10 ml) canola oil
freshly ground pepper to taste
paprika to taste
vegetable oil cooking spray
2 medium-size onions, about ½ pound (225 g), diced
3 medium-size unpeeled potatoes, about 1 pound (450 g), cut

crosswise into ½-inch (2.5 cm) slices
2 carrots, about 6 ounces (180 g), peeled and sliced
3 plum tomatoes, about 1 pound (450 g), peeled and diced
1 cup (236 ml) fish stock (page 46)
juice of 1 lemon

With a pastry brush, paint top of fish with oil; rub with pepper and paprika.

Preheat oven to 350°F (180°C). Lightly spray a 3-quart (2.75 l) casserole with cooking spray. Arrange half the vegetables in casserole. Top with fish, then remaining vegetables. Pour fish stock over top and bake for 45 to 50 minutes, until potatoes are tender. Baste fish twice with pan juices. Carefully transfer fish to a large platter. Surround with vegetables. Add lemon juice to pan juices; boil on top of stove over high heat until reduced to about ¾ cup (177 ml). Pour reduced sauce over fish and vegetables and serve.

MAKES 6 SERVINGS

> **Per serving:** calories, 277 ◆ protein, 29 g ◆ carbohydrate, 24 g ◆ fat, 9 g (calories from fat, 27%) ◆ dietary fiber, 4 g ◆ cholesterol, 96 mg ◆ sodium, 210 mg ◆ potassium, 1,099 mg Joslin Exchanges: 3½ low-fat meat, 1½ bread/starch

Crispy Baked Fish

Breaded fish fillets are great for speedy cool-weather suppers. We gave them a new taste with cumin, minced garlic, and sesame seeds. Serve with Caribbean Spicy Tomato Cabbage (page 342) and parsleyed new potatoes.

olive oil cooking spray
1¼ pounds (570 g) cod, scrod, haddock, or pollack fillets
¼ cup (59 ml) egg substitute
1 tablespoon (15 ml) skim milk
1 teaspoon (5 ml) Worcestershire sauce
1 tablespoon (15 ml) fresh lemon juice

½ cup (69 g) stone-ground cornmeal or cornflake crumbs
½ teaspoon (2.5 ml) ground cumin
1 garlic clove, minced
3 tablespoons (45 ml) sesame seed

Preheat oven to 425°F (220°C). Place a sheet of aluminum foil large enough to hold fillets on a baking sheet. Lightly spray foil with cooking spray. Place fish fillets on foil.

In a small bowl, combine egg substitute, skim milk, Worcestershire sauce, and lemon juice. Using a pastry brush, paint egg mixture onto fillets. Mix together cornmeal, cumin, garlic, and sesame seed. Sprinkle cornmeal mixture onto fillets, covering well. Lightly spray coated fillets with cooking spray. Bake for 10 minutes per inch (2.5 cm) of thickness, about 15 minutes. Serve immediately.

MAKES 4 SERVINGS

Per serving: calories, 200 ◆ protein, 24 g ◆ carbohydrate, 15 g ◆ fat, 5 g (calories from fat, 23%) ◆ dietary fiber, 3 g ◆ cholesterol, 47 mg ◆ sodium, 106 mg ◆ potassium, 595 mg Joslin Exchanges: 3 low-fat meat, 1 bread/starch

Fish Florentine

Delicate fish fillets stuffed with a savory spinach filling. To round out the meal, serve Tomato Focaccia (page 394) and a crisp green salad.

butter-flavored cooking spray
3 scallions, white part and 1 inch (2.5 cm) green, chopped
1 garlic clove, minced
1 10-ounce (285 g) box frozen chopped spinach, defrosted
1/4 cup (59 ml) chopped and seeded fresh tomato
1 tablespoon (15 ml) fresh lemon juice
1/8 teaspoon (.6 ml) ground nutmeg
1/2 tablespoon (7.5 ml) fresh thyme leaves or 1/2 teaspoon (2.5 ml) crushed dried
2 tablespoons (30 ml) low-fat goat cheese
4 5-ounce (140 g) sole, flounder, or orange roughy fillets
1/4 teaspoon (1.25 ml) salt (optional)
freshly ground pepper to taste
paprika to taste
1/4 cup (59 ml) dry white wine

In a small skillet lightly sprayed with cooking spray, sauté scallions and garlic over low heat for 4 minutes, until garlic is wilted but not browned. Remove from heat. Squeeze spinach as dry as possible. Add to scallion mixture along with tomato, lemon juice, nutmeg, thyme, and goat cheese. Mix well.

Preheat oven to 375°F (190°C). Place fish fillets on a piece of wax paper or plastic wrap. Divide spinach mixture among fillets, covering about three-fourths of each fillet. Gently roll each fillet toward the end without filling. Secure rolls with a wooden pick. Place rolled fillets, seam side down, in a shallow baking dish lightly sprayed with cooking spray. Sprinkle with salt, pepper, and paprika. Pour wine over fish. Bake until fish flakes when prodded with a fork, about 15 to 20 minutes.

MAKES 4 SERVINGS

Per serving: calories, 125 ◆ protein, 22 g ◆ carbohydrate, 6 g ◆ fat, 2 g (calories from fat, 14%) ◆ dietary fiber, 1 g ◆ cholesterol, 49 mg ◆ sodium, 279 mg ◆ potassium, 732 mg
Joslin Exchanges: 3 low-fat meat, 1 vegetable

Microwave Method:

Prepare fish as directed. Bake in a covered microwave-safe dish on HIGH power for 4 to 5 minutes, giving the dish a quarter turn every minute until fish is done.

POULTRY

Poultry (but not ducks or geese) is significantly lower in calories and saturated fat than red meat. For example, a 3-ounce (85 g) portion of roasted boneless and skinless chicken breast contains 161 calories and 1 gram of saturated fat, as compared to 351 calories and 12 grams of saturated fat for an equal portion of cooked lean roast beef.

To minimize fat calories even further, most of our recipes concentrate on the white meat of chicken and turkey. We trim away all visible fat and usually remove the skin before cooking. Occasionally, however, the skin is left on to heighten the flavor. As long as you don't actually eat the skin, you won't be getting any extra fat. For roasted whole turkeys and chickens, the skin acts as a flavor-sealing envelope.

A word of caution: be sure to read the label when you purchase ground turkey and ground chicken to determine that this low-fat item is indeed just that—some packaged ground poultry contains the skin, which adds lots of fat. If the label doesn't state the fat content (should be about 7 percent), buy a turkey breast or chicken breasts and have your butcher remove and discard the skin, then grind the turkey or chicken for you.

At the supermarket, check the expiration date and buy only fresh poultry. Once home, remove the chicken or turkey from its wrapping; rinse it thoroughly with cold water. Fresh poultry will have a fresh smell. Remove and discard the package of giblets (organ meats are a high-fat meat exchange and should be eaten only occasionally). Remove and discard any lumps of fat in the cavity and around the openings.

If you aren't cooking the poultry immediately, wrap it loosely in foil and refrigerate for up to 48 hours. Never let poultry sit out at room temperature. To freeze chicken, wrap it airtight in freezer wrap or heavy plastic wrap. Mark the date on the package and freeze for up to 3 months. Thaw frozen poultry in the refrigerator. A whole 3-pound (1.35 kg) chicken will thaw in about a day; a 12-pound (5.5 kg) turkey will take about 3 days. Do not refreeze uncooked poultry.

Wash your hands, cutting knives, and work surfaces with warm soapy water after handling raw poultry to avoid possible cross-contamination.

Most of our recipes are interchangeable—you can use any chicken or turkey you have on hand. For convenience, we keep skinless boneless chicken breasts, pounded flat, in the freezer for impromptu dinners. With the help of a grill or broiler, we can have an interesting entree on the table in a matter of minutes (since they're quite thin, there's no need to thaw before cooking). While the chicken is grilling, we prepare a zesty topping—a sauce, a relish, or salsa. Then we toss a salad, steam a vegetable, and warm some bread. With fresh fruit for dessert, you have a simple but satisfying meal that works as well for company as it does for everyday meals.

Fast and Easy Chicken Breasts

In other sections of the book there are recipes for great accompaniments that would go well with grilled chicken breasts: Red Onion Pineapple Chutney (page 250), Spicy Pipérade (page 152), Roasted Tomatillo Sauce (page 141), Fresh Fruit Relish (page 143), and Sun-Dried Tomato Sauce (page 231), to name a few.

For more inspiration, here are some other "fast and easy" embellishments for four 4-ounce (115 g) boneless, pounded, grilled or broiled chicken breasts. Boneless breats, pounded to $^1/_2$-inch (1.5 cm) thickness will take about 5 minutes per side to grill or broil, 4 to 6 inches (10 to 15 cm) from source of heat. You can also poach the breasts in the microwave in a covered container with 1 cup (236 ml) hot water on HIGH for about 5 minutes or sauté them in a nonstick skillet lightly sprayed with cooking spray.

Basil Cream

In a food processor or blender, combine $^1/_4$ cup (59 ml) packed fresh basil leaves, $1^1/_2$ tablespoons (22.5 ml) white wine vinegar, 2 peeled shallots, and juice of 1 lemon. Process until smooth. Stir in $^3/_4$ cup (177 ml) crème fraîche (page 428), $^1/_8$ teaspoon (.6 ml) freshly ground pepper, and 1 tablespoon (15 ml) minced fresh basil. Spoon onto four 4-ounce (115 g) grilled chicken breasts.

MAKES 4 SERVINGS

Per serving (with chicken): calories, 186 ♦ protein, 30 g ♦ carbohydrate, 7 g ♦ fat, 4 g (calories from fat, 19%) ♦ dietary fiber, trace ♦ cholesterol, 76 mg ♦ sodium, 97 mg ♦ potassium, 421 mg
Joslin Exchanges: 4 low-fat meat, $^1/_2$ nonfat milk

Per serving (cream alone):
calories, 43 ◆ protein, 3 g ◆
carbohydrate, 7 g ◆ fat, 1 g
(calories from fat, 21%) ◆
dietary fiber, trace ◆ cholesterol,
3 mg ◆ sodium, 33 mg ◆
potassium, 207 mg
Joslin Exchanges: ½ nonfat
milk

Dijon-Mustard Sauce

Coarsely grate 1 small onion. Combine with 2 minced garlic cloves, 2 table-spoons (30 ml) Dijon mustard, and 1 cup (236 ml) plain nonfat yogurt. Spoon onto four 4-ounce (115 g) grilled chicken breasts.

MAKES 4 SERVINGS

Per serving (with chicken):
calories, 191 ◆ protein, 31 g ◆
carbohydrate, 7 g ◆ fat, 4 g
(calories from fat, 19%) ◆
dietary fiber, trace ◆ cholesterol,
75 mg ◆ sodium, 207 mg ◆
potassium, 419 mg
Joslin Exchanges: 4 low-fat
meat, ½ nonfat milk

Per serving (sauce alone):
calories, 49 ◆ protein, 4 g ◆
carbohydrate, 7 g ◆ fat, trace
(calories from fat, less than 1%)
◆ dietary fiber, trace ◆
cholesterol, 1 mg ◆ sodium, 142
mg ◆ potassium, 194 mg
Joslin Exchanges: ½ nonfat
milk

Grilled Italian Tomato Relish

Cut 4 medium-size plum tomatoes, about ¾ pound (340 g), in half length-wise. Grill or broil, cut side up, for 3 minutes; turn over and grill for another 3 minutes, until soft to the touch. Meanwhile, sauté 4 chopped scallions, white part only, and 1 minced garlic clove in 2 teaspoons (10 ml) olive oil over low heat until soft, about 4 minutes. Add ½ teaspoon (2.5 ml) dried rosemary and ½ teaspoon (2.5 ml) crushed fennel seed. Add tomatoes; remove from stove and keep warm until chicken is done. Spoon tomato relish over and alongside four 4-ounce (115 g) grilled chicken breasts.

MAKES 4 SERVINGS

Per serving (with chicken):
calories, 178 ◆ protein, 27 g ◆
carbohydrate, 5 g ◆ fat, 6 g
(calories from fat, 30%) ◆
dietary fiber, 1 g ◆ cholesterol,
70 mg ◆ sodium, 69 mg ◆
potassium, ,422 mg
Joslin Exchanges: 3 low-fat
meat, 1 vegetable

Per serving (relish alone):
calories, 42 ◆ protein, 1 g ◆
carbohydrate, 5 g ◆ fat, 3 g
(calories from fat, 64%) ◆
dietary fiber, 1 g ◆ cholesterol,
0 mg ◆ sodium, 8 mg ◆
potassium, 210 mg
Joslin Exchanges: 1 vegetable,
½ fat

Pomegranate Salsa

Free the seeds from 1 pomegranate (page 236). Combine 1 cup (59 ml) seeds with ¼ cup (59 ml) chopped fresh orange sections, ¼ cup (59 ml) chopped fresh ruby grapefruit sections, 2 tablespoons (30 ml) finely minced red onion, 1 tablespoon (15 ml) chopped fresh mint or 1 teaspoon (5 ml) crushed dried, ¼ teaspoon (1.25 ml) crushed dried oregano, ⅛ teaspoon (.6 ml) ground cumin, 1 teaspoon (5 ml) finely minced fresh red serrano chili, and 1 tablespoon (15 ml) fresh lime juice. Toss lightly to mix. Chill until ready to serve. Spoon onto four 4-ounce (115 g) grilled chicken breasts.

MAKES 4 SERVINGS

Per serving (with chicken): calories, 173 ◆ protein, 26 g ◆ carbohydrate, 8 g ◆ fat, 4 g (calories from fat, 20%) ◆ dietary fiber, trace ◆ cholesterol, 72 mg ◆ sodium, 73 mg ◆ potassium, 349 mg Joslin Exchanges: 3 low-fat meat, ½ fruit

Per ¼ cup (59 ml) serving (salsa alone): calories, 33 ◆ protein, 1 g ◆ carbohydrate, 8 g ◆ fat, 1 g (calories from fat, 27%) ◆ dietary fiber, trace ◆ cholesterol, 0 g ◆ sodium, 1 g ◆ potassium, 132 mg Joslin Exchanges: ½ fruit

Roasted Red Pepper Pesto

In a food processor or blender, combine 2 large roasted red bell peppers (page 100) and 2 roasted garlic cloves (roast along with peppers; peel). Process to a smooth puree. With motor running, add 1 tablespoon (15 ml) olive oil, ¼ teaspoon (1.25 ml) ground cumin, ⅛ teaspoon (.6 ml) salt (optional), and ⅛ teaspoon (.6 ml) cayenne pepper. Process until smooth. Spoon over four 4-ounce (115 g) grilled chicken breasts; sprinkle with 2 tablespoons (30 ml) minced cilantro (fresh coriander).

MAKES 4 SERVINGS

Per serving (with chicken): calories, 207 ◆ protein, 28 g ◆ carbohydrate, 8 g ◆ fat, 7 g (calories from fat, 30%) ◆ dietary fiber, 2 g ◆ cholesterol, 73 mg ◆ sodium, 133 mg ◆ potassium, 431 mg Joslin Exchanges: 3½ low-fat meat, 1 vegetable

Per serving (pesto alone): calories, 72 ◆ protein, 1 g ◆ carbohydrate, 8 g ◆ fat, 4 g (calories from fat, 50%) ◆ dietary fiber, 2 g ◆ cholesterol, 0 mg ◆ sodium, 70 mg ◆ potassium, 212 mg Joslin Exchanges: 1 vegetable, 1 fat

Smoky Barbecue Sauce

Sauté 1 minced small onion and 1 minced garlic clove in 2 teaspoons (10 ml) olive oil over low heat until onion is wilted, about 5 minutes. Add 6 table-spoons (90 ml) low-sodium tomato paste, ½ cup (118 ml) water, 1 tablespoon (15 ml) balsamic vinegar, 2 teaspoons (10 ml) Worcestershire sauce, ½ tea-spoon (2.5 ml) liquid smoke, ¼ teaspoon (1.25 ml) dry mustard, ½ tablespoon (7.5 ml) chili powder, and ¼ teaspoon (1.25 ml) salt. Cover and simmer for 10 minutes. Spoon onto four 4-ounce (115 g) grilled chicken breasts.

MAKES 4 SERVINGS

Per serving (with chicken):
calories, 199 ◆ protein, 28 g ◆ carbohydrate, 9 g ◆ fat, 6 g (calories from fat, 27%) ◆ dietary fiber, 1 g ◆ cholesterol, 72 mg ◆ sodium, 248 mg ◆ potassium, 522 mg
Joslin Exchanges: 3 low-fat meat, 2 vegetable

Per serving (sauce alone):
calories, 59 ◆ protein, 1 g ◆ carbohydrate, 9 g ◆ fat, 3 g (calories from fat, 46%) ◆ dietary fiber, 1 g ◆ cholesterol, 0 mg ◆ sodium, 186 mg ◆ potassium, 304 mg
Joslin Exchanges: 2 vegetable

Tomato Confetti

In a large skillet, sauté 2 tablespoons (30 ml) minced shallots, ¼ cup (59 ml) minced green bell pepper, and 1 teaspoon (5 ml) minced garlic in 1 table-spoon (15 ml) olive oil over low heat until wilted, about 4 minutes. Add ½ cup (118 ml) diced and seeded fresh tomato, 6 sliced pimiento-stuffed olives, and 1 tablespoon (15 ml) fresh lemon juice. Continue to cook over low heat for 5 minutes, until slightly thickened. Serve over four 4-ounce (115 g) grilled chicken breasts.

MAKES 4 SERVINGS

Per serving (with chicken):
calories, 198 ◆ protein, 28 g ◆ carbohydrate, 5 g ◆ fat, 7 g (calories from fat, 32%) ◆ dietary fiber, 1 g ◆ cholesterol, 74 mg ◆ sodium, 189 mg ◆ potassium, 366 mg
Joslin Exchanges: 3½ low-fat meat, 1 vegetable

Per serving (confetti alone):
calories, 56 ◆ protein, 1 g ◆ carbohydrate, 5 g ◆ fat, 4 g (calories from fat, 64%) ◆ dietary fiber, 1 g ◆ cholesterol, 0 mg ◆ sodium, 125 mg ◆ potassium, 141 mg
Joslin Exchanges: 1 vegetable, 1 fat

Roast Chicken with Lemon and Oregano

This wonderfully fragrant roast chicken is stuffed with lemons, has lots of fresh oregano tucked under the skin, and roasted with plenty of shallots and garlic. Serve with Buttermilk Mashed Potatoes, flecked with bits of bok choy (page 307). The stuffings would also work with roast turkey.

olive oil cooking spray	freshly ground pepper to taste
1 whole chicken, about 2½ pounds (1.25 kg), well rinsed and patted dry, giblets discarded	4 lemons, rinsed and halved
	24 shallots
	12 garlic cloves
6 small fresh oregano sprigs	½ cup (118 ml) dry white wine

Preheat oven to 350°F (180°C). Line a shallow roasting pan with heavy-duty aluminum foil. Spray lightly with cooking spray.

Remove any visible fat from neck and body cavities of chicken. Starting from neck cavity, with your fingers gently separate skin from breast meat without tearing skin. Tuck oregano sprigs under skin over breast. Rub inside of chicken with pepper. Place 4 lemon halves inside cavity and tie the legs together with kitchen string.

Place chicken, breast side up, on a rack in a shallow heavy roasting pan. Roast for 15 minutes.

Juice remaining lemon halves. Place unpeeled shallots and unpeeled garlic in pan; pour on white wine. Drizzle 3 tablespoons (45 ml) lemon juice over chicken and return pan to oven. Roast for 20 minutes.

Increase oven temperature to 400°F (205°C). Drizzle remaining lemon juice over chicken. Continue to roast for another 20 minutes, or until juices run clear when the leg is pierced with a fork.

Remove chicken from pan. Discard string and lemons. Peel shallots and garlic. Pour pan juices into a small saucepan. Skim fat off surface. Add shallots and garlic to saucepan. Cook over medium heat for about 3 minutes, until liquid reduces slightly, skimming off any fat that rises to the surface.

Carve chicken into 6 equal portions; discard oregano. Serve each portion with 4 shallots and 2 garlic cloves (to squeeze onto the chicken) and 2 tablespoons (30 ml) sauce. (Remember, if you're attempting to lower your fat intake, you shouldn't eat the skin.)

MAKES 6 SERVINGS

Per serving: calories, 245 ◆ protein, 28 g ◆ carbohydrate, 10 g ◆ fat, 11 g (calories from fat, 40%) ◆ dietary fiber, trace ◆ cholesterol, 78 mg ◆ sodium, 51 mg ◆ potassium, 399 mg Joslin Exchanges: 3$\frac{1}{2}$ low-fat meat, 2 vegetable

Stuffing Variations

Instead of lemons and oregano, try these combinations—the calories and exchanges will stay the same:

Orange and Bay Leaves

Tuck 1 unpeeled navel orange, cut into chunks; slices of onion; and 2 bay leaves into body cavity. Position 4 more bay leaves under skin. Roast as directed with garlic and shallots, drizzling chicken with orange juice instead of lemon juice. When chicken is done, discard orange chunks, onion, and bay leaves from body cavity. Prepare pan juices and serve as directed.

Lime, Rosemary, and Thyme

Tuck 4 lime halves, 1 fresh rosemary sprig, and 1 fresh thyme sprig into body cavity. Position small sprigs of additional rosemary and thyme under skin. Roast as directed with garlic and shallots, drizzling chicken with fresh lime juice instead of lemon juice. When chicken is done, discard lime halves and herbs from body cavity. Prepare pan juices and serve as directed.

Lemon and Tarragon

Tuck 1 whole lemon that has been pricked all over with a small metal skewer; 1 whole peeled onion; 1 celery rib, cut into 4 pieces; and 2 fresh tarragon sprigs into the body cavity. Position 4 small tarragon sprigs under skin. Roast as directed with garlic and shallots, drizzling chicken with lemon juice. When chicken is done, discard whole lemon, onion, celery, and tarragon from body cavity. Prepare pan juices and serve as directed.

Sun-Dried Tomatoes and Balsamic Vinegar

Tuck 1 whole peeled onion, 1 bay leaf, and 1 celery rib, cut into 4 pieces, into body cavity. Soak 6 sun-dried tomatoes in warm water for 10 minutes; drain and mince. Combine tomatoes with 2 minced garlic cloves and 2 tablespoons (30 ml) balsamic vinegar. Spread tomato mixture under skin. Roast as directed with garlic and shallots, basting chicken with 1 tablespoon (15 ml) balsamic vinegar mixed with 2 tablespoons (30 ml) water. When chicken is done, discard onion, bay leaf, and celery from body cavity. Prepare pan juices and serve as directed.

Sage

Tuck 1 whole peeled onion; 1 celery rib, cut into 4 pieces; and 4 fresh sage leaves into body cavity. Tuck another 6 whole sage leaves under skin. Roast as directed with garlic and shallots. When chicken is done, discard onion, celery, and sage from body cavity. Prepare pan juices and serve as directed.

SUNDAY DINNER

◆

Roast Chicken with Lemon and Oregano (page 175)

Buttermilk Mashed Potatoes (page 307)

Roasted Asparagus with Parmesan Cheese (page 323)

Fresh Strawberries Splashed with Balsamic Vinegar

Per serving: 544 calories (29% fat)
Joslin Exchanges: 3½ low-fat meat, 3 vegetable, 2 bread/starch, 1 fruit, 1 fat

Chicken Breasts with Balsamic Vinegar Sauce

Almost every French bistro serves a version of this homey dish. Our recipe uses balsamic vinegar and fresh rosemary for a wonderfully simple and slightly Italian variation. Serve with steamed or boiled potatoes and a salad of baby lettuces.

2 whole skinless and boneless chicken breasts, about ½ pound (225 g) each, halved
olive oil cooking spray
1 small onion, about 3 ounces (85 g), finely chopped
1 garlic clove, finely chopped
½ pound (225 g) fresh mushrooms, sliced

⅓ cup (78 ml) balsamic vinegar
½ cup (118 ml) dry white wine
freshly ground pepper to taste
½ teaspoon (2.5 ml) salt (optional)
1 tablespoon (15 ml) fresh rosemary leaves or 1 teaspoon (5 ml) crushed dried
1 teaspoon (2.5 ml) unsalted butter
fresh rosemary sprigs for garnish

Remove all visible fat from chicken. Spray a large nonstick skillet with cooking spray. Brown chicken breasts over medium-high heat for 3 minutes per side. Transfer chicken to a plate. Add onion, garlic, and mushrooms to same skillet. Reduce heat to low and sauté until onion is translucent but not browned, about 3 minutes. Add vinegar, wine, pepper, salt, and rosemary. Bring mixture to a simmer. Return chicken pieces to skillet. Cover and simmer until chicken breasts are cooked through, about 20 minutes.

Transfer chicken to a heated serving platter. Cook sauce over high heat until reduced to about ½ cup (118 ml). Remove from heat and whisk in butter. Pour sauce over chicken; garnish with rosemary sprigs.

MAKES 4 SERVINGS

Per serving: calories, 200 ◆ protein, 28 g ◆ carbohydrate, 11 g ◆ fat, 4 g (calories from fat, 18%) ◆ dietary fiber, 1 g ◆ cholesterol, 74 mg ◆ sodium, 337 mg ◆ potassium, 452 mg Joslin Exchanges: 3 low-fat meat, 2 vegetable

Chicken Lo Mein

We baked whole chicken breasts in the oven for this dish, then discarded the skin and bones. The result is juicier and much more flavorful chicken. You can bake the chicken earlier in the day or a day ahead, shred the chicken, and refrigerate it until dinnertime. The rest goes together rather quickly.

If your market doesn't have dried Asian mushrooms (wood ear, cloud ear, or tree ear), substitute 6 ounces (180 g) fresh cultivated mushrooms.

butter-flavored cooking spray
1½ pounds (675 g) whole chicken breasts
¼ teaspoon (1.25 ml) herb salt substitute (page 115)
freshly ground pepper to taste
juice of 1 lemon
2 tablespoons (30 ml) slivered almonds
1½-ounce (15 g) package Chinese rice stick noodles (Chinese vermicelli)
1 garlic clove, pressed or minced
1 tablespoon (15 ml) minced fresh ginger
3 scallions, white part and 1 inch (2.5 cm) green, thinly sliced
1 stalk of lemongrass, white part only, minced, or 1 teaspoon (5 ml) grated lemon zest
½ pound (225 g) Chinese cabbage, thinly sliced

1 ounce (30 g) dried Asian mushrooms, soaked in lukewarm water for 20 minutes, drained, and sliced
1 carrot, peeled and grated
1 tablespoon (15 ml) cornstarch
¾ cup (177 ml) chicken stock (page 45)
5½ teaspoons (27.5 ml) low-sodium soy sauce
2 tablespoons (30 ml) Chinese rice wine or dry white wine
1 tablespoon (15 ml) white wine vinegar
½ pound (225 g) fresh bean sprouts
⅛ to ¼ teaspoon (.6 to 1.25 ml) hot red pepper flakes or to taste
1 to 2 tablespoons (15 to 30 ml) chopped fresh cilantro (fresh coriander) to taste
⅛ teaspoon (.6 ml) dark sesame oil

Preheat oven to 350°F (180°C). Lightly spray a baking dish with cooking spray.

Place chicken in baking dish skin side up. Sprinkle with salt substitute, pepper, and lemon juice. Cover tightly with aluminum foil. Bake for 25 to 30 minutes. Cool chicken; remove and discard skin and bones. Shred meat and set aside.

While chicken is baking, toast almonds by spreading them in a single layer on a baking sheet and baking for 3 to 5 minutes, shaking pan once or twice, until almonds are golden brown and fragrant. Cool and set aside.

Break rice stick noodles into 6-inch (15 cm) lengths. Soak in warm water according to package directions.

In a large nonstick sauté pan or wok lightly sprayed with cooking spray, sauté garlic, ginger, scallions, and lemongrass over low heat for 1 minute. Add cabbage, mushrooms, and carrot, raise heat to high, and sauté until cabbage starts to wilt, about 2 minutes. Stir cornstarch into stock. Add to skillet along with soy sauce, rice wine, and vinegar. Cook, stirring, until mixture thickens slightly, about 3 minutes. Add bean sprouts, reserved chicken, rice stick noodles, red pepper flakes, and cilantro. Heat through, stirring constantly. Sprinkle with sesame oil; garnish with reserved toasted almonds.

MAKES 4 SERVINGS

Per serving: calories, 257 ◆ protein, 32 g ◆ carbohydrate, 22 g ◆ fat, 6 g (calories from fat, 21%) ◆ dietary fiber, 2 g ◆ cholesterol, 73 mg ◆ sodium, 400 mg ◆ potassium, 757 mg Joslin Exchanges: 3¹/₂ low-fat meat, 2 vegetable, 1 bread/ starch

Chicken Ballottine with Squash Salsa

A ballottine is meat, fish, or fowl that is boned, stuffed, rolled, and tied into a bundle before being cooked. Our method for preparing this elegant entree is easy and quick.

Mark Miller serves a terrific squash salsa at his famed Coyote Cafe in Santa Fe, New Mexico, as a vegetable accompaniment for grilled chicken. Our version adds the crunch of jícama, a bulbous root vegetable with a sweet, nutty flavor. The vegetables should be cut evenly into fine dice, about ¹/₈ inch (.5 cm) square. Serve the salsa at room temperature.

Chicken Ballottine

2 whole skinless and boneless chicken breasts, about ¹/₂ pound (225 g) each, halved and pounded thin

¹/₂ pound (225 g) fresh spinach, washed and stems removed

Remove all visible fat from chicken breasts. Place each breast half on a large piece of plastic wrap.

Cook spinach leaves in boiling water for 1 minute. Drain and squeeze out all moisture. Arrange spinach leaves over chicken pieces, distributing them evenly. Starting at one end, roll up each breast with spinach inside. Wrap each chicken roll in plastic wrap, then in aluminum foil, twisting at each end to seal.

Place sealed chicken bundles in a large pan of boiling water. Reduce heat to a simmer and poach chicken for 15 minutes. Remove from heat, discarding foil and plastic wrap. Slice each chicken bundle into 4 pieces. Arrange on serving plates.

MAKES 4 SERVINGS

> **Per serving:** calories, 152 ◆ protein, 28 g ◆ carbohydrate, 2 g ◆ fat, 3 g (calories from fat, 18%) ◆ dietary fiber, 1 g ◆ cholesterol, 72 mg ◆ sodium, 101 mg ◆ potassium, 478 mg Joslin Exchanges: 3½ low-fat meat

Squash Salsa

¼ cup (59 ml) finely diced zucchini
¼ cup (59 ml) finely diced yellow crookneck squash
¼ cup (59 ml) finely diced carrot
¼ cup (59 ml) finely diced jícama
¼ cup (59 ml) finely diced onion
1 tomatillo, husked and finely diced
1 small tomato, about 3 ounces (85 g), finely diced

1 garlic clove, minced
1 serrano chili, seeded and finely minced
1 tablespoon (15 ml) minced fresh oregano or flat-leaf parsley
1 teaspoon (5 ml) olive oil
1 tablespoon (15 ml) fresh lime juice

Combine all ingredients. Let sit at room temperature for 1 hour before serving.

MAKES 4 SERVINGS

> **Per serving:** calories, 45 ◆ protein, 1 g ◆ carbohydrate, 8 g ◆ fat, 1 g (calories from fat, 20%) ◆ dietary fiber, 1 g ◆ cholesterol, 0 mg ◆ sodium, 10 mg ◆ potassium, 238 mg Joslin Exchanges: 1 vegetable

Diane's White Chili

This excellent chicken chili recipe comes from Diane Glass, a caterer in Tulsa. She serves it in deep chili bowls, topped with chopped red onion, sliced Pickled Okra, and nonfat yogurt. Pickled okra can be purchased in many supermarkets, but it's also easy to make (see page 14).

1 pound (450 g) dried Great Northern beans, rinsed and picked over

7 cups (1.75 l) chicken stock (page 45)

3 garlic cloves, chopped

2 medium-size onions, about ½ pound (225 g), chopped

2 tablespoons (30 ml) chopped fresh cilantro (fresh coriander)

2 tablespoons (30 ml) chopped fresh flat-leaf parsley

1 bay leaf (optional)

1 teaspoon (5 ml) crushed dried oregano

1 teaspoon (5 ml) crushed dried thyme

1 tablespoon (15 ml) ground cumin

2 tablespoons (30 ml) chopped fresh mint or 2 teaspoons (10 ml) crushed dried

1 to 2 small fresh jalapeño chilies, to taste, seeded and chopped

2 pounds (900 g) boneless and skinless chicken breasts

Condiments

chopped red onion
sliced Pickled Okra (page 14) or
    chopped canned green chilies

plain nonfat yogurt

Place beans in a large heavy pot. Add cold water to cover beans by at least 3 inches (8 cm). Bring beans and water to a rapid boil; boil for 2 minutes. Turn off heat and allow to sit, covered, for 1 hour. Or soak beans overnight in water to cover.

Drain beans. Place 5 cups (1.25 l) chicken stock in same pot. Add garlic, onions, cilantro, parsley, bay leaf, oregano, thyme, cumin, mint, jalapeño, and beans. Bring to a boil. Reduce heat and simmer until beans are very tender, stirring occasionally, about 2 hours.

Meanwhile, remove all visible fat from chicken. In a large skillet, poach chicken breasts in remaining 2 cups (472 ml) stock until just tender, about 15 minutes. Cool and cut chicken into cubes. Reserve stock and chicken.

When beans are tender, add chicken and 1 cup (236 ml) reserved stock. Cook for 15 to 20 minutes until chicken is heated through, thinning chili with remaining reserved stock as needed (chili should be thick). Ladle chili into bowls. Serve with chopped red onion, pickled okra, and nonfat yogurt.

MAKES 8 SERVINGS

Per serving (without condiments): calories, 219 ◆ protein, 31 g ◆ carbohydrate, 15 g ◆ fat, 4 g (calories from fat, 15%) ◆ dietary fiber, 4 g ◆ cholesterol, 72 mg ◆ sodium, 108 mg ◆ potassium, 567 mg Joslin Exchanges: 4 low-fat meat, 1 bread/starch

---

CINCO DE MAYO DINNER

◆

Salsa Fresca (page 8) and Flour Tortilla Chips (page 371)

Diane's White Chili (page 182)

Tropical Salad with Chervil Dressing (page 101)

Fresh Pineapple Upside-Down Polenta Cake (page 413)

Per serving: 523 calories (25% fat)
Joslin Exchanges: 4 low-fat meat, 3 bread/starch, 1 fruit

Roast Turkey Breast Jardinière

A roasted turkey breast is wonderful for entertaining—its lean, tasty meat will please your guests. We cooked the turkey breast on a bed of vegetables, which flavor the pan juices to make a delectable sauce. Accompany the turkey with mashed potatoes made with roasted garlic (page 262) and a little skim milk.

1 garlic clove, minced
1 tablespoon (15 ml) chopped
  fresh parsley
2 tablespoons (30 ml) chopped
  fresh tarragon
juice and grated zest of 1 lemon
1 3-pound (1,350 g) turkey breast
  roast, with skin
olive oil cooking spray
3 leeks, white part only, well
  rinsed and thinly sliced
2 garlic cloves, peeled and thinly
  sliced

¼ pound (115 g) fresh mushrooms,
  thinly sliced
½ red bell pepper, seeded and thinly
  sliced
½ yellow bell pepper, seeded and
  thinly sliced
freshly ground pepper, to taste
½ teaspoon (2.5 ml) salt (optional)
2 tablespoons (30 ml) white wine
  (optional)
fresh tarragon sprigs, for garnish

Preheat oven to 350°F (180°C).

In a small bowl, combine minced garlic, parsley, 1 tablespoon (15 ml) tarragon, and lemon zest. Using your fingers, separate skin from breast meat along one side. Spread herb mixture over breast meat and cover with skin.

Place turkey breast in a shallow roasting pan. Squeeze lemon juice over turkey. Cover and roast for 1 hour.

Meanwhile, spray a nonstick sauté pan with cooking spray. Add leeks and garlic; sauté over low heat for 8 minutes or until leeks are wilted. Add mushrooms; sauté for another 4 minutes. Add peppers, remaining 1 tablespoon (15 ml) tarragon, freshly ground pepper, salt, and wine. Cook for another 3 minutes. Set aside.

When turkey has roasted for 1 hour, remove cover and place vegetables around turkey breast. Return to oven and roast, uncovered, for another 40 to 50 minutes, to an internal temperature of 170°F (77°C). Remove from oven and transfer turkey to a carving board or platter. Keep warm.

Remove vegetables from roasting pan. Set aside. Pour pan juices into a heavy skillet; skim off any fat that rises to the surface. Cook over high heat until reduced to a syrup consistency. Add vegetables. Turn heat off; keep warm.

Remove skin from turkey breast. Slice thinly and arrange on a heated serving platter. Spoon sauce and vegetables over turkey; garnish with tarragon sprigs. Serve immediately.

MAKES 10 SERVINGS

Per serving: calories, 172 ◆ protein, 32 g ◆ carbohydrate, 8 g ◆ fat, 1 g (calories from fat, 5%) ◆ dietary fiber, 1 g ◆ cholesterol, 84 mg ◆ sodium, 168 mg ◆ potassium, 467 mg Joslin Exchanges: 4 low-fat meat, 1 vegetable

Variation

Use chopped fresh basil or chopped fresh sage instead of tarragon.

MOTHER'S DAY DINNER

◆

Chilled Cream of Watercress Soup (page 55)

Roast Turkey Breast Jardinière (page 184)

Buttermilk Mashed Potatoes (page 307)

Roasted Asparagus with Lemon and Almonds (page 324)

Strawberry Parfaits (page 430)

Per serving: 592 calories (30% fat)
Joslin Exchanges: 4 low-fat meat, 3 bread/starch, 3 vegetable, 1 fat

Bajan Chicken Brochettes

Almost every island in the West Indies has its own special seasoning mix or hot sauce. The beautiful island of Barbados is no exception, offering a seasoning called *Bajan* that combines fresh herbs and hot peppers.

Here we've marinated chicken breasts in Bajan Hot Sauce, then added cherry tomatoes and pearl onions to make chicken brochettes for a party. While the barbecue's hot, grill some Japanese eggplant to serve alongside.

Bajan Hot Sauce

6 scallions, white part and 2 inches (5 cm) green, coarsely chopped
¼ cup (59 ml) fresh lime juice
2 tablespoons (30 ml) minced flat-leaf parsley
1 tablespoon (15 ml) minced fresh thyme or 1 teaspoon (5 ml) crushed dried
½ tablespoon (7.5 ml) minced fresh rosemary or ½ teaspoon (2.5 ml) crushed dried

1 garlic clove, minced
1 fresh jalapeño chili, seeded and minced
1 teaspoon (5 ml) paprika
⅛ teaspoon (.6 ml) Tabasco sauce or to taste
¼ teaspoon (1.25 ml) salt (optional)
¼ teaspoon (1.25 ml) freshly ground pepper or to taste

In a food processor or blender fitted with a metal blade, combine all ingredients until finely chopped. Refrigerate in a covered container until ready to use.

Chicken Brochettes

2 whole skinless and boneless
  chicken breasts, about ½ pound
  (225 g) each, halved
4 large garlic cloves, peeled

8 large pearl onions
8 large cherry tomatoes, stems
  removed

Remove all visible fat from chicken; slice each half breast into 4 strips lengthwise. Combine with Bajan Hot Sauce and whole garlic cloves; toss well. Cover loosely and marinate in the refrigerator for 4 to 6 hours.

Meanwhile, drop pearl onions into a saucepan filled with gently boiling water. Cook for 5 minutes. Drain, rinse under cold water, and drain again. Slip off skins and set aside.

Prepare barbecue or preheat broiler. Roll up a piece of chicken and slide it onto a long metal skewer. Add an onion, a piece of chicken, a cherry tomato, a piece of chicken, an onion, a piece of chicken, a cherry tomato, and a whole garlic clove from the marinade. Repeat with 3 more skewers.

Place skewers 4 inches (10 cm) from heat source and broil or grill over medium-hot coals for 8 to 10 minutes, turning once.

MAKES 4 SERVINGS

Per serving: calories, 178 ◆ protein, 28 g ◆ carbohydrate, 9 g ◆ fat, 3 g (calories from fat, 15%) ◆ dietary fiber, 1 g ◆ cholesterol, 72 mg ◆ sodium, 204 mg ◆ potassium, 453 mg Joslin Exchanges: 3½ low-fat meat, 2 vegetable

Per serving (hot sauce alone): calories, 38 ◆ protein, 1 gm ◆ carbohydrate, 9 gm ◆ fat, trace (calories from fat, 8%) ◆ dietary fiber, 1 g ◆ cholesterol, 0 mg ◆ sodium, 142 mg ◆ potassium 237 mg Joslin Exchanges: 1 vegetable

Cornish Hens Stuffed with Apples and Cherries

Guests will rave about the winning flavor combination of this dish: fresh cherries, apples, spices, and Rock Cornish hens—made tender and succulent by a long marinade in nonfat yogurt.

3　Rock Cornish hens, about 1 pound (450 g) each, split lengthwise

Yogurt Marinade

1　cup (236 ml) plain nonfat yogurt
1　medium-size onion, about ¼ pound (115 g), chopped
3　garlic cloves, crushed
juice of 1 lime
3　tablespoons (45 ml) red wine vinegar
2　teaspoons (10 ml) chili powder
¾　teaspoon (3.75 ml) ground coriander
¾　teaspoon (3.75 ml) ground cinnamon
dash of ground cloves
⅛　teaspoon (.6 ml) hot red pepper flakes or to taste
1　tablespoon (15 ml) olive oil

Fruit Stuffing

1　medium-size Granny Smith apple, about 5 ounces (140 g), peeled and chopped
1　cup (236 ml) pitted fresh Bing cherries, chopped
1　teaspoon (5 ml) ground cinnamon
dash of ground cloves
1　scallion, white part and 1 inch (2.5 cm) green, thinly sliced
2　tablespoons (30 ml) dry white wine or water
2　tablespoons (30 ml) chicken stock (page 45)
vegetable oil cooking spray

Remove all skin and visible fat from hens. Place in a glass baking dish.

In a food processor or blender, puree marinade ingredients. Pour over hens and turn several times to coat evenly. Cover and refrigerate for at least 6 hours or overnight.

Prepare stuffing at least 45 minutes prior to baking by combining remaining ingredients except cooking spray. Mix well.

Preheat oven to 425°F (220°C).

Remove hens from marinade, scraping off as much of the yogurt mixture as possible. Set marinade aside. Stuff each hen with one-sixth of the fruit stuffing. Line a baking pan with aluminum foil; lightly spray with cooking spray. Place stuffed hens on foil, stuffing side down. Bake for 10 minutes. Reduce oven temperature to 325°F (165°C). Spoon reserved marinade over hens and continue to bake for 35 to 40 minutes, until hens are done.

Transfer hens to heated serving plates, keeping fruit stuffing in place. Skim surface fat off pan juices and spoon some over each hen.

MAKES 6 SERVINGS

Per serving: calories, 316 ◆ protein, 27 g ◆ carbohydrate, 20 g ◆ fat, 15 g (calories from fat, 42%) ◆ dietary fiber, 1 g ◆ cholesterol, 64 mg ◆ sodium, 67 mg ◆ potassium, 303 mg Joslin Exchanges: 3½ low-fat meat, 1 fruit

Per serving (marinade alone): calories, 64 ◆ protein, 3 g ◆ carbohydrate, 8 g ◆ fat, 3 g (calories from fat, 42%) ◆ dietary fiber, 1 g ◆ cholesterol, 1 mg ◆ sodium, 41 mg ◆ potassium, 165 mg Joslin Exchanges: 1 fat

---

SATURDAY NIGHT DINNER PARTY

◆

Fennel and Shiitake Mushroom Crêpes (page 31)

Cornish Hens Stuffed with Apples and Cherries (page 188)

Wehani Rice and Wild Rice (page 288)

Steamed Tiny Green Beans

Filo Tulips with Mixed Berries (page 431)

Per serving: 620 calories (26% fat)
Joslin Exchanges: 4 low-fat meat, 2 bread/starch, 1 vegetable, 2 fruit

Crispy Chicken

A great chicken dish hot from the oven—or room temperature at a picnic. A bit of lemon and fresh thyme adds extra flavor. Offer a vegetable salad as an accompaniment.

Marinade

juice and grated zest of 1 lemon
1/4 cup (59 ml) minced shallot or
    onion
1 teaspoon (5 ml) Worcestershire
    sauce
2 teaspoons (10 ml) dry mustard
1 cup (236 ml) plain low-fat yogurt
1/4 teaspoon (1.25 ml) freshly
    ground pepper
1 tablespoon (15 ml) fresh thyme
    leaves or 1 teaspoon (5 ml)
    crushed dried

Chicken

3 whole skinless and boneless
    chicken breasts, about 1/2 pound
    (225 g) each, halved
1 cup (236 ml) plain dry bread
    crumbs
3 tablespoons (45 ml) stone-ground
    yellow cornmeal
2 tablespoons (30 ml) chopped
    fresh flat-leaf parsley
olive oil cooking spray
paprika
2 teaspoons (10 ml) olive oil

In a large bowl, combine marinade ingredients. Remove all visible fat from chicken breasts. Add breasts to marinade, turning to coat all sides. Cover and refrigerate for at least 2 hours or overnight.

Preheat oven to 350°F (180°C).

Combine bread crumbs, cornmeal, and parsley. Remove chicken breasts from marinade; roll in bread crumb mixture to coat.

Spray a baking sheet with cooking spray. Place chicken pieces on baking sheet. Sprinkle with paprika and drizzle with olive oil. Bake for 35 to 40 minutes, until done.

MAKES 6 SERVINGS

Per serving: calories, 219 ◆ protein, 19 g ◆ carbohydrate, 20 g ◆ fat, 7 g (calories from fat, 29%) ◆ dietary fiber, 1 g ◆ cholesterol, 41 mg ◆ sodium, 193 mg ◆ potassium, 288 mg Joslin Exchanges: 2 1/2 low-fat meat, 2 bread/starch

Per serving (marinade alone): calories, 36 ◆ protein, 2 g ◆ carbohydrate, 5 g ◆ fat, 1 g (calories from fat, 20%) ◆ dietary fiber, trace ◆ cholesterol, 2 mg ◆ sodium, 36 mg ◆ potassium, 131 mg Joslin Exchanges: 1 vegetable

FOURTH OF JULY PICNIC

◆

Crudités and Curry Dip (page 5)

Crispy Chicken (page 190)

Confetti Coleslaw (page 94)

Fresh Fruit Basket

Per serving: 446 calories (29% fat)
Joslin Exchanges: 2¹/₂ low-fat meat, 1¹/₂ vegetable, 2 bread/starch, 1 fruit, 1 fat

Oven-Baked Mexican Chicken with Melon Salsa

Salsa can be made out of just about anything in the refrigerator. This is a great dish, hot or cold, and a gem for picnics.

Make sure that your chili powder is very fresh (it should have a bright brick-red color); stale chili powder will have a dull flavor. Serve with Quinoa Garden Salad (page 292).

Chicken

¹/₂ cup (69 g) stone-ground yellow cornmeal

¹/₃ cup (42 g) unbleached flour

¹/₈ teaspoon (.6 ml) hot red pepper flakes

1 tablespoon (15 ml) chili powder

¹/₂ tablespoon (7.5 ml) ground cumin

¹/₂ tablespoon (7.5 ml) crushed dried oregano leaves

2 whole skinless and boneless chicken breasts, about ¹/₂ pound (225 g) each, halved

¹/₂ cup (118 ml) skim milk

olive oil cooking spray

¹/₂ tablespoon (7.5 ml) olive oil

fresh oregano sprigs, for garnish (optional)

fresh mint sprigs, for garnish (optional)

Preheat oven to 350°F (180°C).

In a shallow bowl, combine cornmeal, flour, red pepper flakes, chili powder, cumin, and oregano. Remove all visible fat from chicken. Dip chicken pieces in milk. Roll in cornmeal mixture to coat lightly. Shake off any excess coating.

Lightly spray a baking pan with cooking spray. Arrange chicken pieces in pan; drizzle with olive oil. Bake for 30 minutes, basting with any juices that accumulate.

Serve with salsa; garnish with oregano and mint.

MAKES 4 SERVINGS

Per serving (chicken alone): calories, 270 ◆ protein, 30 g ◆ carbohydrate, 23 g ◆ fat, 6 g (calories from fat, 20%) ◆ dietary fiber, 1 g ◆ cholesterol, 72 mg ◆ sodium, 105 mg ◆ potassium, 378 mg
Joslin Exchanges: 3 low-fat meat, 1 bread/starch

Melon Salsa

1 navel orange
3/4 cup (177 ml) finely chopped honeydew or cantaloupe
juice of 1 lime
3/4 cup (177 ml) finely chopped red onion
1/4 cup (59 ml) chopped fresh mint
1/4 cup (59 ml) chopped fresh cilantro (fresh coriander)
1 garlic clove, minced
1 jalapeño chili, seeded and minced
1 teaspoon (5 ml) olive oil
4 lettuce leaves, washed and chilled (optional)

With a small sharp knife, remove peel and white pith from the orange and discard. Holding the orange over a bowl, cut between the membranes to remove the sections. Chop sections. Squeeze the membrane to extract all of the juice; discard membrane. Combine all ingredients except lettuce and chill for 30 minutes before serving.

To serve, spoon salsa into lettuce leaves or mound in a small dish.

MAKES 4 SERVINGS

Per serving: calories, 75 ◆ protein, 2 g ◆ carbohydrate, 12 g ◆ fat, 2 g (calories from fat, 24%) ◆ dietary fiber, 1 g ◆ cholesterol, 0 mg ◆ sodium, 10 mg ◆ potassium, 310 mg
Joslin Exchanges: 1 fruit

Chicken Breasts with Nectarines

This fragrant chicken dish has distinctive Indian flavors that are both sweet and spicy. Fortunately good-quality nectarines from South America are readily available during the winter, making this dish possible year-round. (You can also use peaches instead of nectarines.)

Serve with basmati rice (page 288) and a refreshing raita for a spectacular combination of flavors. Raitas are spiced or herbed yogurt sauces traditionally used to cool spicy Indian cuisine.

2 whole skinless and boneless chicken breasts, about ½ pound (225 g) each, halved
olive oil cooking spray
3 shallots, minced
1 tablespoon (15 ml) olive oil
1 tablespoon (15 ml) minced fresh ginger
1 fresh jalapeño chili, seeded and minced

2 teaspoons (10 ml) ground cumin
1½ cups (354 ml) chicken stock (page 45)
½ teaspoon (2.5 ml) freshly ground pepper
2 large nectarines or peaches, about ¾ pound (340 g)

Remove all visible fat from chicken breasts. Lightly spray a large skillet with cooking spray. Place over medium-high heat, add chicken breasts, and cook for 4 minutes per side. Remove chicken from skillet; set aside.

In another large skillet, sauté shallots in olive oil over low heat for 2 to 3 minutes, stirring frequently, until shallots are limp. Stir in ginger and jalapeño. Sauté for 1 minute. Stir in cumin, stock, and pepper. Bring mixture to a boil and cook, stirring constantly, for 2 to 3 minutes, until sauce begins to thicken. Reduce heat to low. Add chicken breasts and simmer gently in the sauce for 3 minutes, basting frequently with sauce.

Slice unpeeled nectarines. Add to saucepan. Cook for another 1 to 2 minutes, until nectarines are heated through.

Arrange chicken and nectarines on a heated serving platter. Pour sauce over chicken and nectarines. Serve immediately.

MAKES 4 SERVINGS

Per serving: calories, 220 ◆ protein, 27 g ◆ carbohydrate, 12 g ◆ fat, 7 g (calories from fat, 28%) ◆ dietary fiber, 2 g ◆ cholesterol, 72 mg ◆ sodium, 81 mg ◆ potassium, 466 mg
Joslin Exchanges: 4 low-fat meat, 1 fruit

Cucumber and Scallion Raita

1 cup (236 ml) plain nonfat yogurt
1 garlic clove, minced
1 large cucumber, about ½ pound (225 g), peeled, seeded, and minced
2 scallions, white part and 1 inch (2.5 cm) green, thinly sliced

¼ cup (59 ml) loosely packed mint leaves, chopped
¼ teaspoon (1.25 ml) salt (optional)
freshly ground pepper to taste
¼ teaspoon (1.25 ml) cumin seed

In a small bowl, combine all ingredients. Refrigerate for at least 1 hour before serving.

MAKES ABOUT 2 CUPS (472 ML)

> **Per ¼-cup (59 ml) serving:** calories, 23 ◆ protein, 2 g ◆ carbohydrate, 4 g ◆ fat, trace (calories from fat, less than 1%) ◆ dietary fiber, trace ◆ cholesterol, 1 mg ◆ sodium 89 mg ◆ potassium, 134 Joslin Exchanges: free

Miniature Turkey Loaves with Fresh Peach Salsa

Meat loaf is standard family fare in most homes. Our sophisticated version, served with a lively peach salsa, is for company too. The salsa is also terrific with grilled fish. Also try slicing the loaves very thinly and serve with French bread and a variety of mustards.

Miniature Turkey Loaves

1½ pounds (675 g) lean ground turkey
3 tablespoons (45 ml) egg substitute or 2 large egg whites
¾ teaspoon (3.75 ml) crushed dried sage

¾ teaspoon (3.75 ml) crushed dried thyme
¾ teaspoon (3.75 ml) crushed dried marjoram
freshly ground pepper to taste

2 scallions, white part only,
chopped
6 fresh mushrooms, about 3
ounces (85 g), chopped

½ tablespoon (7.5 ml) canola oil
½ teaspoon (2.5 ml)
Worcestershire sauce

Preheat oven to 350°F (180°C).

In a large bowl, combine turkey, egg substitute, sage, thyme, marjoram, pepper, scallion, and mushrooms. Mix well. Form into six 4-ounce (115 g) loaves. Place in a baking pan. Combine oil and Worcestershire sauce. Brush oil mixture over loaves and bake for 30 minutes.

MAKES 6 SERVINGS

> **Per serving:** calories, 188 ◆ protein, 19 g ◆ carbohydrate, 2 g ◆ fat, 11 g (calories from fat, 52%) ◆ dietary fiber, trace ◆ cholesterol, 47 mg ◆ sodium, 92 mg ◆ potassium, 304 mg
> Joslin Exchanges: 3 low-fat meat

Fresh Peach Salsa

⅓ cup (78 ml) chopped red bell
pepper
⅓ cup (78 ml) chopped yellow bell
pepper
¼ cup (59 ml) chopped red onion
1 garlic clove, minced
freshly ground pepper to taste
1 fresh jalapeño chili, seeded and
minced

3 tablespoons (45 ml) chopped
fresh mint
3 tablespoons (45 ml) chopped
fresh marjoram
juice of 1 fresh lime
2 large fresh peaches, about ¾
pound (340 g), peeled and
chopped
fresh mint sprigs for garnish

In a large bowl, combine everything but peaches and garnish. Add peaches; toss to mix.

To serve, place 2 tablespoons (30 ml) salsa on each of 6 serving plates. Place baked turkey loaf in middle and garnish with a mint sprig.

MAKES 6 SERVINGS

> **Per serving (salsa alone):** calories, 31 ◆ protein, 1 g ◆ carbohydrate, 7 g ◆ fat, trace (calories from fat, 6%) ◆ dietary fiber, trace ◆ cholesterol, 0 mg ◆ sodium, 2 mg ◆ potassium, 163 mg
> Joslin Exchanges: ½ fruit

Turkey Tonnato

This lightened turkey variation of the classic cold Italian veal dish is excellent for summer entertaining—it can be prepared up to two days ahead, and the ingredients won't wither in the heat. Have your butcher bone, roll, and tie the turkey breast.

The sweetness of the orange slices and the bite of the arugula are excellent complements to the savory tonnato. If you can't get arugula, substitute watercress. You might want to soak the anchovies in milk for 30 minutes to reduce their salty taste if you're not sure how your guests feel about them. Rinse before using.

1 3-pound (1.35 kg) boned, rolled, and tied turkey breast
8 anchovies
1 large garlic clove, slivered
1 small carrot, peeled and cut into chunks
1 celery rib, cut into pieces
1 large onion, about ½ pound (225 g), quartered
3¼ cups (767 ml) chicken stock (page 45)
2 cups (472 ml) dry white wine
4 parsley sprigs
1 bay leaf
1 6½-ounce (195 g) can white tuna packed in water, well drained

2 teaspoons (10 ml) grated lemon zest
3 tablespoons (45 ml) fresh lemon juice
½ teaspoon (2.5 ml) freshly ground pepper or to taste
1 cup (236 ml) reduced-calorie mayonnaise
3 tablespoons (30 ml) drained capers
chopped flat-leaf parsley for garnish
4 large bunches arugula, washed and crisped
2 large navel oranges, about 10 ounces (285 g) each, peeled, all white pith removed, halved, and thinly sliced

Make slits in turkey with tip of a small knife. Cut 3 of the anchovies into ½-inch (1.5 cm) pieces. Insert one anchovy piece and one garlic sliver into each slit. Place turkey, carrot, celery, and onion in a Dutch oven or large covered saucepan. Add 3 cups (708 ml) stock, wine, parsley sprigs, and bay leaf. Bring to a boil over medium heat; reduce heat and simmer, covered, for 1 hour, until an instant-reading meat thermometer inserted in center of turkey registers 140°F (60°C). Remove from heat; let turkey cool in cooking liquid.

To make tonnato sauce, puree tuna, remaining 5 anchovies, lemon zest, lemon juice, and pepper in a food processor or blender until very smooth, occasionally scraping down sides of work bowl. With machine running, add remaining ¼ cup (59 ml) chicken stock. Process until smooth. Add mayonnaise and pulse on and off until just blended (do not overmix, or sauce will separate). Stir in 2 tablespoons (30 ml) capers. Set aside.

Remove turkey from broth; discard broth or reserve for another use (it would make good soup stock). Remove strings from turkey roast; remove and discard turkey skin. Slice thinly.

Spread some tonnato sauce on a very large serving platter, leaving room around edges for arugula. Top with a single layer of turkey. Spread turkey with more sauce. Continue layering turkey and sauce until all turkey is used, ending with sauce. Sprinkle with chopped parsley and remaining 1 tablespoon (15 ml) capers. Cover with plastic wrap and chill for at least 8 hours. Cover and chill any remaining sauce separately. Let stand at room temperature for 1 hour before surrounding edges of platter with arugula. Tuck orange slices between arugula and tonnato. Pass any remaining sauce separately.

MAKES 12 SERVINGS

> **Per serving:** calories, 220 ◆ protein, 32 g ◆ carbohydrate, 7 g ◆ fat, 7 g (calories from fat, 29%) ◆ dietary fiber, trace ◆ cholesterol, 86 mg ◆ sodium, 581 mg* ◆ potassium, 456 mg Joslin Exchanges: 4 low-fat meat, 1 vegetable

*Not recommended for low-sodium diets unless capers are reduced to 2 tablespoons (30 ml) and canned tuna is replaced with low-sodium canned tuna packed in water.

MIDSUMMER DINNER PARTY

◆

Belgian Endive with Goat Cheese and Figs (page 12)

Turkey Tonnato (page 196)

Chive Popovers (page 388)

Cantaloupe and Honeydew Granita (page 435)

Per serving: 611 calories (28% fat)
Joslin Exchanges: 4 low-fat meat, 1 bread/starch, 3 vegetable, 1 fruit, 1 fat

Thai Basil Chicken

The countries of the Pacific Rim cook with lots of fresh basil. Thailand is no exception, although its hot basil has a much stronger taste than our milder sweet basil. An authentic recipe would call for kaffir lime leaves, which are difficult to find except in Asian produce markets. A similar taste is achieved by using grated lime zest in the marinade.

Basil Marinade

1 tablespoon (15 ml) low-sodium soy sauce
¼ cup (59 ml) chicken stock (page 45)
¼ cup (59 ml) dry sherry
1 teaspoon (5 ml) grated lime zest
½ cup (118 ml) chopped fresh basil
1 tablespoon (15 ml) chopped fresh ginger
2 teaspoons (10 ml) cornstarch

Chicken

1 pound (450 g) skinless and boneless chicken breasts
3 garlic cloves, minced
1 large onion, about ½ pound (225 g), halved and thinly sliced
2 fresh red chilies, seeded and chopped, or to taste
2 tablespoons (30 ml) peanut oil
2 cups (472 ml) chopped white cabbage

In a large bowl, combine marinade ingredients. Cut chicken into 2-inch (5 cm) strips. Add chicken to marinade; cover and refrigerate for 30 minutes.

In a wok or large skillet, stir-fry garlic, onion, and chilies in peanut oil over low heat for 2 minutes. Using a slotted spoon, add chicken to wok, reserving marinade. Stir-fry for 4 minutes. Add reserved marinade to wok; cook for another 2 to 3 minutes, until sauce thickens. Serve on a bed of chopped cabbage.

MAKES 4 SERVINGS

Per serving: calories, 255 ◆ protein, 29 g ◆ carbohydrate, 12 g ◆ fat, 10 g (calories from fat, 35%) ◆ dietary fiber, 1 g ◆ cholesterol, 72 mg ◆ sodium, 335 mg ◆ potassium, 557 mg Joslin Exchanges: 3½ low-fat meat, 2 vegetable

Per serving (marinade alone): calories, 17 ◆ protein, 1 g ◆ carbohydrate, 4 g ◆ fat, trace (calories from fat, less than 1%) ◆ dietary fiber, trace ◆ cholesterol, 0 mg ◆ sodium, 261 mg ◆ potassium, 115 mg Joslin Exchanges: free

Chicken Burgundy

This version of *coq au vin* is a splendid meal in itself, using skinless chicken breasts for savings on calories and fat. Be sure to use a good-quality Burgundy.

3 whole skinless and boneless chicken breasts, about ½ pound (225 g) each, halved

30 small frozen pearl onions

1 tablespoon (15 ml) olive oil

¾ pound (340 g) fresh mushrooms, stems trimmed

2 tablespoons (30 ml) cognac (optional)

1½ cups (354 ml) beef stock (page 44)

1½ cups (354 ml) dry red wine

2 tablespoons (30 ml) Dijon mustard

1 tablespoon (15 ml) fresh thyme leaves or 1 teaspoon (5 ml) crushed dried

¼ teaspoon (1.25 ml) freshly ground pepper or to taste

¾ pound (340 g) baby carrots, about 18, scrubbed

2 tablespoons (30 ml) fresh flat-leaf parsley leaves for garnish

Remove all visible fat from chicken breasts. In a large heavy skillet over medium heat, sauté chicken and onions in oil for about 10 minutes, until chicken and onions are well browned on all sides. Transfer chicken and onions to a platter; keep warm.

Add mushrooms (if mushrooms are large, cut into halves or quarters) to same skillet and sauté until mushrooms are lightly browned and all pan juices have evaporated, about 8 minutes. Transfer mushrooms to platter with chicken. Pour cognac into skillet and cook, stirring constantly, over high heat to deglaze pan. Add stock, wine, mustard, thyme, and pepper. Stir to blend.

Return chicken and vegetables to skillet; add carrots. Reduce heat, cover, and simmer until chicken and carrots are tender, about 20 minutes.

To serve, arrange chicken and vegetables on serving plates. Nap with sauce and garnish with a scattering of parsley leaves.

MAKES 6 SERVINGS

Per serving: calories, 233 ◆ protein, 29 g ◆ carbohydrate, 16 g ◆ fat, 6 g (calories from fat, 23%) ◆ dietary fiber, 2 g ◆ cholesterol, 72 mg ◆ sodium, 165 mg ◆ potassium, 791 mg Joslin Exchanges: 3 low-fat meat, 3 vegetable

---

BISTRO DINNER PARTY

◆

Creamed Onion Soup (page 72)

Lemon Pepper Breadsticks (page 396)

Chicken Burgundy (page 199)

Poached Pears with Roasted Plum Sauce (page 436)

Per serving: 558 calories (16% fat)
Joslin Exchanges: 3 low-fat meat, 4 vegetable, 1 bread/starch, 1 nonfat milk, 2 fruit

Grilled Chicken with Yogurt and Herbs

Every Middle Eastern country has a recipe for chicken marinated in seasoned yogurt. Our version is full of bold flavors, with the spices toasted briefly to intensify their aroma. Once marinated—you can do it a day ahead of time—the chicken can be grilled, broiled, or baked.

Although we call for boneless chicken thighs, bone-in thighs can be used.
Serve the chicken on a bed of Kale with Lemon and Cumin (page 350).

Yogurt Marinade

2 teaspoons (10 ml) cumin seed
1 tablespoon (15 ml) coriander seed
½ teaspoon (2.5 ml) mustard seed
2 garlic cloves, quartered
1 small onion, peeled and cut into small pieces
2 tablespoons (30 ml) fresh lemon juice

1 2-inch (5 cm) piece of fresh ginger, peeled and cut into 4 pieces
¼ teaspoon (1.25 ml) hot red pepper flakes
1 cup (236 ml) plain low-fat yogurt

Chicken

6 skinless and boneless chicken
  thighs, about 3½ ounces (99 g)
  each
1 tablespoon (15 ml) finely chopped
  fresh cilantro (fresh coriander)
  for garnish (optional)

1 tablespoon (15 ml) finely chopped
  fresh mint for garnish (optional)
1 tablespoon (15 ml) finely chopped
  fresh flat-leaf parsley for garnish
  (optional)

In a small skillet over medium heat, toast cumin, coriander, and mustard seeds for about 2 minutes, until they become fragrant, shaking the pan constantly.

Place seeds with remaining marinade ingredients in a food processor or blender and process until smooth.

Remove all visible fat from chicken and place it in a glass baking dish. Pour yogurt mixture over chicken; turn chicken to coat. Cover with plastic wrap and chill for at least 4 hours or overnight.

To Grill: Prepare or preheat grill or broiler. Grill or broil chicken pieces about 4 inches (10 cm) from source of heat until juices run clear when pierced with a fork, about 8 minutes per side.

To Bake: Preheat oven to 325°F (165°C). Bake, uncovered, for 40 to 50 minutes. Baste every 15 minutes.

Combine cilantro, mint, and parsley. Sprinkle mixed herbs over chicken pieces; serve immediately.

MAKES 6 SERVINGS

Per serving: calories, 195 ◆ protein, 22 g ◆ carbohydrate, 6 g ◆ fat, 9 g (calories from fat, 41%) ◆ dietary fiber, 1 g ◆ cholesterol, 72 mg ◆ sodium, 96 mg ◆ potassium, 343 mg
Joslin Exchanges: 3 low-fat meat, 1 vegetable

Per serving (marinade alone): calories, 38 ◆ protein, 3 g ◆ carbohydrate, 5 g ◆ fat, 1 g (calories from fat, 24%) ◆ dietary fiber, trace ◆ cholesterol, 2 mg ◆ sodium, 30 mg ◆ potassium, 145 mg
Joslin Exchanges: 1 vegetable

MEDITERRANEAN AUTUMN NIGHT

◆

Grilled Chicken with Yogurt and Herbs (page 200)

Basmati Rice (page 288)

Carrot and Cucumber Chat (page 97)

Kale with Lemon and Cumin (page 350)

Fresh Persimmons on the Half Shell

Per serving: 390 calories (23% fat)
Joslin Exchanges: 3 low-fat meat, 3 vegetable, 1 bread/starch, 1 fruit

Chicken Baked with Quince or Plums

This chicken is easy to make and looks lovely in its puffy parchment paper package. Readily available from early fall through December, quince is a yellow-skinned fruit that looks something like a large pear. Other times of the year, make this subtly spicy and fruity dish with firm pitted plums.

Parchment paper is available in bakery supply stores, gourmet cooking shops, and some supermarkets. You can always substitute aluminum foil from a wide roll.

butter-flavored cooking spray
2 whole skinless and boneless chicken breasts, about ½-pound (225 g) each, halved
2 medium-size quinces, about 1 pound (450 g), or 1 pound (450 g) firm ripe plums, halved and pit removed

1 medium-size onion, about ¼ pound (115 g), chopped
1 large tomato, about 6 ounces (180 g), peeled, seeded, and diced
¼ teaspoon (1.25 ml) ground ginger
½ teaspoon (2.5 ml) ground cinnamon
½ teaspoon (2.5 ml) crushed dried mint

¹/₄ **teaspoon (1.25 ml) salt (optional)**   **2 teaspoons (10 ml) honey**
freshly ground pepper to taste
juice of ¹/₂ lemon

Preheat oven to 350°F (180°C). Cut 4 circles of parchment paper 18 inches (46 cm) in diameter. Lightly spray one side of each circle with cooking spray. Lay each chicken breast on one half of sprayed side of circle. Peel, core, and quarter quinces (they're difficult to cut). Arrange quince pieces, onion, and tomato over the chicken. Sprinkle with ginger, cinnamon, mint, salt, and pepper. Squeeze lemon juice over each chicken breast; drizzle with honey.

   Fold over parchment and crimp edges to seal. Place on a baking sheet; bake for 45 minutes. Place parchment packets on serving plates; break open and serve immediately. (If you're using aluminum foil, open the packets in kitchen and arrange chicken and fruit on a serving platter or individual serving plates.)

MAKES 4 SERVINGS

> **Per serving:** calories, 243 ◆
> protein, 28 g ◆ carbohydrate, 28
> g ◆ fat, 3 g (calories from fat,
> 11%) ◆ dietary fiber, 3 g ◆
> cholesterol, 72 mg ◆ sodium,
> 207 mg ◆ potassium, 632 mg
> Joslin Exchanges: 3 low-fat
> meat, 2 vegetable, 1 fruit

Selecting a Quince

Once a staple in American kitchens (our grandmothers used to make quince jam), this yellow-skinned autumn fruit is now considered uncommon. We love the rich, tart flavor that it develops as it's cooked. Select large, firm quince with little or no sign of green. Refrigerate in a plastic bag until ready to use. Quinces are low in calories and a good source of fiber. Look for them in gourmet produce markets and some supermarkets.

Roasted Capon

A capon is a young rooster grown with an abundance of delicate and tender white meat. Since it's a specialty item and carries a higher price per pound than chicken, serve it for a special dinner. If your market doesn't have a capon, substitute a small turkey or roasting chicken.

1 capon, 6 to 6½ pounds (2.75 to 3 kg)
2 large navel oranges, about 1¼ pounds (570 g)
2 tablespoons (30 ml) chopped parsley
1 scallion, white part and 1 inch (2.5 cm) green, minced
6 fresh sage leaves
4 fresh thyme sprigs

freshly ground pepper to taste
1 large onion, about ½ pound (225 g), peeled and halved
1 head of garlic, separated into cloves
1 cup (236 ml) chicken stock (page 45)
¾ cup (177 ml) dry white wine

Preheat oven to 350°F (180°C). Remove any visible fat from neck and body cavities of capon. Rinse and pat dry. Grate zest from 1 orange; combine zest with parsley and scallion. Cut orange in half.

Starting from neck cavity, with your fingers gently separate skin from breast meat and thighs without tearing skin. Place orange zest mixture under skin. Insert sage leaves and thyme sprigs over orange zest mixture. Rub inside of capon with pepper. Place orange halves and half of onion inside body cavity.

Chop remaining onion half and place in a shallow heavy roasting pan. Place capon, breast side up, on top of chopped onion. Strew garlic cloves around capon; pour chicken stock and wine into pan. Cover with aluminum foil and bake for 2 hours. Remove and discard foil; baste bird with pan juices. Continue to roast for 30 minutes, basting frequently. Remove from oven and transfer capon to a carving board; let stand for 15 minutes.

On top of stove, boil pan juices to reduce to 1 cup (236 ml), skimming off any fat that rises to the surface. Peel and section remaining orange, discarding all peel and white pith. Add orange sections to pan juices; heat through.

Carve breast meat into thin slices (remember not to eat the skin if you're counting fat grams). Pass sauce separately.

MAKES 8 SERVINGS

Per serving (without skin): calories, 272 ◆ protein, 32 g ◆ carbohydrate, 5 g ◆ fat, 13 g (calories from fat, 43%) ◆ dietary fiber, trace ◆ cholesterol, 113 mg ◆ sodium, 114 mg ◆ potassium, 370 mg Joslin Exchanges: 4 low-fat meat, 1 vegetable

THANKSGIVING FEAST

◆

Crudités and Fresh Vegetable Dip (page 6)

Roasted Capon (page 204)

Roasted Mixed Vegetables (page 326)

Sage and Onion Focaccia (page 394)

Apple Cherry Cobbler (page 426)

Per serving: 620 calories (29% fat)
Joslin Exchanges: 4 low-fat meat, 4 vegetable, 3 bread/starch, 1 fat

Slow-Baked Chicken with Tomatoes and Potatoes

Another robust chicken recipe for your repertoire. Round out the meal with Chive Popovers (page 388) and a green salad.

1 medium-size onion, about ¼ pound (115 g), coarsely chopped

2 garlic cloves, minced

2 teaspoons (10 ml) olive oil

2 small bay leaves

½ teaspoon (2.5 ml) chopped fresh thyme or ⅛ teaspoon (.6 ml) crushed dried

½ teaspoon (2.5 ml) chopped fresh rosemary or ⅛ teaspoon (.6 ml) crushed dried

1 small red bell pepper, about 3 ounces (85 g), seeded and cut into thin strips

½ teaspoon (2.5 ml) salt (optional) freshly ground pepper to taste

2 skinless and boneless chicken breasts, about ½-pound (225 g) each, halved

2 medium-size russet potatoes, about ½ pound (225 g), peeled and cut into large dice

1 medium-size tomato, about 5 ounces (140 g), peeled, seeded, and diced

Preheat oven to 300°F (150°C). In a large nonstick skillet, sauté onion and garlic in olive oil over low heat until onion is wilted, about 4 minutes. Add bay leaves, herbs, bell pepper, salt, and pepper. Continue to cook for 5 minutes.

Arrange chicken breasts in a large casserole. Add potatoes, tomatoes, and onion/pepper mixture. Cover and bake for 35 to 40 minutes, until chicken is no longer pink when slashed with a knife.

MAKES 4 SERVINGS

Per serving: calories, 239 ◆ protein, 28 g ◆ carbohydrate, 18 g ◆ fat, 6 g (calories from fat, 23%) ◆ dietary fiber, 1 g ◆ cholesterol, 72 mg ◆ sodium, 337 mg ◆ potassium, 580 mg Joslin Exchanges: 3 low-fat meat, 1 bread/starch, 1 vegetable

Parvine's Persian Chicken

Parvine Latimore, an innkeeper from Newport, Rhode Island, frequently serves this succulent chicken dish—a version of a recipe from her homeland.

Herbed Creamer Potatoes (page 308) would make a savory accompaniment.

2 whole boneless chicken breasts with skin, about ½ pound (225 g) each, halved

4 chicken thighs, with bones and skins, about ¼ pound (115 g) each

8 fresh thyme sprigs or ½ tablespoon (7.5 ml) crushed dried

4 garlic cloves, thinly sliced

16 dried apricots, about ¼ pound (115 g)

¾ pound (340 g) fresh mushrooms, sliced

2 large onions, about 1 pound (450 g), sliced

2 thin-skinned oranges, about 6 ounces (180 g) each

2 lemons

½ teaspoon salt (optional)

freshly ground pepper to taste

1 tablespoon (15 ml) olive oil

Preheat oven to 375°F (190°C). Trim all visible fat from chicken. Using your fingers, carefully separate chicken skin from meat along one side of each piece. Stuff a thyme sprig and several garlic slices under skin. Arrange chicken pieces in a large baking dish. Scatter apricots and mushrooms around chicken. Arrange onions on top.

Thinly slice oranges (do not peel). Using a small sharp knife, remove one-half of the lemon peel by cutting away 2 lengthwise strips on opposite sides of the lemons or use a citrus zester (freeze removed zest for future use). Thinly slice lemons, discarding seeds. Arrange orange and lemon slices over chicken. Season with salt and pepper. Drizzle with olive oil. Cover the pan tightly with aluminum foil and bake for 45 minutes.

To serve, arrange chicken pieces on heated serving platter. Spoon fruit and vegetables on top. (Don't eat chicken skin if you're watching your fat intake.)

MAKES 8 SERVINGS

Per serving (without skin):
calories, 252 ◆ protein, 27 g ◆ carbohydrate, 19 g ◆ fat, 8 g (calories from fat, 29%) ◆ dietary fiber, 1 g ◆ cholesterol, 76 mg ◆ sodium, 207 mg ◆ potassium, 696 mg
Joslin Exchanges: 4 low-fat meat, 1 vegetable, 1 fruit

Chicken with Couscous and Orange Cumin Sauce

Fantastic flavor, easy, make-ahead—that's the essence of a great party dish. This chicken dish is just that. Partially assemble it up to a day ahead, then bake while the sauce simmers and the couscous steams.

Serve with a warm salad of Braised Broccoli Rabe (page 340).

3 whole skinless and boneless chicken breasts, about 1/2 pound (225 g) each, halved and pounded to about 1/4 inch (.75 cm) thick
1 tablespoon (15 ml) fresh thyme leaves or 1 teaspoon (5 ml) crushed dried
freshly ground pepper to taste
4 small fresh purple figs or 9 dried apricots
olive oil cooking spray
2 1/2 cups (590 ml) chicken stock (page 45)
1 cup (184 g) quick-cooking couscous

1/4 cup (1.25 ml) dried currants
1/3 cup (78 ml) finely chopped onion
2 teaspoons (10 ml) olive oil
1 teaspoon (5 ml) grated orange zest
3 tablespoons (45 ml) fresh orange juice
1 teaspoon (5 ml) ground cumin
1 tablespoon (15 ml) toasted pine nuts (page 284)
1/4 cup (59 ml) chopped flat-leaf parsley for garnish

Remove all visible fat from chicken. Sprinkle thyme leaves on chicken breasts. Season with freshly ground pepper. Slice figs lengthwise into 3 pieces, discarding stems (if you're using dried apricots, plump for a few minutes in a little warm water, then slice each in half lengthwise). Arrange 2 fig slices (or 3 apricot halves) in center of each chicken piece, mounding slightly. Lift edges of chicken up and over filling to enclose. Set filled breasts, seam side down, in a 9- by 13-inch (23 by 33 cm) baking dish lightly sprayed with cooking spray. (At this point, you can cover and chill until the next day.)

Preheat oven to 450°F (230°C). Bake uncovered until chicken turns white, about 15 to 18 minutes.

While chicken is baking, bring 1 1/2 cups (354 ml) chicken stock to a rolling boil in a small heavy saucepan. Using a fork, stir in couscous and currants. Cover and remove from stove. Set aside while couscous steams. Garnish with parsley.

In a heavy nonstick skillet, sauté onion in olive oil over low heat for 3 minutes, until onion is translucent. Stir in remaining 1 cup (236 ml) chicken stock, orange zest, orange juice, and cumin. Cook over high heat until sauce is reduced and begins to thicken, stirring frequently. Set aside and keep warm.

Preheat broiler. Broil chicken breasts for about 2 minutes to brown top, about 4 inches (10 cm) from source of heat.

Fluff couscous with a fork; stir in pine nuts. Divide couscous among 6 heated dinner plates. Place a chicken breast alongside and nap with sauce.

MAKES 6 SERVINGS

Per serving: calories, 343 ◆ protein, 31 g ◆ carbohydrate, 41 g ◆ fat, 6 g (calories from fat, 15%) ◆ dietary fiber, 1 g ◆ cholesterol, 72 mg ◆ sodium, 86 mg ◆ potassium, 521 mg Joslin Exchanges: 3 low-fat meat, 1 vegetable, 2 bread/ starch

Updated Chicken Pot Pies

Our new chicken pot pies are both perfect for cold winter nights. One is French style with a rich-tasting broth and a puff pastry lattice crust. The other has Santa Fe seasonings and a savory cornmeal topping.

First, poach the chicken.

Poached Chicken

4½ pounds (2 kg) cut-up chicken pieces, all skin and fat removed
1 onion, stuck with a clove
1 celery rib, cut into 3 pieces
2 large garlic cloves, peeled
1 bay leaf
1 parsley sprig
1 teaspoon (5 ml) crushed dried tarragon leaves (for French version) or 1 teaspoon (5 ml) crushed dried thyme leaves (for Santa Fe pie)

1½ cups (354 ml) chicken stock (page 45)
1 cup (236 ml) dry white wine
1½ cups (354 ml) water
freshly ground pepper to taste

Rinse chicken well; pat dry with paper towels. Place chicken in a large soup pot. Add remaining ingredients and bring to a simmer. Skim off and discard any foam that rises to the surface. Lower heat, cover, and simmer chicken for about 45 minutes, until chicken is tender and cooked through.

Using a slotted spoon, transfer chicken to a platter. Remove and discard bay leaf, onion, and celery. Reduce stock to 2 cups (472 ml). Set aside to cool. Remove and discard any fat that rises to the surface. Set aside.

Meanwhile, when chicken is cool enough to handle, remove chicken meat from bones. Cut into bite-size pieces; discard bones. Set aside.

MAKES 8 SERVINGS

> **Per serving:** calories 165 ◆ protein, 25 g ◆ carbohydrate, 0 g ◆ fat, 6 g (calories from fat, 33%) ◆ dietary fiber, 0 g ◆ cholesterol, 78 mg ◆ sodium, 65 mg ◆ potassium, 168 mg Joslin Exchanges: 4 low-fat meat

French-Style Chicken Pot Pie

1 pound (450 g) small new potatoes
¼ pound (115 g) frozen pearl onions
¼ pound (115 g) carrots, peeled and cut into ⅓-inch (.85 cm) coins
butter-flavored cooking spray
1 garlic clove, minced
½ pound (225 g) fresh mushrooms, sliced
1 cup (236 ml) reduced stock from poaching chicken

½ cup (118 ml) beef stock (page 44)
1 teaspoon (5 ml) crushed dried tarragon leaves
1 tablespoon (15 ml) cornstarch, dissolved in 1 tablespoon (15 ml) Madeira wine or water
1 cup (236 ml) frozen peas
poached chicken pieces (page 209)
½ sheet of frozen puff pastry dough, defrosted

Slice potatoes into ⅛-inch (.5 cm) coins. Steam over boiling water until just tender, about 2 minutes. Set aside. Steam pearl onions and carrots over boiling water until just tender, about 6 minutes. Set aside.

Meanwhile, in a nonstick skillet lightly sprayed with cooking spray, sauté garlic and mushrooms over low heat until mushrooms are limp, about 4 minutes. Transfer mushrooms to a medium-size saucepan. Add stocks and tarragon. Stir in cornstarch and Madeira. Add to saucepan and cook for 5 minutes, stirring, until thickened. Set aside.

Place chicken, potatoes, onions, carrots, and peas in a large ovenproof casserole. Pour on sauce.

Preheat oven to 400°F (205°C). Roll out thawed pastry on a lightly floured surface to ⅛-inch (.5 cm) thickness. Cut into 1-inch (2.5 cm) strips. Weave strips over chicken to form a lattice crust. Lightly spray with cooking spray.

Bake for 20 minutes, until pastry is puffed and golden brown.

MAKES 10 SERVINGS

Per serving: calories, 246 ◆ protein, 24 g ◆ carbohydrate, 21 g ◆ fat, 9 g (calories from fat, 33%) ◆ dietary fiber, 1 g ◆ cholesterol, 62 mg ◆ sodium, 76 mg ◆ potassium, 491 mg Joslin Exchanges: 3 low-fat meat, 1 vegetable, 1 bread/ starch

FALL SUPPER

◆

French-Style Chicken Pot Pie (page 210)

Mâche and Sliced Pear Salad with

Classic Vinaigrette (page 114)

Coeur à la Crème (page 427) with Fresh Raspberries

Per serving: 546 calories (30% fat)
Joslin Exchanges: 3 low-fat meat, 1 vegetable, 1 bread/starch, 2 fruit, 1 milk, 1 fat

Santa Fe Chicken Pot Pie

1 cup (236 ml) canned hominy, drained well

³/₄ pound (340 g) small zucchini, sliced into ¹/₃-inch (.85 cm) coins

¹/₄ pound (115 g) frozen pearl onions

vegetable oil cooking spray

2 to 3 garlic cloves, to taste, pressed or minced

1 fresh serrano chili, seeded and minced

1 pound (450 g) fresh plum tomatoes, peeled, seeded, and coarsely chopped, or 1 16-ounce (450 g) can Italian plum tomatoes, drained and coarsely chopped

1¹/₂ cups (354 ml) reduced stock from poaching chicken

2 tablespoons (30 ml) red wine vinegar

1 teaspoon (5 ml) ground cumin

¹/₂ teaspoon (2.5 ml) crushed dried thyme leaves

¹/₂ teaspoon (2.5 ml) crushed dried oregano leaves

1 tablespoon (15 ml) cornstarch, dissolved in 1 tablespoon (15 ml) stock or water

poached chicken pieces (page 209)

Corn Bread Topping

³/₄ cup (94 g) unbleached flour

¹/₄ cup (59 ml) plus 1 teaspoon (5 ml) stone-ground yellow cornmeal

2 tablespoons (30 ml) finely minced red bell pepper

2 tablespoons (30 ml) finely minced green bell pepper

1 tablespoon (15 ml) finely minced fresh serrano chili (optional)

2 tablespoons (30 g) margarine, softened

¹/₂ tablespoon (7.5 ml) baking powder

6 tablespoons (90 ml) skim milk

Rinse hominy in a colander, drain well, and set aside. Steam zucchini over boiling water until just tender, about 1 minute. Set aside. Steam pearl onions over boiling water until just tender, about 6 minutes. Set aside.

In a large nonstick skillet sprayed with cooking spray, sauté garlic, chili, and tomatoes over low heat until garlic is soft, about 3 minutes. Transfer mixture to a medium-size saucepan. Add stock, vinegar, cumin, thyme, and oregano. Simmer for 10 minutes. Add dissolved cornstarch; simmer, stirring, until thickened. Remove from heat; set aside.

In a large ovenproof casserole, combine chicken pieces, zucchini, onions, and hominy. Toss with prepared tomato sauce.

To prepare corn bread topping, combine all ingredients except 1 teaspoon (5 ml) cornmeal. Mix lightly. Turn out onto a lightly floured surface and knead for a minute or two. Roll out and cut into whimsical shapes (chickens, crescents, stars), using all the dough. Place over chicken. Sprinkle crust with remaining 1 teaspoon (5 ml) cornmeal.

Preheat oven to 425°F (220°C). Bake for 15 to 20 minutes, until crust is browned and filling is bubbling. Serve immediately.

MAKES 8 SERVINGS

Per serving: calories, 297 ◆ protein, 29 g ◆ carbohydrate, 23 g ◆ fat, 10 g (calories from fat, 30%) ◆ dietary fiber, 1 g ◆ cholesterol, 78 mg ◆ sodium, 223 mg ◆ potassium, 505 mg Joslin Exchanges: 3½ low-fat meat, 1 vegetable, 1 bread/starch

Chicken Bouillabaisse

Roasting the tomatoes and red peppers greatly enhances their flavor in this chicken counterpart to the Mediterranean's famous fish stew. This is a very hearty soup meal that needs a knife and fork as well as a soupspoon. If boneless thighs aren't available, you can always use bone-in thighs or legs.

2½ pounds (1.25 kg) fresh tomatoes

2 large red bell peppers, about 1 pound (450 g), seeded

½ pound (225 g) onions, peeled and chopped

1 leek, white part only, well rinsed and thinly sliced

3 garlic cloves, minced

1 tablespoon (15 ml) olive oil

1 small fennel bulb, about ½ pound (225 g), cut into thin crosswise slices

1 tablespoon (15 ml) fresh thyme leaves or 1 teaspoon (5 ml) crushed dried

2 bay leaves

⅛ teaspoon (.6 ml) crushed saffron threads

½ teaspoon salt (2.5 ml) (optional)

¼ teaspoon (1.25 ml) freshly ground pepper or to taste

2 cups (472 ml) chicken stock (page 45)

1 cup (236 ml) dry white wine

6 boneless and skinless chicken thighs, about 3½ ounces (99 g) each

½ cup (93 g) basmati rice, washed well and drained

⅓ cup (78 ml) shredded fresh basil for garnish

Preheat broiler; line a shallow baking pan with aluminum foil. Place tomatoes and peppers in pan. Roast under broiler for about 10 minutes, turning frequently with tongs, until skin begins to blacken. Remove from oven; place tomatoes in cold water and peppers in a plastic bag.

When cool enough to handle, peel blackened skins off tomatoes and peppers; remove seeds. Coarsely chop and set aside.

In a large heavy pot, sauté onions, leeks, and garlic in olive oil over low heat until onions are transparent, about 5 minutes. Add tomatoes, peppers, fennel, thyme, bay leaves, saffron, salt, pepper, stock, and wine. Bring to a boil. Reduce heat and simmer for about 5 minutes.

Remove all visible fat from chicken. Add thighs to pot. Cover and simmer for about 35 to 40 minutes or until chicken is tender. Stir occasionally.

Meanwhile, bring about 2 cups (472 ml) water to a boil in a small saucepan. Add basmati rice, cover, and reduce heat to medium-low. Cook rice for 15 minutes; drain in a colander. Set aside to drain; keep warm.

When soup is done, place 2 tablespoons (30 ml) cooked rice in each of 6 flat-bottomed soup plates. Place a chicken thigh on top of rice and ladle soup over the chicken and rice, discarding bay leaves. Garnish with shredded fresh basil and serve.

MAKES 6 SERVINGS

Per serving: calories, 336 ◆ protein, 24 g ◆ carbohydrate, 36 g ◆ fat, 12 g (calories from fat, 32%) ◆ dietary fiber, 2 g ◆ cholesterol 70 mg ◆ sodium, 284 mg ◆ potassium, 1,057 mg Joslin Exchanges: 3 low-fat meat, 2 bread/starch

Chicken with Apples and Cider Vinegar Sauce

In the Normandy region of France, the area's highly favored apple cider vinegar is used in a reduction sauce for fish. The same ingredients work equally well with chicken. We added tart apples for extra flavor and used a smidgen of unsalted butter to smooth the sauce.

Fresh chanterelles, the mild-flavored trumpet-shaped wild mushrooms, are perfect here, but if they're not available you can use another wild mushroom (shiitake, porcini, morel) or sliced cultivated mushrooms. Serve with Spaghetti Squash with Shallot Butter (page 358) and a green vegetable.

2 whole skinless and boneless chicken breasts, about ½ pound (225 g) each, halved
1 tablespoon (15 ml) olive oil
½ pound (225 g) fresh chanterelles or cultivated mushrooms, chopped
½ cup (118 ml) chopped onion
2 Granny Smith apples, about 6 ounces (180 g) each, peeled, cored, and cut into ¼-inch (.75 cm) slices

juice of ½ lemon
2 tablespoons (30 ml) chopped fresh parsley
1 teaspoon fresh thyme leaves or ¼ teaspoon (1.25 ml) crushed dried
freshly ground pepper to taste
¼ cup (59 ml) cider vinegar
¼ cup (59 ml) chicken stock (page 45)
1 teaspoon (5 g) unsalted butter

Remove all visible fat from chicken breasts. Place each half between 2 sheets of wax paper; pound until very thin.

Heat 2 teaspoons (10 ml) olive oil in a heavy nonstick skillet over medium-high heat. Add chicken breasts and sauté until golden, about 2 minutes on each side. Transfer chicken to a heated platter; keep warm.

Add remaining 1 teaspoon (5 ml) oil to skillet; sauté mushrooms and onion over low heat until onion is soft and transparent, about 5 minutes. Transfer mushrooms and onions to another platter. Add apples, lemon juice, chopped parsley, thyme, and pepper to skillet; sauté for 2 to 4 minutes, until apples are soft but not mushy. Transfer apples to mushroom platter.

Add vinegar to skillet; raise heat and cook until vinegar reduces to a syrup, about 1 minute. Whisk in stock and butter. Return chicken to skillet and cook, basting with sauce, until chicken is done, about 4 minutes. Do not overcook.

Return mushrooms, onion, and apples to skillet. Heat through. Arrange chicken on a heated serving platter. Pour apples and sauce over and around the chicken. Serve immediately.

MAKES 4 SERVINGS

Per serving: calories, 244 ◆ protein, 29 g ◆ carbohydrate, 16 g ◆ fat, 8 g (calories from fat, 29%) ◆ dietary fiber, 1 g ◆ cholesterol, 75 mg ◆ sodium, 167 mg ◆ potassium, 594 mg Joslin Exchanges: 4 low-fat meat, 1 fruit

Chicken Vindaloo

This dish from the southwest coast of India can be made with chicken, lamb, or pork and is usually fiery hot and spicy. We've lightened the recipe and tamed the heat. If you like hot food, add more cumin, chili powder, and red pepper flakes. Serve it with Bulgur Pilaf (page 279), omitting the fresh mint and stirring in 1 tablespoon (15 ml) currants before serving.

1 teaspoon (5 ml) ground cumin
1 teaspoon (5 ml) turmeric
½ tablespoon (7.5 ml) chili powder
3 tablespoons (45 ml) white wine vinegar
2 whole skinless and boneless chicken breasts, ½ pound (225 g) each, halved
½ cup (118 ml) chicken stock (page 45)
2 bay leaves
olive oil cooking spray

1 cup (236 ml) chopped onion
3 garlic cloves, minced
1 tablespoon (15 ml) chopped fresh ginger
1 medium-size tomato, about 5 ounces (140 g), peeled, seeded, and chopped
⅛ teaspoon (.6 ml) hot red pepper flakes or to taste
½ cup (118 ml) chopped cilantro (fresh coriander)

In a small bowl, make a paste of cumin, turmeric, chili powder, and 1 tablespoon (15 ml) vinegar. Cut slits in chicken breasts and rub cumin paste into slits. Place chicken breasts in a nonreactive baking dish. Let stand for 15 minutes. Add stock, bay leaves, and remaining 2 tablespoons (30 ml) vinegar to baking dish. Cover with plastic wrap and refrigerate for 3 to 5 hours.

Lightly spray a large nonstick sauté pan with cooking spray. Place over low heat; add onion, garlic, and ginger. Sauté until onions are wilted, about 4 minutes. Add tomato, red pepper flakes, and chicken with marinade. Bring to a simmer, cover, and cook for 10 to 15 minutes, until chicken is no longer pink when slashed with a knife. Transfer chicken to a heated serving platter; keep warm. Raise heat under pan; boil briefly to reduce sauce. Stir in cilantro. Spoon sauce over chicken.

MAKES 4 SERVINGS

Per serving: calories, 176 ◆ protein, 28 g ◆ carbohydrate, 8 g ◆ fat, 4 g (calories from fat, 20%) ◆ dietary fiber, 1 g ◆ cholesterol, 72 mg ◆ sodium, 84 mg ◆ potassium, 434 mg
Joslin Exchanges: 4 low-fat meat, 1 vegetable

Tandoori-Style Lemon and Tahini Cornish Hens

The tahini-based marinade complements the smokiness of the hen when it's roasted at a high temperature. The cooking technique results in moist meat, similar to poultry that's been cooked in a tandoor—a clay-lined oven. You can prepare the hens a day ahead and simply roast them the next day.

Cool the spiciness with Cilantro Chutney and offer steamed basmati rice (page 288). The recipe comes from Prasad Chirnomula of Kismet, an award-winning Indian restaurant in Connecticut. If you prefer, you can use all mint instead of cilantro in the chutney.

2 fresh hot red chilies, seeded and coarsely chopped
2 garlic cloves, quartered
1 teaspoon (5 ml) ground cumin
½ teaspoon (2.5 ml) ground coriander
½ teaspoon (2.5 ml) salt (optional)
freshly ground pepper to taste
juice of 3 lemons
3 tablespoons (45 ml) tahini
3 Rock Cornish hens, about 1 pound (450 g) each

In a food processor, place chilies, garlic, cumin, coriander, salt, pepper, lemon juice, and tahini. Process to a smooth paste.

Working with one hen at a time, rinse hen, trim off excess fat from neck cavity, and discard giblets and neck. Place hen breast side down on a work surface. Using poultry or kitchen shears, split lengthwise along backbone. Turn hen over and press down with your palm to flatten breastbone. Remove skin from hen. Score meat diagonally at 1-inch (2.5 cm) intervals, making ½-inch-deep (1.5 cm) cuts. Repeat with other hens. Place hens in a glass baking dish.

Rub both sides of each hen with tahini paste; cover and refrigerate for at least 1 hour and up to 24 hours.

Preheat oven to 425°F (220°C). Place hens breast side down in a roasting pan. Roast for 15 minutes. Turn hens over and continue to roast for another 15 minutes, until juices run clear when thighs are pierced with a fork. Transfer to a carving board; let stand for 5 minutes. Split hens in half lengthwise and serve.

MAKES 6 SERVINGS

Per serving: calories, 250 ◆ protein, 24 g ◆ carbohydrate, 5 g ◆ fat, 15 g (calories from fat, 54%) ◆ dietary fiber, trace ◆ cholesterol, 61 mg ◆ sodium, 244 mg ◆ potassium, 88 mg Joslin Exchanges: 3 low-fat meat, 1 fat

Cilantro or Mint Chutney

⅓ cup (78 ml) chopped green bell pepper
1 cup (236 ml) loosely packed cilantro (fresh coriander) or mint leaves
2 tablespoons (30 ml) chopped onion
leaves from 1 fresh mint sprig (omit from mint version)

½ teaspoon (2.5 ml) minced fresh ginger
½ teaspoon (2.5 ml) minced garlic
pinch of salt (optional)
3 cloves
2 cups (472 ml) plain low-fat yogurt

In a food processor or blender, combine everything but the yogurt. Process until finely minced. Stir in yogurt. Cover and refrigerate until ready to use.

MAKES ABOUT 2½ CUPS (590 ML)

Per ¼-cup serving: calories, 34 ◆ protein, 3 g ◆ carbohydrate, 4 g ◆ fat, 1 g (calories from fat, 25%) ◆ dietary fiber, trace ◆ cholesterol, 3 mg ◆ sodium, 33 mg ◆ potassium, 140 mg Joslin Exchanges: ½ low-fat milk

INDIAN SUPPER PARTY

◆

Tandoori-Style Lemon and Tahini Cornish Hens (page 217)

Cilantro Chutney (page 218)

Basmati Rice (page 288)

Spinach with Mint (page 355)

Naan (page 398)

Orange Slices with Pomegranate Seeds (page 236)

Per serving: 608 calories (30% fat)
Joslin Exchanges: 3 low-fat meat, 3 bread/starch, 1 vegetable, 1 fruit, 1/2 low-fat milk, 1 fat

Lion's Head Meatballs

This is a low-fat, low-salt adaptation of a favorite Chinese dish.

The Chinese often include animals in the names of dishes to indicate high quality in the food. The word *lion* signifies not only high quality but also the large size of the meatballs.

4 to 6 dried Asian mushrooms, soaked in water for 15 minutes and finely chopped, discarding soaking liquid

1 pound (450 g) lean ground turkey or chicken

10 canned water chestnuts, finely minced

2 scallions, white part only, finely minced

2 ⅛-inch thick (.5 cm) slices of fresh ginger, peeled and finely minced

2 large egg whites

1½ tablespoons (22.5 ml) cornstarch

dash of freshly ground pepper

1 tablespoon (15 ml) dry sherry (optional)

1 cup (236 ml) chicken stock (page 45)

2 teaspoons (10 ml) peanut oil

1 Chinese cabbage, about 2 pounds (900 g), leaves separated

Combine mushrooms, ground meat, water chestnuts, scallions, ginger, egg whites, cornstarch, pepper, and sherry; mix well. Form into 6 meatballs; brown quickly in a sauté pan in 1 teaspoon (5 ml) oil. Remove meatballs; add remaining 1 teaspoon (5 ml) oil to pan and sauté cabbage leaves until slightly limp. Place meatballs on cabbage leaves; add stock. Cover and simmer for 1 hour. Arrange cabbage and meatballs on a serving platter; keep warm. Reduce chicken stock over high heat until slightly thickened, skimming off any fat. Spoon sauce over meatballs and cabbage. Serve immediately.

MAKES 6 SERVINGS

Per serving: calories, 118 ◆ protein, 11 g ◆ carbohydrate, 7 g ◆ fat, 5 g (calories from fat, 38%) ◆ dietary fiber, trace ◆ cholesterol, 21 mg ◆ sodium, 151 mg ◆ potassium, 497 mg Joslin Exchanges: 1½ low-fat meat, 1 vegetable

Family Turkey Loaf

This recipe was inspired by one of the world's most publicized meat loaves. The original dish, made with ground beef and ground pork and served with a savory gravy, is on the daily menu at 72 Market Street Restaurant in Venice, California.

Serve our homey version with Apple Slaw (page 93) and Mashed Turnips with Roasted Garlic (page 361) for a simple family meal. If you have leftovers, use it for sandwiches the next day.

Turkey Loaf

olive oil cooking spray
3/4 cup (177 ml) minced onion
3/4 cup (177 ml) minced scallion, including some green
1/2 cup (118 ml) minced celery
1/2 cup (118 ml) minced carrot
1/4 cup (59 ml) minced green bell pepper
1/4 cup (59 ml) minced red bell pepper
2 garlic cloves, minced
1/2 teaspoon (2.5 ml) salt (optional)
1/4 teaspoon (1.25 ml) cayenne pepper or to taste

1 teaspoon (5 ml) freshly ground pepper or to taste
1/2 teaspoon (2.5 ml) ground cumin
1/2 teaspoon (2.5 ml) ground nutmeg
1/2 cup (118 ml) evaporated skim milk
1/2 cup (118 ml) low-sodium ketchup
2 pounds (900 g) ground turkey
2 large eggs, beaten
2 large egg whites
3/4 cup (75 g) fine dry bread crumbs

Preheat oven to 350°F (180°C).

Spray a large nonstick skillet with cooking spray. Add onion, scallion, celery, carrot, bell peppers, and garlic. Sauté over low heat until vegetables are tender and liquid is absorbed, about 10 minutes. Cool and set aside.

Combine salt, cayenne, pepper, cumin, and nutmeg. Add to vegetable mixture. Stir in evaporated skim milk, ketchup, turkey, eggs, egg whites, and bread crumbs. Mix well.

Form into a loaf and place on a baking sheet or in a shallow baking dish lightly sprayed with cooking spray. Bake 45 to 50 minutes. Remove from oven and pour off all fat. Let stand for 10 minutes before slicing into 8 portions.

MAKES 8 SERVINGS

Per serving: calories, 202 ◆ protein, 17 g ◆ carbohydrate, 15 g ◆ fat, 8 g (calories from fat, 36%) ◆ dietary fiber, trace ◆ cholesterol, 85 mg ◆ sodium, 404 mg ◆ potassium, 379 mg Joslin Exchanges: 2 low-fat meat, 1 bread/starch

Savory Gravy

4 shallots, minced
1 tablespoon (15 ml) fresh thyme leaves or 1 teaspoon (5 ml) crushed dried
1 bay leaf
freshly ground pepper to taste

1 cup (236 ml) dry white wine
1 cup (236 ml) beef stock (page 44)
1 cup (236 ml) chicken stock (page 45)
2 teaspoons (10 g) unsalted butter

In a heavy saucepan, cook shallots, thyme, bay leaf, pepper, and white wine over medium-high heat for 5 minutes, until mixture is reduced to a glaze.

Add stocks and cook over high heat until mixture is reduced by half. Remove from heat. Whisk in butter. Discard bay leaf. Serve 2 tablespoons (30 ml) gravy with each slice of meat loaf.

MAKES 8 SERVINGS

Per 2-tablespoon (30 ml) serving: calories, 27 ◆ protein, trace ◆ carbohydrate, 2 g ◆ fat, 2 g (calories from fat, 66%) ◆ dietary fiber, trace ◆ cholesterol, 6 mg ◆ sodium, 23 mg ◆ potassium, 100 mg Joslin Exchanges: free

Torta Rustica

This stunning whole-meal pie has been the star at countless picnics, parties, and light suppers with friends. Made one at a time, or by the dozens, our original recipe was made with chorizo, a highly seasoned pork sausage used in Mexican and Spanish cooking, and lots of whole-milk mozzarella.

The slimmed-down dish uses turkey Italian sausage and a modest amount of low-fat cheese, and if it's not quite as deliciously rich, there's a substantial reduction in calories and fat. You could also use the low-fat chicken and turkey sausages (some with sun-dried tomatoes) from New Mexico that are now showing up in the markets. Even if you're not skillful at bread making, the bread dough for this pie goes together quite easily.

1 ¼-ounce (7 g) package active rapid-rise dry yeast
1¼ cups (295 ml) warm water
1 tablespoon (15 g) margarine, melted
1 teaspoon (5 ml) salt (optional)
1 teaspoon (4 g) sugar
3 to 3¼ cups (375 to 406 g) unbleached flour
olive oil cooking spray
1 large white plastic trash bag (with no lettering)
1 pound (450 g) Italian turkey sausage or New Mexican chicken and turkey sausage
1 large onion, about ½ pound (225 g), thinly sliced

2 medium-size fresh tomatoes, about ½ pound (225 g), thinly sliced
1 tablespoon (15 ml) chopped fresh oregano or 1 teaspoon (5 ml) crushed dried
1 tablespoon (15 ml) fresh thyme leaves or 1 teaspoon (5 ml) crushed dried
1 tablespoon (15 ml) chopped fresh basil or 1 teaspoon (5 ml) crushed dried
6 ounces (180 g) nonfat mozzarella cheese or reduced-fat Monterey Jack cheese
2 tablespoons (12 g) grated fresh Parmesan cheese

In a large bowl, combine yeast and ¼ cup (59 ml) warm water. Stir until dissolved. Stir in 1 cup (236 ml) warm water, melted margarine, salt, and sugar. Gradually stir in 2½ cups (313 g) flour, blending until dough is smooth and elastic. Sprinkle half of remaining flour onto a board. Turn out dough and knead dough until smooth and elastic, adding rest of flour as needed.

Place dough in a large bowl sprayed with cooking spray. Turn dough to coat all sides. Place bowl in a large white plastic trash bag. Close with tie and set on kitchen counter for 30 to 40 minutes to allow dough to rise, until doubled.

Punch dough down, squeezing out air bubbles. Shape into a smooth ball. With a sharp knife, divide dough into 2 equal portions. On floured board, roll out one portion to a 9-inch (23 cm) round. Place in a 9- by 1½-inch (23 by 4 cm) cake pan lightly sprayed with cooking spray.

Meanwhile, remove casings from turkey sausage. Coarsely chop and sauté over medium-low heat until sausage is browned. Drain sausage well on paper towels. Place sausage on bread round. Arrange onion and tomato slices over sausage. Sprinkle with herbs. Top with mozzarella and Parmesan cheese.

Preheat oven to 350°F (180°C). Adjust rack to lowest position. Roll out second portion of dough into a 9-inch (23 cm) square. Cut into 1-inch-wide (2.5 cm) strips. Weave strips over filling in a lattice pattern, tucking ends of dough down around filling at the pan rim.

Bake for 35 to 40 minutes or until torta is richly browned. Cool in pan for 5 minutes. Loosen edges with a sharp knife. Remove from pan; cool on a wire rack. Serve warm or at room temperature. When ready to serve, slice into 8 wedges.

MAKES 8 SERVINGS

Per serving: calories, 331 ◆ protein, 19 g ◆ carbohydrate, 42 g ◆ fat, 9 g (calories from fat, 24%) ◆ dietary fiber, 1 g ◆ cholesterol, 5 mg ◆ sodium, 229 mg ◆ potassium, 180 mg Joslin Exchanges: 2 low-fat meat, 2 vegetable, 2 bread/ starch

---

SUPER BOWL BUFFET

◆

Crudités with Chili and Lime (page 4)

Mugs of Hot Tomato Soup (page 49)

Torta Rustica (page 223)

Warm Grapefruit and Orange with Sherry Sauce (page 437)

Per serving: 444 calories (16% fat)
Joslin Exchanges: 2 low-fat meat, 4 vegetable, 2 bread/starch, 1 fruit

LEAN MEATS

A potentially high-fat food, red meat is still one of nature's best sources of complete protein and iron. Eating red meat can be a part of eating light—what's important is to select the leanest cuts, to cook them so that the meat doesn't dry out, and to serve them in modest portions.

When it's trimmed of all fat, today's pork loin can be as lean as veal (and contains less cholesterol), and pork tenderloin now competes with chicken as a lean meat. Lamb, too, has gone on a diet, and today's cuts are quite lean. With its luscious taste and juicy texture, even when a lamb chop is completely trimmed of fat the cooked meat is still moist, tender, and delicious.

Veal is the leanest cut of beef. Milk-fed veal is available nationwide. Look for ivory-colored veal with just a blush of pink. When you're selecting beef, go for the lean—tenderloin, sirloin, flank, rump, or top round. Extra-lean ground beef will have 15 percent or less fat; ground sirloin will have 10 percent or less fat. If you have a food processor, you can grind the beef yourself using the metal chopping blade.

We like our hamburgers so thick that they're like chopped steak. Grilled or broiled to medium-rare, they're juicy and especially good for hearty, casual eating that's deceptively easy on the calories.

Fresh and Light Hamburgers

Cowboy Cheeseburgers

To 1 pound (450 g) extra-lean ground beef, add 1 small minced onion and 1 tablespoon (15 ml) minced fresh jalapeño chili. Form into 4 patties of equal size about 3/4 inch (2 cm) thick without compacting the meat. Mix together 1/4 teaspoon (1.25 ml) ground coriander, 1/4 teaspoon (1.25 ml) ground cumin, 1/4 teaspoon (1.25 ml) salt (optional), and 1/4 teaspoon (1.25 ml) freshly ground pepper. Sprinkle mixture on both sides of patties. Grill or broil, 4 inches (10 cm) from source of heat, for 3 minutes on each side for medium-rare. Place 1 tablespoon (15 ml) shredded nonfat mozzarella cheese on center of each patty. Cook for another minute or until cheese melts. Serve each patty on a warmed 8-inch (20 cm) flour tortilla, topped with a tomato slice, a few cilantro (fresh coriander) sprigs, and 1 tablespoon (15 ml) commercial taco sauce.

MAKES 4 SERVINGS

Per serving: calories, 289 ◆ protein, 21 g ◆ carbohydrate, 23 g ◆ fat, 13 g (calories from fat, 40%) ◆ dietary fiber, 2 g ◆ cholesterol, 54 mg ◆ sodium, 305 mg ◆ potassium, 367 mg Joslin Exchanges: 2½ medium-fat meat, 1½ bread/starch

Greek Burgers

To 1 pound (450 g) extra-lean ground beef, add 1 minced garlic clove, 2 tablespoons (30 ml) fresh lemon juice, 1 teaspoon (5 ml) crushed dried oregano leaves, 1/4 teaspoon (1.25 ml) ground cumin, 1/4 teaspoon (1.25 ml) freshly ground pepper, 1 minced medium-size plum tomato, and 2 tablespoons (30 ml) minced flat-leaf parsley. Form into 4 patties about 3/4 inch (2 cm) thick. Grill or broil, 4 inches (10 cm) from source of heat, for 3 minutes on each side for medium-rare. Cut the top third off each of four 6-inch (15 cm) whole-wheat pita pocket breads. Turn the cut-off piece round side down; tuck inside pocket bread to reinforce bottom. Place a grilled burger in each pocket bread along with a romaine lettuce leaf and paper-thin slices from 1 small red onion. Pass 1/4 cup (59 ml) Cilantro Chutney (page 218) to spoon into burgers.

MAKES 4 SERVINGS

Per serving: calories, 346 ◆ protein, 27 ◆ carbohydrate, 26 g ◆ fat, 15 g (calories from fat, 39%) ◆ dietary fiber, 4 g ◆ cholesterol, 70 mg ◆ sodium, 285 mg ◆ potassium, 441 mg Joslin Exchanges: 3 medium-fat meat, 2 bread/starch

Note: These hamburgers could also be made with lean ground lamb. The exchanges would stay the same, but lamb adds 17 calories and 2 grams of fat (mostly saturated fat) per serving.

BACKYARD BARBECUE

◆

Crudités and Fresh Herb Dip (page 6)

Cucumber Salad (page 89)

Maui Burgers (page 227)

Grilled Corn on the Cob (page 306)

Grilled Peach Halves (page 434) and Fresh Blackberries

Per serving: 465 calories (24% fat)
Joslin Exchanges: 2 medium-fat meat, 2½ bread/starch, 2 vegetable, 1 fruit

Maui Burgers

To 1 pound (450 g) extra-lean ground beef, add 1 minced garlic clove, 2 minced scallions, 1 teaspoon (5 ml) minced fresh ginger, and 1 tablespoon (15 ml) low-sodium soy sauce. Form into 4 patties of equal size about ¾ inch (2 cm) thick. Grill or broil, 4 inches (10 cm) from source of heat, for 7 minutes for medium-rare, turning once. While burgers are grilling, brush 4 slices of fresh or canned water-packed unsweetened pineapple with 1 teaspoon (5 ml) Worcestershire sauce. Grill until pineapple is heated through and seared with grill marks, about 6 minutes (2 minutes for canned pineapple). Serve each patty open-face on a 1-ounce (30 g) toasted slice of French bread, topped with grilled pineapple slice, and garnished with 1 tablespoon (15 ml) minced green bell pepper.

MAKES 4 SERVINGS

Per serving: calories, 282 ◆ protein, 20 g ◆ carbohydrate, 23 g ◆ fat, 13 g (calories from fat, 41%) ◆ dietary fiber, trace ◆ cholesterol, 53 mg ◆ sodium, 401 mg ◆ potassium, 307 mg Joslin Exchanges: 2 medium-fat meat, 1½ bread/starch

Parisian Burgers

To 1 pound (450 g) extra-lean ground beef, add 1 minced garlic clove, 1 tablespoon (15 ml) Dijon mustard, 1 tablespoon (15 ml) minced fresh tarragon or 1 teaspoon (5 ml) crushed dried, and ¼ teaspoon (.6 ml) freshly ground pepper. Form into 4 patties of equal size about ¾ inch (2 cm) thick. Grill or broil, 4 inches (10 cm) from source of heat, for 3 minutes on each side for medium-rare. Place 1 tablespoon (15 ml) crumbled low-fat goat cheese on center of each patty. Cook for another minute or until cheese melts. Serve each patty open-face on a toasted English muffin half, topped with a few alfalfa sprouts.

MAKES 4 SERVINGS

Per serving: calories, 257 ◆ protein, 20 g ◆ carbohydrate, 16 g ◆ fat, 12 g (calories from fat 42%) ◆ dietary fiber, trace ◆ cholesterol, 76 mg ◆ sodium, 340 mg ◆ potassium, 401 mg Joslin Exchanges: 3 medium-fat meat, 1 bread/starch

Reuben Burgers

To 1 pound (450 g) extra-lean ground beef, add 1 small minced onion and ¼ teaspoon (1.25 ml) freshly ground pepper. Form into 4 patties of equal size about ¾ inch (2 cm) thick. Grill or broil, 4 inches (10 cm) from source of heat, for 3 minutes on each side for medium-rare. Place 1 to 2 tablespoons (15 to 30 ml) drained sauerkraut on center of each patty and top with one 1-ounce (30 g) slice of low-fat Swiss cheese. Grill for 1 to 2 minutes, until cheese melts. Serve each patty open-face on a slice of toasted or grilled light rye bread. Top each serving with 1 tablespoon (15 ml) Russian Dressing (page 119).

MAKES 4 SERVINGS

Per serving: calories, 348 ◆ protein, 28 g ◆ carbohydrate, 18 g ◆ fat, 18 g (calories from fat, 46%) ◆ dietary fiber, 1 g ◆ cholesterol, 72 mg ◆ sodium, 460 mg* ◆ potassium, 387 mg Joslin Exchanges: 3 medium-fat meat, 1 vegetable, 1 bread/ starch

* Not recommended for low-sodium diets unless raw shredded cabbage is substituted for sauerkraut.

Beef Burgundy

A light and easy approach to an old favorite. To serve, mold steamed brown rice in a cup or timbale mold. Place in the center of each plate and surround with Beef Burgundy. Serve a crisp green salad on the side.

1¼ pounds (570 g) lean boneless sirloin
1 cup (236 ml) dry red wine
¼ cup (59 ml) beef stock (page 44)
2 shallots, minced
1 teaspoon (5 ml) fresh thyme leaves or ¼ teaspoon (1.25 ml) crushed dried
freshly ground pepper to taste
1 tablespoon (15 ml) olive oil

½ pound (225 g) small fresh mushrooms
½ pound (225 g) frozen pearl onions
1 small fresh plum tomato, about 3 ounces (85 g), peeled, seeded, and diced
2 teaspoons (10 ml) cornstarch
2 tablespoons (30 ml) cognac
chopped fresh flat-leaf parsley for garnish

Trim and discard fat from meat. Cut steak across grain into ⅛-inch (.5 cm) slices. In a medium-size bowl, mix together wine, stock, shallots, thyme, and pepper. Add meat and stir to coat. Let stand at room temperature for 30 minutes or cover and refrigerate for up to 3 hours.

Lift meat from marinade; drain, reserving marinade. In a heavy nonstick skillet, heat oil over medium heat. Add mushrooms and onions. Sauté, stirring frequently, until onions are translucent, about 6 minutes. Add meat and cook, stirring constantly, until meat is no longer pink, 4 to 5 minutes. Add tomatoes and reserved marinade. Cook, stirring, until mixture comes to a boil. Dissolve cornstarch in cognac. Stir into beef mixture. Cook, stirring, until slightly thickened. Garnish with parsley.

MAKES 4 SERVINGS

Per serving: calories, 224 ◆ protein, 22 g ◆ carbohydrate, 10 g ◆ fat, 10 g (calories from fat, 40%) ◆ dietary fiber, 1 g ◆ cholesterol, 60 mg ◆ sodium, 54 mg ◆ potassium, 668 mg
Joslin Exchanges: 2½ medium-fat meat, 2 vegetable

Stir-Fried Beef with Red Pepper Sauce

Tender strips of lean beef are paired with crisp vegetables for a quick Chinese meal that's perfect for a workday supper. Start the meat marinating in the morning; prepare the vegetables and cooking sauce while you steam some rice. Follow the meal with fresh tangerines or mandarin oranges and Chinese tea.

1 pound (450 g) boneless sirloin, trimmed of all fat
vegetable oil cooking spray
1 large onion, quartered and thinly sliced

6 ounces (180 g) fresh snow peas, ends trimmed and strings removed
2 cups (472 ml) bok choy, sliced 1 inch (2.5 cm) thick

Ginger Marinade

2 scallions, white part and 1 inch (2.5 cm) green, minced
1 tablespoon (15 ml) minced fresh ginger
1 garlic clove, minced
1 tablespoon (15 ml) low-sodium soy sauce
1/8 teaspoon (.6 ml) hot red pepper flakes

Cooking Sauce

1 teaspoon (5 ml) cornstarch
1/3 cup (78 ml) beef stock (page 44)
1/2 tablespoon (7.5 ml) grated orange zest
1 tablespoon (15 ml) fresh orange juice
1 tablespoon (15 ml) rice wine
1 tablespoon (15 ml) low-sodium soy sauce
1/8 teaspoon (.6 ml) dark sesame oil
1/8 teaspoon (.6 ml) hot red pepper flakes or to taste

Cut beef across the grain into very thin slanted slices. In a bowl, combine marinade ingredients. Add beef; stir to coat. Cover and refrigerate for at least 30 minutes or up to 9 hours.

To prepare cooking sauce, combine all ingredients. Set aside. Lightly spray a wok or nonstick skillet with cooking spray. Place over high heat. Add beef and stir-fry until meat is browned on the outside but still pink within, about 1½ minutes. Remove from pan and keep warm.

Add onion, snow peas, and bok choy to wok. Stir-fry for 3 minutes, until vegetables begin to wilt but are still crisp. Add a few drops of water if pan appears dry. Return meat to pan. Stir cooking sauce. Add to wok and cook, stirring, until sauce bubbles and thickens.

MAKES 4 SERVINGS

> **Per serving:** calories, 233 ◆ protein, 29 g ◆ carbohydrate, 12 g ◆ fat, 8 g (calories from fat, 30%) ◆ dietary fiber, 2 g ◆ cholesterol, 75 mg ◆ sodium, 364 mg ◆ potassium, 645 mg Joslin Exchanges: 4 medium-fat meat, 1 bread/starch

London Broil with Sun-Dried Tomato Sauce

The Sun-Dried Tomato Sauce is a wonderful piquant counterpoint to lean slices of steak, but since the dish is high in fat, balance it with a low-fat accompaniment such as a Vegetable Terrine (page 315).

Sun-Dried Tomato Sauce

1 ounce (30 g) sun-dried tomatoes (packed dry)
2 tablespoons (30 ml) white wine vinegar
2 tablespoons (30 ml) olive oil
1 tablespoon (15 ml) finely chopped shallot
1 scallion, white part and 1 inch (2.5 cm) green, finely chopped

1 garlic clove, minced
2 tablespoons (30 ml) chopped fresh flat-leaf parsley
1/2 teaspoon (2.5 ml) finely chopped drained capers
1/2 teaspoon (2.5 ml) chopped fresh tarragon or 1/8 teaspoon (.6 ml) crushed dried
freshly ground pepper to taste

London Broil

1 pound (450 g) boneless top round or flank steak, cut about 1 inch (2.5 cm) thick
2 garlic cloves, minced

1/2 teaspoon (2.5 ml) onion powder
1 teaspoon (5 ml) balsamic vinegar
freshly ground pepper to taste

In a small saucepan, simmer tomatoes in water to cover for 10 minutes. Remove from stove and let cool in water until ready to use.

Drain tomatoes, discarding cooking liquid; coarsely chop. Combine with remaining sauce ingredients. Cover and refrigerate sauce until ready to use. (Makes about ³/₄ cup.)

Meanwhile, trim all fat from London broil. In a small bowl, combine garlic, onion powder, balsamic vinegar, and pepper. Rub into meat. Let marinate for 1 hour. Grill or broil, 4 inches (10 cm) from source of heat, to desired doneness, about 5 minutes per side for medium-rare. Allow steak to rest for 10 minutes before cutting into thin slices at a 45° angle. Nap each serving with 1 tablespoon (15 ml) Sun-Dried Tomato Sauce. Cover and refrigerate remaining sauce for another use—such as a topping for grilled chicken, plain pasta, or steamed zucchini.

MAKES 6 SERVINGS

Per serving (with sauce):
calories, 176 ◆ protein, 18 g ◆ carbohydrate, 5 g ◆ fat, 10 g (calories from fat, 51%) ◆ dietary fiber, trace ◆ cholesterol, 50 mg ◆ sodium, 78 mg ◆ potassium, 333 mg
Joslin Exchanges: 3 medium-fat meat

Per serving (sauce alone):
calories, 56 ◆ protein, 1 g ◆ carbohydrate, 4 g ◆ fat, 5 g (calories from fat, 80%) ◆ dietary fiber, trace ◆ cholesterol, 0 mg ◆ sodium, 41 mg ◆ potassium, 100 mg
Joslin Exchanges: 1 fat

Steak Salad with Goat Cheese Croutons

Perfect for a summer day, this dazzling whole-meal salad is a great way to prepare a steak. This dish is also delicious prepared with boneless and skinless chicken breasts instead of beef.

Steak Salad

³/₄ pound (340 g) top sirloin, cut about 1 inch (2.5 cm) thick

2 tablespoons (30 ml) extra-virgin olive oil

1 teaspoon (5 ml) fresh lemon juice

1 teaspoon (5 ml) fresh thyme leaves or ¹/₄ teaspoon (1.25 ml) crushed dried

¹/₂ teaspoon (2.5 ml) chopped fresh rosemary or ¹/₈ teaspoon (.6 ml) crushed dried

¹/₂ teaspoon (2.5 ml) fennel seed

¹/₈ teaspoon (.6 ml) freshly ground pepper or to taste

1 cup (236 ml) chicken stock (page 45)

1 garlic clove, minced

³/₄ cup (177 ml) seedless grape halves, about 15 to 20 grapes

3 small fresh tomatoes, about ¹/₂ pound (225 g), peeled, seeded, and chopped

¹/₄ cup (59 ml) balsamic vinegar

1 quart (1 l) mixed salad greens, such as mâche, arugula, Boston lettuce, radicchio, and frisée

CANDLELIGHT DINNER ON THE DECK

◆

Crudités with Chili and Lime (page 4)

Creamy Gazpacho (page 56)

Steak Salad with Goat Cheese Croutons (page 232)

Fresh Blackberries

Raspberry Thumbprints (page 423)

Per serving: 578 calories (30% fat)
Joslin Exchanges: 2¹/₂ medium-fat meat, 1 vegetable, 2 bread/starch, 2 fruit, 1 fat, ¹/₂ nonfat milk

Goat Cheese Croutons

8 ¹/₄-inch (.75 cm) slices of French bread, cut from a baguette
1 garlic clove, peeled and cut in half

2 ounces (60 g) low-fat goat cheese, cut into 8 equal slices

Trim off all surface fat from sirloin. In a small bowl, mix together ¹/₂ tablespoon (7.5 ml) olive oil, lemon juice, thyme, rosemary, fennel, and pepper to form a paste. Spread over both sides of steak. Refrigerate meat for at least 30 minutes, up to 4 hours.

Grill or broil steak, 4 inches (10 cm) from source of heat, for 5 minutes on each side, until medium-rare. Keep warm.

Meanwhile, boil chicken stock in a medium-size heavy saucepan until reduced to about ¹/₄ cup (59 ml), about 10 minutes. In a medium-size heavy skillet, heat remaining 1¹/₂ tablespoons (22.5 ml) olive oil over medium heat. Add garlic and grapes. Sauté until garlic is soft and grapes begin to cook. Add tomatoes, reduced stock, and vinegar. Continue to cook for 2 minutes, until tomatoes are heated through.

To prepare goat cheese croutons, arrange slices of bread on a heavy baking sheet. Heat a broiler until very hot. Broil croutons until tops are lightly browned. Rub bread with cut garlic. Turn oven temperature to 450° F (230° C). Place a slice of goat cheese on each crouton; bake in oven until cheese begins to melt, about 1 minute.

To serve, mound salad greens in the center of 4 dinner plates. Slice steak thinly on a diagonal. Fan slices around one side of greens. Spoon dressing over steak and greens. Arrange croutons on the opposite side, allowing 2 croutons per person. Serve immediately.

MAKES 4 SERVINGS

Per serving (steak salad alone): calories, 290 ◆ protein, 19 g ◆ carbohydrate, 12 g ◆ fat, 6 g (calories from fat, 18%) ◆ dietary fiber, 1 g ◆ cholesterol, 57 mg ◆ sodium, 66 mg ◆ potassium, 576 mg
Joslin Exchanges: 2½ medium-fat meat, 1 fruit

Per serving (cheese croutons alone): calories, 105 ◆ protein, 4 g ◆ carbohydrate, 15 g ◆ fat, 3 g (calories from fat, 25%) ◆ dietary fiber, trace ◆ cholesterol, 10 mg ◆ sodium, 231 mg ◆ potassium, 27 mg
Joslin Exchanges: 1 bread/starch, 1 fat

Persian Pot Roast

We love this very special beef dish! The combination of spices, citrus, and tomatoes with the essence of walnuts gives the roast a rich, deep flavor—and it smells so terrific as it cooks that everyone will be in the kitchen long before dinner.

Pomegranates are used in meat cookery throughout the Middle East. Since they're in season only part of the year, you might want to freeze some seeds so you can make this dish anytime, adding them to the sauce frozen. You can also substitute chopped orange sections for the pomegranate seeds in the sauce.

1 tablespoon (15 ml) walnut oil
2¾ pounds (1.3 kg) rump roast, trimmed of all fat
2 large onions, about ¾ pound (340 g), sliced and separated into rings
2 garlic cloves, thinly sliced
1 teaspoon (5 ml) ground cinnamon
freshly ground pepper to taste
¼ teaspoon (1.25 ml) ground ginger

1 teaspoon (5 ml) grated orange zest
6 large fresh plum tomatoes, about 1½ pounds (675 g), seeded and finely chopped
1½ cups (354 ml) beef stock (page 44)
seeds from 1 large pomegranate, about ½ pound (225 g)
1 tablespoon (15 ml) ground walnuts for garnish

Preheat oven to 325° F (165° C). In a heavy flameproof casserole or Dutch oven with a lid, heat oil over medium heat. Add rump roast; brown on all sides. When roast is brown, pour off all fat and pan juices. Scatter onion and garlic slices around roast. Season with cinnamon, pepper, ginger, and orange zest. Add tomatoes and stock. Bring to a simmer.

Cover and bake until meat is fork tender, about 2¼ hours. Turn meat and baste with pan juices 2 or 3 times during cooking time. When roast is done, remove meat from casserole; keep warm. Skim any fat from the pan juices. Return casserole to stove. Bring to a boil over medium-high heat and cook until reduced by half. Pour sauce through a sieve, pressing solids to extract their flavor and thicken the sauce. Return strained sauce to casserole. Discard solids. Add pomegranate seeds to sauce. Simmer until heated through.

Transfer roast to a carving board and slice against the grain into ¼-inch (.75 cm) slices. Arrange slices on a heated serving platter. Nap with sauce. Sprinkle with ground walnuts.

MAKES 12 SERVINGS

Per serving: calories, 198 ◆ protein, 22 g ◆ carbohydrate, 9 g ◆ fat, 8 g (calories from fat, 36%) ◆ dietary fiber, 1 g ◆ cholesterol, 64 mg ◆ sodium, 46 mg ◆ potassium, 454 mg Joslin Exchanges: 3 medium-fat meat, 1 bread/starch

---

AUTUMN DINNER

◆

Mixed Greens with Russian Dressing (page 119)

Persian Pot Roast (page 234)

Basmati Rice with Parsley and Chives (page 288)

Roasted Beets Vinaigrette (page 325)

Poached Pears with Crème Fraîche (page 428)

Per serving: 565 calories (27% fat)
Joslin Exchanges: 3 medium-fat meat, 3 vegetable, 2 bread/starch, 1 fruit, ½ nonfat milk

Seeding a Pomegranate

If you work under water when freeing the seeds of a pomegranate, you won't get the bright crimson juice all over you and the kitchen. Cut pomegranate into quarters. Place in a deep bowl of water. While working under water, gently remove the connecting pulp to free the seeds. Discard shell and pulp. Drain seeds on paper towels.

To freeze seeds for future use, pack in a zip-lock freezer bag (use the smallest size possible to minimize the airspace) and place sealed bag in an airtight freezer container. Freeze for up to 6 months. The seeds will separate easily while still frozen.

Picadillo Super Nacho

A popular dish in many Spanish-speaking countries, picadillo is usually made with ground pork and beef, plus tomatoes, onions, olives, nuts, and other regional ingredients. We've modified and lightened a Mexican recipe so we can enjoy it as a supersized nacho over refried beans for a casual family supper.

Scoop up the picadillo with warm Flour Tortilla Chips (page 371) and pass the *Salsa Fresca* (page 8).

Picadillo

¾ pound (340 g) ground lean top round

4 fresh plum tomatoes, about 1 pound (450 g), seeded and chopped, or 2 cups (472 ml) drained canned Italian plum tomatoes, chopped

3 scallions, white part and 1 inch (2.5 cm) green, chopped

2 garlic cloves, minced

1 tart apple, about 6 ounces (180 g), peeled, cored, and chopped

1 medium-size red bell pepper, about 5 ounces (140 g), seeded and chopped

1 tablespoon (15 ml) minced fresh jalapeño chili

½ teaspoon (2.5 ml) crushed dried thyme

½ teaspoon (2.5 ml) crushed dried oregano

½ teaspoon (2.5 ml) ground cumin

Refried Beans

1 medium-size onion, chopped
2 teaspoons (10 ml) olive oil
1 tablespoon (15 ml) minced fresh
  jalapeño chili

1 16-ounce (450 g) can pinto beans,
  drained and rinsed well
3 tablespoons (45 ml) shredded
  Monterey Jack cheese

Place a large nonstick skillet over medium heat and sauté ground round until well browned, breaking up any clumps as it cooks. Drain off any fat. Add tomatoes, scallion, garlic, apple, red pepper, and jalapeño. Reduce heat to low; simmer for 5 minutes. Add herbs and cumin. Simmer for another 10 minutes, until liquid is absorbed.

Meanwhile, in a large nonstick skillet over low heat, sauté onion in olive oil until onion begins to brown, 8 to 10 minutes. Add jalapeño and beans. Stir often, using back of a spoon or a potato masher to coarsely mash beans, until mixture thickens slightly, about 5 minutes.

Preheat oven to 400° F (205° C). Spread beans in a 10-inch (25 cm) round on a large ovenproof platter. Top evenly with picadillo. Cover with aluminum foil. Bake until hot in center, 15 to 20 minutes. Uncover and sprinkle with cheese. Bake, uncovered, until cheese melts, about 5 minutes.

MAKES 6 SERVINGS

Per serving: calories, 287 ♦ protein, 22 g ♦ carbohydrate, 34 g ♦ fat, 7 g (calories from fat, 22%) ♦ dietary fiber, 1 g ♦ cholesterol, 36 mg ♦ sodium, 98 mg ♦ potassium, 441 mg Joslin Exchanges: 2 medium-fat meat, 2 bread/starch

Microwave Browning

The microwave is a great way to brown ground meat quickly, while extracting most of the fat. Crumble the ground meat into a 3-quart (2.75 l) microwave casserole. Cover and cook on HIGH for 5 minutes. Stir to break up meat. Drain meat in a colander to remove any fat.

Beef Tenderloin with Vegetable Medley

A trimmer version of châteaubriand, this is an elegant and delicious way to serve beef to a crowd. With our advance preparation steps, the special dinner goes together the day of the party with a minimum of fuss.

Beef Fillet and Marinade

1 6-pound (2.75 kg) whole fillet of beef
¾ cup (177 ml) dry red wine
1 tablespoon (15 ml) dry sherry
4 to 6 peppercorns, to taste
2 garlic cloves, crushed
2 scallions, white part only, chopped

½ teaspoon (2.5 ml) crushed dried thyme
½ teaspoon (2.5 ml) crushed dried basil
1 bay leaf
fresh herb sprigs for garnish, such as tarragon, rosemary, and thyme

Duchess Potatoes

3 pounds (1.35 kg) potatoes
¾ cup (177 ml) egg substitute
3 large egg whites
2 teaspoons (10 g) unsalted butter

freshly ground pepper to taste
¼ teaspoon (1.25 ml) ground nutmeg

Vegetable Garnish

1 pound (450 g) fresh mushrooms, stems removed
1 pound (450 g) French green beans (very small string beans), trimmed

1 pound (450 g) cherry tomatoes

Trim all fat from fillet. In a saucepan, combine marinade ingredients except fresh herbs for garnish. Simmer for 15 minutes. Cool. Place fillet in a large nonreactive pan. Pour wine mixture over beef, cover, and refrigerate for at least 3 hours. Turn fillet over several times during marination. (You can prepare this up to a day ahead, cover, and refrigerate.)

To prepare Duchess Potatoes; peel and quarter potatoes. Place in a saucepan, cover with cold water, and bring to a boil. Reduce heat slightly and cook until the potatoes are tender, 20 to 30 minutes. Drain potatoes thoroughly. Press potatoes through a ricer or sieve. Add egg substitute, egg whites, butter, pepper, and nutmeg. Beat until smooth, making sure there are no lumps. Lay a sheet of wax paper on a large tray. Pipe potato mixture through a pastry bag or use 2 spoons to make 12 decorative shapes on the paper. Set aside. (You can make these up to a day ahead, cover, and refrigerate.)

Steam mushrooms and French green beans separately until just done, about 3 to 5 minutes. Set aside. (Cook up to a day ahead, cover, and refrigerate.) Wash and stem cherry tomatoes; set aside.

Lift meat from marinade and drain briefly; reserve marinade. Fold thin end of fillet under; tie securely with string to make fillet evenly thick.

To Grill: Place meat on a lightly greased grill 4 to 6 inches over a bed of hot coals. Grill, basting frequently with marinade, turning every 5 minutes, until cooked to desired doneness, about 45 minutes for rare. Let meat stand for 10 minutes.

To Roast: Preheat oven to 425° F (220° C). Roast fillet for 35 minutes for rare meat or to desired doneness, basting occasionally with marinade. You will be reheating meat so undercook it just a bit. Let meat stand for 10 minutes.

Set oven temperature to 450° F (230° C). Place cooked fillet on a large ovenproof platter. Group mushrooms, French green beans, and cherry tomatoes in a decorative arrangement around fillet. Transfer potatoes to platter, placing them around the edge. Bake until vegetables and beef are hot and potatoes are lightly browned, 5 to 8 minutes. Decorate platter with fresh herbs.

Carve the fillet at the table, cutting across the grain on a slight diagonal into thin slices. Serve each portion with some of the potatoes and vegetables.

MAKES ABOUT 12 SERVINGS

Per serving (with vegetables):
calories, 258 ◆ protein, 26 g ◆ carbohydrate, 20 g ◆ fat, 8 g (calories from fat, 28%) ◆ dietary fiber, 1 g ◆ cholesterol, 65 mg ◆ sodium, 84 mg ◆ potassium, 839 mg
Joslin Exchanges: 4½ medium-fat meat, 1 bread/starch, 1 vegetable

Per serving (meat alone):
calories, 157 ◆ protein, 22 g ◆ carbohydrate, trace ◆ fat, 7 g (calories from fat, 40%) ◆ dietary fiber, trace ◆ cholesterol, 64 mg ◆ sodium, 48 mg ◆ potassium, 325 mg
Joslin Exchanges: 3 medium-fat meat

Santa Fe Roast

The eye of round is one of the leanest cuts of beef, and when cooked this way it's very tender and richly flavored. The sauce is not overly hot, despite the amount of chili peppers.

We like this with black beans and white rice.

1 tablespoon (15 ml) olive oil

3 pounds (1.35 kg) beef eye of round, trimmed of all fat

2 large red onions, about ¾ pound (340 g), finely chopped

3 garlic cloves, minced

1 large red bell pepper, about 6 ounces (180 g), seeded and finely chopped

1 large green bell pepper, about 6 ounces (180 g), seeded and finely chopped

3 small jalapeño chilies, seeded and minced

1 28-ounce (790 g) can Italian plum tomatoes, chopped

1 cup (236 ml) beef stock (page 44)

1 teaspoon (5 ml) ground cumin

1 tablespoon (15 ml) chopped fresh oregano or 1 teaspoon (5 ml) crushed dried

½ tablespoon (7.5 ml) fresh thyme leaves or ½ teaspoon (2.5 ml) crushed dried

½ teaspoon (2.5 ml) ground cloves

1 teaspoon (5 ml) paprika

½ teaspoon (2.5 ml) freshly ground pepper

2 tablespoons (30 ml) chopped fresh cilantro (fresh coriander) for garnish (optional)

Preheat oven to 350° F (180° C). In a heavy flameproof casserole or Dutch oven with a lid, heat oil over medium heat. Add eye of round; brown on all sides. When roast is brown, pour off all fat and pan juices. Place pan juices in freezer for a few moments to harden fat. Remove fat and return pan juices to casserole.

Add remaining ingredients except cilantro. Bring to a simmer. Cover and bake for 2½ to 3 hours, until beef is tender, basting with pan juices every 30 minutes.

Transfer beef to a carving board; keep warm. Skim any fat from pan juices. Return casserole to stove and cook over medium-high heat for 15 minutes, until reduced by half.

Carve the beef into thin slices on a diagonal; arrange on a serving platter. Spoon some sauce over meat and garnish with chopped cilantro. Serve any extra sauce in a sauceboat.

MAKES 12 SERVINGS

Per serving: calories, 253 ◆ protein, 30 g ◆ carbohydrate, 10 g ◆ fat, 10 g (calories from fat, 36%) ◆ dietary fiber, 1 g ◆ cholesterol, 86 mg ◆ sodium, 220 mg ◆ potassium, 586 mg Joslin Exchanges: 3½ medium-fat meat, 2 vegetable

Spicy Beef Stew

We've lightened a favorite classic, using leaner beef, more vegetables, and lots of herbs and spices for a contemporary beef stew full of robust flavor. This is a great way to feed a family on a cold winter night.

After a braising period on top of the stove to brown the meat using very little oil, the stew finishes in the oven and needs little attention.

1½ pounds (675 g) boneless lean top round
1 medium-size onion, about ¼ pound (115 g), thinly sliced
2 garlic cloves, minced
½ cup (118 ml) water
1 tablespoon (15 ml) canola oil
1 fresh jalapeño chili, seeded and minced
1 tablespoon (15 ml) ground cumin
1 tablespoon (15 ml) paprika
¼ teaspoon (1.25 ml) hot red pepper flakes or to taste
½ teaspoon (2.5 ml) crushed dried thyme leaves
¼ teaspoon (1.25 ml) crushed dried oregano leaves

6 small leeks, about 2 pounds (900 g), white part plus 2 inches (5 cm) green, well rinsed
3 carrots, about ½ pound (225 g), scraped and cut into 3-inch (8 cm) lengths
¾ cup (177 ml) dry red wine
3 cups (708 ml) beef stock (page 44)
6 small red new potatoes, about ¾ pound (340 g), scrubbed and cut in half
1 pound (450 g) fresh plum tomatoes, peeled, seeded, and chopped, or 1 16-ounce (450 g) can Italian plum tomatoes, drained

Cut meat into 1-inch (2.5 cm) cubes, trimming off and discarding all fat. In a 6-quart (5.5 l) ovenproof pan or flameproof casserole with a tight-fitting lid, combine meat, onion, garlic, water, and oil. Cover pan and simmer on top of the stove over low heat, stirring occasionally, for 30 minutes (add more water if it cooks away). Uncover and cook, stirring often, until almost all liquid is cooked away.

Remove beef cubes from pan; set aside. Add jalapeño, cumin, paprika, red pepper flakes, thyme, and oregano to pan. Cook, stirring, for 30 seconds. Add leeks and carrots. Sauté until vegetables are browned, about 6 minutes. Remove leeks and carrots; set aside. Add red wine and stock; bring to a boil, scraping up any brown bits. Return beef to pan. Add potatoes; stir to combine.

Preheat oven to 350° F (180° C). Transfer pan to oven and bake, covered, for 45 minutes. Remove pan from oven; stir in tomatoes and reserved vegetables. Return pan to oven and bake, uncovered, for another 45 minutes, until beef is very tender when pierced. Serve hot.

MAKES 6 SERVINGS

Per serving: calories, 327 ◆ protein, 24 g ◆ carbohydrate, 40 g ◆ fat, 9 g (calories from fat, 24%) ◆ dietary fiber, 3 g ◆cholesterol, 54 mg ◆ sodium, 390 mg ◆ potassium, 1,167 mg Joslin Exchanges: 2 medium-fat meat, 2 vegetable, 2 bread/ starch

Oven-Roasted Herb-Stuffed Fillet of Beef

An elegant entree for a special dinner. Serve with a variety of vegetables: braised Brussels sprouts, steamed potato balls, and a sauté of yellow and red cherry tomatoes (page 359).

1　6-pound (2.75 kg) whole fillet of beef without tail

Stuffing

½　pound (225 g) mushrooms, minced
9　shallots, minced
1　ounce (30 g) low-salt, no-sugar-added ham, minced
1　tablespoon (15 ml) dry sherry
freshly ground pepper to taste
1　tablespoon (15 ml) fresh thyme leaves or chopped fresh tarragon or 1 teaspoon (5 ml) crushed dried
1　tablespoon (15 ml) olive oil
cheesecloth

Wine Sauce

3　shallots, minced
olive oil cooking spray
½　cup (118 ml) dry red wine
1　cup (236 ml) beef stock (page 44)
1　tablespoon (15 ml) fresh thyme leaves or chopped fresh tarragon (use the same as in stuffing) or 1 teaspoon (5 ml) crushed dried
1　fresh plum tomato, about 3 ounces (85 g), peeled, seeded, and finely chopped
freshly ground pepper to taste

Trim all visible fat from fillet. To prepare stuffing, sauté mushrooms, shallots, ham, sherry, pepper, and thyme in a nonstick sauté pan over low heat until reduced to 1 cup (236 ml).

Slice meat at ½-inch (1.5 cm) intervals not all the way through. Distribute mushroom stuffing equally between slices. Season fillet with pepper and rub with oil. Place fillet on a piece of cheesecloth and wrap, enclosing fillet tightly. Tie ends with kitchen string and at 2-inch (5 cm) intervals along the fillet.

Preheat oven to 425° F (220° C). Place fillet in a shallow roasting pan. Roast fillet for 35 minutes for rare meat or to desired doneness. Let fillet stand for 5 minutes before removing cheesecloth.

Meanwhile, to prepare sauce, sauté shallots in a nonstick sauté pan lightly sprayed with cooking spray over low heat until shallots are wilted, about 4 minutes. Add remaining ingredients and simmer, stirring occasionally until reduced and thickened, about 15 minutes. Keep warm.

To serve, carve fillet and nap with some sauce. Pass remaining sauce separately.

MAKES ABOUT 12 SERVINGS

Per serving: calories, 177 ◆ protein, 22 g ◆ carbohydrate, 3 g ◆ fat, 8 g (calories from fat, 41%) ◆ dietary fiber, trace ◆ cholesterol, 65 mg ◆ sodium, 75 mg ◆ potassium, 433 mg Joslin Exchanges: 3 medium-fat meat

Wine Merchant's Steak

We eat very little red meat these days, but sometimes we get a craving for a good steak. Then we splurge on a well-aged beef fillet, cut into medallions and trimmed of all fat.

If you have a well-seasoned cast-iron skillet, you'll need no oil to prepare this classic bistro dish. A nonstick skillet can also be used, but you won't get a crusty surface on the steak.

Serve this extra-special steak for a holiday party.

6 beef medallions, about ¼ pound (115 g) each, cut ¾ inch (2 cm) thick and trimmed of all fat
½ teaspoon (2.5 ml) salt (optional)
freshly ground pepper to taste
1½ cups (354 ml) dry red wine
½ cup (118 ml) minced shallots
2 large garlic cloves, minced

3 tablespoons (45 ml) tomato paste
2 teaspoons (10 ml) Worcestershire sauce
1 tablespoon (15 ml) Dijon mustard
3 tablespoons (45 ml) snipped fresh chives for garnish

Sprinkle steaks with salt and pepper. Place a heavy well-seasoned iron skillet over medium-high heat. When skillet is very hot, add steaks and sauté for 2¹/₂ to 3 minutes on each side for medium-rare. Transfer steaks to a carving board; keep warm.

Discard fat from skillet. Add wine and increase heat to high. Stir to deglaze pan, scraping the bottom of the skillet to loosen the browned bits. Add shallots and garlic. Boil wine for 1 minute. Reduce heat to medium-low; whisk in tomato paste, Worcestershire sauce, and mustard. Cook, stirring constantly, until sauce thickens and reduces to about ¹/₂ cup (118 ml), about 4 minutes.

Thinly slice steaks on a diagonal. Pour any steak juices into sauce. Arrange steaks on 6 heated serving plates. Spoon 2 tablespoons (30 ml) sauce over steak slices. Sprinkle with snipped chives.

MAKES 6 SERVINGS

Per serving: calories, 246 ◆ protein, 27 g ◆ carbohydrate, 5 g ◆ fat, 13 g (calories from fat, 47%) ◆ dietary fiber, trace ◆ cholesterol, 82 mg ◆ sodium, 333 mg ◆ potassium, 398 mg Joslin Exchanges: 3¹/₂ medium-fat meat, 1 vegetable

---

HOLIDAY DINNER PARTY

◆

Herb Spritzers (page 39) and Pesto-Stuffed Mushroom Caps

(page 352)

Cream of Watercress Soup (page 55)

Wine Merchant's Steak (page 243)

Roasted Garlic Potatoes (page 262)

Steamed Baby Green Beans

Filo Tulips (page 431) with Pear Sorbet (page 432)

Per serving: 539 calories (30% fat)
Joslin Exchanges: 3¹/₂ medium-fat meat, 4 vegetable, 1¹/₂ bread/starch, 1¹/₂ fruit

Roast Pork Stuffed with Mixed Dried Fruits

This luscious pork loin dish can be stuffed with any dried fruit—prunes, pears, apples, peaches, and apricots—or you can purchase a package of already mixed dried fruit.

¼ pound (115 g) mixed dried fruit, chopped into large pieces
3 tablespoons (45 ml) boiling water
1 tablespoon (15 ml) cognac (optional)
½ teaspoon (2.5 ml) grated orange zest
1¾ pounds (790 g) boneless pork loin, trimmed of all fat

1 teaspoon (5 ml) ground cumin
¼ teaspoon (1.25 ml) ground coriander
freshly ground pepper to taste
½ cup (118 ml) dry white wine
1 tablespoon (15 ml) orange zest in thin strips

In a small bowl, combine dried fruits, water, cognac, and grated orange zest. Allow fruit to soak for 20 to 30 minutes. Drain fruit; reserve liquid.

Preheat oven to 350° F (180° C). Using a long thin knife, cut a hole lengthwise through middle of roast. Stuff hole with plumped fruit. Using kitchen string, tie roast at 1½-inch (4 cm) intervals.

Brown roast on all sides in a nonstick skillet over medium heat. Pat browned roast with cumin, coriander, and pepper. Place roast in a covered baking dish just large enough to accommodate roast. Pour on wine and reserved liquid from fruit. Cover and bake for about 60 minutes, until an instant-reading meat thermometer registers 160° F (71° C). Transfer roast to a carving board and let stand while you make sauce.

Pour pan juices into a nonstick skillet. Skim off and discard any surface fat. Bring liquid to a boil and cook to reduce by one-third to thicken slightly. Add orange zest strips. Carve roast into ½-inch (1.5 cm) slices. Nap each serving with 1 tablespoon (15 ml) sauce.

MAKES 6 SERVINGS

Per serving: calories, 172 ◆ protein, 22 g ◆ carbohydrate, 13 g ◆ fat, 4 g (calories from fat, 21%) ◆ dietary fiber, 1 g ◆ cholesterol, 70 mg ◆ sodium, 56 mg ◆ potassium, 564 mg Joslin Exchanges: 3 low-fat meat, 1 fruit

EASTER DINNER

◆

Crudités with Curry Dip (page 5)

Roast Pork Stuffed with Mixed Dried Fruits (page 245)

Roasted Sweet and White Potatoes (page 311)

Steamed Asparagus

Filo Tulips (page 431) with Fresh Strawberries and Crème

Fraîche (page 428)

Per serving: 507 calories (27% fat)
Joslin Exchanges: 3 low-fat meat, 2 vegetable, 3 bread/starch, 2 fruit, ½ milk, 1 fat

Pork Satay with Spicy Peanut Sauce

An Indonesian specialty sold by street vendors in Malaysia and Singapore, satay is traditionally served with a spicy peanut sauce.

While the pork is cooking, grill partially steamed wedges of Chinese cabbage alongside, basting the cabbage with the same marinade (double the marinade recipe). Offer rice, colored yellow with a pinch of turmeric and flavored with chopped mint, to complete the barbecue meal. You can also make the satay using chicken instead of pork.

The Spicy Peanut Sauce can also be used as a dipping sauce for hot steamed vegetables or tossed with cold cooked spaghetti or fettuccine along with pieces of blanched asparagus for a pasta salad.

1 pound (450 g) lean pork
   tenderloin, trimmed of
   all fat

12 long bamboo skewers, soaked in
   hot water to cover for at least 30
   minutes

Marinade

¼ cup (59 ml) fresh lemon juice
1 4-inch (10 cm) piece lemongrass, minced, or 1 teaspoon (5 ml) grated lemon zest
2 tablespoons (30 ml) dry sherry or chicken stock (page 45)

2 tablespoons (30 ml) low-sodium soy sauce
1 teaspoon (5 ml) ground cumin
1 teaspoon (5 ml) ground coriander

Spicy Peanut Sauce

vegetable oil cooking spray
2 garlic cloves, minced
¼ cup (59 ml) minced shallots
3 tablespoons (45 ml) unsalted chunky peanut butter
1 tablespoon (15 ml) low-sodium soy sauce

1 teaspoon (5 ml) hot red pepper flakes
¼ teaspoon (1.25 ml) ground cumin
¼ teaspoon (1.25 ml) ground coriander
½ cup (118 ml) skim milk

Cut pork into 1-inch (2.5 cm) cubes. In a bowl, combine marinade ingredients. Add pork and stir to coat. Cover and refrigerate for at least 2 hours, stirring occasionally.

To prepare sauce, spray a small saucepan with cooking spray. Add garlic and shallots; sauté over low heat until shallots are wilted, about 3 minutes. Add remaining sauce ingredients. Cook, stirring in a small saucepan, until heated through. Transfer sauce to a food processor or blender; process until smooth. Return to stove and keep warm over very low heat. (Makes about 1 cup sauce.)

Thread pork on skewers. Place on a lightly greased grill 4 to 6 inches (10 to 15 cm) above a solid bed of hot coals. Cook pork, turning often and basting occasionally with marinade, until well browned and no longer pink in center, 7 to 10 minutes. Cut to test. Serve with peanut sauce.

MAKES 4 SERVINGS

Per serving: calories, 213 ◆ protein, 24 g ◆ carbohydrate, 9 g ◆ fat, 10 g (calories from fat, 42%) ◆ dietary fiber, 1 g ◆ cholesterol, 61 mg ◆ sodium, 568 mg* ◆ potassium, 589 mg Joslin Exchanges: 4 low-fat meat, 1 vegetable

Per ¼-cup (59 ml) serving (peanut sauce alone): calories, 96 ◆ protein, 5 g ◆ carbohydrate, 6 g ◆ fat, 6 g (calories from fat, 56%) ◆ dietary fiber, 1 g ◆ cholesterol, 1 mg ◆ sodium, 224 mg ◆ potassium, 194 mg Joslin Exchanges: 1 fat

* Recipe not recommended for low-sodium diets.

ASIAN DINNER

◆

Daikon Radish with Chili and Lime (page 4)

Pork Satay with Spicy Peanut Sauce (page 246)

Grilled Chinese Cabbage (page 246)

Rice with Chives, Red Onion, and Fresh Mint (page 289)

Tangerines

Per serving: 445 calories (26% fat)
Joslin Exchanges: 4 low-fat meat, 3 vegetable, 1 bread/starch, 1 fruit

Saffron-Spiced Pork with Prunes and Apricots

Saffron is an expensive spice, but a little goes a long way. You can also achieve a similar yellow color, although a different taste, by using the less expensive turmeric. Serve with Orzo in Hot Baked Tomatoes (page 304) or Bulgur Pilaf (page 279).

4 pork loin chops, cut ½ inch (1.5 cm) thick and trimmed of all fat
1 medium-size onion, chopped
2 garlic cloves, minced
¼ teaspoon (1.25 ml) saffron threads or 1 teaspoon (5 ml) turmeric
¼ cup (59 ml) hot water
¾ teaspoon (3.75 ml) ground cinnamon
¾ teaspoon (3.75 ml) ground ginger

2 tablespoons (30 ml) fresh lemon juice
½ cup (118 ml) water
½ cup (118 ml) dry white wine
¾ cup (177 ml) pitted prunes, chopped
¼ cup (59 ml) dried apricots, chopped
1 tablespoon (15 ml) toasted sesame seeds (page 440)

In a large nonstick sauté pan over medium heat, brown chops on both sides. Remove chops from skillet. Add onion and garlic to skillet; sauté for 3 to 4 minutes, until onion is wilted. Dissolve saffron in hot water. Add to skillet along with cinnamon, ginger, lemon juice, water, and wine. Bring mixture to a boil. Reduce heat to simmer, return chops to pan, and cook, covered, for about 35 to 40 minutes, or until pork springs back when touched. Remove chops; keep warm.

Over high heat, boil pan juices until reduced to the consistency of syrup. Return chops to skillet along with prunes and apricots. Heat through. Serve each chop with a tablespoon (15 ml) of sauce. Sprinkle each serving with sesame seeds.

MAKES 4 SERVINGS

> **Per serving:** calories, 281 ◆ protein, 26 g ◆ carbohydrate, 17 g ◆ fat, 12 g (calories from fat, 38%) ◆ dietary fiber, 1 g ◆ cholesterol, 77 mg ◆ sodium, 64 mg ◆ potassium, 576 mg Joslin Exchanges: 3½ low-fat meat, 1 fruit

South-of-the-Border Grilled Pork Tenderloin

Today's well-trimmed pork tenderloin competes with chicken as a lean, low-cholesterol meat. Already the most tender part of pork, here it's made even more tender and succulent with a brief marinade of marjoram, cilantro, and citrus juices—a typical flavoring for pork in the Yucatán region of Mexico.

Red Onion Pineapple Chutney is just the right condiment to serve alongside. With its natural sweetness and heat, this chutney is spectacular with pork. You can also use chopped peeled Granny Smith apples or chopped peeled Bartlett pears instead of pineapple to make a lively condiment for chicken or turkey.

¼ cup (59 ml) finely chopped fresh marjoram or 1 tablespoon (15 ml) crushed dried
¼ cup (59 ml) finely chopped cilantro (fresh coriander)
¼ cup (59 ml) minced onion
1 garlic clove, minced

juice and grated zest of 1 lime
juice and grated zest of 1 lemon
1 teaspoon (5 ml) freshly ground pepper
1 teaspoon (5 ml) olive oil
2 10-ounce (285 g) pork tenderloins, trimmed of fat

In a small bowl, combine everything but pork. Place tenderloins in a shallow glass baking dish. Pour marinade over them and turn meat to coat evenly. Refrigerate for 30 minutes.

Remove meat from marinade and grill, 4 inches (10 cm) from source of heat, over medium-hot coals for 10 to 12 minutes or broil until internal temperature reaches 140° F (60° C), turning once and basting occasionally with marinade. Slice and serve.

MAKES 4 SERVINGS

Per serving: calories, 199 ◆ protein, 31 g ◆ carbohydrate, 3 g ◆ fat, 6 g (calories from fat, 27%) ◆ dietary fiber, trace ◆ cholesterol, 99 mg ◆ sodium, 74 mg ◆ potassium, 646 mg
Joslin Exchanges: 4 low-fat meat

Red Onion Pineapple Chutney

2 medium-size red onions, about ½ pound (225 g), quartered and thinly sliced
3 garlic cloves, minced
1 cup (236 ml) diced fresh or canned (no sugar added) pineapple
2 fresh hot red chilies, seeded and diced

2 teaspoons (10 ml) light brown sugar
3 tablespoons (45 ml) balsamic vinegar
1 cup (236 ml) water
1 tablespoon (15 ml) chopped fresh marjoram or 1 teaspoon (5 ml) crushed dried

Separate onion slices into rings. Place all ingredients in a heavy stainless-steel saucepan. Bring to a boil; reduce heat and simmer, uncovered, until liquid evaporates, about 30 minutes. Stir frequently. Cool to room temperature before serving.

MAKES 4 SERVINGS

Per serving: calories, 87 ◆ protein, 2 g ◆ carbohydrate, 21 g ◆ fat, trace (calories from fat, less than 1%) ◆ dietary fiber, 1 g ◆ cholesterol, 0 mg ◆ sodium, 9 mg ◆ potassium, 256 mg
Joslin Exchanges: 1½ fruit

Italian Pork with Creamy Polenta

A new "meat and potatoes" kind of meal—except the meat is lean pork cooked with lots of fresh herbs and creamy polenta takes the place of mashed potatoes.

Recently we've been able to buy dried Chilean mushrooms at a fraction of the cost of morels or porcini. They have an intense smoky flavor that's perfect for this dish. If your market doesn't carry them, substitute any dried mushrooms or use sliced fresh mushrooms.

olive oil cooking spray
2 10-ounce (285 g) pork tenderloins, trimmed of all fat
2 garlic cloves, minced
⅓ cup (78 ml) finely diced carrot
1 15-ounce (425 g) can Italian plum tomatoes, drained and chopped
¼ cup (59 ml) dry red wine
2 tablespoons (30 ml) red wine vinegar or balsamic vinegar
1 tablespoon (15 ml) fresh oregano leaves or 1 teaspoon crushed dried
¾ tablespoon (11.25 ml) fresh thyme leaves or ¾ teaspoon (3.75 ml) crushed dried

1 bay leaf
2 ounces (60 g) dried mushrooms or 2 cups (472 ml) sliced fresh
1 small red bell pepper, about 3 ounces (85 g), seeded and chopped
1 small yellow bell pepper, about 3 ounces (85 g), seeded and chopped
1 quart (1 l) chicken stock (page 45)
1 cup (112 g) instant polenta or 1 cup (144 g) stone-ground yellow cornmeal
pinch of salt (optional)
¼ cup (59 ml) finely shredded fresh basil for garnish

In a large nonstick skillet lightly sprayed with cooking spray, brown the tenderloins on all sides over medium heat. Remove pork from skillet; reduce heat to low and sauté garlic and carrot for 1 minute. Return pork to skillet. Add tomatoes, wine, vinegar, oregano, thyme, and bay leaf. Cover and simmer for 40 minutes.

Rinse dried mushrooms thoroughly under warm running water to remove all traces of sand and grit. Slice mushrooms. Place dried mushrooms and peppers in a covered microwave-safe dish and cook on HIGH power for 1 minute. (If you don't have a microwave, cook in ¼ cup boiling water on the stove for 2 minutes; drain.) If you're using fresh mushrooms, sauté in a nonstick pan with 1 tablespoon (15 ml) water over medium heat until tender, about 5 minutes.

Transfer tenderloins to a carving board; keep warm. Boil sauce over high heat until it is reduced enough to coat the back of a wooden spoon. Discard bay leaf; stir in cooked mushrooms and peppers. Add salt, if used. Keep sauce warm.

In a medium-size saucepan, bring stock to a boil. When stock is boiling rapidly,

SOUTHWESTERN BARBECUE

◆

South-of-the-Border Grilled Pork Tenderloin (page 249)

Red Onion Pineapple Chutney (page 250)

Taos Two-Bean and Rice Salad (page 299)

Grilled Summer Squash (page 321)

Watermelon Graníta (page 435)

Per serving: 605 calories (28% fat)
Joslin Exchanges: 4 low-fat meat, 2 bread/starch, 1 vegetable, 2¹/₂ fruit, 1 fat

add polenta while stirring constantly with a wooden spoon. Reduce heat to medium and continue stirring until polenta is cooked and creamy, about 5 minutes.

Spoon polenta onto 4 heated serving plates. Slice tenderloins into ¹/₂-inch (1.5 cm) slices. Arrange pork slices at edges of polenta. Nap with sauce. Sprinkle with shredded basil and serve.

MAKES 4 SERVINGS

Per serving: calories, 252 ◆ protein, 27 g ◆ carbohydrate, 22 g ◆ fat, 6 g (calories from fat, 21%) ◆ dietary fiber, 1 g ◆ cholesterol, 76 mg ◆ sodium, 286 mg ◆ potassium, 982 mg Joslin Exchanges: 3 low-fat meat, 1¹/₂ bread/starch

ITALIAN WINTER EVENING

◆

Crostini with Roasted Peppers (page 18)

Radicchio and Mixed Baby Greens with Classic Vinaigrette

(page 114)

Italian Pork with Creamy Polenta (page 251)

Grilled Eggplant (page 319)

Fresh Pineapple with Balsamic Vinegar (page 430)

Per serving: 632 calories (28% fat)
Joslin Exchanges: 3 low-fat meat, 2 vegetable, 3¹/₂ bread/starch, 1 fruit, 1¹/₂ fat

Pork Tenderloin with Mustard Sauce

This is hearty winter fare generously flavored with fresh sage. We like to serve it with Sautéed Lima Beans (page 298) and a mixed green salad.

20 fresh sage leaves
¹/₄ cup (59 ml) coarsely ground
   prepared mustard
freshly ground pepper
 1 garlic clove, minced
 2 scallions, white part only,
   minced
 2 10-ounce (285 g) pork
   tenderloins, all fat removed

olive oil cooking spray
¹/₄ cup (59 ml) dry white wine
 1 shallot, minced
¹/₄ cup (59 ml) skim milk
¹/₂ teaspoon (2.5 ml) cornstarch
 1 tablespoon (15 ml) water

Mince sage leaves, reserving 4 whole leaves for garnish. In a small bowl, mix together minced sage, 2 tablespoons (30 ml) mustard, pepper, garlic, and scallions.

Place tenderloins on a plate; spread with mustard mixture. Cover tightly with plastic wrap and refrigerate for at least 4 hours or overnight.

Preheat oven to 375° F (190° C). Place tenderloins on a rack in a roasting pan. Lightly spray tenderloins with cooking spray. Bake for 20 to 25 minutes, until an instant-reading meat thermometer registers 160° F (71° C). Baste every 5 minutes with white wine.

Meanwhile, in a nonstick skillet lightly sprayed with cooking spray, sauté minced shallot over low heat until wilted. Add milk and any remaining wine; bring to a slow simmer. Stir cornstarch into water; add to milk. Cook, stirring constantly, until sauce thickens. Add remaining 2 tablespoons (30 ml) mustard and freshly ground pepper. Keep sauce warm.

When pork is done, remove from oven; let stand for 5 minutes. Thinly slice on a diagonal. Arrange 3 to 4 slices on each of 4 heated dinner plates. Top with a reserved sage leaf; nap with some of the sauce.

MAKES 4 SERVINGS

> **Per serving:** calories, 189 ◆ protein, 27 g ◆ carbohydrate, 5 g ◆ fat, 7 g (calories from fat, 33%) ◆ dietary fiber, trace ◆ cholesterol, 76 mg ◆ sodium, 64 mg ◆ potassium, 543 mg Joslin Exchanges: 4 low-fat meat

Deviled Butterflied Lamb Chops

If you're entertaining, have your butcher cut, trim, and butterfly ½-pound (225 g) rib lamb chops—you'll get about ¼ pound (115 g) of edible meat per chop before cooking, which is more than sufficient per person. Or buy two ¼-pound (115 g) baby rib chops, cut about ¾ inch (2 cm) thick, for each person. Just trim the fat and leave the bone in. You'll get the same amount of edible meat.

4 ½-pound (225 g) rib lamb chops, cut about 1½ inches (4 cm) thick, or 8 ¼-pound (115 g) rib lamb chops, cut about ¾ inch (2 cm) thick
¼ cup (59 ml) Dijon mustard
1 shallot, finely minced
1 garlic clove, finely minced

1 tablespoon (15 ml) chopped fresh flat-leaf parsley
½ tablespoon (7.5 ml) chopped fresh rosemary or ½ teaspoon (2.5 ml) crushed dried
¼ teaspoon (1.25 ml) cayenne pepper
2¼ teaspoons (11.25 ml) olive oil

If you're using ½-pound (225 g) chops, have butcher remove bone and all fat from lamb chops; then butterfly. If you're using ¼-pound (115 g) chops, remove all fat. Set aside.

In a small bowl, combine mustard, shallot, garlic, parsley, rosemary, cayenne, and olive oil. Grill or broil 4 inches (10 cm) from source of heat for 3½ minutes. Turn and brush with mustard mixture. Continue grilling for 3½ to 4 minutes for medium-rare or to desired doneness.

MAKES 4 SERVINGS

Per serving: calories, 248 ◆ protein, 25 g ◆ carbohydrate, 2 g ◆ fat, 15 g (calories from fat, 54%) ◆ dietary fiber, trace ◆ cholesterol, 77 mg ◆ sodium, 268 mg ◆ potassium, 307 mg Joslin Exchanges: 3½ medium-fat meat

---

ELEGANT SATURDAY NIGHT DINNER

◆

Carrot Soup (page 48) with Sun-Dried Tomato and Garlic

Breadsticks (page 397)

Deviled Butterflied Lamb Chops (page 254)

Spicy Couscous (page 282)

Grilled Zucchini (page 321)

Fresh Pineapple with Fresh Raspberry Puree

Per serving: 627 calories (30% fat)
Joslin Exchanges: 3½ medium-fat meat, 3½ bread/starch, 1 vegetable, 1 fruit

Veal Sauté with Orange and Capers

Veal scallops cook quickly, so have the side dishes ready. Steamed new potatoes and a simple green vegetable are perfect complements to the savory veal.

1 pound (450 g) veal scallops, pounded ⅛ inch (.5 cm) thick
freshly ground pepper to taste
1 tablespoon (15 ml) olive oil
1 teaspoon (5 g) unsalted butter
¼ cup (59 ml) dry white wine
¼ cup (59 ml) chicken stock (page 45)
3 tablespoons (45 ml) fresh orange juice

1 medium-size orange, about 5 ounces (140 g), peeled and thinly sliced
1 tablespoon (15 ml) drained capers
2 tablespoons (30 ml) chopped fresh parsley

Trim and discard any tough membrane and fat from veal. Sprinkle veal with pepper. Heat oil in a large nonstick skillet over high heat. Add veal a few scallops at a time (do not crowd pan) and cook, turning once, until browned on both sides, 2 to 3 minutes total. Transfer browned veal to a warm platter; continue browning remaining veal.

Add butter to skillet along with wine, stock, and orange juice. Cook, stirring well to combine with pan drippings, until sauce boils. Remove from heat.

Arrange veal on a heated serving platter, tucking orange slices between veal scallops. Return sauce to stove; return to boil. Stir in capers and parsley. Spoon sauce over veal and serve.

MAKES 4 SERVINGS

Per serving: calories, 192 ◆ protein, 25 g ◆ carbohydrate, 6 g ◆ fat, 7 g (calories from fat, 33%) ◆ dietary fiber, trace ◆ cholesterol, 90 mg ◆ sodium, 364 mg ◆ potassium, 434 mg Joslin Exchanges: 3 medium-fat meat, 1 vegetable

Veal Patties au Poivre

A quick and delicious version of a French-inspired dish, using leaner veal and less butter. Serve with White Beans with Tomatoes (page 301) and a steamed green vegetable.

1 pound (450 g) lean ground veal
1 tablespoon (15 ml) fresh thyme leaves or 1 teaspoon (5 ml) crushed dried
¼ teaspoon (1.25 ml) salt (optional)
1 tablespoon (15 ml) cracked black pepper
butter-flavored cooking spray
4 scallions, white part only, thinly sliced
¼ pound (115 g) mushrooms, thinly sliced

1 garlic clove, minced
2 tablespoons (30 ml) cognac
¼ cup (59 ml) dry red wine
¼ cup (59 ml) beef stock (page 44)
2 teaspoons (10 ml) green peppercorns in brine, rinsed and coarsely chopped
1 teaspoon (5 ml) Dijon mustard
1 teaspoon (5 g) unsalted butter

In a bowl, mix together veal, thyme, and salt. Shape into 4 patties of equal size and about ¾ inch (2 cm) thick. Press pepper onto meat.

In a large nonstick skillet over medium-high heat, pan-fry patties for 3 to 4 minutes on one side. Turn patties and cook for another 4 to 5 minutes, to desired doneness. Cut to test.

Transfer patties to a warm serving platter. Discard all fat from skillet. Add scallions, mushrooms, and garlic to pan. Cook, stirring, until mushrooms are soft and lightly browned, about 7 minutes. With a slotted spoon, transfer scallions and mushrooms to the platter. Add cognac and wine to skillet. Cook, stirring, until reduced by half. Add stock. Reduce to about ⅓ cup (78 ml). Whisk in green peppercorns, mustard, and butter. Spoon sauce over patties and mushrooms.

MAKES 4 SERVINGS

Per serving: calories 178 ◆ protein, 22 g ◆ carbohydrate, 3 g ◆ fat, 9 g (calories from fat, 46%) ◆ dietary fiber, 1 g ◆ cholesterol, 92 mg ◆ sodium, 225 mg ◆ potassium, 442 mg
Joslin Exchanges: 3 medium-fat meat

Veal Scallops in Italian Tomato Sauce

We love ossobuco, meaty veal shanks cooked slowly for 2½ hours in a rich tomato sauce. Unfortunately, the traditional recipe uses too many fat exchanges. This light veal dish is done in less than 30 minutes, using lean veal scallops seasoned with garlic, fresh oregano, and parsley. The scallops are served with a light, richly flavored sauce reminiscent of the sauce of ossobuco, but with little fat.

Garnish with gremolata, a combination of chopped parsley, grated lemon zest, and minced garlic. Serve Saffron Risotto (page 292) alongside.

1 pound (450 g) veal scallops,
    pounded thin
3 garlic cloves, minced
leaves from 4 fresh oregano sprigs
    or 1 teaspoon (5 ml) crushed
    dried
leaves from 4 flat-leaf parsley sprigs
    or 1 teaspoon (5 ml) crushed
    dried
½ teaspoon (2.5 ml) salt (optional)
freshly ground pepper to taste
1 tablespoon (15 ml) cornstarch

1 tablespoon (15 ml) olive oil
1 cup (236 ml) white wine
½ cup (118 ml) finely chopped red
    onion
½ cup (118 ml) finely chopped
    carrots
½ cup (118 ml) finely chopped
    celery
1 28-ounce (790 g) can Italian
    plum tomatoes, drained
1 cup (236 ml) beef stock
    (page 44)

Gremolata

2 tablespoons (30 ml) chopped flat-
    leaf parsley
finely grated zest of 1 lemon

2 garlic cloves, minced

Combine half of the chopped garlic with the oregano and parsley leaves. Spread a little on each veal scallop and roll up with garlic mixture inside. Season with salt and pepper. Sprinkle with cornstarch.

In a large nonstick skillet, heat olive oil over high heat. Add veal rolls and sauté for 1 minute on each side. Remove veal rolls from skillet; keep warm.

Deglaze skillet with wine. Add remaining garlic, onion, carrots, and celery. Cook and stir for 2 minutes. Add tomatoes and stock, breaking up tomatoes into small pieces. Cover and simmer for 10 to 15 minutes, until sauce is thickened.

Combine ingredients for gremolata; set aside. Return veal to skillet; heat through. Garnish each serving with some of the gremolata.

MAKES 4 SERVINGS

Per serving: calories, 281 ◆ protein, 33 g ◆ carbohydrate, 15 g ◆ fat, 10 g (calories from fat, 32%) ◆ dietary fiber, 1 g ◆ cholesterol, 113 mg ◆ sodium, 383 mg ◆ potassium, 1,008 mg Joslin Exchanges: 4 medium-fat meat, 1 bread/starch

GRAINS, BEANS, PASTA, POTATOES, AND STARCHY VEGETABLES

Exotic grains, earthy beans, fresh pasta, and other forms of starch have become stylish as health-conscious cooks all over the country focus on these no-cholesterol, high-fiber, complex-carbohydrate foods.

Now supermarkets throughout the country carry packages of quinoa (a 5,000-year-old staple from Peru); prettily packaged bags of more than a dozen kinds of mixed dried beans with odd-sounding names like Tongues of Fire, Christmas Lima, and Appaloosa; sacks of basmati and Italian Arborio rice; boxes of bulgur (cracked wheat), instant polenta, and couscous; packages of red and green lentils—the list goes on and on.

Once upon a time, pasta meant boxes of dried spaghetti, macaroni, or lasagne noodles (all in one flavor—egg). Now fresh and dried pasta is available in more than dozens of shapes and sizes—in flavors ranging from eggless to whole-egg, whole-wheat, spinach, tomato, lemon, red bell pepper, garlic, parsley, tomato and basil, fresh herb, black pepper, and black (squid ink) pasta.

Fresh corn is now available year-round, and freezing brings us little lima beans that rival fresh. Each year's bountiful harvest of hard-shelled winter squash (from the tiny sweet dumpling to the knobby turban and the giant Hubbard and banana squash) offer delectable eating from early fall to the end of winter. Even pumpkins have new uses beyond yesterday's pumpkin pie; they can be baked, pureed, cubed for adding to soups or pasta, or layered in gratins, and the small varieties such as Munchkin and Jack Be Little are showing up filled with savory stuffings to eat along with the sweet pumpkin flesh.

Even the lowly potato has become *haute cuisine* and now comes in a variety of sizes, from the tiny new potatoes called *creamers* to large russets. One of our favorite comfort foods, potatoes also come in a variety of colors—purple, red, orange, and yellow in addition to the familiar white. Potatoes and their skins are loaded with vitamin C and potassium, contain just a trace of fat, and are an excellent source of complex carbohydrates and dietary fiber.

Baked in the microwave, a potato takes only 3 to 5 minutes to cook. But the classic baked spud topped with a hefty helping of butter and sour cream is a calorie- and fat-laden dish of the past. Today's toppings are lean, delicious, and often star at a vegetarian meal. It's our favorite quick-fix dinner when we're dining alone—be sure to eat the skin.

First you must start with the right potato—a russet (sometimes labeled Idaho). One bread/starch exchange (80 calories and 15 grams of carbohydrate) equals ½ medium-size or 1 small (3-ounce/85 g) potato. Scrub the potato and pat dry, then prick the skin several times with a fork. Bake directly on the rack (for the tastiest skin, don't oil it or wrap the potato in foil) at 375° F (190° C) for 45 minutes to 1 hour, until soft when squeezed. Open potato and fluff with a fork.

To microwave 1 medium-size baking potato, scrub, pat dry, then pierce the potato on the top and bottom. Place on a paper towel in the microwave. Cook on HIGH for 3 to 5 minutes, turning over once, until the outside gives slightly when squeezed. Let stand 5 minutes. For 2 potatoes, place the potatoes about 1 inch (2.5 cm) apart on the paper towel; increase cooking time to 5 to 9 minutes, turning over once. Let stand for 5 to 10 minutes. For 4 potatoes, place them in a circle on the paper towel, leaving a 1-inch (2.5 cm) space between them. Increase cooking time to 10 to 13 minutes, turning over once. Let stand for 5 to 10 minutes.

Sweet potatoes are also excellent baked in their skins. You can bake a few, store in the refrigerator, and reheat as needed in a toaster oven. One bread/starch exchange (80 calories and 15 grams carbohydrate) equals ½ medium-size or 1 small (2-ounce/60 g) sweet potato. Scrub the potato and pat dry, then prick the skin several times with a fork. Bake directly on the oven rack (put a piece of aluminum foil underneath to catch the drips) at 400° F (205° C) until soft when squeezed, about 45 minutes.

To microwave sweet potatoes, use the same cooking times as for russet potatoes.

Baked Potato Toppings

Broccoli and Melted Cheese

Fill an opened hot 5-ounce (140 g) baked potato with ½ cup (118 ml) steamed broccoli florets, 1 tablespoon (6 g) grated nonfat mozzarella cheese, and 1 teaspoon (5 ml) chopped fresh dill or ¼ teaspoon (1.25 ml) dried dill weed.

MAKES 1 SERVING

Per serving: calories, 182 ◆ protein, 6 g ◆ carbohydrate, 38 g ◆ fat, 1 g (calories from fat, 6%) ◆ dietary fiber, 5 g ◆ cholesterol, 3 mg ◆ sodium, 52 mg ◆ potassium, 749 mg
Joslin Exchanges: 2 bread/starch, 1 vegetable

Cheese and Chives

Fill an opened hot 5-ounce (140 g) baked potato with ¼ cup (59 ml) low-fat (1%) cottage cheese, 1 tablespoon (15 ml) snipped fresh chives, and 1 teaspoon (5 ml) toasted sesame seeds (page 440).

MAKES 1 SERVING

Per serving: calories, 214 ◆ protein, 11 g ◆ carbohydrate, 38 g ◆ fat, 2 g (calories from fat, 9%) ◆ dietary fiber, 4 g ◆ cholesterol, 3 mg ◆ sodium, 241 mg ◆ potassium, 664 mg
Joslin Exchanges: 2 bread/starch, 1 vegetable

Roasted Garlic Potatoes

Cut the bottom off a medium-size head of garlic, place head on a square of aluminum foil, and drizzle ½ teaspoon (2.5 ml) olive oil over it. Seal and bake along with the potato at 375° F (190° C) for 30 minutes, until the garlic is very soft. Squeeze the pulp out of one or more garlic cloves, to taste, into an opened hot 5-ounce (140 g) potato.

MAKES 1 SERVING

Per serving: calories, 148 ◆ protein, 2 g ◆ carbohydrate, 34 g ◆ fat, trace (calories from fat, less than 1%) ◆ dietary fiber, 3 g ◆ cholesterol, 0 mg ◆ sodium, 11 mg ◆ potassium, 568 mg
Joslin Exchanges: 2 bread/starch

Italian Potato

Top an opened hot 5-ounce (140 g) baked potato with ¹/₂ cup (118 ml) Italian Mushroom Sauce (page 123). Sprinkle with 1 tablespoon (15 ml) chopped fresh basil or parsley.

MAKES 1 SERVING

Per serving: calories, 167 ◆ protein, 4 g ◆ carbohydrate, 38 g ◆ fat, trace (calories from fat, less than 1%) ◆ dietary fiber, 4 g ◆ cholesterol, 0 mg ◆ sodium, 16 mg ◆ potassium, 718 mg
Joslin Exchanges: 2 bread/ starch, 1 vegetable

Onions and Mint

Lightly spray a nonstick sauté pan with butter-flavored cooking spray. Place over low heat, add ¹/₂ cup (118 ml) thinly sliced onion, and sauté for 4 to 5 minutes, until soft but not browned. Add 1 teaspoon (5 ml) balsamic vinegar, 1 teaspoon (5 ml) chopped fresh mint (or flat-leaf parsley), and a generous grinding of pepper. Spoon into an opened hot 5-ounce (140 g) baked potato.

MAKES 1 SERVING

Per serving: calories, 190 ◆ protein, 4 g ◆ carbohydrate, 44 g ◆ fat, trace (calories from fat, less than 1%) ◆ dietary fiber, 5 g ◆ cholesterol, 0 mg ◆ sodium, 15 mg ◆ potassium, 725 mg
Joslin Exchanges: 3 bread/starch

Tijuana Spud

Spoon ¹/₂ cup (118 ml) Microwave Mexican Vegetable Stew (page 351) into an opened hot 5-ounce (140 g) baked potato. Sprinkle with 1 teaspoon (5 ml) fresh chopped cilantro (fresh coriander) and ¹/₂ teaspoon (2.5 ml) dry-roasted sunflower seeds.

MAKES 1 SERVING

Per serving: calories, 208 ◆ protein, 5 g ◆ carbohydrate, 44 g ◆ fat, 2 g (calories from fat, 10%) ◆ dietary fiber, 2 g ◆ cholesterol, 0 mg ◆ sodium, 100 mg ◆ potassium, 885 mg
Joslin Exchanges: 3 bread/starch

Yogurt Primavera

Combine 2 tablespoons (30 ml) plain nonfat yogurt, ¼ teaspoon (1.25 ml) Dijon mustard, 3 tablespoons (45 ml) mixed diced red, green, and yellow bell peppers, and 1 minced scallion, white part and 1 inch (2.5 cm) green. Spoon into an opened hot 5-ounce (140 g) baked potato. Sprinkle with hot red pepper flakes to taste.

MAKES 1 SERVING

Per serving: calories, 189 ◆ protein, 6 g ◆ carbohydrate, 42 g ◆ fat, trace (calories from fat, 2%) ◆ dietary fiber, 5 g ◆ cholesterol, 1 mg ◆ sodium, 52 mg ◆ potassium, 785 mg Joslin Exchanges: 3 bread/starch

QUICK-FIX SUPPER

◆

Cup of Curried Asparagus Soup (page 48)

Baked Potato with Broccoli and Melted Cheese (page 262)

Fresh Fruit

Per serving: 386 calories (13% fat)
Joslin Exchanges: 1 low-fat meat, 3 bread/starch, 1 vegetable, 1 fruit

Potato and Spinach Lasagne

Thinly sliced potatoes are masquerading as pasta in this dish, which takes the humble potato to new culinary heights. In smaller portions, serve the lasagne as a starch accompaniment to grilled fish or meat.

olive oil cooking spray
1 10-ounce (285 g) box frozen chopped spinach, defrosted
1¾ pounds (790 g) russet potatoes
1 medium-size red onion, about 3 ounces (85 g), chopped
1 cup (236 ml) dry white wine
1 cup (236 ml) vegetable stock (page 47) or chicken stock (page 45)
2 shallots, minced
1 medium-size leek, about 5 ounces (140 g), white part only, chopped

2 garlic cloves, minced
juice of ½ lemon
1 tablespoon (15 ml) fresh thyme leaves or 1 teaspoon (5 ml) crushed dried
1 medium-size fresh tomato, about 5 ounces (140 g), peeled, seeded, and diced
3 tablespoons (19 g) freshly grated Parmesan cheese

Lightly spray a 9- by 13-inch (23 by 33 cm) baking dish with cooking spray. Squeeze moisture from spinach. Set aside. Peel potatoes and cut into ⅛-inch (.5 cm) slices. Arrange one-third of the potato slices in baking dish, overlapping slightly, to cover bottom of dish in an even layer. Cover evenly with half the onion and half the spinach. Repeat layers, finishing with the final layer of potatoes.

Preheat oven to 375° F (190° C). In a large saucepan, bring wine and stock to a boil. Add shallots, leek, and garlic. Reduce heat; simmer for 5 minutes. Add lemon juice and thyme. Pour mixture over potatoes. Cover with foil and bake for 30 minutes. Remove cover; continue baking until top is richly browned and potatoes are tender when pierced, another 15 to 20 minutes. Sprinkle diced tomato and Parmesan cheese over lasagne; bake 5 minutes longer. Remove from oven and let stand 10 minutes before cutting into squares.

MAKES 6 SERVINGS

Per serving: calories, 173 ♦ protein, 6 g ♦ carbohydrate, 37 g ♦ fat, 1 g (calories from fat, 5%) ♦ dietary fiber, 2 g ♦ cholesterol, 3 mg ♦ sodium, 121 mg ♦ potassium, 739 mg Joslin Exchanges: 2 bread/ starch, 1 vegetable

MEATLESS WINTER MEAL

◆

Snow Pea and Pearl Onion Salad (page 108)

Potato and Spinach Lasagne (page 265)

Roasted Tomatoes (page 330)

Bartlett Pears and Parmigiano-Reggiano Cheese

Per serving: 447 calories (20% fat)
Joslin Exchanges: 1 medium-fat meat, 3 vegetable, 2 bread/starch, 1 fruit, 1 fat

Peppers Stuffed with Barley and Basil

Barley, a grain from the grass family, dates back to the Stone Age. Whole hulled barley can be found only at natural food stores and needs to be soaked overnight before cooking. We've used pearl barley, which is more readily available and cooks in just 15 minutes.

Lovely as a side dish, these colorful stuffed peppers also work as a main course for lunch or Sunday supper, served with a mixed green salad and fresh fruit for dessert.

1½ cups (354 ml) chicken stock (page 45) or vegetable stock (page 47)
¼ teaspoon (1.25 ml) salt (optional)
½ cup (85 g) pearl barley
1 tablespoon (15 ml) olive oil
½ cup (118 ml) chopped red onion

2 garlic cloves, minced
1 medium-size fresh tomato, about 5 ounces (140 g), peeled, seeded, and diced
¼ cup (59 ml) slivered fresh basil or 4 teaspoons (20 ml) crushed dried

1 tablespoon (15 ml) chopped fresh
  flat-leaf parsley
2 tablespoons (30 ml) golden
  raisins
freshly ground pepper to taste
4 large yellow, red, or green bell
  peppers, about 2 pounds (900 g)

olive oil cooking spray
2 teaspoons (10 ml) grated
  Parmesan cheese
chopped fresh flat-leaf parsley for
  garnish (optional)

Preheat oven to 350° F. (180° C). In a medium-size saucepan, bring stock and salt to a boil. Add barley, reduce heat, and cook, covered, until almost tender, 12 to 15 minutes. Set aside.

In a large skillet, heat 1 teaspoon (5 ml) olive oil over low heat. Add onion and garlic; sauté for 3 minutes, stirring constantly. Stir in cooked barley, tomato, basil, parsley, and raisins. Add pepper.

With a sharp knife, cut the tops off the peppers; remove the cores and seeds. Fill each pepper with the barley mixture, mounding the tops.

Lightly spray a baking dish with a lid with cooking spray. Then arrange peppers in it so that they fit snugly. Sprinkle each pepper with 1/2 teaspoon (2.5 ml) Parmesan cheese and drizzle 1/2 teaspoon (2.5 ml) olive oil over the top. Cover and bake for 35 minutes. Remove cover and bake for another 15 minutes or until the peppers are tender and lightly browned. Remove from oven and sprinkle with parsley.

MAKES 4 SERVINGS

Per serving: calories, 187 ◆ protein, 5 g ◆ carbohydrate, 35 g ◆ fat, 4 g (calories from fat, 19%) ◆ dietary fiber, 1 g ◆ cholesterol, 1 mg ◆ sodium, 179 mg ◆ potassium, 483 mg Joslin Exchanges: 2 bread/starch, 1 vegetable

Tomato Tart in Spinach Crust

This main-course pie teams plum tomatoes, which are good quality year-round, with a savory spinach crust. Serve the tart hot with a salad of thinly sliced radishes, fennel, and red onion piled into green leafy lettuce, lightly dressed with Creamy Orange Dressing (page 116).

1 recipe **Spinach Triangle dough** (page 383)
1 cup (236 ml) evaporated skim milk
½ cup (118 ml) egg substitute
1 egg white
⅛ teaspoon (.6 ml) salt (optional)
1 tablespoon (15 ml) minced fresh basil or 1 teaspoon (5 ml) crushed dried

1 garlic clove, minced
⅓ cup (37 g) grated low-fat Swiss cheese
½ pound (225 g) fresh plum tomatoes, very thinly sliced
freshly ground pepper to taste

Preheat oven to 375° F (190° C). Roll spinach dough into a circle to fit a 9-inch (23 cm) pie pan. Partially bake for 10 to 12 minutes.

Meanwhile, in a bowl, combine milk, egg substitute, egg white, salt, basil, garlic, and cheese. Beat until well blended. Pour into prebaked pie shell. Place tomatoes in concentric circles on top of filling. Sprinkle with pepper. Bake for 35 minutes, until custard is set. Remove from oven. Let stand for 5 minutes before cutting into wedges.

MAKES 6 SERVINGS

Per serving: calories, 235 ◆ protein, 13 g ◆ carbohydrate, 25 g ◆ fat, 10 g (calories from fat, 38%) ◆ dietary fiber, 1 g ◆ cholesterol, 6 mg ◆ sodium, 227 mg ◆ potassium, 493 mg Joslin Exchanges: 1 bread/ starch, 1 medium-fat meat, 1 fat, ½ nonfat milk

Pasta with Ratatouille

A delicious version of pasta primavera. You can use virtually any kind or shape of pasta—fettuccine, linguine, even tubes of macaroni such as ziti or penne. The ratatouille gets better with age. Make it the night before and refrigerate. The next day, reheat the ratatouille while the pasta boils.

Ratatouille

1 large onion, about ½ pound (225 g), sliced
1 tablespoon (15 ml) olive oil
3 garlic cloves, minced
1 medium-size eggplant, about ½ pound (225 g), diced
1 medium-size red bell pepper, about 5 ounces (140 g), seeded and cut into strips
2 medium-size zucchini, about ½ pound (225 g), chopped
1 16-ounce (450 g) can plum tomatoes, drained and chopped

1 tablespoon (15 ml) chopped fresh basil or 1 teaspoon (5 ml) crushed dried
1 small bay leaf
2 tablespoons (30 ml) chopped fresh flat-leaf parsley
1 teaspoon (5 ml) chopped fresh oregano or ¼ teaspoon (1.25 ml) crushed dried
½ teaspoon (2.5 ml) salt (optional)
freshly ground pepper to taste

Pasta

¾ pound (340 g) fresh pasta or ½ pound (225 g) dried

¼ cup (25 g) grated Parmesan cheese

To prepare ratatouille, sauté onion in olive oil in a deep saucepan over low heat for 2 minutes; add garlic and continue to sauté until onion is wilted but not browned, about 4 minutes. Add eggplant, bell pepper, and zucchini. Cook for about 10 minutes, until eggplant begins to soften. Add tomatoes, herbs, salt, and pepper. Cover and simmer for 15 minutes. Remove cover and continue to cook, stirring occasionally, until most of the liquid is gone. If prepared ahead, cover and refrigerate.

Cook pasta in boiling water according to package directions. Drain. Divide cooked pasta among 4 shallow bowls or plates. Top with ratatouille and sprinkle each serving with 1 tablespoon (15 ml) Parmesan cheese.

MAKES 4 SERVINGS

Per serving: calories, 180 ◆ protein, 7 g ◆ carbohydrate, 30 g ◆ fat, 5 g (calories from fat, 25%) ◆ dietary fiber, 4 g ◆ cholesterol, 22 mg ◆ sodium, 395 mg ◆ potassium, 583 mg
Joslin Exchanges: 1 bread/ starch, 2 vegetable, 1 fat

Per serving (ratatouille alone): calories, 86 ◆ protein, 3 g ◆ carbohydrate, 15 g ◆ fat, 3 g (calories from fat, 31%) ◆ dietary fiber, 3 g ◆ cholesterol, 0 mg ◆ sodium, 314 mg ◆ potassium, 565 mg
Joslin Exchanges: 2 vegetable, 1 fat

Penne with Roasted Peppers

A favorite meatless meal. Roast the peppers ahead and refrigerate until ready to use. Serve with a salad of mixed baby greens and offer fresh fruit for dessert, splashed with balsamic vinegar and cracked pepper (page 430).

10 ounces (285 g) penne
 3 quarts (2.75 l) boiling water
 2 tablespoons (30 ml) olive oil
 4 garlic cloves, minced
 1 large red bell pepper, about ½ pound (225 g), roasted (page 100) and cut into thin strips
 1 large yellow bell pepper, about ½ pound (225 g), roasted (page 100) and cut into thin strips
¾ pound (340 g) fresh plum tomatoes, peeled, seeded, and diced

¼ teaspoon (1.25 ml) salt (optional)
⅛ teaspoon (.6 ml) freshly ground pepper or to taste
 3 tablespoons (19 g) grated Parmesan cheese
¼ cup (59 ml) chopped flat-leaf parsley

In a 6-quart (5.5 l) pot, cook penne in boiling water until tender, 10 to 12 minutes.

While pasta is cooking, heat olive oil in a large nonstick sauté pan over low heat. Add garlic; sauté until garlic is wilted but not browned, about 3 minutes. Add bell peppers, tomatoes, and salt. Cook until heated through, about 4 minutes.

Drain pasta; toss with bell pepper mixture. Stir in pepper and Parmesan cheese. Sprinkle with chopped parsley.

MAKES 6 SERVINGS

> **Per serving:** calories, 265 ◆ protein, 9 g ◆ carbohydrate, 44 g ◆ fat, 7 g (calories from fat, 23%) ◆ dietary fiber, 3 g ◆ cholesterol, 3 mg ◆ sodium, 173 mg ◆ potassium, 362 mg Joslin Exchanges: 2½ bread/starch, 1 vegetable, 1 fat

 Spaghetti with Easy Tomato Sauce

Available year-round, ripe plum tomatoes are quick-cooked for a light, fresh-tasting sauce. Angel hair pasta or fettuccine could be used in place of spaghetti for this recipe made from ingredients you probably have on hand. Toss a salad and offer a bowl of seedless grapes for dessert.

 3 quarts (2.75 l) water
10 ounces (285 g) spaghetti
 1 tablespoon (15 ml) olive oil
 2 garlic cloves, minced
12 medium-size plum tomatoes, about 1¾ pounds (790 g), peeled, seeded, and chopped
 1 tablespoon (15 g) margarine
 3 tablespoons (45 ml) chopped fresh flat-leaf parsley

½ cup (118 ml) chopped fresh basil or 2 tablespoons (30 ml) crushed dried
½ teaspoon (2.5 ml) salt (optional)
freshly ground pepper to taste
¼ cup (59 ml) grated Parmesan cheese for garnish
hot red pepper flakes for garnish

In a 6-quart (5.5 l) pot, bring water to a boil over high heat. Add spaghetti and cook, uncovered, until barely tender, 8 to 9 minutes.

Meanwhile, heat oil in a nonreactive saucepan over very low heat. Add garlic; cook until soft but not browned, about 3 minutes. Add tomatoes and raise heat to high. Cook until tomatoes begin to release their juice, about 5 minutes.

Drain pasta. In a warm large serving bowl, combine margarine, parsley, basil, and drained pasta. Toss. Add tomato mixture, salt, and pepper; toss again. Serve with grated Parmesan and red pepper flakes.

MAKES 8 SERVINGS

> **Per 1-cup serving:** calories, 199 ◆ protein, 7 g ◆ carbohydrate, 32 g ◆ fat, 5 g (calories from fat, 23%) ◆ dietary fiber, 1 g ◆ cholesterol, 3 mg ◆ sodium, 233 mg ◆ potassium, 330 mg Joslin Exchanges: 2 bread/starch, 1 fat

Spinach Ravioli in Herbed Tomato Broth

Fresh wonton wrappers are readily available at supermarkets and easy—not to mention fun—to work with. They're great for making fresh ravioli. Here the ravioli are served in a light broth flavored with fresh ginger, chilies, and fresh herbs for a delicious pasta meal.

olive oil cooking spray
2 shallots, minced
1 10-ounce (285 g) box frozen chopped spinach, defrosted
1 cup (236 ml) nonfat ricotta cheese
1 large egg, separated
3 tablespoons (19 g) grated Parmesan cheese
1/4 teaspoon (1.25 ml) freshly ground pepper or to taste
2 tablespoons (30 ml) minced fresh basil
6 dozen wonton wrappers, about 1 pound (450 g)
1 tablespoon (8 g) unbleached flour, approximately

2 cups (472 ml) dry white wine
1 quart (1 l) chicken stock (page 45)
1 medium-size onion, about 5 ounces (140 g), peeled, sliced, and separated into rings
2 tablespoons (30 ml) minced fresh jalapeño chilies
2 tablespoons (30 ml) minced fresh ginger
4 quarts (3.75 l) water
1/4 teaspoon (1.25 ml) salt (optional)
1/2 cup (59 ml) loosely packed fresh basil leaves, shredded
1 small fresh tomato, peeled, seeded and chopped

In a heavy nonstick sauté pan lightly sprayed with cooking spray, sauté shallots over low heat until just wilted, about 4 minutes. Squeeze as much liquid as possible from spinach. Add to sauté pan along with ricotta cheese, egg yolk, grated Parmesan cheese, pepper, and minced basil. Remove from heat; stir until well blended.

Place a wonton wrapper on a flat surface, covering remaining wrappers with a dampened paper towel to prevent them from drying out. Place 1 rounded teaspoon (5 ml) of spinach mixture in the center of the wonton wrapper. Beat egg white with fork to blend. Brush edges of wonton wrapper with egg white. Cover with another wrapper and press edges well to seal. Trim edges with a pastry wheel. Place filled ravioli on a lightly floured cloth. Repeat until all filling is used.

In a large heavy saucepan, bring wine, chicken stock, onion, chili, and ginger to a boil. Reduce heat to medium-low; simmer gently for 5 minutes.

Meanwhile, in another large pot, bring water and salt to a gentle boil. Add ravioli. After they rise to the surface, cook until tender, about 1 minute for al dente. Remove with a slotted spoon; drain well.

Stir shredded basil and tomatoes into hot broth. Arrange 6 cooked ravioli in each of 6 heated soup plates. Ladle hot broth mixture over ravioli. Serve immediately.

MAKES 6 SERVINGS

Per serving: calories, 239 ◆ protein, 16 g ◆ carbohydrate, 28 g ◆ fat, 7 g (calories from fat, 26%) ◆ dietary fiber, 1 g ◆ cholesterol, 77 mg ◆ sodium, 271 mg ◆ potassium, 494 mg Joslin Exchanges: 1 bread/starch, 2 medium-fat meat, 1 vegetable

---

PASTA SUPPER

◆

Arugula and Radicchio Salad with Creamy Italian Dressing

(page 116)

Spinach Ravioli in Herbed Tomato Broth (page 272)

Bowl of Red and Green Seedless Grapes

Per serving: 388 calories (28% fat)
Joslin Exchanges: 2 medium-fat meat, 2 vegetable, 1 bread/starch, 1 fruit

TOFU

Tofu or soybean curd is a bland custardlike Asian product made from soy milk in much the same way that cottage cheese is made from cow's milk. It quickly picks up the flavors of whatever it is cooked with, so you can make it taste like most anything you want. Called "meat without bones" by the Chinese, tofu is high in protein, low in calories, low in fat, free of cholesterol, and low in sodium—and it's also inexpensive. What's more, tofu is a good source of calcium and is recommended for those who are allergic to dairy products.

It comes in forms from soft to extra-firm and can be sliced and eaten (it's already cooked) in sandwiches; stir-fried with vegetables; blended into dips, dressings, or sauces; marinated for salads; and baked in casseroles and quiches.

Tofu is available in most supermarkets (look for it in the produce or deli section). It can also be found in natural food stores and Asian markets. Whether you buy tofu in bulk or in plastic tubs, once home, cover the tofu with fresh water and change the water every day. It should keep fresh for about a week.

Vacuum-packaged tofu will keep unopened for three or four weeks. Once opened, change the water every day and use within a week. You can freeze tofu if you find yourself with a surplus, but we really don't recommend it. Tofu becomes chewy and develops an almost spongelike texture once frozen. It also changes color from a luminous creamy white to an amber while frozen and then to a soft beige when thawed.

We discovered the versatility of tofu years ago, long before we were diagnosed as having diabetes. Our recipes mostly call for extra-firm tofu, which we've further pressed to extract water, thus allowing the tofu to take on more of the flavors of the recipe.

To press tofu, cut the block in half to form two thin rectangles. Place on a clean kitchen towel or four-ply paper towels in a flat-bottomed bowl. Cover with wax paper and more paper towels or the top of the towel. Weight it with a heavy pot or pan for 30 to 45 minutes at room temperature. Dry it off and you're ready to proceed with the recipe.

Tofu Caesar Salad

East meets West in this version of Caesar salad where tofu takes the place of croutons. Substantial enough for a meal, it needs only some crusty French bread and fresh fruit for dessert.

Dressing

3 tablespoons (45 ml) fresh lemon juice
½ tablespoon (7.5 ml) Dijon mustard
1 teaspoon (5 ml) minced garlic
½ teaspoon (2.5 ml) Worcestershire sauce

2 tablespoons (30 ml) olive oil
2 tablespoons (30 ml) water
½ teaspoon (2.5 ml) anchovy paste or 1 anchovy, rinsed and mashed
¼ cup (59 ml) egg substitute
freshly ground pepper to taste

Salad

½ pound (225 g) extra-firm tofu, pressed and cut into 1-inch (2.5 cm) cubes

2 quarts (2 l) torn bite-size pieces of romaine lettuce, washed and crisped

1 19-ounce (535 g) can chick-peas, drained

¼ cup (25 g) freshly grated Parmesan cheese

Whisk together dressing ingredients. Pour over tofu cubes and marinate for 20 to 30 minutes.

Place lettuce in a salad bowl. Add drained chick-peas. Remove tofu cubes from dressing; set aside. Whisk dressing and pour over the lettuce; toss. Top with tofu cubes and Parmesan cheese; toss again. Serve at once.

MAKES 6 SERVINGS

Per serving: calories, 228 ♦ protein, 15 g ♦ carbohydrate, 19 g ♦ fat, 11 g (calories from fat, 43%) ♦ dietary fiber, 6 g ♦ cholesterol, 3 mg ♦ sodium, 543 mg* ♦ potassium, 535 mg Joslin Exchanges: 2 low-fat meat, 1 vegetable, 1 fat

* Recipe not recommended for low-sodium diets, unless ½ pound (225 g) dried chick-peas, cooked in unsalted water until tender, are used instead of canned chick-peas.

Tofu in Chili Garlic Sauce

Serve this savory tofu dish over buckwheat noodles. The chili sauce with garlic, found in Asian markets and some supermarkets, is quite hot, so adjust the amount according to your taste.

If you can't find buckwheat noodles or if you're on a low-sodium diet, substitute 2 cups (472 ml) cooked brown rice for the noodles.

½ pound (225 g) buckwheat noodles

¼ pound (115 g) snow peas, trimmed and strings removed

⅛ teaspoon (.6 ml) dark sesame oil

1 tablespoon (15 ml) peanut oil

Chili Garlic Sauce

1 cup (236 ml) water
¼ cup (59 ml) low-sodium soy
   sauce
1 tablespoon (15 ml) balsamic
   vinegar
1 tablespoon (15 ml) chili sauce
   with garlic or to taste

2 tablespoons (30 ml) minced fresh
   ginger
3 scallions, white part and 1 inch
   (2.5 cm) green, minced
½ tablespoon (7.5 ml) cornstarch

Tofu

1 pound (450 g) extra-firm tofu,
   pressed and cut into ½-inch (1.5
   cm) cubes

1 tablespoon (15 ml) toasted
   sesame seeds (page 440)

Cook noodles in a large pot of boiling water until tender, about 10 minutes. Meanwhile, blanch snow peas in boiling water for 2 minutes; drain and set aside. Drain and rinse noodles under cold running water. Drain again; toss with sesame oil, peanut oil, and snow peas. Set aside.

Combine all sauce ingredients in a medium-size saucepan. Bring to a boil. Cook, stirring, for 1 minute. Add tofu and cook for 2 minutes, stirring carefully to avoid breaking tofu cubes.

Serve tofu and sauce over noodles; sprinkle with toasted sesame seeds. Serve at once.

MAKES 6 SERVINGS

> **Per serving:** calories, 305 ◆ protein, 19 g ◆ carbohydrate, 37 g ◆ fat, 9 g (calories from fat, 27%) ◆ dietary fiber, 2 g ◆ cholesterol, 0 mg ◆ sodium, 745 mg* ◆ potassium, 379 mg Joslin Exchanges: 1½ low-fat meat, 2 bread/starch, 1 vegetable, ½ fat

* Recipe not recommended for low-sodium diets unless served over rice instead of buckwheat noodles and then eaten only occasionally.

Spinach and Tofu Soup

If you're short on time, this hearty soup takes less than 5 minutes to make. Tofu adds a nice texture to the soup.

1 quart (1 l) chicken stock (page 45) or vegetable stock (page 47)
1 pound (450 g) fresh spinach, well washed and ribs removed, or 1 10-ounce (285 g) box frozen leaf spinach, defrosted

juice of ½ lemon
1 cup (236 ml) cubed extra-firm tofu
freshly ground pepper to taste
2 scallions, white part and 1 inch (2.5 cm) green, minced

In a large saucepan, bring stock to a boil. Reduce heat to medium; add spinach and cook for about 1 minute. Add remaining ingredients except scallions; cook for another 30 seconds. Pour into soup bowls. Sprinkle on scallions and serve.

MAKES 4 SERVINGS

Per serving: calories, 134 ◆ protein, 13 g ◆ carbohydrate, 7 g ◆ fat, 6 g (calories from fat, 40%) ◆ dietary fiber, 4 g ◆ cholesterol, 0 mg ◆ sodium, 144 mg ◆ potassium, 858 mg Joslin Exchanges: 2 low-fat meat, 1 vegetable

Tofu Vegetable Stir-Fry

Make this easy dish for a quick after-work supper or Sunday lunch. It's served over bowls of brown rice; offer fresh tangerines for dessert.

Marinade

1 tablespoon (15 ml) Chinese rice wine or dry sherry
½ teaspoon (2.5 ml) five-spice powder
⅛ teaspoon (.6 ml) hot red pepper flakes or to taste

½ teaspoon (2.5 ml) dark sesame oil
2 tablespoons (30 ml) low-sodium soy sauce

Tofu and Vegetables

1 pound (450 g) extra-firm tofu, pressed and cut into ½-inch (1.5 cm) cubes	1 red bell pepper, seeded and diced
2 teaspoons (10 ml) canola oil	½ pound (225 g) broccoli florets
1 or 2 garlic cloves, to taste, minced	½ pound (225 g) cauliflower florets
1 tablespoon (15 ml) minced fresh ginger	¼ pound (115 g) bean sprouts
4 scallions, white part and 2 inches (5 cm) green, cut into 1-inch (2.5 cm) lengths	¼ pound (115 g) snow peas, trimmed
¼ pound (115 g) fresh shiitake or cultivated mushrooms, sliced	¾ teaspoon (3.75 ml) cornstarch
	½ cup (118 ml) chicken stock (page 45) or vegetable stock (47)
	2 cups (472 ml) hot cooked brown rice

Combine marinade ingredients; pour over tofu cubes and marinate for 15 minutes. Drain cubes, reserving marinade.

Heat canola oil in a nonstick wok or sauté pan over medium-high heat. Add garlic, ginger, scallions, and mushrooms. Stir-fry for 2 minutes. Add red pepper, broccoli, and cauliflower. Stir-fry for another 3 minutes. Add bean sprouts and snow peas; cook for another minute. Stir cornstarch into stock. Pour into vegetable mixture along with reserved marinade. Simmer for 1 minute. Add tofu cubes and stir quickly to combine. Divide brown rice among 6 shallow bowls. Top with tofu and vegetables. Serve at once.

MAKES 6 SERVINGS

Per serving: calories, 269 ◆ protein, 17 g ◆ carbohydrate, 30 g ◆ fat, 9 g (calories from fat, 30%) ◆ dietary fiber, 4 g ◆ cholesterol, 0 mg ◆ sodium, 235 mg ◆ potassium, 627 mg Joslin Exchanges: 1½ low-fat meat, 3 vegetable, 1 bread/ starch, 1 fat

Bulgur Pilaf

A staple of the Middle East, bulgur is wheat kernels that have been steamed, dried, and crushed. We love its comforting, nutty flavor and ease of preparation.

1 garlic clove, minced
2 small leeks, white part only, washed well and thinly sliced
2 teaspoons (10 ml) walnut oil
1 cup (140 g) fine bulgur
2½ cups (590 ml) chicken stock (page 45) or vegetable stock (page 47)
juice of ½ lemon

¼ teaspoon (1.25 ml) salt (optional)
freshly ground pepper to taste
2 tablespoons (30 ml) finely chopped fresh mint for garnish

In a heavy nonstick saucepan over low heat, sauté garlic and leeks in walnut oil until garlic is tender but not browned, about 4 minutes. Add bulgur and stock; stir well. Bring to a boil, reduce heat to low, cover, and simmer for 20 to 25 minutes, until bulgur is tender and all the liquid has been absorbed. Turn off heat and let pan stand, covered, for 10 minutes. Add lemon juice, salt, pepper, and mint. Gently toss, fluffing bulgur with a fork.

MAKES 6 SERVINGS

Per ½-cup (118 ml) serving: calories, 130 ◆ protein, 4 g ◆ carbohydrate, 24 g ◆ fat, 2 g (calories from fat, 14%) ◆ dietary fiber, 1 g ◆ cholesterol, 0 mg ◆ sodium, 120 mg ◆ potassium, 197 mg
Joslin Exchanges: 1½ bread/starch

Tabbouleh

This is a favorite in summer when tomatoes are at their peak and the garden is rampant with fresh mint. Bulgur (cracked wheat) is available in specialty food shops and some supermarkets.

For this salad, chop the herbs by hand. Somehow they taste better than when minced in a food processor.

1 cup (140 g) medium bulgur
1 cup (236 ml) cold water
3 tablespoons (45 ml) fresh lemon juice
1 tablespoon (15 ml) olive oil
½ cup (118 ml) finely chopped fresh mint
¾ cup (177 ml) finely chopped flat-leaf parsley
1 medium-size onion, about 5 ounces (140 g), finely chopped
2 garlic cloves, minced

3 large fresh plum tomatoes, about ½ pound (225 g), peeled, seeded, and finely chopped
1 large cucumber, about ½ pound (225 g), peeled, seeded, and finely chopped
1 15-ounce (425 g) can chick-peas, drained
½ teaspoon (2.5 ml) salt (optional)
freshly ground pepper to taste
8 inner leaves of romaine lettuce, washed and crisped

In a large bowl, combine bulgur, water, lemon juice, and olive oil. Mix well; let stand at room temperature for 1 hour. Fluff with a fork. Add remaining ingredients except lettuce leaves, mixing lightly with a fork. Let stand at room temperature for at least 30 minutes to allow flavors to mingle. Arrange lettuce leaves on a serving platter; pile tabbouleh in the center and serve.

MAKES 8 SERVINGS

Per serving: calories, 142 ◆ protein, 4 g ◆ carbohydrate, 18 g ◆ fat, 6 g (calories from fat, 38%) ◆ dietary fiber, 5 g ◆ cholesterol, 0 mg ◆ sodium, 355 mg ◆ potassium, 355 mg Joslin Exchanges: 1 bread/ starch, 1 fat

Confetti Couscous

Couscous, tiny pellets made of semolina flour, is a staple of the North African countries Morocco, Tunisia, and Algeria and offers lots of tasty possibilities for anyone on a special diet. Eaten plain with skim milk, it makes a delicious cereal or snack. Tossed with vegetables and fresh herbs, it becomes a flavorful side dish or salad. Sweetened with fresh fruit, couscous can be served for dessert.

Here we've included the traditional seasonings such as cumin and cinnamon, adding lots of fresh vegetables for a wonderful side dish that can easily be expanded to feed a crowd.

2½ cups (590 ml) chicken stock (page 45) or vegetable stock (page 47)

1 tablespoon (15 ml) olive oil

1 medium-size onion, about ¼ pound (115 g), chopped

1 medium-size red bell pepper, about 5 ounces (140 g), seeded and chopped

2 garlic cloves, minced

1 medium-size carrot, about 3 ounces (85 g), peeled and cut into 1-inch (2.5 cm) chunks

½ teaspoon (2.5 ml) ground cumin

½ teaspoon (2.5 ml) ground coriander

½ teaspoon (2.5 ml) turmeric

¼ teaspoon (1.25 ml) ground cinnamon

1 cup (184 g) quick-cooking couscous

1 medium-size zucchini, about ¼ pound (115 g), cut into 1-inch (2.5 cm) dice

1 small fresh tomato, about 3 ounces (85 g), peeled and cut into 2-inch (5 cm) chunks

juice of ½ lemon

2 tablespoons (30 ml) golden raisins

cayenne pepper to taste

minced fresh parsley for garnish

Basic Quick-Cooking Couscous

In a heavy saucepan, bring 1½ cups (354 ml) water or chicken stock (page 45) and ½ teaspoon (2.5 ml) salt (optional) to a boil over high heat. Stir in 1 cup (184 g) quick-cooking couscous; cover. Remove from heat and let stand 5 minutes. Fluff lightly with a fork.

MAKES SIX ½-CUP (118 ML) SERVINGS

Note: Quick-cooking couscous may be flavored with a variety of herbs and spices—use the same seasonings as for rice (page 289).

In a large saucepan, bring 1 cup (236 ml) stock and olive oil to a boil. Add onion, red bell pepper, garlic, carrot, cumin, coriander, turmeric, and cinnamon. Reduce heat to a simmer; cook, uncovered, until carrots are tender and most of the liquid is absorbed, about 15 minutes.

Meanwhile, in a separate saucepan, bring remaining 1½ cups (354 ml) stock to a boil. Add couscous and stir briefly. Cover and set aside until liquid has been absorbed, about 5 minutes.

Stir zucchini, tomato, and lemon juice into onion mixture. Fluff couscous with a fork and combine with vegetables, tossing lightly. Scatter raisins over couscous and sprinkle with cayenne pepper and minced parsley.

MAKES 8 SERVINGS

Per 1-cup serving: calories, 136 ♦ protein, 4 g ♦ carbohydrate, 26 g ♦ fat, 2 g (calories from fat, 13%) ♦ dietary fiber, 1 g ♦ cholesterol, trace ♦ sodium, 32 mg ♦ potassium, 296 mg
Joslin Exchanges: 2 bread/starch

Spicy Couscous

In Tunisia the couscous is red and seasoned with a fiery pepper puree often used in North African dishes called *harissa*. You'll find tubes of *harissa* in Middle Eastern shops, and it's available by mail order (see Appendix 2). You can also make your own—just be sure to wear rubber gloves when handling the chilies.

The leftover *harissa* can be used to flavor soups or stirred into nonfat yogurt to spoon over steamed vegetables or grated vegetable salads. It's *very hot*, so use it sparingly.

½ cup (118 ml) diced red onion
1 garlic clove, minced
1 teaspoon (5 ml) olive oil
½ teaspoon (2.5 ml) ground cumin
¼ teaspoon (1.25 ml) freshly ground pepper
¼ teaspoon (1.25 ml) salt (optional)
¼ teaspoon (1.25 ml) ground cinnamon
¼ teaspoon (1.25 ml) ground cloves
¼ teaspoon (1.25 ml) ground nutmeg

1½ cups (354 ml) chicken stock (page 45)
¼ teaspoon (1.25 ml) *harissa* (recipe follows) or to taste
1 tablespoon (15 ml) tomato paste
1 cup (184 g) quick-cooking couscous
1 cup (236 ml) drained canned chick-peas
2 tablespoons (30 ml) finely minced fresh mint

In a large nonstick saucepan over low heat, sauté onion and garlic in oil for 5 minutes. Stir in spices, stock, *harissa*, and tomato paste. Bring to a rapid boil. Stir in couscous. Cover and remove from heat. Let stand for 5 minutes. Fluff couscous lightly with a fork. Stir in chick-peas; garnish with mint and serve.

MAKES 8 SERVINGS

> **Per serving:** calories, 127 ◆ protein, 6 g ◆ carbohydrate, 24 g ◆ fat, 1 g (calories from fat, 7%) ◆ dietary fiber, 5 g ◆ cholesterol, trace ◆ sodium, 207 ◆ potassium, 145
> Joslin Exchanges: 1½ bread/starch

Harissa

½ ounce (15 g) dried hot red chilies
½ teaspoon (2.5 ml) caraway seed
¼ teaspoon (1.25 ml) cumin seed
¼ teaspoon (1.25 ml) coriander seed
⅛ teaspoon (.6 ml) salt (optional)
1 garlic clove, peeled
1½ tablespoons (22.5 ml) plus 1 teaspoon (5 ml) olive oil

In a small saucepan, bring chilies to a boil in water to cover. Remove from heat and let stand for 1 hour. Meanwhile, using a spice mill or a mortar and pestle, grind spices. Set aside.

Remove peppers from liquid; pat dry with paper towels and chop. Reserve pepper liquid. Using the spice mill or mortar and pestle, grind or mash together spices, chilies, and garlic until they form a thick paste. Stir in 1½ tablespoons (22.5 ml) olive oil and 1 tablespoon (15 ml) reserved chili-soaking liquid. Store any remaining *harissa* in a small glass jar. Spoon remaining 1 teaspoon (5 ml) olive oil over top. Cover tightly and refrigerate for up to 3 months.

MAKES ABOUT 3 TABLESPOONS (45 ML)

> **Per ¼-teaspoon (1.25 ml) serving:** calories, 7 ◆ protein, trace ◆ carbohydrate, trace ◆ fat, 1 g (calories from fat, 92%) ◆ dietary fiber, 0 g ◆ cholesterol, 0 mg ◆ sodium, 6 mg ◆ potassium, 3 mg
> Joslin Exchanges: free

Couscous Salad

Here we've combined couscous with currants, pine nuts, and a touch of cinnamon for a year-round salad that goes well with almost any chicken, fish, or meat dish.

1½ tablespoons (22.5 g) margarine or unsalted butter
½ teaspoon (2.5 ml) ground cumin
1½ cups (354 ml) chicken stock (page 45)
1½ cups (276 g) quick-cooking couscous
⅔ cup (156 ml) dried currants
¼ cup (59 ml) hot water
1½ cups (354 ml) chopped celery

3 scallions, including some green, chopped
¼ cup (59 ml) chopped flat-leaf parsley
½ teaspoon (2.5 ml) ground cinnamon
2 tablespoons (30 ml) toasted pine nuts (see below)
¼ cup (59 ml) fresh lemon juice
1½ tablespoons (22.5 ml) olive oil

In a large saucepan, melt margarine. Add cumin and stock. Bring to a boil. Add couscous and currants, cover, remove from heat, and let stand for 5 minutes, until liquid is absorbed.

Transfer couscous to a bowl. Fluff with a fork. Add remaining ingredients except lemon juice and oil. Combine lemon juice and olive oil. Pour over couscous mixture. Toss lightly. Chill for at least 2 hours.

MAKES 12 SERVINGS

Per serving: calories, 125 ◆ protein, 3 g ◆ carbohydrate, 20 g ◆ fat, 4 g (calories from fat, 28%) ◆ dietary fiber, 1 g ◆ cholesterol, 0 mg ◆ sodium, 35 mg ◆ potassium, 130 mg Joslin Exchanges: 1 bread/ starch, ½ fruit, 1 fat

Toasting Pine Nuts

In a small sauté pan over medium-low heat, stir pine nuts until lightly browned, about 3 minutes. Watch them carefully.

Kasha with Bow Ties

This is a lightened version of a classic Eastern European Jewish dish that originates from the Ukraine. It's wonderful with pot roast on Friday night.

Kasha (roasted buckwheat groats) is one of the best-known sources of complex carbohydrates in the entire plant kingdom. Some supermarkets carry it, but your best source is a natural food store. Kasha is traditionally coated with beaten egg and then stir-cooked in a skillet until it's dry before being cooked in broth. This "dry" egg polish keeps the nutty-flavored grains separate.

1 large egg, lightly beaten, or ¼ cup (59 ml) egg substitute
1 cup (140 g) medium or coarse kasha
1 shallot or 2 scallions, minced

2 cups (472 ml) beef stock (page 44)
1 cup (236 ml) cooked bow tie pasta, drained

In a small bowl, mix together egg and kasha. Heat a nonstick sauté pan over medium heat. When hot, add kasha/egg mixture, stirring constantly with a wooden spoon until grains are separate and dry. Add shallot and stock. Cover and simmer until liquid is absorbed, about 8 to 10 minutes. Add bow ties and cook for another minute or two, until bow ties are hot. Remove from heat and let stand, covered, for 5 minutes. Fluff with a fork and spoon onto a warmed serving platter.

MAKES 8 SERVINGS

Per serving: calories, 100 ◆ protein, 4 g ◆ carbohydrate, 20 g ◆ fat, 1 g (calories from fat, 9%) ◆ dietary fiber, 2 g ◆ cholesterol, 27 mg ◆ sodium, 21 mg ◆ potassium, 134 mg Joslin Exchanges: 1 bread/ starch, 1 vegetable

---

FRIDAY NIGHT DINNER

◆

Vegetarian Chopped Liver (page 15) on Melba Toast

Persian Pot Roast (page 234)

Kasha with Bow Ties (page 285)

Sliced Tomatoes with Chopped Fresh Herbs

Kugel (page 441)

Per serving: 571 calories (29% fat)
Joslin Exchanges: 3 medium-fat meat, 4 bread/starch, 1 vegetable

Grilled Polenta

Polenta is of course Italian, but here it's combined with fresh chilies for a scrumptious cornmeal side dish to accompany grilled fish or chicken. Serve it with Roasted Tomatillo Sauce (page 141).

If you prefer, the polenta can be sautéed in a skillet.

olive oil cooking spray
2 scallions, white part only, finely chopped
1 tablespoon (15 ml) minced fresh jalapeño chili
1 quart (1 l) water
1/2 teaspoon (2.5 ml) salt (optional)
1/8 teaspoon (.6 ml) cayenne pepper or to taste
1/2 teaspoon (2.5 ml) chili powder
1 1/4 cups (140 g) uncooked instant polenta or 1 1/4 cups (175 g) stone-ground yellow cornmeal
3 tablespoons (19 g) grated Parmesan cheese
1 teaspoon (5 g) unsalted butter
1 tablespoon (15 ml) olive oil

Lightly spray a large nonstick saucepan with cooking spray. Place over low heat. Add scallions and chili. Sauté until scallions are wilted, about 4 minutes. Add water, salt, cayenne, and chili powder. Bring to a simmer. Slowly add polenta. Stir in Parmesan cheese and butter. Cook, stirring constantly, for 4 minutes.

Spray an 8-inch (20 cm) square baking dish with cooking spray. Spread hot polenta mixture evenly in dish. Allow it to cool for at least 30 minutes. Cut cooled polenta into 2-inch (5 cm) squares. Brush each square on both sides with olive oil. Grill or broil until heated through and lightly seared, about 5 minutes per side.

MAKES 8 SERVINGS

Per serving: calories, 100 ◆ protein, 3 g ◆ carbohydrate, 15 g ◆ fat, 4 g (calories from fat, 36%) ◆ dietary fiber, 3 g ◆ cholesterol, 3 mg ◆ sodium, 190 mg ◆ potassium, 68 mg Joslin Exchanges: 1 bread/starch, 1 fat

Rice Basics

Rice is a staple food for more than half the world's population. Yet to most Americans rice is just a starchy side dish to accompany fish, meat, or poultry. We cook rice frequently and find it very versatile for family and company meals. Whenever we cook rice, we make some extra to use later—for stuffing fish, poultry, or vegetables; stirring into soups; tossing with other bits of leftovers for a salad; or mixing with cinnamon, raisins, and skim milk for a quick rice pudding dessert.

Rice that has more bran intact (aromatic rice, brown rice, and wild rice) has less of an impact on blood sugars.

Tips for making light fluffy rice:
- Add a teaspoon (5 ml) of margarine or oil to the cooking water to keep the grains separate.
- When you add the rice to the boiling water, give it a quick stir with a fork, cover, and reduce heat to a simmer. Don't stir again—stirring mashes the grains, making the rice gummy.
- Cook rice in a heavy saucepan to keep the rice from scorching.
- If the rice is cooked but still watery, fluff it with a fork over low heat until the water evaporates.
- To bake rice, add a teaspoon (5 ml) of margarine and the liquid (same proportions as for simmered rice) and stir. Cover tightly and bake at 400° F (205° C) 20 to 25 minutes until tender and liquid is absorbed.

Aromatic Long-Grain Rice (Basmati, Jasmine, Texmati, Wild Pecan, Wehani)

These slender, fragrant, delicate-tasting rices with some bran intact must first be rinsed. Drain, then simmer, covered, 1 part rice to 1½ parts lightly salted (salt optional) water for 15 to 20 minutes.

Brown Long-Grain Rice

This nutty-flavored rice with the bran intact can be soaked ahead to shorten the cooking time. Bring 1 part rice and 2 parts lightly salted (salt optional) water to a boil. Turn off heat, cover, and let stand for 2 hours. Return rice to heat and simmer for 10 minutes. (If not presoaked, brown rice takes 30 to 50 minutes to cook.)

Short-Grain (Carnaroli or Arborio) Rice

These polished white kernels have a bland taste and soft texture and are used for risotto (page 290). Simmer 1 part rice to 2 parts water or broth (adding liquid gradually while stirring for risotto), for 20 minutes.

White Long-Grain Rice

This common rice has a bland taste and firm texture. Simmer, covered, 1 part rice to 2 parts lightly salted (salt optional) water for 15 to 20 minutes.

Wild Rice

This is not a rice but the seed of a native grass with long unpolished kernels, an intense nutty, earthy flavor, and firm, chewy texture. Rinse well and simmer 1 part rice to 3 parts lightly salted (salt optional) water for 45 minutes to 1 hour.

Rice Seasonings

Rice can be cooked with a wide range of seasonings. Here are a few of our favorite combinations for 1 cup (185 g) uncooked rice. These seasonings contain very few calories and may be used freely within your meal plan—1/3 cup (78 ml) cooked rice provides 80 calories and 15 grams of carbohydrate and equals 1 bread/starch exchange:

- 1/4 cup (59 ml) snipped fresh chives, 1/4 cup (59 ml) minced red onion, and 2 tablespoons (30 ml) chopped fresh mint. Stir into cooked rice.
- 2 minced scallions, white part and 1 inch (2.5 cm) green, juice and grated zest of 1/2 lemon, and 1/4 cup (59 ml) minced flat-leaf parsley. Stir into cooked rice.
- 1 teaspoon (5 ml) ground cumin or curry powder and juice of 1/2 lemon. Add to rice before cooking.
- 2 thinly sliced scallions, white part and 1 inch (2.5 cm) green, and 1/8 to 1/4 teaspoon (.6 to 1.25 ml) cayenne pepper. Stir into cooked rice.
- 2 minced scallions, white part and 1 inch (2.5 cm) green, 1/2 cup (118 ml) finely chopped parsley, 1 tablespoon (15 ml) finely chopped dill, 2 tablespoons (30 ml) finely chopped fresh cilantro (fresh coriander), and 1 cup (236 ml) finely chopped raw spinach leaves (stems removed). Stir into cooked rice.
- 1/4 cup (59 ml) minced onion and 1/3 cup (78 ml) chopped pimiento. Add onion to cooking liquid; stir pimiento into cooked rice.
- 1/4 cup (59 ml) chopped parsley, 1 teaspoon (5 ml) chopped fresh tarragon, 1 minced garlic clove, and a generous grinding of pepper. Stir into cooked rice.

Other rice flavorings:
- Basil
- Chilies
- Cinnamon
- Fennel seed
- Ginger
- Mint
- Orange zest
- Paprika
- Saffron
- Thyme

Curried Rice Salad

This salad is fine for a summer picnic and equally good as an accompaniment to poached fish or baked chicken for a winter meal.

2 cups (472 ml) cooked basmati rice (page 288)

1 medium-size green bell pepper, about 5 ounces (140 g), seeded and diced

3 scallions, white part and 1 inch (2.5 cm) green, chopped

¼ cup (59 ml) golden raisins

¼ cup (59 ml) chopped dried apricots

¾ cup (177 ml) plain nonfat yogurt

1 tablespoon (15 ml) fresh lemon juice

1 teaspoon (5 ml) curry powder or to taste

⅛ teaspoon (.6 ml) dry mustard

⅛ teaspoon (.6 ml) ground ginger

⅛ teaspoon (.6 ml) ground cinnamon

⅛ teaspoon (.6 ml) cayenne pepper or to taste

lettuce leaves, washed and crisped

chopped fresh flat-leaf parsley for garnish

In a large bowl, combine rice, bell pepper, scallions, raisins, and apricots. Whisk together remaining ingredients except lettuce leaves and parsley. Pour over rice mixture. Mix lightly until well coated. Chill for at least 2 hours before serving.

Line a salad bowl or serving platter with lettuce. Mound salad on lettuce and garnish with chopped parsley.

MAKES 6 SERVINGS

> **Per serving:** calories, 131 ◆ protein, 4 g ◆ carbohydrate, 28 g ◆ fat, 1 g (calories from fat, 6%) ◆ dietary fiber, 1 g ◆ cholesterol, 1 mg ◆ sodium, 25 mg ◆ potassium, 307 mg Joslin Exchanges: 1 bread/ starch, 1 fruit

RISOTTO

Risotto, the classic rice dish of northern Italy, is made from Italian short-grain rice grown in the Piedmont region that retains its shape while it absorbs the cooking liquid. In our markets, look for Carnaroli or Arborio rice.

Unlike other kinds of rice, Italian short-grain rice is never covered during the cooking period, and it's stirred as it simmers, with the hot cooking broth added gradually. The result is a creamy rice that varies by region and season with the addition of vegetables, wild mushrooms, seafood, bits of poultry or meat, truffles, and fresh herbs.

Depending on the portion, we serve risotto as a sophisticated first course, comforting main course, or scrumptious accompaniment. In the kitchen, risotto can be as versatile as pasta.

Easy Microwaved Lemon Risotto

Barbara Kafka, author of *Microwave Gourmet,* taught us this easy technique for making risotto—the microwave does most of the work. The cooking time is for a 650- to 700-watt oven. If your microwave is less powerful, you will have to allow for more cooking time (approximately another 10 minutes—watch carefully, cooking in additional 1-minute increments).

1 tablespoon (15 ml) olive oil
1 small onion, minced
1 cup (185 g) Italian Carnaroli or Arborio rice
3½ cups (826 ml) chicken stock (page 45)

juice and grated zest of 1 lemon
1 teaspoon (5 ml) fresh thyme leaves or ¼ teaspoon (1.25 ml) crushed dried

In a 2½-quart (2.5 l) microwave-safe casserole, heat oil on HIGH for 30 seconds. Add onion and microwave on HIGH for 2 minutes. Stir in rice. Cook on HIGH for 1 minute. Stir in 2 cups (472 ml) of the stock. Cook, uncovered, on HIGH for 12 minutes. Stir in remaining 1½ cups (354 ml) stock, lemon juice, lemon zest, and thyme. Cook for another 8 minutes. Remove from oven and cover with a cloth kitchen towel. Let stand about 5 minutes until liquid is absorbed.

MAKES 8 SERVINGS

Per ½-cup (118 ml) serving: calories, 108 ♦ protein, 2 g ♦ carbohydrate, 20 g ♦ fat, 2 g (calories from fat, 17%) ♦ dietary fiber, trace ♦ cholesterol, 0 g ♦ sodium, 22 mg ♦ potassium, 110 mg
Joslin Exchanges: 1 bread/starch

Saffron Risotto

A light version of the traditional risotto served in Milan.

1 tablespoon (15 ml) olive oil
½ cup (118 ml) chopped white
  onion
1 cup (185 g) Italian Carnaroli or
  Arborio rice
½ cup (118 ml) dry white wine
3 cups (708 ml) beef stock (page
  44) or vegetable stock (page 47)

¼ teaspoon (1.25 ml) crushed
  saffron threads
freshly ground pepper to taste
2 tablespoons (12 g) grated
  Parmesan cheese

In a heavy nonstick saucepan, heat oil over low heat. Add onion and sauté until soft but not browned, about 5 minutes. Add rice and cook, stirring, for another 4 minutes. Add wine and cook until it evaporates, about 3 minutes.

In another saucepan, bring stock to a boil. Reduce heat and keep it at a simmer. Add 1 cup (236 ml) of the hot broth to the rice, stir, and allow to simmer until broth is absorbed. Add saffron and another ½ cup (118 ml) hot broth; stir gently. Continue adding hot broth, ½ cup (118 ml) at a time, stirring gently, until rice is creamy but just tender (this should take about 25 minutes of total cooking time). Add pepper and Parmesan cheese. Serve immediately.

MAKES 8 SERVINGS

Per ½-cup (118 ml) serving:
calories, 112 ◆ protein, 3 g ◆
carbohydrate, 19 g ◆ fat, 3 g
(calories from fat, 24%) ◆

dietary fiber, trace ◆ cholesterol,
1 mg ◆ sodium, 46 mg ◆
potassium, 151 mg
Joslin Exchanges: 1 bread/starch

Quinoa Garden Salad

Quinoa (pronounced keen-wa) is a mild-flavored Andean high-protein grain now being grown in Colorado and New Mexico. A staple of the ancient Incas, it plays an important part in today's South American cuisine. We love its delicate flavor and ease of preparation. Look for quinoa in your supermarket or health food store.

A basic grain like rice, quinoa can also be made with water. For variety you can use the same flavorings you would for rice (page 289).

Daikon is a crisp and juicy large white radish available in many supermarkets and Asian produce markets. If you can't find it, substitute small red radishes.

1 cup (180 g) quinoa	1 tablespoon (15 ml) balsamic vinegar
2 cups (472 ml) chicken stock (page 45)	1 tablespoon (15 ml) chopped fresh sage or 1 teaspoon (5 ml) crushed dried
1 garlic clove, minced	
2 scallions, including some green, chopped	1 tablespoon (15 ml) fresh thyme leaves or 1 teaspoon (5 ml) crushed dried
1 large fresh tomato, seeded and chopped	
1 large cucumber, peeled, seeded, and thinly sliced	1/2 teaspoon (2.5 ml) salt (optional)
1/2 cup (118 ml) chopped daikon	1/4 teaspoon (1.25 ml) freshly ground pepper or to taste
8 fresh mushrooms, sliced	1 1/2 tablespoons (22.5 ml) olive oil

Rinse quinoa in a strainer, removing any debris. Place in a large nonstick saucepan and toast over medium heat for 3 to 4 minutes, stirring constantly, until it darkens slightly. Add stock. Bring to a boil, cover, reduce heat, and simmer for about 20 minutes, until tender and liquid is absorbed.

Transfer quinoa to a large bowl. Combine with remaining ingredients. Toss lightly to mix. Chill for several hours to allow flavors to blend.

MAKES 8 SERVINGS

Per 1/2-cup (118 ml) serving: calories, 121 ◆ protein, 4 g ◆ carbohydrate, 19 g ◆ fat, 4 g (calories from fat, 30%) ◆ dietary fiber, 2 g ◆ cholesterol, trace ◆ sodium, 155 mg ◆ potassium, 375 mg Joslin Exchanges: 1 bread/starch, 1 fat

Fruited Quinoa Salad

A lovely salad for a winter buffet. Serve any leftovers wrapped in crisped red leaf lettuce for a quick, healthy snack. If you can't find dried cherries with no sugar added, use all apricots.

1 cup (180 g) dry quinoa
2 cups (472 ml) chicken stock (page 45)
1 scallion, finely chopped
½ cup (118 ml) chopped dried cherries (no sugar added), about 3 ounces (85 g)
½ cup (118 ml) chopped dried apricots, about ¼ pound (115 g)
3 tablespoons (45 ml) dry-roasted sunflower seeds

2 tablespoons (30 ml) raspberry vinegar (made without sugar) or 3 tablespoons (45 ml) fresh orange juice
grated zest of 1 orange
½ teaspoon (2.5 ml) dried *herbes de Provence* (see box)
½ teaspoon (2.5 ml) salt (optional)
1½ tablespoons (22.5 ml) canola oil

Rinse quinoa in a strainer, removing any debris. Place in a large nonstick saucepan and toast over medium heat for 3 to 4 minutes, stirring constantly, until it darkens slightly. Add stock. Bring to a boil, cover, reduce heat, and simmer for about 15 minutes, until tender and liquid is absorbed.

Transfer quinoa to a large bowl. Combine with remaining ingredients, tossing lightly to mix. Chill for several hours to allow flavors to mix.

MAKES 8 SERVINGS

Per ½-cup (118 ml) serving: calories, 159 ♦ protein, 4 g ♦ carbohydrate, 25 g ♦ fat, 6 g (calories from fat, 34%) ♦ dietary fiber, 2 g ♦ cholesterol, 0 mg ♦ sodium, 139 mg ♦ potassium, 355 mg
Joslin Exchanges: 1 bread/starch, ½ fruit, 1 fat

Herbes de Provence

Market stalls in southern France sell a mixture of dried herbs known as *herbes de Provence* that are packaged in little cloth sacks, plastic bags, or, as most commonly found in the United States, tiny clay crocks. You can make your own blend for a fraction of the cost of those sold in specialty shops. Sprinkle lightly on fish or poultry before baking or grilling. Mix with steamed vegetables; stir into rice and other grains.

2 tablespoons (30 ml) dried basil
4 teaspoons (40 ml) dried oregano
2 teaspoons (10 ml) dried marjoram
2 teaspoons (10 ml) dried thyme
1 teaspoon (5 ml) dried sage
1 teaspoon (5 ml) dried mint
1 teaspoon (5 ml) dried rosemary
1 teaspoon (5 ml) fennel seed
1 teaspoon (5 ml) dried lavender (optional)

In a food processor or blender, mix to a fine powder. Store in an airtight container away from light and heat for up to 3 months. Makes about 7 tablespoons (105 ml).

Bistro Lentil Salad

This French favorite is a good cool-weather introduction to a dinner of grilled lamb or pork. If your market doesn't have arugula, substitute red or green leaf lettuce.

½ pound (225 g) imported French green or brown lentils
1 medium-size onion, halved and stuck with 2 cloves
1 garlic clove, peeled
1 parsley sprig
1 fresh thyme sprig or ¼ teaspoon (59 ml) crushed dried
1 bay leaf
2 tablespoons (30 ml) olive oil

2 tablespoons (30 ml) red wine vinegar
½ teaspoon (2.5 ml) salt (optional)
2 large bunches arugula, rinsed and crisped
freshly ground pepper to taste
4 shallots, minced
¼ cup (59 ml) chopped fresh chervil or parsley

Rinse lentils, discarding any debris. Place lentils, onion, garlic, parsley, thyme, and bay leaf in a large heavy saucepan. Cover with cold water by 1 inch (2.5 cm). Cover and bring to a boil over medium heat. Reduce heat to a simmer and cook, covered, for 25 to 35 minutes. The lentils are done when they're tender to the bite. Check frequently, adding more water as necessary to keep lentils from drying out.

Drain lentils. Discard onion, garlic, parsley and thyme sprigs, and bay leaf. Cool to room temperature. Toss lentils with oil. Pour vinegar into a large spoon. Sprinkle salt on vinegar; beat with a fork, allowing salted vinegar to flow onto lentils. Toss again.

Spoon lentils onto a bed of arugula. Sprinkle with pepper, shallots, and chervil.

MAKES 8 SERVINGS

Per ½-cup (118 ml) serving: calories, 121 ◆ protein, 6 g ◆ carbohydrate, 17 g ◆ fat, 4 g (calories from fat, 27%) ◆ dietary fiber, 4 g ◆ cholesterol, 0 mg ◆ sodium, 140 mg ◆ potassium, 376 mg
Joslin Exchanges: 1 bread/ starch, 1 fat

Black-Eyed Peas with Tomato Coulis

A coulis is a thick puree or sauce. This coulis is made from fresh tomatoes and is used uncooked. You can also use it as a sauce for steamed asparagus or green beans.

If you use dried black-eyed peas, you'll need to soak them overnight in cold water to cover. Drain and proceed with the recipe. Serve this as a warm salad or starchy side dish. The black-eyed peas are also good without the coulis as a topping for grilled chicken or fish.

olive oil cooking spray
1 cup (236 ml) chopped onion
2 garlic cloves, minced
2 cups (472 ml) frozen black-eyed peas
2 cups (472 ml) beef stock (page 44)
½ teaspoon (2.5 ml) chili powder
½ teaspoon (2.5 ml) ground cumin
¼ cup (59 ml) chopped fresh cilantro (fresh coriander) or flat-leaf parsley
2 tablespoons (30 ml) red wine vinegar
Tomato Coulis (recipe follows)

Lightly spray a large nonstick saucepan with cooking spray. Place over low heat, add onion and garlic, and sauté for 3 to 4 minutes, until onion is wilted but not browned. Add black-eyed peas, stock, spices, cilantro, and vinegar. Cover and simmer for 30 to 45 minutes, until black-eyed peas are tender to the bite.

Spoon black-eyed peas onto serving plates. Top each serving with 2 tablespoons (30 ml) Tomato Coulis.

MAKES 6 SERVINGS

Per serving: calories, 85 ◆ protein, 3 g ◆ carbohydrate, 18 g ◆ fat, 1 g (calories from fat, 11%) ◆ dietary fiber, 2 g ◆ cholesterol, 0 mg ◆ sodium, 38 mg ◆ potassium, 474 mg
Joslin Exchanges: 1 bread/starch

Tomato Coulis

4 fresh plum tomatoes, about ¾ pound (340 g), peeled, seeded, and chopped
1 garlic clove, pressed
⅛ teaspoon (.6 ml) hot red pepper flakes or to taste

⅛ teaspoon (.6 ml) chili powder
3 scallions, white part and 1 inch (2.5 cm) green, chopped
2 tablespoons (30 ml) chopped fresh cilantro (fresh coriander) or flat-leaf parsley

In a food processor or blender, combine all ingredients to make a chunky puree. Refrigerate until ready to serve, up to 3 days (if you're making it ahead, stir in the cilantro just before serving).

MAKES ABOUT 1½ CUPS (354 ML)

Per 2-tablespoon serving (coulis alone): calories, 13 ◆ protein, 1 g ◆ carbohydrate, 3 g ◆ fat, trace (calories from fat, 27%) ◆ dietary fiber, 1 g ◆ cholesterol, 0 mg ◆ sodium, 17 mg ◆ potassium, 125 mg
Joslin Exchanges: free

Sautéed Lima Beans

If fresh lima beans are available, use them. Otherwise, frozen baby limas are an acceptable substitute. Here they're teamed with tomatoes and carrots for a colorful mix.

1 tablespoon (15 ml) olive oil
2 scallions, white part and 1 inch (2.5 cm) green, chopped
1 carrot, about 3 ounces (85 g), peeled and finely diced
1 10-ounce (285 g) box frozen baby lima beans, defrosted
1 medium-size fresh plum tomato, about 5 ounces (140 g), peeled, seeded, and chopped

¼ teaspoon (1.25 ml) salt (optional)
⅛ teaspoon (.6 ml) freshly ground pepper or to taste
1 teaspoon (5 ml) fresh thyme leaves or ¼ teaspoon (1.25 ml) crushed dried

In a large nonstick skillet over medium heat, heat oil. Add scallions, carrot, and lima beans. Sauté for 4 to 5 minutes, until beans are heated through. Add tomato, salt, pepper, and thyme. Toss and sauté for another 1 to 2 minutes, until tomatoes are heated through and lima beans are just tender. Serve hot.

MAKES 4 SERVINGS

Per ½-cup (118 ml) serving: calories, 115 ◆ protein, 5 g ◆ carbohydrate, 17 g ◆ fat, 4 g (calories from fat, 31%) ◆ dietary fiber, 2 g ◆ cholesterol, 0 mg ◆ sodium, 179 mg ◆ potassium, 404 mg
Joslin Exchanges: 1 bread/ starch, 1 fat

Taos Two-Bean and Rice Salad

Offer this piquant salad alongside grilled chicken or fish or stuff it into a tomato or roasted red pepper for lunch.

3 cups (708 ml) cooked long-grain white rice
1 15-ounce (425 g) can black beans, well rinsed and drained
1 15-ounce (425 g) can pinto beans, well rinsed and drained
1 4-ounce (115 g) can diced green chilies, drained

½ cup (118 ml) minced red onion
¼ cup (59 ml) chopped cilantro (fresh coriander)
3 tablespoons (45 ml) white wine vinegar
5 tablespoons (75 ml) canola oil
¼ teaspoon (1.25 ml) salt (optional)

In a large bowl, combine rice, beans, chilies, onion, and cilantro. Whisk together vinegar, oil, and salt. Pour over rice and mix gently. Serve at room temperature or chill.

MAKES 12 SERVINGS

Per ½-cup (118 ml) serving: calories, 200 ◆ protein, 7 g ◆ carbohydrate, 30 g ◆ fat, 6 g (calories from fat, 27%) ◆ dietary fiber, 1 g ◆ cholesterol, 0 mg ◆ sodium, 273 mg ◆ potassium, 270 mg
Joslin Exchanges: 2 bread/ starch, 1 fat

Texas Caviar

Black-eyed peas are a staple in southern pantries. Traditionally served on New Year's Day for good luck, they make a tasty addition to a buffet for the bowl games. Offer Flour Tortilla Chips (page 371) for dipping.

In many supermarkets you can buy frozen black-eyed peas. Follow package instructions for cooking.

½ pound (225 g) dried black-eyed peas, about 1¼ cups (295 ml), or about 4 cups (1 l) cooked
1 quart (1 l) cold water
1 small onion, peeled and stuck with 1 clove
1 parsley sprig
1 fresh thyme sprig or ¼ teaspoon (1.25 ml) crushed dried
1 bay leaf
3 scallions, white part and 1 inch (2.5 cm) green, finely chopped
3 garlic cloves, finely chopped

2 fresh plum tomatoes, about 6 ounces (180 g), seeded and chopped
¼ cup (59 ml) chopped fresh cilantro (fresh coriander)
3 tablespoons (45 ml) olive oil
3 tablespoons (45 ml) red wine vinegar
1 teaspoon (5 ml) salt (optional)
½ teaspoon (2.5 ml) ground cumin
leaves of red leaf lettuce, rinsed and crisped

If you're using dried black-eyed peas, rinse and pick over. Soak overnight in cold water to cover. Drain.

Place black-eyed peas in a large heavy saucepan and add cold water along with onion, parsley, thyme, and bay leaf. Bring to a boil. Reduce heat and simmer until just tender, 30 to 45 minutes.

Drain; discard onion, parsley and thyme sprigs, and bay leaf. Place black-eyed peas in a large bowl. Add remaining ingredients except lettuce leaves. Toss until well blended. Let stand for several hours, stirring occasionally, to develop flavors. Serve at room temperature on a bed of lettuce leaves.

MAKES 8 SERVINGS

Per ½-cup (118 ml) serving: calories, 139 ◆ protein, 3 g ◆ carbohydrate, 20 g ◆ fat, 6 g (calories from fat, 39%) ◆ dietary fiber, 2 g ◆ cholesterol, 0 mg ◆ sodium, 274 mg ◆ potassium, 413 mg
Joslin Exchanges: 1 bread/ starch, 1 fat

White Beans with Tomatoes

Cooked with tomatoes and fresh sage, these beans are good with just about any grilled or roasted main dish. Chilled, they make a savory salad that travels well to a picnic.

½ pound (225 g) dried white beans
olive oil cooking spray
1 cup (236 ml) finely chopped onion
2 garlic cloves, minced
1 tablespoon (15 ml) minced fresh sage or 1 teaspoon (5 ml) crushed dried

1 cup (236 ml) peeled, seeded, and coarsely chopped fresh tomatoes
3 cups (708 ml) cold water
¼ teaspoon (1.25 ml) salt (optional)
2 teaspoons (10 ml) balsamic vinegar
⅛ teaspoon (.6 ml) freshly ground pepper or to taste

Rinse and pick over beans. Soak overnight in cold water to cover. Drain beans and set aside.

In a large heavy saucepan lightly sprayed with cooking spray, sauté onion and garlic over low heat until onion is wilted but not browned, about 4 minutes. Add sage, tomatoes, cold water, and salt. Bring to a boil; reduce heat and simmer for 5 minutes.

Add reserved beans; stir. Cover and cook 50 minutes or until beans are tender, adding more water as necessary as beans cook.

Just before serving, stir in vinegar and pepper.

MAKES 8 SERVINGS

Per 1-cup (236 ml) serving: calories, 103 ◆ protein, 7 g ◆ carbohydrate, 16 g ◆ fat, 1 g (calories from fat, 4%) ◆ dietary fiber, 2 g ◆ cholesterol, 0 mg ◆ sodium, 74 mg ◆ potassium, 448 mg
Joslin Exchanges: 1 bread/starch

PICNIC AT THE PARK

◆

Pickled Vegetables (page 13)

Sliced Cold Miniature Turkey Loaf (page 194) on

Pumpernickel Bread with Assorted Mustards and Greens

White Beans with Tomatoes (page 301)

Fresh Peaches and Figs

Per serving: 468 calories (23% fat)
Joslin Exchanges: 3 low-fat meat, 3 bread/starch, 1 fruit

Orecchiette Pesto Salad

A very tasty alternative to macaroni salad, this version of cold pasta uses orecchiette, which means "little ears." The cup-shaped pasta is perfect for holding the zesty pesto. You can use another fanciful dense pasta such as bow ties or farfalle (butterflies), cappelletti (little hats), conchiglie (conch shells), or rotelle (little wheels).

  3 quarts (2.75 l) water
½ pound (225 g) orecchiette
1½ cups (354 ml) lightly packed
　　fresh basil leaves
  2 tablespoons (12 g) grated
　　Parmesan cheese
  2 garlic cloves, minced

  2 tablespoons (30 ml) white wine
　　vinegar
¼ cup (59 ml) olive oil
⅛ teaspoon (.6 ml) freshly ground
　　pepper or to taste
  1 tablespoon (15 ml) toasted pine
　　nuts (page 284)

In a 6-quart (5.5 l) pan, bring water to a boil over high heat. Add orecchiette; let water return to a boil and cook, uncovered, for 7 to 9 minutes, until just tender. Drain, rinse with cold water, and drain again.

In a food processor or blender, make pesto by combining remaining ingredients except pepper and pine nuts. Process until smooth.

In a large bowl, combine pasta and pesto. Mix gently. Cover and refrigerate for at least 1 hour. Just before serving, sprinkle with pepper and toasted pine nuts.

MAKES 12 SERVINGS

Per ½-cup (118 ml) serving: calories, 121 ◆ protein, 3 g ◆ carbohydrate, 16 g ◆ fat, 5 g (calories from fat, 37%) ◆ dietary fiber, trace ◆ cholesterol, 1 mg ◆ sodium, 29 mg ◆ potassium, 101 mg Joslin Exchanges: 1 bread/ starch, 1 fat

Vegetable Medley Pasta Salad

Sylvia Towner, a dietitian and diabetes educator in Tulsa, Oklahoma, gave us this easy recipe for pasta salad. It's perfect for picnics and potlucks.

1 medium-size zucchini, about 5 ounces (140 g), cut into thin strips
12 large cherry tomatoes, halved
¼ cup (59 ml) sliced pitted ripe olives
2 garlic cloves, minced
½ tablespoon (7.5 ml) minced fresh oregano or ½ teaspoon (2.5 ml) crushed dried
½ tablespoon (7.5 ml) minced fresh basil or ½ teaspoon (2.5 ml) crushed dried

¼ cup (59 ml) chopped fresh flat-leaf parsley
¼ teaspoon (1.25 ml) salt (optional)
⅛ teaspoon (.6 ml) freshly ground pepper
½ cup (118 ml) plain nonfat yogurt
2 teaspoons (10 ml) olive oil
6 ounces (180 g) rotini (little corkscrews)
leaves of green leaf lettuce, washed and crisped

In a large bowl, combine all ingredients except pasta and lettuce. Toss, mixing well. Cover and let stand at room temperature for 1 hour.

In a large saucepan of boiling water, cook pasta for 8 to 10 minutes, until tender. Drain well. Add to vegetable mixture; mix lightly until well coated. Line a salad bowl or serving platter with lettuce; mound salad on lettuce. Chill until ready to serve.

MAKES 12 SERVINGS

Per 1-cup (236 ml) serving: calories, 81 ◆ protein, 3 g ◆ carbohydrate, 13 g ◆ fat, 2 g (calories from fat, 22%) ◆ dietary fiber, trace ◆ cholesterol, 13 mg ◆ sodium, 139 mg ◆ potassium, 144 mg Joslin Exchanges: 1 bread/starch

Orzo in Hot Baked Tomatoes

A simple combination of fresh flavors that makes for good summertime eating. The same orzo stuffing would work equally well with bell peppers or small hollowed-out zucchini.

2 large ripe but firm tomatoes, about 1 pound (450 g)
⅔ cup (120 g) orzo
1 quart (1 l) boiling water
¼ teaspoon (1.25 ml) salt (optional)
1 tablespoon (15 ml) olive oil
2 garlic cloves, minced

2 tablespoons (30 ml) chopped fresh flat-leaf parsley
2 tablespoons (30 ml) chopped fresh basil
¼ teaspoon (1.25 ml) hot red pepper flakes or to taste
olive oil cooking spray

Cut tomatoes in half horizontally. Using a small spoon or melon baller, scoop out seeds. Turn tomatoes upside down on paper towels to drain for 20 minutes.

Cook orzo in boiling salted water until tender, about 10 minutes. Drain. Set aside.

Meanwhile, heat oil in a large nonstick sauté pan over low heat. Add garlic and sauté for 2 to 3 minutes, until garlic is wilted but not browned. Remove from heat. Add parsley, basil, hot pepper flakes, and orzo. Stir gently to blend.

Preheat oven to 350° F (180° C). Stuff orzo mixture into tomatoes, mounding slightly. With cooking spray, lightly spray a baking dish large enough to contain tomatoes without crowding them. Arrange stuffed tomatoes in baking dish. Bake for 12 minutes or until tomatoes begin to soften but before they lose their shape. Serve immediately.

MAKES 4 SERVINGS

Per serving: calories, 169 ◆ protein, 5 g ◆ carbohydrate, 29 g ◆ fat, 4 g (calories from fat, 21%) ◆ dietary fiber, 1 g ◆ cholesterol, 0 mg ◆ sodium, 155 mg ◆ potassium, 340 mg Joslin Exchanges: 2 bread/starch, 1 fat

Corn Pudding

This pudding is almost a soufflé—light and delicious. Bake it in individual 6-ounce (177 ml) custard cups or a 2½-quart (2.5 l) ovenproof casserole.

vegetable oil cooking spray
1⅔ cups (392 ml) fresh or defrosted frozen corn kernels
4 scallions, white part only, chopped
1 cup (236 ml) evaporated skim milk
3 large eggs, separated
1 tablespoon (15 g) margarine, melted

1 tablespoon (15 ml) cornstarch
¼ teaspoon (1.25 ml) salt (optional)
⅛ teaspoon (.6 ml) cayenne pepper
1 medium-size red bell pepper, about 6 ounces (180 g), roasted, peeled, seeded, and cut into thin strips

Preheat oven to 350° F (180° C). Lightly spray 6 custard cups or a casserole with cooking spray.

Puree 1 cup (236 ml) corn in a food processor. Combine with remaining ⅔ cup (156 ml) corn, scallions, milk, egg yolks, margarine, cornstarch, salt, and cayenne pepper. Beat egg whites until stiff but not dry. Fold beaten egg whites into corn mixture. Spoon mixture evenly into custard cups or casserole. Place cups in a 13- by 9- by 2-inch (33 by 23 by 5 cm) baking pan. Pour hot water into baking pan to a depth of 1 inch (2.5 cm). Bake for 50 minutes, until golden. Serve immediately, garnished with roasted red pepper strips.

MAKES 6 SERVINGS

Per serving: calories, 136 ◆ protein, 8 g ◆ carbohydrate, 17 g ◆ fat, 5 g (calories from fat, 33%) ◆ dietary fiber, trace ◆ cholesterol, 108 mg ◆ sodium, 198 mg ◆ potassium, 291 mg Joslin Exchanges: 1 bread/ starch, 1 medium-fat meat

Grilled Corn on the Cob

On the streets of some Middle Eastern and Latin American cities, the sight and smell of fresh corn on the cob being grilled by street vendors is as common as that of roasted-chestnut vendors during the winter months in New York City. In Guatemala they squeeze fresh lime on the roasted corn just before eating it.

   When corn is prepared this way, you won't miss the butter.

fresh corn on the cob
pot of salted water

wedges of fresh lime (optional)

Husk the corn and remove all of the silk. Brush off any stubborn silks with your hand or a soft dry vegetable brush. Grill over medium-hot coals, 4 to 6 inches (10 to 15 cm) from source of heat, turning frequently, for 10 to 15 minutes. When done, dip hot corn briefly into the salted water. Serve at once, squeezing on lime if desired.

> **Per 5-inch ear:** calories, 80 ♦ protein, 3 g ♦ carbohydrate, 17 g ♦ fat, 1 g (calories from fat, 11%) ♦ dietary fiber, 1 g ♦ cholesterol, 0 mg ♦ sodium, 4 mg ♦ potassium, 215 mg
> Joslin Exchanges: 1 bread/starch

Santa Fe Corn Salad

When the farm stands are filled with just-picked fresh corn, we can't have it often enough. This raw corn salad is light and sweet tasting, but it depends on very fresh corn.

crisp inner leaves of romaine
   lettuce, washed
1 cup (236 ml) fresh corn kernels,
   cut from the cob
1 medium-size fresh tomato, about
   5 ounces (140 g), seeded and
   coarsely chopped

1 small jícama, about 1 pound
   (450 g), peeled and coarsely
   chopped
2 small zucchini, about ½ pound
   (225 g), thinly sliced
1 small fresh hot chili, seeded and
   diced

Vinaigrette

2 tablespoons (30 ml) fresh lime
juice
2 tablespoons (30 ml) olive oil
½ teaspoon (2.5 ml) ground cumin
½ tablespoon (7.5 ml) fresh thyme
leaves or ½ teaspoon (2.5 ml)
crushed dried

freshly ground pepper to taste
⅛ teaspoon (.6 ml) Worcestershire
sauce
½ teaspoon salt (2.5 ml) (optional)
1 garlic clove, minced
1 scallion, white part and 1 inch
(2.5 cm) green, chopped

Line a salad bowl with lettuce leaves. Place corn in center and surround with other vegetables in a decorative arrangement. Chill until ready to serve.

In a small bowl, whisk together vinaigrette ingredients. When ready to serve, pour dressing over salad; toss.

MAKES 4 SERVINGS

Per serving: calories, 129 ◆
protein, 3 g ◆ carbohydrate, 16
g ◆ fat, 7 g (calories from fat,
49%) ◆ dietary fiber, 1 g ◆
cholesterol, 0 mg ◆

sodium, 285 mg ◆ potassium,
523 mg
Joslin Exchanges: 1 bread/
starch, 1 fat

Buttermilk Mashed Potatoes

In her book *The Art of Low-Calorie Cooking*, Sally Schneider suggests mashing potatoes with buttermilk as a low-calorie alternative to traditional mashed potatoes loaded with cream and butter. We've used yellow (Yukon Gold or Yellow Finn) potatoes for a more buttery look and added flecks of cooked bok choy for an interesting texture and flavor boost.

If yellow potatoes are not available, substitute russet potatoes.

1¾ pounds (790 g) yellow or russet
potatoes, peeled and cut into
quarters
1 teaspoon (5 ml) salt (optional)
1 tablespoon (15 g) unsalted
butter

1 cup (236 ml) coarsely chopped
bok choy
1¼ cups (295 ml) buttermilk,
warmed
freshly ground pepper to taste

Place potatoes and ¾ teaspoon (3.75 ml) salt in a heavy saucepan with water to cover. Bring to a boil; reduce heat to a simmer and cook, uncovered, until potatoes are tender when pierced with a fork, about 15 minutes. Drain, reserving a few tablespoons of the cooking liquid. Mash potatoes with a potato masher or fork.

In a medium-size sauté pan, melt 2 teaspoons (10 g) butter over medium heat. Add bok choy and sauté until crisp-tender, about 5 minutes. Fold warm buttermilk and bok choy into potatoes, adding reserved cooking liquid to obtain desired consistency. Stir in remaining 1/4 teaspoon (1.25 ml) salt, remaining teaspoon (5 g) butter, and freshly ground pepper to taste.

MAKES 6 SERVINGS

Per 1/2-cup (118 ml) serving: calories, 155 ◆ protein, 4 g ◆ carbohydrate, 29 g ◆ fat, 3 g (calories from fat, 17%) ◆ dietary fiber, 1 g ◆ cholesterol, 7 mg ◆ sodium, 424 mg* ◆ potassium, 545 mg
Joslin Exchanges: 2 bread/starch

* If you're on a low-sodium diet, omit the salt.

Herbed Creamer Potatoes

You'll find diminutive new potatoes about the size of a large marble sometimes labeled "creamer" potatoes in the produce market. They come in several colors— white, red, and purple—and are particularly suited to steaming. Tossed with a little olive oil and lots of fresh herbs, they're extraordinary. Offer lemon wedges to squeeze over the potatoes at the table.

3/4 pound (340 g) tiny new potatoes
1/4 cup (59 ml) chopped fresh flat-leaf parsley
1/4 cup (59 ml) snipped fresh chives
1/4 cup (59 ml) chopped fresh chervil or cilantro (fresh coriander)
1 tablespoon (15 ml) olive oil
lemon wedges

Place potatoes in a steaming basket or on a rack over 1 inch (2.5 cm) of boiling water. Steam, covered, until tender when pierced with a knife, 15 to 20 minutes, depending on size.

Mix herbs. Drizzle oil over potatoes and toss with herbs. Serve hot with lemon wedges.

MAKES 6 SERVINGS

Per serving: calories, 71 ◆ protein, 1 g ◆ carbohydrate, 12 g ◆ fat, 2 g (calories from fat, 25%) ◆ dietary fiber, 1 g ◆ cholesterol, 0 mg ◆ sodium, 4.1 mg ◆ potassium, 210 mg
Joslin Exchanges: 1 bread/starch

Potato and Green Pepper Bake

This is a perfect all-season side dish for a simple supper. We leave the skin on the potatoes for flavor and extra vitamins.

1 teaspoon (5 g) unsalted butter
4 small unpeeled russet potatoes, about ¾ pound (340 g), well scrubbed and very thinly sliced
1 small onion, about 3 ounces (85 g), very thinly sliced
1 large green bell pepper, about ½ pound (225 g), seeded and very thinly sliced

1 tablespoon (15 ml) olive oil
¾ teaspoon (3.75 ml) fresh thyme leaves or ¼ teaspoon (1.25 ml) crushed dried
½ teaspoon salt (2.5 ml) (optional)
freshly ground pepper to taste

Preheat oven to 450° F (230° C). Spread butter on bottom and sides of a shallow round baking dish.

Arrange sliced vegetables in baking dish, forming concentric circles and alternating slices of potato, onion, and pepper. Drizzle with olive oil. Scatter thyme leaves on top. Season with salt and pepper. Bake for 15 minutes. Reduce heat to 400° F (205° C). Continue to bake for 15 to 20 minutes, until vegetables are tender. Cut into 4 wedges. Serve immediately.

MAKES 4 SERVINGS

Per serving: calories, 141 ♦ protein, 2 g ♦ carbohydrate, 24 g ♦ fat, 5 g (calories from fat, 31%) ♦ dietary fiber, 1 g ♦ cholesterol, 3 mg ♦ sodium, 274 mg ♦ potassium, 467 mg Joslin Exchanges: 1½ bread/ starch, 1 fat

Potato and Red Pepper Cakes

Potatoes are the all-time comfort food, and this is a surefire homey way to prepare them. Red bell pepper and fresh rosemary bring sweet and pungent Mediterranean flavors to these crispy potato pancakes.

4 large russet potatoes, about 2 pounds (900 g), peeled
1 medium-size onion, about ¼ pound (115 g), peeled
1 large red bell pepper, about ½ pound (225 g), seeded and finely diced
2 large eggs, slightly beaten
½ teaspoon (2.5 ml) salt (optional)

freshly ground pepper to taste
3 tablespoons (23 g) unbleached flour
½ teaspoon (2.5 ml) baking powder
1 teaspoon (5 ml) minced fresh rosemary or ¼ teaspoon (1.25 ml) crushed dried
1 tablespoon (15 ml) olive oil

Grate the potatoes into a large glass or ceramic bowl. Cover with cold water. Grate onions into another large bowl. Set aside.

Drain potatoes; pat dry with paper towels, squeezing out as much liquid as possible. Add potatoes to grated onions along with remaining ingredients except oil. Mix well.

Heat some of the oil in a large nonstick skillet over medium-high heat. When oil is hot, cook the pancakes in batches, using ½ cup (118 ml) of the potato mixture for each pancake. Sauté until golden brown, about 3 minutes per side. Drain on paper towels. Keep warm while preparing the others, using the remaining oil as needed. Serve hot.

MAKES 8 SERVINGS

Per serving: calories, 149 ◆ protein, 4 g ◆ carbohydrate, 25 g ◆ fat, 3 g (calories from fat, 18%) ◆ dietary fiber, 1 g ◆ cholesterol, 53 mg ◆ sodium, 177 mg ◆ potassium, 466 mg Joslin Exchanges: 2 bread/starch

Roasted Sweet and White Potatoes

These delicious roasted potatoes are a good accompaniment to poultry and fish. If you don't have fresh chervil, substitute flat-leaf parsley.

olive oil cooking spray
½ pound (225 g) unpeeled russet potatoes, scrubbed and cut into 1-inch (2.5 cm) chunks
½ pound (225 g) unpeeled sweet potatoes, scrubbed and cut into 1-inch (2.5 cm) chunks
1 medium-size onion, about ¼ pound (115 gm), peeled and cut into eighths

4 garlic cloves, peeled and cut in half
2 tablespoons (30 ml) olive oil
2 tablespoons (30 ml) fresh lemon juice
¼ teaspoon (1.25 ml) salt
freshly ground pepper to taste
¼ cup (59 ml) loosely packed fresh chervil or flat-leaf parsley leaves

Preheat oven to 425° F (220° C). Lightly spray a 10- by 15-inch (25 by 38 cm) baking pan that's at least 2 inches (5 cm) deep with cooking spray.

Add everything but chervil. Toss to coat potatoes, then spread vegetables out evenly. Bake for 30 to 35 minutes, stirring with a wide spatula after 15 minutes, until tender and well browned. Sprinkle with chervil; serve hot.

MAKES 8 SERVINGS

Per ½-cup (118 ml) serving: calories, 100 ◆ protein, 2 g ◆ carbohydrate, 16 g ◆ fat, 4 g (calories from fat, 36%) ◆ dietary fiber, 1 g ◆ cholesterol, 0 mg ◆ sodium, 73 mg ◆ potassium, 268 mg
Joslin Exchanges: 1 bread/ starch, 1 fat

Warm Red Potato and Green Bean Salad

This satisfying salad is ideal for a casual supper.

1½ pounds (675 g) very small red potatoes, scrubbed
½ pound (225 g) young green beans, trimmed

3 scallions, white part and 2 inches (5 cm) green, thinly sliced

Vinaigrette

3 tablespoons (45 ml) white wine
   vinegar
3 tablespoons (45 ml) olive oil
1 tablespoon (15 ml) minced
   shallot

½ tablespoon (7.5 ml) Dijon
   mustard
1 teaspoon (5 ml) celery seed
1 garlic clove, minced
1 hard-cooked large egg, minced

Cook potatoes in boiling water until tender when pierced with a knife, about 15 minutes. Drain; cut into halves or quarters.

Meanwhile, cook green beans in boiling water until crisp-tender, about 4 minutes. Drain; cut into 2-inch (5 cm) lengths.

In a bowl, combine warm potatoes and beans with scallions. Whisk together vinaigrette ingredients. Pour over potatoes; toss. Serve warm or at room temperature.

MAKES 8 SERVINGS

Per serving: calories, 141 ◆
protein, 3 g ◆ carbohydrate, 21
g ◆ fat, 5 g (calories from fat,
32%) ◆ dietary fiber, 1 g ◆

cholesterol, 27 mg ◆ sodium, 26
mg ◆ potassium, 436 mg
Joslin Exchanges: 1½ bread/
starch, 1 fat

Sicilian Potato Salad

Serve this luscious potato salad with grilled fish, chicken, or hamburgers.

1½ pounds (675 g) small red
   potatoes, well scrubbed
3 tablespoons (45 ml) white wine
   vinegar
2 large garlic cloves, peeled and
   crushed
3 tablespoons (45 ml) olive oil
½ tablespoon (7.5 ml) chopped
   fresh oregano or ½ teaspoon
   (2.5 ml) crushed dried

¼ teaspoon (1.25 ml) salt
   (optional)
freshly ground pepper to taste
1 medium-size red onion, about 3
   ounces (85 g), halved and
   thinly sliced
1 cup (236 ml) chopped fresh
   mint

Slice potatoes into rounds about ¼ inch (.75 cm) thick. Steam in a vegetable steamer over simmering water until just tender, about 15 minutes. Remove from steamer and place in a large bowl.

Combine vinegar and garlic. With the tines of a fork, mash garlic. Let stand for 15 minutes. Remove and discard garlic. Add olive oil, oregano, salt, and pepper; whisk until well blended. Pour over hot potatoes; add onions and toss gently to mix. Cover and cool for at least 1 hour.

Just before serving, toss potatoes with chopped mint.

MAKES 8 SERVINGS

> **Per serving:** calories, 135 ◆ protein, 2 g ◆ carbohydrate, 20 g ◆ fat, 5 g (calories from fat, 34%) ◆ dietary fiber, 2 g ◆ cholesterol, 0 mg ◆ sodium, 71 mg ◆ potassium, 354 mg Joslin Exchanges: 1 bread/ starch, 1 fat

Tzimmes

A marvelous mishmash of vegetables for a Sabbath dinner. We've replaced the flour-and-schmaltz roux traditionally used to thicken the dish with a little cornstarch.

1 large carrot, about 5 ounces (140 g)	2 cups (472 ml) chicken stock (page 45)
2 large russet potatoes, about 1 pound (450 g)	1 tablespoon (15 ml) grated orange zest
1 large sweet potato, about ½ pound (225 g)	½ tablespoon (7.5 ml) cornstarch
	1 teaspoon (5 g) margarine

Peel the carrot and potatoes. Cut into 1-inch (2.5 cm) cubes. Place in a large saucepan with stock. Simmer over low heat for 10 minutes. Add orange zest and continue to cook until vegetables are very tender and liquid is reduced by half, about 15 minutes. Dissolve cornstarch in some of the cooking liquid. Stir cornstarch and margarine into carrot-potato mixture and continue to cook, stirring gently, until thickened.

MAKES 8 SERVINGS

> **Per serving:** calories, 81 ◆ protein, 1 g ◆ carbohydrate, 18 g ◆ fat, 1 g (calories from fat, 5%) ◆ dietary fiber, 2 g ◆ cholesterol, 1 mg ◆ sodium, 20 mg ◆ potassium, 308 mg Joslin Exchanges: 1 bread/starch

Sugar Snaps and Snow Peas

A colorful, quick, and easy side dish with plenty of zest. If fresh sugar snaps are not available, use frozen. Snow peas are a year-round item.

½ pound (225 g) sugar snap peas, trimmed and strings removed
½ pound (225 g) snow peas, trimmed and strings removed
¼ teaspoon (1.25 ml) salt (optional)
1 shallot, minced
2 tablespoons (30 ml) fresh lemon juice
¼ teaspoon (1.25 ml) freshly ground pepper or to taste

1 tablespoon (15 ml) light sesame oil
1 medium-size red bell pepper, about 6 ounces (180 g), cut in half crosswise and then into thin strips
6 fresh water chestnuts, peeled and sliced (optional)
¼ cup (59 ml) shredded fresh basil

Blanch sugar snaps and snow peas in boiling salted water until just tender and still bright green, 2 to 3 minutes. Drain; keep warm. Whisk together shallot, lemon juice, pepper, and oil. Pour over hot peas. Toss. Add bell pepper and water chestnuts; toss again. Arrange vegetables on a serving platter. Scatter basil on top. Serve warm.

MAKES 6 SERVINGS

Per serving: calories, 91 ◆ protein, 3 g ◆ carbohydrate, 14 g ◆ fat, 3 g (calories from fat, 30%) ◆ dietary fiber, 1 g ◆ cholesterol, 0 mg ◆ sodium, 4 mg ◆ potassium, 302 mg
Joslin Exchanges: 1 bread/starch

Vegetable Terrine

Terrines are a glorious way to prepare vegetables without added fat. Here's an easy recipe.

olive oil cooking spray
2 very small Japanese eggplants, about 2 ounces (60 g) each
1 large baking potato, about 1/2 pound (225 g)
1 medium-size zucchini, about 5 ounces (140 g)
1 shallot, minced
1 garlic clove, minced
2 ounces (60 g) fresh mushrooms, thinly sliced

2 large fresh plum tomatoes, about 1/2 pound (225 g), peeled, seeded, and chopped
1/2 teaspoon (2.5 ml) crushed dried basil
1/2 teaspoon (2.5 ml) crushed dried oregano
1/2 cup (118 ml) chicken stock (page 45)
1/4 cup (59 ml) fresh whole-wheat bread crumbs

Preheat oven to 350° F (180° C). Spray an 8- by 4- by 2¹/₂-inch (20 by 10 by 6.5 cm) loaf pan with cooking spray.

Very thinly slice eggplant, potato, and zucchini lengthwise. Pat dry with paper towels. Arrange eggplant slices in bottom of loaf pan. Sprinkle with one-third of shallot and garlic. Top with potato slices and a third of shallot and garlic. Top with zucchini slices and remaining third of shallot and garlic. Arrange mushrooms on top of zucchini. Sprinkle with chopped tomatoes and herbs. Pour chicken stock over vegetables. Cover pan with aluminum foil.

Bake for 30 minutes. Remove foil; refold to fit just over top of vegetables, pressing down slightly. Continue to bake for 30 minutes, until vegetables are tender when pierced with a knife.

Using foil to hold vegetables, drain off all liquid. Discard foil. Top vegetables with bread crumbs. Raise oven temperature to 400° F (205° C). Continue to bake for 5 to 10 minutes, until bread crumbs are browned. Remove from oven and let stand for 10 minutes before cutting into thick slices.

MAKES 4 SERVINGS

Per serving: calories, 120 ◆ protein, 4 g ◆ carbohydrate, 26 g ◆ fat, 1 g (calories from fat, 7%) ◆ dietary fiber, 1 g ◆ cholesterol, 0 mg ◆ sodium, 62 mg ◆ potassium, 630 mg Joslin Exchanges: 1 bread/ starch, 2 vegetable

VEGETABLES

As we turn our focus away from proteins and fats, vegetables of all kinds and colors are taking center stage on our dinner plates. Everyone knows that vegetables are high in vitamins, minerals, and fiber. They're also cholesterol-free and very low in fat, sodium, and calories.

We can't think of a vegetable that we don't like, which is fortunate since our meal plans call for two vegetable exchanges each day, and if we substitute a bread/starch exchange for vegetables (see Exchange Substitutions, Appendix 1), we then have five vegetable exchanges to spread between lunch and dinner.

What's even better is that, when eaten raw, many vegetables are *free food* for people with diabetes, something to remember when you're especially hungry and want more "bulk" in your diet.

Americans who grew up on boiled carrots and canned spinach have a lot to learn about the variety of exciting tastes awaiting them in the produce section of their market. Beyond the supermarket there's a whole world of interesting vegetables in whole-food stores (the best source for organic produce) and ethnic markets. Drive out into the country to the farmer's stands and co-ops (some come into the city one or two days a week). Try new varieties of old favorites.

For example, look for yellow cherry tomatoes, meaty Roma plum tomatoes, and green tomatillos wrapped in their papery husks. Instead of green cabbage, buy ruffled Savoy, bok choy (it resembles Swiss chard), or pearly stalks of Napa (Chinese) cabbage. We buy red and yellow peppers; golden beets (they also come

---

Free Vegetables

Because of their low carbohydrate and calorie content, the following *raw* vegetables may be eaten liberally and are not counted as an exchange (see page 372 for serving ideas):

- Alfalfa sprouts
- Chicory (includes radicchio)
- Chinese cabbage
- Endive
- Escarole
- Lettuce
- Parsley
- Spinach
- Watercress

---

in candy-striped colors of red and creamy white); purple cauliflower; and broccoflower, a brilliant jade-green hybrid of cauliflower and broccoli. Instead of the familiar green or snap bean, look for fresh fava beans, Asian yard-long beans, and tiny French haricots verts that cook in a minute, turning a deep emerald green. Fresh shiitake, porcini, morels, and chanterelles are showing up in more markets each year—their flavor (some are tame, others wild) outshines the more familiar cultivated mushroom. Summer squash doesn't mean just zucchini—the markets are filled with pattypan (which looks like a small flying saucer), yellow squash, baby squash (sometimes with the flower blossom still attached), and from South America, chayote. Instead of iceberg lettuce, choose from any number of interesting and flavorful greens (page 85).

Plant a kitchen garden—whether it's a cluster of clay pots of cherry tomatoes and baby lettuces on the terrace or a backyard garden full of different squashes, rows of sugar snaps, and stands of peppers. Seed catalogs and garden shops are full of new and exciting varieties to try.

Most of the time, however, our fresh vegetables come from the supermarket, and it's important to take time to choose only those that are in perfect condition. Pick ones that are bright in color and crisp or firm in texture. When you're buying root and stem vegetables, select the smaller ones (the larger, more mature specimens will tend to be woody). Buy in quantities that you can use promptly.

Selecting Fresh Vegetables

Experience is the best teacher, but if you're just starting to buy vegetables, here are a few guidelines for finding the freshest:

Check: asparagus, broccoli, cauliflower, celery, and fennel for signs of freshness—look for tightly packed florets or tips, firm stalks, no signs of wilting or browning edges. Beets should look "dusty" with their green tops attached. Pass up Brussels sprouts that are yellowed and withered. Break a green bean—if it doesn't snap, it's not fresh. Don't buy onions with soft or sprouting tops. Spinach should look crisp and dark green with no signs of wilting. Check stem ends of squash and avoid those with soft spots.

Lift: artichokes, cabbage, cucumbers, eggplant, and turnips. All should feel heavy for their size.

Squeeze: cucumbers (should be firm), lettuce (should feel spongy), peppers (should be firm with no soft spots), mushrooms (should be firm and dry to the touch), tomatoes (should give slightly under gentle pressure).

Once purchased, it's best to prepare your vegetables as soon as possible, but if storage is necessary, don't wash the vegetables until you're ready to use them. Perishable vegetables such as leafy greens, asparagus, broccoli, summer squash, and celery will maintain their quality longer if stored in the refrigerator's vegetable crisper. Hardier vegetables such as onions as well as potatoes, sweet potatoes, and winter squash (see the preceding chapter for recipes for these starchy vegetables) require cool, dark, well-ventilated storage. Since most of us don't have a root cellar, a cabinet on an outside wall away from any source of heat is the best substitute. Don't refrigerate tomatoes. Eat the ripe ones within a day or two. If you have more than you can use, roast and freeze them for soups and stews.

Gone are the days of the overcooked and tasteless vegetable. Today's crop is more often served raw or lightly cooked so that its wonderfully sweet, fresh flavor stars. Most vegetables are quick and simple to cook, needing only a little skillful seasoning (fresh herbs, lemon juice, a tart vinegar, freshly ground pepper, and other spices) to bring out their flavor.

Steaming is one of the best ways to cook vegetables without fat while keeping the vitamins and minerals from leaching out into the cooking liquid. We use metal vegetable steamers, but you can easily improvise with a colander or strainer positioned over a covered saucepan.

Sautéing, stir-frying, and grilling (or broiling) are also excellent methods for quick vegetable preparation. And for anyone with a microwave, microwaving is not only one of the quickest and easiest methods for cooking vegetables but also intensifies their color and flavor and preserves their nutrients.

We also endorse the trend of oven-roasting vegetables for up to 2 hours where the cooking is done without any liquid, producing wildly intense flavors without any loss of nutrients.

We use fresh vegetables almost exclusively. Canned vegetables are high in salt and, to our palates, lack in taste and texture (canned Italian plum tomatoes, chipotle and green chilies, water chestnuts, bamboo shoots, and hominy are notable exceptions—all are comparable in quality to fresh and, in the case of hominy, easier to use than the dried). Frozen vegetables are a step forward and closer to fresh in taste. However, with the exception of keeping frozen tiny peas, corn, and chopped spinach on hand for quick stuffings and a few other uses, we opt for fresh vegetables every time.

Grilled Vegetables

While the coals are still hot after barbecuing fish, chicken, or meat, grill some vegetables. There are no hard-and-fast rules for grilling. Most vegetables will benefit from a basting of oil and a free hand with fresh herbs. Experiment with different combinations. Here are some ideas to get you started. (See the preceding chapter for Grilled Corn on the Cob.) In the winter, use your broiler.

Grilled Chile Rellenos: Leaving stems on, slit 4 large Anaheim chilies lengthwise. Discard seeds and ribs. Grill over medium-hot coals, 4 to 6 inches (10 to 15 cm) from source of heat, for 8 to 10 minutes, turning frequently. Remove from grill. Mix together 1/4 cup (59 ml) shredded low-fat cheddar cheese, 1/4 cup (59 ml) shredded nonfat mozzarella cheese, and 2 chopped scallions, white part and 1 inch (2.5 cm) green. Fill each chili with one-quarter of the cheese mixture. Return chilies, stuffed side up, to the grill and continue to cook until cheese melts, about 1 minute.

MAKES 4 SERVINGS

Per serving: calories, 54 ◆ protein, 5 g ◆ carbohydrate, 6 g ◆ fat, 1 g (calories from fat, 16%) ◆ dietary fiber, 1 g ◆ cholesterol, 5 mg ◆ sodium, 81 mg ◆ potassium, 199 mg Joslin Exchanges: 1 vegetable, 1/2 low-fat meat

Grilled Eggplant: Slice a 1-pound (450 g) eggplant lengthwise into 1/4-inch-thick (.75 cm) pieces. Brush with 2 teaspoons (10 ml) olive oil and grill for 3 to 4 minutes per side over medium-hot coals, 4 to 6 inches (10 to 15 cm) from source of heat. Remove from grill and sprinkle with 2 tablespoons (30 ml) fresh lemon juice, 1 teaspoon finely chopped fresh oregano or 1/4 teaspoon (1.25 ml) crushed dried, 1/4 teaspoon (1.25 ml) salt (optional), and freshly ground pepper to taste.

MAKES 4 SERVINGS

> **Per serving:** calories, 48 ◆ protein, 1 g ◆ carbohydrate, 7 g ◆ fat, 3 g (calories from fat, 56%) ◆ dietary fiber, 1 g ◆ cholesterol, 0 mg ◆ sodium, 136 mg ◆ potassium, 239 mg Joslin Exchanges: 1 vegetable, ½ fat

Grilled Leeks: Trim root ends and tops from 4 small leeks. Split leeks lengthwise to within ½ inch (1.5 cm) of root end. Rinse well. Brush with 2 teaspoons (10 g) margarine mixed with 1 teaspoon (5 ml) minced fresh tarragon or ¼ teaspoon (1.25 ml) crushed dried. Grill over medium-hot coals, 4 to 6 inches (10 to 15 cm) from source of heat, for 4 to 6 minutes, turning once.

MAKES 4 SERVINGS

> **Per serving:** calories, 37 ◆ protein, 1 g ◆ carbohydrate, 6 g ◆ fat, 1 g (calories from fat, 24%) ◆ dietary fiber, 3 g ◆ cholesterol, 0 mg ◆ sodium, 25 mg ◆ potassium, 75 mg Joslin Exchanges: 1 vegetable

---

GRILLED SUPPER

◆

Cucumber Buttermilk Soup (page 59)

Grilled Red Snapper with Red and Green Peppercorn Sauce

(page 135)

Grilled Leeks (page 320) and Grilled Mushrooms (page 321)

Grilled Polenta (page 286)

Grilled Bananas (page 434) with Lime and Yogurt Cheese

(page 11)

Per serving: 430 calories (20% fat)
Joslin Exchanges: 3 low-fat meat, 3 vegetable, 1 bread/starch, 1 fruit, ½ nonfat milk

Grilled Mushrooms: Marinate 4 large fresh shiitake or cultivated mushrooms, about 3 inches (8 cm) in diameter, in 2 tablespoons (30 ml) dry sherry or Spanish sherry vinegar, 1¹/₂ teaspoons (7.5 ml) low-sodium soy sauce, and 1 teaspoon (5 ml) dark sesame oil for 30 minutes. Remove from marinade and grill over medium-hot coals, 4 to 6 inches (10 to 15 cm) from source of heat, for 10 to 15 minutes, turning once or twice and brushing with the marinade. Remove mushrooms from grill and sprinkle with 1 tablespoon (15 ml) chopped parsley.

MAKES 4 SERVINGS

Per serving: calories, 33 ◆ protein, 2 g ◆ carbohydrate, 4 g ◆ fat, 1 g (calories from fat, 27%) ◆ dietary fiber, 1 g ◆ cholesterol, 0 mg ◆ sodium, 79 mg ◆ potassium, 320 mg Joslin Exchanges: 1 vegetable

Grilled Radicchio: Place 2 heads of radicchio, about 6 ounces (180 g) each, on a grill rack about 6 inches (15 cm) above a bed of hot coals. Grill for about 3 minutes per side, until leaves are lightly charred and wilted, turning once and brushing with 2 teaspoons (10 ml) olive oil. Transfer to a serving platter and sprinkle with any remaining olive oil, 1 tablespoon (15 ml) balsamic vinegar, 1 teaspoon (5 ml) fresh thyme leaves or ¹/₄ teaspoon (1.25 ml) crushed dried, and freshly ground pepper to taste. Cut in half; serve warm.

MAKES 4 SERVINGS

Per serving: calories, 26 ◆ protein, 1 g ◆ carbohydrate, 1 g ◆ fat, 2 g (calories from fat, 69%) ◆ dietary fiber, 1 g ◆ cholesterol, 0 mg ◆ sodium, 7 mg ◆ potassium, 193 mg Joslin Exchanges: free

Grilled Summer Squash: Cut 4 yellow crookneck, zucchini, or pattypan squash, about 1 pound total (450 g), in half lengthwise. Brush with a mixture of 1 teaspoon (5 g) margarine, melted, 2 tablespoons (30 ml) fresh lemon juice, and 1 teaspoon (5 ml) chopped fresh rosemary or ¹/₄ teaspoon (1.25 ml) crushed dried. Grill over medium-hot coals, 4 to 6 inches (10 to 15 cm) from source of heat, for 15 to 20 minutes, turning every few minutes, until tender when pierced.

MAKES 4 SERVINGS

Per serving: calories, 33 ◆ protein, 1 g ◆ carbohydrate, 6 g ◆ fat, 1 g (calories from fat, 27%) ◆ dietary fiber, trace ◆ cholesterol, 0 mg ◆ sodium, 13 mg ◆ potassium, 238 mg Joslin Exchanges: 1 vegetable

Grilled Tomatoes: Cut 2 medium-size tomatoes in half crosswise. Grill over medium-hot coals, cut side down, 4 to 6 inches (10 to 15 cm) from source of heat, for 4

minutes; turn and brush with a mixture of 1 teaspoon (5 ml) olive oil, 1 teaspoon (5 ml) Dijon mustard, ⅛ teaspoon (.6 ml) salt (optional), and ⅛ teaspoon (.6 ml) freshly ground pepper. Grill for another 4 minutes. Place 1 teaspoon (5 ml) snipped fresh chives and 1 teaspoon (5 ml) grated nonfat mozzarella cheese on each tomato. Grill until cheese melts, about 1 minute.

MAKES 4 SERVINGS

Per serving: calories, 60 ◆ protein, 3 g ◆ carbohydrate, 4 g ◆ fat, 3 g (calories from fat, 45%) ◆ dietary fiber, 1 g ◆ cholesterol, 1 mg ◆ sodium, 137 mg ◆ potassium, 194 mg Joslin Exchanges: 1 vegetable, ½ fat

Roasted Artichokes with Tomatoes and Shallots

Roasting intensifies the wonderful flavor of artichokes, which is complemented by the earthy taste of thyme.

2 medium-size artichokes, 3 to 3½ inches (8 to 9 cm) in diameter
1 lemon, cut in half
1 cup (236 ml) chicken stock (page 45)
½ cup (118 ml) water
½ tablespoon (7.5 ml) chopped fresh thyme leaves or ½ teaspoon (5 ml) crushed dried

4 shallots, minced
1 bay leaf
freshly ground pepper to taste
3 tablespoons (45 ml) balsamic vinegar
1 tablespoon (15 ml) olive oil
2 medium-size fresh plum tomatoes, seeded and chopped
1 teaspoon (5 ml) drained capers

Break off small coarse outer leaves of artichokes. Cut off tops of remaining leaves, leaving about 1 inch (2.5 cm) of leaf. Trim away dark green areas along base. Trim off base of stem. Immerse artichokes in water, swishing up and down to remove any dirt. Shake from stem end to remove water. Cut artichokes in half lengthwise. Using a paring knife, carefully cut away the fuzzy choke. Rub cut portions of artichoke with lemon. Cut artichokes into quarters.

Preheat oven to 450° F (230° C). Place artichokes in a roasting pan. Mix together broth, water, thyme, shallots, bay leaf, and pepper. Pour over artichokes. Cover pan tightly with foil. Bake until artichoke bottoms are tender when pierced, about 30 minutes. Uncover and bake for another 5 minutes, until just tinged with brown. Transfer artichokes to a shallow dish.

Over high heat, boil pan juices, uncovered, until reduced to ¼ cup (59 ml). Remove from heat; discard bay leaf. Whisk in vinegar and oil. Pour liquid over artichokes. Cover and chill for at least 2 hours or overnight.

Transfer artichokes to small individual plates, allowing 2 quarters per serving. Stir tomatoes and capers into artichoke marinade. Spoon about 2 tablespoons (30 ml) marinade over each serving.

MAKES 4 SERVINGS

Per serving: calories, 108 ♦ protein, 3 g ♦ carbohydrate, 15 g ♦ fat, 4 g (calories from fat, 33%) ♦ dietary fiber, 1 g ♦ cholesterol, 0 mg ♦ sodium, 179 mg ♦ potassium, 378 mg
Joslin Exchanges: 3 vegetable, 1 fat, or 1 bread/starch, 1 fat

Roasted Asparagus

Roasting intensifies the flavor of any vegetable. We particularly like the way it brings out the flavor in fresh asparagus. Here are some nifty ways to serve this springtime vegetable.

1 pound (450 g) fresh asparagus, trimmed
2 teaspoons (10 ml) olive oil
2 tablespoons (30 ml) finely shredded Parmesan cheese
1 lemon, cut into wedges

Preheat oven to 500° F (260° C). Arrange asparagus in a single layer in a shallow baking pan. With a pastry brush, paint the oil on the asparagus spears. Roast until tender but still crisp, 8 to 10 minutes, depending on thickness of stalks. Turn spears occasionally for even cooking and to avoid browning.

Place asparagus spears on a serving platter. Sprinkle with cheese. Serve with lemon wedges.

MAKES 4 SERVINGS

Per serving: calories, 76 ♦ protein, 4 g ♦ carbohydrate, 6 g ♦ fat, 4 g (calories from fat, 47%) ♦ dietary fiber, 2 g ♦ cholesterol, 3 mg ♦ sodium, 71 mg ♦ potassium, 205 mg
Joslin Exchanges: 1 vegetable, 1 fat

Roasted Asparagus with Lemon and Almonds

Roast asparagus as directed. Omit Parmesan cheese. Instead, sprinkle roasted spears with grated zest and juice of 1 lemon. Season with freshly ground pepper to taste. Sprinkle with 1 tablespoon (15 ml) sliced almonds. Serve hot.

MAKES 4 SERVINGS

Per serving: calories, 61 ◆ protein, 3 g ◆ carbohydrate, 6 g ◆ fat, 4 g (calories from fat, 59%) ◆ dietary fiber, 2 g ◆ cholesterol, 0 mg ◆ sodium, 13 mg ◆ potassium, 207 mg Joslin Exchanges: 1 vegetable, 1 fat

Roasted Asparagus with Garlic and Sesame

Roast asparagus as directed, painting spears with light sesame oil instead of olive oil. Omit cheese. Instead, in a small bowl, combine 1 tablespoon (15 ml) fresh lemon juice and the pulp from 3 roasted garlic cloves (page 262). Pour over roasted asparagus and toss gently. Sprinkle with 1 teaspoon (5 ml) toasted sesame seeds (page 440).

MAKES 4 SERVINGS

Per serving: calories, 59 ◆ protein, 3 g ◆ carbohydrate, 7 g ◆ fat, 3 g (calories from fat, 40%) ◆ dietary fiber, 2 g ◆ cholesterol, 0 mg ◆ sodium, 14 mg ◆ potassium, 213 mg Joslin Exchanges: 1 vegetable, ½ fat

Roasted Beets with Yogurt Sauce

This vegetable dish is incredibly delicious. The earthy flavor of the beets is intensified by baking. Then they're drizzled with dilled yogurt sauce for a perfect side vegetable with any roasted meat or poultry.

You can roast the beets ahead of time; refrigerate before tossing with the lemon zest and other ingredients. Reheat in the microwave and proceed as directed.

Besides the familiar red beets, you'll also want to try golden beets (they're almost orange in color). And, if you can find them, candy-striped Chioggia beets (cherry red on the outside and red and white striped on the inside) have a very mild flavor. Save the beet greens to cook as for spinach (trim any coarse stems and rinse the leaves well).

8 small beets, about 1 pound
   (450 g)

Yogurt Sauce

finely grated zest of 1 lemon
¼ teaspoon (1.25 ml) salt (optional)
⅛ teaspoon (.6 ml) freshly ground
   pepper or to taste
1 teaspoon (5 ml) cumin seed
½ cup (118 ml) plain nonfat yogurt

1 garlic clove, minced
1 teaspoon (5 ml) balsamic vinegar
2 tablespoons (30 ml) chopped
   fresh dill or 2 teaspoons (10 ml)
   dried dill weed

Preheat oven to 350° F (180° C). Trim beets, leaving 1 inch (2.5 cm) of stem. Scrub well, but do not peel.

Wrap beets in aluminum foil; bake until tender, about 35 to 45 minutes, depending on size. Remove from oven. Cool beets slightly until you can gently slip off skin. Place in a serving bowl. Keep warm.

In a small bowl, combine yogurt sauce ingredients. Drizzle yogurt mixture over beets and serve.

MAKES 6 SERVINGS

> **Per serving:** calories, 38 ◆ protein, 2 g ◆ carbohydrate, 7 g ◆ fat, trace (calories from fat, less than 1%) ◆ dietary fiber, 1 g ◆ cholesterol, trace ◆ sodium, 142 mg ◆ potassium, 304 mg
> Joslin Exchanges: 1 vegetable

Roasted Beets Vinaigrette

Prepare the roasted beets as directed. Instead of Yogurt Sauce, combine ¼ cup (59 ml) raspberry vinegar (no sugar added), 1 teaspoon (5 ml) grated lemon zest, and 1 tablespoon (15 ml) sugar. Heat on top of stove (or in microwave) until sugar dissolves. Pour over peeled beets; toss to coat evenly.

MAKES 6 SERVINGS

> **Per serving:** calories, 41 ◆ protein, 1 g ◆ carbohydrate, 9 g ◆ fat, trace (calories from fat, 1%) ◆ dietary fiber, 2 g ◆ cholesterol, 0 mg ◆ sodium, 39 mg ◆ potassium, 235 mg
> Joslin Exchanges: 2 vegetable

Pureed Roasted Beets Balsamic

Prepare roasted beets using golden beets. Omit Yogurt Sauce. Puree peeled beets in a food processor until smooth. Stir in 1 tablespoon (15 ml) balsamic vinegar, 2 tablespoons (30 ml) crème fraîche (page 428), and 1 teaspoon (5 ml) grated orange zest. Serve warm.

MAKES 6 SERVINGS

Per serving: calories, 24 ◆ protein, 1 g ◆ carbohydrate, 5 g ◆ fat, trace (calories from fat, 2%) ◆ dietary fiber, 2 g ◆ cholesterol, trace ◆ sodium, 35 mg ◆ potassium, 213 mg
Joslin Exchanges: 1 vegetable

Roasted Mixed Vegetables

The flavor of green beans and carrots is also enhanced by the browning that results from oven roasting. Here we've teamed them with other winter vegetables for a colorful mix.

¼ pound (115 g) green beans, stem ends trimmed
2 carrots, about 6 ounces (180 g), scraped and cut into 2-inch-long (5 cm) pieces
½ pound (225 g) small white turnips, peeled and cut into chunks
1 medium-size onion, about 5 ounces (140 g), peeled and cut into eighths
1 medium-size red bell pepper, about 6 ounces (180 g), seeded and cut into thick strips
1 medium-size yellow bell pepper, about 6 ounces (180 g), seeded and cut into thick strips
1 teaspoon (5 ml) fresh thyme leaves or ¼ teaspoon (1.25 ml) crushed dried
½ teaspoon (2.5 ml) salt (optional)
freshly ground pepper to taste
2 teaspoons (10 ml) olive oil
juice of 1 lemon

Preheat oven to 425° F (220° C). Place vegetables in a large roasting pan. Scatter thyme leaves over top; season with salt and pepper. Combine olive oil and lemon juice; drizzle over vegetables and toss to coat evenly. Roast for 30 minutes or until vegetables are tender. Occasionally stir vegetables to ensure even roasting. Serve at once.

MAKES 6 SERVINGS

Per serving: calories, 66 ◆ protein, 2 g ◆ carbohydrate, 12 g ◆ fat, 2 g (calories from fat, 23%) ◆ dietary fiber, 3 g ◆ cholesterol, 0 mg ◆ sodium, 201 mg ◆ potassium, 372 mg ◆ Joslin Exchanges: 2 vegetable

---

WINTER FAMILY SUPPER

◆

Crispy Baked Fish (page 167)

Roasted Mixed Vegetables (page 326)

Mixed Green Salad with Radish Sprouts and Spicy Gazpacho

Dressing (page 119)

Clementines

Per serving: 362 calories (25% fat)
Joslin Exchanges: 3 low-fat meat, 2 vegetable, 1 bread/starch, 1 fruit

Roasted Onions Balsamic

Once you've tasted what this intensely flavored vinegar from Modena, Italy, does to vegetables, you'll wonder how you ever cooked without it. We particularly like it on onions that have been roasted in their skins. Beets, tomatoes, and winter squash are also delicious splashed with balsamic vinegar.

olive oil cooking spray
4 medium-size onions, about 1
    pound (450 g), unpeeled

1 tablespoon (15 ml) olive oil
balsamic vinegar

Preheat oven to 375° F (190° C). Lightly spray a shallow roasting pan with olive oil spray.

Wash onions and remove any loose skins. Rub onions with olive oil. Bake until tender, about 45 minutes to 1 hour. Open onions by cutting in half; drizzle with balsamic vinegar. Serve hot.

MAKES 4 SERVINGS

Per serving: calories, 75 ◆
protein, 1 g ◆ carbohydrate,
11 g ◆ fat, 3 g (calories from fat,
36%) ◆ dietary fiber, 0 g ◆

cholesterol, 0 mg ◆ sodium,
4 mg ◆ potassium, 160 mg
Joslin Exchanges: 2 vegetable

Sauces for Roasted Peppers

Roasted peppers make a very flavorful and attractive vegetable dish, especially when you use a mix of different-colored peppers.

Here are some easy-to-make sauces to finish the dish. Directions for roasting the peppers are on page 100.

One 3-ounce (85 g) roasted pepper provides 24 calories and 6 grams of carbohydrates and equals one vegetable exchange.

Tomato Confit

Cover 1 ounce (30 g) dried porcini with warm water. Let stand for 30 minutes. Drain, discarding soaking liquid, and chop mushrooms. Lightly spray a large nonstick sauté pan with olive oil cooking spray. Place over low heat, add 2 minced garlic cloves and 2 minced shallots, and sauté until vegetables are wilted, about 4 minutes. Peel, seed, and dice 1 pound (450 g) fresh plum tomatoes. Add chopped mushrooms and diced tomatoes to sauté pan along with 1 bay leaf, 2 fresh thyme sprigs or ½ teaspoon (2.25 ml) crushed dried, 2 tablespoons (30 ml) white wine vinegar, and ½ cup (118 ml) beef stock (page 44). Simmer until reduced by one-third. Arrange the roasted peppers on a round serving platter, alternating colors. Spoon some of the sauce in the center; nap peppers with remaining sauce. Garnish with minced fresh herbs (parsley, basil, chervil, or tarragon).

MAKES ABOUT 2 CUPS SAUCE

Per 2-tablespoon serving (confit alone): calories, 13 ◆ protein, 1 g ◆ carbohydrate, 3 g ◆ fat, trace (calories from fat, 7%) ◆ dietary fiber, trace ◆ cholesterol, 0 mg ◆ sodium, 4 mg ◆ potassium, 102 mg
Joslin Exchanges: free

Polonaise

Combine 2 chopped hard-cooked large egg whites, ¼ cup (59 ml) dry bread crumbs, 1 tablespoon (15 ml) fresh lemon juice, freshly ground pepper to taste, 1 tablespoon (15 ml) minced fresh basil or 1 teaspoon (5 ml) crushed dried, and 1 tablespoon (15 ml) grated Parmesan cheese. Sprinkle egg mixture on top of roasted peppers. Place under a preheated broiler until heated through and lightly browned.

MAKES 4 SERVINGS

Per serving (Polonaise topping alone): calories, 42 ◆ protein, 3 g ◆ carbohydrate, 5 g ◆ fat, 1 g (calories from fat, 17%) ◆ dietary fiber, trace ◆ cholesterol, 1 mg ◆ sodium, 103 mg ◆ potassium, 52 mg
Joslin Exchanges: 1 vegetable

Roasted Tomatoes

This is a useful vegetable side dish to have on a cold wintry night when tomatoes are not at their best. The slow roasting at very low heat greatly improves their flavor; by the end of the baking time they are almost caramelized.

For an easy pasta sauce, double the recipe and process in a food processor or blender.

4 garlic cloves, peeled
4 medium-size ripe fresh tomatoes, about 1¼ pounds (570 g), peeled
olive oil cooking spray

¼ teaspoon (1.25 ml) salt (optional)
freshly ground pepper to taste
2 tablespoons (30 ml) minced fresh basil or parsley

Preheat oven to 300° F (150° C). Insert a whole garlic clove in the stem end of each tomato. Place tomatoes stem end down on a small baking sheet lightly sprayed with cooking spray. Spray tomatoes as well; sprinkle with salt and pepper. Bake for 2 hours, until tomatoes begin to caramelize. Remove from oven and transfer tomatoes to serving plates. Sprinkle with fresh basil.

MAKES 4 SERVINGS

Per serving: calories, 31 ◆ protein, 1 g ◆ carbohydrate, 7 g ◆ fat, trace (calories from fat, less than 1%) ◆ dietary fiber, 1 g ◆ cholesterol, 0 mg ◆ sodium, 146 mg ◆ potassium, 296 mg
Joslin Exchanges: 1 vegetable

Roasted Turnips

Turnips' natural sweetness is heightened by a mixture of lime juice, chili powder, cumin, and oregano in this easy oven-roasted dish. Select turnips that are no larger than 2 inches (5 cm) in diameter.

1½ pounds (675 g) small turnips
¼ cup (59 ml) fresh lime juice
2 teaspoons (10 ml) olive oil
1 teaspoon (5 ml) chili powder
½ teaspoon (2.5 ml) ground cumin

½ teaspoon (2.5 ml) crushed dried oregano leaves
¼ teaspoon (1.25 ml) salt (optional)
freshly ground pepper to taste

Preheat oven to 450° F (230° C). Peel turnips and cut into large chunks. Spread in a single layer on a baking sheet.

Combine remaining ingredients, stirring until well blended. Pour mixture over turnips and mix gently until turnips are coated evenly. Roast until turnips are browned and very tender when pierced with a fork, about 45 minutes. Stir turnips every 15 minutes.

MAKES 6 SERVINGS

Per serving: calories, 50 ◆ protein, 1 g ◆ carbohydrate, 7 g ◆ fat, 2 g (calories from fat, 36%) ◆ dietary fiber, trace ◆ cholesterol, 0 mg ◆ sodium, 147 mg ◆ potassium, 169 mg Joslin Exchanges: 1 vegetable

Artichokes with Low-Fat Dipping Sauces

Artichokes are a perfect diet food, high in fiber, low in calories—and they take a long time to eat. If you've never tried microwaving artichokes, you're in for a treat. Cooking time is cut almost in half.

The simplest way to serve them is hot with little bowls of sauce for dipping or chilled with Classic Vinaigrette (page 114).

4 artichokes, ¼ pound (115 g) each   1 lemon, cut in half

Pull off lower leaves of artichokes. With a sharp knife, trim stem end and about 1 inch (2.5 cm) off the top. Using scissors, snip thorny tips off leaves. Immerse artichokes in water, swishing up and down to remove any dirt. Shake from stem end to remove water. Rub cut edges with lemon. Wrap each artichoke in microwave-safe plastic wrap. Arrange in a circle, 1 inch (2.5 cm) apart, on microwave oven floor.

Cook on HIGH for 10 minutes, rotating halfway through cooking. Pierce plastic wrap. Unwrap 1 artichoke and pull off a leaf (it should come away easily). If not done, rewrap artichoke and continue to cook all artichokes on HIGH at 1-minute increments until done. Let stand, still wrapped, for 5 minutes. Carefully unwrap artichokes and cut off stalks (if they're tender, they're edible and delicious; if they're very fibrous, discard). Drain artichokes upside down. Serve artichokes hot, each with ¼ cup (59 ml) sauce for dipping.

MAKES 4 SERVINGS

Per serving (artichoke alone): calories, 60 ◆ protein, 4 g ◆ carbohydrate, 13 g ◆ fat, trace (calories from fat, less than 1%) ◆ dietary fiber, 4 g ◆ cholesterol, 0 mg ◆ sodium, 114 mg ◆ potassium, 425 mg
Joslin Exchanges: 2 vegetable

Note: To cook artichokes on top of the stove, prepare artichokes for cooking as directed. Simmer artichokes in lightly salted boiling water until leaves pull off easily and base can be pierced with the tip of a sharp knife, about 30 minutes. Drain cooked artichokes upside down. Serve as directed.

Orange Sauce

1 tablespoon (15 ml) cornstarch
1 tablespoon (15 ml) water
1 cup (236 ml) fresh orange juice
1 tablespoon (15 ml) grated orange zest

In a small saucepan, stir together cornstarch and water. Add orange juice and bring to a boil over high heat, stirring until slightly thickened. Stir in orange zest. Serve hot or at room temperature.

MAKES 4 SERVINGS

Per ¼-cup (59 ml) serving (sauce alone): calories, 35 ◆ protein, trace ◆ carbohydrate, 9 g ◆ fat, trace (calories from fat, less than 1%) ◆ dietary fiber, 1 g ◆ cholesterol, 0 mg ◆ sodium, 1 mg ◆ potassium, 127 mg
Joslin Exchanges: ½ fruit

Mexican Crème Fraîche

1 cup crème fraîche (page 428)
2 tablespoons (30 ml) minced fresh hot red chili, seeded
1 garlic clove, finely minced
¼ cup lightly packed fresh cilantro (fresh coriander) leaves, chopped
½ teaspoon (2.5 ml) ground cumin
¼ teaspoon (1.25 ml) salt (optional)
⅛ teaspoon (.6 ml) freshly ground pepper or to taste

Combine ingredients. Serve in small bowls for dipping.

MAKES 4 SERVINGS

Per ¼-cup (59 ml) serving
(sauce alone): calories, 42 ◆
protein, 3 g ◆ carbohydrate,
6 g ◆ fat, 1 g (calories from fat,
20%) ◆ dietary fiber, 2 g ◆
cholesterol, 3 mg ◆ sodium,
176 mg ◆ potassium, 180 mg
Joslin Exchanges: ½ low-fat milk

Garlic Yogurt Sauce

3 to 4 garlic cloves, to taste,
    pressed
¼ teaspoon (1.25 ml) salt (optional)

1 cup (236 ml) plain low-fat yogurt

Using a large knife, mince together the pressed garlic and salt until mixture forms a paste. Whisk into yogurt, cover, and refrigerate until ready to serve.

MAKES 4 SERVINGS

Per ¼-cup (59 ml) serving:
calories, 45 ◆ protein, 3 g ◆
carbohydrate, 5 g ◆ fat, 1 g
(calories from fat, 20%) ◆
dietary fiber, 0 g ◆ cholesterol,
4 mg ◆ sodium, 174 mg ◆
potassium, 145 mg
Joslin Exchanges: ½ low-fat milk

Sautéed Baby Artichokes

Tiny artichokes, 2 to 3 inches (5 to 8 cm), are available for a few weeks each spring. Since the choke has not yet developed, you need to trim only the stem and outer leaves. The rest can be eaten.

olive oil cooking spray
2 teaspoons (10 ml) olive oil
8 baby artichokes, about 1 pound
    (450 g), trimmed
1 tablespoon (15 ml) fresh lemon
    juice

⅛ teaspoon (.6 ml) salt (optional)
freshly ground pepper to taste
4 garlic cloves, roasted (page 262)

Lightly spray a large nonstick skillet with cooking spray. Add olive oil and heat over medium heat. When hot, add artichokes and sauté, stirring constantly, for 10 minutes. Add lemon juice, salt, and pepper. Cover and cook for another 10 minutes, stirring occasionally. Squeeze roasted garlic over artichokes; toss well and serve hot.

MAKES 4 SERVINGS

Per serving: calories, 99 ◆ protein, 4 g ◆ carbohydrate, 14 g ◆ fat, 3 g (calories from fat, 27%) ◆ dietary fiber, 4 g ◆ cholesterol, 0 mg ◆ sodium, 175 mg ◆ potassium, 418 mg Joslin Exchanges: 3 vegetable, 1 fat

Stuffed Artichoke Bottoms

Once you've mastered the technique of trimming an artichoke, it's quite easy to prepare artichoke bottoms for unusual side dishes and salads. Here we've stuffed the bottom with tomatoes, mushrooms, and shallots for an interesting accompaniment for chicken or beef.

You can also serve the artichoke bottoms over mixed greens, drizzled with Classic Vinaigrette (page 114) and sprinkled with a teaspoon (5 ml) of chopped walnuts. When fresh artichokes aren't available, you can use frozen or canned (packed in water) artichoke bottoms.

6 artichokes, about 6 ounces (180 g) each
juice of 1 lemon
3 fresh plum tomatoes, about ½ pound (225 g), peeled, seeded, and finely chopped
½ pound (225 g) fresh mushrooms, minced
2 shallots, minced

1 garlic clove, minced
1 tablespoon (15 ml) minced fresh basil
1 tablespoon (15 ml) minced fresh flat-leaf parsley
½ teaspoon (2.5 ml) salt (optional)
freshly ground pepper to taste
1½ tablespoons (9 g) grated Parmesan cheese

To prepare artichoke bottoms, cut stems off artichokes. Pull off outer dark leaves until you reach leaves with a touch of pale yellow (save stems and outer leaves for another use such as steaming to eat with a dipping sauce). Using a sharp knife, slice artichokes in half crosswise. Using a sharp paring knife, trim around bottom to remove outer layer of green skin. This will expose the pale yellow flesh of the bottom.

Place artichoke bottoms in a saucepan full of water and lemon juice. Bring to a boil over medium-high heat. Reduce heat to low and cook until bottoms are tender when pierced with a knife, 30 to 35 minutes. Drain, rinse under running cold water; drain again. Place cooked artichoke bottoms in a baking dish. Set aside.

Meanwhile, in a large nonstick skillet over low heat, sauté tomatoes, mushrooms, shallots, and garlic until vegetables are very soft and all liquid has evaporated, about 25 minutes. Stir frequently. Add herbs, salt, and pepper.

Divide tomato mixture among artichoke bottoms. Sprinkle with cheese. Preheat broiler. Place filled artichoke bottoms under broiler until heated through and lightly browned. Serve at once. (These may be made ahead and reheated in the microwave.)

MAKES 6 SERVINGS

> **Per serving:** calories, 64 ◆ protein, 4 g ◆ carbohydrate, 12 g ◆ fat, 1 g (calories from fat, 11%) ◆ dietary fiber, 3 g ◆ cholesterol, 1 mg ◆ sodium, 271 mg ◆ potassium, 521 mg Joslin Exchanges: 2 vegetable

Main-Course Variation

Add 1 cup (236 ml) minced cooked chicken or veal to tomato mixture. Mix, fill, and broil as directed.

MAKES 6 SERVINGS

> **Per serving:** calories, 103 ◆ protein, 10 g ◆ carbohydrate, 12 g ◆ fat, 3 g (calories from fat, 20%) ◆ dietary fiber, 3 g ◆ cholesterol, 21 mg ◆ sodium, 286 mg ◆ potassium, 526 mg Joslin Exchanges: 1 low-fat meat, 2 vegetable

---

A COZY SUPPER

◆

Mixed Baby Lettuces with Creamy Honey Dijon Dressing

(page 115)

Roast Chicken with Lemon and Tarragon (page 176)

Stuffed Artichoke Bottoms (page 334)

Herbed Creamer Potatoes (page 308)

Fresh Figs

Per serving: 571 calories (27% fat)
Joslin Exchanges: 3½ low-fat meat, 4 vegetable, 2 bread/starch, 1 fruit, 1 fat

Artichokes Stuffed with Corn and Sun-Dried Tomato Salsa

Artichokes stuffed with corn salsa flavored with jalapeño, garlic, and cilantro (coriander) or mint make a terrific first course or main course for a light lunch or supper.

The salsa is good with grilled swordfish or chicken marinated in fresh lemon juice, garlic, and cumin. Prepare the salsa before you start the artichokes. (If you make it earlier in the day, refrigerate and return it to room temperature before stuffing the artichokes.)

kernels from 3 ears of fresh corn
    or 1 10-ounce (285 g) box
    frozen, defrosted
8 sun-dried tomatoes (packed dry),
    soaked in warm water for 10
    minutes, drained, and coarsely
    chopped
4 scallions, white part and 1 inch
    (2.5 cm) green, chopped
1/4 cup (59 ml) chopped red onion
3 garlic cloves, minced
1 fresh jalapeño chili, seeded and
    minced

1 to 2 tablespoons (15 to 30 ml)
    minced fresh cilantro
    (coriander) or fresh mint, to
    taste
juice of 1 lime
1 1/2 tablespoons (22.5 ml) white
    wine vinegar
2 teaspoons (10 ml) olive oil
1 tablespoon (15 ml) water
1/2 teaspoon (2.5 ml) salt (optional)
4 1/4-pound (115 g) artichokes

Cook corn in lightly salted boiling water for 4 minutes. Drain well. Combine with remaining ingredients except artichokes. Let stand at room temperature for at least 30 minutes to allow flavors to mingle. Set aside.

Meanwhile, prepare artichokes according to directions on page 331. After cooking, drain and allow to cool slightly before gently prying centers of artichokes apart and scooping out hairy chokes with a sharp spoon.

Fill cavity of each artichoke with a portion of salsa, mounding it a bit over the top.

MAKES 6 SERVINGS

Per serving: calories, 126 ◆
protein, 5 g ◆ carbohydrate,
22 g ◆ fat, 2 g (calories from fat,
14%) ◆ dietary fiber, 6 g ◆
cholesterol, 0 mg ◆ sodium,
305 mg ◆ potassium, 449 mg
Joslin Exchanges: 2 vegetable, 1
bread/starch

Steamed Green Beans with Shiitake Duxelles

Duxelles is a dry cooked mixture of highly seasoned mushrooms that is used as a vegetable topping here but can also be stuffed into chicken breasts or hollowed-out cherry tomatoes sautéed briefly in a smidgen of olive oil.

If fresh shiitake mushrooms are not available, use 1¼ ounces (37 g) dried or ½ pound (225 g) cultivated mushrooms. The mixture must be used the day it's made. The recipe makes about 1 cup (236 ml) duxelles.

Duxelles

½ pound (225 g) fresh shiitake mushrooms, stems removed and minced

2 tablespoons (30 ml) minced shallot

1 small leek, white part only, well rinsed and minced

2 garlic cloves, minced

½ teaspoon (2.5 ml) olive oil

2 teaspoons (10 ml) fresh thyme leaves or ½ teaspoon (2.5 ml) crushed dried

½ teaspoon (2.5 ml) salt (optional)

¼ cup (59 ml) dry red wine or beef stock (page 44)

¼ cup (59 ml) water

Beans

1 pound (450 g) green beans, stem ends trimmed

1 tablespoon (15 ml) fresh lemon juice

¼ teaspoon (1.25 ml) freshly ground pepper or to taste

In a large nonstick sauté pan over low heat, sauté mushrooms, shallot, leek, and garlic in oil until shallot is translucent, about 5 minutes. Add thyme, salt, wine, and water; cook, stirring often, until liquid evaporates and mushrooms are slightly browned, about 15 minutes.

Meanwhile, in a vegetable steamer or large colander over boiling water, steam beans, covered, until crisp-tender, about 5 to 7 minutes. Transfer beans to a serving platter; toss with lemon juice and pepper. Spoon mushroom duxelles onto beans.

MAKES 6 SERVINGS

Per serving: calories, 81 ◆ protein, 3 g ◆ carbohydrate, 15 g ◆ fat, 1 g (calories from fat, 11%) ◆ dietary fiber, 2 g ◆ cholesterol, 0 mg ◆ sodium, 8 mg ◆ potassium, 374 mg Joslin Exchanges: 3 vegetable or 1 bread/starch

Per 2½-tablespoon (38 ml) serving (duxelles alone): calories, 38 ◆ protein, 1 g ◆ carbohydrate, 8 g ◆ fat, 1 g (calories from fat, 24%) ◆ dietary fiber, 1 g ◆ cholesterol, 0 mg ◆ sodium, 5 mg ◆ potassium, 144 mg Joslin Exchanges: 1 vegetable

Note: If you're using dried shiitake mushrooms, soak in hot water to cover until soft and pliable, about 20 minutes. Rub gently to remove any grit. Drain and pat dry with paper towels; discard soaking liquid. Trim off and discard tough stems; mince caps.

Broiled Tandoori Broccoli and Cauliflower

If you have a grill rack for vegetables and fish that keeps the food from falling into the hot coals, you can grill these vegetables outdoors. The marinade is also delicious as a coating for grilled mushrooms, topping for baked or steamed potatoes, or dip with crudités.

¾ pound (340 g) broccoli florets
¾ pound (340 g) cauliflower florets

chopped fresh mint for garnish (optional)

Marinade

½ cup (118 ml) plain nonfat yogurt
2 garlic cloves, minced
2 teaspoons (10 ml) ground cumin
1 tablespoon (15 ml) chopped fresh mint or 1 teaspoon (5 ml) crushed dried
2 teaspoons (10 ml) olive oil

1 tablespoon (15 ml) fresh lemon juice
1 to 2 fresh jalapeño chilies, to taste, seeded and minced
1 teaspoon (5 ml) fresh thyme leaves or ¼ teaspoon (1.25 ml) crushed dried

Steam broccoli and cauliflower over boiling water for 3 minutes. Remove vegetables from steamer and place in a large nonreactive bowl.

Prepare marinade by placing all ingredients in a food processor or blender. Process until smooth. Pour marinade over vegetables; stir lightly to coat evenly. Marinate for 30 minutes.

Preheat broiler or grill. Drain vegetables and broil or grill about 4 inches (10 cm) from source of heat for 5 to 6 minutes, turning frequently, until crisp-tender and lightly browned. Arrange on serving platter and sprinkle with chopped mint.

MAKES 6 SERVINGS

> **Per serving:** calories, 70 ◆ protein, 4 g ◆ carbohydrate, 9 g ◆ fat, 2 g (calories from fat, 26%) ◆ dietary fiber, 3 g ◆ cholesterol, trace ◆ sodium, 40 mg ◆ potassium, 469 mg Joslin Exchanges: 2 vegetable

Broccoli and Tomato Timbales

Broccoli is the king of vegetables and one of nature's healthiest foods, full of vitamin C and vitamin A as well as goodly amounts of riboflavin, iron, calcium, potassium, and fiber. Prepared this way, it's particularly enjoyable, even for those who aren't fond of its flavor. This is a colorful vegetable to serve with a simple grilled fish or chicken dish.

1 pound (450 g) fresh broccoli, trimmed and chopped
1 scallion, white part only, chopped
1 garlic clove, chopped
1 large egg or 2 large egg whites
splash of fresh lemon juice
1 tablespoon (6 g) grated Parmesan cheese
¼ pound (115 g) soft tofu
freshly ground pepper to taste
vegetable oil cooking spray
¼ pound (115 g) fresh plum tomatoes, peeled, seeded, and chopped
1 tablespoon (15 ml) minced fresh basil for garnish

Steam or microwave broccoli until crisp-tender, about 5 minutes. Place cooked broccoli, scallion, garlic, egg, lemon juice, Parmesan cheese, tofu, and pepper in a food processor or blender. Process until very smooth.

Preheat oven to 350° F (180° C). Lightly spray four 6-ounce (177 ml) timbale molds or custard cups with cooking spray. Place in a baking dish. Half-fill each mold with broccoli mixture. Top with chopped tomatoes, reserving about 1 tablespoon (15 ml) for garnish.

Fill baking dish with hot water until it reaches halfway up sides of molds. Bake for 40 minutes. Remove from oven and let stand for 5 minutes. Unmold onto a serving plate; garnish with reserved chopped tomato and fresh basil.

MAKES 4 SERVINGS

Per serving (using whole egg): calories, 76 ◆ protein, 8 g ◆ carbohydrate, 10 g ◆ fat, 2 g (calories from fat, 23%) ◆ dietary fiber, 2 g ◆ cholesterol, 53 mg ◆ sodium, 94 mg ◆ potassium, 491 mg
Joslin Exchanges: 2 vegetable, ½ low-fat meat

Braised Broccoli Rabe

Until recently, broccoli rabe was an unfamiliar vegetable to anyone not of Italian origin. Now this bright green slightly bitter leafy vegetable is starting to show up on dinner tables throughout the country in place of its more familiar cabbage cousins such as kale and Brussels sprouts.

1½ pounds (675 g) broccoli rabe, washed
2 teaspoons (10 ml) olive oil
2 shallots, minced
⅛ teaspoon (.6 ml) hot red pepper flakes
½ teaspoon (2.5 ml) salt (optional)
juice of 1 lemon

Trim broccoli rabe, discarding any yellow or coarse leaves and the tough stem ends. Cut stems and leaves crosswise into 2-inch (5 cm) pieces. Bring plenty of lightly salted water to a boil in a large saucepan. Add broccoli rabe and cook for 1 minute. Immediately drain into a colander and run under cold water to prevent further cooking. Drain thoroughly; set aside.

In a heavy sauté pan, heat oil over low heat. Add shallots and cook gently for 4 minutes, but do not brown. Add red pepper flakes and broccoli rabe. Toss over medium-high heat until broccoli rabe is wilted, about 3 minutes. Add salt and lemon juice; toss well. Serve hot.

MAKES 6 SERVINGS

Per serving: calories, 58 ◆ protein, 2 g ◆ carbohydrate, 8 g ◆ fat, 2 g (calories from fat, 31%) ◆ dietary fiber, 1 g ◆ cholesterol, 0 mg ◆ sodium, 181 mg ◆ potassium, 16 mg
Joslin Exchanges: 1 vegetable

Brussels Sprouts with Mustard and Lemon

Brussels sprouts are a much maligned vegetable because they are usually over-cooked. In *Quick Cook*, Martha Stewart taught us to prepare them a new way—cook the whole little sprouts until just tender and then peel off the leaves. We toss them in a nippy lemon mustard sauce seasoned with fresh thyme.

½ pound (225 g) fresh Brussels
  sprouts
¼ teaspoon (1.25 ml) salt (optional)
1 teaspoon (5 g) margarine
juice of 1 lemon
1 tablespoon (15 ml) Dijon
  mustard

1 teaspoon (5 ml) fresh thyme
  leaves or ¼ teaspoon (1.25 ml)
  crushed dried
freshly ground pepper to taste

Trim the Brussels sprouts, pulling off any yellowed or withered leaves. Cut an X in the stem of each sprout. Cook in a large pot of boiling salted water until just tender, 10 to 12 minutes. Drain and cool under cold running water. Remove leaves from each Brussels sprout and set aside.

In a large skillet, melt margarine. Add lemon juice, mustard, thyme, and Brussels sprouts leaves. Toss to coat evenly; heat through. Season with pepper and serve hot.

MAKES 6 SERVINGS

Per serving: calories, 25 ◆ protein, 1 g ◆ carbohydrate, 4 g ◆ fat, 1 g (calories from fat, 36%) ◆ dietary fiber, 1 g ◆ cholesterol, 0 mg ◆ sodium, 140 mg ◆ potassium, 133 mg Joslin Exchanges: 1 vegetable

Caribbean Spicy Tomato Cabbage

This unusual spicy cabbage with coconut is frequently served at the Zetlands Plantation & Inn on the island of Nevis, West Indies. You can control the heat of the dish by varying the amount of Tabasco sauce. It's a great side dish for winter meals featuring a simple chicken or fish main course.

4 cups (1 l) tightly packed finely shredded green cabbage, about 1 pound (450 g)
1 large onion, about ½ pound (225 g), chopped
2 garlic cloves, minced
1 large red bell pepper, about ½ pound (225 g), seeded and chopped
1 tablespoon (15 ml) olive oil
1 tablespoon (15 ml) light brown sugar

2 tablespoons (30 ml) fresh lemon juice
1 teaspoon (5 ml) Tabasco sauce or to taste
⅓ cup (78 ml) low-sodium tomato paste
1 cup (236 ml) water
½ teaspoon (2.5 ml) salt (optional)
freshly ground pepper to taste
1 tablespoon (15 ml) grated unsweetened coconut

Place cabbage in the top of a steamer over boiling water. Steam for 7 minutes, until crisp-tender (it may take a little longer if cabbage is old, but do not overcook).

Meanwhile, in a large nonstick skillet, sauté onion, garlic, and pepper in olive oil over low heat until onion is wilted, about 4 minutes. Add sugar, lemon juice, and Tabasco sauce. Cook, stirring, for 1 minute. Add tomato paste, water, salt, and pepper. Stir to blend. Cook over low heat for 5 minutes. Add water as needed to thin sauce.

Toss cabbage with hot tomato sauce. Sprinkle with grated coconut.

MAKES 8 SERVINGS

Per serving: calories, 63 ◆ protein, 2 g ◆ carbohydrate, 11 g ◆ fat, 2 g (calories from fat, 28%) ◆ dietary fiber, 1 g ◆ cholesterol, 0 mg ◆ sodium, 156 mg ◆ potassium, 339 mg Joslin Exchanges: 2 vegetable

TROPICAL DINNER

◆

Jícama with Chili and Lime (page 4)

Grilled Gingered Swordfish (page 142)

Wild Rice (page 288)

Caribbean Spicy Tomato Cabbage (page 342)

Grilled Papaya (page 434)

Per serving: 435 calories (27% fat)
Joslin Exchanges: 4 low-fat meat, 1 bread/starch, 3 vegetable, 1 fruit

Red Cabbage with Apples

A pretty fall vegetable with a delicious mellow flavor, red cabbage is usually used raw—but it's delicious cooked. Green cabbage can also be used, with white wine instead of red.

1 tablespoon (15 g) margarine
1 small onion, about 3 ounces (85 g), thinly sliced and separated into rings
2 garlic cloves, minced
1 medium-size red cabbage, about 1¼ pounds (570 g), cored and thinly sliced
¼ cup (59 ml) dry red wine or 3 tablespoons (45 ml) water plus 1 tablespoon (15 ml) red wine vinegar

1 large Granny Smith apple, about 6 ounces (180 g), cored and thinly sliced
½ teaspoon (2.5 ml) salt (optional)
⅛ teaspoon (.6 ml) freshly ground pepper or to taste

In a large nonstick skillet, melt margarine. Add onion and garlic; sauté over low heat until onion is soft, about 4 minutes. Add cabbage and raise heat to medium-high. Sauté, stirring constantly, until cabbage wilts, about 2 minutes. Add wine; reduce heat to simmer and continue to cook for 6 minutes. Add apple and cook just until apples are soft but not mushy, 2 to 4 minutes. Season with salt and pepper. Serve hot.

MAKES 6 SERVINGS

Per serving: calories, 63 ◆ protein, 1 g ◆ carbohydrate, 11 g ◆ fat, 2 g (calories from fat, 28%) ◆ dietary fiber, 1 g ◆ cholesterol, 0 mg ◆ sodium, 221 mg ◆ potassium, 293 mg Joslin Exchanges: 2 vegetable

Stir-Fried Chayote and Carrots

Cilantro (fresh coriander), lime, and chili powder brighten the mild flavor of this favorite of South American cooks. We teamed it with carrots for added color.

2 **medium-size carrots, about ¼ pound (115 g), scraped**
boiling water
2 **medium-size chayote, about ½ pound (225 g)**
1 **tablespoon (15 g) margarine**
1 **garlic clove, minced**
½ **teaspoon (2.5 ml) chili powder**

¼ **teaspoon (1.25 ml) ground cumin**
¼ **teaspoon (1.25 ml) salt (optional)**
freshly ground pepper to taste
¼ **cup (59 ml) fresh lime juice**
¼ **cup (59 ml) lightly packed cilantro (fresh coriander) leaves, minced**

Cook carrots in boiling water to cover for 3 minutes. Drain and cool under running cold water. Cut into matchsticks. Peel chayote if skin is tough and prickly. Cut into matchsticks.

Melt margarine in a large nonstick skillet over medium heat. Add carrots, chayote, and garlic. Cook, stirring frequently, until vegetables are crisp-tender, about 10 minutes. Add remaining ingredients and stir to mix well. Serve hot.

MAKES 4 SERVINGS

Per serving: calories, 82 ◆ protein, 1 g ◆ carbohydrate, 6 g ◆ fat, 6 g (calories from fat, 66%) ◆ dietary fiber, 1 g ◆ cholesterol, 0 mg ◆ sodium, 189 mg ◆ potassium, 249 mg Joslin Exchanges: 1 vegetable, 1 fat

Sautéed Cucumbers

If you've never tried cooked cucumbers, you're in for a pleasant surprise. Their delicate flavor is enhanced by a quick sauté, which makes them perfect to serve with a quick-cooking main course like fish.

3 cucumbers, about 1 pound (450 g) total
¼ teaspoon (1.25 ml) salt (optional)
1 tablespoon (15 ml) cornstarch
olive oil cooking spray
freshly ground pepper to taste

1 tablespoon (15 ml) fresh lemon juice
1 tablespoon (15 ml) minced fresh dill, basil, or chervil

Peel cucumbers and slice in half lengthwise. With a small spoon, scrape out seeds. Place in a bowl of cold water with salt. Let sit for 15 minutes. Remove cucumber, rinse, and dry on paper towels.

Slice cucumbers into crescents about ¼ inch (.75 cm) thick. Sprinkle with cornstarch. Sauté in a large nonstick skillet lightly sprayed with cooking spray over medium-low heat, tossing occasionally, until cucumbers are cooked but still crisp, about 3 minutes. (Cucumbers will be browned around the edges but still firm.) Sprinkle with pepper, lemon juice, and herbs. Serve at once.

MAKES 4 SERVINGS

Per serving: calories, 24 ◆ protein, 1 g ◆ carbohydrate, 6 g ◆ fat, trace (calories from fat, 5%) ◆ dietary fiber, 1 g ◆ cholesterol, 0 mg ◆ sodium, 137 mg ◆ potassium, 186 mg Joslin Exchanges: 1 vegetable

Curried Eggplant and Lentils

This Indian-style dish is excellent over rice for a vegetarian meal or served as is to accompany grilled fish or meat.

Be sure your curry powder is fresh. It loses its pungency about two months after being opened. Buy small containers and store airtight, away from heat and light.

1 large onion, about ½ pound (225 g), chopped
2 garlic cloves, minced
2 small Italian eggplants, about 5 ounces (140 g) each, cut into 1-inch (2 .5 cm) cubes
1 28-ounce (790 g) can Italian tomatoes with liquid, chopped
½ cup (118 ml) lentils, rinsed and drained

1 teaspoon (5 ml) ground cumin
1 teaspoon (5 ml) curry powder or to taste
½ teaspoon (2.5 ml) turmeric
½ teaspoon (2.5 ml) ground ginger
⅓ cup (78 ml) chopped fresh cilantro (fresh coriander)

In a large nonstick skillet over medium heat, sauté onion and garlic for 1 minute. Add remaining ingredients except cilantro. Stir well. Reduce heat to simmer, cover, and cook for 35 minutes. Stir in cilantro and serve immediately.

MAKES 4 SERVINGS

Per serving: calories, 98 ◆ protein, 4 g ◆ carbohydrate, 19 g ◆ fat, 1 g (calories from fat, 10%) ◆ dietary fiber, 2 g ◆ cholesterol, 0 mg ◆ sodium, 326 mg ◆ potassium, 720 mg Joslin Exchanges: 3 vegetable or 1 bread/starch

Eggplant and Tomato Pie

Serve this savory eggplant pie with a green salad for a light lunch or offer smaller portions as a vegetable side dish for grilled meat or fish.

2 small eggplants or 1 large, about 1 pound (450 g)
½ teaspoon (2.5 ml) salt (optional)
olive oil cooking spray

2 scallions, white part only, minced
1 garlic clove, minced

1 teaspoon (5 ml) fresh thyme
  leaves or ¼ teaspoon (1.25 ml)
  crushed dried
freshly ground pepper to taste
1 large egg, slightly beaten
½ cup (22 g) fresh bread crumbs
1 cup (96 g) grated skim milk
  mozzarella cheese

¼ cup (25 g) freshly grated
  Parmesan cheese
1 tablespoon (15 ml) reduced-
  calorie mayonnaise
3 medium-size tomatoes, about 1
  pound (450 g), thinly sliced
2 tablespoons (12 g) minced fresh
  basil for garnish (optional)

Slice eggplant crosswise into ¼-inch (.75 cm) slices. Lay slices on paper towels, sprinkle with salt, and set aside for 1 hour.

Lightly spray a large nonstick sauté pan with cooking spray. Add scallions and garlic; sauté over low heat for 4 minutes, until scallions are wilted. Meanwhile, pat eggplant dry and finely dice. Add to sauté pan and cook until eggplant is tender, about 10 minutes.

Preheat oven to 350° F (180° C). Add thyme and pepper to eggplant. Stir in egg and bread crumbs; mix thoroughly. Press eggplant mixture into a 9- or 10-inch (23 or 25 cm) pie pan to form a crust. Bake for 10 minutes. Cool.

In a medium-size bowl, mix together cheeses and mayonnaise. Spread evenly into eggplant crust. Place tomatoes on top of cheese mixture in overlapping circles. Lightly spray with cooking spray. Bake for 30 minutes, until bubbly. Just before serving, sprinkle with chopped basil. Cut into wedges to serve.

MAKES 6 SERVINGS

Per serving: calories, 130 ◆ protein, 9 g ◆ carbohydrate, 11 g ◆ fat, 6 g (calories from fat, 42%) ◆ dietary fiber, 1 g ◆ cholesterol, 50 mg ◆ sodium, 382 mg ◆ potassium, 361 mg Joslin Exchanges: 1 medium-fat meat, 2 vegetable

Sicilian Braised Fennel

Braising makes this intriguing vegetable very tender and softens its licoricelike flavor.

 2 fennel bulbs, about 2 pounds
   (900 g) total
olive oil cooking spray
 2 tablespoons (15 ml) snipped
   fresh chives
 1 shallot, minced

¼ teaspoon (1.25 ml) salt (optional)
½ cup (118 ml) chicken stock
   (page 45)
 2 tablespoons (12 ml) grated
   Parmesan cheese

Trim fennel; set aside some of the feathery leaves as a garnish. Cut bulbs into quarters. Rinse and drain well.

In a large nonstick skillet lightly sprayed with cooking spray, sauté chives and shallot over low heat for 1 minute. Add fennel; sprinkle with salt. Cover and cook for 10 minutes. Add stock and braise, covered, for another 10 minutes, until fennel is tender.

Preheat broiler. Transfer fennel to an ovenproof shallow casserole. Sprinkle with cheese. Place under hot broiler until cheese browns, 2 to 3 minutes. Chop reserved fennel leaves; sprinkle over hot fennel. Serve at once.

MAKES 4 SERVINGS

Per serving: calories, 57 ◆ protein, 3 g ◆ carbohydrate, 10 g ◆ fat, 1 g (calories from fat, 17%) ◆ dietary fiber, trace ◆ cholesterol, 3 mg ◆ sodium, 197 mg ◆ potassium, 564 mg Joslin Exchanges: 2 vegetable

Garlic Flan

Garlic, a member of the lily family (along with onions, leeks, scallions, and shallots), is an herb. We often roast it and serve it in place of a vegetable.

Here we've modified Paula Wolfert's recipe for a savory garlic custard, substituting evaporated skim milk for heavy cream and using fewer eggs to lighten the dish. Serve with roasted meat or poultry.

Roasting the garlic mellows its raw taste, giving it a flavor similar to chestnuts. The custard is easy to make, so don't reserve it just for company meals.

olive oil cooking spray
10 garlic cloves, roasted (page 262)
1¼ cups (295 ml) evaporated skim milk
2 large eggs

2 teaspoons (10 ml) fresh thyme leaves or ½ teaspoon (2.5 ml) crushed dried
½ teaspoon (2.5 ml) salt (optional)
freshly ground pepper to taste

Preheat oven to 350° F (180° C). Lightly spray six ½-cup (118 ml) custard cups with cooking spray. Set aside.

Peel and squeeze roasted garlic cloves into a food processor or blender. Puree garlic with milk until smooth. Blend in remaining ingredients; process until smooth.

Divide garlic mixture among prepared custard cups. Place filled custard cups in a large baking pan. Add enough water to pan to come halfway up side of cups. Bake until flans are gently set, about 35 minutes. Allow to cool slightly while custard cups remain in water.

Run a thin-bladed knife around outer edge of each flan and unmold onto serving plates. Serve warm. (Flans can be made ahead and refrigerated for up to a day in a sealed container. Reheat in a 350° F/180° C oven for 5 minutes.)

MAKES 6 SERVINGS

Per serving: calories, 74 ◆ protein, 6 g ◆ carbohydrate, 8 g ◆ fat, 2 g (calories from fat, 24%) ◆ dietary fiber, trace ◆ cholesterol, 73 mg ◆ sodium, 261 mg ◆ potassium, 217 mg Joslin Exchanges: ½ nonfat milk

Kale with Lemon and Cumin

This is a wonderful treatment for an often neglected member of the cabbage family. Kale is at its peak during winter but is available year-round at most produce markets.

The lemon and cumin dressing adds a bold, robust counterpoint to the mild, earthy flavor of the steamed kale.

1½ pounds (675 g) fresh kale, washed and tough stems removed
2 teaspoons (10 ml) olive oil
½ tablespoon (7.5 ml) ground cumin

2 garlic cloves, minced
juice of 1 lemon
½ teaspoon (2.5 ml) salt (optional)
freshly ground pepper to taste

With a large knife or cleaver, cut kale leaves into very fine chiffonade by stacking 4 to 5 leaves and slicing crosswise into thin slivers. Fill a very large skillet with ½ inch (1.5 cm) of water. Bring to a boil; add kale, cover, and steam for 6 to 7 minutes. Drain and keep warm.

In same skillet, warm olive oil and cumin. When cumin begins to smell, add garlic and lemon juice. Add kale, salt, and pepper; toss and serve.

MAKES 8 SERVINGS

Per serving: calories, 41 ◆ protein, 2 g ◆ carbohydrate, 6 g ◆ fat, 2 g (calories from fat, 43%) ◆ dietary fiber, 1 g ◆ cholesterol, 0 mg ◆ sodium, 154 mg ◆ potassium, 212 mg Joslin Exchanges: 1 vegetable

Microwave Mexican Vegetable Stew

A quick and easy microwave recipe that uses the abundant squash and tomatoes that issue from a late-summer garden.

2 medium-size onions, about ½ pound (225 g), peeled and cut into eighths

1 small eggplant, about ½ pound (225 g), cut into 1-inch (2.5 cm) cubes

1 medium-size zucchini, about ¼ pound (115 g), cut into 1-inch (2.5 cm) cubes

1 medium-size yellow summer squash, about ¼ pound (115 g), cut into 1-inch (2.5 cm) cubes

1 medium-size red bell pepper, about 5 ounces (140 g), seeded and cut into 1-inch (2.5 cm) cubes

1 tablespoon (15 ml) seeded and minced fresh jalapeño chili

2 teaspoons (10 ml) olive oil

2 small tomatoes, about 6 ounces (180 g), seeded and chopped

½ teaspoon (2.5 ml) crushed dried oregano

¼ teaspoon (1.25 ml) ground cumin

⅛ teaspoon (.6 ml) freshly ground pepper or to taste

1 tablespoon (15 ml) tomato paste

¼ teaspoon (1.25 ml) salt (optional)

3 tablespoons (45 ml) chopped fresh cilantro (fresh coriander)

In a large deep microwave-size casserole, place onions, eggplant, zucchini, summer squash, red bell pepper, and jalapeño. Drizzle with olive oil; stir to distribute oil.

Cover and microwave on HIGH for 10 minutes, stirring twice during cooking. Remove cover and stir in tomatoes, oregano, cumin, pepper, and tomato paste.

Microwave, uncovered, on HIGH, for 12 to 15 minutes, until vegetables are tender. Stir in salt and cilantro. Let sit for at least 30 minutes before serving to allow flavors to blend.

MAKES 8 SERVINGS

Per ½-cup serving: calories, 45 ♦ protein, 1 g ♦ carbohydrate, 8 g ♦ fat, 1 g (calories from fat, 20%) ♦ dietary fiber, 1 g ♦ cholesterol, 0 mg ♦ sodium, 88 mg ♦ potassium, 280 mg Joslin Exchanges: 1 vegetable

FALL VEGETARIAN SUPPER

◆

Microwave Mexican Vegetable Stew (page 351) over

Spinach Fettuccine

Freshly Grated Parmesan Cheese

Salad of Orange Slices and Pomegranate Seeds with

Balsamic Vinaigrette (page 95)

Per serving: 377 calories (30% fat)
Joslin Exchanges: 1 medium-fat meat, 2 bread/starch, 1 vegetable, 1 fruit, 1½ fat

Pesto-Stuffed Mushroom Caps

These mushrooms are particularly good served with grilled chicken or meat. You can make the pesto, without the cheese, ahead of time and refrigerate for up to several hours. Stir in the cheese just before using.

To serve these for hors d'oeuvres, use 20 to 25 medium-size mushroom caps, about 1 pound (450 g), filling each cap with 1 teaspoon (5 ml) pesto; bake as directed.

6 large fresh mushrooms, about ½ pound (225 g)
olive oil cooking spray
⅔ cup (156 ml) tightly packed fresh basil leaves
3 scallions, including some of the green, coarsely chopped
1 garlic clove, minced

1 teaspoon (5 ml) dry-roasted sunflower seeds
freshly ground pepper to taste
3 to 4 teaspoons (15 to 20 ml) chicken stock (page 45)
½ tablespoon (7.5 ml) grated Parmesan cheese

Preheat oven to 400° F (205° C). Pull the entire stem from each mushroom cap. Discard stems or set aside for another use. Clean mushroom caps. Lightly spray a baking sheet with cooking spray. Arrange mushroom caps on baking sheet.

To make pesto, place basil leaves, scallions, garlic, sunflower seeds, and pepper in a food processor or blender. Pulse on and off until finely minced. Slowly add enough stock to thin to a smooth mixture. Stir in cheese.

Place 1 tablespoon (15 ml) pesto in each mushroom cap. Lightly spray each filled mushroom with cooking spray. Bake for 8 to 10 minutes, until mushrooms are done and pesto is bubbling.

MAKES 6 SERVINGS

Per serving: calories, 23 ◆ protein, 2 g ◆ carbohydrate, 4 g ◆ fat, 1 g (calories from fat, 39%) ◆ dietary fiber, 1 g ◆ cholesterol, trace ◆ sodium, 13 mg ◆ potassium, 237 mg Joslin Exchanges: 1 vegetable

Raw Vegetables

We love vegetables and often serve them raw, embellished with a little chopped shallot, fresh herbs, and a splash of lemon juice or a special vinegar. Here are some good combinations. (See Vegetable Exchanges in Appendix 1 to determine each vegetable exchange.)

Artichokes: Trim artichokes to prepare artichoke bottoms (page 334). Thinly slice and toss with fresh lemon juice. Serve with a few thin shavings of Parmesan cheese—be sure to calculate your meat exchange (Appendix 1).

Asparagus: Drop asparagus into boiling water for 1 minute. Quickly plunge into ice water to stop the cooking. Sprinkle with chopped shallots and balsamic vinegar.

Green Beans: Drop tiny green beans into boiling water for 1 minute. Quickly plunge into ice water to stop the cooking. Toss with minced fresh basil.

Beets: Cover beets with boiling water for 1 minute. Peel and coarsely grate. Top with a little crème fraîche (page 428) mixed with a few drops of red wine vinegar and some chopped fresh tarragon.

Cucumbers: Peel cucumbers and thinly slice. Marinate in a mixture of 1/4 cup (59 ml) white wine vinegar, 1/4 cup (59 ml) water, 1 minced shallot, and 2 tablespoons (30 ml) minced fresh herbs (whatever you have on hand—dill, basil, chives, oregano, or a combination) for at least 30 minutes. Drain and serve.

Fennel: Cut fennel into thin strips. Sprinkle with fresh lemon juice and hot red pepper flakes to taste.

Mushrooms: Trim stem ends from mushrooms. Slice and toss with fresh lemon juice, chopped parsley, and freshly ground pepper to taste.

Onions: Thickly slice a sweet onion such as Vidalia, Maui, Walla Walla, or Texas 1015 Supersweet (taste first to make sure it's sweet) and top with minced red bell pepper. Sprinkle with balsamic vinegar and minced parsley.

Tomatoes: Sprinkle thick slices of tomato with minced shallot and freshly ground pepper. Splash on a few drops of balsamic vinegar or red wine vinegar. Scatter chopped fresh basil, oregano, parsley, or marjoram on top; let marinate about an hour and serve.

Turnips: Peel and cut baby turnips into thin strips. Toss with sliced radishes, a little fresh lime juice, a pinch of ground coriander, and freshly ground pepper to taste.

Zucchini: Cut small zucchini into very thin rounds. Toss with lemon juice, minced garlic, and minced fresh oregano. Season with freshly ground pepper to taste.

Stir-Fried Snow Peas

Try making this dish using Asian yard-long beans, snap green beans, or asparagus instead of snow peas.

1 ounce (30 g) cloud ear or other dried Asian mushrooms

1 scallion, white part and 1 inch (2.5 cm) green, sliced

1 to 2 teaspoons (5 to 10 ml) minced fresh ginger, to taste

1 to 2 garlic cloves, to taste, minced

½ pound (225 g) fresh snow peas, ends trimmed and strings removed

1 6-ounce (180 g) can sliced water chestnuts, well drained

olive oil cooking spray

1 tablespoon (15 ml) rice wine

3 tablespoons (45 ml) low-sodium soy sauces

⅓ cup (78 ml) chicken stock (page 45)

⅛ teaspoon (.6 ml) light sesame oil

Soak mushrooms in warm water for 20 minutes. Rinse well, discarding soaking liquid; slice mushrooms.

Lightly spray a nonstick sauté pan with cooking spray. Add scallion, ginger, garlic, and mushrooms and sauté over low heat for about 2 minutes. Add remaining ingredients and cook, uncovered, over high heat until all vegetables are cooked but crisp, about 2 minutes. Serve at once.

MAKES 4 SERVINGS

> **Per serving:** calories, 93 ◆ protein, 4 g ◆ carbohydrate, 17 g ◆ fat, 1 g (calories from fat, 9%) ◆ dietary fiber, 2 g ◆ cholesterol, 0 mg ◆ sodium, 427 mg* ◆ potassium, 290 mg Joslin Exchanges: 3 vegetable or 1 bread/starch

* Recipe not recommended for low-sodium diets unless low-sodium soy sauce is decreased to 2½ tablespoons (37.5 ml).

Spinach with Mint

A flavorful way to prepare creamed spinach without the fat. Do not let the yogurt boil, or it will separate.

1 pound (450 g) fresh spinach or 1 10-ounce (285 g) box frozen chopped spinach
1 tablespoon (15 ml) chopped fresh mint

½ cup (118 ml) plain nonfat yogurt
¼ teaspoon (1.25 ml) ground nutmeg
freshly ground pepper to taste

Trim stem ends from spinach and rinse thoroughly. Coarsely chop. Place spinach with water still clinging to leaves in a heavy nonstick skillet. Cover and cook over medium heat until wilted, 2 to 3 minutes. (If you're using frozen spinach, cook in a small amount of boiling water for 2 minutes.) Stir once or twice during cooking. Drain off any excess liquid. Add remaining ingredients. Heat through, but do not boil. Serve at once.

MAKES 4 SERVINGS

> **Per serving:** calories, 42 ◆ protein, 5 g ◆ carbohydrate, 6 g ◆ fat, 1 g (calories from fat, 21%) ◆ dietary fiber, 1 g ◆ cholesterol, 1 mg ◆ sodium, 111 mg ◆ potassium, 703 mg Joslin Exchanges: 1 vegetable

Peking Spinach

A delicious new Asian treatment for the classic green vegetable.

1 small carrot, about 3 ounces (85
   g), peeled and cut into thin strips
½ teaspoon (2.5 ml) salt (optional)
1 pound (450 g) fresh spinach,
   washed and stems removed, or 1
   10-ounce (285 g) box frozen leaf
   spinach

1½ tablespoons (22.5 ml) rice wine
    vinegar
½ teaspoon (2.5 ml) sugar
⅛ teaspoon (.6 ml) hot red pepper
   flakes or to taste
½ teaspoon (2.5 ml) five-spice
   powder

Bring a large pot of water to a boil. Add carrot and salt. Cook until almost tender, about 3 minutes. Add spinach; continue cooking for 3 minutes. Transfer to a colander to drain thoroughly. Place spinach and carrots in a serving bowl.

In a small saucepan, bring remaining ingredients to a rapid boil. Pour hot dressing over spinach; toss and serve.

MAKES 4 SERVINGS

Per serving: calories, 25 ◆
protein, 2 g ◆ carbohydrate, 5 g
◆ fat, trace (calories from fat,
less than 1%) ◆ dietary fiber,

1 g ◆ cholesterol, 0 mg ◆
sodium, 32 mg ◆ potassium,
369 mg
Joslin Exchanges: 1 vegetable

Squash Ribbons with Garlic Lemon Sauce

Sometimes just changing the shape of a familiar vegetable elevates it from the everyday to something special. Here zucchini and yellow summer squash are cut into thin ribbons, microwaved, and tossed with garlic lemon sauce and a dusting of nutmeg—a short-order vegetable that always gets raves.

2 medium-size zucchini, about ½
   pound (225 g), washed well
2 medium-size yellow summer
   squash, about ½ pound (225 g),
   washed well
1 teaspoon (5 g) margarine
1 small garlic clove, minced

2 teaspoons (10 ml) fresh lemon
   juice
¼ teaspoon (1.25 ml) salt (optional)
⅛ teaspoon (.6 ml) freshly ground
   pepper or to taste
ground nutmeg to taste

Using a sharp vegetable peeler, cut the squash lengthwise into thin ribbons. Place ribbons in a large microwave-safe dish with a lid. Cook on HIGH for 2 to 3 minutes, until wilted.

In a glass measuring cup, combine margarine, garlic, and lemon juice. Microwave on HIGH for 20 seconds or until margarine is melted. Pour lemon sauce over squash; add salt, pepper, and nutmeg. Toss well and serve.

MAKES 4 SERVINGS

Per serving: calories, 39 ◆ protein, 1 g ◆ carbohydrate, 5 g ◆ fat, 2 g (calories from fat, 46%) ◆ dietary fiber, 1 g ◆ cholesterol, 0 mg ◆ sodium, 174 mg ◆ potassium, 294 mg
Joslin Exchanges: 1 vegetable

Spaghetti Squash Salad

If you're not familiar with spaghetti squash, you'll be surprised to find that the cooked flesh of this watermelon-shaped squash separates into yellow-gold spaghettilike strands that can be served hot as a vegetable or cold in a salad.

1 3¾-pound (1.7 kg) spaghetti squash
1 fennel bulb, about ¾ pound (340 g)
1 medium-size tomato, about 6 ounces (180 g), peeled, seeded, and chopped
1 medium-size red bell pepper, about 5 ounces (140 g), seeded and cut into thin strips
¼ pound (115 g) fresh mushrooms, thinly sliced
¼ pound (115 g) broccoli florets
2 scallions, chopped
1 garlic clove, minced
1 teaspoon (5 ml) curry powder
½ teaspoon (2.5 ml) ground cumin
¼ teaspoon (1.25 ml) ground ginger
¼ to ½ teaspoon (1.25 to 2.5 ml) English hot mustard powder, to taste
freshly ground pepper to taste
¼ cup (59 ml) chopped parsley for garnish

Dressing

2 tablespoons (30 ml) white wine
  vinegar
2 tablespoons (30 ml) olive oil

¼ teaspoon (1.25 ml)
  Worcestershire sauce

Cut squash in half; scoop out seeds. Place squash skin side up in a large saucepan. Cover with 2 inches (5 cm) water; bring to a boil. Reduce heat and simmer, covered, for 20 to 25 minutes, until squash is tender when pierced with a fork. Remove from water; cool. Using a fork, scoop out center of squash to form spaghettilike strands. Place squash strands in a large bowl.

Trim fennel stalks down to white bulb; trim bottom. Peel off any wilted or hard outer stalks. Slice crosswise into thin strips. Add to squash along with remaining ingredients except parsley and dressing. Toss to mix well.

Whisk together vinegar, oil, and Worcestershire sauce. Pour over squash mixture; toss again. Refrigerate for at least 2 hours to allow flavors to blend.

To serve, pile into a pretty salad bowl or onto a serving platter. Garnish with chopped parsley.

MAKES 8 SERVINGS

> **Per serving:** calories, 125 ◆ protein, 4 g ◆ carbohydrate, 20 g ◆ fat, 4 g (calories from fat, 28%) ◆ dietary fiber, 1 g ◆ cholesterol, 0 mg ◆ sodium, 55 mg ◆ potassium, 593 mg Joslin Exchanges: 3 vegetable, 1 fat

Spaghetti Squash with Shallot Butter

1 medium-size spaghetti squash,
  about 1½ pounds (675 g)
2 tablespoons (30 ml) minced
  shallots

2 teaspoons (10 g) unsalted butter

Preheat oven to 350° F (180° C). Pierce squash in several places with a fork. Place on rimmed baking sheet. Bake for 45 minutes to 1 hour, until squash gives when pressed. Turn over after 30 minutes.

Cut squash in half; scrape out and discard seeds. Loosen squash strands; scoop out into a warm serving bowl.

In a small nonstick skillet, sauté shallots in butter over low heat until wilted, about 4 minutes. Pour over spaghetti squash strands and toss lightly.

MAKES 8 SERVINGS

Per serving: calories, 36 ◆ protein, 1 g ◆ carbohydrate, 6 g ◆ fat, 1 g (calories from fat, 25%) ◆ dietary fiber, trace ◆ cholesterol, 3 mg ◆ sodium, 156 mg ◆ potassium, 107 mg

Joslin Exchanges: 1 vegetable

Sautéed Cherry Tomatoes

A lovely dish that's very quick and easy to prepare. It's wonderful with beef or lamb.

olive oil cooking spray
 1 garlic clove, minced
 2 scallions, white part only, minced
32 yellow or red cherry tomatoes, about 1 pound (450 g)
 1 teaspoon (5 ml) fresh lemon juice

 1 tablespoon (15 ml) chopped fresh basil or flat-leaf parsley
 ½ tablespoon (7.5 ml) chopped fresh oregano or ½ teaspoon (2.5 ml) crushed dried
freshly ground pepper to taste

Lightly spray a large nonstick skillet with cooking spray. Place over low heat. Add garlic and scallions; sauté for 2 to 3 minutes, until scallions are wilted. Add tomatoes, increase heat to medium, and cook, rolling tomatoes around constantly, until tomatoes are heated through, about 3 to 4 minutes. Sprinkle with lemon juice, herbs, and pepper. Toss to coat evenly. Serve at once.

MAKES 4 SERVINGS

Per serving: calories, 28 ◆ protein, 1 g ◆ carbohydrate, 6 g ◆ fat, trace (calories from fat, less than 1%) ◆ dietary fiber, 2 g ◆ cholesterol, 0 mg ◆ sodium, 10 mg ◆ potassium, 259 mg

Joslin Exchanges: 1 vegetable

Tian

A tian is actually the vessel this type of dish is cooked in, usually a shallow oval earthenware casserole. Full of the flavors and colors of Provence, tians can be made with layers of whatever vegetables you happen to have—eggplant, zucchini, yellow crookneck squash, tomatoes, sweet bell peppers, potatoes, onions, and lots of fresh garlic and herbs. Garlic cooked this way becomes very mild and sweet.

If you happen to have leftovers, they're delicious eaten cold the next day for lunch.

2 medium-size white onions, about ½ pound (225 g), thinly sliced

2 small Japanese eggplants, about 1 pound (450 g), thinly sliced

2 medium-size yellow or red bell peppers, about ½ pound (225 g), seeded and thinly sliced

4 small tomatoes, about 1 pound (450 g), thinly sliced

½ teaspoon (2.5 ml) salt (optional)

freshly ground pepper to taste

1 tablespoon (15 ml) fresh thyme leaves or 1 teaspoon (5 ml) crushed dried

1 teaspoon (2.5 ml) minced fresh rosemary or ¼ teaspoon (1.25 ml) crushed dried

1 head of garlic

4 teaspoons (20 ml) olive oil

Preheat oven to 350° F (180° C). Arrange vegetables in a shallow baking dish, alternating them. Season with salt, pepper, thyme, and rosemary. Place unpeeled garlic in center of vegetables. Drizzle olive oil over vegetables and garlic.

Bake for 1 hour, until vegetables are very tender. Serve immediately, offering each person several cloves of cooked garlic to squeeze over vegetables.

MAKES 8 SERVINGS

Per serving: calories, 74 ◆ protein, 2 g ◆ carbohydrate, 12 g ◆ fat, 3 g (calories from fat, 36%) ◆ dietary fiber, 1 g ◆ cholesterol, 0 mg ◆ sodium, 146 mg ◆ potassium, 372 mg
Joslin Exchanges: 2 vegetable, ½ fat

Mashed Turnips with Roasted Garlic

We used a pear to sweeten the strong flavor of turnips, then added some roasted garlic for a robust alternative to mashed potatoes.

1½ pounds (675 g) small turnips, peeled and quartered
1 ripe Bartlett pear, about 6 ounces (180 g), peeled, cored, and chopped
4 garlic cloves, roasted (page 262) and peeled

1 tablespoon (15 g) margarine
2 tablespoons (30 ml) skim milk (optional)
¼ teaspoon (1.25 ml) salt (optional)
freshly ground pepper to taste

Steam turnips over boiling water until fork tender, about 15 minutes. Drain turnips and place in a food processor or blender along with pear, garlic, and margarine. Process until smooth, adding skim milk as needed. Season with salt and pepper.

MAKES 8 SERVINGS

Per serving: calories, 41 ◆ protein, 1 g ◆ carbohydrate, 7 g ◆ fat, 2 g (calories from fat, 30%) ◆ dietary fiber, trace ◆ cholesterol, trace ◆ sodium, 129 mg ◆ potassium, 144 mg
Joslin Exchanges: 1 vegetable

Turnips with Apples and Mushrooms

Turnips are a perfect accompaniment for hearty fall and winter dishes. Look for firm turnips no larger than 2 inches in diameter that feel heavy for their size.

Serve this dish with broiled or grilled foods or as part of an all-vegetable meal.

10 ounces (285 g) fresh turnips
butter-flavored cooking spray
1 large Golden Delicious apple, about 6 ounces (180 g), peeled, cored, and sliced
2 scallions, white part and 1 inch (2.5 cm) green, sliced

3 ounces (85 g) fresh mushrooms, sliced
grated zest of 1 orange
1 tablespoon (15 ml) fresh orange juice
freshly ground pepper to taste
chopped fresh parsley for garnish

Peel the turnips; cut in half lengthwise, then into ¼-inch (.75 cm) slices. Boil or steam until crisp-tender, 6 to 8 minutes.

Lightly spray a large nonstick sauté pan with cooking spray. Add apple, scallions, and mushrooms. Sauté over medium heat until apple is partially cooked, about 2 minutes. Add turnips; sauté until turnips are lightly browned, about 4 minutes. Add orange zest and juice. Reduce heat and continue to cook until liquid has evaporated. Season with pepper and sprinkle with parsley.

MAKES 4 SERVINGS

Per serving: calories, 46 ◆ protein, 1 g ◆ carbohydrate, 12 g ◆ fat, trace (calories from fat, less than 1%) ◆ dietary fiber, 1 g ◆ cholesterol, 0 mg ◆ sodium, 32 mg ◆ potassium, 244 mg
Joslin Exchanges: 1 vegetable, ½ fruit

SNACKS

Snacks play an important role in our daily lives, particularly for anyone with type I (insulin-dependent) diabetes, insulin-requiring type II diabetes, and hypoglycemia (low blood sugar), for whom between-meal and bedtime snacks are essential to maintain blood glucose levels as close to normal as possible. For others struggling to keep daily caloric intake low with smaller meals, snacks quiet the midmorning growling stomach and serve as afternoon pick-me-ups and late-night nibbles.

We've provided more than 30 recipes for healthy snacks that you can concoct with ease. And so you won't be tempted by the fat- and sugar-laden offerings of the office coffee cart or vending machines away from home, many of the snacks can be carried in a briefcase, kept in your car or office desk drawer, or tucked into a purse or sports bag.

Seasoned Popcorn

Inexpensive and easy to make, popcorn is one of our favorite snacks. Invest in a hot-air popper, if you don't already own one, so that you can make fluffy popcorn without any fat.

Here are some ideas for good snacking—the seasonings are delicious, dressing up the popcorn with such flavor that you really won't miss the butter.

1 quart (1 l) air-popped corn   butter-flavored cooking spray

Asian Popcorn

2 teaspoons (10 ml) low-sodium
 soy sauce
¹/₂ teaspoon (2.5 ml) garlic powder

¹/₈ teaspoon (.6 ml) onion powder
¹/₄ teaspoon (1.25 ml) ground
 ginger

Italian Popcorn

1 teaspoon (5 ml) dried Italian
 seasoning
¹/₈ teaspoon (.6 ml) cayenne pepper
 or to taste

1 tablespoon (15 ml) finely grated
 Parmesan cheese

Nacho Popcorn

¹/₂ teaspoon (2.5 ml) ground cumin
¹/₂ teaspoon (2.5 ml) garlic powder
¹/₂ teaspoon (2.5 ml) onion powder
¹/₂ teaspoon (2.5 ml) Worcestershire
 sauce

¹/₈ teaspoon (.6 ml) Tabasco sauce
 or to taste

Preheat oven to 300°F (150°C). Place popcorn on a nonstick cookie sheet. Spray lightly with cooking spray and toss with a combination of the seasonings for the flavor you've chosen. Bake for 10 minutes, tossing once. Serve warm.

MAKES 1 SNACK

Per serving of Asian popcorn: calories, 114 ◆ protein, 5 g ◆ carbohydrate, 23 g ◆ fat, trace (calories from fat, less than 1%) ◆ dietary fiber, 1 g ◆ cholesterol, 0 mg ◆ sodium, 371 mg ◆ potassium, 24 mg ◆ Joslin Exchanges: 1¹/₂ bread/starch

Per serving of Italian popcorn: calories, 134 ◆ protein, 7 g ◆ carbohydrate, 21 g ◆ fat, 2 g (calories from fat, 12%) ◆ dietary fiber, 1 g ◆ cholesterol, 5 mg ◆ sodium, 117 mg ◆ potassium, 36 mg ◆ Joslin Exchanges: 1¹/₂ bread/starch

Per serving of nacho popcorn: calories, 111 ◆ protein, 4 g ◆ carbohydrate, 22 g ◆ fat, trace (calories from fat, less than 1%) ◆ dietary fiber, 1 g ◆ cholesterol, 0 mg ◆ sodium, 29 mg ◆ potassium, 51 mg Joslin Exchanges: 1¹/₂ bread/starch

Bagel Chips

These are fun to eat and quite tasty. You can make them at a fraction of the cost of buying them—in both dollars and fat—since the commercial varieties are usually deep-fried.

1 6-ounce (180 g) bagel
olive oil cooking spray
garlic powder, *herbes de Provence* (page 294), onion powder, ground cumin, dried oregano mixed

with an equal amount of Parmesan cheese, chili powder, curry powder, sesame seeds, or poppy seeds

Preheat oven to 400°F (205°C). With a very sharp knife, slice bagel into very thin slices so that you can almost see through them (you'll get about 10 slices). Place slices on a nonstick baking sheet. Lightly spray with vegetable cooking spray. Quickly sprinkle on a small amount of seasoning (a little goes a long way) or leave plain. Bake for 3 to 4 minutes until lightly browned—be careful; they burn easily. Break each slice into 4 chips. Serve warm or store in an airtight container for up to 3 days.

MAKES ABOUT 40 CHIPS

Per 20-chip serving: calories, 89 ◆ protein, 3 g ◆ carbohydrate, 17 g ◆ fat, 1 g (calories from fat, 10%) ◆ dietary fiber, trace ◆ cholesterol, 4 mg ◆ sodium, 108 mg ◆ potassium, 22 mg
Joslin Exchanges: 1 bread/starch

Stuffed Bread Slices

These tasty stuffed breads are made with defrosted frozen white bread dough, readily available at most supermarkets, with a choice of fillings.

unbleached flour
1 1-pound (450 g) frozen white bread dough, thawed
1 apple or pear, cored, peeled, and finely chopped
splash of fresh lemon juice

½ teaspoon (2.5 ml) plus ⅛ teaspoon (.6 ml) ground cinnamon
1 tablespoon (15 ml) finely chopped walnuts
pinch of fructose

On a lightly floured work surface, roll dough into a 12-inch (30 cm) square, about ⅜ inch (1.25 cm) thick. Combine apple, lemon juice, ½ teaspoon (2.5 ml) cinnamon, nuts, and fructose. Using half the apple mixture, place a thin layer of filling, about 3 inches (8 cm) wide, across middle of dough. Fold bottom portion of dough up and over filling. Top with remaining filling. Fold top portion of dough down and over filling, forming a rectangle about 12 by 4 inches (30 by 10 cm). Crimp edges to seal. Do not allow dough to rise. Bake on a large nonstick baking sheet for 35 to 40 minutes, until lightly browned and cooked through. Cool on a wire rack. Cut into ³/₄-inch (2 cm) slices.

MAKES 16 SLICES

Per slice: calories, 84 ◆ protein, 3 g ◆ carbohydrate, 15 g ◆ fat, 2 g (calories from fat, 21%) ◆ dietary fiber, trace ◆ cholesterol, 0 mg ◆ sodium, 156 mg ◆ potassium, 12 mg
Joslin Exchanges: 1 bread/starch

Dried Fruit Variation

On first layer of dough, spread ¹/₃ cup (78 ml) chopped dried fruit (dried apricots, peaches, pears, apples, prunes, or a combination) plumped in ¹/₄ cup (59 ml) warm water for 10 minutes and drained. On second layer, spread 1 tablespoon (15 ml) finely chopped walnuts, ¹/₄ teaspoon (1.25 ml) ground cinnamon, and ¹/₄ teaspoon (1.25 ml) ground ginger. Bake as directed.

MAKES 16 SLICES

Per slice: calories, 86 ◆ protein, 3 g ◆ carbohydrate, 16 g ◆ fat, 2 g (calories from fat, 20%) ◆ dietary fiber, trace ◆ cholesterol, 0 mg ◆ sodium, 156 mg ◆ potassium, 40 mg
Joslin Exchanges: 1 bread/starch

Hoagie Variation

On first layer of dough, spread 2 ounces (60 g) thinly sliced cooked turkey breast. On second layer, spread thin slices of 1 small tomato, 1 small green bell pepper, and 1 scallion, white part and 1 inch (2.5 cm) green. Lightly spray top of filled bread with butter-flavored cooking spray. Top with 1 teaspoon (5 ml) caraway seed. Bake as directed.

MAKES 16 SLICES

Per slice: calories, 84 ◆ protein, 4 g ◆ carbohydrate, 14 g ◆ fat, 1 g (calories from fat, 10%) ◆ dietary fiber, trace ◆ cholesterol, 3 mg ◆ sodium, 158 mg ◆ potassium, 34 mg
Joslin Exchanges: 1 bread/starch

Italian Variation

On first layer of dough, spread 3 tablespoons (45 ml) purchased or homemade pizza sauce, 1 tablespoon (15 ml) minced green bell pepper, and 1 fresh mushroom, thinly sliced. Repeat on second layer. Sprinkle with 1 tablespoon (15 ml) grated Parmesan cheese. Lightly spray top of filled bread with butter-flavored cooking spray. Top with ½ teaspoon (2.5 ml) crushed dried mixed Italian herbs. Bake as directed.

MAKES 16 SLICES

Per slice: calories, 83 ◆ protein, 3 g ◆ carbohydrate, 15 g ◆ fat, 2 g (calories from fat, 21%) ◆ dietary fiber, trace ◆ cholesterol, trace ◆ sodium, 200 mg ◆ potassium, 32 mg
Joslin Exchanges: 1 bread/starch

Mexican Variation

On first layer, spread 3 tablespoons (45 ml) prepared salsa. On second layer, brush with 1 teaspoon (5 ml) hot chili oil and spread with 3 tablespoons (45 ml) chopped fresh hot chili (or sweet bell pepper for a milder flavor) and 1 tablespoon (15 ml) minced scallion. Lightly spray top of filled bread with butter-flavored cooking spray. Sprinkle with ½ teaspoon (2.5 ml) ground cumin. Bake as directed.

MAKES 16 SLICES

Per slice: calories, 80 ◆ protein, 3 g ◆ carbohydrate, 14 g ◆ fat, 2 g (calories from fat, 22%) ◆ dietary fiber, trace ◆ cholesterol, 1 g ◆ sodium, 171 mg ◆ potassium, 9 mg
Joslin Exchanges: 1 bread/starch

Vegetable Variation

On each layer of dough, spread 3 tablespoons (45 ml) finely chopped raw vegetables (chopped spinach, zucchini, mushrooms, seeded tomatoes), or 3 tablespoons (45 ml) homemade ratatouille, or 3 tablespoons (45 ml) leftover vegetables. Sprinkle with 1 tablespoon (15 ml) Parmesan cheese. Lightly spray top of filled bread with butter-flavored cooking spray. Top with 1 teaspoon (5 ml) sesame seed. Bake as directed.

MAKES 16 SLICES

> **Per slice:** calories, 81 ◆ protein, 3 g ◆ carbohydrate, 14 g ◆ fat, 1 g (calories from fat, 11%) ◆ dietary fiber, trace ◆ cholesterol, 1 mg ◆ sodium, 167 mg ◆ potassium, 9 mg
> Joslin Exchanges: 1 bread/starch

Bruschetta

A traditional midday snack for Italian workmen, bruschetta is southern Italy's version of garlic toast. Make it one or two at a time as a snack or in larger quantities for hors d'oeuvres when entertaining and as an accompaniment to soup or salad.

crusty Italian bread, sliced ½ inch (1.5 cm) thick
cut garlic cloves
olive oil

freshly ground pepper to taste
chopped fresh herbs such as arugula, basil, tarragon, or chervil (optional)

Toast bread slices until lightly browned on both sides. Remove from heat and brush each slice with ½ teaspoon (5 ml) olive oil. Rub with a cut clove of garlic. Sprinkle with freshly ground pepper and herbs (if desired), using 1 to 2 teaspoons (5 to 10 ml) chopped herbs per bruschetta. Serve warm.

> **Per 2-slice serving:** calories, 210 ◆ protein, 6 g ◆ carbohydrate, 34 g ◆ fat, 5 g (calories from fat, 20%) ◆ fiber, 2 g ◆ cholesterol, 0 mg ◆ sodium, 304 mg ◆ potassium, 44 mg
> Joslin Exchanges: 2 bread/starch, 1 fat

Zesty Corn Chips

Store any leftover seasoning mix in an airtight container for another time. Use one tortilla for a single snack.

8 6-inch (15 cm) yellow or blue corn tortillas

olive oil cooking spray

Seasoning Mix

1 teaspoon (5 ml) garlic powder
1 teaspoon (5 ml) cumin
1 teaspoon (5 ml) onion powder

¼ teaspoon (1.25 ml) cayenne
   pepper, or to taste
¼ teaspoon (1.25 ml) salt (optional)

Preheat oven to 400°F (205°C). Cut each tortilla into 6 wedges. Lightly spray two 10- by 15-inch (25 by 38 cm) baking pans with cooking spray. Place tortilla wedges close together in a single layer in pans. Lightly spray tortilla wedges with cooking spray.

In an empty saltshaker, combine seasonings. Lightly sprinkle seasoning mixture onto tortilla wedges.

Bake until golden and crisp, 5 to 7 minutes. Switch pan positions after 3 minutes. Pour out chips and repeat until all tortilla chips are baked. Serve warm or cool. Store cooled chips airtight at room temperature for up to 1 day.

MAKES 48 CHIPS

Per 6-chip serving: calories, 93 ◆ protein, 3 g ◆ carbohydrate, 18 g ◆ fat, 2 g (calories from fat, 19%) ◆ dietary fiber, 1 g ◆ cholesterol, 0 mg ◆ sodium, 161 mg ◆ potassium, 81 mg
Joslin Exchanges: 1 bread/starch

Fruited Couscous

Wrap this mixture in a crisped lettuce leaf for a quick, healthy snack.

¼ cup (59 ml) chicken stock
   (page 45)
2 teaspoons (10 ml) fresh lemon
   juice
⅛ teaspoon (.6 ml) ground cumin

2 tablespoons (30 ml) quick-
   cooking couscous
1 teaspoon (5 ml) dried currants
2 leaves of red leaf lettuce, washed
   and crisped

In a small saucepan, bring stock, lemon juice, and cumin to a boil over high heat. Stir in couscous and currants. Remove from heat, cover, and let stand until liquid is absorbed, about 5 minutes. Fluff with a fork, breaking up any clumps. Scoop into lettuce leaves. Wrap or roll lettuce around couscous to eat.

MAKES 1 SNACK

Per serving: calories, 99 ◆ protein, 3 g ◆ carbohydrate, 21 g ◆ fat, trace (calories from fat, 1%) ◆ dietary fiber, 4 g ◆ cholesterol, 0 mg ◆ sodium, 14 mg ◆ potassium, 98 mg Joslin Exchanges: 1½ bread/ starch

Cucumber Mint Lassi

Lassi is a refreshing Indian frothy yogurt drink, sometimes sweet (with fruit) and sometimes not, like this one.

⅓ cup (78 ml) plain low-fat yogurt
4 teaspoons (20 ml) water
1 tablespoon (15 ml) finely minced cucumber
1 tablespoon (15 ml) finely chopped fresh mint or 1 teaspoon (5 ml) crushed dried

4 ice cubes
⅛ teaspoon (.6 ml) salt (optional)
freshly ground pepper to taste
3 thin slices of cucumber for garnish
1 fresh mint sprig for garnish

In a food processor or blender, combine yogurt, water, cucumber, mint, ice cubes, salt, and pepper. Process until smooth. Pour into a glass; garnish with cucumber slices and mint sprig.

MAKES 1 SNACK

Per serving: calories, 50 ◆ protein, 4 g ◆ carbohydrate, 6 g ◆ fat, 1 g (calories from fat, 18%) ◆ dietary fiber, trace ◆ cholesterol, 5 mg ◆ sodium, 319 mg ◆ potassium, 185 mg Joslin Exchanges: ½ low-fat milk

Mango Lassi

Omit cucumber and mint. Add ¼ cup (59 ml) chopped mango and 1 teaspoon (5 ml) minced fresh ginger or a dash of ground ginger. Process as directed and garnish with a mint sprig.

Per serving: calories, 81 ◆ protein, 4 g ◆ carbohydrate, 14 g ◆ fat, 1 g (calories from fat, 11%) ◆ dietary fiber, 1 g ◆ cholesterol, 5 mg ◆ sodium, 267 mg ◆ potassium, 266 mg Joslin Exchanges: ½ low-fat milk, ½ fruit

Flour Tortilla Chips

Low in calories and high in crunch, these tortilla chips are not fried or salted, so they're a nutritious snack at a fraction of the cost and calories of a store-bought chip. When you get the tortillas home from the store, separate them with a piece of plastic wrap and freeze in a zip-lock bag. (They'll keep for up to two months.) This way you can remove one at a time for a single snack serving.

8 8-inch (20 cm) flour tortillas   chili powder (optional)
olive oil cooking spray

Preheat oven to 400°F (205°C). Cut each tortilla into 8 wedges. Lightly spray two 10- by 15-inch (25 by 38 cm) baking pans with cooking spray. Place tortilla wedges close together in a single layer in pans. Lightly spray tortilla with cooking spray. If desired, sprinkle lightly with chili powder.

   Bake until golden and crisp, 5 to 7 minutes. (If you're using one oven, switch pan positions after 3 minutes.) Pour out chips and repeat until all tortilla chips are baked. Serve warm or cool. Store cooled chips airtight at room temperature for up to 1 day.

MAKES 64 CHIPS

Per 8-chip serving: calories, 95 ◆ protein, 3 g ◆ carbohydrate, 17 g ◆ fat, 2 g (calories from fat, 18%) ◆ dietary fiber, 1 g ◆ cholesterol, 0 mg ◆ sodium, n/a ◆ potassium, n/a Joslin Exchanges: 1 bread/starch

Creative Free Foods

Because of their low carbohydrate and calorie content, these raw vegetables are free foods and may be eaten in either unlimited quantities or very liberally. (For the full list of free foods, see the Joslin Exchanges in Appendix 1.)

If you're especially hungry, indulge in these combinations:

- alfalfa sprouts—dip in taco sauce
- Chinese cabbage, endive, and romaine lettuce—dip in a mixture of taco sauce, minced cucumber, Tabasco sauce (make it as hot as you like it), and minced garlic
- cucumber—dip in lemon juice and then chili powder or marinate in a mixture of red wine vinegar, water, freshly ground pepper, and minced fresh dill
- endive—dip in lemon juice and then dill
- lettuce—use as a wrapper for sliced cucumbers and pieces of pimiento
- green and red cabbage—shred and sprinkle with balsamic vinegar, caraway seed, and chopped parsley
- spinach—use as a wrapper for a mixture of chopped cucumber, minced shallots, and minced pimiento moistened with a little balsamic vinegar

Frittata Snacks

This makes enough snacks for a crew. It's also good served cold as picnic hors d'oeuvres.

1 large baking potato, about ½ pound (225 g), well scrubbed
vegetable oil cooking spray
2 scallions, white part and 1 inch (2.5 cm) green, chopped
¼ pound (115 g) fresh mushrooms, chopped

1 small red bell pepper, about 3 ounces (85 g), seeded and chopped
2 cups (472 ml) egg substitute
3 slices of turkey bacon, cooked until crisp and chopped

¼ cup (59 ml) chopped fresh basil
or 1¼ teaspoons (6.25 ml)
crushed dried
1 10-ounce (285 g) package fresh
spinach, well washed, stems
removed, and coarsely chopped,
or 1 10-ounce (285 g) box frozen
chopped spinach, defrosted and
well drained
freshly ground pepper to taste
1 tablespoon (6 g) grated
Parmesan cheese

Pierce the potato on top and bottom. Place on a paper towel in microwave. Cook on HIGH for 3 to 5 minutes, turning over once. Remove from microwave oven and let cool slightly. Cut potato into small cubes.

In a 12-inch (30 cm) nonstick ovenproof sauté pan lightly sprayed with cooking spray, sauté potatoes over medium heat until browned, about 4 minutes. Add scallions, mushrooms, and bell pepper. Sauté for 2 to 3 minutes, until scallions are wilted but peppers are still crisp. Add egg substitute, turkey bacon, basil, spinach, and black pepper. Reduce heat to low to allow frittata to cook for about 12 minutes, until set and bottom is browned.

Preheat broiler. Sprinkle cheese on top of frittata. Place under broiler for 2 to 3 minutes to brown top. Cut into 8 wedges.

MAKES 8 SNACKS

Per serving: calories, 109 ◆ protein, 11 g ◆ carbohydrate, 10 g ◆ fat, 3 g (calories from fat, 25%) ◆ dietary fiber, 1 g ◆ cholesterol, 5 mg ◆ sodium, 231 mg ◆ potassium, 598 mg Joslin Exchanges: 1½ low-fat meat, ½ bread/starch

PICNIC AT THE BEACH

◆

Frittata Snacks (page 372)

Carrot and Cucumber Chat (page 97) in Pita Bread

Pickled Green Beans (page 14)

Bing Cherries

Per serving: 292 calories (18% fat)
Joslin Exchanges: 1½ low-fat meat, 1 vegetable, 1½ bread/starch, 1 fruit

Granola

This granola is not only a nourishing breakfast cereal but also a great snack that travels well. Fill a zip-lock bag and tuck it into your briefcase or purse.

1 cup (156 g) rolled oats
1 tablespoon (15 ml) sesame seed
1 cup (60 g) crumbled shredded wheat cereal
½ teaspoon (2.5 ml) vanilla extract

2 tablespoons (30 ml) unsalted dry-roasted sunflower seeds
1½ tablespoons (22.5 ml) frozen peach or pear juice concentrate
⅛ teaspoon (.6 ml) salt (optional)

Preheat oven to 325°F (165°C). Combine all ingredients in a shallow baking pan. Bake for 15 minutes, stirring every 5 minutes. Cool and store in an airtight container for up to 1 week or freeze individual portions in zip-lock bags for longer storage.

MAKES 4 SNACKS

Per ¾-cup (177 ml) serving: calories, 186 ◆ protein, 6 g ◆ carbohydrate, 31 g ◆ fat, 5 g (calories from fat, 24%) ◆ dietary fiber, 1 g ◆ sodium, 60 mg ◆ potassium, 199 mg Joslin Exchanges: 2 bread/ starch, ½ fat

Date Granola

Naturally sweet, this granola is also delicious sprinkled over plain nonfat yogurt.

2 cups (312 g) rolled oats
½ cup (60 g) wheat germ
½ cup (118 ml) chopped pitted dates, softened in ¼ cup (59 ml) hot water

2 tablespoons (30 ml) sesame seeds
3 tablespoons (45 ml) blanched almonds, chopped

Preheat oven to 325°F (165°C). Combine all ingredients in a shallow baking pan. Bake for 15 minutes, stirring every 5 minutes. Cool and store in an airtight container for up to 1 week or freeze individual portions in zip-lock bags for longer storage.

MAKES 6 SNACKS

Per ½-cup (118 ml) serving:
calories, 220 ◆ protein,
8 g ◆ carbohydrate, 36 g ◆ fat,
6 g (calories from fat, 24%) ◆
dietary fiber, 1 g ◆ cholesterol,
0 mg ◆ sodium, 4 mg ◆
potassium, 321 mg
Joslin Exchanges: 2 bread/
starch, 1 fat

Date Granola Bars

Packed with flavor, these bars are satisfying, healthy, and quick to make.

1 recipe cooked Date Granola
(preceding recipe)
6 tablespoons (90 ml) egg
substitute
¼ cup (59 ml) fruit juice (peach,
white grape, apple, or orange)

½ teaspoon (2.5 ml) ground
cinnamon
dash of ground nutmeg
1 tablespoon (15 g) margarine,
melted
butter-flavored cooking spray

Preheat oven to 350°F (180°C). Combine all ingredients; pat into a 9-inch (23 cm) square nonstick baking pan lightly sprayed with cooking spray. Press down firmly. Bake for 20 to 25 minutes. Cut into 2-inch (5 cm) squares. Cool.

MAKES 16 BARS

Per 1-bar serving: calories,
95 ◆ protein, 4 g ◆ carbohydrate,
14 g ◆ fat, 3 g (calories from fat,
28%) ◆ dietary fiber, 1 g ◆
cholesterol, trace ◆ sodium,
20 mg ◆ potassium, 145 mg
Joslin Exchanges: 1 bread/starch

Huevos Rancheros for One

On a cold night this makes a fine late-evening snack, with no added fat.

butter-flavored cooking spray
½ fresh hot chili, seeded and
  chopped
1 scallion, white part and 1 inch
  (2.5 cm) green, chopped
1 mushroom, thinly sliced
¼ cup (59 ml) egg substitute
1 6-inch (15 cm) corn tortilla,
  crisped in the microwave on a
  paper towel for 30 seconds just
  before serving

1 tablespoon (15 ml) prepared salsa
1 teaspoon (5 ml) chopped fresh
  cilantro (fresh coriander) for
  garnish

In a nonstick skillet lightly sprayed with cooking spray, sauté chili, scallion, and mushroom over low heat for 3 to 4 minutes, until scallion is wilted. Add egg substitute and cook, gently lifting cooked portion to allow uncooked portion to flow underneath, until mixture is softly set. Spoon egg mixture onto crisped tortilla. Top with salsa and sprinkle with cilantro.

MAKES 1 SNACK

Per serving: calories, 139 ◆ protein, 11 g ◆ carbohydrate, 17 g ◆ fat, 4 g (calories from fat, 26%) ◆ dietary fiber, 2 g ◆ cholesterol, 1 mg ◆ sodium, 222 mg ◆ potassium, 438 mg Joslin Exchange: 1 bread/starch, 1 low-fat meat

Quick Pissaladière

Almost every bistro and pastry shop in the south of France makes pissaladière, a rich flaky tart covered with anchovies, black olives, and onions. Here we use a flour tortilla as the crust base and judicious amounts of toppings for great taste without the fat.

1 8-inch (20 cm) flour tortilla
olive oil cooking spray
1 small onion, thinly sliced
1 garlic clove, minced
½ teaspoon (2.5 ml) crushed dried mixed Italian herbs

½ teaspoon (2.5 ml) anchovy paste
1 small fresh plum tomato, cut crosswise into thin slices
1 pitted ripe olive, very thinly sliced
½ teaspoon (2.5 ml) olive oil

Preheat oven to 500°F (260°C). Prick tortilla with a fork and brush lightly with water. Set on a 12- by 15-inch (30 by 38 cm) baking sheet. Bake until tortilla is almost crisp, about 4 minutes. Remove from oven; keep warm.

Meanwhile, lightly spray a small nonstick sauté pan with cooking spray. Add onion and garlic; sauté over medium heat until onion is very soft, about 10 minutes. Add Italian herbs and anchovy paste.

Arrange tomato slices on baked tortilla. Spoon onion mixture over tomatoes, top with olive slices, and drizzle with olive oil. Return to oven and bake until heated through, about 2 minutes. Cut into wedges.

MAKES 1 SNACK

Per serving: calories, 176 ◆ protein, 5 g ◆ carbohydrate, 29 g ◆ fat, 5 g (calories from fat, 26%) ◆ dietary fiber, 1 g ◆ cholesterol, 0 mg ◆ sodium, 563 mg* ◆ potassium, 314 mg Joslin Exchanges: 2 bread/ starch, 1 fat

* Not recommended for low-sodium diets unless anchovy paste is omitted.

Pita Sandwich

A quintessential vegetarian snack—tofu and vegetables combined with the flavors of the Middle East.

1 1-inch (3 cm) cube of firm tofu, thinly sliced
2 radishes, thinly sliced
3 tablespoons (45 ml) diced yellow summer squash
¾ cup (177 ml) chopped fresh spinach or romaine lettuce, washed and crisped
¾ teaspoon (3.75 ml) olive oil
¾ teaspoon (3.75 ml) fresh lemon juice
⅛ teaspoon (.6 ml) ground cumin

⅛ teaspoon (.6 ml) garlic powder
pinch of turmeric
pinch of dried thyme
pinch of ground ginger
freshly ground pepper to taste
½ whole-wheat pita bread (cut 1 pita bread in half crosswise, reserving second half for another use)
1 tablespoon (15 ml) dried currants

In a medium-size bowl, combine all ingredients except pita bread and currants; toss to mix well. Stuff pita half with mixture; top with currants.

MAKES 1 SNACK

> **Per serving:** calories, 148 ◆ protein, 6 g ◆ carbohydrate, 22 g ◆ fat, 5 g (calories from fat, 30%) ◆ dietary fiber, 1 g ◆ cholesterol, 0 mg ◆ sodium, 146 mg ◆ potassium, 466 mg Joslin Exchanges: 1 bread/ starch, 1½ vegetable, 1 fat

Mushroom Pita Pizza

Mushrooms, basil, and goat cheese make this an earthy but sophisticated pizza.

1 teaspoon (5 ml) olive oil
½ cup (118 ml) diced onion
½ cup (118 ml) sliced wild (chanterelles, cèpes, or shiitake) or cultivated mushrooms
1 6-inch whole-wheat pita bread
2 fresh plum tomatoes, thinly sliced

8 small fresh basil leaves
2 teaspoons (10 ml) chopped fresh oregano or ½ teaspoon (2.5 ml) crushed dried
1 ounce (30 g) fresh low-fat goat cheese, crumbled

Preheat oven (or toaster oven) to 400°F (205°C). In a heavy skillet over medium heat, heat oil. Add onion and mushrooms; sauté for 5 minutes, until onions and mushrooms are tender.

Meanwhile, split pita bread in half horizontally. Place pita halves directly on oven rack and bake for 5 minutes or until lightly toasted. Arrange tomato slices and basil leaves on bread. Scatter cooked onions and mushrooms over top. Sprinkle with oregano and goat cheese.

Bake for 5 to 8 minutes or until crust begins to brown around the edges. Remove from oven and cut each pita half into 4 wedges.

MAKES 4 SERVINGS

Per 2-wedge serving: calories, 66 ◆ protein, 2 g ◆ carbohydrate, 9 g ◆ fat, 2 g (calories from fat, 27%) ◆ dietary fiber, trace ◆ cholesterol, 5 mg ◆ sodium, 95 mg ◆ potassium, 148 mg Joslin Exchanges: ½ bread/ starch

Zucchini Variation

Substitute ½ cup (118 ml) thinly sliced small zucchini for mushrooms and 3 tablespoons (45 ml) grated Parmesan cheese for goat cheese. Proceed as directed.

MAKES 4 SERVINGS

Per 2-wedge serving: calories, 65 ◆ protein, 2 g ◆ carbohydrate, 10 g ◆ fat, 2 g (calories from fat, 27%) ◆ dietary fiber, trace ◆ cholesterol, 5 mg ◆ sodium, 105 mg ◆ potassium, 154 mg Joslin Exchanges: ½ bread/ starch

Pita Stuffed with Red Lentils

Red or orange lentils cook in just 15 minutes; look for them in Indian and specialty food markets.

2 tablespoons (30 ml) cooked red or orange lentils

⅛ teaspoon (.6 ml) minced garlic

1 scallion, white part only, chopped

½ teaspoon (2.5 ml) balsamic vinegar

freshly ground pepper to taste

½ teaspoon (2.5 ml) fresh thyme leaves or ⅛ teaspoon (.6 ml) crushed dried

⅛ teaspoon (.6 ml) ground cumin

½ 6-inch whole-wheat pita bread (cut 1 pita bread in half crosswise, reserving second half for another use)

½ cup (118 ml) alfalfa sprouts

1 tablespoon (15 ml) chopped fresh tomato

Mix together lentils, garlic, scallion, vinegar, pepper, thyme, and cumin. Stuff pita pocket with mixture. Top with alfalfa sprouts and tomato.

MAKES 1 SNACK

Per serving: calories, 91 ◆ protein, 5 g ◆ carbohydrate, 17 g ◆ fat 1 g (calories from fat, 10%) ◆ dietary fiber, 1 g ◆ cholesterol, 0 mg ◆ sodium, 110 mg ◆ potassium, 144 mg Joslin Exchanges: 1 bread/starch

Easy Polenta

Put together in minutes, this makes a warm, tasty snack for cold, blustery days. If your store doesn't sell instant polenta, use stone-ground cornmeal.

1 cup (236 ml) chicken stock (page 45)

¼ cup (28 g) instant polenta

1 tablespoon (15 ml) chopped parsley

1 scallion, white part only, finely minced

½ tablespoon (3 g) grated Parmesan cheese

In a small saucepan, bring chicken stock to a rapid boil. Add polenta, stirring constantly. Continue stirring while polenta cooks, about 5 minutes. Stir in parsley and scallion. Spoon into a small bowl. Sprinkle with Parmesan cheese. Serve warm.

MAKES 1 SNACK

Per serving: calories, 78 ◆ protein, 5 g ◆ carbohydrate, 10 g ◆ fat, 2 g (calories from fat, 23%) ◆ dietary fiber, trace ◆ cholesterol, 8 mg ◆ sodium, 113 mg ◆ potassium, 104 mg Joslin Exchanges: 1 bread/starch

Dilled Potato-Cheese Soup

This hearty microwaved soup has satisfying midmorning or soothing late-night snack potential year-round. It's ready in less than 10 minutes.

1 small russet potato, scrubbed and diced
½ cup (118 ml) chicken stock (page 45)
½ cup (118 ml) skim milk

¼ teaspoon (1.25 ml) dried dill weed
freshly ground pepper to taste
1 tablespoon (6 g) grated cheddar cheese

In a 1-quart (1 l) glass measuring cup or deep microwave-safe bowl, combine potato and ¼ cup (59 ml) chicken stock. Cover and microwave on HIGH for 4 to 6 minutes, stirring once or twice, until potato is tender when pierced with a fork. Mash potato coarsely with a fork. Stir in remaining chicken stock, skim milk, and dill. Cook on HIGH for 4 to 5 minutes, until soup is hot. Season with pepper. Pour into a soup mug or bowl. Stir in grated cheese.

MAKES 1 SNACK

Per serving: calories, 174 ◆ protein, 9 g ◆ carbohydrate, 23 g ◆ fat, 5 g (calories from fat, 26%) ◆ dietary fiber, trace ◆ cholesterol, 17 mg ◆ sodium, 178 mg ◆ potassium, 579 mg Joslin Exchanges: ½ nonfat milk, 1 bread/starch

Soft Pretzels

Although not an exact replica of the pretzels you can purchase from street vendors on the streets of New York and other cities, these pretzels are pleasing and can be tucked handily into a purse or briefcase for snacking on the go.

1 ¼-ounce (7 g) package active dry yeast
1½ cups (354 ml) warm water
4 to 4½ cups (500 g to 560 g) unbleached flour
½ teaspoon (2.5 ml) salt (optional)
2 teaspoons (10 ml) sugar
butter-flavored cooking spray

4 teaspoons (20 ml) baking soda
1 quart (1 l) water
1 large egg yolk mixed with 1 tablespoon (15 ml) water
1 teaspoon (5 ml) kosher salt (optional)
Dijon mustard (optional)

In a small bowl, mix together yeast and ¼ cup (59 ml) warm water. Let stand for 5 minutes, until yeast dissolves. In a large bowl, mix together 3 cups (375 g) flour, salt, and sugar. Add dissolved yeast and remaining warm water. Add enough additional flour to make a stiff dough.

Turn out onto a floured surface; knead for 10 minutes, until dough feels smooth and elastic. Form dough into a ball. Place in a bowl lightly sprayed with cooking spray. Cover with a clean kitchen towel and let rise in a warm place until doubled in bulk, about 45 minutes.

Shape dough into an evenly shaped log about 24 inches (61 cm) long. Cut log into 12 equal pieces. Roll each piece between your hands to form a rope about 20 inches (50 cm) long. Shape each rope into a pretzel shape, tapering the ends slightly. Let rise for 15 minutes, until slightly puffy.

Preheat oven to 475°F (245°C). Dissolve soda in 1 quart (1 l) water; bring to a boil. Drop pretzels into boiling water one at a time and boil for 1 minute or until pretzels float to top. Lift pretzel out with a skimmer; drain briefly on a clean kitchen towel.

Transfer drained pretzels to a baking sheet lightly sprayed with cooking spray. Brush with egg yolk; sprinkle with a few grains of salt. Bake for 15 to 20 minutes, until golden brown. Transfer to a wire rack to cool. Serve warm or at room temperature, with mustard if desired. Store in an airtight container for up to 1 week or wrap and freeze for longer storage.

MAKES 12 PRETZELS

Per pretzel: calories, 157 ◆ protein, 4 g ◆ carbohydrate, 33 g ◆ fat, 1 g (calories from fat, 6%) ◆ fiber, trace ◆ cholesterol, 18 mg ◆ sodium, 365 mg ◆ potassium, 56 mg Joslin Exchanges: 2 bread/starch

Spinach Triangles

These unusual crackers make a good party hors d'oeuvre, decorated with strips of roasted red peppers and a dab of yogurt cheese.

1 **10-ounce (285 g) box frozen chopped spinach, defrosted**
1½ **cups (185 g) unbleached flour**
1 **scallion, white part only, chopped**
1 **garlic clove, minced**
⅛ **teaspoon (.6 ml) ground nutmeg**

¼ **teaspoon (1.25 ml) salt (optional)**
3 **tablespoons (45 g) margarine, melted**
1½ **tablespoons (22.5 ml) sesame seed, divided**
6 **tablespoons (90 ml) cold water olive oil cooking spray**

Preheat oven to 375°F (190°C).

Squeeze as much water out of spinach as possible. In a large bowl, combine spinach, flour, scallion, garlic, nutmeg, salt, margarine, and 1 tablespoon (15 ml) sesame seed. Mix in water to form a soft dough. Place dough on a nonstick cookie sheet. Pat and press dough to form an 11½-inch (29 cm) circle. With a knife, score the circle into quarters. Score each quarter into thirds, making 12 triangles. Sprinkle with remaining ½ tablespoon (7.5 ml) sesame seed. Lightly spray with cooking spray. Bake for 20 to 25 minutes, until bottom is lightly browned and dough is cooked through. Serve warm or cold. Store in an airtight container for up to 4 days. Wrap and freeze for longer storage.

MAKES 12 TRIANGLES

Per cracker: calories, 91 ◆ protein, 3 g ◆ carbohydrate, 13 g ◆ fat, 4 g (calories from fat, 35%) ◆ dietary fiber, 1 g ◆ cholesterol, 0 mg ◆ sodium, 103 mg ◆ potassium, 95 mg Joslin Exchanges: 1 bread/ starch, ½ fat

Tofu Pita Snack

This is a wonderful pick-me-up snack. The tofu soaks up the seasonings of the quick marinade.

1 ounce (30 g) firm tofu, chopped into small cubes
1 scallion, white part only, chopped
1 tablespoon (15 ml) chopped red bell pepper
½ teaspoon (2.5 ml) Dijon mustard
½ tablespoon (7.5 ml) reduced-calorie mayonnaise
½ tablespoon (7.5 ml) white wine vinegar
freshly ground pepper to taste
½ whole-wheat pita bread (cut 1 pita bread in half crosswise, reserving second half for another use)
½ cup (118 ml) shredded lettuce
1 tablespoon (15 ml) chopped tomato

In a small bowl, combine tofu, scallion, red pepper, mustard, mayonnaise, vinegar, and pepper. Let sit for 5 minutes. Stuff pita pocket with mixture; top with lettuce and tomato.

MAKES 1 SNACK

Per serving: calories, 131 ◆ protein, 7 g ◆ carbohydrate, 16 g ◆ fat, 5 g (calories from fat, 34%) ◆ dietary fiber, 1 g ◆ cholesterol, 3 mg ◆ sodium, 150 mg ◆ potassium, 234 mg
Joslin Exchanges: 1 bread/ starch, 1 fat

Tunisian Pita Sandwich

This is a typical North African vegetable salad, turned into a hearty sandwich snack.

3 tablespoons (45 ml) roasted red bell pepper (page 100), chopped
2 tablespoons (30 ml) chopped red onion
½ small tomato, peeled, seeded, and diced
½ small apple, peeled, cored, and diced
1 teaspoon (5 ml) minced fresh hot green chili
1 teaspoon (5 ml) fresh lemon juice

1 teaspoon (5 ml) minced fresh
  mint or ¼ teaspoon (1.25 ml)
  crushed dried
1 ounce (30 g) feta cheese,
  crumbled

½ whole-wheat pita bread (cut 1
  pita bread in half crosswise,
  reserving second half for
  another use)

Mix together all ingredients except pita bread. Stuff into pita.

MAKES 1 SNACK

> **Per serving:** calories, 204 ◆
> protein, 8 g ◆ carbohydrate, 30 g
> ◆ fat, 7 g (calories from fat, 31%)
> ◆ dietary fiber, 1 g ◆ cholesterol,
> 25 mg ◆ sodium, 431 mg ◆
> potassium, 413 mg
> Joslin Exchanges: 2 bread/
> starch, 1 fat

Vegetable Crisps

These savory crackers are perfect for snacking away from home. Keep a small tin of
them in your car or office desk drawer. Dehydrated vegetable flakes are available in
the spice section of supermarkets.

1 cup (125 g) unbleached flour
1 teaspoon (5 ml) sesame seeds
3 tablespoons (45 ml) dehydrated
  vegetable flakes
½ cup (118 ml) rolled oats
½ teaspoon (2.5 ml) *herbes de
  Provence* (page 294)
1 small garlic clove, minced

¼ teaspoon (1.25 ml) salt (optional)
⅛ teaspoon (.6 ml) freshly ground
  pepper or to taste
⅓ cup (78 ml) plus 1 to 2
  tablespoons (15 to 30 ml) water
3 tablespoons (45 ml) olive oil
olive oil cooking spray

Preheat oven to 350°F (180°C). In a medium-size mixing bowl, combine flour,
sesame seed, vegetable flakes, oats, *herbes de Provence*, garlic, salt, and pepper. Stir
in enough water and the oil to form a soft dough. Using a level teaspoon (5 ml), drop
dough onto a nonstick cookie sheet lightly sprayed with cooking spray. With a

floured finger, press dough into a thin circle or square. Prick crisps with tines of a fork. Lightly spray with cooking spray. Bake for 10 to 15 minutes, until lightly browned on the bottom. Store in an airtight container for up to 4 days. Wrap and freeze for longer storage.

MAKES ABOUT 36 CRISPS

Per 4-crisp serving: calories, 116 ◆ protein, 2 g ◆ carbohydrate, 15 g ◆ fat, 5 g (calories from fat, 38%) ◆ dietary fiber, trace ◆ cholesterol, 0 mg ◆ sodium, 65 mg ◆ potassium, 61 mg
Joslin Exchanges: 1 bread/ starch, 1 fat

Onion Crisps

Substitute caraway seeds for sesame seeds and dehydrated onion flakes for vegetable flakes. Proceed as directed.

MAKES ABOUT 36 CRISPS

Per 4-crisp serving: calories, 114 ◆ protein, 2 g ◆ carbohydrate, 15 g ◆ fat, 5 g (calories from fat, 39%) ◆ dietary fiber, trace ◆ cholesterol, 0 mg ◆ sodium, 65 mg ◆ potassium, 63 mg
Joslin Exchanges: 1 bread/ starch, 1 fat

Cajun Crisps

Substitute poppy seeds for sesame seeds and sprinkle very lightly with cayenne pepper before baking.

MAKES ABOUT 36 CRISPS

Per 4-crisp serving: calories, 115 ◆ protein, 2 g ◆ carbohydrate, 15 g ◆ fat, 5 g (calories from fat, 39%) ◆ dietary fiber, trace ◆ cholesterol, 0 mg ◆ sodium, 65 mg ◆ potassium, 62 g
Joslin Exchanges: 1 bread/ starch, 1 fat

BREADS

No aroma is more appealing than that of bread baking, and when you can produce homemade bread that tastes so good you can enjoy it without having to smother it with spreads, it's well worth the effort.

We offer many kinds of bread recipes—some are perfect for backyard family gatherings; others are fancy enough for company fare. Some are made with a bubbly sponge of yeast, requiring time and a gentle hand. A few use purchased frozen bread dough to speed the process; you add flavorings, shape the loaf, and bake it.

Quick breads can be stirred up in minutes, with no waiting for the mixture to rise. Popovers are easy to make and as light as a feather. Whatever your choice, all of our breads are delicious, full of complex carbohydrates, and made with a minimum of fat.

Banana Tea Loaf

A fragrant tea bread that makes good use of too many ripe bananas. It's also great for breakfast, spread with a little margarine mixed with grated orange zest.

2 very ripe bananas, mashed
½ cup (118 ml) canola oil
1 large egg white
6 tablespoons (90 ml) egg substitute
⅛ teaspoon (.6 ml) almond extract
2 tablespoons (30 ml) frozen orange juice concentrate, defrosted

2 cups (250 g) unbleached flour
2 teaspoons (10 ml) baking powder
¼ teaspoon (1.25 ml) baking soda
butter-flavored cooking spray

Preheat oven to 350°F (180°C). In a large bowl, combine bananas, oil, egg white, egg substitute, almond extract, and orange juice concentrate. Sift together flour, baking powder, and baking soda. Gradually stir into banana mixture, mixing until just well blended (do not overmix).

Spread batter into a 9¹/₂- by 5-inch (24 by 13 cm) loaf pan lightly sprayed with cooking spray. Bake for 50 to 60 minutes, until golden brown. Cool in pan for 5 minutes. Transfer bread to a wire rack to continue cooling. When cool, slice into ¹/₂-inch (1.5 cm) slices. Keeps well, wrapped airtight, in refrigerator; freezes well.

MAKES 18 SERVINGS

Per serving: calories, 122 ◆ protein, 2 g ◆ carbohydrate, 14 g ◆ fat, 6 g (calories from fat, 44%) ◆ dietary fiber, trace ◆ cholesterol, trace ◆ sodium, 61 mg ◆ potassium, 105 mg Joslin Exchanges: 1 bread/ starch, 1 fat

Chive Popovers

These chive-laced popovers are easy to make and dramatic to serve. You can bake them in cast-iron popover pans, regular muffin pans, or ¹/₂ cup (118 ml) glass or ceramic custard cups.

butter-flavored cooking spray
2 large eggs
1 cup (125 g) unbleached flour
¹/₄ teaspoon (1.25 ml) salt

freshly ground pepper to taste
1 cup (236 ml) low-fat (2%) milk
¹/₄ cup (59 ml) snipped fresh chives

Preheat oven to 400°F (205°C). Spray 8 muffin cups, popover cups, or custard cups with cooking spray.

In a food processor or blender, combine eggs, flour, salt, and pepper. Process until well blended, 10 seconds. With the machine running, pour in milk through the feed tube. Process until smooth. Stir in chives. Fill prepared baking cups with batter, filling to no more than ¹/₄ inch (.75 cm) below rim. If you're using individual cups, set them well apart on a baking sheet.

Bake for 35 minutes, until puffed and golden brown. (Don't open the oven door while the popovers are baking, or they will fall.) Remove from oven and run a knife around the edge of each popover to loosen. Invert and remove popovers. Serve immediately.

For crispier popovers, or to gain a little extra time before they're served, cut a short slit in the side of each popover and return to turned-off oven for 5 to 10 minutes. Serve immediately.

MAKES 8 POPOVERS

Per 1-popover serving:
calories, 87 ◆ protein, 4 g ◆ carbohydrate, 13 g ◆ fat, 2 g (calories from fat, 21%) ◆ dietary fiber, trace ◆ cholesterol, 56 mg ◆ sodium, 98 mg ◆ potassium, 83 mg Joslin Exchanges: 1 bread/starch

Corn and Chili Pepper Muffins

Baking these muffins in corn husks intensifies their rustic flavor—and adds a bit of whimsy to your brunch or dinner. Dry corn husks are available at Mexican grocers, specialty food stores, and many supermarkets. Any leftover corn husks will keep indefinitely for future use. Of course you can always bake these directly in the muffin cups, without the corn husks.

12 dry corn husks, 6 to 8 inches (15 to 20 cm) long (optional)
 1 cup (125 g) unbleached flour
 1 cup (144 g) stone-ground yellow cornmeal
½ teaspoon (2.5 ml) salt (optional)
 1 tablespoon (15 ml) baking powder
 1 teaspoon (5 ml) baking soda

⅔ cup (156 ml) buttermilk
 1 large egg, beaten
¼ cup (59 ml) canola oil
 1 tablespoon (15 ml) honey
¾ cup (177 ml) frozen corn kernels
 1 tablespoon (15 ml) minced fresh jalapeño chili

Separate corn husks. In a large bowl, pour boiling water over husks to cover. Let soak until soft and pliable, about 10 minutes. Drain husks; pat dry with paper towels. Tear lengthwise into strips 2 inches (5 cm) wide.

In a large bowl, combine flour, cornmeal, salt, baking powder, and baking soda. Make a well in center. In another bowl, beat together buttermilk, egg, oil, honey, corn, and chili. Pour into well in flour mixture. Stir just enough to moisten dry ingredients.

Preheat oven to 375°F (190°C). In each of 12 greased 2½-inch (6.5 cm) muffin cups, place 2 or 3 strips of corn husk, crossing centers in bottom of each cup, allowing husks to extend up around sides. Fill each cup about two-thirds full of batter.

Bake until a toothpick inserted in center comes out clean, about 25 minutes. Lift muffins and corn husks out of pan; cool on a wire rack. Serve warm or cool. Best eaten same day; freeze for longer storage.

MAKES 12 MUFFINS

> **Per muffin:** calories, 140 ◆ protein, 3 g ◆ carbohydrate, 20 g ◆ fat, 6 g (calories from fat, 39%) ◆ dietary fiber, 2 g ◆ cholesterol, 18 mg ◆ sodium, 263 mg ◆ potassium, 94 mg Joslin Exchanges: 1 bread/ starch, 1 fat

Green Chili Scones

These savory scones are great for breakfast or brunch, as a robust accompaniment to soups or salads, or split and filled with thin slices of roasted turkey breast and a few radish sprouts for a great lunch.

1 cup (125 g) unbleached flour
1 cup (144 g) stone-ground yellow cornmeal
1 tablespoon (15 ml) baking powder
½ teaspoon (2.5 ml) ground cumin
4 tablespoons (60 g) cold margarine, cut into ½-inch (1.5 cm) pieces

1 Anaheim or poblano chili, roasted (page 100), seeded, and chopped, or 1 4-ounce (115 g) can chopped green chilies
2 large eggs
½ cup (118 ml) skim milk
olive oil cooking spray

Preheat oven to 400°F (205°C). In a large bowl, mix together flour, cornmeal, baking powder, and cumin. Using a pastry blender or 2 forks, cut in margarine until mixture forms coarse crumbs. Stir in chilies.

Beat together eggs and milk until well blended. Set aside 2 tablespoons (30 ml) of the mixture. Add remaining egg mixture to flour mixture, stirring until dough is evenly moistened. Transfer dough to a floured board; knead lightly until dough holds together. Divide dough in half. Pat each half into a 6-inch (15 cm) round about ¾ inch (2 cm) thick. Place rounds far apart on a baking sheet lightly sprayed with cooking spray. With a sharp knife, cut each round into 6 wedges. Slightly separate wedges on baking sheet. Brush with reserved egg mixture.

Bake for 16 to 18 minutes, until golden brown. Serve hot or warm. Best eaten same day; freeze for longer storage.

MAKES 12 SCONES

> **Per scone:** calories, 129 ◆ protein, 3 g ◆ carbohydrate, 17 g ◆ fat, 5 g (calories from fat, 34%) ◆ dietary fiber, trace ◆ cholesterol, 36 mg ◆ sodium, 143 mg ◆ potassium, 65 mg Joslin Exchanges: 1 bread/starch, 1 fat

Irish Oatmeal Scones with Dried Cherries

These are beautiful for a lazy Sunday brunch or holiday tea table. If you can't find dried cherries that are processed without added sugar, substitute dried currants, apples, or apricots. Buy the date sugar at a health food store.

  1 cup (156 g) rolled oats
1½ cups (185 g) unbleached flour
 ¼ cup (59 ml) egg substitute
  1 tablespoon (14 g) date sugar or granulated sugar
 ¼ cup (59 ml) finely chopped dried cherries (no sugar added)
 ¼ teaspoon (1.25 ml) ground nutmeg
 ¼ teaspoon (1.25 ml) ground cinnamon
  3 tablespoons (45 g) margarine, melted
2½ teaspoons (12.5 ml) baking powder
 ¾ cup (177 ml) skim milk
butter-flavored cooking spray

Preheat oven to 400°F (205°C). In a large bowl, combine all ingredients except cooking spray, mixing until just moistened. Flour your hands and form dough into two 8-inch (20 cm) circles about ½ inch (1.5 cm) thick. Place on a nonstick cookie sheet lightly sprayed with cooking spray.

Dip a sharp knife in flour and cut each circle into 8 pie-shaped wedges. Separate the wedges, leaving about ½ inch (1.5 cm) between edges. Bake for 12 to 15 minutes, until golden brown. Serve warm. Store in airtight container for up to 3 days or freeze for longer storage.

MAKES 16 SCONES

Per scone: calories, 92 ◆
protein, 3 g ◆ carbohydrate,
14 g ◆ fat, 3 g (calories from fat,
29%) ◆ dietary fiber, trace ◆

cholesterol, trace ◆ sodium,
90 mg ◆ potassium, 167 mg
Joslin Exchanges: 1 bread/starch

Irish Soda Bread

This old-fashioned bread makes a lovely addition to a tea table. If there's any left, it's wonderful toasted the next morning with coffee.

2 cups (250 g) unbleached flour,
  sifted
1½ tablespoons (22.5 ml) baking
  powder
¾ teaspoon (3.75 ml) baking soda
¼ cup (59 ml) dried currants

½ tablespoon (7.5 ml) caraway
  seed
1 cup (236 ml) buttermilk
1 large egg
butter-flavored cooking spray

Preheat oven to 350°F (180°C). In a large bowl, combine flour, baking powder, baking soda, currants, and caraway seed. In a small bowl, combine buttermilk and egg. Pour over dry ingredients; mix well. Turn out onto a floured board and lightly knead to form a smooth, soft dough. Form into a round loaf. Make an X on top with the back of a knife. Place on a nonstick baking sheet lightly sprayed with cooking spray. Bake for 40 to 45 minutes, until lightly browned. Cool on a wire rack. Cut into wedges when cool. To store, wrap wedges airtight and freeze.

MAKES 18 SERVINGS

Per serving: calories, 63 ◆
protein, 2 g ◆ carbohydrate,
12 g ◆ fat, 1 g (calories from fat,
14%) ◆ dietary fiber, trace ◆

cholesterol, 12 mg ◆ sodium,
80 mg ◆ potassium, 58 mg
Joslin Exchanges: 1 bread/starch

Orange Applesauce Tea Bread

One of our favorites for tea time or spread with a smidgen of low-fat goat cheese for breakfast.

1 cup (236 ml) unsweetened applesauce
1 heaped teaspoon (5 ml) baking soda
juice and grated zest of 1 orange
1¾ cups (219 g) unbleached flour
1 teaspoon (5 ml) ground cinnamon

½ teaspoon (2.5 ml) ground nutmeg
½ teaspoon (2.5 ml) ground allspice
⅓ cup (78 ml) raisins
4 teaspoons (20 g) margarine, melted
butter-flavored cooking spray

Preheat oven to 350°F (180°C). In a large bowl, combine applesauce and baking soda. Stir in orange juice and zest, flour, cinnamon, nutmeg, allspice, raisins, and melted margarine. Blend well. Spread the batter into a 9½- by 5-inch (24 by 13 cm) loaf pan lightly sprayed with cooking spray. Bake for 40 minutes, until golden brown. Cool in pan for 5 minutes. Transfer to a wire rack to cool. Slice into ½-inch (1.5 cm) slices. To store, wrap slices individually and freeze.

MAKES 18 SERVINGS

Per serving: calories, 65 ◆ protein, 1 g ◆ carbohydrate, 13 g ◆ fat, 1 g (calories from fat, 14%) ◆ dietary fiber, trace ◆ cholesterol, 0 mg ◆ sodium, 56 mg ◆ potassium, 55 mg Joslin Exchanges: 1 bread/starch

Focaccia—Four Ways

This version of the popular Italian flatbread gets a head start from thawed frozen bread dough. It takes 25 minutes to prepare and bakes in 8 minutes.

1 pound (450 g) frozen white bread dough, thawed
olive oil cooking spray

1 tablespoon (15 ml) olive oil
choice of topping (recipes follow)

Cut dough into 6 equal pieces. On a lightly floured board, roll each piece into a 5- to 6-inch (13 to 15 cm) circle. Lightly spray three 12- by 15-inch (30 by 38 cm) baking sheets with cooking spray. Place 2 circles of dough far apart on each sheet. Brush circles with olive oil. Sprinkle with topping. Lightly cover with plastic wrap and let stand in a warm place until dough rises and appears puffy, about 20 minutes.

Preheat oven to 475°F (245°C). Bake until puffed and golden, 8 to 10 minutes. Serve warm. Best eaten same day; freeze for longer storage.

MAKES 6 BREADS

Sage and Onion Topping

1 medium-size onion, thinly sliced
1 tablespoon (15 ml) chopped fresh sage or 1 teaspoon (5 ml) crushed dried

¼ teaspoon (1.25 ml) coarse salt

> **Per ½-bread serving:** calories, 106 ◆ protein, 4 g ◆ carbohydrate, 19 g ◆ fat, 2 g (calories from fat, 17%) ◆ dietary fiber, trace ◆ cholesterol, 0 mg ◆ sodium, 252 mg ◆ potassium, 19 mg Joslin Exchanges: 1 bread/starch

Rosemary and Raisin Topping

⅓ cup (78 ml) golden raisins, plumped in ¼ cup (59 ml) fresh orange juice for 30 minutes

1 tablespoon (15 ml) chopped fresh rosemary or 1 teaspoon (5 ml) crushed dried

> **Per ½-bread serving:** calories, 116 ◆ protein, 4 g ◆ carbohydrate, 22 g ◆ fat, 2 g (calories from fat, 15%) ◆ dietary fiber, trace ◆ cholesterol, 0 mg ◆ sodium, 208 mg ◆ potassium, 41 mg Joslin Exchanges: 1½ bread/ starch

Tomato Topping

1 fresh plum tomato, about ¼ pound (115 g), sliced crosswise into paper-thin slices
1 ounce (30 g) sun-dried tomatoes (packed dry), plumped in ⅓ cup (78 ml) hot water for 5 minutes, drained, and chopped

1 tablespoon (15 ml) chopped fresh oregano or 1 teaspoon (5 ml) crushed dried
¼ teaspoon (1.25 ml) coarse salt

Per ½-bread serving: calories, 110 ◆ protein, 4 g ◆ carbohydrate, 21 g ◆ fat, 2 g (calories from fat, 16%) ◆ dietary fiber, trace ◆ cholesterol, 0 mg ◆ sodium, 256 mg ◆ potassium, 64 mg Joslin Exchanges: 1½ bread/ starch

Southwestern Topping

4 garlic cloves, slivered
¼ cup (59 ml) chopped fresh cilantro (fresh coriander)

¼ cup (59 ml) dry-roasted sunflower seeds

Per ½-bread serving: calories, 120 ◆ protein, 5 g ◆ carbohydrate, 19 g ◆ fat, 3 g (calories from fat, 23%) ◆ dietary fiber, trace ◆ cholesterol, 0 mg ◆ sodium, 202 mg ◆ potassium, 24 mg Joslin Exchanges: 1 bread/starch

---

ITALIAN BREAD AND SOUP PARTY

◆

Basket of Focaccia (page 393)

Pickled Vegetables (page 13)

Spicy Seafood Gazpacho (page 58)

Fresh Figs with Low-Fat Goat Cheese and Cracked Pepper

Per serving: 380 calories (28% fat)
Joslin Exchanges: 2 low-fat meat, 1 medium-fat meat, 2 vegetable, 1 bread/ starch, 1 fruit

Lemon Pepper Breadsticks

Playing the sweetness of lemon zest against the spiciness of coarse pepper, these breadsticks are full of flavor. They're also easy to make—just a quick cut and a stretch, and they're ready to bake.

1 ¼-ounce (7 g) package active dry yeast
1 cup (236 ml) warm water (110°F/43°C)
1 teaspoon (4 g) granulated sugar
1 tablespoon (15 ml) grated lemon zest
2 teaspoons (10 ml) coarsely ground pepper
1 teaspoon (5 ml) salt (optional)

2 tablespoons (30 ml) nonfat dry milk
2 tablespoons (30 ml) canola oil
2¾ cups (344 g) unbleached flour, approximately
vegetable oil cooking spray
2 tablespoons (30 ml) stone-ground yellow cornmeal

In a large bowl, combine yeast, water, and sugar. Let stand until yeast is foamy, about 5 minutes. Stir in lemon zest, pepper, salt, dry milk, 2 tablespoons (30 ml) oil, and 1½ cups (185 g) flour. Beat with a heavy spoon or an electric mixer until dough is sticky, 1 to 2 minutes. Mix in another cup (125 g) of flour to make a soft dough. Turn dough out onto a floured surface and knead for 5 to 10 minutes, until dough is smooth and elastic. Add more flour as necessary to prevent sticking. Pat dough into a 6-inch (15 cm) square. Cover with plastic wrap. Let stand until dough rises and appears puffy, about 45 minutes.

Preheat oven to 350°F (180°C). Lightly spray three 12- by 15-inch (30 by 38 cm) baking sheets with cooking spray.

Sprinkle dough with cornmeal. Cut dough into quarters. Working with 1 quarter at a time, cut quarter lengthwise into 8 equal pieces. Pick up 1 piece and stretch it to length of pan. Repeat, placing breadsticks at least ½ inch (1.5 cm) apart. Bake for 20 to 25 minutes, until crisp and golden brown. Store in an airtight container for up to 4 days. Freeze for longer storage.

MAKES 32 BREADSTICKS

Per 2-stick serving: calories, 99 ◆ protein, 3 g ◆ carbohydrate, 17 g ◆ fat, 2 g (calories from fat, 18%) ◆ dietary fiber, trace ◆ cholesterol, trace ◆ sodium, 137 mg ◆ potassium, 47 mg
Joslin Exchanges: 1 bread/starch

Sun-Dried Tomato and Garlic Breadsticks

Omit lemon zest and pepper. Add 1 garlic clove, minced, to yeast/water mixture when you add salt. Proceed as directed, but at the end of kneading, work in ½ ounce (15 g) sun-dried tomatoes (packed dry) plumped in hot water for 5 minutes, drained, and finely chopped.

MAKES 32 BREADSTICKS

Per 2-stick serving: calories, 99 ◆ protein, 3 g ◆ carbohydrate, 17 g ◆ fat, 2 g (calories from fat, 18%) ◆ dietary fiber, 1 g ◆ cholesterol, trace ◆ sodium, 138 mg ◆ potassium, 57 mg
Joslin Exchanges: 1 bread/starch

Herb Bread

A friend taught us this trick of using a clean white plastic trash bag (with no lettering) to create an ideal warm, draft-free environment for the rising of this no-knead bread. If you don't have a plastic bag, you can cover the bowl with a clean kitchen towel, but the bread won't rise as quickly. It's a dense bread that's also good without the herbs.

1 teaspoon (5 ml) crushed dried oregano
1 teaspoon (5 ml) crushed dried basil
1 teaspoon (5 ml) crushed dried thyme
1 teaspoon (5 ml) freshly ground pepper
1 tablespoon (15 ml) olive oil
1 ¼-ounce (7 g) package rapid-rise dry yeast

1¼ cups (295 ml) warm water (100°F/43°C)
1 tablespoon (15 ml) sugar
1½ teaspoons (7.5 ml) salt (optional)
about 3 cups (375 g) unbleached flour
olive oil cooking spray

In a small bowl, combine herbs, pepper, and oil. Let stand for 10 minutes. In a large bowl, dissolve yeast in warm water; let stand for 5 minutes. Stir in sugar, salt, and herb mixture. Stir in enough flour, 1 cup (125 g) at a time, to make a soft dough.

Transfer dough to a clean bowl lightly sprayed with cooking spray. Cover bowl with a large white plastic trash bag (with no lettering). Secure with tie. Let dough rise in a warm place until doubled in bulk, about 40 minutes. Punch down and form into 2 rounded loaves of equal size. With your fingers, press dough down around the edges of each loaf, forming what resembles the rim of a hat.

Place oven rack on the next-to-top rack position and preheat oven to 450°F (230°C). Place a double layer of heavy-duty aluminum foil on the rack. Place formed loaves directly on the foil; bake for 12 to 15 minutes, until browned. Flip loaves over and bake for another 5 to 10 minutes. Serve warm or at room temperature. Best eaten same day; freeze for longer storage.

MAKES 2 LOAVES; 16 SERVINGS

> **Per serving:** calories, 73 ◆ protein, 2 g ◆ carbohydrate, 14 g ◆ fat, 1 g (calories from fat, 12%) ◆ dietary fiber, trace ◆ cholesterol, 0 mg ◆ sodium, 54 mg ◆ potassium, 32 mg Joslin Exchanges: 1 bread/starch

Naan

Naan is a puffy Indian bread baked in a tandoor oven. Los Angeles chefs Susan Feniger and Mary Sue Milliken adapted the recipe for home ovens, sacrificing the puffiness but keeping the taste. We've added some changes of our own.

1 ¼-ounce (7 g) package active dry yeast
1 tablespoon (15 ml) sugar
1 cup (236 ml) warm water (110°F/43°C)
1⅓ cups (314 ml) plain nonfat yogurt
2 teaspoons (10 ml) salt (optional)

4¾ cups (594 g) unbleached flour vegetable oil cooking spray
6 garlic cloves, peeled
2 tablespoons (30 ml) minced cilantro (fresh coriander)
2 tablespoons (30 ml) minced fresh hot red chilies
2 tablespoons (30 ml) cumin seed

In a large bowl, dissolve yeast and sugar in warm water. Let stand until foamy, about 5 minutes. Stir in 1 cup (236 ml) yogurt and salt. Gradually add enough flour to form a soft dough. Turn dough out onto a floured surface and knead until dough is elastic and no longer sticky, adding more flour if necessary. Place dough in a bowl lightly sprayed with cooking spray. Cover with plastic wrap and set aside to rise in a warm, draft-free place for 45 minutes to 1 hour, until dough has doubled in size.

Punch dough down; divide into 16 equal pieces. Knead each by hand to form a ball. Place balls on a baking sheet lightly sprayed with cooking spray. Cover with plastic wrap and let rise for another 15 minutes, until doubled in size.

Preheat oven to 400°F (205°C). Thinly slice garlic; cut lengthwise into thin slivers. Place in a bowl and cover with boiling water. Let stand for 2 minutes; drain and pat dry with paper towels. Set aside.

Stretch each ball into a 4-inch (10 cm) oblong; let rise for another 5 minutes. Transfer oblongs to an ungreased baking pan. Spread 1 teaspoon (5 ml) of remaining yogurt onto center of each oblong. Sprinkle each with garlic slivers, cilantro, chilies, and cumin. Bake for 12 minutes, until golden brown. Serve warm or at room temperature. Does not keep well—use same day.

MAKES 16 BREADS

> **Per bread:** calories, 146 ◆ protein, 5 g ◆ carbohydrate, 30 g ◆ fat, 1 g (calories from fat, 6%) ◆ dietary fiber, trace ◆ cholesterol, trace ◆ sodium, 309 mg ◆ potassium, 107 mg Joslin Exchanges: 2 bread/starch

Walnut Raisin Whole-Wheat Peasant Bread

This bread makes great toast for breakfast. The recipe comes from Linda Benincasa, who owns a pastry shop in Connecticut.

1 ¼-ounce (7 g) package active dry yeast
¼ cup (59 ml) warm water (110°F/43°C)
1 teaspoon (5 ml) sugar
1½ cups (354 ml) low-fat (2%) milk
¼ teaspoon (1.25 ml) salt (optional)

1¾ cups (219 g) whole-wheat flour
1¾ cups (219 g) unbleached flour
vegetable oil cooking spray
½ cup (118 ml) raisins
½ cup (118 ml) coarsely chopped walnuts

In a large bowl, sprinkle yeast over warm water. Whisk in sugar; let stand for 5 minutes, until foamy.

Meanwhile, scald milk by heating to just below boiling point until small bubbles form around the edges. Remove milk from stove; cool to lukewarm. Add cooled milk to yeast mixture.

In medium-size bowl, combine salt and flours. Add enough of the flour mixture to milk mixture to form a soft dough. Turn dough out onto a floured surface and knead until dough is elastic and no longer sticky, adding more flour if necessary. Place dough in a bowl lightly sprayed with cooking spray. Cover with plastic wrap; let rise in a warm, draft-free place for 1½ to 2 hours or until doubled in volume.

Punch down dough; knead in raisins and walnuts. Shape into 2 round loaves. Place loaves on a baking sheet and let rise for 30 to 45 minutes or until doubled in volume.

Preheat oven to 350°F (180°C). Dust tops of loaves with flour. Using a sharp knife, cut a crosshatch design on top. Bake for 30 to 35 minutes or until loaves sound hollow when bottoms are tapped. Transfer loaves to a wire rack; cool before slicing. Best eaten same day; freeze for longer storage.

MAKES 2 LOAVES; 32 SERVINGS

Per serving: calories, 71; protein, 2 g ◆ carbohydrate, 12 g ◆ fat, 2 g (calories from fat, 25%) ◆ dietary fiber, trace ◆ cholesterol, trace ◆ sodium, 23 mg ◆ potassium, 83 mg Joslin Exchanges: 1 bread/starch

---

SUNDAY BRUNCH

◆

Eggplant and Tomato Pie (page 346)

Walnut Raisin Whole-Wheat Peasant Bread (page 399)

Star Fruits (Carambolas) with Neufchâtel and Gingersnaps

Per serving: 424 calories (25% fat)
Joslin Exchanges: 2 medium-fat meat, 2 bread/starch, 2 vegetable, 1 fruit

DESSERTS

Desserts, almost always high in simple carbohydrates and fats, pose a potential problem for those of us with diabetes: we love them! But since we both have diabetes and must adhere to our daily exchanges, dessert is not an everyday event—it's reserved for special occasions.

You can imagine our astonishment, however, when one of our doctors suggested that for those whose blood sugars are in good control an occasional scoop of vanilla ice cream will not raise the blood glucose level precipitously. That suggestion, however, does not give us carte blanche to eat all sweets, nor are we suggesting that everyone with diabetes can occasionally eat vanilla ice cream. While you, too, may be able to include ice cream as an occasional treat in your meal plan, it should be avoided totally until you have discussed it with your dietitian or physician.

Most of the time we end our meal with a piece of fruit. But of course when we have company we like to offer a sweet to top off the meal. Toward that end we have created some desserts that are truly beautiful and delicious—special enough for company and yet nutritionally acceptable for those of us on special diets.

In this cookbook we used fructose, frozen fruit juice concentrates, fresh fruit, date sugar, and sugar-free spreads and jams as sweeteners because we feel they produce a better product. Occasionally we have used granulated sugar (sucrose), honey, or brown sugar—keeping these amounts to less than the 1 teaspoon (5 ml) per reasonable serving of the finished dish, the amount of sugar that may be allowed when one's blood glucose level is in good control. Note, however, that all of these sweeteners do add calories and raise blood glucose levels, although somewhat more slowly than sucrose.

If you must or prefer to use only noncaloric sweeteners, we have indicated substitutions for some of the recipes. Keep in mind that noncaloric sweeteners will not produce an end product identical to caloric sweeteners. Although still quite tasty, they will differ somewhat in flavor, texture, and appearance. The results will also vary according to the type of noncaloric sweetener used. Noncaloric sweeteners are discussed on page 446.

CAKES FOR ENTERTAINING

An elegantly decorated birthday cake aglow with candles, a beautiful bûche de Noël finale to the Christmas Eve feast, a luscious chocolate cake atop an antique cake pedestal—as a rule, cakes like these have been "look but do not eat" desserts for anyone with diabetes, or if they were made from recipes written for our special diets, the resulting flat, dense cake would be unacceptable to everyone.

We want to be able to enjoy the cakes that we serve on special occasions, so we developed a terrific recipe for a sponge cake (génoise) using both egg and egg substitutes as well as fructose. Beaten egg whites are also used to make the cake as light as possible, and the fructose, nature's alternative to ordinary table sugar, is whirled in a food processor to break it down and further lighten the cake. The cake can be baked in two 9-inch (23 cm) round cake pans or in a 10-inch (25 cm) tube pan.

A word of caution from the nutrition experts at Joslin: fructose is converted into glucose, thus raising blood sugar precipitously, albeit at a slower rate than sucrose does.

These cakes are for special occasions. They're appropriate only when one's blood sugars are under good control and then only in small portions. Check with your doctor before you decide to indulge.

Basic Sponge Cake (Génoise)

butter-flavored cooking spray
 2 cups (218 g) sifted cake flour
 ¾ cup (177 ml) fructose, whirled in a food processor for 10 seconds
 1 tablespoon (15 ml) baking powder
 ½ teaspoon (2.5 ml) salt (optional)
 ⅓ cup (78 ml) canola oil
 2 large eggs, separated
 ½ cup (118 ml) egg substitute

 ½ cup (118 ml) water
1½ teaspoons (7.5 ml) vanilla extract
grated zest of 1 lemon, 1 orange, or a combination (optional)
1 cup (236 ml) egg whites (the whites from the 2 eggs plus 6–7 more) at room temperature
 ½ teaspoon (2.5 ml) cream of tartar

Preheat oven to 325°F (165°C). Lightly spray two 9-inch (23 cm) round cake pans or a 10-inch (25 cm) tube pan with cooking spray. Dust with flour.

In a large bowl, sift together cake flour, fructose, baking powder, and salt. Make a well in the middle. Beat together oil, egg yolks, egg substitute, water, vanilla, and lemon zest. Pour into flour mixture; blend well. In a large mixing bowl, beat egg whites until frothy. Add cream of tartar; beat until egg whites form stiff peaks.

Stir about ½ cup (118 ml) beaten egg whites into flour and egg mixture to lighten it. Gently fold in remaining egg whites. When blended, divide batter between prepared cake pans. Bake for 25 to 30 minutes (50 to 55 minutes for tube pan), until cake is golden brown and begins to pull away slightly from sides. Do *not* open oven door until cake is almost done, or it may fall. Run spatula around edges and turn out at once onto a wire rack. Cool completely. Cakes can be made ahead, wrapped well, and frozen for up to 1 month.

MAKES 16 SERVINGS

Per serving: calories, 144 ◆ protein, 4 g ◆ carbohydrate, 19 g ◆ fat, 6 g (calories from fat, 37%) ◆ dietary fiber, trace ◆ cholesterol, 27 mg ◆ sodium, 208 mg ◆ potassium, 100 mg Joslin Exchanges: 1 bread/starch, 1 fat

Note: See page 405 for frostings and fillings.

Chocolate Almond Génoise

Omit citrus zest and add ¼ teaspoon (1.25 ml) almond extract along with 1 ounce (30 g) melted bitter chocolate to flour and egg mixture before adding beaten egg whites.

MAKES 16 SERVINGS

Per serving: calories, 153 ◆ protein, 5 g ◆ carbohydrate, 19 g ◆ fat, 6 g (calories from fat, 35%) ◆ dietary fiber, trace ◆ cholesterol, 27 mg ◆ sodium, 194 mg ◆ potassium, 87 mg Joslin Exchanges: 1 bread/starch, 1 fat

Chocolate Génoise

Omit citrus zest. Stir 1 ounce (30 g) melted bitter chocolate into flour and egg mixture before adding beaten egg whites.

MAKES 16 SERVINGS

Per serving: calories, 153 ◆ protein, 5 g ◆ carbohydrate, 19 g ◆ fat, 6 g (calories from fat, 35%) ◆ dietary fiber, trace ◆ cholesterol, 27 mg ◆ sodium, 194 mg ◆ potassium, 87 mg Joslin Exchanges: 1 bread/ starch, 1 fat

Mocha Génoise

Omit citrus zest. Dissolve 2 teaspoons (10 ml) instant coffee in 1 tablespoon (15 ml) hot water. Add to flour and egg mixture along with 1 ounce (30 g) melted bitter chocolate before adding beaten egg whites.

MAKES 16 SERVINGS

Per serving: calories, 145 ◆ protein, 4 g ◆ carbohydrate, 19 g ◆ fat, 6 g (calories from fat, 37%) ◆ dietary fiber, trace ◆ cholesterol, 27 mg ◆ sodium, 194 mg ◆ potassium, 86 mg Joslin Exchanges: 1 bread/ starch, 1 fat

Nut Génoise

Omit citrus zest. Fold in ⅓ cup (78 ml) finely chopped nuts just before pouring batter into pan. If you're using almonds, add ¼ teaspoon (1.25 ml) almond extract.

MAKES 16 SERVINGS

Per serving: calories, 160 ◆ protein, 5 g ◆ carbohydrate, 19 g ◆ fat, 7 g (calories from fat, 39%) ◆ dietary fiber, trace ◆ cholesterol, 27 mg ◆ sodium, 194 mg ◆ potassium, 94 mg Joslin Exchanges: 1 bread/ starch, 1 fat

Orange Génoise

Use only orange zest and substitute fresh orange juice for ¼ cup (59 ml) of the water.

MAKES 16 SERVINGS

Per serving: calories, 146 ◆ protein, 4 g ◆ carbohydrate, 19 g ◆ fat, 6 g (calories from fat, 37%) ◆ dietary fiber, trace ◆ cholesterol, 27 mg ◆ sodium, 194 mg ◆ potassium, 83 mg Joslin Exchanges: 1 bread/ starch, 1 fat

EXTRA SPECIAL TOUCHES

Sponge cakes are the basis for many fancy desserts. Here are a few special fillings and frostings to try.

Chocolate Hazelnut Cake

1 cup (225 g) part-skim ricotta cheese
1 tablespoon (15 ml) hazelnut-flavored liqueur or water
1 tablespoon (15 ml) unsweetened cocoa powder

1 baked Chocolate Génoise (page 404), cooled
16 hazelnuts

Set a sieve over a small mixing bowl; press ricotta cheese through sieve. Blend with liqueur and cocoa. Spread half of the mixture between the cake layers. Spread top and sides with remaining ricotta mixture. Place hazelnuts around outer rim of cake.

MAKES 16 SERVINGS

Per serving: calories, 181 ◆ protein, 7 g ◆ carbohydrate, 20 g ◆ fat, 8 g (calories from fat, 41%) ◆ dietary fiber, trace ◆ cholesterol, 32 mg ◆ sodium, 213 mg ◆ potassium, 132 mg Joslin Exchanges: 1 bread/ starch, 1 fat

European Nut Cake

1 cup (123 g) fresh raspberries
1 teaspoon (5 ml) cornstarch
1 teaspoon (5 ml) water
1 baked Nut Génoise (page 404),
  cooled

1 tablespoon (6 g) confectioners'
  sugar

Puree raspberries in a blender or food processor. Strain into a small saucepan. Combine cornstarch and water. Stir into raspberry puree and place over low heat. Cook, stirring constantly, just until cornstarch is dissolved and mixture thickens slightly.

Spread raspberry puree between cake layers. Sift confectioners' sugar over top.

MAKES 16 SERVINGS

Per serving: calories, 166 ◆ protein, 5 g ◆ carbohydrate, 21 g ◆ fat, 7 g (calories from fat, 38%) ◆ dietary fiber, trace ◆ cholesterol, 27 mg ◆ sodium, 194 mg ◆ potassium, 105 mg Joslin Exchanges: 1 bread/ starch, 1 fat

Génoise with Fresh Fruit

1 baked basic sponge cake
  (page 402)
1 cup (236 ml) low-fat yogurt
  cheese (page 11)
½ teaspoon (2.5 ml) almond extract

1 pint (298 g) fresh strawberries,
  raspberries, cherries,
  blackberries, or blueberries

Place a cooled cake layer on a flat plate. Combine yogurt cheese and almond extract. Spread one-third on cake. Top with half the berries (if you're using strawberries, remove stems and slice half of the berries, reserving the nicest berries for the top). Place second cake layer on top, holding it in place with a couple of toothpicks if necessary. Spread remaining yogurt cheese on top; decorate with remaining whole berries. Refrigerate until ready to serve.

Note: If cake has been baked in a 10-inch (25 cm) tube pan, slice in half horizontally.

MAKES 16 SERVINGS

Per serving: calories, 175 ◆ protein, 5 g ◆ carbohydrate, 20 g ◆ fat, 8 g (calories from fat, 41%) ◆ dietary fiber, trace ◆ cholesterol, 29 mg ◆ sodium, 201 mg ◆ potassium, 105 mg Joslin Exchanges: 1 bread/ starch, 1 fat

Lemon Chiffon Cake

Lemon Topping

2 teaspoons (10 ml) fructose
2 tablespoons (30 ml) cornstarch
⅓ cup (78 ml) water
2½ tablespoons (37.5 ml) fresh lemon juice

1 tablespoon (15 ml) egg substitute or 1 teaspoon (5 ml) egg yolk

Cake

⅓ cup (78 ml) raspberry fruit spread (no sugar added)
1 baked basic sponge cake (page 402), cooled

1 lemon, thinly sliced, for garnish

In a small saucepan, combine topping ingredients. Cook over low heat, stirring constantly, until mixture thickens and coats the back of a wooden spoon, about 10 minutes. Remove from heat and cover with plastic wrap, touching surface to prevent a skin from forming. Cool.

Place fruit spread in a glass cup and melt in microwave on HIGH power for 30 seconds (or place in a small saucepan and melt on top of stove over low heat).

Spread melted fruit spread on bottom layer of cake. Top with second layer and spread with lemon topping. Decorate with lemon slices.

MAKES 16 SERVINGS

Per serving: calories, 165 ◆ protein, 5 g ◆ carbohydrate, 24 g ◆ fat, 6 g (calories from fat, 32%) ◆ dietary fiber, trace ◆ cholesterol, 27 mg ◆ sodium, 196 mg ◆ potassium, 81 mg Joslin Exchanges: 1½ bread/ starch, 1 fat

Chocolate Buttercream Frosting

½ cup (118 ml) fructose
3 tablespoons (45 ml) skim milk
2 tablespoons (30 ml) cornstarch
2 tablespoons (30 ml)
  unsweetened cocoa powder
1 large egg yolk

½ teaspoon (2.5 ml) vanilla extract
½ teaspoon (2.5 ml) salt (optional)
4 tablespoons (60 g) cold unsalted
  butter
4 tablespoons (60 g) cold
  margarine

In a small saucepan, combine fructose, milk, cornstarch, and cocoa powder. Bring to a boil, stirring constantly. Remove from heat and stir until smooth and thick, about 3 minutes.

Using an electric mixer, beat egg yolk, vanilla, and salt. Add chocolate mixture; beat until smooth. Add butter and margarine, 1 tablespoon (15 ml) at a time, beating after each addition until frosting has consistency of whipped butter. Use to frost one cake; refrigerate until ready to serve.

MAKES ABOUT 1 CUP; 16 SERVINGS

Per serving: calories, 96 ◆ protein, trace ◆ carbohydrate, 10 g ◆ fat 6 g (calories from fat, 56%) ◆ dietary fiber, trace ◆ cholesterol, trace ◆ sodium, 52 mg ◆ potassium, 41 mg Joslin Exchanges: 1 bread/ starch, 1 fat

Mocha Buttercream Frosting

Decrease skim milk to 2 tablespoons (30 ml) and cocoa powder to 1 tablespoon (15 ml). Add 1 heaped teaspoon (heaped 5 ml) instant coffee dissolved in 1 tablespoon (15 ml) boiling water to chocolate mixture.

MAKES ABOUT 1 CUP; 16 SERVINGS

Per serving: calories, 42 ◆ protein, trace ◆ carbohydrate, 6 g ◆ fat, 2 g (calories from fat, 32%) ◆ dietary fiber, trace ◆ cholesterol, 16 mg ◆ sodium, 77 mg ◆ potassium, 41 mg Joslin Exchanges: ½ bread/ starch

Bûche de Noël

It would not be Christmas at either of our homes without a French Yule log cake, complete with meringue mushrooms and fresh holiday greens for a beautiful rich-tasting finale to the feast.

Cake

5 large egg whites
½ cup (118 ml) fructose, whirled in a blender or processor for 10 seconds
½ cup (55 g) sifted cake flour
½ teaspoon (2.5 ml) baking powder

¼ teaspoon (1.25 ml) salt (optional)
2 large egg yolks
¼ teaspoon (1.25 ml) almond extract
2 teaspoons (4 g) confectioners' sugar

Filling

1 cup (236 ml) heavy cream, whipped
2 tablespoons (30 ml) unsweetened cocoa powder

1 tablespoon (15 ml) fructose

Meringue Mushrooms

1 large egg white
pinch of cream of tartar

¼ cup (50 g) superfine sugar

Garnish

holly sprigs or other fresh Christmas greens

Preheat oven to 400°F (205°C). Grease a 15- by 10- by 1-inch (38 by 25 by 2.5 cm) jelly-roll pan. Line bottom with wax paper.

In a large mixing bowl, beat 5 egg whites until stiff. Add ¼ (59 ml) cup fructose; beat well. Sift together remaining ¼ (59 ml) cup fructose, flour, baking powder, and salt.

In a separate bowl, beat egg yolks and almond extract until very light and thick. Fold egg yolks into beaten egg whites. Gently fold in dry ingredients a little at a time. Spread batter evenly in prepared pan. Bake for 12 to 15 minutes or until cake springs back when touched lightly.

Sift confectioners' sugar over a clean kitchen towel. Loosen edges of cake; turn out onto towel. Remove wax paper carefully. Roll up cake and towel from short side. Cool on a wire rack.

Gently combine whipped cream, cocoa, and fructose. Unroll cake and remove towel. Spread a third of the filling on cake. Reroll cake. Cut off a 1-inch (2.5 cm) slice from one end; set aside. Place cake, seam side down, on an oval or rectangular serving platter. Gently press the cut off slice into the side of the "trunk" to simulate a sawed-off branch.

Spread remaining cream mixture on the "trunk" and "branch," with long strokes from one end to the other. Use tines of a fork to simulate bark. Chill cake.

Note: If you are making meringue mushrooms, reserve 3 tablespoons (45 ml) of the cream mixture to use when assembling mushrooms. Chill until ready to use.

To make mushrooms: preheat oven to 250°F (120°C). Grease and flour a cookie sheet.

In a small mixing bowl, beat 1 egg white and cream of tartar until foamy. Gradually beat in sugar until it forms stiff, glossy peaks. Spoon into a pastry bag (page 411) fitted with a large round tip. (Don't fill the bag too full.) Holding the pastry bag fairly close to the cookie sheet, press out ¾-inch-wide (2 cm) mushroom caps. Smooth top if peaked. For stems, hold the bag vertically; press out the meringue. Pull straight up until short stem forms. Continue to make mushroom stems. (Or, using 2 small spoons, form rounded mushroom caps and straight short stems, smoothing out rough edges with the back of a spoon.)

Bake for 30 to 40 minutes, until dry and ivory colored. Loosen with spatula. Cool on a wire rack.

To assemble, make a small hole in the underside of caps. Put in some of the reserved cream. Insert pointed stem end.

Top frosted cake with mushrooms. Decorate platter with holly sprigs. Refrigerate cake until serving time.

MAKES 12 SERVINGS

Per serving (without meringue mushrooms): calories, 124 ♦ protein, 3 g ♦ carbohydrate, 10 g ♦ fat, 8 g (calories from fat, 58%) ♦ dietary fiber, trace ♦ cholesterol, 63 mg ♦ sodium, 102 mg ♦ potassium, 67 mg
Joslin Exchanges: 1 bread/starch, 1 fat

Per serving (with 2 meringue mushrooms): calories, 150 ♦ protein, 3 g ♦ carbohydrate, 16 g ♦ fat, 8 g (calories from fat, 48%) ♦ dietary fiber, trace ♦ cholesterol, 63 mg ♦ sodium, 107 mg ♦ potassium, 70 mg
Joslin Exchanges: 1 bread/starch, 1 fat

Pastry Bag

You can make a pastry bag out of wax paper or parchment paper. Cut a square of paper. Fold it double into a triangle. Roll that into a cone, using a paper clip to hold it in shape. Cut off the tip with a pair of scissors, creating a hole of the desired size.

Fresh Peach Cake

This summer treat is bursting with peach flavor; it's equally delicious made with apricots, nectarines, or plums. When fall arrives, make the cake with apples or pears.

Since this cake is high in simple carbohydrates, it's appropriate only for special occasions.

3 tablespoons (45 g) margarine
2 tablespoons (30 ml) egg substitute
1 large egg white
1 teaspoon (5 ml) fructose*
juice and grated zest of 1 lemon
1 cup (125 g) unbleached flour
½ tablespoon (7.5 ml) baking powder
¼ cup (59 ml) skim milk
butter-flavored cooking spray
3 fresh peaches, about 6 ounces (180 g) each
¼ cup (59 ml) apricot fruit spread (no sugar added)
dash of ground ginger
dash of ground cinnamon

Preheat oven to 400°F (205°C). In a food processor, combine margarine, egg substitute, egg white, fructose, and lemon zest. Process until well blended. Add flour and baking powder alternately with milk. Mix well. Spread batter into a 9-inch (23-cm) cake pan lightly sprayed with cooking spray.

* Substitute ⅓ teaspoon (1.7 ml) saccharin or 1¼ packets acesulfame-K for the fructose. It will not change the exchanges.

Peel peaches, slice in half, and discard pits. Place each half, cut side down, on a cutting board and cut crosswise into thin slices, taking care not to cut all the way through so as to retain shape of peach. Sprinkle with lemon juice. Arrange peaches on batter. Bake for 25 minutes.

Mix together apricot spread, ginger, and cinnamon. Brush onto peaches. Continue baking for 5 to 10 minutes, until top is lightly golden. Remove cake from pan as soon as it is cool and firm enough to handle. Serve lukewarm or cold.

MAKES 12 SERVINGS

Per serving: calories, 104 ◆ protein, 2 g ◆ carbohydrate, 18 g ◆ fat, 3 g (calories from fat, 25%) ◆ dietary fiber, trace ◆ cholesterol, trace ◆ sodium, 88 mg ◆ potassium, 127 mg Joslin Exchanges: 1 bread/starch

Plum or Apricot Tea Cake

A dream of a cake that will become a family favorite. It's a very dense cake that's equally good made with plums or fresh apricots.

1 large egg white	2 teaspoons (10 ml) baking powder
6 tablespoons (90 ml) fresh orange juice	1 tablespoon (15 g) margarine, softened
6 tablespoons (90 ml) skim milk	2 tablespoons (30 ml) fructose*
1 tablespoon (15 ml) grated orange zest	2 large fresh plums or apricots, diced
1½ cups (185 g) unbleached flour, sifted	butter-flavored cooking spray

Preheat oven to 350°F (180°C). In a large bowl, combine egg white, orange juice, milk, and orange zest. Sift together flour and baking powder. Gradually add to egg mixture, mixing well. Stir in margarine, fructose, and apricots or plums. Spread batter into an 8½- by 4½-inch (22 by 11 cm) loaf pan lightly sprayed with cooking spray. Bake for 55 to 65 minutes or until a toothpick inserted in the center comes out clean. Cool in pan for 10 minutes. Transfer cake to a wire rack to finish cooling.

* Substitute 5 packets saccharin or 10 packets aspartame (if you're using aspartame, bake in two loaf pans that are 5 inches (13 cm) in length for 25 to 30 minutes) or 5 packets acesulfame-K for the fructose. It will not change the exchanges.

Wrap cooled cake in plastic wrap or aluminum foil and refrigerate until ready to serve. Cut into ¹/₃-inch (.85 cm) slices.

MAKES ABOUT 10 SERVINGS

Per slice: calories, 96 ◆ protein, 3 g ◆ carbohydrate, 18 g ◆ fat, 1 g (calories from fat, 9%) ◆ dietary fiber, trace ◆ cholesterol, 1 mg ◆ sodium, 93 mg ◆ potassium, 93 mg
Joslin Exchanges: 1 bread/starch

Fresh Pineapple Upside-Down Polenta Cake

We like to bake this light and luscious version of the classic pineapple cake in a cast-iron skillet, but a lightly oiled 10-inch (25 cm) cake pan can also be used.

Instant polenta, available in specialty food stores and many supermarkets, replaces the traditional wheat flour in this recipe for an interesting change in texture and flavor.

Pineapple Layer

1 tablespoon (15 g) margarine
1 tablespoon (13 g) dark brown sugar*
2 tablespoons (30 ml) dark rum or orange juice

1 small fresh pineapple, peeled, cored, and cut into 8 rings

Polenta Cake Layer

2 tablespoons (30 ml) milk
1 teaspoon (4 g) granulated sugar*
¹/₂ ¹/₄-ounce (7 g) package active dry yeast
2 large eggs, separated
5 tablespoons (75 ml) fructose*, whirled in a food processor for 10 seconds

2 teaspoons (10 ml) vanilla extract
²/₃ cup (75 g) instant polenta
2 additional large egg whites

* Substitute ¹/₃ teaspoon (1.7 ml) saccharin or 1¹/₄ packets acesulfame-K for the brown sugar and 10 packets saccharin or 10 packets acesulfame-K for the fructose. It will not change the exchanges.

Preheat oven to 350°F (180°C). Place margarine, dark brown sugar, and rum in the bottom of an 11-inch (28 cm) cast-iron skillet. Place in oven until margarine and sugar melt, about 8 minutes. Mix well.

Arrange pineapple slices over bottom of skillet, cutting some in thirds to fill in gaps between whole slices. Set aside.

In a small saucepan, warm milk. Remove from stove; add granulated sugar and yeast, stirring until yeast is dissolved.

In a large bowl, beat together egg yolks and fructose until mixture is pale yellow. Add vanilla; mix well. Sift polenta into egg mixture, stirring constantly. Add yeast mixture and mix well.

Beat all 4 egg whites until they form stiff peaks. Stir a third of the egg whites into polenta mixture. Carefully fold in remaining egg whites. Pour batter over pineapple layer and smooth top.

Bake for 25 to 30 minutes or until a toothpick inserted in the center comes out clean. Cool cake on a rack, then turn out onto a serving plate.

MAKES 12 SERVINGS

> **Per serving:** calories, 94 ◆ protein, 2 g ◆ carbohydrate, 17 g ◆ fat, 2 g (calories from fat, 19%) ◆ dietary fiber, 0 g ◆ cholesterol, 36 mg ◆ sodium, 41 mg ◆ potassium, 95 mg Joslin Exchanges: 1 bread/starch

Gingerbread

What's autumn without the smell of gingerbread baking? Our slimmed-down version is an easy one-bowl recipe. Just remember: this cake is high in simple carbohydrates, so it's served in very small pieces for special occasions. Date sugar is available at health food stores.

1½ cups (354 ml) water
 1 cup (225 g) date sugar
 4 tablespoons (60 g) margarine, softened
 2 teaspoons (10 ml) ground ginger
 1 teaspoon (5 ml) ground cinnamon

½ teaspoon (2.5 ml) ground cloves
 2 cups (250 g) unbleached flour
 1 teaspoon (5 ml) baking soda
 1 teaspoon (5 ml) baking powder
 1 large egg, slightly beaten
 butter-flavored cooking spray

Preheat oven to 350°F (180°C). In a heavy saucepan, simmer water and date sugar for 5 minutes. Cool. In a large bowl, combine margarine, spices, and cooled date sugar mixture. Add flour, baking powder, baking soda, and egg. Mix until just blended. Pour batter into a 9-inch (23 cm) square baking pan lightly sprayed with cooking spray. Bake for 25 to 35 minutes or until gingerbread pulls away from pan and springs back when touched. Cool in pan for 5 minutes. Transfer cake to a wire rack to continue cooling. Cut into 1½-inch (4 cm) squares.

MAKES ABOUT 25 SERVINGS

> **Per serving:** calories, 84 ◆ protein, 2 g ◆ carbohydrate, 16 g ◆ fat, 2 g (calories from fat, 21%) ◆ dietary fiber, trace ◆ cholesterol, 9 mg ◆ sodium, 71 mg ◆ potassium, 88 mg
> Joslin Exchanges: 1 bread/starch

Key Lime Cheesecake

This dense and creamy cheesecake has the refreshing flavor of Key lime throughout. The Key lime, which is indigenous to the Florida Keys, has a milder, more delicate flavor than the dark green Persian limes we buy all the time. In winter, Key limes are available in some produce markets, or you can buy bottled Key lime juice from specialty markets.

Also try making this cheesecake with the juice of Persian limes or Meyer lemons.

½ tablespoon (7.5 g) margarine
⅓ cup (35 g) graham cracker crumbs, about 5 crackers, crushed
2 cups (450 g) nonfat cottage cheese, drained
14 ounces (400 g) soft tofu, drained
1 cup (236 ml) nonfat yogurt cheese (page 11)
grated zest of 1 Key lime, Persian lime, or lemon

¼ cup (59 ml) Key lime juice, fresh lime juice, or fresh lemon juice
½ teaspoon (2.5 ml) vanilla extract
2 large egg whites
½ cup (118 ml) egg substitute
3 tablespoons (45 ml) fructose*
2 tablespoons (16 g) unbleached flour
1 cup (150 g) fresh strawberries

Grease sides and bottom of a 9-inch (23 cm) springform pan with margarine. Dust with graham cracker crumbs. Refrigerate until ready to fill.

Preheat oven to 350°F (180°C). In a food processor or blender, process cottage cheese and tofu until smooth. Add everything but the strawberries. Process for 3 minutes until very smooth and light. Pour into prepared springform pan. Place a

* Substitute 7 packets saccharin or 7 packets acesulfame-K for the fructose. It will not change the exchanges.

sheet of aluminum foil on the middle rack of the oven under the springform pan to protect oven from any possible leakage. Bake for 1½ to 1¾ hours, until filling is set, slightly puffed, and golden brown on the edges. Cool on a wire rack for 45 minutes. Refrigerate until chilled, 2 hours. Remove the sides of the springform pan. Slice into 16 portions.

Whirl strawberries in a food processor to make a puree. Spoon over each serving.

MAKES 16 SERVINGS

> **Per serving:** calories, 117 ◆ protein, 10 g ◆ carbohydrate, 8 g ◆ fat, 4 g (calories from fat, 30%) ◆ dietary fiber, trace ◆ cholesterol, 1 mg ◆ sodium, 165 mg ◆ potassium, 145 mg Joslin Exchanges: ½ bread/ starch, 1 low-fat meat

COOKIES TO TREASURE

Butter, sugar, eggs, some nuts, or bits of chocolate—all simple enough ingredients that form the basis for hundreds of delicious cookie recipes, except when you're trying to limit the consumption of these everyday items.

We're cookie mavens who think that tea time and "come for a cup of coffee and . . ." means cookies. We've reworked some old favorites that will likely bring back heartwarming memories of your childhood—except our cookies are more wholesome and okay for special occasions if your blood sugars are in good control, as part of your meal plan.

Almond Sugar Cookies

5 tablespoons (75 g) margarine	1 cup (125 g) unbleached flour
1½ tablespoons (22.5 ml) fructose*	⅛ teaspoon (.6 ml) baking soda
1 tablespoon (15 ml) egg white	pinch of cream of tartar
¼ teaspoon (1.25 ml) almond, vanilla, or lemon extract	32 almond slices

Preheat oven to 350°F (180°C). In a medium-size bowl, combine margarine and fructose, beating until light and fluffy. Mix in egg white and almond extract. Gradually stir in flour, baking soda, and cream of tartar; mix well. Form into ½-inch (1.5 cm) balls. Place on a nonstick cookie sheet. Dip a flat-bottomed glass into flour and press down on each ball to flatten cookie. Top each cookie with an almond

---

* Substitute 4 packets saccharin or 8 packets aspartame or 4 packets acesulfame-K for the fructose. It will not change the exchanges.

slice. Bake for 8 to 10 minutes, until lightly browned. Transfer to parchment or wax paper to cool.

MAKES ABOUT 32 COOKIES

> **Per 2-cookie serving:** calories, 90 ◆ protein, 2 g ◆ carbohydrate, 10 g ◆ fat, 4 g (calories from fat, 40%) ◆ dietary fiber, trace ◆ cholesterol, 0 mg ◆ sodium, 49 mg ◆ potassium, 33 mg Joslin Exchanges: 1 bread/ starch, 1 fat

Austrian Apple Bars

½ cup (120 g) margarine
2 cups (250 g) unbleached flour
6 tablespoons (90 ml) fructose
3 tablespoons (45 ml) plain low-fat yogurt
½ teaspoon (2.5 ml) grated lemon zest
4 medium-size Granny Smith apples, peeled and thinly sliced, about 1 pound (450 g)

1 tablespoon (15 ml) dried currants
1 large egg yolk, mixed with 1 teaspoon (5 ml) cold water
4 teaspoons (8 g) confectioners' sugar (optional)

Using a pastry blender or 2 forks, work together margarine and flour. Add 3 tablespoons fructose, yogurt, and lemon zest. Knead to form a dough. Form into a ball, wrap in plastic wrap, and refrigerate for at least 30 minutes.

Preheat oven to 325°F (165°C).

Divide dough into 2 parts. On a lightly floured surface, roll out one part to fit a 9-inch (23 cm) square pan. Arrange apple slices on dough and sprinkle with currants and remaining 3 tablespoons fructose. Roll out remaining dough and cut into ½-inch (1.5 cm) strips. Arrange strips to form a lattice pattern on top of apples. Brush with egg wash. Bake for 20 minutes, until golden brown. Dust with confectioners' sugar while still warm. Cut into 1- by 2-inch (2.5 by 5 cm) bars.

MAKES ABOUT 30 BARS

> **Per bar:** calories, 76 ◆ protein, 1 g ◆ carbohydrate, 11 g ◆ fat, 3 g (calories from fat, 36%) ◆ dietary fiber, trace ◆ cholesterol, 7 mg ◆ sodium, 40 mg ◆ potassium, 33 mg Joslin Exchanges: 1 bread/ starch, ½ fat

Chocolate and Vanilla Swirl Cookies

½ cup (120 g) margarine, softened
2 tablespoons (30 ml) fructose*
2 teaspoons (10 ml) vanilla
   extract
6 tablespoons (90 ml) egg
   substitute or 3 large egg whites
1½ cups (173 g) sifted unbleached
   flour
½ teaspoon (2.5 ml) baking
   powder

¼ cup (59 ml) skim milk, warmed
   to room temperature
1 teaspoon (5 ml) unsweetened
   cocoa powder
⅛ teaspoon (.6 ml) chocolate
   extract
butter-flavored cooking spray

Combine margarine and fructose; add vanilla, egg, flour, baking powder, and 3 tablespoons (45 ml) milk. Divide batter into 2 parts. Add cocoa and chocolate extract to one part, stirring until well blended. Chill both halves for at least an hour. Roll out each part to a rectangle about 3 inches (8 cm) wide. Place chocolate dough on top of plain dough. Press together lightly with a rolling pin. Brush chocolate dough with remaining tablespoon (15 ml) of milk. Roll up like a jelly roll to make a log about 1½ inches (4 cm) in diameter. Wrap in wax paper; chill until firm, about 2 hours.

    Preheat oven to 375°F (190°C). Slice cookies ⅛ inch (.5 cm) thick. Bake on a nonstick cookie sheet lightly sprayed with cooking spray for 8 minutes. Cool on a wire rack.

MAKES ABOUT 60 COOKIES

Ribbon Cookies Variation

Roll out 2 vanilla and 2 chocolate rectangles. Starting with vanilla layer, brush with milk. Top with chocolate layer; brush with warm milk. Add second vanilla layer and second chocolate layer. Press together lightly. Chill for 1 hour. Slice into thin ribbons and bake as directed.

MAKES ABOUT 60 COOKIES

Per 3-cookie serving: calories, 85 ◆ protein, 2 g ◆ carbohydrate, 8 g ◆ fat, 5 g (calories from fat, 53%) ◆ dietary fiber, trace ◆ cholesterol, trace ◆ sodium, 73 mg ◆ potassium, 37 mg Joslin Exchanges: 1 bread/ starch, 1 fat

*Substitute 5 packets saccharin or 10 packets aspartame or 5 packets acesulfame-K for the fructose. It will not change the exchanges.

Chocolate Meringue Kisses

4 large egg whites at room temperature
¼ teaspoon (1.25 ml) cream of tartar

2 tablespoons (30 ml) honey
1 teaspoon (5 ml) almond extract
¼ cup (43 g) semisweet chocolate pieces

Preheat oven to 375°F (190°C). Line 2 baking sheets with parchment paper.

In a large bowl, beat egg whites and cream of tartar until foamy. Beat in honey and almond extract until egg whites form stiff peaks. Drop by tablespoonfuls onto prepared baking sheets. Place 1 baking sheet on the middle shelf of the oven. Close oven door and immediately turn oven off. Leave baking sheet in the oven for 1½ hours. Transfer cookies to a wire rack.

Again, preheat oven to 375°F (190°C). Bake second sheet of cookies in the same manner. Transfer cookies to a wire rack.

Place chocolate pieces in a plastic bag. Microwave on HIGH for 1 to 1½ minutes, until chocolate is melted. Snip one corner of bag; drizzle chocolate over meringue kisses with zigzag motions.

MAKES ABOUT 48 COOKIES

> **Per 6-cookie serving:** calories, 52 ◆ protein, 2 g ◆ carbohydrate, 8 g ◆ fat, 2 g (calories from fat, 34%) ◆ dietary fiber, trace ◆ cholesterol, 0 mg ◆ sodium, 35 mg ◆ potassium, 48 mg Joslin Exchanges: ½ bread/ starch

Note: Meringue can be tricky; don't make these on a rainy day—humidity prevents proper drying.

Dried Cherry Oatmeal Delights

½ cup (78 g) dried cherries, chopped (no sugar added)
2 tablespoons (30 ml) frozen orange juice concentrate, defrosted
1½ cups (234 g) rolled oats
½ cup (60 g) unbleached flour

½ tablespoon (7.5 ml) ground cinnamon
½ teaspoon (2.5 ml) baking soda
1 teaspoon (5 ml) fructose
½ cup (120 g) margarine, melted
1 large egg white

In a small bowl, combine cherries and orange juice concentrate. Set aside to soak for 30 minutes.

Preheat oven to 375° F (190° C). In a large bowl, combine oats, flour, cinnamon, baking soda, and fructose. Stir in melted margarine, egg white, and cherries with juice. Drop by rounded teaspoons onto a nonstick cookie sheet. Bake for 10 minutes, until lightly browned. Let sit on baking sheet for a few moments; transfer to parchment paper to cool.

MAKES ABOUT 30 COOKIES

Per 2-cookie serving: calories, 118 ◆ protein, 2 g ◆ carbohydrate, 13 g ◆ fat, 7 g (calories from fat, 50%) ◆ dietary fiber, 1 g ◆ cholesterol, 0 mg ◆ sodium, 103 mg ◆ potassium, 125 mg
Joslin Exchanges: 1 bread/starch, 1 fat

Note: These cookies are equally delicious made with dried apricots.

Fruited Meringue Drops

1 cup (130 g) mixed dried fruit
3 tablespoons (45 ml) chopped pecans
2 large egg whites at room temperature
1/8 teaspoon (.6 ml) cream of tartar
1 tablespoon (15 ml) honey
1/2 teaspoon (2.5 ml) vanilla extract

Preheat oven to 375° F (190° C). Line a cookie sheet with parchment paper.

Place dried fruit and pecans in a food processor and process until finely minced.

In a large bowl, beat egg whites and cream of tartar until foamy. Beat in honey and vanilla until egg whites form stiff peaks. Gently fold in fruit mixture. Drop by tablespoonfuls onto prepared cookie sheet. Place cookie sheet on middle shelf of oven. Close oven door and immediately turn oven off. Leave baking sheet in the oven for 1 1/2 hours. Transfer cookies to a wire rack.

MAKES 30 COOKIES

Per 4-cookie serving: calories, 74 ◆ protein, 2 g ◆ carbohydrate, 14 g ◆ fat, 2 g (calories from fat, 25%) ◆ dietary fiber, trace ◆ cholesterol, 0 mg ◆ sodium, 20 mg ◆ potassium, 266 mg
Joslin Exchanges: 1 fruit

Note: Meringue can be tricky; don't make these on a rainy day—humidity prevents proper drying.

German Loaf Cookies

2½ tablespoons (37.5 ml) fructose
½ cup (118 ml) egg substitute or 1 large egg plus 2 large egg whites
4 tablespoons (60 g) softened margarine
juice and grated zest of 1 lemon
⅛ teaspoon (.6 ml) almond extract
1½ cups (173 g) sifted unbleached flour

2¾ teaspoons (13.75 ml) baking powder
½ tablespoon (7.5 ml) unsweetened cocoa powder
½ teaspoon (2.5 ml) ground cinnamon

Preheat oven to 350° F (180° C). Combine fructose and egg substitute; beat until light and fluffy. Add margarine, lemon juice, lemon zest, almond extract, flour, and baking powder. Mix well. Place three-quarters of the dough mixture on a floured board. Form into a rectangle about ¾ inch (2 cm) thick.

Add cocoa and cinnamon to remaining dough and spread over rectangle. Fold both sides of dough into the middle to make a long, flattened log. Place on ungreased baking sheet and bake for 40 minutes, until lightly browned.

Remove from oven and slice with a very sharp knife into ½-inch (1.5 cm) slices. Preheat broiler. Place slices on an ungreased baking sheet and broil for a few moments on each side (be careful; these burn easily). Cool on a wire rack. Store in an airtight container.

MAKES ABOUT 30 COOKIES

Per 2-cookie serving: calories, 85 ◆ protein, 2 g ◆ carbohydrate, 11 g ◆ fat, 4 g (calories from fat, 42%) ◆ dietary fiber, trace ◆ cholesterol, trace ◆ sodium, 92 mg ◆ potassium, 56 mg Joslin Exchanges: 1 bread/starch, ½ fat

Oatmeal Cookies

1½ cups (234 g) rolled oats
½ cup (60 g) unbleached flour
½ tablespoon (7.5 ml) ground cinnamon
½ teaspoon (2.5 ml) baking soda
1 teaspoon (5 ml) fructose (optional)

2½ tablespoons (37.5 ml) frozen peach juice concentrate, defrosted
½ cup (120 g) margarine, melted
butter-flavored cooking spray

Preheat oven to 375° F (190° C). In a large bowl, combine oats, flour, cinnamon, baking soda, and fructose. Add defrosted peach juice concentrate and margarine; mix well. Drop by rounded teaspoons onto a nonstick cookie sheet lightly sprayed with cooking spray. Bake for 10 minutes, until lightly browned. Let sit on baking sheet for a minute or two, then transfer to parchment paper to cool.

MAKES ABOUT 30 COOKIES

Per 2-cookie serving: calories, 102 ◆ protein, 2 g ◆ carbohydrate, 9 g ◆ fat, 7 g (calories from fat, 61%) ◆ dietary fiber, trace ◆ cholesterol, 0 mg ◆ sodium, 99 mg ◆ potassium, 37 mg Joslin Exchanges: ½ bread/ starch, 1 fat

Poppy Seed Cookies

½ cup (120 g) margarine, softened
1 tablespoon (15 ml) fructose*
½ cup (118 ml) warm skim milk
1 ounce (30 g) poppy seeds
1 teaspoon (5 ml) ground cinnamon
½ teaspoon (2.5 ml) ground cloves

⅛ teaspoon (.6 ml) ground nutmeg
1¼ cups (144 g) sifted unbleached flour
1 teaspoon (5 ml) baking powder
¼ cup (59 ml) dried currants

Preheat oven to 350° F (180° C). Cream together margarine and fructose. Add everything but the currants; mix well. Stir in currants. Drop by rounded teaspoons onto a nonstick cookie sheet. Bake for 15 minutes, until lightly browned. Cool on a wire rack.

MAKES ABOUT 36 COOKIES

Per 2-cookie serving: calories, 105 ◆ protein, 2 g ◆ carbohydrate, 10 g ◆ fat 7 g (calories from fat, 60%) ◆ dietary fiber, trace ◆ cholesterol, trace ◆ sodium, 86 mg ◆ potassium, 76 mg Joslin Exchanges: 1 bread/ starch, 1 fat

* Substitute 3 packets saccharin or 6 packets aspartame or 3 packets acesulfame-K for the fructose. It will not change the exchanges.

Raspberry Thumbprints

¼ cup (60 g) margarine, softened
3 tablespoons (45 ml) fructose*
1 large egg white
1 teaspoon (5 ml) vanilla extract

1⅓ cups (142 g) sifted cake flour
butter-flavored cooking spray
5 tablespoons (75 ml) raspberry
   fruit spread (no sugar added)

In a large bowl, cream together margarine and fructose until light and fluffy. Add egg white and vanilla; beat well. Stir in flour. Using your hands, form dough into a ball. Wrap in plastic wrap and chill for at least 30 minutes.

Preheat oven to 350° F (180° C). Shape dough into 1-inch (2.5 cm) balls. Place 2 inches (5 cm) apart on cookie sheet lightly sprayed with cooking spray. Using your thumb, press a hole in the center of each cookie. Bake for 8 to 10 minutes, until golden. Cool completely on wire racks.

Spoon ½ teaspoon (2.5 ml) fruit spread into center of each cookie. Store cookies in tightly covered container.

MAKES 16 COOKIES

Per 1-cookie serving: calories, 85 ♦ protein, 1 g ♦ carbohydrate, 14 g ♦ fat, 3 g (calories from fat, 31%) ♦ dietary fiber, trace ♦ cholesterol, 0 mg ♦ sodium, 43 mg ♦ potassium, 15 mg Joslin Exchanges: 1 bread/starch

* Substitute 7 packets saccharin or 14 packets aspartame or 7 packets acesulfame-K for the fructose. It will not change the exchanges.

FIRESIDE TEA*

◆

Quartered Open-Face Sliced Turkey Sandwiches with Cold

Cucumber Sauce (page 122) on Walnut Raisin Whole-Wheat

Peasant Bread (page 399)

Quartered Open-Face Tomato, Arugula, and Low-fat Goat

Cheese Sandwiches on Herb Bread (page 397)

Irish Oatmeal Scones with Dried Cherries (page 391)

All-Fruit Jam

Cookie and Tea Bread Tray

Fresh Strawberries and Crème Fraîche (page 428)

Tea

* Caution: This special menu is high in calories and exchanges—if you have diabetes, carefully watch your exchanges and make sure they are worked into your meal plan. Since you'll likely be counting this as a snack (typically 2 bread/starch and 1 meat exchange), your plate could include 2 quartered turkey sandwiches, 2 quartered tomato, arugula, and goat cheese sandwiches, and 1 scone with 1½ teaspoons of the all-fruit jam (or the sandwiches and 2 cookies or the sandwiches and 1 slice of tea bread). The strawberries and crème fraîche are for the guests.

Basic Pie Pastry

A secret to making good piecrust is to work in a cool kitchen and to have your ingredients very cold—the margarine frozen and the water ice cold.

Our lightened recipe is made in a food processor, but you can also cut in the margarine with a pastry blender or your fingertips. Although the crust has less fat than most recipes, it's quite flaky and tender.

Pie dough will keep in the refrigerator for up to three days or in the freezer for six months.

½ teaspoon (1 g) sugar
1 cup (125 g) unbleached flour
½ teaspoon (2.5 ml) lemon zest
4 tablespoons (60 g) frozen margarine, cut into ½-inch (1.5 cm) pieces

2 tablespoons (30 ml) plus 2 teaspoons (10 ml) ice water

In a food processor, process sugar, flour, lemon zest, and margarine for 5 seconds. Add water and process for another 5 seconds. Remove dough (even if not completely mixed) and press it between 2 sheets of plastic wrap. Pat into a 4-inch (10 cm) circle. Wrap securely and chill for at least 1 hour.

Preheat oven to 375° F (190° C). Roll dough out on a lightly floured board to ⅛-inch (.5 cm) thickness. Fit loosely into an 8- or 9-inch (20 or 23 cm) pie or tart pan. Prick bottom and sides with a fork. Bake for 8 minutes before filling.

Note: For a 10-inch (25 cm) tart shell, make 1½ times the recipe.

MAKES 12 SERVINGS

Per serving: calories, 70 ◆ protein, 1 g ◆ carbohydrate, 8 g ◆ fat, 4 g (calories from fat, 51%) ◆ dietary fiber, trace ◆ cholesterol, 0 mg ◆ sodium, 51 mg ◆ potassium, 12 mg Joslin Exchanges: ½ bread/ starch, 1 fat

Apple Cherry Cobbler

Apples are a year-round staple in our kitchens. This homey dessert rises to company status with the addition of dried cherries macerated in Calvados. Choose a tart apple with good baking quality such as Granny Smith, Gravenstein, or Jonathan.

Dried cherries with no sugar added are available by mail order (see Appendix 2) or use all apples and sprinkle the Calvados over the apples.

6 ounces (180 g) dried cherries (no sugar added)

3 tablespoons (45 ml) Calvados, apple brandy, or unsweetened apple juice

3 tart apples, about 1 pound (450 g)

2 tablespoons (30 ml) fresh lemon juice

½ teaspoon (2.5 ml) ground cardamom

1 basic pie pastry (page 425)

2 tablespoons (12 g) sugar

Preheat oven to 350° F (180° C). Combine dried cherries with Calvados: set aside for 15 minutes. Meanwhile, peel and core the apples; slice thinly lengthwise. Sprinkle apples with lemon juice and cardamom. Combine macerated cherries and apples.

Roll out dough into a large, ragged circle about 14 inches (35 cm) in diameter. Fit dough into an 8-inch (20 cm) round ovenproof dish at least 2 inches (5 cm) deep, allowing excess pastry to drape over the edge. Place apples and cherries in the prepared dish, mounding slightly in the middle. Bring pastry up and over apples and cherries. (It will not quite cover the fruit.) Sprinkle with sugar.

Bake for 45 minutes, or until the crust is brown and filling is bubbling.

MAKES 10 SERVINGS

Per serving: calories, 173 ◆ protein, 2 g ◆ carbohydrate, 28 g ◆ fat, 7 g (calories from fat, 36%) ◆ dietary fiber, 1 g ◆ cholesterol, 18 mg ◆ sodium, 74 mg ◆ potassium, 323 mg Joslin Exchanges: 2 bread/ starch, 1 fat

Fresh Peach Tart

Fruits for tarts are generally interchangeable. This tart could also be filled with nectarines, plums, apricots, apples, or pears. Choose fruit that is blemishless and firm yet ripe.

4 peaches, about 1 pound (450 g), peeled and thinly sliced
1 tablespoon (8 g) unbleached flour
dash of ground cinnamon or nutmeg
1 partially baked 9-inch (23 cm) basic pie pastry shell (page 425)
1 tablespoon (15 g) butter or margarine

½ cup (118 ml) apricot fruit spread (no sugar added), thinned with 1 tablespoon (15 ml) fresh lemon juice and melted
1 tablespoon (15 ml) finely ground almonds or hazelnuts for garnish

Preheat oven to 375° F (190° C). Toss peaches with flour and cinnamon; arrange in concentric circles in partially baked pastry shell. Dot with butter. Bake for 45 minutes, until crust is golden brown and peaches are tender. Brush with melted fruit spread; sprinkle with finely ground almonds.

MAKES 12 SERVINGS

Per serving: calories, 151 ◆ protein, 2 g ◆ carbohydrate, 20 g ◆ fat, 8 g (calories from fat, 47%) ◆ dietary fiber, trace ◆ cholesterol, 18 mg ◆ sodium, 84 mg ◆ potassium, 98 mg Joslin Exchanges: 1 bread/ starch, 1 fat

Coeur à la Crème

This classic French summer dessert, literally "heart of the cream," is easy to make even if you don't own the traditional porcelain heart-shaped mold for draining the cheese. We use a double layer of cheesecloth in a colander or basket to allow the whey to drain out, then shape the fresh cheese in a heart-shaped mold. A basket shape is pretty too; you can mold it in the draining basket.

Fresh strawberries are usually served with this luscious dessert, but raspberries, blueberries, blackberries, or a berry mixture is equally delicious. Remember to start this dessert the day before you plan to serve it.

2 cups (472 ml) plain nonfat yogurt
2 cups (450 g) nonfat ricotta cheese
grated zest of 1 lemon or 1 orange

¼ teaspoon (1.25 ml) vanilla
  extract
3 cups (450 g) strawberries, hulled
  and sliced

Using a food processor or electric mixer, combine yogurt and ricotta cheese; process until smooth. Line a colander or basket with a double layer of cheesecloth, letting cloth hang over edges. Spoon cheese mixture into colander. Fold cheesecloth over top and place colander over a bowl or baking dish to catch the whey. Refrigerate for 24 hours. Scrape cheese from cheesecloth; add lemon zest and vanilla.

Line a 3-cup (708 ml) heart-shaped mold (or the draining basket) with cheesecloth, again allowing cloth to hang over edges. Spoon cheese mixture into mold, smoothing the top. Fold cheesecloth over cheese; chill for 3 hours.

To serve, unfold cheesecloth and invert mold onto a serving platter. Remove cheesecloth. Surround cheese with sliced berries.

MAKES 8 SERVINGS

Per serving: calories, 90 ◆ protein, 11 g ◆ carbohydrate, 10 g ◆ fat, 1 g (calories from fat, 10%) ◆ dietary fiber, trace ◆ cholesterol, 4 mg ◆ sodium, 274 mg ◆ potassium, 286 mg
Joslin Exchanges: 1 low-fat milk

Crème Fraîche

By adding cultured buttermilk to plain low-fat yogurt you'll get a lightened version of crème fraîche, the cultured, slightly acidic cream. It's wonderful spooned on berries and other fresh fruit for a quick dessert. We also keep it on hand for topping vegetables, stirring into soups and sauces, or thinning with a little raspberry vinegar as a delicious dressing for watercress or sliced tomato salads. It will keep in the refrigerator for at least a week. If a little water accumulates on the surface, just stir it in.

¼ cup (59 ml) cultured buttermilk   4 cups (1 l) plain low-fat yogurt

In a large saucepan, combine buttermilk and yogurt; heat until lukewarm, about 1 minute (do not overheat). Remove from heat, cover, and let stand at room temperature for 24 hours. Refrigerate until ready to use.

MAKES 4¼ CUPS

Per ¼-cup (59 ml) serving: calories, 35 ◆ protein, 3 g ◆ carbohydrate, 4 g ◆ fat, 1 g (calories from fat, 25%) ◆ dietary fiber, 0 g ◆ cholesterol, 4 mg ◆ sodium, 42 mg ◆ potassium, 130 mg Joslin Exchanges: ½ nonfat milk

Nectarine Mousse

When you're looking for a light summer dessert, try this delicious concoction spooned into pretty glasses. A bit of crème fraîche (page 428) could be used as a topping.

¼ cup (59 ml) plus 2 tablespoons (30 ml) water
¼ cup (59 ml) dry white wine or unsweetened apple juice
juice of ½ lemon
2 tablespoons (30 ml) frozen peach juice concentrate

1 pound (450 g) fresh nectarines, peeled, pitted, and coarsely chopped
1 ¼-ounce (7 g) envelope unflavored gelatin
6 large whole strawberries, unhulled

In a large saucepan, bring ¼ cup (59 ml) water, wine, lemon juice, and frozen peach concentrate to a boil. Add nectarines and simmer until fruit is soft.

Meanwhile, soften gelatin in 2 tablespoons (30 ml) water. Add to fruit mixture, stirring until gelatin has dissolved. Remove from stove and cool for 5 minutes. Place mixture in a food processor or blender; process until smooth.

Spoon into 6 parfait glasses. Chill for at least 2 hours. Make 5 lengthwise cuts in each strawberry, taking care not to cut through stem. Garnish each serving with a strawberry, gently spreading berry to resemble a fan.

MAKES 6 SERVINGS

Per serving: calories, 60 ◆ protein, 2 g ◆ carbohydrate, 14 g ◆ fat, trace (calories from fat, less than 1%) ◆ dietary fiber, trace ◆ cholesterol, 0 mg ◆ sodium, 2 mg ◆ potassium, 263 mg Joslin Exchanges: 1 fruit

Strawberry Parfaits

Try a combination of raspberries, blackberries, and strawberries instead of just strawberries for variety.

1 cup (236 ml) unsweetened apple juice	½ cup (118 ml) crème fraîche (page 428)
2 tablespoons (30 ml) cornstarch	6 almond slices
1 tablespoon (15 ml) grated lemon or orange zest	2 tablespoons (30 ml) graham cracker crumbs or crushed gingersnaps
4 cups (1 l) fresh strawberries, washed, hulled, and sliced	

Combine ¼ cup (59 ml) of the apple juice with cornstarch. Stir into remaining apple juice and simmer over low heat until a thick syrup forms. Remove from heat; add lemon zest. Set aside to cool. When cool, toss with fruit.

Divide half the strawberry mixture among 6 decorative glasses. Top each with 1 tablespoon (15 ml) crème fraîche. Cover with remaining strawberry mixture. Chill.

Just before serving, top each parfait with 1 teaspoon (5 ml) crème fraîche, an almond slice, and some of the graham cracker crumbs.

MAKES 6 SERVINGS

Per serving: calories, 107 ◆ protein, 3 g ◆ carbohydrate, 17 g ◆ fat, 3 g (calories from fat, 25%) ◆ dietary fiber, 3 g ◆ cholesterol, 1 mg ◆ sodium, 24 mg ◆ potassium, 300 mg
Joslin Exchanges: 1 bread/starch

Balsamic Vinegar

Sprinkle balsamic vinegar over fresh fruit—sliced peaches, whole strawberries, raspberries, chunks of fresh pineapple, or melon—with a little cracked black pepper. Couldn't be simpler or more wonderful to eat.

Filo Tulips

Greek filo dough is a godsend for those in search of low-fat desserts. It takes almost any shape and holds almost anything—we use it often for light, special desserts. The parchmentlike dough is sold fresh or frozen in most supermarkets and Middle Eastern specialty food shops. It comes in 1-pound packages containing about 24 to 32 sheets. Keep it in your freezer for impromptu desserts. (See page 159 for defrosting instructions.)

butter-flavored cooking spray   choice of fillings (recipes follow)
2 14- by 18-inch (35 x 46 cm) filo
   dough

Preheat oven to 375° F (190° C). Spray four 1-cup (236 ml) custard cups with cooking spray.

With a sharp knife, trim off and discard 4 inches (10 cm) from the top of each filo sheet, leaving two 14-inch (35 cm) squares. Cut each sheet into quarters.

Spray 1 quarter with cooking spray. Spray a second quarter with cooking spray and place it catercorner on top of first quarter to form an 8-pointed star. Lift both quarters off work surface and press them into a custard cup to form a tulip shape. Repeat, making 3 more tulips.

Place filled custard cups on a baking sheet. Bake for 8 to 10 minutes, until golden. Carefully remove tulips from custard cups (the filo will be brittle). Cool on wire racks.

To serve, place filo tulips on individual dessert plates. Fill with selected filling.

MAKES 4 SERVINGS

Per serving: calories, 23 ◆ protein, 1 g ◆ carbohydrate, 5 g ◆ fat, trace (calories from fat, less than 1%) ◆ dietary fiber, 0 g ◆ cholesterol, 0 mg ◆ sodium, 0 mg ◆ potassium, 0 mg
Joslin Exchanges: ½ bread/starch

Here are some of our favorite fillings:

Mixed Summer Fruits

1 cup (236 ml) fresh raspberries
1 cup (236 ml) blueberries
1 cup (236 ml) strawberries
1 cup (236 ml) diced cantaloupe
1 cup (236 ml) blackberries
2 kiwifruit, sliced

Mix fruits and fill filo cups with them.

MAKES 4 SERVINGS

Per serving (filo cup and filling): calories, 69 ◆ protein, 1 g ◆ carbohydrate, 16 g ◆ fat, 1 g (calories from fat, 13%) ◆ dietary fiber, 2 g ◆ cholesterol, 0 mg ◆ sodium, 3 mg ◆ potassium, 141 mg Joslin Exchanges: 1 fruit

Frozen Yogurt

1 pint nonfat, sugar-free commercial frozen yogurt

Fill filo cups with frozen yogurt.

MAKES 4 SERVINGS

Per serving (filo cup and ½ cup/118 ml filling): calories, 96 ◆ protein, 6 g ◆ carbohydrate, 18 g ◆ fat, 0 g (calories from fat, 0%) ◆ dietary fiber, trace ◆ cholesterol, 0 mg ◆ sodium, 240 mg ◆ potassium, n/a Joslin Exchanges: 1 bread/starch

Raspberry Sorbet

3 cups (375 g) fresh raspberries
⅓ to ½ cup (78 to 118 ml) water

¼ cup (59 ml) fructose or frozen apple juice concentrate

Puree berries in a food processor. Force through a strainer to remove most of the seeds, forming a thick juice of about 1⅓ to 1½ cups (314 to 354 ml). In a heavy saucepan, bring water and fructose to a boil; stir until fructose is dissolved. Add berry puree; blend well. Transfer to a bowl, cover, and chill in the refrigerator.

Freeze mixture in an electric or hand-cranked ice cream maker, following manufacturer's instructions.

MAKES ABOUT 2 CUPS (472 ML)

Per ½-cup serving: calories, 97 ◆ protein, 1 g ◆ carbohydrate, 23 g ◆ fat, 1 g (calories from fat, 9%) ◆ dietary fiber, 3 g ◆ cholesterol, 0 mg ◆ sodium, 1 mg ◆ potassium, 219 mg Joslin Exchanges: 1½ fruit

Note: Other fruits can be used instead of raspberries—pears, strawberries, blackberries, peaches, nectarines, mango, kiwifruit, apples.

Sautéed Peaches with Apricot Sauce

Dessert in minutes. Try nectarines instead of peaches.

10 dried apricots
¼ cup (59 ml) dry white wine or
  unsweetened apple juice
2 tablespoons (30 ml) fresh lemon
  juice
⅓ cup (78 ml) water
1 teaspoon (5 ml) grated lemon or
  orange zest

4 large fresh peaches
butter-flavored cooking spray
½ teaspoon (2.5 g) unsalted butter
6 tablespoons (90 ml) nonfat
  yogurt cheese (page 11)
  (optional)

In a small saucepan, combine apricots, wine, lemon juice, and water. Simmer until apricots are soft and most of the liquid has evaporated, about 10 minutes. Add lemon zest and puree mixture in a food processor or blender until smooth. Set aside.

Peel and pit peaches. Lightly spray a nonstick skillet with cooking spray. Add peaches and sauté over low heat, stirring constantly, until peaches are warmed through. Add butter and stir.

Divide peaches among 6 dessert plates. Top with 1 tablespoon (15 ml) apricot puree and 1 tablespoon (15 ml) yogurt cheese if desired.

MAKES 6 SERVINGS

Per serving: calories, 64 ◆ protein, 2 g ◆ carbohydrate, 14 g ◆ fat, trace (calories from fat, 7%) ◆ dietary fiber, 2 g ◆ cholesterol, 1 mg ◆ sodium, 16 mg ◆ potassium, 251 mg
Joslin Exchanges: 1 fruit

Grilled Bananas

Often when we're grilling we throw some fresh fruit on the barbecue for a quick dessert. Bananas are a particular favorite—and very easy. To prepare, do not peel. Cut bananas in half lengthwise. Grill, cut side down, 4 to 6 inches (10 to 15 cm) from source of heat, for 4 to 6 minutes. When done, squeeze fresh lime juice over cooked banana. Serve in its skin. (^{1}/$_2$ 9-inch/23 cm banana equals one fruit exchange).

Note: You can also grill peeled cantaloupe wedges (3 to 4 minutes), unpeeled nectarines and peach halves (6 to 8 minutes), seeded papaya rings (5 to 8 minutes), and peeled, cored fresh pineapple rings (6 to 8 minutes). Squeeze lime juice over cooked fruit.

Check fruit exchanges (Appendix 1) to determine serving size for one exchange.

Dessert Fruit Combinations

Fresh fruit is our favorite and most frequent dessert. Here are some combinations that we like—all equal one fruit exchange.

- star fruit/carambola (^{1}/$_2$ large star fruit), cut into slices, and fresh blackberries (^{1}/$_3$ cup/78 ml), topped with grated lemon zest and freshly grated nutmeg
- banana (^{1}/$_4$ 9-inch banana), cut in half lengthwise, and fresh raspberries (^{1}/$_2$ cup/236 ml), topped with grated lemon zest and minced fresh basil
- peach (^{1}/$_2$ small peach) and fresh blueberries (^{1}/$_3$ cup/78 ml), topped with grated lemon zest and a sprinkling of chopped fresh ginger
- diced watermelon (^{1}/$_2$ cup/118 ml) and fresh boysenberries (^{1}/$_3$ cup/78 ml), topped with grated lemon zest and chopped fresh mint
- diced fresh pineapple (^{1}/$_3$ cup/78 ml), topped with a puree (use a food processor or blender) of fresh raspberries (^{1}/$_2$ cup/118 ml) and 1 tablespoon (15 ml) fresh lemon juice and sprinkled with freshly grated nutmeg

Cantaloupe Graníta

Similar to a sorbet, but more granular in texture, this graníta freezes easily in a metal pan or bowl. This is also lovely made with honeydew. Sometimes we make both kinds and serve a ¼-cup (59 ml) scoop of each, side by side, in a stemmed glass.

2 cantaloupes or 1 honeydew melon	¼ cup (59 ml) fresh lime juice

Seed and peel melon; cut into chunks. Whirl enough of the fruit in a food processor or blender to make 3 cups (708 ml) puree. Add lime juice. Pour into a shallow metal pan or bowl. Freeze firm. Let stand at room temperature until soft enough to break up with a wooden spoon. Transfer to a large bowl and smash into small pieces. Beat until slushy and fairly smooth. Cover and refreeze. Soften at room temperature for about 5 minutes before serving.

MAKES 6 SERVINGS

Per ½-cup (118 ml) serving: calories, 46 ◆ protein, 1 g ◆ carbohydrate, 11 g ◆ fat, 0 g (calories from fat, 0%) ◆ dietary fiber, 1 g ◆ cholesterol, 0 mg ◆ sodium, 11 mg ◆ potassium, 382 mg Joslin Exchanges: 1 fruit

Pear Clafouti

Our version of this country-French dessert has a rich custard pudding topping. You can substitute sliced apples for the pears and raspberries or blackberries for the strawberries.

1 pound (450 g) Bartlett pears	2 large egg whites
butter-flavored cooking spray	1 teaspoon (5 ml) dry sherry or dry port (optional)
⅔ cup (85 g) sliced fresh strawberries	½ teaspoon (2.5 ml) ground ginger
juice of ½ lemon	2 to 3 drops almond extract, to taste (optional)
¾ cup (177 ml) skim milk	2 tablespoons (30 ml) fructose*
3 tablespoons (23 g) unbleached flour	1½ tablespoons (22 g) margarine
¼ cup (59 ml) egg substitute	

* Substitute 5 packets saccharin or 5 packets acesulfame-K for the fructose. It will not change the exchanges.

Preheat oven to 400° F (205° C). Peel pears, cut in half, and scoop out core and seeds. Cut each pear into 8 equal-size pieces. Arrange in a pretty 12-cup (2.75 l) round baking dish lightly sprayed with cooking spray. Arrange strawberries between pears. Sprinkle with lemon juice.

In a food processor or blender, place milk, flour, egg substitute, egg whites, sherry, ginger, almond extract, and fructose. Process until smooth. Pour batter over fruit. Dot with margarine. Bake for 30 to 40 minutes, until golden in color and custard has set. Cool for 15 minutes before serving.

MAKES 8 SERVINGS

Per serving: calories, 95 ◆ protein, 3 g ◆ carbohydrate, 15 g ◆ fat, 3 g (calories from fat, 28%) ◆ dietary fiber, 1 g ◆

cholesterol, 1 mg ◆ sodium, 69 mg ◆ potassium, 171 mg
Joslin Exchanges: 1 fruit, ½ fat

Poached Pears with Roasted Plum Sauce

Poached pears, standing upright in a pool of plum sauce and sprinkled with pistachios, are visually stunning. This easy-to-make dessert is absolutely delicious.

4 small, firm Bosc pears, about 1 pound (450 g)
2 cups (472 ml) dry white wine or unsweetened apple juice
3¼ cups (767 ml) water
5 peppercorns
2 cloves
1 cinnamon stick, 3 inches (8 cm) long
½ pound (225 g) fresh purple plums, halved and pitted

vegetable oil cooking spray
¼ cup (59 ml) unsweetened apple juice
1 tablespoon (15 ml) fructose (optional)
1 tablespoon (15 ml) finely chopped pistachio nuts for garnish
fresh mint sprigs for garnish

Core pears from bottom with a melon baller; peel, leaving stems on. In a medium-size saucepan, bring wine, 3 cups (708 ml) water, peppercorns, cloves, and cinnamon to a boil over high heat. Add pears. If necessary, add enough water to cover pears completely. Reduce heat to simmer, cover pan, and cook for 10 to 15 minutes, until pears are tender but not mushy. Remove from stove, uncover pan, and let pears cool in poaching liquid; refrigerate pears in poaching liquid overnight.

Meanwhile, preheat oven to 275° F (135° C). Place plums on a baking sheet cut side down. Lightly spray with cooking spray. Bake for 30 minutes, until plums are soft and juicy. Remove plums from oven. In a small saucepan, bring apple juice and remaining 1/4 cup (59 ml) water to a boil. Boil until reduced by half. Add plums and cook for another 10 minutes. Transfer mixture to a food processor; puree until smooth. Force through a sieve to remove any bit of peel. Stir in fructose if needed; chill.

When you're ready to serve, divide plum puree among 4 dessert plates. Top with a pear, standing upright. Sprinkle with pistachio nuts and garnish with mint sprigs.

MAKES 4 SERVINGS

Per serving: calories, 128 ◆ protein, 1 g ◆ carbohydrate, 27 g ◆ fat, 2 g (calories from fat, 14%) ◆ dietary fiber, 2 g ◆ cholesterol, 0 mg ◆ sodium, 6 mg ◆ potassium, 286 mg Joslin Exchanges: 2 fruit

 Warm Grapefruit and Orange with Sherry Sauce

A pretty dessert to pile into glass dessert cups or short-stemmed goblets.

2 large ruby grapefruits, about 3/4 pound (340 g) each
2 large navel oranges, about 10 ounces (285 g) each
1/4 cup (59 ml) dry sherry or unsweetened grapefruit juice

1 tablespoon (15 ml) grated orange zest
1 tablespoon (15 ml) sliced almonds

With a very sharp knife, remove rind and white pith from grapefruits and oranges. Working over a bowl, section fruits carefully, cutting between membranes so sections come out whole. Place sections in a covered microwave dish. Reserve juice.

In a small saucepan, combine sherry, 1/4 cup (59 ml) reserved juice, and orange zest. Simmer to reduce by half. Set aside.

Microwave fruit sections on HIGH for 1 to 1½ minutes, until heated through. Toss with sauce.

Pile fruit sections into dessert dishes; sprinkle with nuts.

MAKES 6 SERVINGS

> **Per serving:** calories, 52 ◆ protein, 1 g ◆ carbohydrate, 12 g ◆ fat, 1 g (calories from fat, 12%) ◆ dietary fiber, 2 g ◆ cholesterol, 0 mg ◆ sodium, trace ◆ potassium, 194 mg Joslin Exchanges: 1 fruit

Lemon Sponge Pudding

The rage of the fifties, pudding cakes frequently showed up at our family gatherings and potluck church suppers. As teenagers we loved the overly sweet taste of the sponge cake on top with lemon pudding underneath.

Our lightened version is refreshing and not as sweet, with a delicious lemony flavor.

3 tablespoons (45 g) margarine, melted
5 tablespoons (75 ml) fructose*
6 tablespoons (90 ml) egg substitute
grated zest of 1 lemon
½ cup (118 ml) fresh lemon juice

1 cup (236 ml) skim milk
⅓ cup (42 g) unbleached flour
3 large egg whites at room temperature
pinch of cream of tartar

Preheat oven to 325° F (165° C). In a medium-size bowl, beat melted margarine, fructose, and egg substitute until creamy and light. Add lemon zest, juice, and milk. Gradually stir in flour; mix until well blended.

In a medium-size bowl, beat egg whites with cream of tartar until egg whites hold stiff peaks. Stir one-quarter of the egg whites into lemon mixture to lighten it. Gently fold in remaining egg whites; mix until just incorporated. Pour batter into a 1-quart (1 l) soufflé dish. Set dish in a larger baking dish and pour water into pan to reach halfway up sides of soufflé dish. Bake until set, about 35 to 40 minutes. Serve warm, spooning some pudding over cake.

MAKES 8 SERVINGS

* Substitute 11 packets saccharin or 11 packets acesulfame-K for the fructose.

Per serving: calories, 109 ◆ protein, 4 g ◆ carbohydrate, 12 g ◆ fat, 5 g (calories from fat, 39%) ◆ dietary fiber, trace ◆ cholesterol, 1 mg ◆ sodium, 117 mg ◆ potassium, 135 mg
Joslin Exchanges: 1 bread/ starch, 1 fat

Per serving (made with noncaloric sweetener): calories, 92 ◆ protein, 4 g ◆ carbohydrate, 8 g ◆ fat, 5 g (calories from fat, 46%) ◆ dietary fiber, trace ◆ cholesterol, 1 mg ◆ sodium, 113 mg ◆ potassium, 139 mg
Joslin Exchanges: ½ bread/ starch, 1 fat

Lemon Tuiles with Apricot Mousse

The tuile (a tulip-shaped molded cookie) part of this dessert is a bit tricky to make, but it makes such a lovely presentation that it's well worth the extra effort. Tuiles should be baked a few at a time since they must be molded while still warm.

The apricot mousse is quickly made from pantry staples and is also good alone or layered with plain low-fat yogurt as a parfait.

Lemon Tuiles

1 tablespoon (15 g) margarine, melted
1 tablespoon (15 ml) canola oil
1 large egg white
½ teaspoon (2.5 ml) lemon extract
1 teaspoon (5 ml) grated lemon zest

3 tablespoons (23 g) unbleached flour
3 tablespoons (18 g) confectioners' sugar
butter-flavored cooking spray

Preheat oven to 375° F (190° C). In a small bowl, whisk together everything but cooking spray. Mix until smooth. Drop batter 1 tablespoon (15 ml) at a time at least 3 inches (8 cm) apart on a baking sheet lightly sprayed with butter-flavored spray (you will fit 4 on the baking sheet). Using the back of a spoon dipped in cold water, spread each mound of batter out slightly to form a 5-inch (13 cm) circle. Bake until tuiles are golden brown, 6 to 8 minutes.

Using a large spatula, immediately remove cookies one at a time, drape each cookie over an inverted custard cup, pressing it against the bottom and sides so that it takes the shape of the cup. Allow the tuiles to cool on the cup. Remove the cooled shaped cookies very carefully.

Repeat with remaining batter. (If made ahead, store cool cookies in an airtight tin at room temperature for up to a week.)

MAKES 8 SERVINGS

Per serving (tuile alone): calories, 48 ◆ protein, 1 g ◆ carbohydrate, 5 g ◆ fat, 3 g (calories from fat, 56%) ◆ dietary fiber, trace ◆ cholesterol, 0 mg ◆ sodium, 24 mg ◆ potassium, 10 mg Joslin Exchanges: ½ bread/ starch, ½ fat

Apricot Mousse

6 ounces (180 g) dried apricots
3 tablespoons (45 ml) water
3 tablespoons (45 ml) Amaretto liqueur or fresh lemon juice
5 large egg whites at room temperature
grated zest of ½ lemon

¼ teaspoon (1.25 ml) vanilla extract
¼ cup (60 ml) sliced almonds, toasted

Soak apricots in water and Amaretto for 30 minutes. Place apricots and any liquid in a food processor or blender. Process to a puree. Transfer to a small saucepan and cook over low heat, uncovered, to form a thick puree; stir frequently. Chill.

Beat egg whites until stiff. Fold in puree, lemon zest, and vanilla. Spoon ½ cup (118 ml) of apricot mousse into each tuille. Sprinkle with toasted almonds. Serve at once.

MAKES 8 SERVINGS

Per serving (apricot mousse alone): calories, 83 ◆ protein, 4 g ◆ carbohydrate, 14 g ◆ fat, 2 g (calories from fat, 21%) ◆ dietary fiber, 1 g ◆ cholesterol, 0 mg ◆ sodium, 37 mg ◆ potassium, 350 mg Joslin Exchanges: 1 fruit, ½ low-fat meat

Toasting Nuts and Seeds

Preheat oven to 350°F (180°C). Spread nuts in a single layer on a baking sheet. Toast for 3 to 5 minutes, shaking pan once or twice, until nuts are fragrant and golden brown. Be sure to not let the nuts get too brown—pine nuts, particularly, will burn quickly.

To toast seeds (sesame, sunflower, coriander, cumin), heat a nonstick sauté pan over medium-low heat and add seeds. Toast, stirring very often, until lightly browned. Be careful to not let the seeds burn.

Baked Apples

An old favorite made without sugar. Pears can be baked in the same manner.

⅓ cup (78 ml) unsweetened apple juice

⅓ cup (78 ml) dry white wine or water

⅓ cup (78 ml) water

2 tablespoons (30 ml) grated orange zest

4 medium-size baking apples (Jonathan or Rome Beauty)

ground cinnamon to taste

¼ cup (59 ml) crème fraîche (page 428)

1 tablespoon (15 ml) chopped walnuts

In a small saucepan over low heat, simmer apple juice, wine, and water for 10 minutes. Add zest and set aside.

Preheat oven to 375° F (190° C). Using a small paring knife, core and peel apples halfway down from stem end. Place in a small nonreactive baking pan just large enough for the apples and reserved apple liquid. Generously sprinkle apples with cinnamon. Bake, basting with pan juices every 10 minutes, until apples are tender but still hold their shape, about 25 to 30 minutes.

Serve apples warm with 1 tablespoon (15 ml) of the pan juices spooned into the cored center. Top each serving with 1 tablespoon (15 ml) crème fraîche and sprinkle with chopped walnuts.

MAKES 4 SERVINGS

Per serving: calories, 106 ◆ protein, 1 g ◆ carbohydrate, 21 g ◆ fat, 2 g (calories from fat, 17%) ◆ dietary fiber, 3 g ◆ cholesterol, trace ◆ sodium, 12 mg ◆ potassium, 200 mg Joslin Exchanges: 1½ fruit

Kugel

This delicious kugel is made without dairy products, making it a perfect sweet to end a meat meal for special Jewish holidays. We offer winter and summer recipes.

Apple Kugel

½ pound (225 g) broad noodles
½ tablespoon (7 g) margarine
½ cup (118 ml) egg substitute
½ teaspoon (2.5 ml) fructose
  (optional)
 1 teaspoon (5 ml) ground
  cinnamon
⅛ teaspoon (.6 ml) ground nutmeg
 1 small tart apple such as Granny
  Smith, peeled, cored, and thinly
  sliced

¼ cup (59 ml) golden raisins
 1 tablespoon (15 ml) chopped
  toasted almonds (page 440)
butter-flavored cooking spray
½ tablespoon (22.5 ml) dry bread
  crumbs

Add noodles to rapidly boiling water and cook according to package directions until tender. Drain. Toss with margarine. Mix together remaining ingredients except cooking spray and bread crumbs. Toss with noodles.

Preheat oven to 325°F (165°C). Lightly spray a 9-inch square baking pan with cooking spray. Pour noodle mixture into pan. Top with bread crumbs. Bake for 40 to 45 minutes, until a knife inserted in center comes out clean. Serve warm.

MAKES 12 SERVINGS

> **Per serving:** calories, 107 ◆ protein, 4 g ◆ carbohydrate, 18 g ◆ fat, 2 g (calories from fat, 17%) ◆ dietary fiber, trace ◆ cholesterol, 18 mg ◆ sodium, 32 mg ◆ potassium, 121 mg
> Joslin Exchanges: 1 bread/starch

Summer Variation

Omit cinnamon, nutmeg, apples, and raisins. Substitute 1 tablespoon (15 ml) grated orange zest and 1 cup (236 ml) pitted and chopped fresh cherries, apricots, peaches, or nectarines. Bake as directed.

MAKES 12 SERVINGS

> **Per serving:** calories, 104 ◆ protein, 4 g ◆ carbohydrate, 17 g ◆ fat, 2 g (calories from fat, 16%) ◆ dietary fiber, trace ◆ cholesterol, 18 mg ◆ sodium, 31 mg ◆ potassium, 128 mg
> Joslin Exchanges: 1 bread/starch

FIBER: THE ESSENTIAL ELEMENT

Fiber—the part of whole grains, beans, vegetables, fruits, nuts, and seeds that is not digested or absorbed by the body—is of particular help to people with diabetes.

There are two different types of fiber. *Water-insoluble fiber* holds on to but doesn't dissolve in water. This type of fiber helps food move faster through the digestive tract. Sources of insoluble fiber are whole-grain breads and cereals (wheat, barley, and rye), vegetables, fruits (especially when eaten with the skin on), and seeds. *Water-soluble fiber* dissolves in water. Oat bran has been touted in the media as a type of water-soluble fiber that can lower cholesterol. While the verdict is still out on just how effective it is in doing that, we do know that water-soluble fiber is particularly good for people with diabetes because it blunts the rise of blood sugar after meals. In addition to oat bran, water-soluble fiber is found in dried beans, peas, and rice bran. Some foods—apples, potatoes and bananas, for example—are a combination of both insoluble and soluble fibers and are especially beneficial inclusions in your diet.

Both fibers help you feel full without overloading on calories. Eating more fiber on a daily basis may lead to an overall reduction in blood glucose levels so that the need for insulin or an oral agent to control blood sugar may be lessened. As you add more fiber to your diet, be sure that you drink at least eight glasses of fluids each day to help your body use fiber effectively and prevent constipation. Don't count coffee, tea, and other diuretics toward those eight glasses, however, as they can actually deplete body fluids.

Seven Ways to Add More Fiber to Your Diet

- Eat more vegetables, especially raw vegetables such as broccoli, carrots, cauliflower, zucchini, and green beans.
- Eat fruit with skins—apples, pears, peaches, etc.—instead of juice or peeled canned fruits. Especially high in fiber: strawberries, blackberries, blueberries, raspberries, nectarines, and pomegranates.
- Choose whole-grain breads and cereals like whole wheat, corn tortillas, corn bread, rye, and pumpernickel bread and cereals such as oatmeal, bran cereals, and wheat germ.
- Have legumes (dried beans and peas: lima beans, lentils, etc.) several times a week in soups, pilafs, and salads.
- Eat the edible skins and seeds of vegetables—the skin of a baked or steamed potato, the seeds of a cucumber.
- Eat brown rice instead of white rice; eat plenty of other grains (couscous, bulgur, quinoa, etc.).

SUGAR AND SUGAR SUBSTITUTES

To most of us the word *sugar* means white table sugar or brown sugar. If you have diabetes, you have probably thought that these are forbidden. You are probably also aware that sugar has many forms and names, and manufacturers can add it to foods without having to use the word *sugar* on the label.

A product label might state "contains no sugar" yet lists corn syrup, dextrose, fructose, glucose, honey, lactose, maltose, mannitol, sorbitol, xylitol, maple sugar, or molasses as an ingredient. All of these add sweetness to the product, and all have calories and could affect your blood glucose level. So take the label that says "sugar free" with the proverbial grain of salt.

Let's Try to Sort This Out

Sweeteners are grouped into two categories: caloric and noncaloric. Although caloric sweeteners have essentially no nutritional value, they do provide four calories per gram, or approximately 120 calories per ounce of weight.

Recent research has shown that if your blood sugars are in good control and your triglycerides are within the normal range, a small amount of sugar (simple carbohydrate) or caloric sweetener may not cause as significant a rise in blood sugar as once thought. Some caloric sweeteners, like fructose, also will cause less of a blood sugar increase than others, like sucrose (table sugar).

Whether and which caloric sweeteners you use is a decision that should be based on your blood sugar control, lipid levels, and weight. Discuss this with your health-care team. The dessert recipes in this cookbook comply with the American Diabetes Association recommendations for allowable sugar content. Also, the following section provides some guidelines for lowering the sugar content in recipes.

The chart on page 446 describes the most common caloric and noncaloric sweeteners and their pros and cons.

Cutting Back on Sugar

One way to keep sweetness in your diet without causing high blood sugar levels is to cut back on the amount of sugar used. Sometimes you can add sweetness to a food by using nutmeg, cinnamon, vanilla, or almond extract in place of some of the sugar.

Sugar provides cakes and cookies with sweetness, tenderness, and color. But with most recipes you can reduce the sugar by at least one-third without changing the taste and texture. For example, if a recipe calls for 1 cup (236 ml) sugar, try using ⅔ cup (156 ml); then, the next time, try ½ cup (118 ml).

You may use 1 teaspoon (5 ml/4 grams) of sucrose (table sugar, brown sugar, honey, syrup, molasses, corn syrup, or other caloric sweetener) per reasonable serving size. The caloric sweetener should be used only within a balanced meal, once a day, if blood sugars are in good control. One cup (236 ml) sugar equals 48 teaspoons.

Noncaloric Sweeteners

You can also reduce sugar intake by using artificial, noncaloric sweeteners. They provide almost no calories and will not affect your blood sugar level. While we prefer to use caloric sweeteners in preparing the recipes in this book, we do offer noncaloric equivalents for some of the recipes for those who must cook with only noncaloric sweeteners. The chart on page 446 provides additional information on these noncaloric sweeteners in comparison to caloric sweeteners.

Using Artificial Sweeteners in Cooking

We do not recommend substituting artificial sweeteners for all the sugar in cakes and cookies. Not only does sugar provide sweetness, but its chemical interaction with the other ingredients is what gives these baked goods their lightness, tenderness, and nicely browned appearance. As a rule noncaloric sweeteners can replace up to half the sugar in most recipes. However, in sweetened sauces or beverages all the sugar can be replaced by a noncaloric sweetener.

You can use the following chart as a guideline for further replacing sugar or fructose in other recipes with noncaloric sweeteners, thereby lowering calories, the amount of simple sugar, and carbohydrate content.

Sugar Substitutes in Place of Sugar

Sugar	Fructose	Saccharin	Aspartame	Acesulfame-K
2 tsp (10 ml)	⅔ tsp (3.3 ml)	⅕ tsp (1 ml)	1 packet	1 packet
1 T (15 ml)	1 tsp (5 ml)	⅓ tsp (1.7 ml)	1½ packets	1¼ packets
¼ c (59 ml)	4 tsp (20 ml)	3 packets	6 packets	3 packets
⅓ c (78 ml)	5⅓ tsp (26.7 ml)	4 packets	8 packets	4 packets
½ c (118 ml)	8 tsp (40 ml)	6 packets	12 packets	6 packets
⅔ c (156 ml)	3½ T (52.5 ml)	8 packets	16 packets	8 packets
¾ c (177 ml)	¼ c (59 ml)	9 packets	18 packets	9 packets
1 c (236 ml)	⅓ c (78 ml)	12 packets	24 packets	12 packets

Note: During pregnancy, limited amounts of aspartame are the recommended noncaloric sweetener.

Sugar and Sweeteners

Sweetener (Noncaloric)	Trade Name	Comments
Saccharin	Sucaryl Sugar Twin Sweet Magic Sweet'n Low Zero-Cal	375 times sweeter than sucrose. Can be used in cooking and baking. Sold as tablets, as liquid, and in granular form.
Aspartame	Equal Sweetmate Spoonfuls	180 times sweeter than sucrose. Loses sweetening effect when heated. Not acceptable for use in recipes cooked longer than 20 minutes. People with PKU need to discuss use with their physician.
Acesulfame-K	Sweet One	200 times sweeter than sucrose. Can be used in baking and cooking.

Sweetener (Caloric)	Generic Name	Comments
Fructose	Estee Fructose	100% fruit sugar. Discuss use with your physician or dietitian.
Glucose	Date sugar	Not as sweet as sucrose. Discuss use with your physician or dietitian.
Honey	Honey Honey Comb	About 35% glucose and 40% fructose plus water. Discuss use with your physician or dietitian.
Molasses	Black strap	50–75% sucrose and invert sugar. Discuss use with your physician or dietitian.

Sucrose	Barley malt
	Beet sugar
	Brown sugar
	Cane sugar
	Powdered sugar
	  or
	Confectioners'
	  sugar
	Raw sugar
	Table sugar
	Turbinado
	  sugar
		50% glucose and 50% fructose. Discuss use with your physician or dietitian.

Syrups	Corn syrup Fruit syrups Maple syrup Rice syrup	Primarily glucose. Discuss use with your physician or dietitian.

FACTS ON FATS AND CHOLESTEROL

People with diabetes are more likely to develop heart disease, stroke, and atherosclerosis (plaque formation and thickening of the arteries) and will develop them earlier than people without diabetes. Research shows that the types and quantity of dietary fat and cholesterol eaten are related directly to the development of these complications. A high-fat diet also impedes successful weight management since fat contains more than twice the number of calories that protein and carbohydrates contain. Decreasing your fat intake aids in weight loss, which in turn helps you achieve better blood sugar control. Better blood sugar control in turn will lower the levels of certain bad fats in your bloodstream.

For all these reasons people with diabetes should pay attention to how much and what kind of fat and cholesterol they eat.

Saturated fats, found mainly in meats, whole-milk dairy products, and tropical oils (palm and coconut oil), raise your blood cholesterol level more than anything else in your diet.

We hear more in the media about cholesterol because it has been most closely associated with increased risk of heart disease. Cholesterol and "fat" are not synonymous, however. The body produces some cholesterol, and cholesterol is present in many of the foods we eat. Cholesterol then combines with substances called *fatty acids* plus certain proteins to form substances called *lipoproteins*, which float around in the bloodstream.

Health experts are now focusing their efforts on how to increase the levels of certain good lipoproteins (good fats) and decrease the levels of certain bad lipoproteins (bad fats). By doing this you can in turn keep blood cholesterol levels down below the recommended level of 200 mg/dl and lower the risk of clogged arteries.

High-density lipoproteins (HDLs), which are high in protein and low in cholesterol, are "good fats" because they are thought to sweep out undesirable cholesterol, preventing it from clogging the arteries. People who have higher levels of HDLs in their blood actually have a reduced risk of heart disease.

Low-density lipoproteins (LDLs) are low in protein and high in cholesterol. They are "bad fats" and are thought to be responsible for keeping cholesterol circulating in the body and depositing it in the arteries. People with high levels of LDLs have a higher risk of heart disease.

People can also have problems with *triglycerides* in their blood. Triglycerides are a form of fat. Your body produces more of them when you consume too many simple sugars or carbohydrate foods or drink too much alcohol. When people with diabetes have not had proper blood sugar control, the level of triglycerides may also be elevated.

CONTROLLING THE GOOD FATS AND BAD FATS

Low-density lipoproteins (LDLs) are "bad fats." Most of the cholesterol that deposits in the arteries is carried by this lipoprotein.

- Keep your level of LDLs under 130 mg/dl.
- To lower your level of LDLs:

  Reduce total fat intake.
  Reduce the amount of saturated fat you eat.

Use unsaturated fat (polyunsaturated and/or monounsaturated fat) when you do use fat.

Reduce the amount of high-cholesterol foods you eat.

Increase the amount of high-fiber foods you eat.

Keep your blood sugars under control. High blood sugars increase LDLs in the blood.

High-density lipoproteins (HDLs) are "good fats," sweeping cholesterol out of the arteries.

- Keep your level of HDL greater than 35–45 mg/dl.
- To increase your level of HDLs:

  Exercise regularly (five or more times per week; aerobic exercise is best).
  Lose weight.
  Keep your blood sugars under control. High blood sugars decrease HDLs in the blood.

Triglycerides are "bad fats." While they increase the risk of heart disease, they do not increase it as much as high cholesterol levels do.

- Keep your level of triglycerides below 200 mg/dl.
- To lower triglyceride levels:
  Lose weight if overweight.
  Exercise regularly.
  Avoid alcohol.
  Reduce the amount of simple sugars you eat so that you keep your blood sugars under control.

Eat Less of These

- *Saturated fats*
  They raise cholesterol levels by triggering the body to produce more LDLs and less HDLs. Found primarily in meats and whole-milk dairy products, with the exception of tropical oils (palm and coconut oils) and are solid at room temperature.
- *Cholesterol-rich foods*
  They raise cholesterol levels in the blood. Found primarily in animal sources, such as meats, poultry, some seafood, egg yolks, and whole-milk dairy products. Shellfish, once thought to be taboo because of its high cholesterol content, can be used in moderation because it is lower in saturated fat than most meats.

Eat More of These

- *Polyunsaturated fats*
  They lower cholesterol levels by lowering LDL levels. They also lower HDL levels. Found primarily in foods of plant origin, such as corn, sunflower, cottonseed, safflower, and soybean oil.
- *Monounsaturated fats*
  They lower cholesterol levels by lowering LDL levels. Some studies suggest they also raise HDL levels, but this has not been proven conclusively. Primarily found in olive, canola, peanut, macadamia, walnut, and avocado oils.

The experts at Joslin Diabetes Center and other health organizations recommend that you limit your intake of dietary cholesterol to no more than 300 mg per day (as a reference, one large egg has 213 mg cholesterol) and your dietary fat intake to 30 percent of your total daily calorie intake (see page xxiv).

This means an entire day's meal plan may not derive more than 30 percent of the calories from fat—not 30 percent of the calories per recipe or per meal. In our nutrition calculations we have given you the percentage (%) of calories derived from fat as a guideline to alert you when a recipe contains a high percentage of fat. If you plan to eat that dish, the rest of the meal and that day's meals should be lower in fat to compensate for this fat-heavy dish.

The following chart lists grams of total fat recommended per day at different calorie levels.

Grams of Total Fat to Stay Within 30 Percent Limit

Calories	Fat Recommendation
1,200	40 g
1,500	50 g
1,800	60 g
2,000	67 g
2,200	73 g
2,500	83 g
2,800	93 g
3,000	100 g

PRACTICAL TIPS TO REDUCE DIETARY FAT AND CHOLESTEROL

- Limit red meats to occasional use; instead choose fish or poultry, removing the skin from poultry before eating it.
- Limit egg yolks to no more than four per week.
- Drink skim or 1% milk instead of whole milk. Substitute canned evaporated skim milk for heavy cream. Use plain low-fat yogurt or plain nonfat yogurt instead of sour cream or mayonnaise.
- When cooking with yogurt, add 1 tablespoon (15 ml) cornstarch to each cup (236 ml) of yogurt to keep it from separating.
- Substitute tub margarine for butter and reduced-fat or nonfat cheese for whole-milk cheese.
- Use vegetable cooking sprays, a small amount of stock, or a minimum of oil or margarine in a nonstick pan. Avoid bacon fat, shortening, and lard.
- Eat more foods rich in soluble fiber—oat bran, rice bran, dried beans, and peas.
- Use fruit spread (no sugar added) instead of butter or margarine on bread and toast.
- Stock your refrigerator and pantry with foods that are naturally low in fat and cholesterol-free, like fresh fruits, vegetables, pasta, potatoes, and grains.
- Use 2 egg whites or ¼ cup (59 ml) egg substitute for each whole egg called for in most recipes.
- If a recipe calls for chocolate, substitute 3 tablespoons (45 ml) unsweetened cocoa powder plus 1 tablespoon (15 ml) canola oil for each ounce (30 g) of chocolate. The total fat will not be much different, but the fat is unsaturated.

LOW-FAT COOKING TIPS

- Roast, grill, broil, braise using vegetable cooking spray, poach, or bake poultry, fish, and meat.
- Sauté or stir-fry in nonstick cookware, using stock, wine, vegetable cooking spray, or a minimum of polyunsaturated or monounsaturated oil.
- Remove fats from soups, sauces, and gravy using a fat separator (a small pitcher with a specially designed spout available at kitchen and discount stores). Refrigerate stews and one-pot meals; scoop off the fat that rises to the top.
- Trim fat from meat before cooking and buy the leanest cuts you can find. Remove all visible fat from poultry.
- Create sauces by adding stock or wine to pan juices and boil rapidly for a few minutes, until reduced and thickened. The longer heat is applied, the more alcohol evaporates, leaving negligible calories and mainly just flavor.

- Instead of making butter sauces with herbs, make herb sauces with a smidgen of unsalted butter.
- Use marinades of special vinegars, lemon juice, or fruit juice to flavor your food before cooking, rather than flavoring food by adding a rich sauce after the food has been cooked.
- Baste poultry and meats with stock instead of butter or margarine.
- Steam dishes to concentrate a food's natural flavor, eliminating the need for rich sauces or basting with fat-loaded oil, margarine, or butter. Works well with fish, poultry, meat, vegetables, and fruit.
- Cook food *en papillote*, in a sealed pouch of parchment paper or aluminum foil with a little wine, herbs, and lemon juice.
- Use your microwave to cook virtually fat-free; a microwave cooks so quickly that foods are naturally flavorful, juicy, and tender.

SHAKING THE SALT HABIT

While reducing salt in your diet is not a standard part of diabetes treatment, many people with diabetes develop high blood pressure for the reasons mentioned earlier in this book. For many years the recommendation was to put people with high blood pressure on a sodium-restricted diet because sodium was thought to encourage fluid retention, which in turn caused blood pressure to rise. While new research suggests that cutting back on salt may help lower blood pressure only if you are salt sensitive, most clinicians will encourage their hypertensive patients to try a low-salt diet to see if it helps bring their blood pressure down.

Everyone—whether you have high blood pressure or not—should limit intake of sodium to 3,000 milligrams per day. Canned and prepackaged foods contain so much sodium (mostly as salt) that it isn't hard to exceed that 3,000-milligram limit. For that reason—and because so many people with diabetes do find themselves on sodium-restricted diets at one time or another—our recipes use reduced amounts of salt and use salt only in those recipes that would have lacked in flavor without it. Salt is always an optional ingredient. With the exception of a few dishes, all of the recipes are within the suggested 400 milligrams of sodium per serving. Those that are not are clearly marked with a cautionary footnote.

If your doctor recommends cutting back on salt, here are some tips to help you reduce your salt intake when you're eating foods other than the recipes in this book.

TIPS FOR CUTTING SALT

- Taste the food before adding salt. Once you've cut back on salt, you'll discover that most foods need very little salt, if any.
- Use fewer canned, packaged, and convenience foods. About two-thirds of the salt in most American diets comes from processed foods.

- Look for sodium-free products. If you're using canned stock (chicken or beef) instead of our salt-free stock recipes, use sodium-free canned broth.
- Use herbs as a salt substitute. On page 115 we've given a wonderful and easy-to-make salt-free herb seasoning that can be used on most foods. Also try fresh lemon juice or lime juice, flavored vinegars, and spices such as cayenne pepper, black pepper, mace, cumin, nutmeg, allspice, turmeric, coriander, fenugreek, ginger, and celery seeds as salt substitutes.
- Limit your consumption of smoked or cured meats, such as bacon, hot dogs, and cold cuts. Instead, eat sliced turkey, chicken, and lean roast beef.
- Use low-sodium ketchup, soy sauce, tomato paste, tomato juice, and vegetable juice.

WHAT ABOUT ALCOHOL?

If you want to drink alcohol, you should limit your intake to no more than one or two alcoholic drinks at a time and then only with your physician's permission. There are two reasons to do this.

First, if you are trying to reduce your weight, alcohol contains calories that may slow your efforts. It will also stimulate your appetite.

Second, alcohol initially raises the blood sugar, but then the blood sugar level drops. If you are on insulin, you should not omit food calories for alcohol—make sure you always have some food with your alcoholic beverage.

We both cook with wine, considering it as basic to good cooking as garlic and fresh herbs. Depending on the amount and intensity of heat, the alcohol and its calories will be lost due to evaporation, leaving only the flavor. The nutritional analysis of the recipes has been adjusted to compensate for this loss.

However, if you don't use wine in cooking, here are some substitutions to try (check the seasoning of the finished dish—you may wish to add more herbs and/or spices to compensate for the flavor that would have come from the wine).

SUBSTITUTIONS FOR WINE IN RECIPES

- For white wine used in cooking fish: substitute an equal amount of fish stock or bottled clam juice (both are high in salt—adjust the salt in the recipe). *If you are on a low-sodium diet,* substitute an equal amount of plain water and 1 tablespoon (15 ml) fresh lemon juice.
- For white wine used in cooking chicken: substitute an equal amount of chicken stock (page 45) or plain water and 1 tablespoon (15 ml) fresh lemon juice, champagne vinegar, or Spanish sherry vinegar.

• For red wine used in cooking chicken or beef: substitute an equal amount of beef stock (page 44) or plain water and 1 tablespoon (15 ml) red wine vinegar or balsamic vinegar. Or replace three-quarters of the amount with low-calorie cranberry juice and 1 tablespoon (15 ml) balsamic vinegar. Make up the rest of the volume with plain water.

THE HEALTHY PANTRY

Cooking for yourself if you have diabetes or cooking for someone with diabetes is a lifetime, day-by-day commitment to healthy eating. As we changed our diet and cooking habits to control our diabetes, our pantries also changed. We threw out the high-sodium soy sauce, solid vegetable shortening, packaged foods with hidden sugars, emulsifiers, and stabilizers, oils with highly saturated fat such as palm and coconut oils, high-calorie mayonnaise, bottles of high-sugar and high-fat condiments, and bottled salad dressings from specialty food shops. In their place we opted for healthy grains—six or seven varieties of rice, kasha, bulgur, couscous, barley, and polenta; eight or more kinds of tart vinegars; dried mushrooms from Chile, Asia, and Italy; sun-dried tomatoes (packed dry without oil) from California; and cans of low-sodium tomato paste and Italian plum tomatoes.

As we focused on flavor instead of fat in our food, we can truly say that we and our families have never eaten better or enjoyed our food more—and we've gained better control of our blood sugars.

Once you've stocked your pantry with healthy staples, shopping becomes simple. Each week you have to buy only the fresh foods—fish, chicken, vegetables, and a few dairy products. Here's what we keep on hand.

FOR SHELF STORAGE

Vinegars

White wine—sprinkle on salads; frequently our only dressing
Red wine—wonderful sprinkled over chicken or cold vegetables
Balsamic—an exquisite dark vinegar from Modena, Italy. A godsend to diabetic cooking as its pungent sweetness doesn't affect blood sugars. Use on salads, in marinades and sauces, over cooked vegetables, sprinkled on fresh fruit for

dessert. Look for balsamic vinegar that's been aged for at least 12 years—it's worth the price.

Champagne—delicious for dressing greens and adding a mild acidity to sauces

Cider—use it to make Pickled Vegetables (page 13)

Fruit vinegars: blueberry and raspberry (no sugar added)—sprinkle over fruit or shredded vegetables (see page 459 for directions for making your own)

Japanese rice wine—a very mild vinegar for delicate sauces and dressings

Spanish sherry—mild flavor with a hint of sweetness and taste of sherry; use for salads and to deglaze a pan

Herb vinegars (tarragon, opal basil, etc.)—you can buy these or make your own for a fraction of the cost

Herb Vinegars

Using about 1 cup (236 ml) clean, fresh herbs per quart (1 l) of vinegar, loosely place the dry herbs in a clean glass bottle or jar—recycled olive oil and wine bottles are pretty—along with other flavorings as desired. Fill the bottle with unflavored vinegar of your choice and cap the bottle. Let the vinegar stand in a cool, dark place for 4 weeks (or until you like the flavor). After a few days, check the bottles and add more vinegar as needed to make sure the herbs are still covered. Use the vinegar within 12 months.

Here are some of our favorite homemade vinegars:

Dill: Fill jar or bottle loosely to two-thirds full with fresh dill. Add white wine vinegar. Wonderful on fish and salads.

Garlic: Impale 6 peeled large garlic cloves on a thin bamboo skewer. Place in jar or bottle along with white or red wine vinegar. Excellent for marinades; use in salads and sauces.

Lemon Herb: Fill jar or bottle loosely with a mixture of fresh lemon-flavored herbs (lemon basil, lemon verbena, lemon balm, lemon thyme) and a continuous spiral of zest from 1 lemon. Add white wine vinegar. Especially nice with fish or sprinkled over cooked broccoli.

Opal Basil: Place three 3-inch (8 cm) clusters of fresh opal basil in a jar or bottle. Cover with white wine vinegar. In two to three days, a lovely pink color will begin to show. Sprinkle over sliced tomatoes or cucumbers; splash into ratatouille.

Tarragon: Place 2 long sprigs of fresh tarragon and 4 peeled whole shallots in a jar or bottle. Add white wine vinegar. Use for deglazing pan juices after sautéing fish or chicken. Add to chicken or fish salad; use in fish marinades.

Note: Remove the herb sprigs and spirals of fruit zest as soon as they're no longer completely covered with vinegar. Otherwise, when exposed to the air in the bottle, they will mold.

Fruit Vinegars

Fruit vinegars are also easily made without the added sugar so often found in commercial fruit vinegars.

Blueberry: Place rinsed and dried fresh blueberries, a stick of cinnamon, and a whole nutmeg in a glass jar or bottle, filling the jar to within 2 inches (5 cm) of the top. Heat white wine vinegar until it begins to bubble. Pour it over the blueberries, filling the container. Cover the opening with plastic wrap and screw on the top. Store in a dark, cool place for 48 hours. Strain the vinegar and rebottle, discarding the blueberries and spices. Use within three months on fruit salads, fish salads, grilled fish or chicken, or steamed vegetables.

Raspberry: Gently wash fresh raspberries; drain well. Loosely fill a glass jar or bottle with raspberries to within 2 inches (5 cm) of the top. Heat white wine vinegar until it begins to bubble. Pour it over the raspberries, filling the jar. Cover the jar with plastic wrap and screw on the top. Store in a dark, cool place for six weeks. Strain the vinegar through a tea strainer lined with a coffee filter to remove all debris. Pour the vinegar into a clean bottle, cap, and seal. Use within three months on spinach salad, splashed onto baked pears or apples, in marinades for chicken or fish, or stirred into plain nonfat yogurt for dressing fruit salads.

Oils

Olive (for sautéing)—imparts excellent flavor.

Extra-virgin olive (for salads)—more expensive but more flavorful than 100 percent pure olive oil.

Canola—lowest saturated-fat content (6 percent) of all of the oils. Acceptable for cooking; imparts no taste.

Dark sesame—use sparingly for flavor (has a rich amber color and intense taste of roasted sesame seeds); buy small bottles and refrigerate once opened to prevent spoiling.

Light sesame—a bland oil that can be used for sautéing. Once opened, refrigerate to prevent spoiling.

Walnut—smokes when heated and therefore inappropriate for sautéing; use in uncooked foods for excellent nutty taste. Once opened, refrigerate to prevent spoiling.

Peanut—use sparingly for stir-frying, where its higher smoking point and flavor are desirable. Store in the refrigerator once opened to prevent spoiling.

Macadamia—lovely nutty flavor; smokes when heated, so inappropriate for cooking. Refrigerate once opened to prevent spoiling.

Cooking Sprays

Many of our recipes call for cooking sprays. These vegetable-based sprays add virtually no calories and are useful for sautéing, coating baking pans, and spritzing on filo dough instead of painting the layers of dough with butter. Cooking sprays come in three flavors—olive oil, vegetable, and butter. Experiment with different brands and decide which you like best.

Grains

We store our grains in glass jars (along with cooking instructions and/or serving charts, cut from the box).

Brown rice
Basmati rice—an aromatic long-grain rice with a fragrant, delicate taste and light fluffy texture. Look for basmati from India and Pakistan. U.S. produces Texmati.
Long-grain white rice
Italian short-grain rice—for risotto. Look for Carnaroli or Italian Arborio.
Wild rice
Wehani rice—a basmati-type hybrid grown in California that turns a deep russet color when cooked.
Quick-cooking couscous
Bulgur
Kasha
Pearl barley
Quick-cooking oats
Quick grits
Instant polenta
Stone-ground cornmeal (white and yellow)

Legumes

Dried black beans
Dried navy beans
Dried chick peas
Dried black-eyed peas
Dried split peas
Dried lentils

Pasta

Linguine
Capellini (angel hair)
Fettuccine
Spaghetti
Rotini (corkscrews)
Lasagne
Penne
Bow ties
Rice stick noodles
Orzo—tiny rice-shaped pasta and a good substitute for rice

Baking Needs

Unbleached flour
Whole-wheat flour
Rye flour
Cornstarch
Dry bread crumbs
Rolled oats
Wheat bran
Oat bran
Baking powder
Baking soda
Cream of tartar
Yeast (dry active and rapid-rise)
Unflavored gelatin
Tapioca
Instant espresso granules
Cocoa powder
Semisweet chocolate chips
Baking chocolate (unsweetened and semisweet)
Salt
Vanilla (beans and extract)
Almond extract
Maple extract
Lemon extract
Mint extract
Fructose
Granulated sugar
Honey
Molasses
Date sugar

Canned and Packaged Goods

Cornichons
Olives (Greek and black)
Water chestnuts
Anchovies and anchovy paste
Low-sodium tomato paste
Low-sodium canned Italian tomatoes
Low-sodium canned stock
Canned pumpkin
Capers
Low-sodium soy sauce
Sun-dried tomatoes (dry—not packed in oil)
Low-sodium ketchup
Fruit spreads (no sugar added)
Peanut butter (no sugar added)
Dried mushrooms (porcini, morels, shiitake, Asian)
Dried chilies
Dried fruits (no sugar added—cherries, apples, peaches, apricots)
Evaporated skim milk
Nonfat dry milk
Dry buttermilk
Worcestershire sauce
Mustard (Dijon, coarse-grain)
Unsweetened pineapple juice
Unsweetened apple juice
Red and white wine (for cooking)
Cognac (for cooking)
Dry sherry (for cooking)

Spices

Coarse salt
Peppercorns
Cayenne pepper
Cinnamon (ground and sticks)
Cumin (ground and seeds)
Ground ginger
Ground allspice
Mace
Nutmeg (ground and whole)
Cloves (ground and whole)
Curry powder

Turmeric
Coriander (ground and seeds)
Paprika
Juniper berries
Sesame seed
Fennel seed
Cardamom (ground and whole)
Celery seed
Dill (weed and seed)
Chili powder
Mustard (powder and seed)
Caraway seed
Pickling spice
Poppy seed
Chinese five-spice powder
Hot red pepper flakes
Cajun spice mixture (no sugar added)
Homemade salt-substitute herb seasoning (page 115)

IN THE FREEZER

Fresh-frozen fruits (blueberries, blackberries, raspberries)
Fruit juice concentrates (no sugar added)
Pastry dough (ready to roll out)
Breads
Homemade bread crumbs
Crêpes
Homemade stocks
Margarine
Unsalted butter
Raisins (golden, muscat)
Currants (dried, either red or black)
Pounded boneless and skinless chicken breasts
Fresh pasta (fettuccine, linguine, angel hair)
Filo dough
Egg substitute
Sliced almonds
Walnuts
Vegetables—spinach, corn, and peas

Note: Remember, everything must be properly packaged for freezer storage and labeled with the date it was frozen.

ON THE REFRIGERATOR SHELF

Part-skim Parmesan cheese
Nonfat mozzarella cheese
Nonfat ricotta cheese
Low-fat goat cheese
Prepared horseradish
A piece of fresh ginger
Lemons
Limes
Oranges
Grapefruits
Scallions
Fresh parsley
Fresh dill
Plain yogurt (low-fat and nonfat)
Fruit juices (no sugar added)
Carrots
Celery
Sweet bell peppers (green, red)
Fresh chilies
Skim milk
Eggs
Buttermilk
Homemade crème fraîche (page 428)

GROWING FRESH HERBS

Fresh herbs have become so essential to our cooking style that we cannot imagine cooking (or eating) without them. We both have extensive herb gardens, outdoors during the growing season and indoors in pots during the winter. For those who don't grow their own, fresh herbs are now available year-round in major supermarkets from coast to coast.

Herbs are a joy to grow and an inspiration to the cook, adding zest and flavor to our food and changing simple ingredients into interesting dishes. Herbs are also an excellent substitute for salt.

You don't need a garden to grow herbs; even a sunny apartment windowsill can produce plenty of sage, thyme, basil, rosemary, and savory for cooking.

Almost any pot is suitable for growing herbs—clay pots, barrels, strawberry jars, ceramic pots, wooden boxes, even old wooden nursery flats and recycled grape flats from your produce market. More important are the potting mixture, good drainage, and lots of sun.

In the garden, pick a site that has good air circulation (herbs are susceptible to fungus) and at least six hours of sunlight. The ideal soil mixture contains two parts sterilized topsoil to one part perlite (crushed volcanic ash), two parts peat moss or compost, and two parts sand or fine gravel.

Herbs growing in pots dry out quickly and must be kept well watered. During the hottest part of the summer, this may mean watering every day. Check the soil for moisture; if the top inch is dry, water.

In the summer we grow basil (sweet bush, lettuce leaf or Italian, dark opal), chervil, chives, cilantro (coriander), dill, sweet marjoram, mint (spearmint, peppermint, orange), oregano, parsley (curly, Italian flat-leaf), rosemary, sage (gray, golden, tricolor, purple, pineapple), tarragon (French), and thyme (English, lemon). If you have room, you might also want to try these herbs: borage, burnet, lemon balm, lemon verbena, lovage, savory (summer, winter), and sorrel.

At the first threat of frost, potted herbs are moved indoors, and herbs from the garden are cut in bunches and hung upside down to dry in the kitchen.

Fresh herbs are not as strong as their dried counterparts. Use 1 tablespoon fresh for each teaspoon of the dried herb, a ratio of three to one.

Also remember that dried herbs lose much of their pungency when stored near heat and light. Store them in a dim, cool place in tightly sealed containers. Their flavor will start to fade after six months.

SAVVY SHOPPING

In this book we've provided you with more than 500 healthy recipes, but a lifetime of healthy eating doesn't start in the kitchen. It starts at the grocery store, and for many of us it means changing the way we shop and becoming more aware of what we're buying.

We've all been told to increase our consumption of vegetables, fruits, and other complex carbohydrates while reducing our intake of meat and dairy products. So it makes sense to select the items from the vegetable and plant kingdoms first. After your cart is filled with fresh vegetables, fruits, grains, dried beans, and pasta, select fish, poultry, meat, and dairy products.

Our recipes call for very few processed foods, but all of us buy them occasionally to save time or cut corners, so it's important to know how to read labels.

NEW REGULATIONS FOR FOOD LABELS

Many of the sweeping reforms in food labeling are especially important for people with diabetes. Since these new regulations, the first big update of food labels in nearly 20 years, are scheduled to go into effect in May 1994. You can obtain updated information from a regional Joslin Diabetes Center Affiliate or by writing to Nutrition Services, Joslin Diabetes Center, One Joslin Place, Boston, MA 02215.

Current government regulations mandate that every can or package of food carry a list of ingredients in descending order by weight. For example, if you see *water* at the top of a list of ingredients for low-fat margarine, it means, by weight, there is more water than other ingredients in that margarine.

Under the new regulations, nearly all packaged foods will be required to carry nutrition labeling—printed values for calories, fat (including a breakout of saturated fat), carbohydrates (complex carbohydrates and sugar separately), cholesterol, calcium, fiber, Vitamins A and C, protein, sodium, and iron. The listing of niacin, riboflavin, and thiamine—the three B vitamins—will become optional.

Although your supermarket may carry as many as 12,000 items, only fortified foods and those foods making a nutritional claim are presently required to carry nutritional labeling.

The FDA has proposed standard serving portions for 131 categories of food. Until these regulations go into effect, a manufacturer can choose the serving size and often opts for unrealistically small portion sizes to make a product look lower in fat and calories than it actually is.

ALTERNATIVES TO THE SUPERMARKET

A savvy shopper will take advantage of alternatives to one-stop supermarket shopping—other markets that offer variety.

Farm markets: In the summer, roadside stands are the best source of field-fresh produce. In most cities, farmers bring their produce into the city two or three times a week during the growing season and set up stalls to sell their fruits and vegetables. Check your local newspaper for the location of these "greenmarkets" in your area or your yellow pages for the locations of year-round produce markets.

Ethnic markets: In many of our recipes we've suggested sources for specialty foods. These markets offer a treasure of wholesome foods. We frequent the Asian (Chinese, Japanese, and Korean), Italian, Middle Eastern, Indian, and Mexican markets for everything from tofu to dried mushrooms, pasta, and dried chilies. Ethnic markets are often an excellent source of unusual vegetables and fruits.

Health food stores: The best source for grains, dried fruits, nuts, seeds, and other staples. Health food stores are also excellent sources of organic produce and whole-grain breads.

Mail-order shopping: Look in Appendix 2 for sources of top-quality fresh, canned, and dried foods, spices, and herbs—even sources of seeds for growing your own. Most have free catalogs or will apply the cost of the catalog to your first order.

EQUIPPING THE KITCHEN

For these recipes, you'll need only a few basics: nonstick cookware and bakeware, a soup pot, a Dutch oven, and a variety of casseroles. We also use a wok, vegetable steamer, and a cast-iron skillet for flash-in-the-pan cooking without fat.

Microwave cooking can save time and be virtually fat- and salt-free (salt is actually inadvisable in microwave cooking because of its tendency to draw moisture out of food). The microwave cooks so quickly that foods are naturally flavorful, juicy, and tender.

The recipes in this book were tested in microwave ovens with power ranging from 600 to 700 watts. You'll need to determine the power of your oven since ovens vary significantly by manufacturer and model. The higher your oven's wattage, the more quickly it cooks food.

What Watt?

Here's an easy way to determine approximate wattage of your microwave. Fill a glass measuring cup with 1 cup (236 ml) of cold tap water. Heat the water in your microwave on HIGH (100% power). Note when the water comes to a rolling boil. If it takes 2½ to 3 minutes, your oven's power output is 600 to 700 watts; 3½ to 4 minutes, 400 to 500 watts; 4½ to 5½ minutes, 300 to 350 watts. If your oven is lower than 600 to 700 watts, you'll need to increase the cooking time given in the recipe.

Other kitchen essentials:
- food processor or blender
- kitchen scale sensitive to ¼ ounce (7 grams)

469

- a good set of knives and a knife sharpener
- a couple of sets of measuring spoons; glass and metal measuring cups in assorted sizes
- wooden spoons, rubber scrapers, and wire whisks
- stainless-steel, glass, and pottery mixing bowls
- citrus zester, kitchen shears, potato peeler, potato masher, pastry brush, rolling pin, melon baller, garlic press, and small hand-held grater

Handy, but not essential:
- electric mixer
- spice grinder

EXCHANGES

EXCHANGE SUBSTITUTIONS

The Joslin experts believe that there are circumstances in which an exchange from one food group can be substituted for an exchange in another food group, if they both provide approximately the same amount of carbohydrate, protein, and fat. This increases flexibility with your food choices.

Here are some guidelines to follow:
- Replace one fruit exchange with one bread/starch exchange. But do not do this more than once a day, or you will be eliminating vitamins A and C present in the fruit.
- Replace one bread/starch exchange with three vegetable exchanges. Use this substitution to provide yourself with more fiber and "bulk" when you are especially hungry.
- Replace one skim or 1% low-fat milk exchange with one bread/starch exchange *and* one low-fat meat exchange or ½ cup milk for one low-fat meat. This substitution should be made only occasionally, or you will be eliminating too much of the calcium present in milk from your meal plan.

JOSLIN DIABETES CENTER EXCHANGE LIST FOR MEAL PLANNING

Brand-name items and prepared foods are not included in the following list. If you wish to purchase a complete Joslin food list, which includes these ever-changing items, write to Publications, Joslin Diabetes Center, One Joslin Place, Boston, MA 02215, or call (617) 732-2695 for ordering information.

Milk List

Best Choices: Nonfat or low-fat
Be Sure: You take calcium supplements if you use less than 2 cups per day for adults, 3 to 4 cups per day for children.

Nonfat Selections

One choice provides:
Calories: 80
Protein: 8 grams
Carbohydrate: 12 grams
Fat: 0 grams

Item	Portion
Nonfat milk (skim)	1 cup
Low-fat milk (1/2%)	1 cup
Nonfat yogurt:	
plain	1 cup
made with nonnutritive sweeteners	6-8 ounces
Lactaid milk (skim)	1 cup
Powdered nonfat milk	
(before adding liquid)	1/3 cup
Canned evaporated skim milk	1/2 cup
* Sugar-free hot cocoa mix	
plus 6 ounces water	1 cup

* Most cocoa mixes do not provide the same amount of calcium as 1 cup milk. Mixes that do provide the same amount should indicate on the label that the product contains 30% Reference Daily Intakes (RDIs) for calcium.

Low-Fat Selections

One choice provides:
Calories: 107
Protein: 8 grams
Carbohydrate: 12 grams
Fat: 3 grams

Item	Portion
Low-fat milk (1%)	1 cup
Yogurt, plain, unflavored	1 cup
Lactaid milk (1%)	1 cup

Medium- and High-Fat Selections

Be Sure: You use the following milk items sparingly due to their high saturated fat and cholesterol content.

One choice provides:
Calories: 125–150
Protein: 8 grams
Carbohydrate: 12 grams
Fat: 5–8 grams

Item	Portion
Low-fat milk (2%)	1 cup
Whole milk	1 cup

Vegetable List

Best Choices: Fresh or raw vegetables: dark green, leafy, or orange
Be Sure: To choose at least two vegetables each day
We Encourage: Steaming with a minimum amount of water

One choice provides:
Calories: 28
Protein: 2 grams
Carbohydrate: 5 grams
Fat: 0 grams

Item	Portion
Artichoke	½
Asparagus	1 cup
Bamboo shoots	½ cup
Bean sprouts	½ cup
Beets	½ cup
Beet greens	1 cup
Broccoli	½ cup
Broccoli rabe	½ cup
Brussels sprouts	½ cup
Cabbage	1 cup
Carrots	½ cup
Cauliflower	1 cup

Item	Portion
Celery	1 cup
Chayote	1/2 cup
Chili peppers (hot)	4 small
Collard greens	1 cup
Eggplant	1/2 cup
Fennel, bulb	1/2 cup
Garlic	5 cloves
Green beans	1 cup
Kale	1/2 cup
Kohlrabi	1/2 cup
Leeks	1/2 cup
Mushrooms, fresh	1 cup
Mustard greens, cooked	1 cup
Okra	1/2 cup
Onion	1/2 cup
Pea pods, Chinese (snow peas)	1/2 cup
Peppers, red, green, and yellow	1 cup
Radishes	1 cup
Rutabagas	1/2 cup
*Sauerkraut	1/2 cup
Scallions	1/2 cup (4 to 5 whole)
Spinach, cooked	1/2 cup
Squash:	
spaghetti	1/2 cup
summer	1 cup
zucchini	1 cup
Swiss chard	1 cup
Tomatillos	1/2 cup
Tomato (ripe)	1 medium
*Tomato juice	1/2 cup
Tomato paste	1 1/2 tablespoons
*Tomato sauce, canned	1/3 cup
Turnips	1/2 cup
Vegetables, mixed	1/4 cup
*Vegetable juice	1/2 cup
Wax beans	1 cup
Water chestnuts	5 whole

* These vegetables are high in sodium (salt). Low-sodium vegetables, juices, and sauces should be purchased if you are following a sodium-restricted diet. Fresh and frozen vegetables are lower in sodium than canned vegetables unless the canned product states "low-sodium."

Because of their low carbohydrate and calorie content, the following *raw* vegetables may be used liberally.

Alfalfa sprouts
Chicory
Chinese cabbage
Cucumber
Endive
Escarole
Lettuce
Parsley
*Pickles (unsweetened)
Pimiento
Spinach
Watercress

Fruit List

Best Choices: Fresh whole fruit
Be Sure: To choose fresh, frozen, or canned fruit packed in its own juice or
water, with no added sugar

One choice provides:
Calories: 60
Protein: 0 grams
Carbohydrate: 15 grams
Fat: 0 grams

Item	Portion
Apple, 2-inch diameter	1 small
Apple, dried	1/4 cup
Applesauce	1/2 cup
Apricots:	
fresh	4 medium
canned	4 halves
dried	7 halves
Banana, 9-inch length, peeled	1/2
Banana flakes or chips	3 tablespoons
Blackberries	3/4 cup
Blueberries	3/4 cup
Boysenberries	1 cup

Item	Portion
Canned fruit, unless otherwise stated	$\frac{1}{2}$ cup
Cantaloupe, 5-inch diameter	
sectioned	$\frac{1}{3}$ melon
cubed	1 cup
Carambola (star fruit)	$1\frac{1}{2}$
Casaba, 7-inch diameter	
sectioned	$\frac{1}{6}$ melon
cubed	$1\frac{1}{3}$ cups
Cherries, sweet fresh	12
Dates	3
Figs	2 small
Granadilla (passion fruit)	4
Grapefruit, 4-inch diameter	$\frac{1}{2}$
Grapes	15 small
Guava	$1\frac{1}{2}$ small
Honeydew melon, $6\frac{1}{2}$-inch diameter:	
sectioned	$\frac{1}{8}$ melon
cubed	1 cup
Kiwifruit (3-ounce)	1 large
Kumquat	5 medium
Lemon	1 large
Litchis, fresh or dried	10
Loquats, fresh	12
Mango	$\frac{1}{2}$ small
sliced	$\frac{1}{2}$ cup
Nectarine, $2\frac{1}{2}$-inch diameter	1 cup
Orange, 3-inch diameter	1
Papaya, $3\frac{1}{2}$-inch diameter:	
sectioned	$\frac{1}{2}$
cubed	1 cup
Peach, $2\frac{1}{2}$-inch diameter	1
Pear	1 small
Persimmon:	
native	2
Japanese, $2\frac{1}{2}$-inch diameter	$\frac{1}{2}$
Pineapple:	
diced fresh	$\frac{3}{4}$ cup
canned	$\frac{1}{3}$ cup
Plum, 2-inch diameter	2
Pomegranate, $3\frac{1}{2}$-inch diameter	$\frac{1}{2}$
Prunes, medium	3

Item	Portion
Raisins	2 tablespoons
Raspberries	1 cup
Rhubarb, diced fresh	3 cups
Strawberries	1⅓ cups
Tangerine, 2½-inch diameter	2
Watermelon, diced	1¼ cups

Fruit Juice

Because fruit juice contains little of the fiber found in whole fruits, it may elevate blood glucose rapidly, especially when consumed on an empty stomach or with a small amount of food such as a snack. Limit your intake of juice to no more than one meal each day or to times when you are engaging in vigorous activity or treating low blood sugar.

Item	Portion
Apple juice, unsweetened	½ cup
Cranapple juice, low-calorie	1½ cups
Cranberry juice, low-calorie	1¼ cups
Grape juice, unsweetened	½ cup
Grapefruit juice, unsweetened	5 fluid ounces
Lemon juice, unsweetened	¾ cup
Orange juice, unsweetened	½ cup
Pineapple juice, unsweetened	½ cup
Prune juice, unsweetened	3 fluid ounces

Bread/Starch List

Best Choices: Whole-grain breads and cereals, dried beans, and peas
Be Sure: Cereals contain less than 5 grams of sucrose per serving. (In general, one bread choice equals 1 ounce bread.)

Breads

One choice provides:
Calories: 80
Protein: 3 grams
Carbohydrate: 15 grams
Fat: trace

Item	Portion
White, whole wheat, rye, etc.	1 slice
Raisin	1 slice
Italian and French	1 slice
Reduced-calorie (1 slice equals 40 calories)	2 slices
Syrian:	
pocket, 6-inch diameter	$\frac{1}{2}$ pocket
diet size	1 pocket
Bagel	$\frac{1}{2}$ medium
English muffin	$\frac{1}{2}$ medium
Rolls:	
kaiser, hard	$\frac{1}{2}$ small
dinner, plain	1 small
frankfurter	$\frac{1}{2}$ medium
hamburger	$\frac{1}{2}$ medium
Taco shell	2 = 1 bread + 1 fat
Tortilla:	
Corn, 6-inch diameter	2 = 1 bread + 1 fat
Flour, 7-inch diameter	1 = 1 bread + 1 fat
Bread crumbs	3 tablespoons

Cereals

Item	Portion
Cooked cereals	$\frac{1}{2}$ cup
Bran, concentrated	$\frac{1}{3}$ cup

Starchy Vegetables

Item	Portion
Corn, kernels	$\frac{1}{2}$ cup
Corn on the cob, 5- by $1\frac{3}{4}$-inch ear	1
Lima beans	$\frac{1}{2}$ cup
Parsnips	$\frac{1}{2}$ cup
Peas, green	$\frac{2}{3}$ cup
Plantain, cooked	$\frac{1}{3}$ cup

Item	Portion
Potato, white:	
mashed	½ cup
baked	½ medium
	or 1 small
	(3 ounces)
Potato, sweet:	
mashed	⅓ cup
baked	½ medium
	(2 ounces)
Pumpkin	¾ cup
Winter squash, acorn, butternut	¾ cup

Pasta, Cooked

Item	Portion
Macaroni, noodles, orzo, spaghetti, etc.	½ cup

Legumes, Cooked

Item	Portion
Beans, split peas, lentils	⅓ cup

Grains

Item	Portion
Barley, cooked	¼ cup
Bulgur, cooked	⅓ cup
Cornmeal, polenta, uncooked	2½ tablespoons
Cornstarch	2 tablespoons
Couscous, cooked	½ cup
Flour	3 tablespoons
Kasha, cooked	⅓ cup
Quinoa, uncooked	2 tablespoons
Rice, white, wild, basmati, Arborio, cooked	⅓ cup
Wheat germ	¼ cup =
	1 bread +
	1 lean meat

Crackers Equal to One Bread Choice

Best Choices: Low-sodium products; e.g., saltines with unsalted tops

Item	Portion
Gingersnaps	3
Graham crackers, 2½ squares	3
Matzo or matzo with bran, ¾ ounce	1
Whole-wheat matzo	7
Melba toast rectangles	5
Melba toast rounds	10
Norwegian flatbread	
thin	3
thick	2
Popcorn:	
Popped, no fat added	3 cups
Popped, microwave light	3 cups = 1 bread + 1 fat
*Pretzels	¾ ounce
Rice cakes, popcorn cakes	2
mini rice cakes	8
*Saltines	6

*High in sodium.

Miscellaneous

Item	Portion
***Ice cream	½ cup = 1 bread + 2 fat
***Frozen ice milk	½ cup = 1 bread + 1 fat
Frozen Yogurt:	
Soft serve, nonfat, sugar free	½ cup = 1 bread

***Due to the high fat and/or sugar content, these foods should be used only occasionally, i.e., not more than once or twice a week.

Meat List

Best Choices: Nonfat or low-fat selections
Be Sure: To trim off visible fat. Bake, broil, grill, or steam selections with no added fat. Weigh your portion *after* cooking.

Nonfat Selections

One choice provides:
Calories: 40–45
Protein: 7 grams
Carbohydrate: 0 grams
Fat: 0 grams

Item	Portion
Nonfat cheese products:	
sliced	1 ounce
cottage cheese	1/4 cup
100% skim ricotta	1 ounce

Low-Fat Selections

One choice provides:
Calories: 55
Protein: 7 grams
Carbohydrate: 0 grams
Fat: 3 grams

Item	Portion
Cheese:	
Cottage, 1% fat	1/4 cup
Low-fat cheese	1 ounce
Cooked dried beans	1/2 cup = 1 meat + 1 bread
Egg substitute with fewer than 55 calories per 1/4 cup	1/2 cup
Fish and shellfish, fresh or frozen	1 ounce

Item	Portion
Canned fish and shellfish:	
Anchovies	1 ounce
Anchovy paste	2 tablespoons
Herring, uncreamed or *smoked	1 ounce
Imitation crab	1 ounce
Sardines, drained	3
Water-packed clams, oysters, scallops, **shrimp	1 ounce
Water-packed salmon, tuna, crab, **lobster	$\frac{1}{4}$ cup
*Luncheon meat, 95% fat free	1 ounce
Pork tenderloin, trimmed of all fat	1 ounce
Poultry: chicken, turkey, Rock Cornish hen, or capon, without skin	1 ounce
Ground chicken or turkey	1 ounce
*Canadian bacon	1 ounce
Tofu	3 ounces

* High in sodium.

** People trying to reduce dietary cholesterol may need to limit these. For additional information, ask your dietitian.

Medium-Fat Selections

One choice provides:
Calories: 75
Protein: 7 grams
Carbohydrate: 0 grams
Fat: 5 grams

Item	Portion
Beef, chipped, chuck, flank steak, hamburger with 15% fat, rib-eye, rump, sirloin, tenderloin, top and bottom round	1 ounce
Lamb, except for breast	1 ounce
Pork, except for deviled ham, ground pork, spareribs, and tenderloin	1 ounce
Veal, except for breast	1 ounce
Cheese:	
Part-skim mozzarella, part-skim ricotta, farmer, Neufchâtel, processed light, natural light	1 ounce
Parmesan, *Romano	3 tablespoons

Item	Portion
**Egg	1
Egg substitute with 56–80 calories per ¼ cup	¼ cup
*Luncheon meat, 86% fat free	1 ounce
Turkey bacon	2 slices
Peanut butter	1 tablespoon = 1 meat + 1 fat

* High in sodium.
** High in cholesterol. Limit consumption to 3–4 per week.

High-Fat Selections

Be Sure: Due to the high saturated fat and cholesterol content, the meat choices listed should be used sparingly.

One choice provides:
Calories: 100
Protein: 7 grams
Carbohydrate: 0 grams
Fat: 8 grams

Item	Portion
Beef:	
brisket, club, and rib steak, *corned beef, regular hamburger with 20% fat, rib roast, short ribs	1 ounce
Lamb: breast	1 ounce
Pork:	
*deviled ham, ground pork, spareribs, *sausage (patty or link)	1 ounce
Veal: breast	1 ounce
Poultry: duck, goose	1 ounce
Regular cheese:	
*blue, Brie, cheddar, Colby, *feta, Monterey Jack, provolone, Swiss, *pasteurized process	1 ounce
low-fat goat cheese	2 ounces
Organ meats: liver, heart, kidney	1 ounce
Fried fish	1 ounce

* High in sodium.

Fat List

Best Choices: More unsaturated selections
Be Sure: When using low-calorie version of fat choices, use amounts equal to 45 calories for one serving.

One choice provides:
Calories: 45
Protein: 0 grams
Carbohydrate: 0 grams
Fat: 5 grams

More Unsaturated

Item	Portion
Avocado, 4-inch diameter	1/8
Margarine, soft tub or *stick	1 teaspoon
Reduced-calorie	1 tablespoon
**Mayonnaise	1 teaspoon
Reduced-calorie	1 tablespoon
Nondairy creamer, liquid	2 tablespoons
Nondairy creamer, light, liquid	5 tablespoons
Nuts	
Almonds	6 whole
Brazil	2 medium
Cashews	5–8 whole
Filberts (hazelnuts)	5 whole
Macadamia	3 whole
Peanuts	
Spanish	20 whole
Virginia	10 whole
Pecans	2 whole
Pignoli (pine nuts)	1 tablespoon
Pistachio	12 whole
Walnuts	2 whole
Other	1 tablespoon
Oils:	
corn, cottonseed, safflower, soy, sunflower, canola, olive, macadamia, walnut, peanut (monounsaturated)	1 teaspoon
*Olives:	
green	5 small
black	2 large

Item	Portion
Salad dressings (commercial):	
*French, Italian	1 tablespoon
Mayonnaise type	2 teaspoons
*Seeds (without shells)	
Sesame, sunflower	1 tablespoon
Pumpkin	2 teaspoons

* High in sodium.

** Can be used in a cholesterol-reducing diet if made with corn, cottonseed, safflower, soy, or sunflower oil as the first ingredient.

More Saturated

Item	Portion
Butter	1 teaspoon
Bacon, crisp	1 strip
Chitterlings	1/2 ounce
Coconut, shredded	2 tablespoons
Coffee whitener, liquid	2 tablespoons
Coffee whitener, powder	1/4 cup
Nondairy whipped topping	3 tablespoons
Cream:	
Half-and-half	2 tablespoons
Heavy	1 tablespoon
Light	1 1/2 tablespoons
Sour	2 tablespoons
Whipped, fluid	1 tablespoon
Whipped, pressurized topping	1/3 cup
Cream cheese	1 tablespoon
Whipped	2 tablespoons
Margarine, stick (oil not listed as first ingredient)	1 teaspoon
Oils: palm, coconut	1 teaspoon
Salad dressings: (oil not listed as first ingredient)	
*French, Italian	1 tablespoon
Mayonnaise type	2 teaspoons
Salt pork	1/4 ounce

* High in sodium.

Free Foods

The following foods contain very few calories and may be used freely in your meal plan. Items marked with an asterisk(*) should not be used, however, if you are on a salt- (sodium-) restricted diet. (See page 372 for some creative uses of these free foods.)

General

*Bouillon cubes
*Broth (clear)
Calorie-free soft drinks
Coffee
*Consommé
Cranberries (unsweetened)
Decaffeinated coffee
Extracts (see list)
Herbs (see list)
Horseradish
*Ketchup (1 tablespoon daily, calculated as part of the total daily calories)
Lemon/lime rind
Lime juice
*Mustard (prepared)
Noncaloric sugar substitute
Orange rind
*Pickles (unsweetened)
Rennet tablets
Seasonings and condiments (see following list)
*Soy sauce
Spices (see following list)
*Steak sauce
Tabasco sauce
Taco sauce
Tea
Unprocessed bran (1 tablespoon)
Vinegar (cider, white, apple, wine, balsamic)
Yeast (dry or cake)

Spices, Herbs, and Extracts

Allspice
Almond extract
Anise extract
Anise seed
Baking powder
*Baking soda
Basil
Bay leaf
Black cherry extract
*Bouillon cube
Butter flavoring
*Butter salt
Caraway seed
Cardamom
*Celery salt (seeds, leaves)
Chives
Chocolate extract
Cilantro (fresh coriander)
Cinnamon
Cloves
Cream of tartar
Cumin
Curry
Dill

Fennel
Ginger
Hot red pepper flakes
Lemon extract
Mace
Maple extract
Mint
Mustard (dry)
Nutmeg
Onion (1 tablespoon)
Orange extract
Oregano
Paprika
Parsley
Pepper
Peppermint extract
Pimiento
Poppy seed
Poultry seasonings
Saffron
Sage
*Salt
Savory
Shallots

* High in sodium.

MAIL-ORDER SOURCES OF INGREDIENTS

If you are unable to locate some of the ingredients used in the recipes in this book, you can order many of them through the mail-order sources listed below.

Apple Pie Farm, Inc.
1 Arlington Ave.
Malvern, PA 19355
(215) 933-9696
fresh and dried herbs, flavored vinegars

American Spoon Foods Inc.
1668 Clarion Ave., P.O. Box 566
Petoskey, MI 49770-0566
(800) 222-5886
no-sugar fruit butters, jams, and pie fillings; dried cherries

Birkett Mills
Penn Yan, NY 14527
(315) 536-3311
stone-ground flours

Laura Chenel's Chèvre
1550 Ridley Ave.
Santa Rosa, CA 95401
(707) 575-8888
low-fat goat cheese

Cook's Garden
Post Office Box 535
Londonderry, VT 05148
(802) 824-3400
seeds

Coyote Kitchens
102 West San Francisco St., Suite 1
Santa Fe, NM 87501
(800) 866-HOWL
dried chilies, southwestern spices, and specialty foods

Dean and Deluca
Mail Order Department
560 Broadway
New York, NY 10012
(800) 221-7714
grains, beans, dried chilies, canned chipotle peppers, specialty foods

Ideal Cheese
1205 Second Ave.
New York, NY 10021
(212) 688-7579
low-fat cheeses, low-fat goat cheese

Josie's
2600 Camino Entrada
Santa Fe, NM 87505
(505) 473-3437
dried chilies, blue cornmeal

Just Tomatoes
P.O. Box 807
Westley, CA 95387
(209) 894-5371
no-oil domestic sun-dried tomatoes

Le Marché
P.O. Box 190
Dixon, CA 95620
(916) 678-9244
seeds

Los Chileros de Nuevo Mexico
P.O. Box 6215
Santa Fe, NM 87502
(505) 471-6967
dried chilies, white posole, blue popcorn

Malibu Greens
P.O. Box 6286
Malibu, CA 90264
(800) 383-1414
fresh baby vegetables, fresh exotic fruits

Meadowbrook Herb Gardens
R.R. Box 138
Wyoming, RI 02898
(401) 539-7603
dried herbs and seasonings, peppercorns

Organic Foods Warehouse
4399 A Henniger Ct.
Chantilly, VA 22021
(703) 631-0881
*organic fruits, vegetables, grains, flours,
dried beans, dried fruits, seeds*

Rafal Spice Co.
2521 Russell St.
Detroit, MI 48207
(313) 259-6373
spices, seasoning mixes, peppercorns

G. B. Ratto & Co.
821 Washington St.
Oakland, CA 94607
(800) 325-3483
*dried mushrooms, vinegars, ethnic in-
gredients*

San Francisco Herb Co.
250 Fourteenth Street
San Francisco, CA 94103
(800) 227-4530
dried herbs, spices

Select Origins
Box N
Southampton, NY 11968
(516) 288-1382, (800) 822-2092
vinegar, oils, rice, dried mushrooms

Timber Crest Farms
4791 Dry Creek Rd.
Healdsburg, CA 95448
(707) 433-8251
no-oil domestic sun-dried tomatoes

Uwajimaya
519 Sixth Ave. S.
Seattle, WA 98104
(206) 624-6248
Asian specialty foods

Vanilla Saffron Imports, Inc.
949 Valencia St.
San Francisco, CA 04110
(415) 648-8990
dried mushrooms, herbs, peppercorns

Walnut Acres
Penns Creek, PA 17862
(717) 837-0601
stone-ground flours, oils, exotic rice

Wax Orchards
22744 Wax Orchards Rd. SW
Vashon, WA 98070
(206) 463-9735, (800) 634-6132
no-sugar condiments, chutneys, fruit jams, fruit syrups, fruit butters; low-fat, no-cholesterol, no-sugar fudge toppings

Williams-Sonoma
P.O. Box 7456
San Francisco, CA 94120-7456
(800) 541-2233
oils, vinegars, specialty foods

This list of mail-order sources is provided as a service and is not an endorsement of these manufacturers by the Joslin Diabetes Center or the authors. You may need to obtain nutrition information regarding the products listed before including them in your meal plan.

JOSLIN DIABETES CENTER AND ITS AFFILIATES

Joslin Diabetes Center
One Joslin Place
Boston, MA 02215
(617) 732-2440

Joslin Diabetes Center at
    Framingham
161 Worcester Road
Framingham, MA 01701
(508) 620-9600

Joslin Center for Diabetes
Methodist Hospital of Indiana and
    Endocrinology Associates
1701 North Senate Boulevard
Indianapolis, IN 46206
(317) 924-8866

Joslin Center for Diabetes
St. Barnabas Medical Center
101 Old Short Hills Road
West Orange, NJ 07052
(201) 325-6555

Joslin Center for Diabetes
West Penn Hospital
5140 Liberty Avenue
Pittsburgh, PA 15224
(412) 578-1724

Joslin Center for Diabetes
Morton Plant Hospital
323 Jeffords Street
Clearwater, FL 34616
(813) 461-8300

Joslin Center for Diabetes
Baptist Hospital of Miami
8900 North Kendall Drive
Miami, FL 33176
(800) 992-1879

Nalle Clinic Diabetes Center
    an Affiliate of Joslin Diabetes
    Center
1350 S. Kings Drive
Charlotte, NC 28207
(704) 342-8000

Joslin Center for Diabetes
MacNeal Hospital
3249 So. Oak Park Avenue
Berwyn, IL 60402
(708) 430-0730

Joslin Center for Diabetes
St. Luke's-Roosevelt Hospital
    Center
Amsterdam Avenue at 114th Street
New York, NY 10025
(212) 523-4000

INDEX OF RECIPE TITLES

GENERAL INDEX

498